Between Cross and Crescent

The History of African-American Religions

Florida A&M University, Tallahassee
Florida Atlantic University, Boca Raton
Florida Gulf Coast University, Ft. Myers
Florida International University, Miami
Florida State University, Tallahassee
University of Central Florida, Orlando
University of Florida, Gainesville
University of North Florida, Jacksonville
University of South Florida, Tampa
University of West Florida, Pensacola

The History of African-American Religions
Edited by Stephen W. Angell and Anthony Pinn

This series will further historical investigations into African religions in the Americas, encourage the development of new paradigms and methodologies, and explore cultural influences upon African-American religious institutions, including the roles of gender, race, leadership, regionalism, and folkways.

Laborers in the Vineyard of the Lord: The Beginnings of the AME Church in Florida, 1865–1895, by Larry Eugene Rivers and Canter Brown, Jr. (2001)
Between Cross and Crescent: Christian and Muslim Perspectives on Malcolm and Martin, by Lewis V. Baldwin and Amiri YaSin Al-Hadid (2002)

Between Cross and Crescent

Christian and Muslim Perspectives on Malcolm and Martin

Lewis V. Baldwin and Amiri YaSin Al-Hadid

University Press of Florida

Gainesville · Tallahassee · Tampa · Boca Raton

Pensacola · Orlando · Miami · Jacksonville · Ft. Myers

07 06 05 04 03 02   6 5 4 3 2 1

Library of Congress Cataloging-in-Publication Data
Baldwin, Lewis V., 1949–
Between cross and crescent: Christian and Muslim perspectives
on Malcolm and Martin / Lewis V. Baldwin and Amiri YaSin Al-Hadid.
p. cm. — (The history of African-American religions)
Includes bibliographical references (p.) and index.
ISBN 0-8130-2457-9 (c.: alk. paper)
1. X, Malcolm, 1925–1965—Religion. 2. King, Martin Luther, Jr., 1929–1968—
Religion. 3. Black Muslims. 4. Afro-Americans—Religion. 5. Islam—Relations—
Christianity. 6. Christianity and other religions—Islam. I. Al-Hadid, Amiri YaSin.
II. Title. III. Series.
BP222.B35 2002
323'.092'2—dc21 2001043721

The University Press of Florida is the scholarly publishing agency for the State University System of Florida, comprising Florida A&M University, Florida Atlantic University, Florida Gulf Coast University, Florida International University, Florida State University, University of Central Florida, University of Florida, University of North Florida, University of South Florida, and University of West Florida.

University Press of Florida
15 Northwest 15th Street
Gainesville, FL 32611–2079
http://www.upf.com

For the Baldwin and Jackson families
and in memory of our ancestors
Fannie Bell Baldwin
Lacy Leon Holt
Artes Jackson
Annie Knox

Contents

Foreword

We seek, through the texts selected for this series, to present African-American religiosity in all its complexity and experiential thickness. This book, the second in our series, furthers our concern with exploring new and expanded paradigms and methodologies through attention to the interplay between Christianity and Islam. While many scholars have written on the importance of the Christian faith to African-American communities, few have explored the longstanding presence of Islam within these same communities, and even less attention has been given to the interplay between these two traditions.

It is safe to say that, as Allan Austin notes, many Africans brought to North America were practicing Muslims. Their practices—including prayer habits and diet—have been expressed and documented by their descendants. Yet, although present for centuries, Islam's impact on African-American life is primarily explored with respect to the emergence of the Nation of Islam as a sociocultural organization during the early twentieth century. With the emergence of this organization, the African-American perspective on religious life as well as social, economic, political, and cultural realities was forever changed. The vocal and confrontational nature of the Nation of Islam made their presence difficult to ignore, and the charisma of many of the leaders, especially Malcolm X, made their growing influence a concern to many. The conflict between the teachings of most black churches and the Nation of Islam was apparent quite early, but their differences portended major consequences during the period of the civil rights movement when the struggle for full inclusion in American society drew heavily on religious principles for its rationale and method. As Lewis V. Baldwin and Amiri YaSin Al-Hadid suggest, this conflict is most clearly symbolized by two figures—Martin Luther King, Jr., and Malcolm X.

King was the spokesperson for the civil rights movement, the architect who blended the black Christian tradition with the teachings of Gandhi to develop an approach to social transformation built upon the foundation of nonviolent direct action. Malcolm X, whose version of Islamic theology and social theory, in the view of many, illuminated the weaknesses of nonviolent direct action, has come to be seen as King's major opponent. Neither could be dismissed easily because each spoke the thoughts and concerns of particular segments of the African-American collective community. In the late 1960s some African-American scholars and ministers attempted to bring these two figures and their philosophies into a somewhat creative tension. What resulted from this was a black theology that maintained King's radical reading of scripture but blended it with Malcolm X's biting social critique. The development of black theology, unfortunately, represents one of the few efforts to bring these two vital twentieth-century leaders into conversation. While this has been important, it is not enough.

Historian Lewis V. Baldwin and sociologist Amiri YaSin Al-Hadid address this gap in black religious studies. Growing out of better than ten years of conversation and discussion regarding King and Malcolm X, *Between Cross and Crescent* moves beyond simple prescription of mere antagonism between these leaders. It pushes for a more thoughtful presentation that recognizes both the conflict and connection between the two and, of particular merit, it pushes an academic dialogue on this relationship that recognizes the *religious* nature of the Nation of Islam. Based on themes related to the importance of prophetic critique of American culture—the necessity of interfaith dialogue, the urgency of articulating a Pan-African perspective, and the celebration of community as the highest ideal—the authors unpack the underlying threads of continuity found in the social vision of both leaders. This approach is unique in that it is perhaps the first treatment of King and Malcolm X that explicitly opens up their religious sensibilities through a multidisciplinary method.

Readers are encouraged to appreciate the possibilities inherent in both traditions and to hold them in creative tension. Baldwin and Al-Hadid provide the groundwork for an interdisciplinary and religiously complex discussion of two major religious leaders of the twentieth century. Students of American and African-American religious life will appreciate the thoughtfulness and detail of this project. The authors' careful discussion of important issues such as freedom, family, gender roles, democracy, and globalization within the thought of Malcolm X and King will challenge readers to think about these figures in new and complex terms. We are delighted to offer this text, and we believe students, scholars, and general readers will enjoy this book for its contribution to African-American religious thought and interreligious dialogue.

Stephen W. Angell and Anthony Pinn,
Series Editors

Acknowledgments

It is our pleasure to acknowledge gratefully those persons who helped make this book possible. We have been inspired by the many students who have taken our classes on Malcolm and Martin over the years, and to them we offer a strong word of gratitude. We are also indebted to those Tennessee State and Vanderbilt students who have participated in the Great Debate Series, an annual event initiated by Professor Al-Hadid in 1985 to keep Malcolm's and Martin's legacies of ideas alive and to assist students in refining their own intellectual skills. Having worked together from time to time in staging this event, we can speak personally and jointly to the intellectual stimulation we have received through its encouragement of the free play of ideas.

Stephen Angell and Anthony Pinn were very supportive of this project, and both offered useful advice and insights at a critical stage in its development. We are deeply indebted to them and others at the University Press of Florida for their patience and understanding and for including this volume in their series, History of African-American Religions.

Betsy Cagle, the secretary in the Religious Studies Department at Vanderbilt University, deserves our praise and gratitude for editing and typing this work. She assumed these responsibilities at a point when this work required numerous corrections, and she, too, provided much-needed advice and suggestions. Her contributions helped make the effort all the more exciting and productive.

The completion of this book is due in great part to small research grants received from the Vanderbilt University Research Council. We owe a special word of thanks to Russell G. Hamilton, who once chaired that council, and who has a deep interest in scholarship on Malcolm and Martin. Without the assistance he provided, research trips to the King Center in Atlanta, the Schomburg Center in New York, and the Amistad Center at Tulane University would have been virtually impossible to finance. Unfortunately, since he relinquished his position in the VURC, it has been virtually impossible to get strong university support for scholarship on any subject.

We acknowledge the assistance of Jacqueline Loretta Laws-Baldwin, Lewis Baldwin's wife, who read most of the manuscript and offered advice on corrections and revisions. She was always willing to discuss the work while it was in progress and frequently said that she would not rest until it appeared in published form.

Our heartfelt gratitude goes out to Nathan Jackson Sr., the father of Al-Hadid and a close friend of E. D. Nixon Sr., for his wise and rare insights about Martin Luther King Jr., and the Montgomery bus protest (1955–56). Special appreciation is also extended to Fatma Mohamed Athman Al-Bakery, Al-Hadid's wife, and his children, Yasmine Nefertiti and Yasin Amiri, for their devotion, love, and inspiration.

This volume is dedicated to our immediate families and ancestors. Their support and spirits kept us from giving up on what we know is an enormously important enterprise.

Introduction

Christians and Muslims in the African-American community almost never meet for serious reflection and dialogue on any subject. Although both groups proclaim God's unconditional love for everyone, the kinship of all humanity, and the need to create bridges of understanding and goodwill between people, they seldom listen to one another and are actually kept apart by bigotry, self-righteousness, competitiveness, and a lack of open-mindedness on both sides. This book has arisen out of the recognition that black Christians and Muslims must learn not only to affirm and respect one another but also to work together for a more peaceful and inclusive society.[1]

Between Cross and Crescent is the product of a collaborative effort between a Christian and a Muslim who have learned to listen to and respect each other. Lewis V. Baldwin is a highly regarded church historian with deep roots in the African-American Christian tradition, and Amiri YaSin Al-Hadid is a Sunni Muslim and a sociologist. For more than a decade, we have discussed and debated the lives, ideas, activities, and legacies of Malcolm X and Martin Luther King Jr. We have also participated together in Tennessee State University's Great Debate series and in debates in other public forums, appearing before audiences of black Christians and Muslims. Our experiences lead us to believe that extensive and meaningful dialogue between these faith communities hinges in part on their willingness to take Malcolm and Martin seriously as religious figures, as social activists, and as cultural heroes who provide rich insights into the relationship between spirituality and social transformation.

This volume treats Malcolm and Martin as powerful sources of dialogue for Christians and Muslims who are interested in the kind of interfaith cooperation that results in the improvement of culture and the liberation of humans across the barriers of race, religion, and geography. At the same time, we contend that ethical and theological dialogue with Malcolm and Martin can be rewarding for all people who struggle for genuine peace and community. While sharing this contention, we sometime differ in the ways in which we advance it within the context of this work. We know that no single perspective on Malcolm and Martin can clarify the complexities underlying their images as race leaders, religious figures, national icons, and world symbols. Therefore, our goal in this volume was never to achieve complete uniformity in our treatments of these two great men.

Mass confusion about their significance exists among both academics and the public at large. Multiple and competing images of both men linger in the minds of people of different backgrounds and religious and political persuasions, images created in the public imagination by the American mass media, reinforced in the works of misinformed scholars, and widely promoted by profit-seeking business entrepreneurs and commercial artists.[2] Some portray Malcolm and Martin as antagonists in a bitter conflict, the forces of evil against the forces of good, suggesting that the Muslim imam is less acceptable than the Christian pastor.[3] Following the same nondialectical approach to reasoning, many young African Americans reject Martin while embracing Malcolm.[4] Only in rare cases have both Malcolm and Martin been viewed as great political-religious theoreticians who learned from each other, received impelling intellectual, spiritual, and moral power from each other, and complemented and corrected each other to the benefit of the human liberation cause.[5]

The content of this work reflects both a dialectical ("both-and") and a nondialectical ("either-or") approach to reasoning regarding Malcolm and Martin. Al-Hadid's approach is considerably more nondialectical than Baldwin's. But we believe that both approaches hold some merit in our continuing efforts to understand those forces which separated Malcolm and Martin and those which drew them together in what Gayraud S. Wilmore calls "a dialectic of social action" that was, "at one and the same time, cultural and political, Christian and non-Christian, separatist and integrationist."[6] To assume that one or the other approach alone is sufficient is to ignore the different levels of creativity that Malcolm and Martin brought to their tasks as ministers, theologians, and agents of cultural and social change. Both men were products of essentially the same sociohistorical forces, but it is a mistake to assume that they ultimately found common ground on all matters pertinent to the human condition and struggle.

Four central themes in this volume give it a certain flavor and direction. One is the significance of the prophetic critique and transformation of culture. We hold that Malcolm and Martin were not only interpreters, theoreticians, and fashioners of culture but also profound critics and transformers of it. We also contend that they were in some ways ethical prophets who were compelled by their understandings of God and of the divine-human relationship to subject the prevailing institutions, values, and practices of the United States and Western society as a whole to critical scrutiny and analysis.[7] At the same time, Malcolm and Martin remained captive in some respects to the standards of the very culture they so strongly criticized and zealously sought to transform, a point clearly substantiated by our discussions of their attitudes toward and relationships with women and children.

The essentiality of interfaith dialogue and cooperation as an avenue to human liberation and survival is a second prominent theme in this volume. While not ecumenists in the strongest sense of the word, Malcolm and Martin ultimately felt that people of diverse religious traditions in the United States, and especially in the African-American community, had to interact and work together to create a society based on genuinely democratic and spiritual values.[8] Both came to see religious bigotry and intolerance as merely another barrier to human community, a position that came naturally as Malcolm and Martin read widely, traveled the world, and encountered people from numerous faith traditions. Thus they were "religious revolutionists" in that they transcended much of the spiritual blindness and narrowness so typical of large numbers of people in both Christianity and Islam even today.[9]

The recognition of strong links and obligations between people of color everywhere is a third theme developed here. Malcolm and Martin realized that people of color throughout the world suffered politically, economically, and otherwise from the effects of white supremacist ideas and practices. This explains the passion and the consistency with which they attacked racism, colonialism, and wars of aggression by the major Western powers against people in Vietnam, southern Africa, and other parts of the so-called dark world. Convinced that people of color worldwide were engaged in a common struggle, they never doubted the need for them to support one another physically, financially, morally, emotionally, and otherwise.[10] In order to establish closer links with people of color in other parts of the world, Malcolm founded the Organization of Afro-American Unity (OAAU) and the Muslim Mosques, Inc., and Martin worked with agencies such as the American Committee on Africa (ACOA) and the American Negro Leadership Conference on Africa (ANLCA).[11]

The final theme explored is the absolute necessity for world peace and community as the highest human ideal. Malcolm and Martin felt that each person should commit to peace and community as regulating ideals, and both insisted that the survival of the human family depended ultimately upon the elimination of racism, poverty and economic injustice, and violence and human destruction.[12] This is why Malcolm, after traveling to Africa and the Middle East in the summer of 1964, urged his people to "understand the problems of the world and where you fit into that world picture."[13] Martin spoke in similar terms, admonishing the African American to develop "a growing awareness of his world citizenship."[14] Malcolm envisioned the possibility of a world that "practices brotherhood," and Martin saw a totally integrated world or what he labeled "the beloved community." Both leaders became international symbols of peace and community, despite the different ways in which they articulated and pursued their visions on practical levels. Martin's importance in this regard is widely acknowledged both in the academy and in the broader public arena, but many in both circles persist in viewing Malcolm as a racial fanatic and separatist who never embraced an explicit and enlightened globalism.[15] We reject that contention wholeheartedly, concluding instead that there was no essential difference between the world visions of Malcolm and Martin by the time each met his death.

This book consists of nine chapters. Chapter 1 discusses Malcolm and Martin in relationship to African-American culture and the broader American culture. Baldwin argues that the two leaders were the products of essentially the same culture, despite Malcolm's claim that he knew "nothing about the South."[16] In this chapter Baldwin refutes the common view that the culture to which Malcolm was exposed from childhood in the North was different from what Martin experienced growing up in Georgia, especially since southern black culture moved North with Malcolm's Georgia-born father and other African-American migrants whom Malcolm associated with as a child and later as a hustler in the streets of Boston and New York. Baldwin also asserts that Malcolm and Martin were exposed to the full range of this culture from their earliest years—from its folklore and culinary customs to its musical and religious dimensions. Thus, the claim that regionalism and geography are important factors in explaining Malcolm and Martin is strongly refuted.[17] Much of this chapter also treats Malcolm's and Martin's developing understanding of African-American culture, their views on the importance of culture to liberation, and their continuing significance as cultural icons in American society.

Chapter 2 explores Malcolm's religious pilgrimage from the Nation of Islam to Sunni Islam. Here Al-Hadid underscores the critical roles of the Qur'an and the traditions of the Prophet Muhammad (pbuh) in Malcolm's transition from Elijah Muhammad's brand of black religious nationalism to a more traditional and universal expression of the Muslim faith. Some hold that this shift created a serious tension within Malcolm between the demands of *asabiya* (black nation-building) and the commitment to the *ummah* (world community of Islamic believers), a position Al-Hadid essentially rejects.[18] Al-Hadid suggests that Malcolm experienced virtually no difficulty in reconciling his black nationalism and Pan-Africanism with his devotion to Islam worldwide. Moreover, he contends that the name Malcolm X was rendered spiritually insignificant after the Muslim leader's pilgrimage to Mecca in 1964, when he changed his name to El-Hajj Malik El-Shabazz. This chapter goes on to explain how Malcolm's Muslim Mosque, Inc., founded in New York in that same year, became symbolic of how he had turned the corner in his spiritual journey.

Chapter 3 examines the place of religion in the lives of Malcolm and Martin. Particular attention is given to their religious backgrounds, their efforts to understand Christianity and Islam in intellectual terms, their dependence on religion and spiritual values in their struggles for freedom, and the significance of their religious attitudes and practices for interreligious dialogue and cooperation today. In contrast to Al-Hadid, who emphasizes Malcolm's reliance on the Qur'an, Baldwin points to Malcolm's and Martin's use of stories, characters, and images from the Bible to explain black suffering and the destiny of their people. The conclusion is that they saw no disjunction between the religious and the political, social, and economic dimensions of life.[19]

Al-Hadid discusses Malcolm's and Martin's concepts of manhood and family in chapter 4. He considers Earl Little's and Elijah Muhammad's impact on Malcolm's life and perspective, as well as Martin Luther King Sr.'s influence on the younger Martin. It is clear from Al-Hadid's discussion that both the Muslim activist and the civil rights leader attached great significance to manhood, partly because they lived in a society that had long sought to deny black males the privilege of being strong husbands and fathers. Malcolm and Martin respected each other as a vital symbol of manhood, and both associated manhood not only with the ability to protect and provide for family but also with the capacity to afford courageous and effective leadership for their people.[20] Their perspectives on the separate and distinct arenas of activity for men and women in the home and in society are revealed in subtle ways in this chapter, but Al-Hadid considers their views to be traditional and not necessarily marred by sexism and the centuries-old standards of patriarchy.

A different point of view surfaces in chapter 5 with Baldwin's treatment of Malcolm's and Martin's perceptions of and relationships with black women. Much of the focus is on the development of their earliest attitudes toward women within the contexts of their home and family environments. Attention is also devoted to their relationships with their wives and with Fannie Lou Hamer, Gloria Richardson, Ella Baker, and other activists in the freedom movement of the 1950s and 1960s. The chapter ends with some reflections on how feminists and womanists have analyzed the roles and contributions of Malcolm and Martin. An extensive and trenchant critique of the two leaders' sexism is afforded, with some recognition of how their conceptions of female subordination limited the success of their freedom movements.[21]

In chapter 6, Baldwin gives careful consideration to Malcolm's and Martin's roles as fathers and to their attitudes toward children and youth generally. Their views on student involvement in the freedom movement of the 1950s and 1960s are highlighted. Attention is also given to the various images of Malcolm and Martin that have existed in the minds of youngsters over the last half century.[22] This chapter closes with some discussion of the relevance and implications of their legacies of ideas and struggle for youngsters who find it virtually impossible to escape poverty, drugs, crime, and violence.

In chapter 7, Al-Hadid turns to what he terms the Great Debate between Malcolm and Martin. Taking an approach that appears more nondialectical than dialectical, Al-Hadid employs the "double consciousness" idea of W.E.B. Du Bois in contrasting the philosophies and methods of Malcolm and Martin. This approach is also utilized in James H. Cone's celebrated study of the two figures.[23] Al-Hadid claims that Malcolm represented the fullest evolution of the emigration/self-determination philosophy and Martin the highest expression of the assimilation/integration philosophy. Al-Hadid also feels that this debate reached classic proportions between Du Bois and Booker T. Washington at the beginning of the twentieth century, before being popularized and advanced in somewhat different ways by Malcolm and Martin.[24] The chapter concludes with references to how these two apparently opposite positions might be juxtaposed to arrive at a synthesis or unity of the opposites.[25] Al-Hadid's insights bear the influence of working with students in the

Great Debate series, which he started in memory of Malcolm and Martin at Tennessee State University in 1985.

We are not in complete agreement about the viability of the Cartesian model for interpreting and understanding Malcolm and Martin. For Baldwin, this interpretive model, which portrays Malcolm and Martin as polar opposites, or as religious leaders and social activists who stood on opposite sides of the ideological spectrum, is somewhat problematic and inadequate for capturing the essence of these phenomenal figures. Unlike Al-Hadid, Baldwin rejects the use of neatly defined categories such as North vs. South, Christianity vs. Islam, lower class vs. middle class, nationalism vs. integrationism, and racial separatism vs. universalism to distinguish Malcolm from Martin.[26] In Baldwin's estimation, the use of such categories, when viewed as mutually exclusive, actually results in rank oversimplifications and leads to a distortion of the two leaders' ideologies and programs. According to Baldwin, the powerlessness of African Americans in a hypocritical nation, in a country proclaiming equality of opportunity while sanctioning racism and segregation, led Malcolm and Martin to combine aspects of nationalism, integrationism, and other seemingly contradictory philosophical streams in their approaches to liberation.[27] The different interpretive models and conceptual frameworks employed by Baldwin and Al-Hadid become clear as one moves through this volume.

Malcolm's and Martin's views on each other are highlighted by Baldwin in chapter 8. The central claim is that their disagreements over violence and nonviolence, separatism and integration, Christianity and Islam, and other matters kept them from becoming close friends and associates and actually determined in large measure how they viewed and related to each other.[28] Attention is devoted to their critiques of each other's philosophy and methods, to their differences over the significance and outcome of various civil rights campaigns, to their movement toward common ground on a range of issues, and to Martin's reflections on Malcolm's death. This chapter shows that the relationship between them advanced through two stages, the first covering the period from 1957 to March 1964 and the second from March 26, 1964, to Malcolm's assassination on February 21, 1965.

Chapter 9 explains how Malcolm's and Martin's visions of community transcended the particularities of the African-American experience to assume global significance. We explore their perspectives on the African-American condition, their attitudes toward the so-called white world, their thoughts on the bonds and obligations between people of color worldwide, and their belief in and pursuit of world peace and community. Malcolm's belief in a peaceful and harmonious world is equated essentially with Martin's devotion to the creation of the beloved community on a global scale. We conclude that their assessments of racism, poverty, war, and religious bigotry as barriers to world community are as meaningful and relevant today as they were in the 1950s and 1960s.

This is the first major work produced on Malcolm and Martin by a Christian scholar and a Muslim scholar. We have tried to present our different perspectives honestly and forthrightly, while making clear those areas on which we agree. Furthermore, we have tried to bring a sensitive and critical focus to our treatments of Malcolm and Martin without doing violence to their rich lives and powerful legacies. We hope that this volume will testify to the beauty of what can happen when people of different faiths engage in charitable debate and authentic dialogue and cooperation.

I

Out of the Dark Past

Malcolm, Martin, and Black Cultural Reality

Sing a song full of the faith that the dark past has taught us.
Negro National Anthem[1]

Culture is an indispensable weapon in the freedom struggle. We must take
hold of it and forge the future with the past.
Malcolm X[2]

Negroes are learning that their dignity is not a matter of manners. It is not
a pattern of behavior possessed by white people to be imitated by Negroes;
it is unborn in a sense because they live in a culture their fathers made as
part of the whole community of creators.
Martin Luther King Jr.[3]

Malcolm X and Martin Luther King Jr. contributed enormously to the transformation of American culture in the 1950s and 1960s. Through the scope of
their social activism and the arresting power of their messages, they challenged white Americans who subscribed uncritically to established social and
political mores, forcing them to reexamine their prevailing institutions, values, and practices. But in black America their cultural contributions carried
an added dimension. Here Malcolm and Martin became cultural spokesmen,
interpreters and theorists of culture, and advocates and promoters of radical
responses to white cultural domination. Consequently, they have become not
only prototypes for civil rights leadership but prototypical cultural heroes as
well.[4]

Cultural Roots: Malcolm and Martin in Context

Malcolm and Martin came from backgrounds that were different in some
ways and similar in others. Malcolm was born to Earl and Louise Little in
Omaha, Nebraska, on May 19, 1925, the fourth of eight children. The family

moved to Milwaukee before settling on the outskirts of East Lansing, Michigan. Martin was born to Alberta and Martin Luther King in Atlanta on January 15, 1929, the second of three children.[5] The security and coherence of Martin's childhood contrasted sharply with the poverty and insecurity of Malcolm's. Even so, growing up during the worst years of the Great Depression, when joblessness and the relief rolls soared to unprecedented levels, exposed both to some of the most tragic realities of the black experience, thus contributing to their sense of identification and solidarity with all African Americans. Recalling those years, Martin wrote, "I was much too young to remember the beginning of this depression, but I do recall how I questioned my parents about the numerous people standing in bread lines when I was about five years of age. I can see the effects of this early childhood experience on my present anti-capitalistic feelings."[6]

Such an experience would have been more familiar to Malcolm, who recounted that "we would be so hungry we were dizzy." Added to the grinding poverty was the terrible specter of racism, which loomed large and in graphic detail in the consciousness of African Americans during the Great Depression. The fact that in some places there was "as much as a six-dollar differential in the monthly aid given to white and black families" would not have been surprising to young Malcolm and Martin, especially since they suffered the indignities of being called "nigger" and of being physically attacked and barred from facilities that whites frequented. The relationship between poverty, economic injustice, and racism had emerged clearly in their thinking when they reached adolescence, thus fertilizing their minds for the seeds of democratic socialism that would sprout later.[7]

Because African Americans were perhaps the most oppressed group in the land in the 1930s and 1940s, Malcolm and Martin could not have survived childhood unscathed. While it is doubtful that they seriously questioned their worth as human beings, living in a society where blacks were consistently treated differently from whites must have caused some inner conflict on their parts. Malcolm's autobiographical reflections are the best testimony to the conflicting impulses that raged within him, especially since his contacts with whites as a youngster were generally more extensive than Martin's. As a seventh grader in an integrated school in Lansing, Michigan, Malcolm was a leader among his peers, a privilege not available to Martin in the rigidly segregated schools of Atlanta. Martin lost a white playmate at age six due to racism, was slapped by a white woman when he was only eight, and was forced to surrender a bus seat to a white passenger at age fourteen—experiences that clearly contrasted with the affirmation and acceptance he enjoyed in Atlanta's larger black community.[8] Martin later reflected on his struggle to deal with such experiences in terms that Malcolm would have easily understood: "As I look back over those early years, I did have something of an inner tension. On the one hand my mother taught me that I should feel a sense of somebodiness. . . . On the other hand, I had to go out and face the system, which stared me in the face every day saying, 'You are less than, you are not equal to.' So this was a real tension within me."[9]

The shared experience of oppression based on race united the Littles and the Kings in spirit even as material possessions and educational levels marked off boundaries between them. It made no difference that the Littles were significantly less educated and affluent than the Kings. The fact that one family lived in the Midwest and the other in the more segregated South held no significance. Growing up in settings where all blacks suffered on the basis of race and where whites were constantly belligerent in their dealings with all people of color, it was only natural for Malcolm and Martin to sense the need for black unity. Their early awareness of oppression, of being black in a hostile white world, precluded any possibility of the kind of regional self-consciousness that, under different circumstances, would have undermined racial solidarity. Also, that awareness stimulated their curiosity and ultimately led them to think of African Americans as essentially a single people with their own institutions, values, and ways of thinking and living.[10]

That sense of the essential oneness of the folk was reinforced by a potent black culture that became all the more vital as African Americans from the Deep South moved North and interacted with their people from various regions of the country. Malcolm and Martin were nurtured in the essentials of that culture, despite their initial inability to understand it in theoretical terms. African influences on that culture, particularly in the areas of folklore and religion, remained evident in the North and the South throughout the 1930s and 1940s, due mainly to persistent patterns of segregation and to the continuing presence and influence of ex-slaves and their immediate descendants. Under such influences, Malcolm and Martin found values that informed their earliest conceptions of freedom and community.[11] Moreover, they discovered not only the foundation for what became a lifelong interest in the fate of African Americans but also vital sources on which they would later draw as religious leaders and as theorists and transformers of culture.

A greater foundation could hardly have been laid, especially since their fathers were Baptist preachers with deep roots in the South. The experiences that both Earl Little and Martin Luther King Sr. had known while growing up in rural Georgia, when memories of slavery and the realities of Jim Crow loomed large, and the spiritual values they subsequently brought to their art as preachers and their activities as freedom fighters, strengthened young Malcolm and Martin as they struggled to understand the world and their place in it. The boys saw their fathers not only as men of courage who had not been demoralized and spiritually diminished by oppression but also as living examples of how the younger generations could best meet the challenges of racism and white domination.[12]

Malcolm's and Martin's early exposure to the currents of Africanity in black culture proved only natural. Earl Little's roots in Georgia and Louise Little's background in the West Indies, together with their Garveyism and teachings about Africa, virtually ensured young Malcolm's exposure to the cultural symbols and traditions of people from various parts of Africa. While not having the same advantages in relation to black culture, Martin did find in his parents, the preacher and the musician, spiritual and artistic values that people of African descent anywhere in the world would have claimed as their own.[13]

The richness of black culture was such that young Martin and Malcolm were exposed to folk practices and beliefs dating back more than a century in slavery and many more in Africa. The youngsters observed the lingering remnants of a powerful tradition that included voodoo, ghostlore, herbalism, witchcraft, and fortune-telling. Such beliefs and practices could be found wherever ex-slaves and their immediate offspring resided. Remembering some of his experiences as a boy in church, Malcolm declared, "It was spooky, with ghosts and spirituals and 'hants' seeming to be in the very atmosphere." His mother, "who always had a strong intuition of things about to happen," had a vision of the death of her husband, Earl Little, a few hours before he was actually killed, an experience not altogether surprising because visions, dreams, and signs that foretold imminent death had pervaded the sacred world not only of native Africans for generations but also that of the slaves and their descendants in the United States, Latin America, and the Caribbean. Louise Little's children inherited her belief in visions, omens, and signs. Malcolm once remarked, "When something is about to happen, I can feel something, sense something."[14]

The Kings' belief in the surviving spirits of ancestors was as much African in character as the Littles' propensity toward visions, omens, and signs. Martin Sr. and Alberta assured their twelve-year-old son Martin, upon the death of his maternal grandmother in 1941, that "somehow" she "still lived," thus easing the pain of the loss. For the Kings, as for their slave forebears, the spirits of ancestors lessened the hardship of the living and linked the world of the living with the other world, thus explaining why respect for ancestors and elders remained at the core of black culture.[15]

Traditions that valued the experiences and wisdom of the aged as sources of insight and instruction were strongly embraced by the Littles and the Kings, thus recalling Africa and slave culture in significant ways. Exposed to such traditions, Malcolm and Martin became quite conscious of the central place of the ancestors and elders as bearers of culture and as transmitters of cultural values from generation to generation, a consciousness heightened by the strict discipline imposed by their parents.[16]

Malcolm and Martin also witnessed in their own families variants of African spirit possession that took the forms of "shouting" and "holy dancing." Malcolm's recollection of his father "jumping and shouting as he preached, with the congregation jumping and shouting behind him, their souls and bodies devoted to singing and praying," clearly squares with Martin's memories of his father "prancing" and "walking the benches" with his parishioners.[17] Such ceremonies afforded ample proof that Malcolm's early Nebraska and Michigan environments shared many similarities with Martin's Georgia setting.[18] Moreover, they showed that Earl Little and Martin Luther King Sr., while different in terms of educational level, wealth, and influence, became essentially one in their affirmation of forms of sacred dance.[19]

Discussions about the many positive and creative contributions of the slaves to the fashioning of African-American culture probably never surfaced in any serious ways in the Little and King households. This would not have been unusual in the 1930s and 1940s, when the slave experience was viewed in the most negative terms and when images of a history of primitive savagery in Africa found wide acceptance even in parts of the African-American community. Negative images of Africa invariably translated into distorted pictures of slave culture. As a youngster, Malcolm was not prone to reject such images, despite his father's frequent references to the glories of Africa in the centuries before the establishment of slavery. "My image of Africa, at that time," Malcolm reminisced, "was of naked savages, cannibals, monkeys and tigers and steaming jungles." Martin's earliest perception was hardly different. Confronted with false portrayals of Africa, and with his mother's reflections on the horrors of slavery and its tragic legacy of segregation, he, as was the case with Malcolm, was not prepared to think of a rich slave culture grounded in the ring shout and other African ceremonial forms—a culture that was the basis of so much of what he witnessed and experienced in black Atlanta.[20]

The murder of Earl Little in 1931 deprived Malcolm of perhaps the most powerful cultural symbol of his childhood. Only six at the time, Malcolm would endure a series of tragedies over the next four years, highlighted by his mother's mental breakdown and the disintegration of his family. A sense of homelessness and a longing for family stability followed, causing pain beyond anything Martin could have imagined in his more secure and stable world. Shuttling between different homes, Malcolm moved in with the Gohannas family, whom he later described as "nice, older people, and great churchgoers." Here he was continuously exposed to cultural values and practices that reflected Africa and the slave experience on many levels and that would have been commonplace in the church environment Martin knew as a child. Malcolm recounted: "The Gohannas were very religious people. Big Boy and I attended church with them. They were sanctified Holy Rollers now. The preachers and congregations jumped even higher and shouted even louder than the Baptists I had known. They sang at the top of their lungs, and swayed back and forth and cried and moaned and beat on tambourines and chanted." His description of the Gohannas mirrors Martin's account of having grown up in a community where "most of our neighbors were deeply religious."[21]

The two boys responded similarly to what they perceived as the excessively emotional character of African-American religion. Malcolm recalled that the church "confused and amazed me," and Martin recounted that "the shouting and stamping in Negro Churches embarrassed me."[22] Apparently, both failed initially to grasp the artistic, spiritual, and therapeutic value of African-American religion as well as the extent to which the church served as the fountainhead of culture in the black community. This would have been only natural for them at a time when images of black religion as an unenlightened, superficial caricature of the Christian faith pervaded media sources and the works of misinformed scholars.

Even so, religion and the church figured prominently in Malcolm and Martin's earliest conceptions of "place," "freedom," and "community." Malcolm frequently alluded to the presence of churches and to the numerous occasions on which he accompanied his mother and siblings in worshiping with Baptists, Pentecostals, Seventh Day Adventists, and Jehovah's Witnesses. Exposure to the church continued to some degree when fourteen-year-old Malcolm moved to Boston to live with his sister Ella. He found that "the Boston Negroes, like all other Negroes I had seen at church, threw their souls and bodies wholly into worship." Unimpressed with his experiences, Malcolm drifted from the Christian faith in ways that remained untypical of Martin, who always claimed the church as his "second home." For Martin, the Ebenezer Baptist Church in Atlanta, pastored by his father and located near the Kings' home on Auburn Avenue, remained enormously important. Ebenezer Church and the King family became extensions of each other, especially since Martin's maternal grandfather, A. D. Williams, had pastored the church for thirty-seven years (1894–1931) before Martin Sr. took over.[23]

A genuine spirit of cooperation characterized the communities in which Malcolm and Martin were raised. Both experienced acceptance, affirmation, and support from neighbors and relatives alike, experiences that were perhaps even more meaningful for Malcolm, whose immediate family was rocked by a tyrannical father, spousal abuse, and brutal poverty. Malcolm vividly remembered the assistance and reinforcement his family received from the Gohannas, the Lyons, the McGuires, the Walkers, and other friends and neighbors after Earl Little died, generosity that must have given the young man a feeling of kinship with these people that transcended blood lines.[24] The expressions of love and concern Malcolm shared with Ella, and his determination to stay in touch with his mother and siblings after the Little family had been separated, easily call to mind the intimacy and security Martin felt in a home filled with parents, aunts, uncles, cousins, a "saintly grandmother," and others who were not actual relatives at all.[25]

Affirmed and supported by African Americans who were not blood relatives, Malcolm and Martin were not likely to be totally oblivious, even as children, to the power of the extended family as a preserver and promoter of cultural values. This sense of the extended family must have been stronger with Martin than with Malcolm, especially since the Kings shared a long generational bond with their elders and ancestors through the church and naming practices, and also because family, church, and neighborhood, in their case, formed a network far more powerful than anything Malcolm experienced in his youth.[26]

Communal values found poignant expression through art, particularly in the sphere of music. Malcolm and Martin recognized this very early. Many African Americans in the communities in which they lived readily accepted black music in its various sacred and secular forms, and vocal and instrumental music was inseparable from dance. Malcolm and Martin witnessed the singing of spirituals in church and in the sermons of their fathers, the phrasings and rhythms of which left indelible marks on their thinking. Malcolm's failure to grasp the artistic value of this music, a tendency that persisted throughout his life, stemmed mostly from its connection to slavery and from the seeming excesses of his people while testifying, singing, and shouting in church. In contrast, Martin sang the spirituals and gospel songs as early as age four, and black sacred music became increasingly important to him years later as he pondered the links between art and the struggle for freedom.[27]

Secular music revealed the distinctiveness of mass culture in ways both typical and untypical of the spirituals and gospel songs. Malcolm and Martin grew up in atmospheres charged with the sounds and the emotive force of jazz and the blues—music ringing through the open doors of bars, taverns, nightclubs, and poolrooms and heard blocks away. The rising and falling of secular musical forms with their peculiar cadence and perfect melody struck a responsive chord in both. Traveling back and forth between New York and Boston in the early 1940s, Malcolm found his growing sense of the cultural significance of this music as he associated with band leaders like Cab Calloway and Fess Williams, blues artists such as Jimmie Rushing and Dinah Washington, and a parade of other great musicians, among whom were Sonny Greer, Ray Nance, and Eddie "Cleanhead" Vinson. As a teenager, Malcolm affirmed jazz, the blues, and other forms of black secular music with absolutely no objections on religious grounds, a point that cannot be made of Martin, who reflected to some degree the tensions within the church over the value of secular music. Growing up in southern black Baptist fundamentalism, where distinctions between the secular and the sacred were sometimes taken seriously, and where jazz, the blues, worksongs, and other secular forms were commonly called "the devil's music," young Martin sometimes found it very difficult to justify his apparent love for that music in light of the objections and teachings of the church.[28]

The rejection of secular music by the church appeared only logical in a time when even gospel songs were dismissed by many black Christians as being too "jazzy" and "bluesy." For some, jazz and the blues became all the more sinful because of their relation to secular dance, which involved flexed, fluid positions, shuffling steps, gliding, movement from the pelvic region, close contact, and other characteristics viewed as lewd and sacrilegious. Being more inclined toward the liberal rather than the fundamentalist approach to religion, Martin never completely embraced this perspective. While studying at Atlanta's all-black Morehouse College from 1944 to 1948, he was known to dance to the tunes of secular music, a habit he maintained even after becoming a minister at eighteen and one frowned upon by his father and others at Ebenezer Baptist Church.[29]

This struggle between two seemingly disparate realms, between the secular musical scene and the sacred life of the church, seemed foreign to young Malcolm, who enjoyed the nightclubs and dance halls as part of the center of his world. From the nightclubs of Boston to the Savoy Ballroom and the Apollo Theater in Harlem, "where great bands played and famous songs and dance steps and Negro stars originated," Malcolm lindy-hopped and performed other dance styles, often into the morning. He later spoke of those times with a measure of pride, noting how his "long-suppressed African instincts broke through," the "dancing instincts of my African heritage," an admission quite puzzling in view of his attitude toward shouting and holy dancing in black churches.[30]

Skill in dance reinforced the belief, rooted deeply in the culture, that African Americans were endowed with physical strength, bodily coordination, and a rhythm-consciousness far superior to that of whites.[31] Malcolm and Martin subscribed to some variant of this conviction as youngsters, one that had immeasurable implications in a society where images of black inferiority shimmered before their people at virtually every turn. Their great love for sports, particularly boxing, in which fighters like Jack Johnson and Joe Louis had inspired race pride by demonstrating their ability to defeat whites, emerged out of this context. Growing up in environments where sports were essential to a consideration of culture, Malcolm and Martin played football and basketball, and they understood the embarrassment that could result from losing in any one-on-one competition with whites their age and size. At thirteen, Malcolm actually endured the pain of such an experience when a white boy named Bill Peterson knocked him down "fifty times if he did once" in a boxing match. Humiliated in the presence of his younger brother Reginald, who looked up to him, and convinced that he had let his people down, Malcolm later said of Peterson: "He did such a job on my reputation in the Negro neighborhood that I practically went into hiding. A Negro just can't be whipped by somebody white and return with his head up to the neighborhood, especially in those days, when sports and, to a lesser extent show business, were the only fields open to Negroes, and when the ring was the only place a Negro could whip a white man and not be lynched. When I did show my face again, the Negroes I knew rode me so badly I knew I had to do something."[32]

The rematch proved equally damaging to Malcolm's pride, as he was knocked to the canvas by Peterson "the moment the bell rang," perhaps "the shortest 'fight' in history." Malcolm's reaction to the defeat would have been readily understood by Martin, who, at age fifteen, in a speech called "The Negro and the Constitution," implied that his people's struggle involved the capacity to withstand whatever whites handed out without being totally demoralized. In fact, African Americans had to show that they were capable of even superhuman feats of strength, a capacity more than adequately illustrated in folktales like "Stagolee," who was "so bad" that he "whupped" the U.S. Army, and "High John the Conqueror," in which the main character defeated the devil, eloped with his daughter, and turned the dampers of Hell down so that the place would not be so hot when he returned to visit his in-laws.[33]

Tales of this nature had a direct appeal to the black communities that Malcolm and Martin came to know so well. Both delighted in listening to the stories of their elders, who introduced them to a folkloric tradition that extended back generations into slavery. Malcolm's brother Philbert remembered that "at night before we would go to bed, we would all gather around the stove, and my mother would tell us stories about our ancestry." Sitting at the feet of Louise Little as a child, and at those of "the real old-timers" in Harlem in the early 1940s, Malcolm undoubtedly became familiar with a rich mine of tales, folk wit, and humor which had informed the works of Sterling Brown, Langston Hughes, Zora Neale Hurston, Jean Toomer, and other poets, fiction writers, and playwrights of the so-called Harlem Renaissance. Martin's experiences were hardly different, for he recalled the artistic genius of his maternal grandmother, Jennie C. Parks Williams, who "spent many evenings telling us interesting stories."[34]

The core values of resistance, freedom, self-reliance, and community in the tales must have been quite clear to Malcolm and Martin, though it is highly unlikely that they, in their youthfulness, understood the extent to which generations of blacks had employed wit and humor as a means of dealing with their plight and of exerting some control over an often hostile and unpredictable world.[35] In any case, they found in the folklore and humor of their people reservoirs of wisdom and inspiration which later helped them to achieve remarkable creativity as pulpiteers and to skillfully articulate the black pain predicament at all levels of society.

For young and inquisitive minds like those of Malcolm and Martin, folk-lore must have opened new avenues for understanding the survival ethics and instincts of African Americans. The determination to resist and survive in a violently antiblack society finds powerful expression in the trickster tales, and especially in the adventures of Brer Rabbit, sources to which Malcolm and Martin must have had some exposure.[36] While working as a shoeshine boy in Boston and a food salesman in New York, Malcolm, in ways reminiscent of generations of his forebears, employed the techniques of the trickster as a means of outsmarting whites and of ensuring his own survival and well-being. "It didn't take me a week to learn that all you had to do was give white people a show and they'd buy anything you offered them," Malcolm recalled. "It was like popping your shoeshine rag. The dining car waiters and Pullman porters knew it, too, and they faked their Uncle Tomming to get bigger tips. We were in that world of Negroes who are both servants and psychologists, aware that white people are so obsessed with their own importance that they will pay liberally, even dearly, for the impression of being catered to and entertained."[37]

Martin appeared equally mindful of the ways in which his people utilized the techniques of deception to survive and even triumph in the face of white racism. In the South he knew so well as a youngster, untold numbers of African Americans had escaped lynching by outwitting and manipulating whites.[38] Martin's sense of the importance of deception as a defense mechanism grew as he reached manhood. In terms that Malcolm would have immediately grasped, Martin once wrote: "The extensive use of violence, ridicule, and distortion often required that Negroes develop skill in the pretense of self-deprecation. Frequently they played the fool to make fools of their oppressors."[39] By mastering the art of deception, African Americans gave further evidence of their ability to fashion norms of behavior and a set of values—a cultural ethos—which allowed them to survive, to obtain psychic relief, and to assert their humanity in a society that sought to reduce them to nonpersons.

The social significance of food and eating was as much a part of this cultural ethos as sacred folk beliefs, religion, music, dance, and the tales. Malcolm and Martin's development occurred in communities where food was a constant preoccupation and where delicious food and feasts were associated with friends, neighborhood block parties, family reunions, funerals, and church meetings. Attitudes toward food and eating formed the basis of much of Malcolm's and Martin's initial cultural bond with their ancestry and with the mass of black people in America, not only because culinary traditions had informed folk literature and art dating back to slavery but also because they afforded yet another example of how southern black culture merged with the culture of the black North.[40]

Malcolm's cultural ties to the South came primarily through his father, who had migrated with other blacks to the North, bringing with him a keen sense of the spiritual and ritualistic value of food. Earl Little believed in eating plenty of soul food, a habit that often led to conflict with his wife, Louise, who, because of her Seventh Day Adventist faith, insisted that the family should not eat pork or rabbit. Malcolm's father re-created a southern sense of place in Michigan by maintaining big gardens and raising chickens and rabbits. Like so many boys in the South, Malcolm was permitted to have his own garden, and he felt immensely proud when his peas reached the family table. This deep appreciation for food and its connection to place and family also resonated in profound ways with young Martin, who knew the pleasures of southern cooking, who heard secular and sacred songs replete with language pertaining to food and drink, and who lived in a neighborhood where patches of peas, corn, greens, okra, and tomatoes crowded backyards.[41]

The lingering effects of the Great Depression reinforced Malcolm's and Martin's views of food and eating as basic to life and community. Earl Little's death in 1931 plunged his family into an economic crisis far more painful than anything the Kings experienced in those years. "The day was to come," recounted Malcolm, "when our family was so poor that we would eat the hole out of a doughnut." By contrast, the Kings ate well and never missed a meal. But easy access to food did not keep young Martin from identifying with a black world larger than his own, one marked by starvation, malnutrition, and disease. The South of his childhood was the poorest region of the country, and many of his own playmates were economically insecure. Surrounded by poverty, and sensitive to the struggles of his ancestors in slavery and under sharecropping arrangements, it was impossible for Martin, as it was for Malcolm, to ignore food as a symbol of culture and of the determination of African Americans to survive while enjoying the fullness of life.[42]

The festive and celebrative side of black culture must have been most evident to both whenever relatives gathered before a spread of native food and drink. For Malcolm and Martin, eating large quantities of soul food became a consuming passion. As a teenager, Malcolm "worked out" at his sister "Ella's kitchen table like there was no tomorrow," for she was known to "heap up your plate with such as ham hock, greens, black-eyed peas, fried chicken, cabbage, sweet potatoes, grits and gravy, and cornbread." Martin had the same moments of pleasure, growing up with a grandmother and a mother who were, as Malcolm said of Ella, "truly Georgia black women when they entered the kitchen with their pots and pans." Whereas Malcolm's eventual conversion to Islam turned him against soul food, Martin never broke with that part of the culture. In any event, both remained ever mindful of the significance of food and eating as a social and cultural phenomenon, and their conceptions of the economic and political aspects of this phenomenon ultimately matured as they confronted laws and customs that denied their people service at lunch counters.[43]

Although steeped in the full range of African-American cultural traditions, Malcolm and Martin did not escape the influence of the white communities that surrounded them. Malcolm attended school with whites, worshiped with whites, lived and dined with whites, and actually considered some to be his friends. "I grew up with white people," he once observed. "I was integrated before they even invented the word." Such relationships undoubtedly accounted for Malcolm's early struggle with his own blackness, as well as his initial tendency to see whites as individuals, not as a monolith. This was not possible for Martin, who rarely associated positively and openly with whites during his childhood and who, by his own admission, came "perilously close to resenting all white people."[44] When all is considered, the rigidly segregated South put Martin in a better position than Malcolm to escape the cultural influences of whites, a point that helps explain why Martin remained more firmly rooted in the black church.

But the lure of materialism and the ethnocentric standards of white society proved too strong for the young men to resist. While in his teens, Malcolm conked his hair, dressed in zoot suits, and dated white women, actions he later regarded as steps toward self-degradation. Martin seemed equally susceptible to some of the standards of the larger culture, despite the fact that he never shared Malcolm's wish to be shaped after the image of whites. He, too, dated a white girl and dressed sharply, often sporting his fine blue suits and fancy wide-brimmed hats.[45] Both Malcolm and Martin reflected the tendency to put on a show by conspicuous consumption, a tendency quite typical of oppressed people in a culture that cherishes materialism.[46] Even so, the attractions of the larger society did not diminish their desire to remain rooted in the communities and culture of black America.

The struggle to establish positive relationships with whites seems to have been more difficult for Martin than for Malcolm. Martin was fifteen before he seriously embraced the possibility that there were whites who did not subscribe to racism and segregation. In a letter to his mother, Alberta, in 1944, the young man, who had taken a summer job on a tobacco plantation in Simsbury, Connecticut, expressed amazement that "Negroes and whites go to the same church." In another letter Martin declared that after passing through Washington, D.C., he witnessed "no discrimination at all"—that "all the white people here are very nice." In yet another letter, he spoke of having dined at a fine white restaurant, noting, "I never thought that a person of my race could eat anywhere."[47] These and other experiences reinforced Martin's early sense that human community at its best is not confined by racial barriers.

Such experiences also blinded Martin initially to the subtle but vicious racism of whites in the North. This was not so characteristic of Malcolm, who, upon entering the eighth grade, began to experience "a restlessness with being around white people," feelings fueled largely by a white teacher who dismissed his expressed desire to become a lawyer as "no realistic goal for a nigger."[48] A sobering experience of this nature occurred for Martin in June 1950, when he and three of his black friends were denied service by a white tavern owner in New Jersey. Although the tavern owner faced the charge of violating a state civil rights law, the case was dropped when three white witnesses refused to testify on behalf of Martin and the other complainants.[49] This undoubtedly taught Martin something about the painful ways in which whites, however mean-spirited or well-meaning, collaborated in preserving the structures of racism.

Rejected and abused due to the color of their skin, Malcolm and Martin, despite their youthfulness, were not apt to embrace white cultural values uncritically. Unpleasant encounters with whites deepened their consciousness regarding the centrality of race in American life. Moreover, such encounters ultimately helped them come to terms with their own unique identities as persons of African descent, thus preparing them to become not only perceptive critics and effective transformers of culture but also strong leaders of their people.[50]

Understanding Black Culture: The Theoretical Side

The struggle to understand African Americans and their culture on a theoretical plane began with Martin long before Malcolm gave the matter serious consideration. At an oratorical contest sponsored by the black Elks in Dublin, Georgia, in April 1944, the fifteen-year-old Martin traced his people's struggle for freedom back to slavery in a speech called "The Negro and the Constitution." A junior at Atlanta's Booker T. Washington High School at the time, the young man alluded to concert singer Marian Anderson's remarkable struggle to overcome white society's rejection through her art, through skillful renditions of the folksongs, but he gave no indication that he saw slave culture as the foundation for that art. Failing to grasp that connection, Martin was ill-prepared at that juncture to articulate a theory of culture for the empowerment of his people and for the enhancement of their collective drive toward liberation. In fact, he was almost as devoid of such a theory as the nineteen-year-old Malcolm, who, fascinated with the underworld, had turned to alcohol, drugs, pimping, the numbers racket, and other vices that reflected the shady side of black life in the nation's largest cities.[51]

Greater cultural awareness came as Martin moved through college and seminary and as Malcolm obtained his "homemade education" in the streets and later in prison. While studying at Morehouse College, an institution related closely to his family, Martin sang in the choir and studied with gifted preacher-intellectuals such as Benjamin E. Mays and George D. Kelsey, experiences which, along with his heavy involvements in the black church, heightened his sense of the spiritual and the artistic and their relationship to the struggle for freedom. Martin's writings, speeches, and sermons in those days suggested that his people had a set core of values—freedom, education, economic justice, race pride, and self-determination—that conflicted on some levels with the cultural ethos embraced by white Americans. In a letter to the *Atlanta Constitution,* the Morehouse sophomore denied that his people's quest for "basic rights and opportunities" resulted from an insatiable appetite for "social mingling and intermarriage" with whites, a point that would eventually become classic in Malcolm's rhetoric.[52]

But Martin stopped short of saying that African Americans had nothing to gain in the realm of values from the larger culture. During his last two years at Morehouse, he appeared as a speaker before the Negro Cultural League in Atlanta, and he wrote at least two essays which suggested that his people had much to gain from the Western intellectual tradition in their struggle for liberation, a position consistent with his growing belief in interracial cooperation. In "The Purpose of Education," which appeared in the January/February 1947 issue of the *Maroon Tiger,* a Morehouse periodical, Martin referred to intellectual freedom as the most reliable path to moral improvement and cultural enrichment, a view that Malcolm later espoused, and one that had significant implications for the character development of African Americans. In another essay, "The Economic Basis of Cultural Conflict," Martin suggested an inseparable link between class and race as cultural norms in America.[53] Evidently, he had come to see that the interrelated problems of racism and economic exploitation provided the key to understanding most of the undesirable aspects of black culture and American culture generally.

The Massachusetts prison system benefited Malcolm in ways that recall Martin's Morehouse experience. Sentenced to ten years for robbery in February 1946 and moved from one state prison to another, Malcolm found in the Norfolk Prison Colony "a culture" that stimulated his thinking around the many critical issues regarding his people's identity and struggle.[54] The young man read voraciously, devoting considerable attention to ancient African history, slavery, and the Negro's historic crusade for equal rights and social justice. Carter G. Woodson's 1922 book, *The Negro in Our History,* and J. A. Rogers's three volumes on *Sex and Race* (1942), gave Malcolm his first sense that human life and civilization had begun with Africans, a perception that grounded him in a certain understanding of African-American culture, one that was not so obvious in the writings of Martin Luther King Jr. at Morehouse.[55]

In their different settings, Malcolm and Martin read some of the same works but arrived at different cultural understandings. A prime source for both was *The Souls of Black Folk* by W.E.B. Du Bois (1903), a work known for its deep probing into the richest veins of black culture. From this source, in conjunction with the writings of Frederick L. Olmstead, Frances Kemble, and Harriet Beecher Stowe, Malcolm learned about the slave experience and about the historical and cultural ties shared by people of African ancestry over time and across geographical lines, but there is no reason to believe that he was influenced in any significant way by Du Bois's affirmation of the African background of the black church and the slave priest. Malcolm the convict, to a much greater degree than Martin the Morehouse student, was prone to view slave religion and the slave preacher as merely products of a brutal system of oppression and not as dimensions of a vital culture with deep roots in Africa. Significantly, Malcolm's trenchant critique of the black church and its leadership and potential actually crystallized and found a sharper focus after he apparently read Du Bois's comments on the artistic, spiritual, and social significance of slave music, the preacher, and the frenzy.[56]

Although surrounded at Morehouse by professors and students who reflected and affirmed the best in black culture, Martin probably would have had as many questions as Malcolm when confronted with Du Bois's claims concerning the African roots of slave religion and art. This would not have been unusual for a young black intellectual at a time when leading scholars saw virtually nothing of intrinsic value in African societies, and when Melville J. Herskovits's groundbreaking research and findings on African survivals in the New World evoked silence in many circles and a barrage of criticism and denial in others.[57] Martin studied both Du Bois's and Herskovits's conclusions on the persistence of African cultural practices and values among his people, and in a paper written at Morehouse he commented on Herskovits's analysis of the ritualistic value of vodun dance in Haitian culture but apparently did not subscribe to any pronounced view of the African cultural heritage. However, Martin clearly responded more affirmatively than Malcolm to the power of folk culture as discussed in *The Souls of Black Folk,* and Martin was particularly intrigued, as he said later, with Du Bois's assertion that his people had "learned to sing that most original of all American music, the Negro spiritual."[58] Martin's more positive response owed much to Du Bois's affirmation of what became essentially "Christian" about black religion and art, a matter that would not have generated any serious interest or pride on Malcolm's part.[59]

The fact that Martin became a Christian minister while still in his teens suggests that he was swept up in the vortex of a culture that Malcolm observed, experienced, and read about but refused to accept on its own terms. Martin's decision to honor "the call to preach" emerged out of a recognition that the church and its leadership were absolutely essential in his people's struggle for human dignity, liberation, and survival. Rejecting this outlook, Malcolm, while still in prison, decided to join Elijah Muhammad's Black Muslim Movement, a nationalistic religion that had rivaled black churches since its origin in 1930. In time, Malcolm, too, became a minister, devoting much time and energy to the Muslims' program for the salvation of black America.[60] The different religions Malcolm and Martin embraced became pivotal forces not only in their analyses of African-American culture but also in the philosophies and methods they later brought to their assault on white cultural domination.

Prison life gave Malcolm a critical perspective on culture that matured and assumed greater clarity through his involvement with the Black Muslims, a perspective that Martin did not get in academic and church settings. Converted to the Black Muslim Movement, commonly called the Nation of Islam, in 1948, Malcolm subjected the whole American system of values to sustained and withering attack, noting that "the average so-called Negro in prison has had experiences enough to make him realize the hypocrisy of everything in this society." Martin was more deeply influenced by Western thought, especially Christian theology and ethics, and this explains why his earliest assessments of culture lacked the critical edge so characteristic of Malcolm's. Steeped in the traditions of the academy and the church, Martin proved more apt than Malcolm to identify the attractive and redeeming features of American culture and, more specifically, African-American culture. This became increasingly clear as Malcolm, after his release from prison, denounced the "Christian" foundations upon which so much of black and white culture was supposedly based.[61]

Martin's travels and studies in the North enlarged his cultural perspective in ways that would not have been possible in Malcolm's more confined prison existence. From the fall of 1948 to the spring of 1951, Martin studied at Crozer Theological Seminary in Chester, Pennsylvania. After graduating from Crozer, he pursued graduate work at Boston University, completing the residential requirements for the doctorate in 1953. Life in Chester and Boston did not lead to a culture shock for Martin, mainly because he lived among blacks who had migrated from the South and who had re-created a southern sense of place in their new environments. Homes rocked with the honest joy of laughter; the elderly delighted in the gifts of folk wit and story; churches shook under the impact of powerful preaching, lively music, personal testifying, and shouting; the rhythms and sounds of jazz and the sorrowful notes of the blues could be heard on sidewalks; and small gardens existed in full view of passersby. Like Malcolm, who benefited from his contacts with black southerners in the North, Martin found much of what he needed for his material well-being and for the quality of his own mind and spirit. Despite the otherwise cautious and impersonal climate of the North, blacks in Chester and Boston gave him a sense of being culturally located in the South.[62]

Martin's experiences and studies in the North helped him to better understand the complex cultural region of the American South, particularly the ambivalent side of southern culture. As he thought about his upbringing in the South, it was clear that he had rarely experienced anything without also encountering its opposite. His family, church, and neighborhood had affirmed his worth and dignity, but white southerners had consistently treated him as if he lacked significance. He had been blessed with an economically secure and comfortable childhood, but he remembered playmates who had endured a life of poverty and insecurity similar to Malcolm's. His father had preached against segregation, while white preachers had sanctioned it even in the church. Memories of a life fraught with such contradictions easily bring to mind the cultural paradox Malcolm faced while growing up among whites in Michigan.[63] But Martin resolved this dialectic in his own experiences in intellectual terms at Crozer Seminary and Boston University, where he read Heraclitus, Georg W. F. Hegel, the Existentialist philosophers, Frederick Douglass, and W.E.B. Du Bois, sources with which Malcolm became somewhat familiar as an inmate and later as a Muslim minister.

The struggle to understand the cultural contradictions and the inner tension Martin had endured as a child proved successful because he interpreted and appropriated Heraclitus, Hegel, and the Existentialists, these white Western sources, in light of his own cultural traditions and experiences as an African American. Heraclitus's contention that justice emerges from the strife of opposites reminded Martin that genuine integration ultimately results from a struggle between the builders of community and the promoters of segregation. Further confirmation of this contention came from Hegel's idea that the path to truth is a progression based on opposites in conflict, thesis and antithesis, an idea that also proved useful to Martin as he reflected on his early experiences of community among blacks and noncommunity with southern whites. The Existentialists provided other answers to the inner tension and confusion Martin felt as a child in the segregated South, for they explained how the existential situation of humans (segregation) so often conflicts with their essential nature (community). The use to which Martin put these sources in developing an understanding of himself and his culture and of the entire history of his people probably would not have been fully understood by a rebellious young man like Malcolm, who approached Western intellectual traditions with much skepticism, particularly in cases where they were employed to explain black people.[64]

It is important to note that Martin did not ignore African-American sources in his effort to grasp in theoretical terms the dialectic that characterized life and culture from his childhood. In Frederick Douglass's claim that struggle is a precondition for progress, Martin discovered echoes of what he learned from Heraclitus and Hegel. Du Bois added to the young man's sense of the dual nature of African-American consciousness in a society that proclaimed freedom and equality of opportunity while upholding inequality and injustice.[65] Malcolm, too, must have found in Du Bois a brilliant explanation for a certain tension with which African Americans had long struggled, but his analysis of the dialectic which had marked his own experiences did not rest heavily on intellectual sources.

Martin's "serious intellectual quest for a method to eliminate social evil" began at Crozer when he was only nineteen. That quest grew directly out of his studies and especially out of the example of his parents and the experiences he had had in the black community of Atlanta. In his application for admission to Crozer in February 1948, Martin spoke of "an inescapable urge to serve society," a longing instilled largely by Morehouse College and the Ebenezer Baptist Church, and one Malcolm never really expressed before becoming a Muslim minister at twenty-eight. In any case, Martin's search for a method to get rid of social evil led him to sources as varied as the philosophy of Friedrich Nietzsche, the ethics of Mohandas Gandhi, and the theologies of Paul Tillich, Anders Nygren, and George W. Davis, but these initially left him with as many questions as they did answers. Martin graduated from Crozer in the spring of 1951, and his intellectual quest became even more serious when he entered the doctoral program in philosophical theology at Boston University in the fall of that year.[66]

That quest was further fueled by Martin's relatives' and friends' expectation that he would achieve greatness and that his future would be linked to better times for his people. His parents had hints of their son's "developing greatness" as early as 1946, when seventeen-year-old Martin "wrote a letter to the editor" of an Atlanta newspaper "which received widespread and favorable comment." In 1950, a Crozer Theological Seminary Placement Committee referred to Martin as "very personable," "a man of high character," and one who "makes a good impression in public in speaking and discussion," and the report concluded that he "should make an excellent minister or teacher." Another version of that same report described Martin as "hardworking" and "fertile minded," and it predicted that he would "probably become a strong man among his people." In 1952, during Martin's second year at Boston, he received a letter from a friend declaring that "we are expecting great things from you."[67] This sense of being the instrument of a special destiny, which for obvious reasons was never associated with young Malcolm, reinforced Martin's sense of obligation toward his people, and it also figured into his perspective on the possible role his people as a whole could play in enlarging the perimeters of the human endeavor.

Questions concerning the ways in which African Americans might best

meet the challenges of racist oppression confronted Martin at Crozer and
Boston with an intensity analogous to Malcolm's intellectual struggle behind
bars. Indeed, Martin's view of his own obligations as a black preacher, and of
his people's capabilities as a humanizing force in the world, assumed greater
clarity as he recalled the writings of W.E.B. Du Bois and as he delved deeper
into Christian theology and ethics. He reacted strongly to Du Bois's contention that African Americans have much to contribute to a better world,
particularly in terms of the spiritual and the artistic. Convinced that "the
character of the Negro race is its best and greatest hope," Du Bois, who
recognized creativity in its highest form in black music and folklore, had
prophesied in 1915 that "the future world will, in all reasonable probability,
be what colored men make it."[68] Du Bois's thoughts on the redeeming power
of black humanity, a feature more than adequately revealed in the folktales,
made far more sense to Martin than they did to Malcolm, who felt, certainly
by the beginning of his ministry in the Nation of Islam, that too many of his
people had surrendered to an inferiority complex that made it impossible for
them to lead the way in the shaping of a new world order.

The messianic role of African Americans, a recurring theme in Du Bois's
works, must have registered with greater force as Martin read and reread
Henry David Thoreau's "Essay on Civil Disobedience" (1848), a treatise
which promoted the idea that history, in the final analysis, is saved by a
creative minority who resists an evil system with the goal of ameliorating it.
Moreover, Thoreau's essay was Martin's "first intellectual contact with the
theory of nonviolent resistance." In time, Martin related Thoreau's ideas to
those of other major thinkers who theorized that the potential of African
Americans as a humanizing force could be actualized through a categorical
rejection of violence. He turned naturally to Gandhi, who speculated that "it
may be through the Negroes that the unadulterated message of nonviolence
will be delivered to the world."[69] A similar perspective emerged through
Martin's reading of Reinhold Niebuhr, who stated in 1932 that the liberation
of black America depended on the adequate development of nonviolent strategy within her ranks.[70] Such ideas would have been casually dismissed by
Malcolm, who was always suspicious of sources that encouraged his people
to be nonviolent in the face of violent oppression.

Be that as it may, reinforcement for Gandhi's and Niebuhr's views came as
Martin studied the writings of the British historian Arnold Toynbee, who
concluded that African Americans had rediscovered "in Christianity certain
original meanings and values" that rendered them capable of injecting "a

new spiritual dynamic into Western civilization."[71] Significantly, the thoughts of Du Bois, Thoreau, Gandhi, Niebuhr, and Toynbee came together in Martin's consciousness at a time when he and Malcolm were not that far apart when considering the best means to achieve black liberation. Questions about the relevance of nonviolence were entertained on some levels by both, thus explaining Martin's refusal to fully commit to that method before 1955.[72]

While at odds over the transforming role African Americans could possibly assume in the world under the power of the Christian faith, Malcolm and Martin, certainly by the mid-1950s, were convinced that their people had to take primary responsibility for liberating themselves. This conviction came naturally to both, despite the fact that Martin was more open than Malcolm to the possibility of white allies in the struggle. The belief that blacks should form the vanguard in their own struggle loomed, along with cultural factors, as vividly in Malcolm's determination to reestablish roots in the black North as they did in Martin's desire to return to the South.[73] These young men had a sense of place and of social responsibility that developed out of their encounters with the folk and with the whole sweep of folk culture. They preferred to return to the environments that they called "home" and to reshape and redefine the institutions and values that gave their lives personal identity and a feeling of being a part of the fullness of African-American peoplehood. But ultimately, Malcolm and Martin were driven not simply by a sense of regional identity and responsibility, the pull of culture, or the need for cultural change, but also by a spiritual bond they shared with black people across generations and geographical boundaries.

On Culture and Liberation: From Theory to Praxis

There was much evidence in the first twenty years of Malcolm's and Martin's lives to indicate that they might become champions of the oppressed. Both showed flashes of brilliance and leadership potential when competing with classmates, and the racial insults they sustained contributed to a restlessness of spirit and an ability to empathize with all who suffered from injustice. Moreover, both demonstrated a critical and questioning attitude toward the established order of things. Such attributes of mind and spirit, which became more evident when they became ministers, all but assured them leadership roles in black America.

Their greatest cultural contributions came in their capacities as religious leaders. Both had established themselves as socially conscious and progressive young ministers when the Supreme Court decision in *Brown v. Board of Education* opened a new era in black protest in 1954. Malcolm was serving Temple Twelve in Philadelphia, and Martin had only recently been named pastor of the Dexter Avenue Baptist Church in Montgomery, Alabama.[74] Malcolm discovered in the temple what Martin found in the church, namely, an arena through which to articulate a fresh cultural vision while encouraging a new social awareness and a sense of the need for cultural transformation. Their impeccable reputations, keen intellects, and deep spiritual lives conspired to make them cultural protagonists among their people and in the society as a whole, but Malcolm's and Martin's activities must be understood in social and political terms as well.[75]

The black freedom struggle of the 1950s and 1960s signaled a shift toward a more vital culture of resistance on the part of African Americans. Possible approaches and solutions to the race problem were widely discussed, leading some to adopt peaceful means and others the idea of armed resistance. This provided the context out of which Martin embraced nonviolence as a personal and social ethic, and Malcolm adopted a more flexible "by any means necessary" ethic, one that sanctioned self-defense or counterviolence in the face of aggressive, unprovoked violence from whites.[76] Their different methods and philosophies seemed inspired chiefly by their contacts over time with black communities. The "Christian stoicism" of the southern Negro community became "the traditional base" on which Martin's message of nonviolence and universal agape love was engrafted, and Malcolm's gospel of retaliatory violence and black self-love arose primarily out of the anguish and impatience of what he labeled "the ghetto-created Negro" in the North, though it is equally true that the values of the black South and the black North came together at many points in the consciousness of both men.[77]

Broad exposure to African Americans from the North and South, and to white racism in its most blatant and subtle forms in both contexts, convinced Malcolm and Martin that the only meaningful freedom is that which a whole people achieve for themselves. Toward this end, they called for broad racial unity and cooperation, a concern raised more consistently by Malcolm given the Nation of Islam's claim that there was no place for whites in the black struggle.[78] Martin translated his call for racial solidarity into practical action through the Montgomery Improvement Association (1955–59), the Southern Christian Leadership Conference (1957–68), and numerous other church-related and secular organizations that accepted contributions from white sources.

Martin and Malcolm carefully considered the range of resources that had to be drawn upon for the liberation of African Americans. They believed that blacks of talent—especially religious leaders, educators, and artists—had a special responsibility to pursue freedom for their people. As they embraced more firmly the view that spiritual values constitute the foundation of black culture, Martin and Malcolm insisted that men of religion, especially those with integrity and vision, had special leadership roles to adopt in the salvation of the masses. Martin's thoughts on this matter centered naturally on black preachers, "men of the cloth" who touched base with the spirituality of their people, and who symbolized the union of the sacred and the secular in black culture. From the beginning of the Montgomery bus boycott in 1955 until his death thirteen years later, the civil rights leader challenged black preachers, through his message and example, to use the pulpit and the spoken word to promote the values of freedom and equality of opportunity, and to lead boycotts, mass demonstrations, civil disobedience campaigns, prayer vigils, and other organized nonviolent movements aimed at the social and economic improvement of the society.[79] Rejecting Martin's perspective on the importance of black preachers in the culture and the struggle, Malcolm focused instead on the benefits of Elijah Muhammad and the Nation of Islam's program of racial separatism, group solidarity, and self-reliance, a program he sought to implement through his own Muslim Mosque, Inc. and the Organization of Afro-American Unity after breaking with Muhammad in 1964.[80]

This emphasis on religious leadership in the struggle grew out of a certain understanding of black history and culture. Both Martin and Malcolm knew that the hopes, aspirations, and sense of destiny of the folk had long been invested largely in the preacher, a premier cultural figure who discovered in Moses, the Hebrew prophets, and Jesus of Nazareth the primary paradigms for his leadership.[81] However, Martin's perception of the black preacher as a powerful, historic symbol of unity and hope, one he struggled to exemplify in his own nonviolent activism against racism, poverty, and war, stirred the imaginations and inspired the activities of African Americans in ways that Malcolm found difficult to accept and, at times, to imagine. Even so, Malcolm's view of the preacher as more of a liability than an asset to his people was not likely to be casually dismissed in a culture where attitudes toward "men of the cloth" ranged from deep admiration to suspicion to outright hostility.[82]

Martin's image of the preacher as an activist and unifying influence recalled not only the reflections of W.E.B. Du Bois and James Weldon Johnson on that phenomenal figure, but also slave tales in which Brer Rabbit frequently personified the religious leader, "the defender of the interests of the weak and defenseless."[83] Despite their different religious affiliations, Martin and Malcolm stood squarely in the tradition of the Negro preacher. Using persuasive and fluent discourse and an amazing sweep of images and symbols, they related the Bible, the most cherished book in the culture, to the contemporary realities of black existence, thus reflecting Johnson's image of the preacher as "a master of all the modes of eloquence" and Du Bois's portrait of that figure as "one who rudely but picturesquely expressed the longing, disappointment, and resentment of a stolen and oppressed people." Like the preacher in the works of Johnson and Du Bois, and like Brer Rabbit in the tales of the Reverend William John Faulkner, Martin and Malcolm spoke the language of the disenfranchised, articulated concerns that were primarily ethical in nature, and assumed functions that principally involved the advancement of communal consciousness and liberation. In a real sense, both personified Du Bois's challenge to African Americans to become "missionaries of culture."[84]

Martin's and Malcolm's charge to black intellectuals appeared all the more meaningful in view of their own roles as educators. They knew the value of education as an avenue to freedom, and both included a strong educational component in their strategies for cultural revitalization and social change.[85] Convinced that racial discrimination contributed tremendously to a poor quality of education for blacks and whites, Martin declared in 1964 that the Negro "must press unrelentingly for quality, integrated education or his whole drive for freedom will be undermined by the absence of a most vital and indispensable element—learning." A year later he labeled education "a primary concern of the civil rights movement," and counseled black intellectuals to show loyalty to their people. Malcolm fully agreed, indicating, as Martin often did, that the lack of education accounted in large measure for the disunity and self-hatred among African Americans. The two leaders clearly understood the dilemma confronting black intellectuals in the culture, but Malcolm complained that the small number of African Americans in this category, due to their own miseducation, class consciousness, and fear of economic reprisals, were ill prepared to devote themselves whole-heartedly and in creative ways to the struggle. While offering his own assessment of the dilemma, Malcolm asked, "Do you realize this is one of the major reasons why America's white man has so easily contained and oppressed America's black man? Because until just lately, among the few educated Negroes scarcely any applied their education, as I am forced to say the white man does—in searching and creative thinking, to further themselves and their own kind in this competitive, materialistic, dog-eat-dog white man's world."[86]

For Malcolm and Martin, black intellectuals had to accept as a primary obligation the rewriting of history, especially since white scholars had for so long denied black humanity and the rich and varied contributions of people of African ancestry to world civilization. Both had an intense interest in history, particularly the history of their people. Convinced that "the number one thing that makes us differ from other people is our lack of knowledge concerning the past," Malcolm held that a proper reexamination of history, beginning with Africa and not with American slavery, would show that his ancestors were the first to forge high levels of culture and civilization, particularly "in Egypt along the banks of the Nile." His conclusions concerning the place of the Negro in Egyptian civilization reinforced the earlier findings of W.E.B. Du Bois and Cheikh Anta Diop and anticipated the arguments of contemporary Afrocentrists and some Egyptologists.[87]

The extent to which Martin embraced this view of human civilization is not known, but he did share Malcolm's view that a reinterpretation of Africa's role in ancient history is essential for black self-esteem and elevation. Both men knew that Du Bois, who epitomized for them the intellectual-activist type, had pioneered in recapturing Africa's importance in world history and civilization, a contribution that made him a model for younger scholars seeking their place in the struggle. But Malcolm appeared at times to be less optimistic than Martin regarding the possibility of young black scholars assuming vital and productive roles in the quest for liberation and uplift.[88] Referring to black intellectuals as "trained black puppets" and "Ph.D. house and yard Negroes," the Black Muslim leader questioned the depth of their knowledge and their ability to inspire the type of critical thinking needed to enhance black self-confidence and autonomy:

History has been so "whitened" by the white man that even black professors have known little more than the most ignorant black man about the talents and rich civilizations and cultures of the black man of millenniums ago. I have lectured in Negro colleges and some of these brainwashed Ph.D.'s, with their suspenders dragging the ground with degrees, have run to the white man's newspapers calling me a "black fanatic." Why, a lot of them are fifty years behind the times. If I were president of one of these black colleges, I'd hock the campus if I had to, to send a bunch of black students off digging in Africa for more, more and more proof of the black race's historical greatness.[89]

The need for a new culture of learning consistent with the emerging spirit of resistance led Malcolm and Martin to advocate that black studies programs be instituted in the nation's colleges and universities. Each had carefully studied and reappraised the intellectual climate by the mid-1960s, and each felt that programs of this nature could be enormously beneficial for both blacks and whites. But Malcolm insisted that such programs had to move far beyond the focus on the traditional Negro History Week, which "reminds us only of the achievements we made in the Western Hemisphere under the tutelage of the white man."[90] In keeping with Malcolm's concern and with the idea that no American should be deprived of knowledge of African-American history, Martin called for "freedom schools" and "black cultural events" as a part of his proposed Poor People's Campaign in early 1968. He desired to educate the whole country concerning poets like Countee Cullen and Langston Hughes, philosophers such as Alaine Locke and W.E.B. Du Bois, scientists like George Washington Carver, and the "great jazz, blues," and other forms of music that "made America beautiful." For Martin, such efforts were necessary to counter the arguments of those who "have made us feel that we haven't done anything for the history and culture of the world." In their support for a black studies movement, Martin and Malcolm prefigured later debates concerning the merits of diversity and multicultural education.[91]

For black artists, the two leaders envisioned roles not far removed from those expected of religious leaders and educators in the community. Both saw black artists as potential jewels in the arsenal of social protest, a view which explains in large measure the admiration and respect that both had for James Baldwin, Dick Gregory, and Harry Belafonte. Martin saw the need for writers, singers, dancers, actors, and other artists to be involved at all levels of the freedom movement, for it was evident to him that art could not be logically separated from the moral, spiritual, and intellectual resources required to overcome oppression. For Martin, those resources were present in abundance in the church and in the literature, music, and oral traditions of the folk.[92] While agreeing that black artists on the whole represented some hope for their people, Malcolm thought nevertheless that too many had bowed to habits and roles imposed on them by white society, instead of relying on their own special genius. This is why he characterized some of the most celebrated black comics, musicians, and dancers in his time as "not leaders" but "puppets and clowns who are put before the Negro by white liberals." As far as Malcolm was concerned, African Americans deserved more:

> Our artists—we have artists who are geniuses; they don't have to act the Stepin Fetchit role. But as long as they're looking for white support instead of black support, they've got to act like the old white supporter wants them to. When you and I begin to support the black artists, then the black artists can play that black role. As long as the black artist has to sing and dance to please the white man, he'll be a clown, he'll be clowning, just another clown. But when he can sing and dance to please black men, he sings a different song and dances a different step. When we get together, we've got a step all our own. We have a step that nobody can do but us, because we have a reason for doing it that nobody can understand but us.[93]

The talents of black artists had to find a more independent, practical, and effective means of expression, considering the realities of oppression before them. Malcolm and Martin did not differ substantially on this point. For both, the need for black artists to be true to themselves and to set their own standards could not have been more pressing, especially since culture was the one sphere in which African Americans had the freedom to excel as creators and protagonists. Convinced that there was no great reward in "copying some European cultural pattern or some European cultural standard," Malcolm insisted, as did Martin at times, that the Negro needed "an atmosphere of complete freedom where he has the right, the leeway, to bring out of himself all of that dormant, hidden talent that has been there for so long." He continued:

> And in that atmosphere, brothers and sisters, you'd be surprised what will come out of the bosom of this black man. I've seen it happen. I've seen black musicians when they'd be jamming at a jam session with white musicians—a whole lot of difference. The white musician can jam if he's got some sheet music in front of him. He can jam on something that he's heard jammed before. If he's heard it, then he can duplicate it or he can imitate it or he can read it. But that black musician, he

picks up his horn and starts blowing some sounds that he never thought of before. He improvises, he creates, it comes from within. It's his soul, it's that soul music. It's the only area on the American scene where the black man has been free to create. And he has mastered it.[94]

But Malcolm's problems with the black church and the more celebrational aspects of folk culture, particularly during his years with the Black Muslims, made it impossible for him to fully accept black art on its own terms, a struggle Martin never really had as a civil rights leader. Malcolm often proved less receptive than Martin to black people's keen sense and gift of rhythm, their love of music and dance, and their tendency toward emotional and expressive religiosity, which was ironic since Martin was more the polished intellectual-type so commonly associated with a rejection of the emotive and aesthetic qualities of the black masses. Even so, Martin agreed with Malcolm concerning the need for African Americans to "improve our cultural standards."[95]

Occasionally, Malcolm displayed a strong tendency to identify some of the most vital aspects of black art with mere entertainment and not with activities designed to force revolutionary change, a propensity quite understandable for one so sensitive to stereotypes aimed at black people. This could explain why he scoffed at African Americans who dared to sing their anthems and spirituals while participating in mass demonstrations for justice. "Whoever heard of a revolution where they lock arms" singing "We Shall Overcome"? Malcolm lamented in his "Message to the Grassroots" in Detroit in November 1963. And in words that Martin would have found disturbing, he added: "You don't do any singing; you're too busy swinging."[96] A few months later, Malcolm was equally blunt at a party given in his honor in Ghana, where he and others "arrived to warm hand shakes, drum rolls, shouts of praise and music from the open air dance floor." Apparently perturbed as he witnessed Africans and black Americans "moving sensually to the rhythms of the High Life, West Africa's most popular dance," Malcolm, when asked to speak, commented: "I do not want you to think that because I have been sitting here quietly, that I do not appreciate your invitation. The fact is, I am in no mood to dance. I think of our brothers and sisters at home, squirming under the heel of racial oppression, and I do not care to dance. I think of our brothers and sisters in the Congo, squirming under the heel of imperialist invasion, and I do not care to dance. I think of our brothers and sisters in Southern Africa squirming under the heel of apartheid, and I do not care to dance."[97]

Seeing no necessary disjunction between their gaiety and their devotion to the struggle, the crowd greeted Malcolm's words with astonishment, and "a few disapproving murmurs could be heard." "Fortunately, Malcolm's speech was brief," recounts Maya Angelou, the gifted writer who was also present, "and when the orchestra returned the celebrants crowded again onto the floor, dancing, flirting, wiggling and inviting."[98] Malcolm's seemingly ambivalent attitude toward the more celebrative or festive side of black culture, and his occasional failure to properly connect this with the spirit of freedom and with the ongoing quest for racial pride, uplift, and autonomy, were factors that kept him from clearly comprehending the struggle in its wholeness. This was not so true of Martin, who, despite his ties to the church, came to see dance as one expression of black freedom—as another aspect of that determination of the body and soul to break free and to express themselves despite what white society thinks. This explains why the civil rights leader, even in the heat of battle, took time to attend parties, to dance, and to celebrate in other ways.[99]

The rich store of artistic, spiritual, and intellectual resources that empowered the drive toward freedom in the 1950s and 1960s owed much to the wisdom literature and the spiritual and emotional heritage of the slaves. Martin became more convinced of this than Malcolm, who exemplified the ironic tendency that Sterling Stuckey attributes to most black nationalists in our history, namely, the tendency to underestimate the depths of African culture in black society and the sophistication of the slave community from which it developed.[100] Unlike Malcolm, who felt that the tragic circumstances of slavery could not have led to great creativity in the cultural sphere, Martin saw the massive protests of the 1950s and 1960s as essentially an affirmation and extension of the artistic and spiritual values of the slaves, whose pain and struggle are "mirrored artistically in the unique work songs, protest songs, and spirituals of the Negro." For Martin, the relationship between art and freedom, like that between art and labor, could not be comprehended apart from a serious consideration of the creative genius of his slave forebears, whose songs inspired the modern civil rights movement:

In a sense the freedom songs are the soul of the movement. They are more than just incantations of clever phrases designed to invigorate a campaign; they are as old as the history of the Negro in America. They are adaptations of the songs the slaves sang—the sorrow songs, the shouts for joy, the battle hymns and the anthems of our movement. I have heard people talk of their beat and rhythm, but we in the movement are as inspired by their words. "Woke Up This Morning with My Mind Stayed on Freedom" is a sentence that needs no music to make its point. We sing the freedom songs today for the same reason the slaves sang them, because we too are in bondage and the songs add hope to our determination that "We shall overcome, Black and white together, we shall overcome someday."[101]

Malcolm never fully comprehended the powerful and intimate relationship between slave art and the more contemporary movement for black liberation. He seemingly assumed a necessary dichotomy between tragedy and creativity, that pain cannot be the catalyst for great art, particularly in the case of the slaves, whose African identity and culture were, in his estimation, completely obliterated. Small wonder that Malcolm, again in striking contrast to Martin, failed to grasp the full significance of the gospel songs of Mahalia Jackson and Thomas Dorsey, and the soul music and dance of performers like James Brown and Aretha Franklin, as critical aspects of the spiritual and cultural thrust of the freedom movement. This was most obvious during Malcolm's years with the Black Muslims, who were known to listen to jazz "without ostensible response to the rhythm."[102]

Malcolm seemed considerably more perceptive when assessing the value of black literature as an inspiration in the freedom struggle. His lofty view of James Baldwin, W.E.B. Du Bois, Ralph Ellison, Langston Hughes, J. A. Rogers, and countless others, whose ideas became a weapon in the assault on social injustice, owed much to the Nation of Islam's tendency to assign a higher value to the intellectual than to black art and institutions. Malcolm and Martin treasured these writers' perspectives on the black condition. Both found innovative and sustaining power through appeals to the works of black literary giants, works which treated questions of race and civil rights with candor and prophetic insight.[103]

Malcolm was often more adamant than Martin in stressing the need for African Americans to pursue a more viable cultural path in their struggle. The Muslim leader had in mind a more liberating existence and a means of transmitting the values of freedom, resistance, self-defense, and self-determination from one generation to another, a vision he sought to actualize first through the Nation of Islam and later through his Muslim Mosque, Inc. and the Organization of Afro-American Unity. "Such a cultural revolution," as Malcolm termed it in 1964, had to be centered in the black community, "for it is our home" and "the base of our power." Malcolm continued: "It must begin in the community and be based on community participation. Afro-

Americans will be free to create only when they can depend on the Afro-American community for support, and Afro-American artists must realize that they depend on the Afro-American community for inspiration."[104]

This essential link between group solidarity and culture seemed no less important to Martin, though he did acknowledge a shared history and culture with whites around him, despite the physical barriers imposed by racism and segregation. But Malcolm, determined to overcome white cultural hegemony and to reach black cultural independence, called for the development of a more positive black identity and race consciousness. "A race of people is like an individual man," he observed. "Until it uses its own talents, takes pride in its own history, expresses its own culture, affirms its own selfhood, it can never fulfill itself." And, further on, as part of his program for the Organization of Afro-American Unity, Malcolm stated, "We must recapture our heritage and our identity if we are to liberate ourselves from the bonds of white supremacy. . . . This cultural revolution will be the journey to our rediscovery of ourselves." This charge to the race, made as the smoldering fires of discontent erupted in America's ghettoes, evoked full agreement from Martin, whose Southern Christian Leadership Conference stood as a symbol of black awareness and of the strengths of the folk heritage. "We have a rich and noble heritage," Martin explained in 1966, and "I think it's absolutely necessary for the Negro to have an appreciation of his heritage."[105]

But the ultimate objective of the cultural revolution, as Malcolm understood it, presented problems for moderate civil rights leaders like Martin. That objective required blacks in America to assume roles truly reflective of their African heritage, a process which Malcolm, as a Black Muslim minister, deemed possible only if his people emigrated to Africa or established a separate nation within the boundaries of the United States. Malcolm was not always clear on what constituted the essentials of that heritage, although he had begun to say, by 1964, when he had severed his link with the Black Muslims, that his people should take on African names, hairstyles, dress codes, and ways of viewing themselves and the world. This was his idea of blacks migrating "back to Africa culturally, philosophically and psychologically, while remaining here physically."[106] The idea that black Americans could return to Africa in any fashion at all seemed improbable and perhaps even impractical for Martin, who held that black nationalism was "based on an unrealistic and sectional perspective" that he had "condemned both publicly and privately." Moreover, Martin insisted that his people had established deep roots in the United States and that they should press their claims as Americans by continuing the struggle to eliminate racism.[107]

Although Martin and Malcolm regarded the African-American community and its culture as the source of their identity, they often clashed over what this meant in terms of their cultural relationship with whites. Martin stressed the biracial aspects of American culture as a product of the interactions of blacks and whites, insisting that each had influenced the other in the areas of religion, language, literature, art, material culture, and values in general, a position that undergirded his rejection of back-to-Africa movements as well as his efforts to move America from a segregated to an integrated and culturally inclusive society. This does not negate the fact that Martin believed that "in so many respects, the quality of the black people's scale of values was far superior to that of the white culture which attempted to enslave us."[108] Less comfortable with the notion of a shared culture with white people, Malcolm was more likely to argue that African Americans, when true to themselves, are closer to Africa culturally than to their oppressors. Thus he counseled his people to "hold fast to and nurture their own black culture, and not have it 'integrated out of existence.'" He wanted his people to find their place in a unified African culture, a culture that drew on the best sensibilities, talents, and values of African people throughout the world. And, as suggested already, Malcolm never realized the degree to which the foundation for such a Pan-African culture existed in New World slavery.[109]

Despite their differences over how African Americans should view themselves in relation to the larger society and culture, Malcolm and Martin found affinity in their prophetic critiques of white culture. Both rejected in principle and practice the white supremacist doctrines, the violence, and the excessive individualism, secularism, and materialism of that culture. In their estimation, sweeping cultural changes were necessary to save white America from tragic self-destruction. Malcolm ultimately decided that perhaps such changes would be possible if whites embraced Islam, a religion which he felt respected cultural diversity and encouraged a more genuine spirit of human community than Christianity. In a different vein, Martin believed that the salvation of white culture depended upon a deeper and more conscious devotion to the democratic ideal and to the practical application of Christian principles in daily life.[110]

Martin and Malcolm knew that the cultural changes of the 1950s and 1960s did not stem from their activities alone. They realized that they were part of a movement much larger than themselves and that the rise of blacks and whites to new heights of maturation testified to the contributions of many who went unnoticed and unrewarded. They were constantly reminded of local, grassroots figures, organizations, and institutions that sustained black protest even when the goal of freedom seemed hopelessly out of reach. And perhaps more important, they understood that the courage they displayed and the resources they expended in challenging America's racism were not unprecedented in history—that they stood on the shoulders of generations of black men and women who had died for the cause. Martin's "sense of history was both keen and intense," writes John Hope Franklin. "Even as he spurned Nat Turner's recourse to physical violence, he knew how to channel the outrage on which it fed into the massive but peaceful protests" of his own time. By contrast, Malcolm proudly identified with Turner's use of violence to win freedom, and he knew how to transform the anger and frustration that motivated Turner and other nationalists who preceded him into fearless rhetoric and militant action in the ghettoes, thus preparing the ground for the rise of black power in the late 1960s.[111]

The cultural perspectives of Martin and Malcolm were never limited to the particularities of the African-American experience. The range of their perspectives covered the world, for both believed that their people should play a part in the reshaping of cultural systems wherever injustice existed. They knew the plight of the oppressed worldwide, and they wanted ultimately to see humans striving for cultural and spiritual values that would not be confined by narrow considerations of race, class, and nationality.[112]

Preeminent Symbols of the Nation: Malcolm and Martin as Cultural Icons

Death at the hands of assassins clothed Malcolm and Martin in martyrdom and earned them a secure place in history. Malcolm was killed on February 21, 1965, and Martin on April 4, 1968, and the eventual rise of both to cult-figure status could only be expected in a capitalist society where the competitive spirit is encouraged and where heroes are indispensable. But despite the strong tendencies of many toward the veneration of both men, there is no clear public understanding of their meaning and significance for us today.[113]

Many competing images of Malcolm and Martin have emerged over time in the media, the academy, and the public imagination. Among the most prominent are Malcolm and Martin as heroes and saints, as public moralists, as victims and vehicles of psychohistorical and psychosocial forces, and as revolutionary figures. But the personalities of the two men were too complex, the messages they shared too broad, the movements they led too challenging and controversial, and the places they hold in history too important to be subjected to any narrow cultural definitions.[114]

The problems involved in defining Malcolm and Martin remain most evident in black America. Nothing could be expected more in a culture that embraces a range of opinions, traditions, and practices. From the points of Malcolm's and Martin's assassinations, African Americans have differed over the question of their intellectual meaning and cultural significance. Conservative black voices have emerged over time to distort the meaning of their ideas and to question their motives, the relevance of their activities, the wisdom of their tactics, and the value and extent of their contributions to society. This trend is vividly reflected in the writings of the noted columnist Carl T. Rowan, who denounced Malcolm as "a racial fanatic," as "no great hero of mine," as one who "saw the salvation of blacks in 'separatism,'" and as the godfather of "a feeble 'revolution' run by the likes of Rap Brown and Stokely Carmichael."[115] Unfortunately, the same levels of misunderstanding and lack of comprehension are apparent not only in Joseph H. Jackson's portrait of Martin as one who carried on a militant campaign "against his own denomination and his own race" but also in Glenn C. Loury's, Ward Connerly's, and Supreme Court Justice Clarence Thomas's tendency to invoke Martin's famous exhortation to judge individuals by the content of their character rather than race as a profound rejection of affirmative action.[116]

The ideological chasms between black militants and black conservatives have so often been reflected in the different ways in which both view Malcolm and Martin. Since the mid-1960s, some militants in the African-American community have delighted in casting Malcolm and Martin in the antagonistic roles of fearless black revolutionary and impotent Uncle Tom. Black conservatives have countered by portraying Malcolm as a classic demagogue who expounded outlandish theories of race in a period of renewed optimism and cultural change and Martin as a responsible leader who freed many Americans from a narrow racial provincialism. While such images do not capture the spirits of these phenomenal figures, they do speak to Malcolm's and Martin's remarkable ability to enter the minds and emotions of the black masses.[117]

Most African Americans have developed more positive and realistic images of Malcolm and Martin as cultural spokesmen and as critics of culture, and they appeal to Malcolm's and Martin's blackness and bouts with racism as the basis of their strict identification with them. Throughout black America, streets, parks, schools, libraries, community centers, public housing developments, social service and cultural centers, and works of art bear Malcolm's and Martin's names.[118] Their pictures hang on the walls of countless homes in black neighborhoods, lines from their speeches are included in rap and gospel lyrics, and their names and words are marketed in numerous business ventures and branded on hats and T-shirts worn by African Americans of every age and gender. They are commemorated with worship services, speeches, workshops, and political action, and their birthdays are considered occasions for sober reflections on and serious recommitment to the cause of freedom.[119] For so many African Americans, Malcolm and Martin have achieved mythic stature because they advocated and fought for the reshaping of a culture that had long been seriously marred by racist oppression and bloodsucking capitalism.

The ways in which Malcolm and Martin continue to stir emotions of African Americans should be expected in a culture where many have always called metaphorically for a Moses to lead their people out of bondage. For so many of their people, Malcolm and Martin are not simply great, charismatic leaders who stand in a grand tradition of black heroism dating back to slavery and beyond; they are also messiahs who appeal to their ethnic chauvinism and their millennial enthusiasm and hope.[120] In other words, they were men called and commissioned by God to contribute to the fulfillment of the black messianic hope.

The symbolic meaning and significance of Malcolm and Martin for America as a whole remain largely unrecognized because of the mass confusion and ambiguity that exist among whites regarding their identities. For most white Americans, Malcolm was a curious, rather mad black leader preoccupied with a hatred that bordered on the pathological, an image not easily shattered despite mountains of evidence to the contrary.[121] Although most whites regard Martin as less extreme, he, too, remains controversial because of his persistent assault on white supremacy and capitalism. Furthermore, white society is still determined to forget his challenge to America's economic injustice and wars of aggression, even as it honors him as an official national hero. Because of the confusing and ambiguous message surrounding white America's celebration of Martin's birthday, Vincent Harding labels the civil rights leader "the inconvenient hero."[122]

But Martin has become in some ways white America's "convenient hero." While publicly despising and ridiculing Malcolm, representatives of the feminist movement, the peace movement, and gay rights continue to appeal to the power of Martin's movement and the magic of his words to advance their cause. Pro-life advocates on the religious and political right proudly claim that their protests against abortion "follow in the tradition of Martin Luther King Jr.'s civil rights movement," a claim quite ironic given their tendency to support the death penalty and to ignore the problem of racism and its impact on society.[123] White ministers, who questioned the wisdom of Martin's activism in the 1950s and 1960s, now uphold the validity of church involvement in public affairs, even if that involvement requires acts of civil disobedience. Conservative white politicians even draw on Martin's ideas in their attacks on affirmative action, noting that "skin color should make no difference in this country."[124] As Theodore Pappas has noted, there are neoconservatives "who tolerate no criticism of King, no matter how tempered or just, because King is their new-found champion of conservatism."[125] Concerned about both the conservative and liberal views of the civil rights leader, William R. Jones has said the following concerning white America's "bewildering way of praising King," its "ideological abuse of King's deeds and doctrine" while negating his dream, and its tendency to stress "King's mystical authority as the Black Messiah" when confronted with militants like Malcolm:

> Black leaders are indexed as militant or violent, not on the basis of their actual thought and deeds but by virtue of how far they strayed from King's footsteps. Because he localized nonviolence and vicarious suffering as the heart of Christian faith, other black interpretations of the gospel are suspect. Whites incessantly pressed his philosophy of non-violence upon blacks—when faced with the alternative of a Malcolm X—as the exclusive strategy for economic, social and political change. Yet when King was consistent and advanced the same policy for Americans in Vietnam, he was dropped like a hot potato. This ideological abuse of King's thought should be a hint to all to scrutinize carefully the heroines and heroes that those in seats of power place on a pedestal for us. Behind the facade of praise may be another Trojan horse to further the oppression of those for whom King gave his life to liberate. All this generates for me the nagging suspicion that white America desires to perpetuate a black hero who fits its special needs of oppression and not those of black liberation. White adoration of King secures him more as a guardian of white interest than as a black Moses to lead his people to freedom. Moreover, and here I must be blunt, there are serious, indeed fatal defects in King's thought that sabotage any hope that he can be the theological alpha and omega for blacks.[126]

For many African Americans, this tendency to choose Martin over Malcolm is still reflective of the white power structure's approach to black leadership. Those like Ward Connerly, Clarence Thomas, and J. C. Watts, who oppose affirmative action and support a white conservative political agenda, are embraced and applauded, while those such as Al Sharpton and Louis Farrakhan, who are uncompromising and prophetic in their work for black liberation, are shunned and unmercifully castigated.[127]

All celebrations of Malcolm's and Martin's heroism should be inspired by a sense of how fundamentally *American* they were in their outlooks and aspirations, despite their basic disagreements with the American society. Both struggled for the expansion of American democracy. Both represented the brightest and best in the American tradition of dissent and protest, and they showed the nation, through the beauty of their social witness, the hideous and inhuman face of racism. Special recognition of Martin's significance along these lines came in October 1983, when the U.S. Senate voted overwhelmingly to make his birthday a federal holiday. Efforts to secure such a holiday in Malcolm's honor have not materialized, despite the fact that he was as zealous as Martin in challenging America to live out the true meaning of her creed.[128]

In the late 1980s, renewed interest in Malcolm and Martin surfaced as part of a larger reexamination of the modern civil rights movement and its continuing impact on American life and culture. Malcolm finally received recognition previously denied, and Martin was subjected to more intense levels of critical scrutiny. Writers described in glowing and sometimes painful terms Malcolm's "cultural rebirth," a renaissance clearly witnessed by 1990 by personalities as varied as filmmakers, politicians, and artists in hip-hop culture.[129] While Martin still evoked admiration and reverence in numerous circles, Malcolm became "the liberator of black pride," "a prophet of rage," "a symbol of achievement for the black underclass," or "the romantic hero that young African Americans of spirit" were encouraged to emulate. In the early 1990s, persons of every age, race, gender, and class studied Malcolm's life and work, rap artists evoked his words, his image flashed in music videos, his face peered sternly from bags, T-shirts, and jackets, the X symbol appeared on buttons and baseball and knitted caps, and his slogans "No sellout" and "By any means necessary" assumed the dimensions of commandments. This display of Malcolmania had clearly faded by the end of the century, when Michael E. Dyson raised eyebrows with his strong claim that Martin had much in common with Tupac Shakur, Biggie Smalls, and others in the hip-hop culture and generation.[130]

Significantly, this revived interest in and focus on Malcolm undermined emerging efforts by the press and misguided scholars to further discredit him.[131] Moreover, "Malcolm's cultural renaissance" came at the very time that Martin's symbolic importance was being questioned due to mounting charges of promiscuity and plagiarism.[132] As critics raved about Malcolm's dubious impact in life and Martin's moral and intellectual failures, some Americans engaged in the senseless endeavor of trying to make one man better and more acceptable than the other. Such efforts were obviously driven by a curious and complex mixture of crass commercialism and power politics. According to some scholars, this strange mixture has become glaringly evident in the King family's commercialization of Martin. In the late 1980s and the 1990s, the King family was accused of trying to control Martin's life story and legacy by engaging in a legal battle to get his personal papers returned to the King Center in Atlanta from Boston University, by legally campaigning to enforce strict copyrights on his intellectual property, by collecting exorbitant fees for commercial use of his image, by publicly breaking with the National Park Service over how best to celebrate his legacy, and by making a deal with Time Warner to promote his legacy in multimedia sources ranging from books and audiotapes to cyberspace. Accused of reducing Martin to a commodity for profit, the Kings are still at odds with critics over how to preserve the civil rights leader's cultural significance. But criticism of the Kings is not likely to gain wide support in a racist society that has long exploited the talents and contributions of black athletes and musicians. The feeling among many is that some will automatically profit from Martin's legacy and that no one is more worthy of this than his family.[133]

Malcolm's surge in popularity in the early 1990s appealed to black cultural artists in ways that have never been so evident in the case of Martin. This was especially true of young black filmmakers. Spike Lee's $34 million film biography of Malcolm illustrates the point. Michael Dyson is right in saying that "Lee's film has contributed significantly to the renewed heroism of Malcolm X among black and other Americans." But the portrayal of Malcolm in the film, despite Denzel Washington's "riveting performance," has caused far more controversy than Paul Winfield's dramatic representation of Martin in an earlier movie. Writers, social critics, and cultural pacesetters such as Amiri Baraka and Nikki Giovanni have denied the value of Lee's film not only as a depiction of Malcolm's life but also as a cultural and educational vehicle.[134] At the other extreme, some black writers and educators have praised the film as "a powerful message from Malcolm X," a device to "stimulate black studies," and a possible "impetus for a cinematic movement for black directors."[135]

Considering the many artistic and political barriers Spike Lee had to transcend in order to achieve his goal, one might agree with Dyson's assertion that the Malcolm film is "the most important cultural representation of the black cultural hero yet created." It added fervor to the phenomenon of "Malcolmania" and inspired other efforts to capture Malcolm on film. It encouraged a strong but brief flurry of interest in Malcolm. Unfortunately, the hype for the film has faded, reinforcing fears that Malcolm would "become a fad."[136] Even so, artists in the film industry must dedicate themselves to building on Spike Lee's work, not by demonizing Malcolm and sanitizing Martin, but by offering portrayals of both that will enlighten all Americans and lead them to recommit themselves to the achievement of the democratic ideal. This is part of the challenge that America faces at the beginning of this new century and millennium.

The nation must move beyond celebrations of Malcolm's and Martin's memory to achieve the ends for which they so gallantly fought. Anything less will amount to a failure to truly honor them. While recognizing that Malcolm and Martin did not provide solutions to all of our problems, Americans who believe in freedom must ask themselves continuously: What are the enduring lessons of Malcolm's and Martin's lives? In what vital, liberating ways can we learn from and build on their legacies? How relevant will their visions of freedom and justice be in the twenty-first century? Solid answers to these questions will come only if we approach Malcolm and Martin discerningly and critically, and if we resolve to remain true to their cherished dreams and their brave and invincible spirits.

Malcolm and Martin will always have different meanings for different people. Fixed one-dimensional images of them are not possible in a nation where both are viewed with a strange mixture of respect and disdain and where the mere mention of their names will continue to ignite deep, conflicting passions. Some will continue to regard Malcolm and Martin as great heroic figures, and others will reduce them to tragic enigmas. For many, Malcolm will remain the misguided, raving lunatic, and Martin the gentle, harmless crusader.[137] Still others will refuse to judge them on anything less than their entire lives. As symbols, they will remain as fluid or mutable as the culture that produced them.

2

Al-Qur'an and Sunnah

From Malcolm X to El-Hajj Malik El-Shabazz

O humankind, we have created you from a single pair of a male and a female and made you into families and nations that ye may know each other (not that you may despise each other). Verily, the most honored of you in the sight of Allah is the one who is the most righteous.
Al-Qur'an[1]

My religious pilgrimage (Hajj) to Mecca has given me a new insight into the true brotherhood of Islam, which encompasses all races of mankind. The pilgrimage broadened my scope, my outlook, and made me more flexible in approaching life's many complexities and in my reactions to its paradoxes.
El Hajj Malik El-Shabazz[2]

Through our scientific genius we have made of the world a neighborhood; now through our moral and spiritual genius we must make of it a brotherhood.
Martin Luther King Jr.[3]

In the Name of Allah, Most Gracious, Most Merciful. . . . There is no god but Allah. The God of Absolute and Pure Monotheism with no associates: "Say: He is Allah, The One and Only; Allah, the Eternal, Absolute; He begets not, Nor is He begotten; And there is none Like unto Him."
Al-Qur'an[4]

On January 20, 1999, the U.S. Postal Service introduced a stamp commemorating an influential leader, Malcolm X, whose "controversial ideas sharpened America's debate about racial relations and strategies for social change." Postal bulletin 21988 noted that the photograph featured on the stamp had been taken by the Associated Press on May 21, 1964. The stamp had the name Malcolm X in large letters and El-Hajj Malik El-Shabazz in small letters, which demonstrates an awareness of the transformation of his religious beliefs and his cultural and political ideology. Also, the photograph was taken after he had left the Nation of Islam (NOI) and completed his famous Hajj, or pilgrimage to Mecca, in April 1964.[5] El-Shabazz has finally received the mainstream recognition that Martin Luther King Jr. has always enjoyed. Perhaps this symbolic statement will generate a new and broader dialogue about his universal Islamic beliefs, thoughts, and values.[6]

Malcolm and the Islamic Faith in Proper Context

This chapter will examine the life of Malcolm X through the lenses of the Qur'an and the Sunnah. The Qur'an, the sacred text revealed to Prophet Muhammad Ibn Abdullah (pbuh)[7] between 610 and 632, and the Sunnah, or the methodology used by the Prophet (pbuh) in the application of these divine and universal principles, are the absolute primary sources for defining and interpreting the religion of Islam and the prescribed codes of conduct for Muslims. Therefore, these authoritative canons will be used as the interpretive model to analyze the religious evolution of Malcolm X from his stage of false consciousness in the Nation of Islam to his conversion to Sunni or mainstream Islam.[8] Moreover, this standard will be used to evaluate Malcolm's personality, intellect, behavior, and spirituality.

Islam is an Arabic word that means "total submission to the Will of Allah." According to the Islamic scholar Abul A'La Mawdudi, "It is derived from two root-words: one 'Salm,' meaning peace, and the other 'Silm,' meaning submission. Islam stands for 'a commitment to surrender one's will to the Will of God,' and thus to be at peace with the Creator and with all that has been created by Him. It is through submission to the Will of God that peace is brought about."[9]

Malcolm's consciousness evolved in three distinct stages: (1) Jahiliyah (Days of Ignorance), (2) False Consciousness (Nation of Islam), and (3) Allah Consciousness (Taqwa) or True Consciousness. Each stage was marked by a name change. Malcolm Little was the stage of Jahiliyah, Malcolm X the stage of False Consciousness, and El-Hajj Malik El-Shabazz the stage of Allah Consciousness. It is important that scholars and admirers of Malcolm X begin referring to him as El-Shabazz because he left the Nation of Islam, absolutely and totally repudiated and rejected its theology, and is believed to have been assassinated by individuals affiliated with the NOI.[10] Moreover, his wife, Betty, and their six daughters—Attallah, Qubilah, Ilyasah, Gamilah Lamumbah, Malikah Saban, and Malaak Saban—all assumed the family name Shabazz. Therefore, out of respect for Malcolm's legacy, he should be referred to as El-Hajj Malik El-Shabazz. His Hajj or pilgrimage earned him the title El-Hajj and elevated him to the status of an international statesman for the Muslim ummah (the global community of Muslims).

In the streets of Boston, Chicago, Detroit, and New York, Malcolm Little or "Detroit Red" was notorious as a con man, hustler, drug dealer, numbers runner, and pimp.[11] He earned respect in the criminal world while descending deeper into the abyss of decadence and immorality. This aberrant behavior was in sharp contrast to the religious beliefs and family values of Malcolm's parents. They were Baptists and followers of the Pan-African philosophy of Marcus Garvey. Garvey envisioned a free and united Africa in harmony with the African diaspora around the world. He formed the Universal Negro Improvement Association (UNIA) in 1914 in order to realize his vision of "Africa for the Africans at home and abroad." Garvey wrote, "Day by day we hear the cry of 'AFRICA FOR THE AFRICANS.' This cry has become a positive, determined one. It is a cry that is raised simultaneously the world over, because of the universal oppression that affects the Negro. All of us may not live to see the higher accomplishments of an African Empire—strong and powerful, as to compel the respect of mankind, but we in our life-time can so work and act as to make the dream a possibility within another generation."[12] Malcolm's family was totally committed to Garvey's vision and worked diligently to achieve the objectives of the UNIA, which embraced "One God, One Aim, and One Destiny."[13]

In 1948, while serving a ten-year prison term for burglary, Malcolm Little converted to the theology of the Nation of Islam. This conversion initiated him into the moral codes of Islam, knowledge of self, and knowledge of his African and Muslim ancestry. Furthermore, it reconnected him with the core Garveyite values of his parents. Upon release from prison in 1952, Malcolm rapidly rose into the upper echelon of Elijah Muhammad's ministers and became his national spokesman. His main base of operation was Mosque #7 in Harlem. This international and cosmopolitan city gave Malcolm access to Muslim diplomats from Africa, the Arabian Peninsula, and Asia. He was also in contact with a wide range of indigenous African-American Muslims. Famous for the Harlem Renaissance, Harlem was the headquarters of Marcus Garvey and the capital of black nationalism. Therefore, Malcolm's contacts extended to African, Caribbean, and African-American activists, artists, intellectuals, and scholars who were not Muslims.

Malcolm's conversion to mainstream Islam broadened his understanding of the universal religion that he professed. It also helped him to appreciate the cultural, economic, moral, political, religious, and social wisdom of Islam. He came to realize that the Nation of Islam had some Islamic beliefs and values, but many of its beliefs and practices were shirk or blasphemy according to the Qur'an and the Sunnah of Prophet Muhammad (pbuh).[14] Once Malcolm discovered the essence and purity of Islam, he concluded that there are no distinctions based on class, color, ethnicity, gender, nationality, or race in true Islam. He further noted that Islam advocates a healthy and positive respect for other religions, as the following excerpts from the Qur'an indicate: "And among His Signs is the creation of the heavens and the earth, and the variations in your languages and your colours; verily in that are Signs for those who know (Sura Rum). . . . O humankind! We created you from a single (pair) of a male and a female, and made you into nations and tribes, that ye may know each other (not that ye may despise each other). Verily the most honoured of you in the sight of Allah is (the one who is) the most righteous of you. And Allah has full knowledge and is well acquainted (with all things) (Sura Hujurat)."[15]

This true Allah consciousness and perspective endeared Malcolm to the leaders of African and Muslim nations. It elevated him to the status of an international celebrity with access to presidents and kings. It also gave him a new appreciation for human differences and for the need for people to reach across the artificial barriers that fragmented humanity. His character and mentality were transformed, and his universal Islamic consciousness allowed him to see the plight of African Americans in an international context.

Few scholars have carefully and perceptively analyzed Malcolm's religious development and transformation. To get a Muslim perspective on the subject, one must read books written by his widow, Betty Shabazz, and his nephew, Rodnell P. Collins. Heshaam Jaaber's *The Final Chapter: I Buried Malcolm* and Benjamin Karim's *Remembering Malcolm* are also representative of Muslim scholarship on this colorful but controversial figure. Non-Muslim scholarship on Malcolm is represented by Louis A. DeCaro Jr.'s *On the Side of My People: A Religious Life of Malcolm X* and *Malcolm and the Cross: The Nation of Islam, Malcolm X, and Christianity,* as well as Alex Haley's account in *The Autobiography of Malcolm X*. Most scholars in this category have focused almost exclusively on the secular dimensions of Malcolm's philosophy.[16] From a Muslim perspective, these secular interpretations have disconnected Malcolm from his core Islamic beliefs, values, cosmology, moral codes, and spirituality, which are prescribed by the canons of the Qur'an and Sunnah.

The few scholars who have devoted serious attention to his religious beliefs can be placed in one of three categories: mainstream Muslim interpreters, Nation of Islam interpreters, and non-Muslim interpreters. Malcolm participated in the NOI movement for about fifteen years, but he was secretly turning toward orthodox Islam as early as 1961. He publicly began practicing Sunni Islam in 1964. Therefore, his Islamic metamorphosis evolved over eighteen years. Ordinarily it takes a long time to transform the conscious and subconscious beliefs acquired from years of socialization in American culture and society. Whether one is initiated into the international family of Muslims from the perspectives of the Nation of Islam or mainstream Islam, the transformative journey and metamorphosis are arduous, challenging, and developmental.

The mainstream Muslim interpreters are Malcolm's widow, his oldest daughter, Attallah Shabazz, his friends Imam Warith Deen Mohammed and Imam Benjamin Karriem, his siblings, and Heshaam Jaaber, who performed his Jinaza, or funeral rites.[17] The main NOI interpreter is his protégé, Minister Louis Farrakhan, whose perspective is influenced by his loyalty to Elijah Muhammad and his criticism of Malcolm's separation from the Nation of Islam. Some non-Muslim interpreters are Louis E. Lomax, C. Eric Lincoln, and E. U. Essien-Udom.

A close examination of the life of El-Shabazz will reveal some fundamental contradictions and paradoxes. As an intellectual and activist, he experienced cognitive dissonance between the theology of Fard Muhammad and the teachings of the Qur'an and the Sunnah. These two theologies fundamentally contradict each other in their concepts of God, the Messenger of God, and the human race. El-Shabazz also passionately identified with, and had unconditional love for, the estimated 22 million African Americans (1960s estimate). Again, mainstream Islam is fundamentally opposed in principle to nationalism, racism, and tribalism.

Muslims believe human beings were created for the sole purpose of worshiping Allah. Islam is the religion created and revealed by Allah. It means total submission to the Will of Allah, with no reservations. The Holy Qur'an states: "Let there be no compulsion in religion. Truth stands out Clear from Error: whoever Rejects Evil and believes in Allah hath grasped the most trustworthy Handhold, that never breaks."[18] El-Shabazz took these words to heart as he struggled to understand and practice Islam in its most authentic form.

Muslims also believe the religion of Islam is as old as time and space, for it is the Divine and Universal Principle of the submission of creation to the Creator. Everything in the universe submits to the Will of Allah. Human behavior does not obey fixed laws such as the nonhuman elements of the universe. Humans have free will and can choose to submit or not to submit. Submission is the path of peace, happiness, and success, as El-Shabazz often said. Nonsubmission is the path of chaos, misery, and failure. True religion brings the human ego and will into a state of humility (submission), thus giving the individual a peaceful state of mind, harmony with the whole of creation, and union with Allah. This explains why El-Shabazz could not maintain a racial separatist philosophy and a race-based theology after establishing links with Sunni Islam.

The religion of Islam is based on five pillars: (1) Kalimah or Shahadah—bearing witness that there is no god but Allah and Muhammad Ibn Abdullah is Allah's Last and Final Messenger; (2) Salat—praying five times a day at the designated times of fajr (dawn), zuhr (early afternoon), asr (late afternoon), maghrib (sunset), and isha (night); (3) Zakat—charity (2.5 percent of one's gross annual income); (4) Sawm—obligatory fasting during the month of Ramadan (fasting from dawn to sunset for the duration of the ninth lunar month of the Islamic calendar); and (5) Hajj—pilgrimage to Mecca (if one's health, family obligations, and finances will permit this sacred journey).[19] Obviously, Sunni Islam provided a much more positive and vital context than the Nation of Islam for El-Shabazz to live out the true meaning of each of these pillars of faith.

The Kalimah is a declaration of the Tauhid, or the Oneness of Allah, which is the quintessential idea of God in the religion of Islam. Mainstream Islam is based on what its practitioners view as absolute and pure Monotheism. The Monotheism of Islam is parallel to the description of Yahweh or Jehovah in the Old Testament or Torah. As a logical extension from the belief in One God, Muslims believe in One Universe, One World, One Creation, and the Oneness of the Human Family.[20] Moreover, Muslims agree with the contention of Mohandas Gandhi and Martin Luther King Jr. that the universe, the world, and the human family are indivisible.[21] In other words, we are interrelated and interdependent, and what affects one individual directly affects everyone indirectly. During the final year of his life, El-Shabazz also embraced this principle as he subscribed to a faith he felt challenged all barriers to the achievement of human community and social solidarity.

Prayer is the heart and soul of Islam. Muslims organize each day around the performance of the five obligatory prayers. They can be performed alone or in a Jamaat (group). The Islamic form of prayer functions as a spiritual compass and social unifier of the local Muslim community and the ummah. Before the prayer can be performed, Muslims must make wudu (ablution), using clean water to wash their hands, mouth, nose, and feet. After wudu, a prayer rug, mosque, or clean area is selected for the performance of the prayer. Then Muslims must stand and face the Qibla (direction of the Kaaba in Mecca, Arabia) for the performance of the prayer. The prayer is performed in units called rak'a, which consists of standing erect (qiyaam), bowing at the waist ninety degrees (ruku), prostration with the forehead touching the floor (sujud), and sitting on the heels (juluus). The levels of seriousness that El-Shabazz attached to the performance of prayer has not yet been captured, even in works that explore the broader dimensions of his Islamic faith. Although he was familiar with the Islamic form of prayer, he was still learning the correct postures of salat and the Arabic recitation while on the Hajj in 1964:

> Two Egyptian Muslims and a Persian roused and also stared as my guide moved us over into the corner. With gestures, he indicated that he would demonstrate to me the proper prayer ritual postures. Imagine, being a Muslim minister, a leader in Elijah Muhammad's Nation of Islam, and not knowing the prayer ritual. . . . I tried to do what he did. I wasn't doing it right. I could feel the other Muslims' eyes on me. Western ankles won't do what Muslim ankles have done for a lifetime. Asians squat when they sit. Westerners sit upright in chairs. When my guide was down in a posture, I tried everything I could to get down as he was, but there I was, sticking up. . . . In Elijah Muhammad's Nation of Islam, we hadn't prayed in Arabic. About a dozen or more years before, when I was in prison, a member of the orthodox Muslim movement in Boston, named Abdul Hamed, had visited me and later sent me prayers in Arabic. At that time, I had learned those prayers phonetically. But I hadn't used them since.[22]

Prostration is an ancient form of prayer performed by the Prophets who lived before the Prophet Muhammad (pbuh). This was the mode of prayer used by Abraham, Moses, and Jesus. Passages in the Bible depict prophets praying in the same manner as Muslims still pray today: "And Abram fell on his face; and God talked with him" (Genesis 17:3). Another states, "And Moses made haste, and bowed his head toward the earth and worshiped" (Exodus 34:8). There are also these words: "Then cometh Jesus with them unto a place called Gethsemane, and saith unto the disciples, 'Sit ye here, while I go and pray yonder.' . . . And he went a little farther, and fell on his face, and prayed" (Matthew 26:36, 39). It is reported by scholars that the act of prostration is an ancient spiritual ritual that produces peace of mind, tranquillity, and harmony. Therefore, this act of placing the forehead on the ground eliminates stress and induces relaxation.[23] The performance of the five daily prayers is a discipline combining spiritual purification, mental concentration, Islamic education, personal hygiene, and physical exercise. El-Shabazz came to a greater understanding of this as he seriously studied Sunni Islam between 1961 and 1965. He came to see that the highly disciplined life is, for Muslims, the best and most productive life.

Finally, salat is an orientation toward the Kaaba and the Muslim world. Prayers are offered at fixed times on a twenty-four-hour cycle. Due to the differences in time zones, Muslims in various parts of the world offer different prayers at different times. For example, when the fajr or dawn prayer is offered in the United States, the zuhr or noon prayer is being offered in Africa and the Middle East. However, this diversity also creates global uniformity because at any given prayer time, most Muslims around the world are praying different prayers at the same time. They are also facing in the same direction, which is a powerful symbol of unity. Also, the Muslim prayer involves physical movements of the body through the postures of standing, bowing, prostration, sitting, and moving back to a standing position. Such movements mean that Muslims around the world are moving in concert in a global spirit of unity and harmony. El-Shabazz became more mindful of this during his Hajj in 1964, and this made him even more conscious of the need to transcend the sectarianism that the Nation of Islam had sought to instill in him.

The payment of zakat, or the poor tax, is required of every able-bodied Muslim. Muslims are taxed about 2.5 percent of their gross income, and this is used for the relief of the poor, the support of Muslim education, the maintenance of the mosques, the funding of Islamic projects, and the support of liberation struggles. Charity is a method by which acquired money and wealth are purified. It also has as its goal the leveling of the class and socioeconomic inequities in society. In the final analysis, Islam attempts to create a classless and egalitarian society. This helps explain why El-Shabazz saw capitalism as an evil and vulturistic system. The socialist interpreters view this critique as a movement toward socialism. However, Islam is a communalistic religion that predated Karl Marx (1818–83) and Friedrich Engels (1820–95) by more than a thousand years. Moreover, Ibn Khaldun (1332–1406), the Muslim founder of sociology, anticipated Marx's labor theory of value and surplus value by more than four hundred years in his magnum opus, *maqqadimmah*.

Ramadan is the obligatory month of fasting. It occurs during the ninth lunar month of the Islamic calendar. By Islamic tradition, fasting begins with the sighting of the new moon of Ramadan. The commandment to fast during Ramadan is revealed in the Qur'an as follows: "'O ye who believe! Fasting is prescribed to you as it was prescribed to those before you, that ye may learn self-restraint.'" The main goal of fasting is the cultivation of self-control, a point that El-Shabazz entertained seriously as he sought the type of transforming encounter with Allah that only a true Muslim experiences. If one can control the consumption of those things which are lawful, then it should be easier to abstain from sin and crime. Ramadan is an inner pilgrimage of self-discovery. It is a time of self-purification, introspection, extra prayers, and meditation on the Oneness and Greatness of Allah.

Ramadan comes earlier each year by ten to twelve days. It also travels over the seasons of spring, summer, fall, and winter. Ideally, it becomes easier to fast as one grows older in Islam, because the days are shorter and cooler each Ramadan. The principle of equality operates in this natural cycle, because no Muslim community or country is stuck with the extremes of hot and long days. Fasting during Ramadan is an obligation for all Muslims, and El-Shabazz took this practice seriously. In the NOI he was told that Ramadan occurs each year in the month of December, but this is not the custom of Sunni Muslims and the Muslim world. Muslims are required to fast from dawn to sunset for twenty-nine or thirty days. Moreover, they must avoid food, drink, and conjugal relations during these daylight hours. After the sun sets, those observing the fast can return to their normal routine of lawful drink, food, and conjugal relations. Fasting resumes each day at dawn until the new moon of Shawwal is sighted. Ramadan is an observance and celebration of the revelation of the Holy Qur'an to Prophet Muhammad (pbuh). Therefore, Muslims are encouraged to read one-thirtieth of the Qur'an during the days of fasting. Muslims who are pregnant, ill, or elderly are exempted from fasting. However, if the illness is not chronic, one has to make up the missed days or feed an indigent person.

The Hajj or pilgrimage to the holy city of Mecca is a duty incumbent on every Muslim. It is an annual gathering of two to three million out of a global population of 1,099,634,000 Muslims.[24] This means that approximately 1/1000 of the Muslim world goes on pilgrimage. It is tantamount to three million Muslims pollinating the flower of Mecca and then returning home to cross-pollinate their families, friends, local masjids, and communities with the spiritual nectars of Mecca. Malcolm was transformed from Malcolm X to El-Hajj Malik El-Shabazz by the experience of the Hajj. But what is the essence and purpose of this annual pilgrimage by millions of Muslims from around the world? Heshaam Jaaber says: "In essence, Hajj is man's approach toward Allah. Suffice it to say that Hajj is a great show; a show of creation, of history, of unity, of the Islamic ideology and the ummah. In this 'show,' Adam, Abraham, Hagar, and Satan are the main characters, while Allah is the stage manager. The scenes are Masjid ul Haram (the sacred mosque house), Masa (the distance between the two mountains of Safa and Marwa), Arafat (the 'mount of recognition' located twelve miles from Mecca), and Mina (a sacred valley near Mecca where the symbolic idols are located)."[25] Imam Jamil Al-Amin (formerly H. Rap Brown) elaborates further: "In many ways, the pilgrimage to Mecca is comprised of the first four pillars of Islam: the unity of God (Tauheed); worship of God (Salaat); giving of your wealth for the pleasure of God (Zakaat); and fasting for God (Saum). Hajj includes elements of all these practices."[26]

In a certain way, Malik's concept of black nationalism was challenged by the rituals and spirit of the Hajj. Imam Al-Amin raises these considerations:

What was it that Brother Malcolm saw? What did Allah allow him to see on the Hajj that made him make the transition from nationalism to something much higher? ... To be black is vital but it isn't sufficient. It's just not sufficient. It is basic but it is not sufficient. You have to go beyond the whole concept of nationalism when you are talking about successful struggle. If we follow the logic that Allah has given us, which says that all come from two, you lose the whole sense of lineage, when you go back to Adam; because we all come from two. So, race becomes something that is insignificant when you try to trace it all the way back; because you can't go any further than Adam.[27]

Ali Shariati, in his excellent scholarship on the meanings, rituals, and symbols of Hajj, makes the case in the following manner: "Regardless of whether you are a man or a woman, young or old, black or white, you are the main feature of the performance. The role of Adam, Ibrahim and Hajar in the confrontation between 'Allah and Satan' is played by you. As a result, you, individually, are the hero of the 'show.' Annually, Muslims from all over the world are encouraged to participate in this great 'show' (Hajj). Everyone is considered equal. No discrimination on the basis of race, sex, or social status is made. In accordance to the teachings of Islam, all are one and one is all."[28]

The above discussion on the five pillars of Islam is an attempt to define Islam. It is also an attempt to define and elaborate a Muslim or Islamic perspective for an analysis of El-Shabazz's spiritual pilgrimage. Most Americans have heard of the Nation of Islam, but the ideology of this group would be inadequate for such an analysis because it does not represent the beliefs, practices, and values of more than one billion Muslims around the world. The three most fundamental flaws in the Nation of Islam's ideology are that Allah is a man by the name of Fard Muhammad, the Honorable Elijah Muhammad is the Messenger of Allah, and all whites or Europeans are genetically devils. What is presented as religion is more black nationalism than Islam, as El-Shabazz ultimately came to see, although it is fair to say that there are some basic elements of Islam within the NOI theology. This perhaps accounts for its strong program of moral reformation and economic development, to which El-Shabazz often referred in the years before his break with Elijah Muhammad.

Whether one is Muslim or non-Muslim is determined by the canons of the Holy Qur'an and the Sunnah, or traditions of the Prophet Muhammad (pbuh). Fard Muhammad, the founder of the Nation of Islam, and his most dedicated disciple, Elijah Muhammad, advocated beliefs, practices, and rituals that remain alien to the teachings of mainstream and universal Islam. Their doctrine amounted to a customized amalgam of religious black nationalism, free masonry, and some elementary principles of orthodox Islam.[29] It was C. Eric Lincoln who first labeled the Nation of Islam "Black Muslims." He coined this name to make a distinction between indigenous and immigrant orthodox Muslims and the Nation of Islam.[30] El-Shabazz once criticized this label in an interview with Kenneth B. Clark: "We're not even Black Muslims. We are black people in a sense that 'black' is an adjective. We are black people who are Muslims because we have accepted the religion of Islam, but . . . Eric Lincoln . . . made 'black' an adjectival noun and then attached it to 'Muslim,' and now it is used by the press to make it appear that this is the name of an organization. It has no religious connotations or religious motivation or religious objectives."[31]

Unfortunately, the name became a stigma and has given the Nation of Islam a racial overtone since the initial publication of Lincoln's *Black Muslims in America* in 1961. This image has been further reinforced by the language, rhetoric, and theology of the Nation of Islam, which now seem to be gradually fading as Louis Farrakhan interacts more and more with representatives of mainstream Islam. This pattern of change will undoubtedly continue, especially since Farrakhan has approached imams from orthodox Islam about teaching his followers in the Nation of Islam. Strangely, this step is in line with the legacy of El-Shabazz.

Malcolm X was indoctrinated into the ideology of the Nation of Islam at a time when he needed discipline and stability in his life. However, over time, he outgrew the NOI and embraced Sunni Islam.[32] Any scholarly study of Malcolm X must come to terms with his core beliefs and values as a minister in the NOI and also with his metamorphosis from this cocoon of religious black nationalism to universal Sunni Islam. This cultural, economic, political, and spiritual metamorphosis has given rise to a body of conflicting and diverging scholarship among the interpreters of the last years of Malcolm X (1963–65). The parameters of these diverging interpretations can be defined in terms of the perspectives of five distinct schools of thought: mainstream Muslims, the Nation of Islam, black nationalists, socialists, and integrationists, all of whom employ their own perspective in interpreting the life and legacy of El-Shabazz.

Mainstream Muslims maintain that El-Shabazz abandoned all of his black nationalist proclivities. They passionately argue that he stopped viewing white people as "a race of devils" and came to see them as human beings with the capacity to accept true Islam and to practice brotherhood with people of African descent. El-Shabazz's observations and testimony about his Hajj are cited as irrefutable evidence of his spiritual transformation. When El-Shabazz returned from Mecca, three aspects of his life had dramatically changed: his name, his views on race, and his methodology for achieving liberation.[33] Malcolm's letter from Mecca serves as the capstone for the orthodox Muslim position: "Throughout my travels in the Muslim world, I have met, talked to, and even eaten with, people who would have been considered 'white' in America, but the religion of Islam in their hearts has removed the 'white' from their minds. They practice sincere and true brotherhood with other people irrespective of their color."[34] This tendency to analyze El-Shabazz's personality, philosophy, and methods within the orthodox Islamic framework should gain increasing acceptability as scholars focus more on his internationalism.

Black nationalist interpreters of Malcolm X believe that he was beginning to move away from Islam. They are convinced that Islam is an Arab religion and "the deification of Arab culture and nationalism." Black nationalists passionately argue that "Islam is not an African religion and that the Arabs were among the first slave-traders in Africa."[35] From the black nationalist perspective, there is no fundamental difference between Arab Muslims transporting African slaves across the hot Sahara desert and Indian Ocean to be enslaved in Arabia, and European Christians transporting African slaves across the Atlantic Ocean to be enslaved in the Americas and the Caribbean. This approach to the study of El-Shabazz concentrates almost exclusively on his advocacy of black nationalism and Pan-Africanism. Black nationalists do not take into account the cultural and historical links between Islam and Pan-African nationalism. Scholars will undoubtedly continue the debate over the extent to which El-Shabazz remained wedded to both black nationalist and Sunni Islamic principles.

After his pilgrimages to Mecca and Africa, El-Shabazz was invited by the Militant Labor Forum, a socialist organization, to express his views on the struggle and to present the goals and objectives of his new organizations, the Muslim Mosque, Inc. and the Organization of African Unity (OAAU). George Breitman has edited and written several books on Malcolm X, and Pathfinder Press has published several volumes of his speeches and interviews. Both Breitman and Pathfinder have given these works a socialist slant. In the tradition of Karl Marx, socialist interpreters believe Malcolm was becoming less religious and more revolutionary in the political sense. With this in mind, they recall Karl Marx's conclusion: "Man makes religion, religion does not make man. . . . Religion is the sigh of the oppressed creature, the heart of a heartless world, just as it is the spirit of a spiritless situation. It is the opium of the people. The abolition of religion as the illusory of happiness of the people is required for their real happiness. The demand to give up the illusions about its condition is the demand to give up a condition which needs illusions. The criticism of religion is therefore in embryo the criticism of the vale of woe, the halo of which is religion."[36] El-Shabazz was apt to use similar language in his critique of Christianity, but he did not embrace Marx's atheism, and he was becoming more religious, not less religious, in the last three years of his life. Thus, a socialist analysis of El-Shabazz is at best inadequate and quite erroneous in view of his own reflections on his faith journey.

According to socialists, El-Shabazz was becoming more class-conscious and political. Thus, his new humanitarian and international perspectives were moving him closer to socialism. Huey Newton and Bobby Seale, founders of the Black Panther Party, have concurred with these conclusions as put forth by white socialists.[37] They were fixated on Malcolm's concepts of the "ballot or the bullet" and "by any means necessary," which led them to embrace Malcolm's call for armed self-defense and revolutionary change. Based on their understanding of El-Shabazz, Frantz Fanon, and other critics of capitalism and white supremacy, they made a cognitive leap of political consciousness and strongly embraced Marxist-Leninism. This is all the more intriguing in view of Malcolm's claim that he knew essentially nothing about Marx.

When Malcolm made a sincere effort to re-create himself, by getting involved with the civil rights movement, he wanted to elevate it to the level of human rights. Some have interpreted this as a sign that Malcolm was becoming an integrationist. Integrationists were cognizant of the fact that he had radically modified his views on racism and whites. As members of the Nation of Islam, the followers of Elijah Muhammad were discouraged from voting, a practice linked to the quest for what King called "the beloved community" or "the truly integrative society." Malcolm initially conformed to Muhammad's policy, but his later support for the right to vote became a positive sign for the integrationists in the civil rights movement. Malcolm went to Selma, Alabama, during the period of the march to Montgomery for the right to vote. At a press conference in Selma, conducted February 4, 1965, Malcolm announced: "I might point out that I am 100 percent for any effort put forth by black people in this country to have access to the ballot. And I frankly believe that since the ballot is our right, that we are within our right to use whatever means are necessary to secure those rights. And I think that the people in this part of the country would do well to listen to Dr. Martin Luther King and give him what he's asking for, and give it to him fast, before some other factions come along and try to do it another way. What he's asking for is right. That's the ballot."[38] Malcolm did not mean to suggest that he had embraced uncritically a full-blown integrationism. He merely meant to suggest that his people had a right to enjoy the fruits of democracy, a right enshrined in the U.S. Constitution.

Michael Dyson has "identified at least four Malcolms who emerge in the intellectual investigations of his life and career: Malcolm as hero and saint, Malcolm as public moralist, Malcolm as victim and vehicle of psychohistorical forces, and Malcolm as revolutionary figure as judged by his career trajectory from nationalist to alleged socialist."[39] Dyson's comments are clearly reflective of the continuing struggle, in both the intellectual world and the public square, to place El-Shabazz in proper context.

As a subject of historical, political, and religious analysis, he has been reinvented in the images of many activists, revolutionaries, and scholars. Ostensibly, this image-making mode of analysis seeks to legitimize a certain ideological agenda that is imported into the analysis by these interpreters of the so-called Malcolm X phenomenon. Adib Rashad makes a poignant observation:

> Malcolm means many things to many people; in addition, many people have given the impression that they have captured the historical essence of Malcolm. Many books and articles have been written about him that almost always extol his revolutionary character. Orthodox Muslims, both immigrants and indigenous, extol his Sunni Islamic assertiveness. Socialists declare that once he renounced black nationalism for internationalism, he made an overture to socialism and subsequently discussed the ideological evil of capitalism versus the ideological goodness of socialism. Because these themes repeat themselves, it seems Malcolm is only written about or discussed within the context of one's ideological persuasion.[40]

But the contention here is that El-Shabazz's Muslim faith affords the best analytical framework for understanding this complex and phenomenal figure. Indeed, Islam was the crucible out of which his social, cultural, political, and economic views emerged.

The difficulty with the scholarship and the activist rhetoric about Malcolm is that each interpreter seeks to describe him using an image with which they are comfortable. Various representatives interpret him in a manner designed to legitimize their version of Islam, of nationalism, of Pan-Africanism, of socialism, and of integrationism. But Malcolm is too complex to be boxed into any label. Even so, this study supports the view that orthodox Islam affords one of the significant keys to a proper analysis of who and what he ultimately became. Because Malcolm spoke so eloquently and profoundly from the soul and spirit of the African masses around the world, most people who identify with him speak as though they knew him personally. Since Spike Lee commemorated his life in a movie, Malcolm X has become an icon, a cult hero, and a saint to some. With this in mind, the rest of this chapter will focus on the spiritual evolution and metamorphosis that marked his pilgrimage from Malcolm X to El-Hajj Malik El-Shabazz.

El-Shabazz was "Muslim to the soul and African to the bone." If our analysis is accurate and true to his legacy, then the most definitive generalizations we can make about his new ideology are that he declared himself a

Sunni Muslim while also claiming to be a black nationalist and Pan-Africanist. His Sunni Islamic theology and his cultural, economic, political, and social ideology of Pan-African Nationalism merged in the "heart of Africa." The reconciliation of Sunni Islam (his sacred cosmology) and Pan-Africanism (his secular epistemology) did not create anxiety, cognitive dissonance, or an existential dilemma for him. Thus, his Sunni Islamic beliefs and values were institutionalized in the Muslim Mosque, Inc. and his Pan-African ideology in the Organization of Afro-American Unity.

Advent of Islam in Arabia: The Significance of This History for Malcolm X

"Arabia can be defined as that land mass located between the Nile and the Euphrates rivers in the Middle East. . . . A more accurate description would simply be 'Northeast Africa.'"[41] The story of Islam goes back to the marriage between the Prophet Abraham (pbuh) and Hagar. She was an Egyptian of royal lineage and was of course African.[42] This genealogical marking is significant because the first child born to the marriage, Ishmael, is considered the original Ancestor of the Ishmaelite or Arabized Arab nation.[43] Ishmael was the offspring of a Semitic father and an African mother. This historiography suggests that the Arabized Arab nation is genealogically connected to the indigenous people of ancient Kemet (Egypt). "So we have seen that the entire Arab people, including the Prophet, is mixed with Negro blood."[44] El-Shabazz knew this history quite well, and he often referred to it when making distinctions between the Muslim world and the Western Christian world.

With the birth of the Prophet Muhammad in the seventh century, a direct descendant of Prophet Abraham and Ishmael, the stage was set for a series of revelations that revived Islam in the Arabian peninsula.[45] Abraham and his son Ishmael built the Kaaba, a shrine for the worship of One God. After Abraham's death, the Arabs degenerated into a polytheistic nation worshiping 360 pagan gods. Muslims refer to this period as the Jahiliyah, or "the Days of Ignorance."[46] This history must have figured prominently in El-Shabazz's consciousness at a time when he was rejecting the man-God of the Nation of Islam in favor of the orthodox Islamic conception of Allah.

In addition to these acts of shirk or blasphemy, the birth of a female child was considered a curse by the chauvinistic Arab males. Female babies were buried alive in the desert sands in order to expiate the "curse of the devil." As the Qur'an explains, "When news is brought to one of them, of (the birth of) a female (child), his face darkens, and is filled with inward grief. With shame does he hide himself from his people, because of the bad news he has had! Shall he retain it on (sufferance and) contempt, or bury it in the dust? Ah! what an evil (choice) they decide on."[47] Historical accounts of this nature must have registered in profound ways in El-Shabazz's consciousness as he ultimately turned to Islamic traditions that he felt rejected sexism and discrimination on all grounds.

Wine, women, lewd poetry, and parading around the Kaaba naked were symptomatic of the *Jahiliyah* into which the Arab nation had degenerated. Morals and mores were almost nonexistent. Unfortunately, this was the sad state of affairs that existed in the Arabian peninsula when the Prophet Muhammad (pbuh) was born in 570 and at the advent of Islam in 610.[48] Islam came as a "mercy and healing." While meditating in the Cave of Hira, the first revelation came to Prophet Muhammad: "Read in the name of thy Lord! Read in the name of thy Lord Who creates!"[49] Echoes of this remained with El-Shabazz as he struggled to gain a sense of his own calling as a Muslim.

It is significant to note that early followers of the Prophet Muhammad (pbuh) were of a heterogeneous background. The first community of Muslims were of a multiethnic, multicultural, and multiracial background, a point El-Shabazz often made. Islam became the transcendent cement that bonded these diverse groups of humanity together. Based on the tribal instincts of the Arab nation, the Prophet could have chosen to preach a message of religious Arab nationalism, but this was not the case. According to Sayyid Qutb, "In this great Islamic society Arabs, Persians, Syrians, Egyptians, Moroccans, Turks, Chinese, Indians, Romans, Greeks, Indonesians, Africans were gathered together—in short, peoples of all nations and all races. Their various characteristics were united, and with mutual cooperation, harmony and unity, they took part in the construction of the Islamic community and Islamic culture. This marvellous civilisation was not an 'Arabic civilisation,' even for a single day; it was purely an 'Islamic civilisation.' It was never a 'nationality' but always a 'community of belief.'"[50]

Hence, the ummah or beloved community of the Muslims was created. The ummah became a society that respected and tolerated differences of race, class, and gender. There is no room in Islam for nationalism, racism, and sexism, especially as understood by Muslims. Brotherhood and Sisterhood are derived from iman (belief) and amal (practice). Islam is not a theory but a complete way of life or civilization. The observations of J. A. Rogers on this issue coincide with those of Sayyid Qutb: "One fact about Islam stands glowingly forth through the centuries: Its almost total freedom from race and class prejudice; the opportunity it gave to every capable and aspiring follower, regardless of color or social status, to rise to the highest possible rank. Slaves rose to be sultans, and slave women to be favorites of the ruler, and mothers of heirs to the throne. At times the slave, himself, became a master while still enslaved and held freeborn men of wealth and power in dread of him."[51]

Malcolm X read J. A. Rogers's *Sex and Race* while trying to validate the mythological theology of Fard Muhammad. One must wonder why he ignored or rejected clear evidence of race-mixing in Islamic societies. In the *Autobiography,* Malcolm shared the following information about the books that he read while in prison: "J. A. Rogers's three volumes of *Sex and Race* told about race-mixing before Christ's time; about Aesop being a black man who told fables; about Egypt's Pharaohs; about the great Coptic Christian Empires; about Ethiopia, the earth's oldest continuous black civilization, as China is the oldest continuous civilization."[52] The Hajj allowed Malcolm to revisit these pages of culture, history, and religion which he had previously read with a racial bias. Now he was able to take a fresh look through the lens of mainstream Islam.

Malcolm and Islam in the United States

Islam first came to the United States on slave ships. Between 1492 and 1865, millions of Muslims from the coast and interior of North West Africa were captured, sold, and transported. Conflicts of class, culture, ethnicity, race, and religion produced an industry driven by corruption and greed.[53] Such tragic episodes stood at the center of El-Shabazz's critique of capitalism and colonialism in its various forms.

African Muslims were chained to the decks of the slave ships along with Africans who practiced traditional African religions and Christianity. No one knows how many Muslims were enslaved and brought to North America; estimates range between 10 and 40 percent.[54] African Muslims also made the historic voyage with Christopher Columbus as he claimed to discover the "New World."[55] Hence, the Islamic/Muslim roots among African Americans go very deep. In *Message to the Blackman in America,* Elijah Muhammad took these facts and stretched them to conclude that "the original religion of the Ancestors of African Americans was Islam."[56] Muslims believe all human beings are born Muslims and become otherwise due to the religious practices of their parents or other influences.[57] El-Shabazz expressed these convictions on numerous occasions, and they became the centerpiece of his efforts to attract increasing numbers of African Americans from Christianity to Islam.

Today Islam is the fastest growing religion on the African continent and the second largest religion in the United States. One-fifth of the world's population is Muslim. Approximately six million Muslims live in the United States. Of this number, one to two million are black.[58] With such a dynamic growth of Islam, particularly among African Americans, who are embracing Islam faster than any other segment of American society, a study of the Islamic consciousness and the development of the ideology of Malcolm X can greatly inform our understanding of this phenomenon. It is significant to note that Malcolm X was largely responsible for the conversion of Muhammad Ali, Louis Farrakhan, and thousands of others to Islam. Indeed, the tremendous growth of Islam among African Americans since 1965 must be viewed as part of his legacy.

This chapter is guided by some critical questions and issues: Did Malcolm X really change after his pilgrimage to Mecca? What was his attitude toward white people after his spiritual experience and enlightenment? Because Malcolm X's assassination left his emerging ideology in a seminal stage, controversy and debate continue to exist about his ideology and direction. It is important to bear in mind that Malcolm X's ideology went through a cultural, economic, political, religious, and social maturation, a process that was still occurring at the time of his assassination.

The so-called Lost-Found Nation of Islam is a religious variety of black nationalism. E. U. Essien-Udom defines nationalism as "the belief of a group that it possesses, or ought to possess, a country; that it shares, or ought to share, a common heritage of language, culture, and religion; and that its heritage, way of life, and ethnic identity are distinct from those of other groups. Nationalists believe that they ought to rule themselves and shape their own destinies, and that they should therefore be in control of their social, economic, and political institutions."[59] Therefore, the key to understanding the theophilosophical orientation of the Nation of Islam is cultural and psychological identity. Slavery eliminated the specific ethnic identity of most African Americans. Many of the problems of cultural identity, economic development, political empowerment, and unity are rooted in slavery. Members of the Nation of Islam believe the ancestors of African Americans were Muslims. The slave trade, according to Elijah Muhammad, separated the African Muslims from the international Nation of Islam. Thus, the NOI members believe that African Americans are lost until they discover and reclaim their true Muslim identity and unite with the Nation of Islam. Hence the name "Lost-Found Nation of Islam" was frequently used in Malcolm's speeches.

The Nation of Islam first appeared in Detroit on July 4, 1930, at a time when thousands of African Americans were turning to new forms of religion and alternative and unconventional avenues to spirituality. The NOI members believe that Allah "appeared in the Person of Master W. Fard Muhammad, July 1930; the long-awaited 'Messiah' of the Christians and the 'Mahdi' of the Muslims." W. Fard Muhammad is actually the founder of the Nation of Islam. He is regarded as God and Elijah Muhammad as his messenger. This belief has no foundation or support in the Qur'an and the Sunnah, the sacred text of Islam and of its authoritative traditions, respectively.[60] Islam considers such beliefs to be shirk or blasphemy. The correct Kalimah (Declaration of Faith) is "There is no God but Allah, and Mohammed is His Last and Final Messenger." Fard Muhammad's motives for corrupting the belief system of Islam are not totally clear, and Malcolm never really addressed this in any serious way. Imam Warith Deen Mohammed suggests that Fard created the Nation of Islam as a "satire" on American racism and white supremacy.[61] There is reason to believe that Malcolm would have said the same after becoming a Sunni Muslim.

In addition to these exotic ideas of God and the Messenger of God, the Nation of Islam preached that "the white man is the devil." Again, there is no foundation for this idea in the Qur'an and the Sunnah. While this idea is theologically untenable, there is a sense in which it was used as a technique of "reverse psychology," a point Malcolm apparently realized before he left the Nation of Islam. Be that as it may, the NOI's use of race in its "reverse psychology" technique clearly called to mind the racist so-called Christian theologians and scholars who used the "curse of Canaan" to justify and rationalize slavery and the system of white supremacy. The "curse of Canaan" is a Judeo-Christian belief that has no foundation in Islamic theology or epistemology, and even many Christians either reject or attach different interpretations to this curse.

According to this myth, the prophet Noah became intoxicated while building the Ark and got naked in public. Ham laughed when he saw his father drunk and naked. As a punishment, Noah put a curse on Canaan, the son of Ham.[62] This alleged "curse" was translated by the racist scholars and theologians in Christianity to mean that the Hamites, or the people of Africa, were cursed. The curse stated that Canaanites should be "the hewers of wood and the drawers of water for Shem and Japheth." In other words, Ham's descendants would be in bondage to the descendants of Shem and Japheth, who symbolize the Asiatic and Caucasian peoples, respectively. El-Shabazz and Martin Luther King Jr. rejected the racist interpretations of this story for many of the same reasons.

King did an analysis of the white supremacy mythology as it sought to manifest itself in the form of logic. With the Hamitic myth and other types of racist mythology in mind, King asserted: "Logic was manipulated to give intellectual credence to the system of slavery. Someone formulated the argument for the inferiority of the Negro in the shape of a syllogism: 'All men are made in the image of God; God, as everybody knows, is not a Negro; therefore the Negro is not a man.'"[63] Mindful of how both history and language were used to keep African Americans in psychological bondage, El-Shabazz and King ultimately called for a process of reeducation that would lead both blacks and whites away from the racist mythology that some claimed to be biblically grounded.

Fard Muhammad used "reverse psychology" by putting the "curse" on the Caucasians and by labeling them a "race of devils." The belief system of white supremacy maintains that whites are a race of gods and goddesses and that Africans are a race of devils and pagans. Over time, this ideology created feelings of superiority among whites who accepted this myth and feelings of inferiority among blacks who consciously or subconsciously accepted it as well. Fard reversed the equation and argued that whites personified evil and blacks were gods, that it was the whites who were really inferior and the blacks who were superior.[64] Malcolm became widely known for his ability to articulate these views while denying that the Nation of Islam was fundamentally racist.

From Satan to Malcolm X

After the death of Malcolm's father, Earl Little, Louise Little and her eight children were separated due to poverty and hunger. Mrs. Little suffered an emotional breakdown resulting from the dehumanizing treatment she received from the Michigan Welfare Department.[65] This trauma remained with Malcolm X for the rest of his life. He was always guarded when talking about his mother. One can only imagine the various ways that this influenced his religious outlook and his approach to injustice. Thus, his opposition to systems of oppression cannot be divorced from his childhood experiences, an opposition that was reinforced over time as he studied racism and subscribed to various forms of Islam.

With the separation of his family, Malcolm descended into a world of juvenile delinquency and crime. He became a hustler, pimp, thief, and drug addict. This deviant behavior was terminated with his arrest and incarceration in 1946. He was sentenced in Massachusetts to eight to ten years for burglary. Malcolm served six and a half years of this sentence. When he entered prison, he was functionally illiterate. He began educating himself through correspondence courses and by reading voraciously, and he mastered the art of debating. In time he would become perhaps the most feared and respected debater of the modern civil rights era.

Malcolm's brothers Philbert and Reginald introduced him to the teachings of Elijah Muhammad. This brand of Islam was mystical and esoteric. It used symbolism and signs that paralleled the teachings of Freemasonry. According to the eschatology of the Nation of Islam, "God has 360 degrees of knowledge . . . known as Masonry." Members of the Nation further assert that a Mason is a Muslim's son, which in essence is the meaning of Mason.[66]

When Reginald told Malcolm that he could get out of prison by not eating pork or smoking cigarettes, Malcolm wanted to learn all there was to know about "the Black man's religion." To add to the mystery, Malcolm saw an apparition very much like a scene out of Shakespeare's *Hamlet:* "It was the next night, as I lay on the bed, suddenly, with a start, I became aware of a man sitting beside me in my chair. . . . I could see him as plainly as I see anyone I look at. . . . I couldn't move, I didn't speak, and he didn't. I couldn't place him racially other than that I knew he was a non-European."[67] Malcolm had been preconditioned by his mother not to eat pork. However, the beliefs and practices of Islam, which reinforced this view, were a cognitive leap for him, if not a form of cultural shock.

What attracted Malcolm to black Islam were its moral codes, its program of personal discipline, and the fact that it represented a way out of prison. The demonology ascribed to white people as a "race of devils" probably appealed to his animosity toward whites. After all, whites had murdered his father and uncles and had committed his mother to an insane asylum. Moreover, a white woman had betrayed Malcolm, landing him in prison. These experiences, and the many other bouts Malcolm had with white racism, helped prepare the young man to accept teachings that glorified blacks and demonized whites.

In corresponding with Elijah Muhammad, Malcolm came to learn of the original man, the Asiatic black man from the tribe of Shabazz. Echoing Muhammad, Malcolm said on one occasion: "He has declared that we are descendants of the Asian black nation and of the tribe of Shabazz. You might ask, who is the tribe of Shabazz? Originally, they were the tribe that came with the earth (or this part) 60 trillion years ago when a great explosion on our planet divided it into two parts. One we call earth and the other moon. . . . We, the tribe of Shabazz, says Allah, were the first to discover the best part of our planet to live on. The rich Nile Valley of Egypt and the present seat of the Holy City, Mecca, Arabia."[68] Elijah Muhammad also taught that Islam was the original religion of the black man. "There is no doubt about it, according to the meaning of Islam and what the Holy Qur'an Sharrieff teaches us of it. Islam means peace and submission to the will of Allah, who is the Author of Islam."[69]

Of course, this claim that Islam was exclusive to black mankind is in conflict with the Qur'an and the Sunnah. By presenting Islam in a black costume, it was apparently made psychologically more appealing to the working-class African Americans who had migrated from the South and to those who were convicts and ex-offenders. One other misrepresentation of Islam helps us to understand the "reverse psychology" of the racial superiority that Elijah Muhammad used to awaken the masses. The whites were a "race of devils" created by a mad scientist named Mr. Yakub. "Yakub made devils who were really pale white, with really blue eyes; which we think are the ugliest of colors for a human eye. They were called Caucasian—which means, according to some of the Arab scholars, one whose evil effect is not confined to one's self alone, but affects others."[70] Elijah Muhammad was taught by Fard Muhammad that the white race was grafted from the black race, or the original race. This is to say that the white race is essentially an albino race of black people, a position impossible to defend on biological and theological grounds. Even so, Malcolm employed the Yakub myth in order to counter much of the self-hatred and low self-esteem that afflicted his people.

Minister Malcolm X

Malcolm was paroled from prison on August 7, 1952, and he received his X from Elijah Muhammad a month later. This meant that he would never again use the slave name "Little." Between June 1953 and June 1954, Malcolm X established himself as one of the most effective and promising ministers in the

Nation of Islam. According to one source, "he was named the assistant minister of Detroit Temple No. 1, became the first minister of Boston Temple No. 11 in the winter of 1953, then in March 1954, acting minister of Philadelphia Temple No. 12. In June 1954 he became minister of New York Temple No. 7."[71]

Elijah Muhammad became Malcolm's mentor and spiritual guide. Also Malcolm quickly became the most charismatic and recognized minister in the Nation of Islam. This set the stage for a high level of visibility and popularity that would follow Malcolm for more than a decade and that would launch him into the international arena. This proved to be quite positive for the Nation of Islam from the standpoint of growth and influence, but somewhat negative in the sense that the vulnerabilities of that organization and of Elijah Muhammad were made clearer to a curious world.

On August 28, 1963, the March on Washington attracted more than 200,000 people, and Martin Luther King Jr. gave his famous "I Have a Dream" speech. The marchers rallied around the issues of freedom and jobs. It was a magnificent appeal to the government and the nation to deliver on the promise of democracy for all Americans. Malcolm was in Washington, D.C., at the time, and his description of the event as "a circus" or "a farce on Washington" conflicted sharply with King's account. In any case, eighteen days after the marchers returned home, racists bombed a Baptist church in Birmingham, Alabama, killing four girls. The spiral of violence escalated, reaching a peak with the assassination of John F. Kennedy on November 22, 1963. Muhammad instructed his ministers not to make any statements concerning the assassination. He felt that African Americans truly mourned Kennedy's death and that negative comments would only invite unwelcome scrutiny of the Nation of Islam.

On December 1, 1963, at a rally in New York, Malcolm X delivered a speech entitled "God's Judgment of White America." His major point was that white America needed to make amends for its sins against African Americans. Malcolm further criticized Negro integrationists as "sell-outs." In the classic language of the Nation of Islam, he demanded that the U.S. government provide financial compensation and arable land in the African homeland or inside of the United States: "How can America atone for her crimes? The Honorable Elijah Muhammad teaches us that a desegregated theater or lunch counter won't solve our problems. An integrated cup of coffee isn't sufficient pay for four hundred years of slave labor, and a better job in the white man's factory or position in his business is, at best, only a temporary solution. The only lasting or permanent solution is complete separation on some land that we can call our own."[72] Nothing in this speech deviated from the standard position of "What the Muslims Believe" and "What the Muslims Want."[73] However, an unwise remark in the question-and-answer period set the stage for Malcolm's permanent excommunication from the Nation of Islam. When asked to comment on the assassination of President Kennedy, Malcolm observed, "I said what I honestly felt—that it was, as I saw it, a case of 'the chickens coming home to roost.' I said that the hate in white men had not stopped with the killing of defenseless black people, but that hate, allowed to spread unchecked, finally had struck down this country's Chief of State. I said it was the same thing as had happened with Medgar Evers, with Patrice Lumumba, with Madame Nhu's husband." The newspapers captured the comments in bold headlines: "Black Muslims' Malcolm X: 'Chickens Come Home to Roost.'"[74]

Obviously, the correct response to this question should have been "no comment," as Elijah Muhammad had instructed. Perhaps without thinking about the consequences, Malcolm gave a controversial answer. This not only angered the NOI leader but prompted Malcolm's adversaries in the NOI to question his loyalty to Elijah Muhammad. Some of the other ministers and national staff members were jealous of Malcolm's closeness to their leader and his public visibility. Imam Warith Deen Mohammed, in an exclusive interview, observed: "They were jealous of his acceptance in the black community. He wasn't accepted just by Muslims. A lot of black nationalists had begun to admire Malcolm in New York City and Harlem. He was very strong in Harlem. He was becoming very popular in many other big cities. It was because the Honorable Elijah Muhammad encouraged him to take advantage of the media. He was skillful and a very witty person. He was clever, calculating, and a strategist. He knew just how to organize a big, massive team of people."[75] Malcolm identified these tensions in the press conference in which he made a formal declaration of his break from the Nation of Islam. "Internal differences within the Nation of Islam forced me out of it. I did not leave of my own free will. But now that it has happened I intend to make the most of it. Now that I have more independence of action, I intend to use a more flexible approach toward working with others to get a solution to this problem."[76] In other words, for the first time in his career as a Muslim, Malcolm seriously entertained the possibility of working with Martin Luther King Jr. and other more moderate civil rights leaders.

Imam Warith Deen Mohammed explained, "Malcolm was just so popular that all the other ministers were almost like invisible. They were eclipsed by Malcolm. He eclipsed the other ministers. He did. And he made the national staff fear that he, his very person, threatened to eclipse the Nation of Islam. That is what they began to tell the Honorable Elijah Muhammad."[77] In any case, Malcolm declared himself "independent" on March 8, 1964, and he took a series of steps that more closely linked him to the Muslim world. Establishing links with Sunni Islam invariably meant that he had to become more global in his approach to matters of race, religion, and politics.

Conversion to Sunni Islam

Malcolm X was always sincere and open-minded. As he often stated, his sincerity was his only credential. From his days in the Nation of Islam and the hard life that he led before converting, Malcolm learned to face life from a realistic perspective. He changed according to the unfolding of new facts and realities. Imam Warith Deen Mohammed stated that Malcolm had long had some reservations about the teachings of the NOI: "He wanted to believe in everything that the Honorable Elijah Muhammad said. But he had great difficulty making sense of some of the myths that we thought were actual facts in the teachings of the Honorable Elijah Muhammad's language of religion."[78]

The separation from the Nation of Islam was both cathartic and liberating for Malcolm. It liberated his mind and soul from the cognitive dissonance of a belief system that was absolutely in conflict with Islam and the Sunnah. Malcolm always wanted to have a closer relationship with the world community of Islam. His passion for this level of brotherhood was ignited when he traveled to Egypt, Ghana, and the Sudan in 1959 to make arrangements for Elijah Muhammad's pilgrimage. Malcolm's 1964 trip to parts of Africa and the Middle East was quite different in that he went voluntarily, determined to learn more about orthodox Islam and to have a greater impact on the human condition worldwide.

As indicated earlier, the core of the Nation of Islam is black nationalism. Moreover, this variety of black nationalism is similar in some ways to the Universal Negro Improvement Association (UNIA) created by Marcus Garvey. As a hybrid of Islamic principles and black nationalism, the Nation of Islam alienated itself from the ummah. Because of its castigation of whites as "devils" and its deification of blacks as "gods," it alienated itself not only from the Muslim world but from the integrationism of the civil rights movement as well. The civil rights movement sought to bring about fundamental social change through the process of interracial cooperation. Fully aware of these differences, Martin Luther King Jr. strongly disagreed with the theology of the NOI. His opinion of the NOI echoed through parts of his famous "Letter from Birmingham Jail":

> I stand in the middle of two opposing forces in the Negro community. One is a force of complacency, made up in part of Negroes who, as a result of long years of oppression, are so drained of self-respect and a sense of "somebodiness" that they have adjusted to segregation; and in part of a few middle-class Negroes who, because of a degree of academic and economic security and because in some ways they profit by segregation, have become insensitive to the problems of the masses. The other force is one of bitterness and hatred, and it comes perilously close to advocating violence. It is expressed in the various black nationalist groups that are springing up across the nation, the largest and best-known being Elijah Muhammad's Muslim movement. Nourished by the Negro's frustration over the continued existence of racial discrimination, this movement is made up of people who have lost faith in America, who have absolutely repudiated Christianity, and who have concluded that the white man is an incorrigible "devil."[79]

While he strongly disagreed with the theology of the Nation of Islam, King commended the Nation of Islam for its rehabilitation programs. But the civil rights leader felt that the Nation of Islam's approach to moral reform had to be matched by an equally positive and progressive stand on the race question, especially if that movement hoped to contribute to the total liberation of Americans.[80]

The break from Elijah Muhammad and the Nation of Islam was actually a blessing in disguise for Malcolm. He would no longer be restricted by its dogmatic and fanatical ideology and leadership. Since his release from prison in 1952, this was the second time that Malcolm was truly free to think for himself and to act upon the world stage with the passion of his own convictions and vision. He stated his intentions in these terms: "I am going to organize and head a new mosque in New York City, known as the Muslim Mosque, Inc. This gives us a religious base, and the spiritual force necessary to rid our people of the vices that destroy the moral fiber of our community.

Our political philosophy will be black nationalism. Our economic and social philosophy will be black nationalism. Our cultural emphasis will be black nationalism."[81]

Malcolm's plan was to have a Muslim mosque inclusive enough to embrace the philosophy of black nationalism in all its dimensions. His liberation strategy was the brotherhood and unity of all peoples of African descent. The Nation of Islam had not afforded the proper context for implementing this strategy, for it was not recognized in the Muslim world as a legitimate Muslim community. Therefore, the advocacy of Sunni Islam helped to overcome the perception that Malcolm's new Muslim Mosque, Inc. was merely an extension of the Nation of Islam.

According to the Qur'an, the foundation of a mosque should meet the following specifications: "a mosque whose foundation was laid from the first day on piety is more worthy of your standing forth for prayer therein. In it are men who love to be purified; and Allah loves those who make themselves pure."[82] Imam Warith Deen Mohammed said Malcolm invited him to assist in the development of the Muslim Mosque, Inc. Because Imam Muhammad's understanding of Sunni Islam and religion were more advanced than Malcolm's at that time, Malcolm wanted him to provide the religious leadership while he himself focused on the cultural and political leadership.[83]

Ideally, Malcolm wanted the Muslim Mosque, Inc. to accommodate NOI members who left with him, Sunni Muslims, black nationalists, socialists, integrationists, and revolutionaries. Over time, however, the ideological chasms between these different groups proved too wide to bridge. Malcolm eventually had to form the Organization of Afro-American Unity in order to accommodate his non-Muslim followers, including militant Christians who found the philosophy and methods of Martin Luther King Jr. unacceptable.

The Holy Qur'an gives specific guidance on the etiquette and protocols of the mosque: "The mosque of Allah shall be visited and maintained by such as believe in Allah and the Last Day, establish regular prayers, practice regular charity, and fear none (at all) except Allah. It is they who are expected to be on true guidance."[84] Malcolm remained mindful of this as he sought to keep before his followers a clear sense of the differences between the mission of the Muslim Mosque, Inc. and the goals of the OAAU.

The Hajj, or pilgrimage to Mecca, is a religious obligation for all Muslims. It serves as a metaphor or epiphany in understanding the spiritual transformation of Malcolm X to a new identity as El-Hajj Malik El-Shabazz. His pilgrimage to Mecca and Medina had essentially the same spiritual enlightenment as King's pilgrimage to Jerusalem and India. The Qur'an proclaims the following concerning the Hajj:

> And proclaim the Pilgrimage
> Among men: they will come
> To thee on foot and (mounted)
> On every kind of camel,
> Lean on account of journeys
> Through deep and distant
> Mountain highways; . . .
> Then let them complete
> The rites prescribed
> For them, perform their vows,
> And (again) circumambulate.
> The Ancient House.[85]

Muslims are exempted from this obligation of the Hajj if they do not have the financial means to do so or if it will impose a burden on their health or family.[86] After Malcolm left the Nation of Islam, his financial resources were limited. His sister Ella, who had already become a Sunni Muslim, loaned him the money needed for the Hajj. He reported, "She was saving up to make the pilgrimage. . . . She told me there was no question about it; it was more important that I go. . . . I had brought Ella into Islam, and now she was financing me to Mecca."[87]

The transition and conversion of Malcolm X to El-Hajj Malik El-Shabazz did not come easily. He had to unlearn the incorrect beliefs and practices of the Nation of Islam and to internalize a new belief system with different customs, practices, and rituals. He had to take on a new perspective and orientation toward the universal religion of Islam. This resocialization process involved study, new thought patterns, new attitudes, new behavior, and new values. Most of all, he had to learn how to think for himself and to put his ultimate faith not in a "man god" but in the true Muslim God, Allah. Malcolm X was hypnotized by Elijah Muhammad, but El-Hajj Malik El-Shabazz was in total submission to the Will of Allah.

Malcolm X's conversion to Sunni Islam began under the guidance of Dr. Mahmoud Youssef Shawarbi, who was on leave from Cairo University and serving as director of the Islamic Center of New York. Malcolm's first lesson started with Dr. Shawarbi reading an ayat (verse or sign) from the Qur'an in Arabic and then translating it into English: "Muslims are all brothers regardless of their color and race." Dr. Shawarbi observed that "Malcolm jumped to his feet and asked him to repeat the reading. He did, and suddenly standing there, Malcolm was shivering and weeping."[88] Dr. Shawarbi gave Malcolm X Shahadah (the verbal commitment and pledge that there is no God but Allah and Muhammad [pbuh] is the Last and Final Messenger of Allah) and was instrumental in paving the way for Malcolm's Hajj.[89]

What actually happened during the performance of Hajj that broadened and reoriented El-Shabazz's thought patterns and actions? The power of the Hajj is in the congregational prayers, unity, rituals, and reenactment of the Old Testament story of Abraham, Sarah, Hagar, and Ishmael. The Hajj is a dramatic play, and the pilgrim is an actor. The story is from the Book of Genesis. Abraham's elderly wife, Sarah, is childless. Because Abraham desires a son, Sarah offers her Egyptian handmaiden, Hagar, as a concubine. Hagar bears Abraham's beloved son, Ishmael. When Ishmael reaches the age of thirteen, Sarah miraculously bears a son, Isaac. Long jealous of Abraham's affection for Hagar and Ishmael, Sarah demands that he banish them to the desert to die. Abraham reluctantly does so, but only after God promises him that Ishmael will begin a new nation. When they run out of water, Hagar begins wandering between the two hills of Safa and Marwa. After her seventh journey back and forth, an angel appears and leads her to the well of Zam Zam. Thus, the mother and son are able to survive the cruelty of the desert. Malcolm must have revisited this story many times as he struggled to come to terms with his new identity and fresh sense of mission.

The real test of faith for Abraham comes when Allah commands him to sacrifice his firstborn son. In the Torah and the Book of Genesis, the son who is offered for sacrifice is Isaac. But Muslims believe Abraham offered to sacrifice Ishmael.[90] The devil tries to persuade Abraham not to obey Allah. Abraham ignores the devil's advice and prepares to slay his son, but Allah suddenly intervenes and allows Abraham to sacrifice a ram instead. During the Hajj, stones are thrown at three statues of different heights. These statues represent the three temptations offered by the devil. In the Nation of Islam, Malcolm was taught that the white man is the devil, but in mainstream Islam the devil is Satan. The stoning of the devil also represents a rejection of all negative thoughts, words, and deeds. Before the stones are cast, the pilgrims say: "I seek refuge in Allah from the rejected Satan."

Malik El-Shabazz's testimonies concerning his changed religious beliefs were grounded in his spiritual transformation during the performance of the Hajj. The Hajj was a defining moment for him. On the Mount of Arafat, which is the Mount of Mercy, Allah gave him true guidance. The full essence of his sincerity was made manifest. Thus, one might conclude that Malcolm X's Hajj in 1964 was perhaps as historically significant as the celebrated Hajj of Mansa Musa, the king of the Mali Empire, in 1324.[91] It was the custom of African Muslim rulers to make the Hajj once they were inaugurated into power. The Hajj anointed the ruler with knowledge and wisdom. Malcolm X's Hajj anointed him with the wisdom necessary for him to return to the United States to wage a successful jihad (struggle) against classism, racism, and gender oppression.[92]

According to Essien-Udom, "Apart from the personal religious duty, Malcolm had a twofold purpose in making the Hajj. First, he wished to establish links between the Muslim Mosque, Inc. which he had founded, and the estimated 750 million orthodox Muslims of the world. Second, he wished to win support of his effort to bring a charge of the violation of the Afro-Americans' human rights before the attention of the world at the United Nations. The Hajj would, of course, offer a very favorable opportunity for making valuable contacts, especially since important Muslim political and religious leaders from all over the world make this pilgrimage."[93] These contacts and linkages were made. Malik El-Shabazz created an international network of Muslim and African allies that gave him access to powerful leaders and resources on a world scale. Thus, any serious effort to internationalize his people's struggle through the United Nations would have put the United States in a bad light, and Malcolm's move in this direction undoubtedly contributed to his assassination.

A Paradigm Shift

Sunni Islam changed Malik's belief system, thought patterns, attitudes, values, and behavior patterns. In a word, he underwent both a spiritual transformation and an ideological paradigm shift. This fundamental and axiomatic shift in his model of the universe, society, and the human family caused him to rethink his positions on issues that he took as a member of the Nation of Islam. The Hajj challenged his black nationalist beliefs and ideology, but his fundamental commitment to the total liberation of the 22 million African Americans in the United States did not change. His mode of analysis shifted from rigid racial categories to more flexible class, cultural, political, and religious categories. The world could no longer be defined in Manichean categories of white supremacy and black inferiority. In fact, his new class analysis led him to an intense critique of capitalism and imperialism: "It is impossible for capitalism to survive, primarily because the system of capitalism needs blood to suck. Capitalism used to be like an eagle, but now it's more like a vulture. It used to be strong enough to go and suck anybody's blood whether they were strong or not. But now it has become more cowardly, like the vulture, and it can only suck the blood of the helpless. As the nations of the world free themselves, then capitalism has less victims, less to suck, and it becomes weaker and weaker. It's only a matter of time in my opinion before it will collapse completely."[94]

Malcolm's analysis of the African and African diaspora situation was based on the tenets of Islam. He saw the Pan-African paradigm as parallel to the Muslim paradigm. By this, we mean Muslims view themselves as members of a global nation or ummah.[95] While they are differentiated by nationality, culture, language, color, gender, education, social class, and lineage, they are integrated by a shared belief in the Oneness of Allah and in the absolute and eternal truths of the Qur'an and Sunnah.[96]

Mecca is a cosmic magnet that draws all Muslims toward the center of the Muslim world in an array of radiating and unfolding concentric circles. It symbolizes the spiritual and cosmic unity of all Muslims. Because of its location in the Arabian Peninsula, Mecca does not connote the cultural hegemony of Arabs over the Muslim ummah. Moreover, Mecca is the fountainhead of Islam because it is the birthplace of Prophet Muhammad (pbuh) and the rebirth place of Islam in the seventh century. It does not empower Arab Muslims above non-Arab Muslims. In his farewell address on Mount Arafat, the Prophet Muhammad (pbuh) said: "O people! Your God is one, and your ancestor is also one. You are all the progeny of Adam who was created from earth. The most respected before God amongst you is one who is most God-fearing. No Arab has preference over a non-Arab or a non-Arab over an Arab. Preference, if any, is on the basis of the fear of God."[97] It is important to stress this point because some black nationalists seem to think Islam is the deification of Arab nationalism, a view impossible to sustain under a close examination of its history and one that El-Shabazz categorically rejected.

In an analogous way, Malcolm related the Islamic paradigm to the Africana paradigm. Hence, Africa was to African descendants what Mecca was to Muslims. Africa was the motherland that symbolized the primordial genetic pool and the historiography of all Africans. Pan-Africanism represented the asabiya or the ideology and sentiment that bonded all Africans in a global community.[98] Hence El-Shabazz saw an interconnection between

Pan-Islam and Pan-Africanism. Many of his admirers and followers could not reconcile this Malcolm with the one with whom they identified. So in a certain way, this aspect of El-Shabazz's personality was either ignored or denied. This perceptual transformation was not so problematic in the case of Martin Luther King Jr. King is consistently seen as a Christian minister. His secular philosophy of nonviolence is seen as an extension of his Christian beliefs. However, this is not the case with Malcolm. In the last years of his life, Malcolm was perceived as becoming more of an integrationist, more of a socialist, or more of a nationalist, and less of a Sunni Muslim, when in fact his economic, political, and social philosophy was an extension of his Sunni Islamic beliefs and values.

When Malcolm left the Nation of Islam, he immediately created the Muslim Mosque, Inc. This religious organization was parallel to the Nation of Islam; however, it was designed to teach mainstream Islam and not the theology of the Nation of Islam. Some followers of Elijah Muhammad left the Nation of Islam and joined Malcolm in this new venture. At that point, the black nationalists felt that they could work more closely with Malcolm, while not being concerned about being pressured to convert to Islam.

Malcolm's analysis of the oppression of African Americans included moral issues. In order to wage a serious struggle against the system of oppression, Malcolm felt it was absolutely necessary to abstain from gambling and consuming alcohol, drugs, and pork. He also advocated celibacy for single African Americans. These moral codes were too demanding for many of the nationalists, integrationists, and socialists who wanted to join Malcolm in the liberation struggle. Therefore, it was easier to approach these activists with a secular ideology rather than one based on Islam.

El-Shabazz and the Enduring Islamic Legacy

The cultural and spiritual transformations that moved a man from Malcolm Little to Malcolm X, and ultimately to El-Hajj Malik El-Shabazz, are magnificent odysseys in the triumph of the human spirit. A child born to a strong father and loving mother made these transformations, thus reflecting an emerging consciousness that put him at odds with the religious traditions of both his parents and Elijah Muhammad. Malcolm was nurtured in the spirit of Marcus Garvey and orphaned at the tender age of six. The Qur'an says of the orphan: "Thy Lord has not forsaken thee, nor is He displeased. . . . Did He not find thee an orphan and give thee shelter (and care)? And He found thee wandering, and He gave thee guidance. And He found thee in need, and made thee independent. Therefore, treat not the orphan with harshness."[99] Because of the trauma of being an orphan, Malcolm subconsciously desired a father surrogate. Elijah Muhammad became an infallible father figure for him. This situation involved expressions of agapic or unconditional love that proved both his salvation and his tragedy. For many years, Malcolm ignored and repressed what he perceived to be Muhammad's character flaws. But the contradictions that precipitated his cognitive dissonance were rationalized or repressed.

While El-Shabazz is often criticized for attempting to strike a proper balance between Islam and black nationalism, he and King both felt that religion was useless if it failed to address the economic, political, and social evils of society. El-Shabazz fundamentally wanted Islam to do the same thing for Africans that it had done for the Arabs. Islam took the Arabs from a backward, decadent, and pagan nation to a world empire. El-Shabazz was disinclined to assimilate into Arab culture in order to achieve this objective. He believed that Marcus Garvey held the key to the redemption of African Americans. Thus, he felt that Islamization was a correct process, but not Arabization. He believed too much in the dignity and integrity of African and African-American cultures to make a personal claim to another culture in order to achieve a truly Islamic identity.

Finally, El-Shabazz came full circle to meet Martin in a spiritual climax of universal beliefs. His study of Al-Qur'an and the Sunnah of Prophet Muhammad (pbuh) before Mecca, and his celebrated Hajj (pilgrimage), led him to reject the false doctrines of the Nation of Islam and embrace Sunni Islam. The Islam of Prophet Muhammad (pbuh) is based on six cardinal beliefs: the Oneness of Allah, the existence of Angels, the acceptance of the Prophets of Allah and the Scriptures revealed to these Prophets, the Day of Judgment, and Divine Preordainment. These fundamental beliefs linked El-Shabazz to the three Abrahamic faiths—Judaism, Christianity, and Islam.

3

Of Their Spiritual Strivings

Malcolm and Martin on Religion and Freedom

> Out of the nation's heart we have called all that was best to throttle and
> subdue all that was worst; fire and blood, prayer and sacrifice, have bil-
> lowed over this people, and they have found peace only in the altars of the
> God of Right. Nor has our gift of the Spirit been merely passive.
> W.E.B. Du Bois[1]

> I believe in a religion that believes in freedom. Anytime I have to accept a
> religion that won't let me fight a battle for my people, I say to hell with
> that religion.
> Malcolm X[2]

> The belief that God will do everything for man is as untenable as the belief
> that man can do everything for himself. It, too, is based on a lack of faith.
> We must learn that to expect God to do everything while we do nothing is
> not faith but superstition.
> Martin Luther King Jr.[3]

Religion assumed a pivotal role in the lives and activities of both Malcolm X
and Martin Luther King Jr. While they drew on different sets of religious
values at critical points in their lives, both refused to reduce religion to the
passive acceptance of abstract concepts and formal creeds. Convinced that
religion should be activistic as well as spiritually and intellectually satisfying,
they offered compelling insights into many of the unappealing aspects of
American religious life and institutions.[4]

What appeared above all in the phenomena of Malcolm and Martin was
religion becoming creative in the struggle to expand human rights and social
justice. Religion provided the supporting framework for their years of service
to humanity. They were exemplars of an active spirituality that discouraged
any dichotomy between piety and ethics, one with deep roots in what

Gayraud S. Wilmore terms "the fecund soil of the Black folk tradition."[5] Thus, they symbolized the search for genuine spirituality and the interplay between religion and other spheres of African-American culture.

Years of Doubt and Decision: The Religious Backgrounds of Malcolm and Martin

Both Malcolm and Martin were inevitably immersed in the atmosphere of their parents' religion. The sons of Baptist preachers and deeply pious women, their earliest awareness of religion centered around dynamic sermons and spiritual and gospel songs that often swelled and overflowed into joyous shouts, recalling the slave church and spirit possession among Africans. Malcolm clearly remembered his father, Earl Little, proclaiming, "That little *black* train is a-comin' . . . an' you better get all your business right," a sermon that probably reflected "his association with the back-to-Africa movement, with Marcus Garvey's 'Black Train Homeward.'" Martin also recalled vividly the sermons of his father, Martin Sr., whose "preaching was rooted in the emotional appeal that country Baptists understood better than anybody in the world."[6] Although Malcolm and Martin developed an antipathy toward what they saw as the emotional extravagance of the black church, that institution, so important in fostering group cohesion and self-respect among the folk, helped shape their earliest conceptions of themselves and the world around them.

But the Little family's church life lacked the stability and direction that existed in the case of the Kings. The difference here resulted partly from the fact that Earl Little "was always a 'visiting preacher'" who "never pastored in any regular church of his own," and Martin Sr. served as the full-time pastor of Ebenezer Baptist Church, "one of black Atlanta's most prominent institutions."[7] Consequently, Malcolm's sense of identification with the church as a child was not as intense as Martin's, a situation that became all the more evident after Malcolm's father was murdered and as his mother exposed her children to many churches, sects, and cultic movements, including Seventh Day Adventists and Jehovah's Witnesses. Although Martin eventually moved far beyond "his Auburn Avenue origins" in Atlanta, "his basic identity remained rooted in Baptist Church traditions that were intertwined with his family's history."[8]

The absence of a definite conversion experience during childhood courses through some of Malcolm's and Martin's autobiographical statements. Malcolm did not have the kind of spiritual crisis or transforming encounter with the supernatural that traditionally established one's place in the faith community, but the values of freedom and self-expression he inherited from his parents and others around him undoubtedly reflected the influence of the black church. This was more the case with Martin, who described his religion as the "largely unconscious" and "gradual intaking of the noble ideals set forth in my family and my environment," and who remembered that "all of my childhood playmates were regular Sunday School goers."[9] But it was sibling rivalry, and not so much this "inherited religion," that compelled Martin to join the Ebenezer Baptist Church at age five, an experience he highlighted later in his "Autobiography of Religious Development":

> I well remember how this event occurred. Our church was in the midst of the spring revival, and a guest evangelist had come down from Virginia. On Sunday morning the guest evangelist came into our Sunday School to talk to us about salvation, and after a short talk on this point he extended an invitation to any of us who wanted to join the church. My sister was the first one to join the church that morning, and after seeing her join I decided that I would not let her get ahead of me, so I was the next. I had never given this matter a thought, and even at the time of my baptism I was unaware of what was taking place. From this it seems quite clear that I joined the church not out of any dynamic conviction, but out of a childhood desire to keep up with my sister.[10]

Competition of this nature did not occur in the Little family, for Malcolm stood in stark contrast to his older brother Philbert, who "loved the church." Far from being an enthusiastic participant in the worship life of the black church, young Malcolm associated its more dramatic, emotive outpourings with religious confusion and irrationalism, a tendency not unusual in a culture where high levels of emotionalism were so often equated with the absence of reason. Although Martin was singing and reciting Bible passages in church at age five, by the time he reached his teens he "wondered whether religion, with its emotionalism in Negro Churches, could be intellectually respectable as well as emotionally satisfying."[11]

Malcolm's disdain for religious emotionalism made it difficult for him to accept his father's image as a Baptist preacher. "I knew that the collections my father got for his preaching were mainly what fed and clothed us," he reminisced, "but still the image of him that made me proudest was his crusading and militantly campaigning with the words of Marcus Garvey."

Malcolm's mistake at this juncture was in failing to see the inseparable link between Earl Little's preaching and his Garveyite activities, for both were extensions of his ministry. This tendency was not as evident with young Martin, who never separated his father's pastoral role from his protests against segregation, and who reported that the elder King "had a great deal to do with my going into the ministry." "He set forth a noble example that I didn't mind following."[12] The different perspectives Malcolm and Martin held toward their fathers' roles as preachers raise interesting questions, because both saw that the ministry provided one of the very few opportunities for leadership and recognition open to black men in those days.

Basic Christian teachings were routinely shared with the children in the Little and King homes. This was only natural in communities where most people were Christians. Malcolm and his siblings were taught to obey God, to follow the Golden Rule and the Ten Commandments, and to be open-minded in their approach to religion. Martin learned some of the same lessons in his home, though he was taught to conform to the doctrines of the black Baptist Church. In one of his autobiographical statements, he referred to two incidents that "had a tremendous effect on my religious development." The first occurred when Martin, at age six, was told by his white playmates that they could no longer play together because he was black. Shocked and deeply hurt, Martin "was determined to hate every white person," a feeling tempered only by his parents' insistence that it was his "duty as a Christian" to love people irrespective of their race. The second incident was the death of his maternal grandmother, Jennie C. Parks Williams, in 1941, an experience that caused even deeper pain and one that forced the boy to struggle with "the doctrine of immortality." "My parents attempted to explain it to me and I was assured that somehow my grandmother still lived," Martin recalled, an assurance that made him "a strong believer in personal immortality."[13]

Displaying intelligence far beyond their years, Malcolm and Martin did not accept uncritically the doctrinal conservatism they heard in churches. Both passed through periods of skepticism before finally embracing a religion that suited their spiritual and intellectual needs. Even at a "young age," Malcolm once declared, "I just couldn't believe in the Christian concept of Jesus as someone divine." Martin's youthful struggle at this level was virtually the same, as he recalled: "I guess I accepted Biblical studies uncritically until I was about twelve years old. But this uncritical attitude could not last long, for it was contrary to the very nature of my being. I had always been the questioning and precocious type. At the age of 13 I shocked my Sunday School class by denying the bodily resurrection of Jesus."[14]

Malcolm's early struggle with church teachings extended beyond claims regarding Jesus' divinity to include more practical considerations. He had difficulty understanding how his father could affirm Garveyism and the glories of Africa while favoring his light-skinned children over the darker ones.[15] Malcolm would later attribute Earl Little's tendency to "the white man's brainwashing of Negroes," a problem which, for Malcolm, was more than adequately revealed in some of the Christian symbolism embraced by his parents:

> My mother was a Christian and my father was a Christian and I used to hear them when I was a little child sing the song "Wash Me White as Snow." My father was a black man and my mother was a black woman, but yet the songs that they sang in their church were designed to fill their hearts with the desire to be white. So many people, especially our people, get resentful when they hear me say something like this. But rather than get resentful all they have to do is think back on many of the songs and much of the teachings and the doctrines that they were taught while they were going to church and they'll have to agree that it was all designed to make us look down on black and up at white.[16]

Malcolm's recollections would have been easily understood by Martin, who most certainly heard his people singing "Wash Me White as Snow" at one time or another and who frequented black churches where pictures of the white Jesus and white angels hung from the walls of sanctuaries. Martin would later note how "even semantics have conspired to make that which is black seem ugly and degrading," a point he found illustrated in *Roget's Thesaurus,* where at least half of the "synonyms for 'blackness'" are "offensive," and all of the "synonyms for 'whiteness'" are "favorable."[17]

Growing up in worlds filled with ambiguities, it was natural for Malcolm and Martin to question religion and the church. Malcolm asserted that "no religious person, until I was a man in my twenties—and then in prison— could tell me anything" because "I had very little respect for most people who represented religion." While Martin was more willing to listen to religious people, his doubts about much of what he had been taught in church haunted him until he went to Morehouse College, where "the shackles of fundamentalism [were] removed from my body." Martin reminisced: "From the age of thirteen on doubts began to spring forth unrelentingly. At the age of fifteen I entered college and more and more I could see a gap between what I had learned in Sunday School and what I was learning in college. The conflict continued until I studied a course in Bible in which I came to see that behind the legends and myths of the Book were many profound truths which one could not escape."[18]

While mindful of the many shortcomings of the black church as young-sters, Malcolm and Martin had more problems with the glaring contradic-tions inherent in the white church. The memory of whites burning the Littles' homes in Omaha and Lansing in the late 1920s hovered over Malcolm like a menacing cloud, giving the boy his first lessons about the racism of white Christians. "It was Christians who burned the home in both places—people who teach, you know, religious tolerance and brotherhood and all of them," he angrily reflected years later. Although the Kings never suffered this fate at the hands of whites, Martin, growing up in an environment where segrega-tion existed even in white churches, could have easily identified with Malcolm's bitterness. Moreover, both attended white churches in the North while in their early teens, experiences that must have triggered further re-minders of the tragic ambivalence in the souls of white Christians.[19]

Malcolm's declining interest in Christianity became increasingly obvious after he moved from Michigan to live with his sister Ella in Boston. Fourteen at the time, Malcolm attended church with Ella for a brief period, but he soon found more excitement and affirmation in the streets and the nightclubs. During his escapades as a hustler, pimp, dope addict, drug pusher, and bur-glar, he continued to meet both black and white Christians who compelled him to raise critical questions about the viability or practicality of religion. As Malcolm penetrated deeper into the underworld in Boston and New York, he encountered "Evangelists who on Sundays peddled Jesus," "mystics" who prayed "a lucky number for you for a fee," and even white clergymen whom he steered toward prostitutes or "whatever kind of sin they wanted in Harlem." There is reason to take seriously his conviction that had he not gone to Boston, he probably would have remained "a brainwashed black Christian."[20] But the hypocrisy Malcolm witnessed made him less receptive to the Christian faith than Martin, who, at age fifteen, expressed a keen interest in the practical application of "the central teachings of Jesus" and who conveyed "an intimate knowledge of Baptist church life, including such details as congregational governance, ward meetings, church finances, and social events."[21]

The underworld instilled in Malcolm values that Martin could never have accepted given his strong church ties and deep sense of inner spiritual security. Up to age nineteen, Martin operated in a southern setting where *right* and *wrong* behaviors were clearly defined within the framework of church teachings, whereas Malcolm functioned in criminal circles in northern ghettoes under a different system of ethics. He quickly learned that "the ghetto hustler" at his worst knows no sacred creed. "He has no religion, no concept of morality, no civic responsibility, no fear—nothing," Malcolm once observed. "To survive, he is out there constantly preying upon others, probing for any human weakness like a ferret."[22] Memories of exposure to this kind of world surfaced in powerful ways when Malcolm, as a Muslim minister, began to develop a perspective on the relationship between religion and life that was similar in many ways to Martin's.

The ten-year prison sentence that twenty-year-old Malcolm received for burglary in 1946 clearly signaled a turning point in his faith pilgrimage. An avowed "atheist" long before he was convicted, Malcolm found it impossible to escape the spiritual and intellectual search that prisoners typically experienced. As an inmate in the Massachusetts State Prison system, he had more time to read and think about his spiritual life than Martin ever envisioned for himself at Morehouse College, Crozer Theological Seminary, and Boston University. Malcolm's attitude toward the Christian Church in those years was anything but favorable. After receiving a letter "from my religious brother Philbert in Detroit, telling me his 'holiness' church was going to pray for me," he remembered, "I scrawled him a reply I'm ashamed to think of today." The young man's "anti-religious attitude" was such that fellow inmates dubbed him "Satan," an image that contrasted sharply with the "polished preacher" demeanor Martin would develop in some circles before graduating from Morehouse.[23]

Malcolm's turn toward religion began in 1948, the year Martin graduated from Morehouse and became an ordained Baptist minister. The greatest inspiration for this gradual shift came from his brother Reginald, who communicated with Malcolm concerning the Nation of Islam, or what he labeled "the natural religion for the black man." Malcolm, who "had graduated from Christianity to agnosticism on into atheism," gave this account of what happened:

My family became Muslims; accepted the religion of Islam, and one of them who had spent pretty much—had spent quite a bit of time with me on the streets of New York out here in Harlem had been exposed to the religion of Islam. He accepted it, and it made such a profound change in him. He wrote to me and was telling me about it. Well, I had completely eliminated Christianity. After getting into prison and having time to think, I could see the hypocrisy of Christianity. Even before I went to prison, I had already become an atheist. . . . Most of my associates were white; they were either Jews or Christians, and I saw hypocrisy on both sides. None of them really practiced what they preached.[24]

The Islam that Malcolm embraced differed in many ways from the Christianity to which Martin had long subscribed. While both religions upheld the necessity for high standards of morality and personal ethics, the Nation of Islam's affirmation of Allah as the Supreme Black Man, of the divinity of black men and women, of whites as "blue-eyed devils" by nature, and of heaven and hell as strictly earthly realities clashed with the fundamental teachings of the black church. Even before officially becoming a member of the Nation of Islam, later known as the Black Muslims, Malcolm had accepted its ban on smoking, drinking alcohol, cursing, sexual promiscuity, and eating pork, and he eagerly affirmed the group's theology and anthropology after communicating with its leader, Elijah Muhammad. Malcolm never forgot how "Mister Muhammad came along with his religious gospel and introduced the religion of Islam and showed the honesty of Islam, the freedom in Islam. Why naturally, just comparing the two, Christianity had already eliminated itself, so all I had to do was accept the religion of Islam."[25]

From the point of his conversion to Islam, Malcolm blamed "the white man's Christian world" for the problems that had led to his imprisonment. "I firmly believe that it was the Christian society, as you call it, the Judaic-Christian society, that created all of the factors that send so many so-called Negroes to prison," he observed. Although there was a measure of truth in this claim, Malcolm's crimes in youth stood primarily as an indictment against his own character and not Christianity. If challenged, he would have been hard-pressed to explain how his and Martin's exposure to the same so-called Christian society accounted for the radically different directions they took as teenagers. Martin would have been the first to acknowledge the role of white Christianity in establishing the structures, values, and practices that encouraged criminal behavior among his people, but he also would have admitted, without any hesitation, that he himself was able to avoid crime and imprisonment mainly because of the constant affirmation and reinforcement he received in the church.[26]

The Nation of Islam was relatively unknown and located almost exclusively in the North when Malcolm joined it. The movement had emerged as part of the diversification of African-American religion in the early twentieth century, when a range of new Islamic and Jewish sects originated in reaction to the perceived dysfunctionality and bourgeoisification of established black churches, and as a response to racism and social stratification in the larger society.[27] These new developments struck a responsive chord in the hearts of black youngsters like Malcolm, who, unlike Martin, found essentially no hope for salvation in the faith and church traditions of their elders. While Martin disagreed theologically with his father, his religious heritage remained dear to him. "At present I still feel the effects of the noble moral and ethical ideals that I grew up under," he declared as a seminary student. "They have been real and precious to me, and even in moments of theological doubt I could never turn away from them."[28]

Christianity and Islam: Putting Religion in Perspective

Both Malcolm and Martin saw the need to understand religion in intellectual as well as practical terms. Efforts toward this end escalated in the late 1940s, as Malcolm served time in prisons in Massachusetts and as Martin matriculated at Morehouse College. In their different settings, each man found role models who taught him by words and example that religion in its truest sense is not only intellectually challenging and stimulating but also socially aware and committed to positive change. Malcolm undoubtedly learned this from Bimbi, a fellow inmate whom he highly respected. Martin found his chief role models in his father, who "always stood out in social reform," and in Benjamin E. Mays and George D. Kelsey, Morehouse College president and professor, respectively, both of whom were ministers, "deeply religious," and yet "learned men, aware of all the trends of modern thinking." Concerning Mays and Kelsey, Martin noted, "I could see in their lives the ideal of what I wanted a minister to be," a point he also made frequently regarding his father, despite the differences between them theologically.[29]

Malcolm's and Martin's understandings of religion benefitted from sources other than their role models. Their intellectual sources on the subject included the Bible. As an inmate, Malcolm studied the Bible with an intensity that matched Martin's persistent questioning of literal interpretations of that resource at Morehouse. Martin was first introduced to historical-critical approaches to scripture in a Bible class taught by George Kelsey, and the result was the beginnings of a "liberalizing process" that continued with his studies at Crozer and Boston, leading him to question much of what he had learned in Christian churches and particularly among black Baptists.[30] The critical approaches he and Malcolm took to Bible study in those days were immensely significant, especially since that document would later figure prominently in the shaping of many of their insights into the meaning of the black experience and the destiny of their people.

The prison libraries enabled Malcolm to read some of the same authors that Martin studied at Morehouse and Crozer Theological Seminary. Among such sources were the nineteenth-century American social critic Henry David Thoreau and the Indian leader Mohandas Gandhi, both of whom appealed to spiritual values in their literary and physical challenges to some of the abuses of power and privilege in their particular societies. Malcolm was led to Thoreau through Bimbi, and he also read "Gandhi's accounts of the struggle to drive the British out of India." Martin read Thoreau's *Essay on Civil Disobedience* (1848) at Morehouse and several works by and about Gandhi at Crozer.[31] While it is clear that Thoreau and Gandhi did not influence Malcolm as they did Martin, Malcolm would have been no less intrigued by their insistence that noncooperation with an evil system constitutes a truly moral and spiritual act, especially since Thoreau and Gandhi applied this principle in their opposition to unjust governmental structures.

Malcolm's and Martin's emerging perspectives on religion owed much to their experiences in the church and their readings concerning the history of Christianity. Aside from the teaching of Elijah Muhammad, Malcolm's views on the history of Christianity drew not only on the works of Will Durant, H. G. Wells, and J. A. Rogers but also on the free exchange of ideas that often occurred between him and other prison inmates. Having advantages in relation to Christianity not consciously shared by Malcolm, Martin's writings at Morehouse reveal a keen grasp of the history and traditions of various branches of Christianity. His broader exposure to and knowledge of Christianity made his insights into the limitations of that faith more informed and constructive than Malcolm's, particularly at this point in their lives.[32] In time, Malcolm's views on Christianity were influenced almost exclusively by his increasing familiarity with the teachings of Elijah Muhammad and the Nation of Islam. Converted to Islam while still in prison, his assault on Christian teachings and practices soon echoed Muhammad's:

> And where the religion of every other people on earth taught its believers of a God with whom they could identify, a God who at least looked

like one of their own kind, the slavemaster injected his religion into this "Negro." This "Negro" was taught to worship an alien God having the same blond hair, pale skin, and blue eyes as the slavemaster. . . . This religion taught the "Negro" that black was a curse. It taught him to hate everything black, including himself. It taught him that everything white was good, to be admired, respected, and loved. It brainwashed this "Negro" to think he was superior if his complexion showed more of the white pollution of the slavemaster. This white man's Christian religion further deceived and brainwashed this "Negro" to always turn the other cheek, and grin, and scrape, and bow, and be humble, and to sing, and to pray, and to take whatever was dished out by the devilish white man; and to look for his pie in the sky, and for his heaven in the hereafter, while right here on earth the slavemaster white man enjoyed his heaven.[33]

Although Martin recognized the shortcomings of Christianity as practiced by whites and blacks over time, he, as a college and seminary student, did not subject the church to the kind of penetrating criticism for which he would become known in later years.[34] He saw clearly that the oppression of his people resulted not from the Christian faith itself, as critics like Malcolm often suggested, but from the essentially anti-Christian values and practices of white Western society. This helps explain Martin's refusal to break with Christianity, even as he witnessed racism and segregation in white churches. He was always able to separate the evil actions of those who claimed to be Christians from Christianity in its purest and most powerful expression.

But Martin had to experience an intellectual and spiritual crisis at Crozer before the Christian ethics of love and nonviolence became "the dominant force in his life." This crisis was precipitated by his reading of the nineteenth-century German philosopher Friedrich Nietzsche, who equated the Hebraic-Christian ethic with weakness and a resignation of power. After reading Nietzsche's *The Genealogy of Morals* (1887) and *The Will to Power* (1901), Martin seriously questioned the efficacy of Jesus' ethical message of "turn the other cheek" and "love thine enemies" in resolving social conflict. At this juncture, he quite likely believed in the necessity and inevitability of violence and even war in resolving conflicts between racial groups and nations, a point that would have applied even more to Malcolm the inmate. Malcolm read Nietzsche while in prison, but he gave no indication of being influenced by that philosopher's critique of Christianity, an omission that raises many questions since Nietzsche's views on the subject were frighteningly close to his own. Malcolm felt that Nietzsche, like the German philosophers Imman-uel Kant and Arthur Schopenhauer, spent too much time "arguing about things that are not really important."[35]

There was a direction to Malcolm's and Martin's studies that grew out of their encounters with racism and with the need to make religion relevant to their people's struggle against oppression. Unfortunately, the "culture" in prison interfered with any desire Malcolm may have had to commit his cre-ative ideas to paper. In contrast, Crozer Theological Seminary afforded the ideal setting for Martin to write about religion and its applicability to human needs. The young man wrote extensively on such topics as the ancient mys-tery religions, the Hebrew prophets, the views of Jesus, the problems of God and evil, neo-Reformed thought, fundamentalist and liberal trends in theol-ogy, and the social roles of religion.[36] His writings were consistent with his search for answers to the problem of social evil, a quest Malcolm pursued in his own way behind bars.

They came to share the perception that religion could not be separated from politics and daily life, a view that appeared only natural given their roots in a culture where there was often no bifurcation of the sacred and the secular. During his last three years in prison, the inseparability of religion and politics became increasingly clear for Malcolm as he considered the contribu-tions Islam might make to the empowerment of his people and to their free-dom from white domination. The Western tendency to divorce religion from politics never registered well with Martin, who lived in a world where the functions of the church were never limited to the spiritual and the ecclesias-tical, and who consistently witnessed manipulative power politics at work in many areas of black Baptist church life. In a paper at Crozer, Martin de-scribed his religion as "closely knitted to life. . . . In fact, the two cannot be separated; religion for me is life." He obviously understood that "religion is something broad and universal covering the whole of life."[37] This view found complete vindication years later as spirituality became the basis of both his and Malcolm's efforts to transform society and to create human community.

The perspectives of Malcolm and Martin on religion found further refine-ment in the 1950s as each confronted with mounting urgency his own role as a spiritual leader in the African-American community. This experience could not have been more significant for Malcolm, who, when freed from prison in 1952, resolved to spread Elijah Muhammad's "religious message" of free-dom and independence as a cure to the multitude of problems afflicting his people in a racist society.[38] Malcolm's goal at this juncture differed substantially from the vision of Martin, who was in his second year as a doctoral student in philosophical theology at Boston University and not yet very vocal about the concrete problems and challenges facing religion and religious institutions around the issue of race. The politics involved in obtaining a doctoral degree from a white university did not allow Martin the kind of freedom and flexibility Malcolm enjoyed when it came to raising critical questions about the vast gulf between the Christian creed and what white Christians practiced.

But Martin's studies at Boston were perhaps more important than his training at Morehouse and Crozer in providing him with the intellectual categories and language to relate religion and theology to racial polarization and other areas of social conflict. His search for philosophical and theological answers to the problem of race and other social and political barriers to human community was more intense at this point than that of Malcolm, who had found "substantiation for the Black Muslim creed in *Paradise Lost* and in Herodotus" while incarcerated. Martin wrote much concerning the perfectibility of human nature, the need to rediscover the moral laws of the universe, the relationship between spirituality and social transformation, the meaning of faith and conversion, Christian hope and responsibility, the problems of evil and suffering, the tension between individual and corporate ethics, personal idealism, and the meaning of God in the human struggle—topics that would have intrigued Malcolm in varying degrees given his continuing quest for knowledge. Less concerned with the study of religion and theology as academic disciplines, Malcolm, who quickly rose as a Black Muslim minister, would have agreed nonetheless with Martin's insistence that justice between humans "is one of the divine foundations of society" and "an ethical ideal" at "the root of all true religion."[39]

Fundamental to their theories of religion was the belief that the Bible speaks to the plight of the oppressed. This had become abundantly clear to both men by the mid-1950s, as they moved to the forefront of the African-American struggle for freedom. Ironically, Malcolm drew more heavily on the Bible than on the Qur'an in advancing his conviction that Islam offered far more than Christianity in terms of a spiritual solution to the social, economic, and political problems confronting black people.[40] While occasionally referring to the Bible as a "poison book" used by white Christians to control "the minds of Negroes throughout the centuries," he insisted, on the other hand, that the Bible foretold everything that had happened to his people since slavery.[41] "The Honorable Elijah Muhammad teaches us that these so-called American Negroes are God's long-lost people who are symbolically described in the Bible as the Lost Sheep or the Lost Tribe of Israel," Malcolm declared. He was even more specific in a speech at Atlanta University in 1961:

The Bible speaks of how we were purposely cut off from our own kind after being robbed of our identity by the cruel Christian slavemaster (Ezekiel 37.11; Psalms 137.1–9, 83.4). The slave master then took our names, language, and religion from us so we would have to accept his, obey him, and worship him (Dan. 1.6–7). . . . Messenger Muhammad has given us many Scriptures to prove his teachings to us are true and in accord with the prophecies of the Bible. He says it is we (so-called Negroes) in America who were robbed and made deaf, dumb, and blind to the knowledge of our own God and our own selves; so that today we are like DRY BONES IN THE VALLEY (spiritually dead, and in a mental grave of ignorance).[42]

For Malcolm, the biblical accounts of the Babylonian Captivity and the Exodus affirmed the past and future of African Americans in no uncertain terms. Although slave traders had brought them to Egypt land, where they suffered enslavement under a new pharaoh, God's liberation of His people, as told in the stories of Egypt and Babylon, would one day be reenacted in the United States under the leadership of a new Moses. According to Malcolm:

The same solution that God has given the Honorable Elijah Muhammad is the same solution that God gave to Moses when the Hebrews in the Bible were in a predicament similar to the predicament of the so-called Negroes here in America today, which is nothing other than a modern house of bondage, a modern Egypt, or a modern Babylon. And Moses' answer was to separate these slaves from their slave master and show the slaves how to go to a land of their own where they would serve a God of their own and a religion of their own and have a country of their own in which they could feed themselves, clothe themselves, and shelter themselves.[43]

Martin shared Malcolm's view that the story of the Exodus provided a powerful store of metaphors to illustrate the unfolding history and destiny of African Americans, but the civil rights leader categorically rejected the claim that Muhammad was the new Moses called by God to separate blacks from whites. Even so, he, like Malcolm, repeated the story of the Exodus many times as a historical reality that paralleled the black experience, asserting that God's hand had guided his people through the Egypt of slavery into the wilderness of segregation, only to prepare them for a triumphant entrance into the Promised Land of freedom, justice, and equality of opportunity.[44] It was in their use of the Exodus story to explain their people's historic struggle, sense of peoplehood, and destiny that Malcolm and Martin reflected most profoundly the traditions of their slave forebears.[45]

The same could be said, at least on some levels, of the images of Jesus Christ that Malcolm and Martin found in the Scriptures. While both concluded that the very essence of Jesus' power and authority rested in his identification with the despised and rejected, the two men arrived at such a conclusion without coming to full agreement about who Jesus really *was*. The situation could not have been otherwise, especially since they interpreted Jesus in light of their different faith traditions. Malcolm pictured Jesus as a religious reformer, as a wise man who advocated separating the "lost sheep" from the Gentiles, and as one who "died on the cross because the Pharisees of his day were upholding their law, not the spirit." Disturbed by the image of the blond, blue-eyed Jesus displayed and affirmed in black churches, Malcolm maintained that "Christ wasn't white, Christ was a black man. Only the poor, brainwashed American Negro has been made to believe that Christ was white to maneuver him into worshiping the white man."[46]

Martin did not entirely accept this portrait of Jesus. He commonly referred to Jesus as a great teacher and philosopher, as "an extremist for love," as "the world's most dedicated nonconformist," and as one who, through his social outreach and death on the cross, embodied to the fullest the ethic of altruism. But the very notion that Jesus was a black man who preached racial segregation struck Martin as absurd, as evidenced by a remark he made in 1957:

The color of Jesus' skin is of little or no consequence. The whiteness or blackness of one's skin is a biological quality which has nothing to do with the intrinsic value of personality. The significance of Jesus lay not in His skin color, but in His unique God-consciousness and His willingness to surrender His will to God's will. He was the Son of God, not because of His external biological make-up, but because of his internal spiritual commitment. He would have been no more significant if His skin had been black. He is no less significant because His skin was white.[47]

After some rethinking of the person and significance of Jesus in the decade that followed, Martin adopted a view on the color of that figure that more closely approximated Malcolm's. Interestingly enough, Martin contended in 1968 that "Jesus Christ was not a white man."[48] This shift in perspective owed much to the black awareness thrust that accompanied the cry for black power in the late 1960s, though Martin, despite becoming increasingly radical, stopped short of identifying Jesus as a black man. This was not surprising, since he attached far more significance to the universal love ethic that the man from Nazareth embodied. In any case, in raising the matter of Jesus' skin color, he and Malcolm anticipated debates that would later occur among black theologians in the academy and the church.[49]

Viewing the Bible as a book of prophecies, Malcolm and Martin naturally included Jesus among the great prophets of all times. As a Black Muslim minister, Malcolm frequently likened Elijah Muhammad's role as prophet to that of Jesus, which was significant because Malcolm, unlike Martin, rejected images of Jesus as Messiah and Savior of the world. Malcolm also refused to accept Martin's characterizations of Jesus as one who fully embodied the nonviolent ethic and the command to "love thine enemies." Convinced that Jesus' prophetic task involved separating the sheep from the goats, or the oppressed from the oppressor, Malcolm "was drawn more and more in his last years to the wild apocalyptic visions of the Book of Revelation, in which the righteous make war against the wicked and even Jesus takes up the sword."[50]

But Malcolm was less receptive than Martin to the idea that Jesus stood in the traditions of the ancient Hebrew prophets. Malcolm argued that Jesus practiced Islam, "the religion of Moses, Noah, and Abraham."[51] This view conflicted sharply with the most reputable scholarship on the subject, which held that Jesus lived and died a Jew and that Abraham and the core of his descendants were adherents of the Jewish rather than the Muslim faith. Martin subscribed to the standard view set forth in the scholarship on Jesus, reflecting his wide exposure to Western Christian theology and ethics. Having read works such as Walter Rauschenbusch's *Christianity and the Social Crisis* (1907), Martin developed a keen understanding of how ancient Jewish prophecy constituted the chief religious heritage of Jesus and his nation. Moreover, Martin's training and background in the black church help explain why his thought was more traditionally Christocentric than Malcolm's.[52]

Malcolm's insistence that Jesus was a black man and a devoted Muslim was part of a broader effort to convince African Americans that their ancestral roots and their ultimate salvation as a people inhered in Islam and not Christianity. He did not hesitate to challenge those blacks who suggested, on the basis of antiquity, that their ancestral background was more authentically Christian than Islamic. While maintaining that "the genesis of Christianity as we know it" was "conceived in Africa" by the "Desert Fathers," Malcolm denied that ancient Egypt and Ethiopia were Christian before Islam was organized, a position he arrived at quite naturally given his belief that "all of the prophets were Muslims." Having immersed himself thoroughly in the writings of J. A. Rogers concerning ancient African Christianity, Malcolm was more apt than Martin to talk about "the great Coptic Christian Empires" and about early Christian thinkers like Augustine, "that black African saint who saved Catholicism from Heresy." But due to the heavy Greek and Roman influences on ancient Christianity in Egypt and Ethiopia and the contamination of the church with racism "when it entered white Europe," Malcolm readily dismissed Christianity as the religion of his ancestors. Said he: "But when you go back, you'll find that there were large Muslim empires that stretched all the way down into equatorial Africa, the Mali Empire, Guinea. All these places—their religion was Islam. . . . So here in America today when you find many of us who are accepting Islam as our religion, we are only going back to the religion of our forefathers."[53]

Malcolm's claim that Islam is the natural religion of African Americans and their ancestors was unacceptable to Martin, who knew that tribal religions, Judaism, Christianity, and other faiths existed in Africa long before Islam appeared on that continent in the seventh century. Furthermore, Martin knew that Africans had figured prominently in the origins and expansion of the Christian Church, and he praised the ancient Christians for their great courage and devotion amidst persecution, but he limited his perspective primarily to the United States when identifying the Christian roots of African Americans.[54]

While essentially agreeing that religion at its best embraces the totality of human existence, Malcolm and Martin could not have been more divided when it came to the question of the relationship between religion and race. As a Black Muslim minister, Malcolm taught what many considered a race-centered religion, proclaiming that Islam corresponded more to the values of the dark world than to those of the white world: "Muhammad was in Arabia fourteen hundred years ago and he taught that all men are brothers. If you notice, the spread of that religion of brotherhood went rapidly in Asia and Africa where the dark people of the earth believed by nature in being hospitable, friendly, and brotherly toward everyone. But when that religion of brotherhood reached Europe it ran into a stone wall, because the white man by nature cannot practice brotherhood even with another white man."[55]

Convinced that tendencies toward good and evil exist in some measure within all races and ethnic groups, Martin did not agree with Malcolm. Martin felt that under the power of a genuinely religious experience, a white person could become as congenial and as open to the possibilities of human community as the most dedicated black Christian. While he believed that higher human values and virtues were extremely rare in the great mass of white people, Martin refused to accept Malcolm's claim that the white race was created devils by nature by a mad black scientist named Yacub, "the central myth of the Black Muslim movement." Until 1963, Malcolm fervently preached the idea that all whites are irredeemable, but it struck Martin as absurd and quite alien to the spirit of human community as taught by all the world's great religions.[56] Less problematic for Martin was Malcolm's view that the Christian Church is inseparable from whiteness and white supremacy as a world problem, a position Malcolm advanced with disturbing clarity:

> Your Christian countries, if I am correct, are the countries of Europe and North and South America. Predominantly, this is where you find Christianity, or at least people who represent themselves as Christians. Whether they practice what Jesus taught is something we won't go into. The Christian world is what we usually call the Western world. . . . The colonization of the dark people in the rest of the world was done by Christian powers. The number one problem that most people face in the world today is how to get freedom from Christians. Wherever you find non-white people today they are trying to get back their freedom from people who represent themselves as Christians, and if you ask these (subject) people their picture of a Christian, they will tell you "a white man—a Slave-master."[57]

The belief that "Christianity is the white man's religion" helps explain why Malcolm, as a Black Muslim minister, found virtually no redeeming features in the black church. In fact, that belief contributed enormously to his aggressive and unyielding assault on the black church. At times, Malcolm reduced that institution to a poor carbon copy or a pale facsimile of the white church, and he stressed the sobriety and reasonableness of Islam as a more attractive alternative to what he saw as the unbridled emotionalism, the misguided otherworldliness, and the fierce irrationalism of black Christians.[58] This became a part of Malcolm's strategy to win all African Americans to Elijah Muhammad's brand of Islam. Conversely, Martin had no desire to convert all African Americans to Christianity, as evidenced by his lack of both a strong proselytizing spirit and a need to consistently stress the superiority of his religion over Islam.

In highlighting what he deemed the absurdity of the black Christian experience, Malcolm boasted that the Muslims engaged in no music, shouting, or emotive outbursts even during funerals. This failure to grasp the spiritual, artistic, and therapeutic value of the black church perplexed Martin, who increasingly identified with the emotive features and the otherworldly outlook of that institution. Frequently exposed to lively singing, fervent prayers, and shouts of joy in black churches during the mass meetings, Martin acknowledged those times when he was overpowered by spurts of emotion that he could not control, and he insisted, "Religion deals with both earth and heaven, both time and eternity." Martin felt that much of the power of the black church rested in its amazing spirituality and in its tendency to combine this-worldly concerns with the compensatory hope for otherworldly pleasure, and he was not persuaded by Malcolm's insistence that Islam was a more intelligent option for African Americans. Martin also dismissed Malcolm's view that white oppressors had rendered Christianity impotent and meaningless and, therefore, counterproductive and perhaps even self-defeating for black people. According to Coretta Scott King, Martin "felt that it was not the Christian ethic which must be rejected, but that those who failed Christianity must be brought—through love, to brotherhood, for their own redemption as well as ours. He believed that there was a great opportunity for black people to redeem Christianity in America."[59]

For Martin, the nonviolent movement stood as ample proof that his people had redefined and reshaped the Christian faith in conformity with a higher morality and a more perfect human ideal. The black church's powerful prophetic vision of love, justice, hope, and community, and the centrality of the exodus and cross events, were finding fulfillment through church-centered civil rights campaigns. Indeed, African Americans were demonstrating that Christianity in its truest form is not "the white man's religion" or a tool of oppression but, rather, a faith that dethrones the high and mighty while exalting the meek and the deprived. In contrast to Malcolm, who consistently predicted the impending death of Christianity, Martin believed that Christianity was becoming once again the living faith of a rapidly declining civilization. Thus, he urged African Americans not to abandon that faith which brought "our mothers and fathers" through "the dark days of slavery."[60]

Malcolm's perspective on Christianity and the black church in particular expanded and became less critical after his departure from the Nation of Islam in early 1964. He no longer felt compelled to advance Elijah Muhammad's diatribes against the Christian faith, and he knew that strong and persistent attacks on the black church would undermine his growing desire to work with Martin and others on the front line of the freedom movement. Also, as Malcolm observed the increasing radicalization of Martin, and as he associated with militant preachers like Adam Clayton Powell Jr. and Albert B. Cleage Jr., he must have realized that black Christianity embodied revolutionary teachings and a rebellious spirit remarkably similar to what existed in Islam, though he never publicly said so.[61]

Although Malcolm sought to establish an orthodox Islamic movement among his people through the Muslim Mosque, Inc., his efforts to bring black Muslims and Christians together in the Organization of Afro-American Unity (OAAU) showed that he was moving away from a narrow conception of religion. His growth in this regard was further stimulated by his travels abroad in 1964 and also by the freedom he now had to study and think for himself. Martin sensed Malcolm's maturing perspective on religion, and identified it as a much-needed step on his part toward internationalism, especially since the Muslim leader no longer understood religion strictly in racial terms.[62]

But the two men never agreed entirely on the roles that Christianity and Islam might play in eroding racism from the minds and the thought patterns of human beings. Highlighting the need for his people to "forget about higher denominations" because "these things divide us," Martin insisted that the answer to the race problem inhered in a more rigid adherence to the Christian principles of love, forgiveness, and reconciliation. He always believed in the redemptive and transforming power of Christianity and the black church. But Malcolm's exposure to orthodox Islam in the Middle East, particularly during his pilgrimage to Mecca in the spring of 1964, reinforced his doubts about Christianity and convinced him that the Muslim faith held the solution to the problem. "America needs to understand Islam," he wrote, "because this is the one religion that erases the race problem from its society." The experience of sharing to the fullest with "tens of thousands of pilgrims from all over the world," who dressed similarly and chanted as one in the name of Allah, overwhelmed Malcolm, as his testimony suggested: "Throughout my travels in the Muslim world, I have met, talked to, and even eaten with, people who would have been considered 'white' in America, but the religion of Islam in their hearts has removed the 'white' from their minds. They practice sincere and true brotherhood with other people irrespective of their color. . . . The whites as well as the non-whites who accept true Islam become a changed people."[63]

One source raises the strong possibility that Malcolm "was misled by the fictitious picture of 'colorless' Islamic 'brotherhood,' waved constantly before his eyes by white Arabs who obtain thousands of Black slaves from Africa every year." According to this source, millions of black people were "subjected to the most degrading forms of oppression in the various Arab-dominated portions of the Middle East and North Africa." Be that as it may, Malcolm's belief that racism would simply vanish under the power of Islam was amazingly naive, and it showed the limitations of his perspective on religion as a transforming force. Malcolm never really explained how Islam could solve a racial dilemma that Christianity, with all of its stress on love and the communitarian ideal, had failed to resolve over many centuries. Moreover, he seemed unaware that Muslims, like Christians, were guilty of promoting prejudice and oppression based on skin color and religious and cultural differences.[64] Malcolm's essentially uncritical attitude toward orthodox Islam blinded him to a problem that became increasingly obvious to Martin, namely, that no religion can transform a people as long as they benefit from and are truly determined to maintain structures of evil and injustice.

The essence of religion for both men involved self-sacrifice and complete submission to the will of God. This is why they cared little for material possessions. While he never subscribed to Martin's view that the co-worker with God must be willing to "suffer peacefully," Malcolm did believe that obedience to God invariably means a readiness to die for a just and noble cause.[65] Martin viewed the sacrificial life in terms of the redemptive quality of unearned suffering, and he often said that his personal ordeals afforded opportunities to transform himself and to heal others involved in the tragic racial situation. Convinced that suffering is part of the very essence of being spiritual, he sought to transform the violence and the threats of death, to which he was so often subjected, into a creative force. Of his cross-bearing,

Martin, undoubtedly with critics like Malcolm in mind, commented in 1960: "There are some who still find the cross a stumbling block, and others consider it foolishness, but I am more convinced than ever before that it is the power of God unto social and individual salvation. So like the Apostle Paul I can now humbly yet proudly say, 'I bear in my body the marks of the Lord Jesus.' The suffering and agonizing moments through which I have passed over the last few years have also drawn me closer to God. More than ever before I am convinced of the reality of a personal God."[66]

Malcolm and Martin challenged Americans with a new awareness of the possibilities inherent in religion, particularly when it is not relegated to the sphere of the private. They demonstrated that overcoming the worst in America, especially in terms of racial oppression and economic injustice, involves not only the outer physical person but also the inner spiritual person. In so doing, they influenced conceptions of religion and its relationship to culture. They also impacted scholarly treatments of American religion in ways that have not been sufficiently acknowledged and documented. Of particular concern for some are their contributions to the shaping of black liberation theology as an intellectual discipline, a development that occurred in the United States in the late 1960s. Those contributions became most evident in black theology's effort to reconcile black identity with the demands of the Christian faith. Malcolm's unqualified affirmation of blackness and Martin's devotion to the Christian gospel of liberation gave black theology much of its central core.[67] The impact of these men on other trends in American religious and theological thought will become clearer as scholars develop more appreciation for them as keen, innovative thinkers.

The God of War and Peace: On Religion and the Struggle for Freedom

Martin and Malcolm affirmed with undeviating conviction that their people's drive for freedom could not be sustained without a continuing reliance on religious values and institutions. They knew that religion had long provided their people with a context of meaning and building blocks for a structured social and institutional life, but they disagreed in their assessments of the role of Christianity in the African-American struggle for freedom since slavery. As a Black Muslim minister, Malcolm equated Christianity and its symbol of the cross with "Slavery, Suffering, and Death," and Islam and its flag, crescent, and star with "Freedom, Justice, and Equality." In contrast, Martin closely identified the Christian faith with the African-American freedom struggle from its origins, and he insisted that Islam, with its philosophy of an eye for an eye and a tooth for a tooth, could only lead to more racial conflict and bloodshed.[68] These two perspectives competed for dominance, as much of black America was consumed with a paroxysm of anger and rebelliousness.

The role of religion in the struggle against slavery was of particular interest to Malcolm and Martin as they considered the means most suitable for eliminating racism and segregation in their own time. Malcolm knew that "some slaves brought from Africa spoke Arabic, and were Islamic in their religion," but he never mentioned the ways in which they put their faith to the service of resistance to bondage.[69] He was more specific when discussing Nat Turner, the slave preacher who led the most successful slave revolt in antebellum America:

> I read about the slave preacher Nat Turner, who put the fear of God into the white slavemaster. Nat Turner wasn't going around preaching pie-in-the-sky and "nonviolent" freedom for the black man. There in Virginia one night in 1831, Nat and seven other slaves started out at his master's home and through the night they went from one plantation "big house" to the next, killing, until by the next morning 57 white people were dead and Nat had about 70 slaves following him. White people, terrified for their lives, fled from their homes, locked themselves up in public buildings, hid in the woods, and some even left the state. A small army of soldiers took two months to catch and hang Nat Turner. Somewhere I have read where Nat Turner's example is said to have inspired John Brown to invade Virginia and attack Harpers Ferry nearly thirty years later, with thirteen white men and five Negroes.[70]

Malcolm seems to have attributed Turner's militancy to a deep African spirituality and a certain sturdiness on his part, rather than to any strong Christian influences. This tendency flowed logically from Malcolm's view that Christianity made slaves docile and accommodating, which is not surprising, since his methods for eliminating social injustice grew out of religio-political foundations that were foreign to Martin. While agreeing to some extent with Malcolm's thoughts on Christianity's potential as a pacifying force, Martin knew that Turner's rebellion, like that of numerous other slaves, was inspired by a radical reading of the Christian faith. Moreover, Martin too extolled Turner's "courageous efforts," but maintained that the insurrections of slaves like Turner and Denmark Vesey "should be eternal reminders to us that violent rebellion is doomed from the start."[71] The civil rights leader never wavered in his conviction that Christianity is incompatible with violence.

The strange amalgam of religion and resistance to oppression is unmistakable in slave art. Both Malcolm and Martin saw this as they probed the deeper meanings of the spirituals. It is ironic that Malcolm could reduce the spirituals to merely comforting rhythms in troubled times in one voice, while suggesting in another that they spoke of the slaves' condition and of their deep yearning for the unfettered freedom they associated with Africa. On one occasion, he noted: "Slaves used to sing that song about 'My Lord's going to move this wicked race and raise up a righteous nation that will obey.' They knew what they were talking about—they were talking about the man. They used to sing a song, 'Good news, a chariot is coming.' If you notice, every thing they sang in those spirituals was talking about going to get away from here. None of them wanted to stay here. . . . Everything they sang, every song, had a hint in it that they weren't satisfied here, that they weren't being treated right, that somebody had to go."[72] In another statement, Malcolm elaborated the point in more precise terms, implying that the slave spirituals were far more militant and charged with the message of freedom than the songs heard in the contemporary black church:

> The slaves had an old spiritual which they sang, "Steal away to Jesus, steal away home." You think that they were talking about some man that got hung on the cross two thousand years ago, whereas they were talking about a ship. They wanted to steal away and get on board that ship that was named Jesus, so that they could go back home on the mother continent, the African continent, where they had been tricked and brought from. But you've got poor Negroes today, who have been brainwashed, still sitting in church talking about stealing away to Jesus; they talk about going up yonder, dying, if they're going somewhere. Showing you how your mind is all messed up. They were talking about a boat. . . . Or, they used to sing a song, "You can have all this world, but give me Jesus." They weren't talking about that man that died supposedly on the cross, they were talking about a boat. "You can have this world—this Western world, this evil, corrupt, run-down, low-down Western world—but give me Jesus the boat, but give me the ship Jesus, so I can go back home where I'll be among my own kind. This is what the spiritual came from. But they've got it in the church today, and that old dumb preacher has your and my—yes, dumb preacher—has

your and my mind so messed up we think that Jesus is somebody that died on a cross, and we sit there foaming at the mouth talking about you can have all this world, but give me Jesus. And the man took all this world, and gave you Jesus, and that's all you've got is Jesus.[73]

Malcolm's analysis of the themes of resistance and freedom in the slave spirituals was similar in many ways to Martin's. Both echoed Harold Courlander's claim that the songs were "full of hidden meanings, hints, messages, and signals for slaves looking toward escape," an assertion also made by ex-slaves such as Frederick Douglass and Harriet Tubman. Malcolm and Martin also identified the essentials of a liberation ethic in the spirituals, but Martin was less apt to stress that this art necessarily reflected an intense desire on the part of slaves to physically return to Africa. Also unlike Malcolm, Martin affirmed the Christian roots and outlook of the spirituals. The nonviolent activist's perspective on the meaning of "heaven" in slave songs clearly paralleled views held a century earlier by Douglass and Tubman:

Our spirituals, now so widely admired around the world, were often codes. We sang of "heaven" that awaited us, and the slave masters listened in innocence, not realizing that we were not speaking of the hereafter. Heaven was the word for Canada, and the Negro sang of the hope that his escape on the Underground Railroad would carry him there. One of our spirituals, "Follow the Drinking Gourd," in its lyrics contained disguised directions for escape. The gourd was the Big Dipper, and the North Star to which its handle pointed gave the celestial map that directed the flight to the Canadian border.[74]

There was virtually no agreement between Malcolm and Martin concerning the extent to which the black church was keeping alive this tradition of struggle and resistance to oppression in the 1950s and 1960s. Malcolm consistently attacked that institution for inhibiting civil rights militancy and for failing to use the vast resources at its disposal for the intellectual, social, and economic advancement of the folk. Constantly confronting black Christians who ignored the condition of their people while wrapping themselves in an aura of personal piety could not have disturbed Malcolm more, especially since the church was the source of many of the cultural values of the African-American community.[75] Seeing few instances of radical Christian practice among his people, Malcolm, in a manner untypical of Martin, lamented what he regarded as the enslavement of the black church to the dominant culture. Consequently, the greatest possibilities for black liberation were embodied in

Islam, and particularly the Black Muslims, who counseled African Americans to separate completely from their oppressors and who exemplified moral discipline while operating their own factories, farms, restaurants, and other enterprises.[76]

Malcolm's blistering assault on what he perceived to be the passivity, apathy, indifference, and otherworldliness of black congregations was shared in some measure by Martin. Martin constantly criticized those in the black church who gave only token support to civil rights and who refused to assume a prophetic posture in the battle against racism, poverty, war, and other social evils. He, too, felt that black churches were among that range of institutions that had to take a leading role in empowering the masses, so that African Americans, "as a group, can hold their own in a society where, instead of a melting pot, separate peoples function beside each other, exchanging the power they control for the power the other fellow has." But Martin differed from Malcolm in that he saw redeeming qualities in the black church, a tendency not altogether surprising since that institution served as his chief source of inspiration, power, and validation.[77] Martin praised black churches in Montgomery for "becoming militant" during the bus boycott in 1955–56 and for serving as "dispatch centers where the people gather to wait for rides."[78] In his "Letter from the Birmingham City Jail" (1963), he thanked God "that, through the influence of the Negro church, the way of nonviolence became an integral part of our struggle."[79] The mere thought of church bombings and of black Christians suffering and dying in the streets, while uniting song and the prayer circle with the picket line, moved Martin to compare the black church to the Apostolic Church: "The role of the Negro church today, by and large, is a glorious example in the history of Christendom. For never in Christian history, within a Christian country, have Christian churches been on the receiving end of such naked brutality and violence as we are witnessing here in America today. Not since the days of the Christians in the catacombs has God's house, as a symbol, weathered such attack as the Negro churches."[80]

Thus Martin did not embrace Malcolm's hope for a time when the moral and spiritual authority of the church among African Americans would erode. Furthermore, Martin rejected Malcolm's insistence that black Christianity could not match up in any way with the standards of Islam when it came to movements for the general improvement of the black condition. At the same time, Martin commended the Nation of Islam for its contribution to the moral elevation of the folk, suggesting that Christians and Muslims in the African-American community had much to learn from each other in the continuing drive toward freedom: "While I strongly disagree with their separatist black supremacy philosophy, I have nothing but admiration for what our Muslim brothers have done to rehabilitate ex-convicts, dope addicts and men and women who, through despair and self-hatred, have sunk to moral degeneracy. This must be attempted on a much larger scale and without the negative overtones that accompany Black Muslimism."[81]

Apparently, the role that religion could possibly play in freeing African Americans from mental enslavement and self-destructive behavior was as important for Malcolm as it was for Martin. Both felt that religion had as much to offer as education in this regard. But here again, Malcolm clearly preferred the Muslim faith over Christianity, especially since the "fantastic" teachings of Elijah Muhammad, with the stress on blacks as divine and whites as evil, were "superbly suited to the task of shaking off the feeling of niggerness." Thus, blacks who joined the Nation of Islam found new badges of respectability. Malcolm insisted that this was clearly not the case with Christianity, which was designed to keep his people in psychological bondage. "The black masses that are waking up don't believe in Christianity anymore," Malcolm declared. "All it's done for black men is to help keep them slaves." For the Muslim spokesman, the best evidence of this was the religious images embraced by both black and white churches—the white Jesus, a white Virgin, white angels, all of which upheld white supremacy and black inferiority. Such an observation proved impossible for Martin to refute, even as he recognized the subtle nuances of God language and symbolism in his people's culture. Even so, he still insisted that Christianity in its truest sense had the power to mentally and physically liberate both blacks and whites. Indeed, he believed that the black church, despite its limitations, had become an instrument of God's salvific and liberative purposes for both races.[82]

This unyielding confidence in the redemptive and reconciliatory power of Christianity required a rare depth of conviction and insight at a time when the faith was being dismissed as obsolete by the death of God theologians and other cultural critics. But Martin saw that the church-based civil rights struggle in America and other Christian movements against injustice abroad were contributing a lot in terms of restoring the credibility of the faith.[83] He was particularly encouraged by the rich contributions that the black church was making to the vitality of Christianity, both through its adherence to disciplined nonviolence and its displays of artistic genius. This optimistic view of Christianity made virtually no sense to Malcolm, who never ceased to talk about the awful and unspeakable horrors perpetrated by that religion.

Malcolm blamed the Christian churches for the enslavement of Africans, the slaughter of the Jews, and countless other crimes against humanity. "The white man," he observed, "never has gone among the non-white peoples bearing the Cross in the true manner and spirit of Christ's teachings—meek, humble, and Christ-like." Thus, he concluded that Islam held the key to both the elimination of oppression and the shaping of a new humanity: "The only true world solution today is governments guided by true religion—of the spirit. Here in race-torn America, I am convinced that the Islamic religion is desperately needed, particularly by the American black man. The black man needs to reflect that he has been America's most fervent Christian—and where has it gotten him? In fact, in the white man's hands, in the white man's interpretation . . . , where has Christianity brought this *world*? It has brought the non-white two-thirds of the human population to rebellion."[84]

The linking of slavery and oppression with the theology and practices of the white church became a standard line for both Malcolm and Martin. They were particularly critical of white fundamentalists and evangelicals, who exemplified the tendency to sanction both white supremacy and the oppression of people of color. Malcolm reduced the evangelist Billy Graham's gospel to merely "white nationalism." Martin would not have made this claim regarding Graham, with whom he associated at times, but the civil rights leader knew as well as Malcolm that conservative Christianity actually desensitized Graham and many other whites to the need for militant action against social evil.[85] In his "Letter from the Birmingham City Jail," Martin addressed this problem in clear terms: "In the midst of blatant injustices inflicted upon the Negro, I have watched white churches stand on the sideline and merely mouth pious irrelevancies and sanctimonious trivialities. In the midst of a mighty struggle to rid our nation of racial and economic injustice, I have heard so many ministers say, 'Those are social issues with which the gospel has no real concern,' and I have watched so many churches commit themselves to a completely otherworldly religion which make a strange distinction between body and soul, the sacred and the secular."[86]

Both Malcolm and Martin proclaimed that the white Western world would reap a bitter harvest, that God's wrath would be visited upon it, because of its distortion of the Christian faith.[87] Black Christians could avoid this fate only by acting in the servant style of Jesus Christ. But Malcolm felt that as long as African Americans embraced Christianity, they would remain enslaved to the values of white Western society and thus ill-prepared for solidarity with other peoples of color across the globe. In Malcolm's estimation, it was impossible for Christianity to engender the type of radical ideological shift his people needed to be a force in the total liberation of dark humanity. For him, such a revolution in consciousness could only come with Islam, a position Martin adamantly rejected.

Much of Malcolm's critique of Christianity targeted black preachers, whose power and authority as spiritual leaders in folk culture were well established and largely unchallenged. Referring to black preachers as "the white man's puppet Negro leaders," Malcolm denounced these "men of the cloth" for ignoring the needs of their people while teaching them that after death they will "float up to some city with golden streets and milk and honey on a cloud somewhere." He complained, "Every black man in North America has heard black Christian preachers shouting about 'tomorrow in good old Beulah's Land.' But the thinking black masses today are interested in Muhammad's Land. The Promised Land that the Honorable Elijah Muhammad talks about is right here on earth."[88] Martin, too, had problems with these "pie-in-the-sky" fundamentalist teachings and the "soul-saving" narrowness of fellow clergymen. He lashed out at those "Negro preachers that have never opened their mouths about the freedom movement," a tendency he found all the more disturbing since these figures were "freer, more independent, than any other person in the community." Martin reminded black preachers that any gospel which speaks of the joys of heaven to the exclusion of human needs on earth is irrelevant: "It's all right to talk about 'silver slippers over yonder,' but men need 'shoes' to wear down here. It's all right to talk about streets flowing with 'milk and honey' over yonder, but let's get some food to eat for people down here in Asia and Africa and South America and in our own nation who go to bed hungry at night. It's all right to talk about 'mansions in the sky,' but I'm thinking about these ghettoes and slums right down here."[89]

The superficiality of narrowly focused proclamations about salvation in the afterlife could not have been clearer, since many ministers lived in luxury here on earth. Malcolm spoke disparagingly of "the hustling preacher-pimps to be found in every black ghetto, the ones with some little storefront churches of mostly hardworking, older women, who kept their 'pretty boy' young preacher dressed in 'sharp' clothes and driving a fancy car." The "ignorant greedy Negro preachers," as he and his fellow Black Muslims put it, were to be compared to Judas, especially since they were paid and brain-washed to parrot the white man's "religious lies to us." In 1960, several black preachers "hot-footed it out of a meeting" at which Malcolm blamed them for "the Negro's deplorable economic condition" and for collaborating with whites in keeping black Christians in poverty. One source reported: "He said $90,000,000 is spent annually in Los Angeles in up-keeping Negro preachers and churches, while [only] $60,000,000 is spent for houses and furniture combined. . . . Malcolm X then pleaded with the Negro preachers to return to their churches and put their members' money to work 'for these members' . . . building factories and supermarkets instead of [more] churches."[90]

Martin joined Malcolm in pouring special venom on black ministers who proved to be nothing more than rogues and charlatans. In a tone of voice indicating his annoyance and disappointment, the civil rights leader asserted: "I'm sick and tired of seeing Negro preachers riding around in big cars and living in big houses and not concerned about the problems of the people who made it possible for them to get these things. It seems that I can hear the Almighty God say 'stop preaching your loud sermons and hooping your irrelevant mess in my face, for your hands are full of tar for the people that I sent you to serve, . . . and you are doing nothing but being concerned about yourself.'"[91]

But Martin knew better than Malcolm that there were black ministers who did preach a relevant social gospel and who were not exploiting their people. As stated previously, the fact that there had always been some preach-ers at the forefront in creating positive change in their local communities and in the society at large was a major factor in Martin's decision to pursue ministry as a life vocation. Martin proudly pointed to James Bevel, Bernard Lee, Wyatt Walker, Ralph Abernathy, T. Y. Rogers, Hosea Williams, Jesse Jackson, C. T. Vivian, and others as "brilliant young men who could make, I'm sure, much larger salaries elsewhere," but who "stay here, and they work because of their commitment to this struggle." Malcolm would ultimately agree with this assessment, but he never forgave Martin and other black preachers for teaching African Americans to be nonviolent when physically and verbally attacked by whites, especially since, as he saw it, learning the methods of self-defense or counterviolence is essential to the experience of freedom. In Malcolm's view, the damage done by such teachings was often impossible to repair: "No one can react to persecution like this but the Ne-gro, and he does it under the counseling of the Negro preacher. . . . Were it not for the Negro pastor, our people would be just like the Hungarians, we'd be fighters. . . . The Negro is a fighting man all right. He fought in Korea; he fought in Germany; he fought in the jungles of Iwo Jima. But that same Negro will come back here, and the white man will hang his mother on a tree, and he will take the Bible and say, 'Forgive them Lord, for they know not what they do.' This Negro preacher makes them that way. . . . Where there is a slave like that, why you have a slave-making religion."[92]

Malcolm always noted that his criticism of black preachers came only after they attacked him and the Nation of Islam. The Muslim leader's forthright and confrontational style made him not simply a curiosity but a serious annoyance to some ministers in the black community. Occasionally, Martin and other preachers in the movement blasted what they termed "the extremism" of the Black Muslims, a charge that Malcolm always denied. "These preachers" attack Muhammad "out of self-defense," he claimed in 1963, "because they know he's waking up Negroes." Malcolm added: "No one believes what the Negro preacher preaches except those who are mentally asleep, or in the darkness of ignorance about the true situation of the black man here today in this wilderness of North America."[93] Perplexed and amused by images of the black preacher as a powerful symbol in the culture, Malcolm reduced that figure to the buffoon portrayed in much of society's folklore, literature, and film.

There was a certain irony about Malcolm's attacks on black preachers, for two reasons. The first was because Elijah Muhammad failed to participate in the struggle for civil rights and was known for his lavish lifestyle. Malcolm would acknowledge as much and more after his break with the Black Muslims. In an interview given in early 1965, he stated: "Muhammad is the man with the house in Phoenix, his $200 suits, and his harem. He didn't believe in the Black state or in getting anything for the people. That's why I got out."[94] Martin saw this as clearly as Malcolm but refused to comment. In any case, it was quite a serious blow to Malcolm to discover that Muhammad and some of his top ministers were virtually no different from the black preachers he had castigated for years.

Second, Malcolm's attacks on black preachers were ironic in that he, perhaps unconsciously at times, adopted much of the preaching style, the pulpit manner, and the language of the African-American preaching tradition. His discourse was full of rich metaphors and parables that were rooted both in the Scriptures and in the tradition transmitted by black preachers. Like Martin, Malcolm, a man of imposing stature, piercing eyes, and penetrating voice, held audiences spellbound with his ability to fuse acting and biting humor with dynamic oratory. The manner in which Malcolm combined these qualities with a strong social outlook recalled Martin and other black preacher-activists. Milton Henry must have known this when he called Malcolm "a prophet in the tradition of Moses and Jesus who will in time be central to the development of a newer, fuller and more vibrant Islam in America and to the development of a code of conduct and a strategy by which black people, now oppressed, can become free."[95]

Malcolm's tendency to make blanket characterizations of all black preachers waned after his travels abroad and conversion to Sunni Islam in 1964. His growing admiration for Martin became more evident, for he came to realize the great extent to which Martin was "fighting for the civil rights of black people in this country." Malcolm also spoke highly of Eugene L. Callender, a Presbyterian preacher in Harlem, who had once cautioned him privately about "his general attacks upon the Negro clergy." Said Malcolm of Callender: "He's a preacher, but he's a fighter for the black man." Malcolm actually supported Milton Galamison, another Presbyterian minister, who was "deeply involved in the school boycotts to eliminate segregated education" in New York. Of his boundless respect for Adam Clayton Powell Jr., Malcolm made no secret. He called Powell, the Baptist preacher and congressman from Harlem, "the loudest thing in this country" when it came to the race question, and his working relationship with Powell was much closer than that which existed between Martin and Powell. Malcolm's admiration for the Reverend Albert B. Cleage Jr. of the Black Christian Nationalist Church was well known in some circles, for he included Cleage as part of a brain trust responsible for establishing his Organization of Afro-American Unity.[96] Other preachers who made Malcolm's approval list were Franklin Florence and C. Eric Lincoln. Many of these preachers demonstrated a spirit of militancy that must have reminded Malcolm of his father, Earl Little.

Sunni Islam taught Malcolm what Martin learned well through an adherence to the Christian faith, namely, that the movement for black freedom could not be logically separated from the liberation struggles of all oppressed people. Moreover, it taught Malcolm that the destinies of the oppressed and the oppressors are ultimately inseparable because both stand in need of liberation. Thus, he overcame the Nation of Islam's narrow conception of religion and how it might relate to human freedom. This is yet another example of how Malcolm and Martin found common ground, even as one remained a Muslim and the other a Christian.

Overcoming Religious Barriers: Malcolm, Martin, and Interreligious Dialogue

The development of a rich tolerance and respect for religious diversity occurred over time for both Malcolm and Martin. Malcolm had considerable exposure to "ecumenical" religion during his childhood, spending time with mainline Christian congregations, sectarian groups such as the Seventh Day Adventists, and cultic or new religious movements such as the Jehovah's Witnesses. But in those early years, Malcolm did not develop a lasting appreciation for the truths and values embodied in different faiths. In fact, he had rejected all religions by the time he was imprisoned in 1946. This strong anti-religious attitude changed when he joined the Nation of Islam two years later, but affiliation with that group encouraged a deep intolerance for Christians and Jews. Having grown up with a more receptive spirit toward religion and religious diversity, Martin addressed the subject with surprising objectivity in some of the papers he wrote as a seminarian.[97] Even so, he and Malcolm had to experience spiritual and intellectual crises before they concluded that an unwavering preference for one's own faith tradition should never make one blind to the broader truths conveyed through others, and that devotion to one's religion must never outweigh the need for persons to struggle collectively for freedom and community. Both believed in interfaith cooperation among blacks to achieve liberation by the time of their deaths, and their plan to meet and discuss the issue in early 1965 was thwarted only by the murder of Malcolm X. Thus, Martin and Malcolm might be considered sources of dialogue for Islam and Christianity in the African-American community.[98]

Such a conclusion would have been difficult to sustain in the 1950s because each stated at times that his religion was more valid than other faiths. Malcolm often echoed Elijah Muhammad's claim that Islam is "God's religion," a tendency he displayed until his break with the Black Muslims. For Malcolm, such an argument was easy to support given his belief that Islam existed from the very beginning of time itself and is the only religion not founded by and named after a human being: "Buddhism is named after a man called Buddha; Confucianism is named after a man called Confucius. . . . Likewise with Judaism and Christianity. But Islam is not connected with any name. Islam is independent of any name. . . . If your religion is Christianity you're following Christ, if your religion is Judaism you're following Judah, if your religion is Buddhism you're following Buddha."[99]

Martin would have casually dismissed such contentions as utterly false, for he knew that all the major religions originated with men who struggled for some sense of and connection with a supernatural force. Although Martin was more prone than Malcolm to see validity in all the great world religions, his tendency to attach more validity to Christianity undermines any suggestion that he rejected Western notions of the superiority of that faith over others or that he was totally different from the Muslim leader on the question of religious pluralism and toleration. The civil rights leader put his perspective in these terms in 1958:

> I believe that God reveals Himself in all religions. Wherever we find truth we find the revelation of God, and there is some element of truth in all religions. This does not mean, however, that God reveals Himself equally in all religions. Christianity is an expression of the highest revelation of God. It is the synthesis of the best in all religions. In this sense Christianity is more valid than the tribal religions practiced by our African ancestors. This does not mean that these tribal religions are totally devoid of truth. It simply means that Christianity, while flowing through the stream of history, has incorporated the truths of all other religions and brought them together in a meaningful and coherent system. Moreover, at the center of Christianity stands the Christ who is now and ever shall be the highest revelation of God. He, more than any other person that has ever lived in history, reveals the true nature of God. Through his life, death, and resurrection the power of eternity broke forth into time.[100]

Such a view should not have been surprising at a time when most Americans accepted uncritically the Christian doctrine of the exclusivity of salvation and when vast numbers of Christians were known for their inflexibility and unchanging code of absolutes. Both Malcolm and Martin found it virtually impossible in the 1950s to relinquish some of the biases instilled by their particular faith communities. They had tremendous difficulty discussing their different religions without assuming the rightness of one over the other, a point that is not diminished by the fact that Martin, from the time of the Montgomery bus boycott in the mid-1950s, "contributed to the broader meaning of interfaith dialogue" by engaging in "distinctly ecumenical enterprises," by supporting "social activism that reflected interfaith cooperation," and by condemning and challenging "sectors of the black community that he, for theological reasons, understood as racially and religiously intolerant of others."[101]

Muslim-Christian interactions in the African-American community had often been antagonistic and seldom congenial and cooperative up to the late 1950s. Malcolm and the Nation of Islam sought to change this in 1957 when they tried unsuccessfully to start a dialogue with Martin and other Christian ministers concerning strategies and goals for the black freedom movement. A similar effort was made by the leadership of the Nation of Islam in 1958, an effort quite significant, since Malcolm was known to attack Christianity while emphasizing the intellectual integrity and rational defensibility of Islam. Although Martin worked in the movement with Protestants, Catholics, and Jews, he saw no need at this time to converse with Malcolm and the Black Muslims concerning issues on which they obviously took widely different positions. Martin's reluctance stemmed from both an intolerant attitude toward the Black Muslim faith and a determination to avoid pointless discussions and debates that he felt would have harmed rather than enhanced the civil rights cause. Even so, it is difficult to avoid the conclusion that Martin was somewhat ambivalent in his attitude toward religious diversity, especially since he frequently stated that Gandhi, a Hindu and consistent critic of Western Christianity, was "more than a saint" and "the greatest Christian of the modern world."[102]

The failure of Malcolm and Martin to develop "clear ecumenical dialogues" in the late 1950s and early 1960s was rooted in doctrinal and theological issues on which Black Muslims and Christians could never have agreed. As stated earlier, insurmountable differences existed in their images of God, their perceptions of humanity, and their beliefs concerning the relationship of the divine to the human. Moreover, the Muslims strongly rejected the view, consistently advanced by Martin and other black Christian ministers, that the ultimate success of the African-American freedom movement hinged on strong ecumenical activities spearheaded by Jews and black and white churches. Denouncing Jews and white Christians as racists and exploiters of black people, Malcolm scoffed at the "interfaith religious conference of Protestant, Catholic, and Jewish groups" held in Chicago in 1963 to deal with the race question, noting that "it broke up with the problems of racism still unsolved." "In fact, when one reads the results of that religious conference," Malcolm further observed, "one has to agree that it succeeded only in highlighting their inability to eliminate white racism from their own churches and synagogues." At this juncture, Malcolm was convinced that "no group or council or conference would ever solve the race problem" until they recognized Elijah Muhammad "as an active participant in all of their discussions and in all of their plans."[103]

Martin never lost faith in the power and potential of ecumenical cooperation of a biracial nature. Even as he expressed disappointment with the white church for its silence and indifference around the issues of race, this prophet of the civil rights movement conceded that the National Council of Churches and the Roman Catholic Church had condemned segregation as immoral and sinful. This was for Martin a hopeful sign, one that reinforced his view that, "by common sharing," the black and white "church communities" would build "significant bridges of mutuality which will better equip both for resolving the troublous times in which we live." But Martin essentially ignored Malcolm's insistence that no interfaith effort across racial lines would work as long as Elijah Muhammad and his Muslims were excluded. To the contrary, Martin felt that the anti-white, anti-Christian, and anti-Semitic language of the Nation of Islam rendered it an undesirable entity in any biracial and ecumenical venture to destroy bigotry and inequity.[104]

But Martin did not escape completely the very charge of religious intolerance that he so adamantly made against Malcolm and the Nation of Islam. It was often difficult for Martin to defend the normativity and finality of Jesus Christ as God's self-disclosure for Christians without making seemingly arrogant claims suggesting the superiority of his faith tradition over others. In the summer of 1961, Martin insisted in a speech that America had to become a "Christian nation" in order to overcome racism and segregation, a comment that evoked a negative response from a Jewish man in New Jersey. In an apologetic tone, Martin assured the man that his remark was not meant to insult persons who embraced religions other than Christianity:

> I regret so much that you misinterpreted a statement that I made in Miami, Florida, some weeks ago. When I referred to America becoming a Christian nation, I was not referring to Christianity as an organized institutional religion. I was referring more to the principles of Christ, which I think are sound and valid for any nation and civilization. I have never been a victim of religious bigotry. I have never condemned any of the great religions of the world, for it is my sincere conviction that no religion has a monopoly on truth and that God has revealed Himself in all of the religions of mankind. So let me assure you that when I speak of America rising to the heights of a Democratic and Christian nation, I am referring to the need of rising to the heights of noble ethical and moral principles. I am sure that you are aware of the fact that many

people, Christians and non-Christians, theists and humanists, have found within the Sermon on the Mount and other insights of Jesus Christ, great ethical principles that they can adhere to even though they would not accept institutionalized Christianity. . . . I am very sorry that you are so offended by the word Christian. Maybe it is due to the fact that we Christians have not always been Christian in our dealing with people of other religions, and sometimes in our dealings with people of our own religion.[105]

Although Jews were sensitive to any suggestion of the supremacy of Christianity over Judaism, and understandably so, some of them, like white Christians, exploited the differences between black Christians and the Nation of Islam and thus prevented Malcolm and Martin from working together.[106] Clearly, this hurt the black freedom cause and undermined the fact that the black church and the Black Muslims had much to learn from each other about the relationship of faith to life.

The relationships Malcolm and Martin had with Jews were reflected to some extent in the different positions they took concerning the so-called Middle East crisis in their time. Malcolm tended to be strongly pro-Palestinian, feeling that Europeans had assisted white Jews in setting up a nation "in the middle of a dark-skinned people's territory" in 1948. This perspective, which remained essentially unchanged after Malcolm's break with the Black Muslims, took both race and religion seriously, especially given the prominence of Islam among the Palestinians. Rejecting the position of "the so-called young militants," who "condemned" anything that was "non-colored," Martin affirmed "Israel's right to exist" as "incontestable," and he also insisted that "the great powers have the obligation to recognize that the Arab world is in a state of imposed poverty and backwardness that must threaten peace and harmony." Having worked with Jews in the movement from the very beginning of the bus boycott in Montgomery (1955–56), and having emphasized the importance of interfaith cooperation as a means to overcome racial discrimination, Martin found it impossible to be as rigid and one-sided as Malcolm and the militants on the Israeli-Arab conflict.[107] Even so, the positions taken by Malcolm and Martin revealed much concerning their approaches to interfaith issues.

Martin's struggle to remain open-minded on the religion question sometimes led to tension between him and more conservative white ministers. After contributing to the organization of the Gandhi Society, "an educational fund or foundation" established to "serve as a crucible for new ideas and nonviolent direct action," Martin felt compelled to defend his actions against the claims of two white ministers who implied that he was "now forsaking the Christian church in order to turn to a *new* kind of American sectarianism." Denying that the Gandhi Society was set up to "displace the church or repudiate the Christian gospel," Martin asserted in June 1962:

> How anyone could interpret my relation with the Gandhi Society as a turn away from the Church is a real mystery to me. As far as my Christology goes, I believe as firmly now as ever that God revealed himself uniquely and completely through Jesus Christ. Like Thomas of old, I, too, can affirm in the presence of Christ, "My Lord, and my God." I believe with every Christian in the Lordship of Jesus Christ and I am more convinced than ever before that we will only find the solutions to the problems of the world through Christ and his way. One's commitment to Jesus Christ as Lord and Savior, however, should not mean that one cannot be inspired by another great personality that enters the stage of history. I must confess that I saw in your statement and that of Mr. Morris a narrow sectarianism and a degree of religious intolerance that causes me real concern. While I firmly agree that God reveals himself more completely and uniquely in Christianity than any other religion, I cannot make myself believe that God did not reveal himself in other religions. I believe that in some marvelous way, God worked through Gandhi, and the spirit of Jesus Christ saturated his life. It is ironic, yet inescapably true, that the greatest Christian of the modern world was a man who never embraced Christianity. This is not an indictment on Christ but a tribute to him—a tribute to His universality and His Lordship. When I think of Gandhi, I think of the Master's way in the words of the fourth gospel: "I have other sheep that are not of this fold."[108]

Despite the claims made in this letter, Martin never reduced religion to doctrinal conformity. For him, as for Malcolm, religion was essentially about relationships. Clearly, when it came to orthodox Christianity, Martin stood between the highly conservative fundamentalists and evangelicals and the ultraliberal Christians, without embracing the views of either side completely and uncritically. This was only natural for one who was Hegelian, for one who took a dialectical approach to reasoning, and for one who looked for limited truths in opposing faiths and ideologies. "I am always seeking dialogue," he stated emphatically in 1967. "I am always seeking to communicate with those that I cannot agree with entirely."[109]

Martin seemed more apt than Malcolm to celebrate great men who embodied the spirit of interfaith dialogue and cooperation. The civil rights leader delighted in recalling Gandhi's "decision to fast until the Hindu temples in India were open to Untouchables, and until Hindus and Moslems agreed to co-exist peacefully." Martin apparently recognized in Gandhi a living example of how dialogue and communication might best occur between persons from various religious traditions. In fact, Gandhi could not have been a better example for African Americans, since they, like the Indian leader, had suffered enough "to be instinctively intolerant of intolerance."[110] The same could be said of the Vietnamese Buddhist monk and peace advocate Thick Nhat Hanh, whom Martin met and admired greatly. Convinced that there were parallels between the civil rights movement and Buddhism, particularly in terms of the concept of human community, Martin nominated Thick Nhat Hanh for the Nobel Peace Prize in 1967, calling him a "gentle Buddhist monk" whose "ideas for peace, if applied, would build a monument to ecumenism, to world brotherhood, to humanity." The work of Gandhi and Hanh came together in Martin's consciousness as he considered the enormous contributions that Hinduism, Buddhism, and other religions could make to the shaping of a new humanity.

The religious barriers that separated Malcolm and Martin began to crumble as both moved increasingly and more consciously toward international perspectives. Malcolm's break with the Nation of Islam in 1964 freed him to engage in the kind of traveling, observation, and critical and analytical thinking that inevitably leads to a more positive outlook on human differences. His discovery of what he termed "true Islam" impacted his consciousness on two levels. First, it compelled him to move increasingly beyond an exclusive emphasis on black nation-building (asabiya) to a stronger commitment to the global community of Islamic believers (ummah). Second, it led him to accept the idea that human community across the boundaries of color could exist, and this realization led to a greater toleration of other religions and cultures. Of particular importance was Malcolm's broader and more positive view of black Christianity. He began to refer to blacks as America's most dedicated Christians, to solicit the support of black church persons for his OAAU, and to express a strong desire to work with Martin and other Christian leaders in the struggle.[111]

Martin's respect and tolerance for different religions grew over time as he witnessed multifaith dialogue and cooperation in the civil rights movement. Religious ineptness and intolerance were part of what he had in mind when he accused Christians of "a high blood pressure of creeds and an anemia of deeds." Convinced that "the struggle for freedom and human dignity rises above the communions of Catholic and Protestant," Martin called the Selma campaign of 1965 "the warmest expression of religious unity of Catholic, Protestant, and Jew in the nation's history." After the Selma campaign, which brought together Jews and black and white Christians in the struggle for the right to vote, Martin began to speak more emphatically of a "world house" in which Jews, Catholics and Protestants, and Moslems and Hindus learn to coexist peacefully. While recognizing that these faiths were different at many levels, Martin remained open to their truth claims and to the possibilities that God was at work through them. This helps explain his changing attitude toward Malcolm and his plans to meet with him in early 1965.[112] The movement of Malcolm and Martin toward each other in 1964–65 occurred in part because they came to understand each other's religion in more than superficial ways.

They developed a concern for values that transcended religious barriers. For both men, religious differences became far less important than the need for African Americans to forge a trusting and cooperative relationship in the interest of their liberation and survival. "We have to forget our religious differences," Malcolm declared, "and come to some kind of conclusions of what we can do to solve the problem of our ever increasing number of black people across the nation." "When we come together, we don't come together as Baptists or Methodists," he continued. "You don't catch hell because you're a Baptist, and you don't catch hell because you're a Methodist. . . . You catch hell because you're a black man." Malcolm was fully convinced by the last year of his life that "religion is not enough," because "today the problems of the Negro go beyond religion."[113] Martin could not have agreed more, for his struggles with Christian fundamentalists in the black and white communities had taught him just how difficult it is to launch a social movement when people are self-righteous and unwilling to submerge their religious differences for a higher human ideal.

Martin and Malcolm became equally convinced that black freedom would remain a distant dream as long as Christians, Muslims, and adherents of other religions in the black community fail to exchange ideas and to engage in collective action. Moreover, both men reached the conclusion that the liberation of oppressed peoples worldwide could not possibly occur devoid of multifaith cooperation. Martin sought to advance this view through his emphasis on the ideal of the "world house." In more specific terms, Malcolm spoke of multifaith activity that would benefit people of color globally in their battle against the white Christian world, a development which, in his view, could be seen with the United Nations:

> Right after the black man, brown man, red man, yellow man agreed to submerge their differences and come together in unity, their unified force was sufficient to make it almost impossible today for a white man to be elected to the helm of the United Nations, or for a Christian to be elected to the helm of the United Nations, or for a European to be elected to the helm of the United Nations. Everyone that you see now sitting in the top seat of authority in the UN is either an African, an Asian, or an Arab, or he is either a Hindu, a Buddhist, or a Muslim. And all of this is the result of the ability of these black, brown, red, and yellow people to forget their little differences and come together against the common foe, against the common enemy, the oppressor.[114]

The sense that Islam and Christianity shared much despite their differences undergirded Malcolm's and Martin's belief in the potential benefits of interreligious dialogue and cooperation among African Americans. Malcolm noted at times that the story of Joseph being sold into slavery appeared in both the Bible and the Qur'an, and, like Martin, he frequently spoke of the faith of Abraham, the message of the prophets, the Exodus, and other biblical stories in explaining the context and the destiny of his people. Furthermore, Malcolm and Martin saw that the language of faith is essentially the same for the major religions of the world. As Malcolm put it,

> I am a Muslim and there is nothing wrong with being a Muslim, nothing wrong with the religion of Islam. It just teaches us to believe in Allah as the God. Those of you who are Christians probably believe in the same God, because I think you believe in the God who created the universe. That's the one we believe in, the one who created the universe—the only difference being you call him God and we call him Allah. The Jews call him Jehovah. If you could understand Hebrew, you would probably call him Jehovah, too. If you could understand Arabic, you would probably call him Allah.[115]

Martin was even more forceful in making the claim that the great religions of the world shared a language of faith. The civil rights leader, in words not commonly used by Malcolm, insisted that language surfaces most prominently in the idea of God as the supreme embodiment of the idea of universal and unconditional love. Said Martin: "I am speaking of that force which all of the great religions have seen as the supreme unifying principle of life. This Hindu-Moslem-Christian-Jewish-Buddhist belief about ultimate reality is beautifully summed up in the first epistle of Saint John: 'Let us love one another; for love is God and everyone that loveth is born of God and knoweth God. He that loveth not knoweth not God; for God is love. If we love one another God dwelleth in us, and his love is perfected in us.'" Martin made essentially the same point in an interfaith prayer as early as 1950. After delivering an address on Gandhi's religion, he declared: "We thank thee for the fact that you have deified men and women in all nations; in all cultures, we call you this name; some call thee Allah, some call you Elohenu, some call you Jehovah, some call you Brahma, some call you the Unmoved Mover, some call you architectonic, but we know that these are all names for one and the same God. And we know you are one."[116]

When Malcolm and Martin agreed to meet in New York in February 1965 to discuss areas of mutual concern, it is doubtful that they consciously meant to set an example for Muslims and Christians in the African-American community who followed them. Although Malcolm was assassinated two days before the scheduled meeting, some Muslims and Christians were inspired by the fact that he was converging rapidly with the strategies of Martin.[117] Recollections of this growing relationship between the two men sprouted in the early 1980s when Malcolm's protégé, Louis Farrakhan, participated in the presidential campaign of Martin's protégé, Jesse Jackson. Such recollections were also stirred in the early and mid-1990s when Farrakhan and Benjamin F. Chavis, then a black Christian preacher and a well-known civil rights activist, took the lead in planning and implementing the Million Man March as "a National Day of Atonement, calling Black men to spiritual repentance and responsibility and promoting reconciliation within the Black Community." Occurring in Washington, D.C., on October 16, 1995, this event inspired many black men to join Islamic groups and Christian churches, and it led to an even greater display of interfaith cooperation at the Million Family March in Washington in October 2000. At the Million Family March, Farrakhan, Al Sharpton, and other Muslim and Christian leaders brought families of various races together to celebrate their oneness in creation and destiny despite their religious differences. This event clearly called to mind Martin's efforts to bring people of various faiths together in the cause of human freedom and community.[118]

Memories of Martin and Malcolm could not have been stronger in the summer and fall of 1995, when Farrakhan and Chavis toured the country gathering physical and financial support for the march. A private luncheon was held with over fifty black Christian pastors at the Ebenezer Baptist Church in Atlanta, where Martin Luther King Jr. and others had founded the SCLC and had staged many critical planning sessions. Several of the clergy present had worked with Martin, including Joseph Lowery, Hosea Williams, and Andrew Young. In his speech to the clergy, Farrakhan, the convener of the march, seemingly set the stage for a new era of positive Christian-Muslim interaction in the black community. In a reference to Martin's civil rights campaigns, Farrakhan noted that "the Nation of Islam was not always in support of marching and sometimes even antagonized the church for their theological differences." He went on to explain that plans for the march would be incomplete if they were not first "sanctified" by Ebenezer Church, and he called upon Christian and Muslim leaders to build on the legacies of Martin and Malcolm: "What we have to understand is there is nothing wrong with two points of view. In our immaturity we missed the value of Dr. King. And the civil rights movement missed the value of . . . Malcolm X and other nationalist leaders. However, time and circumstances have caused us all to mature. Maturing is part of the struggle, and when you mature you see the value that you missed yesterday."[119]

Chavis, executive director of the march, echoed Farrakhan's appeal for dialogue and cooperation between Christians and Muslims: "I am a Jesus man, and a Christian minister. My faith in Jesus has been strengthened through working with Minister Farrakhan. If we serve the same God, and we do, we should be united."[120] Such expressions of unity and goodwill were unprecedented in the history of Christian-Muslim interaction among African Americans. Strangely enough, Chavis later left the Christian church, becoming a member of Farrakhan's Nation of Islam and changing his name to Benjamin Chavis Muhammad, but he also insisted that he would continue to support Christian-Muslim coalitions for much-needed change in the African-American community.

The very idea of the Million Man March was conceived in the spirit and tradition of Martin. "There could be no march today," Farrakhan insisted, "if the march of the '60s did not lay a foundation for us to stand on." The powerful symbolism surrounding the Atlanta visit reached a fitting climax as Farrakhan and Chavis walked to the Martin Luther King Jr. Center for Nonviolent Social Change, laid a wreath on Martin's tomb together, and listened to "wise counsel and advice on the dynamics of marching" from King's former associates.[121]

The vast crowd that participated in the Million Man March was perceived as "standing tall on the shoulders" of Malcolm, Martin, and other great leaders. Muslim and Christian men stood together, prayed together, and made pledges together, and Farrakhan and a parade of church leaders urged those present to return to their communities and get involved in both religious and secular organizations.[122] Vincent Harding graphically described how Farrakhan returned again and again to Martin's "hallmark visions," obviously "identifying himself with King's vision in a way that would have seemed impossible less than a decade before":

> In those often well-meaning comments, especially before the men's march, it was assumed that King and his spirit would not be present this time. But just as many of us were wrong about most of our predictions concerning the 1995 march, we were also wrong in our statements concerning the absence of Martin Luther King. Indeed, one of the most powerful signs of an uncontrollable spirit at work in the march was the constant appearance of King all through that day. . . . On certain levels his presence was obvious and explicit. Many of the speakers made reference to him, and it is likely that Minister Louis Farrakhan surprised millions of participants and viewers when he brought King into the heart of his rambling but often moving presentation. At one point, not only did Farrakhan quote his supposed opposite number, he actually quoted God quoting King, surely the highest form of recognition.[123]

Contrary to the expectations of many, the Million Man March did not take Muslim-Christian dialogue in the African-American community to a more advanced level. The first reason is that the white-controlled media frantically tried to discourage support for the event by identifying it solely with Farrakhan and not with the concerns of black men in general. Second, the march failed to generate full support from black Islamic and Christian communities. Muslim groups under the leadership of Warith D. Mohammed and others were not heavily involved, and the march divided the black Christian community. Black preachers in the National Baptist Convention, the Progressive National Baptist Convention, and other major African-American church organizations lined up for or against the march. Ironically, many black preachers who had had absolutely no problem fellowshipping with white clergy and their congregations refused to become involved because of the Muslim connection. Consequently, Malcolm and Martin's dream of inter-religious dialogue and cooperation based on a shared commitment to promoting black liberation and survival was not fully realized.[124]

But the rich and vital legacies of the two men still challenge the African-American religious community on the issue of Muslim-Christian interaction. Malcolm and Martin taught us that interreligious dialogue and action presuppose more than an intellectual interest in what Islam and Christianity have to say about particular theological matters. Their attempts to converse and to work toward common goals in a unified fashion had moral credibility because they transcended the dimensions of the academic and the religious to embrace the physical and psychic sufferings of their people. In other words, they showed us that different faiths can be formed around a core of collective praxis—that collective responsibility is an ethical task that persons of different religious persuasions can assume together. This lesson is as important for the United States as it is for China, India, Iran, the Sudan, or any country where religious persecution still exists on an alarming scale.[125] Thus, the message emerging out of Malcolm's and Martin's legacies is that interreligious dialogue and cooperation in the black community and indeed the whole world is authentic to the degree that it is concerned with the socioeconomic and political liberation of individuals and communities.

Malcolm and Martin brought us closer to the view that because no religion exhausts truth, different traditions can complement and enrich each other rather than being mutually exclusive rivals. Their different faiths complemented each other because they ultimately shared a common goal, namely, to embrace the essential "oneness" of humanity, among which the many religions, while upholding their own truth claims, will also affirm their individual obligations to contribute to the shaping of a shared universal ethic. There is no greater legacy for the twenty-first century.

4

In the Matter of Faith

Malcolm and Martin on Family and Manhood

Hazrat Abu Hurairah (RAA) relates that the Holy Prophet (pbuh) said:
"The most perfect Muslim in the matter of faith is one who has excellent
behavior; and the best among you are those who behave best toward their
wives."
Abu Hurairah Tirmzi[1]

When I speak of love I am not speaking of some sentimental and weak response. I am speaking of that force which all of the great religions have
seen as the supreme unifying principle of life. Love is somehow the key
that unlocks the door which leads to ultimate reality.
Martin Luther King Jr.[2]

I'm the man you think you are. And if it doesn't take legislation to make
you a man and get your rights recognized, don't even talk that legislative
talk to me. No, if we're both human beings, we'll both do the same thing.
And if you want to know what I'll do, figure out what you'll do. I'll do the
same thing—only more of it.
Malcolm X[3]

What manner of men were Martin Luther King Jr. and Malcolm X? They
stand out as icons of character, courage, intelligence, and manhood. They are
recognized and respected by freedom-loving people all over the world. We
can learn much by analyzing their "rites of passage" or socialization into
manhood. Boys and men today are in dire need of culturally and morally
appropriate role models. These two men can be viewed as standard-bearers
of religious sincerity, cultural dignity, and world citizenship, qualities that are
associated with manhood at its best in many cultures.

What lessons did they teach us about family life and values? Through
words and example, they taught us that family life is a dress rehearsal for the

drama that each individual participates in on the stage of culture and society. It determines the character and quality of primary and secondary relationships. As such, the family is the basic unit of social organization. Its primary function is the socialization of individuals into the culture, language, norms, and values of the society. Therefore, the answers to Martin's philosophical question "Where do we go from here: chaos or community?" must start with the dynamics of the African-American family. There is an integral and intimate relationship between manhood, family, and community dynamics. The macro conflicts and contradictions in society are a direct reflection of the micro conflicts and contradictions in the family. Unresolved conflicts in the family are "acted out" in society. Hence, any permanent and profound remedy to the macro conflicts, contradictions, and problems in society must intervene at the micro level of the family and the individual. Malcolm and Martin said this and more as they considered the various forms of oppression, external and internal, that prevented total liberation for their people.

The Qur'an says, "Verily never will Allah change the condition of a people until they change themselves." On this same point, Mohandas Gandhi said, "Whatever you want to change in society, you must first change it in yourself." This same principle found expression in the many remarks Malcolm and Martin made about advancing the quality of both individual and family life. Both knew that a people are only as strong and resilient as the individuals and families that shape their values and traditions.

This chapter will examine the family values and practices represented by the legacies and lives of Malcolm and Martin. It is hoped that such an examination will provide guidance and inspiration for the living and the unborn who will participate in the just and egalitarian transformation of the United States. The primary focus here is on their respective concepts of family values, manhood, and human liberation as a "consistent way of life." Their relationships with their fathers and other significant male role models are also examined. This profile will be complemented by an examination of their roles as fathers and husbands. Both men were deeply religious figures and spiritual humanitarians, and their religious beliefs and values defined and determined their character, purpose, strategies, tactics, and vision for the liberation of humanity. Malcolm and Martin were both empowered by their boundless faith in divine power, divine guidance, and the divine fulfillment of prophecy.

A holistic and systematic examination of the cultural wisdom found in the ideas and practices of Martin and Malcolm can provide a blueprint for the reconstruction of the African-American family system. This cultural blue-print can indicate the moral codes needed to establish strong family tradi-tions. Perhaps these new traditions will give rise to a new moral and social order that can transform the dysfunctions in the family and the pathologies in the community. Anger, abuse, crime, disrespect, and violence are spiraling at alarming rates in the black community, in part because 50 percent or more of black children grow up without a father in the home. This results from high rates of so-called illegitimate births and divorces. Obviously, radical intervention is needed to treat the root causes of the problem rather than the myriad symptoms. The ideas of Malcolm and Martin are relevant to any such effort along these lines.

Nonviolence and the Family: Relying on Malcolm and Martin

Each year on Martin Luther King's birthday, many think about his philoso-phy of nonviolence at the societal and institutional levels. Their images of Martin's manhood and approach to social change are associated with boy-cotts, demonstrations, marches, sit-ins, and other nonviolent methods. Rarely do they reflect on how his philosophy and methods can be applied in addressing the range of problems that confront men, the family, and small groups. When Gandhi conceived the philosophy of nonviolence, he was more concerned about the transformation of individuals and families than nations. As he put it, "The best field for the operation of nonviolence [is] the family or institution regarded as a family. Nonviolence between the members of such families should be easy to practice. If that fails, it means we have not devel-oped the capacity for pure nonviolence."[4] In a biography of Gandhi, one gets a sense of how family taught the Indian leader the power of nonviolence as a personal ethic, a development quite significant in his maturation as a man and a leader:

> I learnt the lesson of nonviolence from my wife, when I tried to bend her to my will. Her determined resistance to my will, on the one hand, and her quiet submission to the suffering my stupidity involved, on the other, ultimately made me ashamed of myself and cured me of my stu-pidity. . . . In the end, she became my teacher in nonviolence. . . . With-out knowing it, Kasturbai had used satyagraha's foremost weapons to win over her husband: a readiness to suffer rather than retaliate, and an implacable will. Family satyagraha is founded, like all satyagraha, on this delicate balance of patience and determination, which, when

rightly practiced, can become a cornerstone for deep personal relations between men and women.[5]

Gandhi defined satyagraha as "holding on to truth" or "soul force." *Satya* means "truth" in Sanskrit, and comes from *sat,* which means simply "that which is."[6] Gandhi's concept of family satyagraha calls to mind Martin's and Malcolm's perspectives on the importance of familial solidarity and cooperation in building strong black manhood and in establishing peaceful coexistence within the context of the larger black community.

Martin's nonviolent approach is explored here to resolve conflicts and to decrease incidents of violence between black men and in black families and communities. A similar approach is taken to the views of Malcolm, who took the position that African Americans need to be taught not how to love their enemies but how to love themselves. While a Black Muslim, he noted:

> Mr. Muhammad teaches us to love each other, and when I say love each other—love our own kind. This is all black people need to be taught in this country because the only ones whom we don't love are our own kind. Most of the Negroes you see running around here talking about "love everybody"—they don't have any love whatsoever for their own kind. When they say, "Love everybody," what they are doing is setting up a situation for us to love white people. This is what their philosophy is. Or when they say, "Suffer peacefully," they mean suffer peacefully at the hands of the white man, because the same nonviolent Negroes are the advocators of nonviolence. If a Negro attacks one of them, they'll fight that Negro all over Harlem. It's only when the white man attacks them that they believe in nonviolence, all of them.[7]

In the language of Islam, Malcolm was calling for a greater asabiya, or collective group sentiment, among African Americans, a development essential to the building of strong bonds and a sense of social responsibility at all levels, especially in the family.[8] As a Black Muslim, Malcolm found that Elijah Muhammad's teachings and program of self-determination were ideal for instilling in black men and families a deep sense of personal and social responsibility. Muhammad urged black men to take care of their families and black families to forge the kinds of values that discourage welfare dependency, matriarchy, juvenile delinquency, crime, and other problems.

Martin saw agape as necessary to the unity of the male personality and the human family. He defined agape in "Love, Law, and Civil Disobedience," a speech he delivered November 16, 1961:

Agape is more than romantic love, agape is more than friendship. Agape is understanding, creative, and redemptive good will toward all men. It is an overflowing love which seeks nothing in return. Theologians would say that it is the love of God operating in the human heart. So that when one rises to love on this level, he loves men not because he likes them, not because their ways appeal to him, but he loves every man because God loves him. And he rises to the point of loving the person who does an evil deed while hating the deed that the person does. I think this is what Jesus meant when he said, "Love your enemies."[9]

In short, Martin emphasized unconditional love for everyone, and Malcolm stressed unconditional love for black and Muslim families. But both knew that love in all of these cases had to begin with a healthy self-love. This is why Malcolm and the Black Muslims uplifted and even glorified blackness. Malcolm and Martin made self-esteem and self-confidence central themes in their quests for the kind of extended family system and values that result in strong peoplehood and nationhood.

One theological and sociological task for the future, as it relates to black manhood and family life, is the reconciliation of Martin's concept of agape with Malcolm's concept of asabiya. Dialectically, each principle of love represents a partial "yes" and a partial "no." What are the connections and unities between one's love for self and one's love for family, between one's love for a particular people and one's love for the whole of the human family? The contradiction is between the particular and the universal. Mao Tse-tung, in *Four Essays on Philosophy*, speaks to this in an essay on contradictions, noting that "they do not understand that it is precisely in the particularity of contradiction that the universality of contradiction resides." Malcolm was the epitome of the particularity of contradictions, and Martin epitomized the universality of contradictions. Both contradictions are interrelated and derived one from the other in a symbiotic relationship. Even though Martin started with the universality of contradictions, and Malcolm with the particularity of contradictions, they would eventually arrive at the same position. Their protracted struggles around the issues of culture, economics, politics, morality, poverty, racism, and war brought them face to face with the same social reality.

In Martin's mind there was no Manichean dualism.[10] The Manichean dualism existed for Malcolm during his tenure with the Nation of Islam;

however, once he left the NOI and made his sacred Hajj or pilgrimage to Mecca, he ceased to think of the world strictly in terms of a radical dualism that categorically equated some people with evil and others with good. Moreover, he ceased to rely on the Black Muslim model of manhood and family and turned instead to the Sunni Muslim model, which embraced a monotheistic God concept as the basis of a healthy concept of maleness, of family, and of humanity as a whole:

> I'm a Muslim, which only means that my religion is Islam. I believe in God, the Supreme Being, the creator of the universe. This is a very simple form of religion, easy to understand. I believe in one God. It's just a whole lot better. But I believe in one God, and I believe that God had one religion, has one religion, always will have one religion. And that God taught all of the prophets the same religion, so there is no argument about who was greater or who was better: Moses, Jesus, Muhammad, or some of the others. All of them were prophets who came from one God. They had one doctrine, and that doctrine was designed to give clarification of humanity, so that all of humanity would see that it was one and have some kind of brotherhood that would be practiced here on this earth. I believe that.[11]

Any serious and scientific examination of the theology and philosophy of Martin and Malcolm will discover agapic or altruistic love operating in theory and practice. Both men were practitioners of agapic love in their dealings with people at all levels of society. However, Martin defined the universe as the entire human family, and Malcolm thought of it primarily in terms of the people of African descent and the Muslim world. Malcolm's selective identification represents a microcosm of the entire human family. Martin was an idealist and eternal optimist who showed compassion for the entire human race. Moreover, it is important to note that Martin demonstrated an unconditional love tempered by "a tough mind and a tender heart,"[12] the kind of love he saw as necessary in raising children, in turning boys into men, and in insuring the welfare, survival, and vitality of families, neighborhoods, and communities.

Malcolm, on the other hand, was compassionate with all blacks and Muslims, but firm and often uncompromising with anyone else. His covenant with his extended family by blood and faith was based on love, peace, and harmony. The social contract with groups outside of this circle was one of respect and peaceful coexistence. The world community of Islam is a microcosm of the entire human family. Its members include peoples of African, Asian, European, and Native American descent. Significantly, Malcolm's sense of the extended family expanded to include European Muslims after his Hajj experience. He explained this personal transformation on his part this way:

> When I got over there and went to Mecca and saw these people who were blond and blue-eyed and pale-skinned and all those things, I said, "Well," but I watched them closely. And I noticed that though they were white, and they would call themselves white, there was a difference between them and the white ones over here. And that basic difference was this: In Asia or the Arab world or in Africa, where the Muslims are, if you find one who says he's white, all he's doing is using an adjective to describe something that's incidental about him, one of his incidental characteristics; there is nothing else to it, he's just white. . . . But when you get the white man over here in America and he says he's white, he means something else. You can listen to the sound of his voice—when he says he's white, he means he's boss.[13]

Malcolm demonstrated no unconditional love for whites outside of the context of the Muslim ummah. Moreover, he dealt with non-Muslim whites on an individual basis and not as a group. He distrusted the collective white world because, historically and sociologically, white supremacy loomed as a collective and global phenomenon.[14] However, Malcolm was prepared to enter into limited alliances with whites who were progressive, radical, and revolutionary. The possibility that increasing numbers of whites would reach such a state was, for him, not beyond the realm of possibility, especially since he saw more and more white students who recognized and acknowledged that their lives and destinies were linked to those of African Americans. He reasoned, "So when the day comes when the whites who are *really* fed up— I don't mean these jive whites, who pose as liberals and who are not, but those who are fed up with what is going on—when *they* learn how to really establish the proper type of communication with those uptown who are fed up, and they get some coordinated action going, you'll get some changes. You'll get some changes. And it will take both, it will take everything that you've got, it will take that."[15]

Manchild in America: The Family Ties of Malcolm and Martin

Malcolm Little was born in Omaha on May 19, 1925, and Martin Luther King Jr. in Atlanta on January 15, 1929. Malcolm was born in the Midwest and Martin in the Deep South. These geographical differences were mediated by the chronological fact that both men were born in an era of racial turmoil and national reconstruction. Both were children during the Great Depression. However, their families adapted differently to this national crisis based on their socioeconomic status. Malcolm was born into the working class, and Martin into the middle class. These class differences would come to define their conceptions of manhood and family and also their ideologies as religious and human rights leaders. Martin was the epitome of progressive leadership from the African-American middle class, standing firmly in the tradition of W.E.B. Du Bois, Asa Philip Randolph, and Bayard Rustin. Malcolm was the quintessential leader from the African-American masses and one who identified fully with the tradition of Martin Delany, Noble Drew Ali, and Marcus Garvey. But despite the class distinctions, Malcolm and Martin associated manhood and family at their best with loyalty, determination, and achievement.

While there were class, ideological, and formal educational differences between Malcolm and Martin, both men converged in the mainstream of African-American culture. They connected to the cultural soul force at the heart of African-American society, especially as they encouraged the transmission of the values of freedom and self-reliance from one generation of their people to another. In essence, they were able to captivate the minds, hearts, and spirits of their people as few past or present leaders have been able to do, mainly because they gave them a sense of being involved in a communal struggle. On these matters, the two men found common ground even as circumstances, some of which were beyond their control, kept them from forming a close alliance or working with the same organizations.

Malcolm's father was a Baptist minister from Reynolds, Georgia. His spiritual father, Elijah Muhammad, was from Sandersville, Georgia, and was also a Baptist minister before converting to the Nation of Islam. Martin's father was a Baptist minister from Stockbridge, Georgia. In this context, Baptist faith traditions and the state of Georgia proved to be common denominators in the spirituality and sociology of both men's fathers, a consideration quite relevant to any serious study of the positions Malcolm and Martin took on family issues and values.

Earl Little was a tall black man with one eye. His perspective on manhood led him to rule his wives and children with an iron hand. He was also an authoritarian who equated self-reliance with manhood and strong family life. His second wife, Louise Little, bore him eight children and was a house-wife. She did not work outside of the home until after her husband's death. Malcolm had a very light complexion like his mother, who could almost "pass" for white. He was the seventh child and his father's favorite son. His mother was very strict in rearing him and tended to be more permissive with the other children.[16] It was in this context that Malcolm developed his earliest sense of the role of the father and the mother as the cementing force in family life.

The Reverend Martin Luther King Sr. was also authoritarian.[17] Alberta Williams King was a housewife. Daddy King, as he was affectionately called in the Atlanta community, graduated from Morehouse College, and Alberta graduated from Spelman College. These two institutions were among the elite black colleges, and their traditions became closely intertwined with the values and traditions of the King family. Before the advent of black power and black pride, middle-class African Americans thought of Morehouse as the "Negro Harvard" and Spelman as the "Negro Radcliffe." The Kings thought of these institutions as part of their extended family, for it was here that they were reminded that they had responsibilities toward blacks less fortunate than themselves.

Both Malcolm and Martin were blessed with strong father figures, worthy of honor and respect. This was significant in view of the findings of behav-ioral psychologists, who suggest that the first seven years of a child's life set the mold for his or her adult personality. Unfortunately, Earl Little was mur-dered by the Black Legion, a white supremacist organization, when Malcolm was only six years old. Malcolm no longer had what had been a towering symbol of manhood, and this loss, in addition to tremendous pressure from the racist society, threw his family into a state of turmoil from which it never fully recovered. Martin's life within the context of family proved to be quite different. Daddy King, Martin's father, lived to see his son become a famous civil and human rights leader. Therefore, the father/son bonding and inter-generational transmission of culture, knowledge, and wisdom from father to son was completed in Martin's case. Malcolm, on the other hand, was left with a deep desire for a father surrogate, a void later filled by Elijah Muham-mad. In any case, Malcolm's fatherlessness created a psychological and spiri-tual need that Martin never felt.

Malcolm's and Martin's Expanding Sense of Family: Leadership, Courtship, and Marriage

Both Malcolm and Martin viewed themselves as leaders with a mission and a vision, perceptions reinforced by family expectations. One might also suggest that they viewed themselves as men of destiny. In order to achieve their mission and realize their destiny, they both accepted the need for unconditional love for their people, commitment, discipline, loyalty, and sacrifice, which involved the uplifting of their people. In other words, they knew that they had to think of their whole people in familial terms. Moreover, they also realized that they had to select the right spouse or soul mate if they were going to stay on course, a realization that led Malcolm to be slow and very deliberate in his search for a wife. Malcolm stated the case: "I wouldn't have considered it possible for me to love any woman. I'd had too much experience that women were only tricky, deceitful, untrustworthy flesh. I had seen too many men ruined, or at least tied down, or in some other way messed up by women. . . . And for anyone in any kind of leadership position, such as I was, the worst thing in the world that he could have was the wrong woman. Even Samson, the world's strongest man, was destroyed by the woman who slept in his arms. She was the one whose words hurt him."[18]

But Malcolm and Martin further realized that they needed wives who were devoted to the cause and who could accept their levels of commitment, discipline, loyalty, and sacrifice for the movement. During the 1950s and 1960s, women were expected to be housewives by both Muslim and Christian men. Male authority and leadership were the norms that supported the traditional family. The American nuclear family was patriarchal and patrilineal, and some black families conformed to this model. Any family that did not fit this description was considered to be abnormal if not pathological, and this helps explain the excessive focus on black families that were considered matriarchal and matrilineal.[19] This is even more the case today, when the women's movement is redefining gender roles in the family, and when patriarchal structures are under attack in the academy, in religious institutions, in government, and in the public square.

Malcolm and Martin both had college-educated wives with career goals, but their manhood was never threatened. Coretta Scott was trained to be a concert singer, and Betty Sanders was in nursing school. Before their conversions to the same faiths as their husbands, Coretta and Betty were both Methodist. Coretta converted to the Baptist denomination, and Betty converted to

Islam. Her conversion took place before her marriage. She changed her name to Betty X, based on the practices of the Nation of Islam. Her foster parents were not pleased, and they refused to continue paying her tuition.[20] In any case, Coretta and Betty embraced their husbands' faith traditions and assumed the roles of supportive wives, thus keeping their immediate families secure and functional in the absence of Martin and Malcolm.

At the time of Martin and Coretta's courtship, Martin had completed both a bachelor's degree in English and sociology at Morehouse College and a master of divinity degree at Crozer Theological Seminary and was working on a doctorate in theology at Boston University. Coretta had completed a bachelor's degree at Antioch College and was attending the New England Conservatory of Music.[21] Malcolm had completed the eighth grade at Mason High School in Michigan. But he had taken correspondence courses from Harvard University, was on the prison debate team, and had been mentored by Elijah Muhammad. Betty had received a bachelor's degree from Tuskegee Institute. She clearly had more Western formal education than her husband. However, the Nation of Islam's education equipped Malcolm to be an awesome husband, father, and leader of his people.

While formal education and social status are good indicators of compatibility, the Prophet Muhammad (pbuh) offered careful and wise counsel in matters of marriage. Abu Hurairah reported Allah's Messenger as saying: "A woman may be married for four reasons: for her property, her status, her beauty and her religion; so try to get one who is religious, and prosper."[22] According to the Prophet Muhammad (pbuh), of all the qualities a man should seek in a wife, religious virtue is the most important. It is more important than education, socioeconomic status, physical beauty, family background, or romance skills. Religious faith and practice, discipline, and moral character are the backbone and cornerstone of a virtuous wife in Islam. A morally upright wife will teach and rear morally upright children. A virtuous woman is trustworthy, loyal, devoted, supportive, sensitive, wise, and devoted to family welfare. In the words of King Solomon, "A virtuous woman is a crown to her husband; but she that maketh ashamed is a rottenness in his bones."[23]

Mary Powell, a mutual friend of Martin and Coretta, introduced them in January 1952. On their first date, their conversation reflected concerns to which they would later devote their public lives. Martin recounted: "She talked about things other than music. I never will forget, the first discussion we had was about the question of racial and economic injustice and the question of peace. She had been actively engaged in movements dealing with these problems. . . . After an hour, my mind was made up. I said, 'So you can do something else besides sing? You've got a good mind also. You have everything I ever wanted in a woman. We ought to get married someday.'"[24] In his matrimonial conversations with Coretta, Martin told her, "The four things that I look for in a wife are character, intelligence, personality, and beauty. And you have them all." This model of the ideal wife owed much to Martin's lifelong exposure to black church culture. Be that as it may, he and Coretta were married on June 18, 1953, in Marion, Alabama.[25]

Malcolm's concept of an ideal wife was initially based on the teachings of Elijah Muhammad. Referring to those teachings, Malcolm stated, "A wife's ideal age was half the man's age, plus seven. He taught that women are physiologically ahead of men. Mr. Muhammad taught that no marriage could succeed where the woman did not look up with respect to the man. And that the man had to have something above and beyond the wife in order for her to be able to look to him for psychological security."[26] Malcolm never really abandoned this conception of manhood, even as he changed his mind about male-female relationships and the place of women in religion and society.

It is clear from the descriptions afforded above that both Malcolm and Martin expected their wives to play traditional roles in both the private and public spheres. They were expected to support their husbands' public leadership and to be homemakers. Both Coretta and Betty were known to rebel against such views of marital relationships and family at times, but they refused to make their concerns public. Although they challenged their husbands in private, they supported them in public. This was significant in a racist culture that sought to highlight weak black males, to divide black men and women, and to define black families as dysfunctional.

The courtship between Malcolm and Betty was based on Islamic etiquette and protocol. In Islam there is no concept of dating. According to one source, "During the process of courtship (Khitbah), and before performing the marriage ceremony (Nikah), the two individuals are to know one another. However, there should be no privacy between them. The members of the two families are to be included also."[27] Betty Shabazz described her courtship with Malcolm as follows: "I never 'dated' Malcolm as we think of it because at the time single men and women in the Muslims[28] did not 'fraternize,' as they called it. Men and women always went out in groups. Whenever I went out in a group with Malcolm he would always drive, and I always sat in the backseat directly behind him. I never understood why I was supposed to sit behind him, until one day I was talking and happened to look up into the rearview mirror. I saw him looking at me. When he saw me looking, he smiled and I smiled back. That was as much as we could do."[29]

Muslims are not permitted to meet in private with members of the opposite gender. In situations where a man and a woman are alone, it is believed that Satan will be the third party and perhaps will tempt the couple to do something that is unlawful.[30] When the man and the woman are together, there must be a chaperon. The ages of the individuals do not matter, nor whether they have been married before. These standards defined the premarital relationship between Malcolm and Betty.

During those times when Malcolm took Betty out to dinner or entertainment, he had a chaperon. Betty reported, "Malcolm would always take me to dinner accompanied by another Muslim brother. For me, it was a whole new way of living and learning and eating and being. Malcolm treated me really special, but he treated everybody special. But what most attracted me to him was his nobility. He always made me feel very comfortable. If he said he was going to call, you could bank on it. If he said he was going to do something, you could be assured that it would be done. He did not play games."[31] Before the wedding, Malcolm was in a state of strict celibacy: "From the time I entered prison until I married, about twelve years later, because of Mr. Muhammad's influence upon me, I had never touched a woman."[32] In an American culture where there are free interactions between males and females and a mass media saturated with sex, it is extremely difficult for the average black male, or any male for that matter, to practice sexual abstinence. Malcolm's observance of this strict moral code of sexual abstinence speaks volumes about his level of commitment to Islam and Elijah Muhammad.

Betty and Malcolm were married on January 14, 1958, in Lansing, Michigan. They had known each other for about a year. In his memoir of Malcolm's family, nephew Rodnell Collins revealed some interesting circumstances that influenced Malcolm's decision to get married:

> Mr. Muhammad wanted him to get married. Sisters in the Nation considered him prime husband material, as did many women outside the Nation. Ma and her good friend, Sister Saoud Muhammad, concerned about his eating and sleeping habits, strongly believed that he needed a wife. In fact, Ma said that she and Sister Saoud, knowing that he

planned to travel to Africa and the Middle East in 1959, were already preparing the way for him to find an African wife on his trip. Malcolm, they knew, had no interest in an arranged marriage, but if he suspected they were involved in such plans, he might make a move on his own. That's exactly what he did. Before leaving for Africa, he married Sister Betty X, a nursing student who lectured on hygiene and medical facts to the Muslim girls' and women's classes.[33]

Theologian James Cone believes that Malcolm and Martin were both sexist. For Cone, this attitude not only interfered with their effectiveness as husbands and fathers; it also limited their success as leaders and activists:

The most glaring and detrimental limitation of Martin's and Malcolm's leadership was not seeing sexism as a major problem connected with and as evil as racism. Like most white and black men of the 1960s, their attitude toward women was shaped by their acceptance of patriarchal values as the norm for the family and society. Following the pattern of white religious bodies, the black church and the Nation of Islam provided religious justification for the subordination of women. While Martin and Malcolm challenged white values regarding race, their acceptance of male privilege prevented them from seeing the connection between racism and sexism. . . . Both believed that the woman's place was in the home, the private sphere, and the man's place was in society, the public arena, fighting for justice on behalf of women and children.[34]

As indicated earlier, Malcolm and Martin were operating out of their traditional Islamic and Christian perspectives on the issues of gender and the rights and roles of women. As their concerns became more global, their positions on manhood, womanhood, and family shifted and became more flexible.

After Malcolm left the Nation of Islam, his views on women became more progressive, a development that embodied significant implications for his emerging perspective on manhood and family:

In every Middle East or African country I have visited, I noticed the country is as "advanced" as its women are, or as backward as its women. By this I mean, in areas where the women have been pushed into the background and kept without education, the whole area or country is just as backward, uneducated, and "underdeveloped." Where the women are encouraged to get education and play a more active role in the all-around affairs of the community and the country, the entire people are more active, more enlightened, and more progressive. Thus, in my opinion, the Muslim religious leaders of today must reevaluate and spell out with clarity the Muslim position on education in general and education for women in particular. And then a vast program must be launched to elevate the standard of education in the Muslim world. An old African proverb states: "Educate a man and you educate an individual; educate a woman and you educate an entire family."[35]

In many of the Middle Eastern and African countries, Muslims in general and Muslim women in particular did not attend the missionary schools. They did not want their Islamic culture and values to be compromised or diluted by the influences of Western education. In the postcolonial era, Muslim governments and communities are trying to provide quality formal education for the women and children. This position is more consistent with the more inclusive educational system that Malcolm and Martin had in mind as they considered means by which family ties could be significantly strengthened.

Slavery and the Extended Family: The Views of Malcolm and Martin

In 1974, archaeologists working in Ethiopia in a place called Hadsar found sufficient fossil remains to piece together the most complete skeleton of a two-legged upright walking human ancestor ever unearthed. It was a female they named Lucy. "She was about three feet tall, weighed about sixty pounds as an adult, and was approximately 3.5 million years old. It was the oldest complete skeleton of a human ancestor ever found. It was also the latest in a long line of discoveries pioneered by Louis and Mary Leakey, who first discovered East African man in 1959. . . . The next year in the same location they found enough fossils to represent thirteen individuals: men, women, and at least four children. They named this "The First Family."[36] The evolution of the African extended family created the first civilizations.[37] Agriculture, the city, religion, science, and technology were the hallmarks of these ancient civilizations. The slave traders did cultural, economic, political, and spiritual violence to many of these African extended families and societies. The extended family or kinship system, based on shared ancestors, marriage, culture, and language, was disrupted. Genealogically and culturally dislocated Africans were alienated from their society. Malcolm and Martin took this history into account as they identified the challenges confronting black families in their own time.

Many African Americans are descended from the victims of the transatlantic slave trade. Today, the African-American family is in a state of crisis, much as the African family structure was during the slave trade and slavery. The roots of this crisis extend back to the oppression and trauma of centuries of chattel slavery and the disruption of the extended family. For Malcolm and Martin, this could not have been more devastating, since the family structure was the foundation upon which the quest for racial solidarity rested.

Sociologically, the modern-day crisis is rooted in economic problems associated with absentee fathers and single mothers. These historical and sociological conflicts, operating in an environment of capitalist exploitation and racism, have produced psychological problems of cultural alienation, anger, aggression, and violence. Therefore, attempts should be made to extract from the thoughts and actions of Malcolm and Martin some remedies for the family crisis and gender issues confronting Africans in America.

If we could project ourselves back to the days of slavery and witness the hopes and prayers of the enslaved Africans, we would no doubt observe their constant concern for freedom and family. The African slaves prayed for freedom from the cruel conditions of chattel slavery. They also prayed to keep their families together in order to nurture, educate, and protect each other. Slaveowners consistently sought to deny these precious human needs and values to the slaves for almost four hundred years.

Martin Luther King Jr. presented a graphic account of slavery in the New World, giving special attention to how it has affected the African-American family structure over time:

> The Negro family for three hundred years has been on the tracks of the racing locomotives of American history and was dragged along mangled and crippled. Pettigrew has pointed out that American slavery is distinguished from all other forms because it consciously dehumanized the Negro. In other cultures slaves preserved dignity and a measure of personality and family life. Our institution of slavery began on the coasts of Africa and because the middle passage was long and expensive, African families were torn apart in the selective process as if the members were beasts. On the voyages millions died in holds into which blacks were packed spoon fashion to live on a journey often of 2 to 6 months with approximately the room for each equivalent to a coffin.

The sheer physical torture was sufficient to murder millions of men, women, and children. But even more incalculable was the psychological damage. For those who survived as a family group, once more on the auction block many families were ripped apart.[38]

The ripping apart of extended families was one of the tactics used by slaveowners to "divide and conquer" the race as a whole. Alienation and devaluation of the cultural identity of the African captives was another tactic. Moreover, the circumstances of Africans left them with the options of reconstructing their kinship system or assimilating into the culture created by their slave masters. King addressed this dilemma in these terms:

On the plantation the institution of legal marriage for slaves did not exist. The masters directed mating, or if they did not intervene, marriage occurred without sanctions. There were polygamous relationships, fragile monogamous relationships, illegitimacies, abandonment, and the repetitive tearing apart of families as children, husbands, or wives were sold to other plantations. But these cruel conditions were not yet the whole story. Masters and their sons used Negro women to satisfy their spontaneous lust or, when more humane attitudes prevailed, as concubines. The depths were reached in Virginia, which we sentimentally call the State of Presidents. There slaves were bred for sale, not casually or incidentally, but in a vast deliberate program that produced enormous wealth for slaveowners. This breeding program was one answer to the legal halting of the slave traffic early in the nineteenth century.[39]

As both Martin and Malcolm realized, the stigma of color and race made assimilation into the dominant white society impossible for most and problematic for those few who could "pass" for white. African Americans with African phenotypical traits were prevented from assimilating into white society. A caste system based on color and race was created in America, thus increasing the burdens placed on black men and their families. This caste system defined a matrix of power relationships that permanently relegated African Americans to the bottom of society. On the other hand, the power relationships in white society were premised on economic and social class arrangements, all of which impacted the African-American family structure in strange and destructive ways.[40]

Assimilation into the culture and social life of white society for the vast majority of African Americans has been almost impossible. For decades, historians and sociologists have debated the degree of assimilation versus the persistence of African cultural survivals. Malcolm and Martin were not oblivious to this debate as they wrestled with questions about black identity. While they failed to publicly identify with any particular school of thought on this matter, they knew that the most important mode of social and cultural organization in traditional African society remains the extended family. Hence, a study of African-American family life and structure can reveal much concerning the African retentions debate. In the United States, Melville J. Herskovits has argued in support of the African survivals thesis, and E. Franklin Frazier has argued in support of the non-African survivals antithesis.[41] Both positions are relevant to any discussion of Malcolm and Martin in relation to the black family.

The African-American community has enjoyed its highest level of peace and stability in times when its three primary institutions—church/mosque, family, and neighborhood school—were healthy. Such a state has also existed when business and economic activities in the community were dynamic. Ironically, the peace, stability, and economic viability existed under the hegemony of a segregated society for decades. With the imposition of court-ordered desegregation and the increasing number of family households without the physical presence of the father, the African-American community started drifting from what Martin would call "community to chaos." The extent to which Malcolm and Martin anticipated such an outcome is not clear, but Malcolm always denied that African Americans had much to gain as individuals, as families, and as a people through an integrated social order.

The Moynihan Report: What Did It Say about the Black Family?

In 1965, the U.S. Department of Labor released a document entitled *The Negro Family: The Case for National Action*. The principal investigator was Daniel Patrick Moynihan, a white sociologist at Harvard University who later became a prominent senator from New York. The study is also known as the Moynihan Report. Perhaps the most penetrating finding of the study was that 23 percent of black families were headed by single mothers. Moynihan concluded that if the trend continued, the African-American family would be in a state of crisis. The report presented nothing that was strikingly new to black leaders, but it provided Martin with additional evidence to draw on in his struggle for an end to racial segregation and economic injustice. Malcolm died before seeing the report, but he too probably would have used it to support claims that the African-American family was in trouble.

Martin expressed his reaction to the Moynihan Report in an address at Abbot House in Westchester County, New York, on October 29, 1965:

A recent study offers the alarming conclusion that the Negro family in the urban ghettos is crumbling and disintegrating. It suggests that the progress in civil rights can be negated by the dissolving of family structure and therefore social justice and tranquility can be delayed for generations. The statistics are alarming. They show that in urban cities nearly 25 percent of Negro women, who were married, are divorced, in contrast to a rate of 8 percent among whites. The rate of illegitimacy in the past twenty years rose slightly more for whites than Negroes, but the number of Negro illegitimacies in proportion to its population is substantially higher than whites. The number of Negro families headed by a woman is two and a half times that of whites and as a consequence 14 percent of all Negro children receive aid and 56 percent of Negro children at some point in their lives have been recipients of public aid.[42]

The Moynihan Report proved useful to Martin as he pushed for more government expenditures to enhance broken families and deprived communities. It was also a reminder that African-American men and women necessarily had to recommit themselves to each other and to the shaping of wholesome family life.

Malcolm, speaking in a somewhat similar vein, saw the problems of black families in historical context, attributing them to a system of enslavement that robbed both African-American women and men of their capacity to be strong family figures. In his reflections on the problem, he anticipated some of the findings of the Moynihan Report:

Even right now you read some of the conclusions reached by some of these so-called sociologists. They admit that the tendency of our women to have babies born out of wedlock is a throwback right to a habit that was born during slavery. In slavery, it was nothing for a Black woman to have a baby—she was supposed to have a baby. And the father, the Black man who fathered the baby, was never permitted to have the responsibility of a father. . . . And that came right down from slavery to the Black community today. You'll find many men who are married and have two or three children, walk away from that woman like she didn't even exist, and leave those children in the house without a second thought, without a second thought. Well, you wouldn't find an African doing this. We weren't like this in Africa.[43]

While Martin acknowledged the alarming findings of the report, he put forward a powerful caveat to the policymakers. His thoughts echoed in these words: "As public awareness increases there will be dangers and opportunities. The opportunity will be to deal fully rather than haphazardly with the problem as a whole—to see it as a social catastrophe and meet it as other disasters are met with an adequacy of resources. The danger will be that the problems will be attributed to innate Negro weaknesses and used to justify neglect and rationalize oppression."[44] Martin's caveat was on target in light of the fact that the Moynihan Report defined the crisis as a "tangle of pathology."

While most African-American leaders and scholars disagreed with much of the Moynihan Report, the disturbing trend regarding weak male figures did continue, and twenty years later, half of all African-American families were headed by the mother.[45] Based on the 1960s data, Moynihan had defined African-American families as a matriarchy, because so many children grew up without a father in the house. He used statistics to suggest that the mother was the primary authority figure in the household. This contrasted with the traditional white American nuclear family with respect to demography and function.[46] In his analysis of African-American family life, Martin came to a similar conclusion:

> Moreover, the women, being more generally in the house and charged with the care of the white master's children, were more often exposed to some education and a sense—though minimal—of personal worth. Hence a matriarchy had early developed. After slavery it persisted because in the cities there was more employment for women than for men. Though both were unskilled, the women could be used in domestic service at low wages. The woman became the support of the household and the matriarchy was reinforced. The Negro male existed in a larger society dominated by men, but he was subordinated to women in his own society.[47]

During the 1960s, the father was the authority figure and disciplinarian in the traditional American nuclear family. Similarly, the mother nurtured the children and managed the household. Some scholars of this period suggested that the African-American family functioned more like the traditional African extended family. In this context, elders, grandmothers, mothers, and even those not related by blood were in fact authority figures. Their authority did not abrogate the authority of the father but reinforced the African principle that "it takes a whole village to raise a child."[48]

In May 1984, the National Association for the Advancement of Colored People (NAACP) and the National Urban League convened a summit conference at Fisk University in Nashville in response to the crisis of the family. Leaders of national organizations, representatives from governmental agencies, and recognized scholars were invited. The Fisk University Black Family Summit highlighted many of the issues and themes that surrounded the crisis of the African-American family as Malcolm and Martin had seen them a generation earlier. Asa Hilliard, one of the keynote speakers, presented a discussion on the ancient African families in Kemet (Egypt) and other parts of Africa before slavery and colonization. This classical cultural paradigm set a powerful tone for the summit, as it directed the discussion of the African-American family in the context of African culture and kinship systems. According to Hilliard,

> In that southern cradle, certain types of family patterns were produced. Cheikh Anta Diop calls them matrilineal, as opposed to patrilineal. In matrilineal families, the line of succession is reckoned through the mother. . . . We suddenly find that this extended family pattern we have talked about has a foundation in our history. . . . We have a clear African culture. . . The healthy black family is a family that has a common memory. The healthy black family is a family that has common values. The healthy black family is a family that cooperates because of its common memory and common values. The healthy black family is a family that has a formal and informal educational system that takes place outside the public schools or anywhere else and is conducted by the family.

Hilliard stressed the importance of the cultural unity of Africans on the continent and in the diaspora. And on the strengths of the African culture and values, he felt that the African-American family could be resurrected to a living and healthy state of existence. Malcolm and Martin said as much and more as they articulated their visions of the greatness their people were capable of achieving.

Church and Mosque: Reinforcing Black Family Life

Saul D. Alinsky observed in 1965 that Martin's leadership had a stronger appeal in the South and was less effective in the urban North. As he put it, "Dr. King's appeal has always been much greater among southern than among northern Negroes—and greater among northern whites than among northern Negroes. His philosophy of nonviolence has reassured whites; it has tended to anger lower-class Negroes, who see it as coming too close to the image of the docile Negro they have rejected. And the Negroes of the North—particularly the men—have moved pretty far away from the Negro churches, which provide Dr. King's base in the South."[49] Despite the abandonment of the church by increasing numbers of African Americans in King's time, the civil rights leader always stressed the need for the values of the church and family in the creation of black unity and in the progress of the freedom struggle.

Malcolm's appeal was the reciprocal of Martin's geographical leadership. Malcolm was more effective in the urban North and less effective in the South. The black South is a strong Christian region of the country. Historically, Islam in the United States is largely a twentieth-century phenomenon, and it has also been associated with the urban areas of the North, Midwest, and more recently the West Coast and the South.[50] This helps explain why black churches had a greater impact than other religious institutions on black family networks and values up to the 1950s and 1960s, when Malcolm and Martin were obsessed with the relationship between black family life and the broader struggle for liberation.

The African-American father, or male authority figure, is conspicuously absent today not only in the family but in the church as well. There has been a sharp decline in black male church attendance. Churches are starting to experience the same phenomenon as the African-American family. C. Eric Lincoln and Lawrence H. Mamiya offer the following observations: "Any casual observer of a Sunday worship service in the typical black church is immediately struck by the predominance of female members. Depending on the congregation, between 66 to 80 percent of its membership is usually composed of women. In our survey of 2,150 churches, male membership averaged 30 percent. There are about 2.5–3 females to every male member. The usual anguished lament and questions heard from pastors and laity are: 'Where have all the black men gone?' 'Why don't more black men attend church?'"[51] Fifty percent of African-American families are headed by females, and the church is predominantly female and in most instances headed by a male pastor. Historically, the family and church have been the cultural, spiritual, and economic backbone of the black community. Moreover, the church has been an institution for the cultivation of character, discipline, leadership, responsibility, and talents among young boys who aspire toward manhood. Also, if young women are looking for good husbands, the church has been one of the best places to find suitable candidates for marriage and family life. For African Americans, the church and the mosque are parallel institutions to the African extended family or kinship system. The pastor and imam are analogous to the Babalawo, chief, emir, and oba in the African context. Malcolm and Martin would undoubtedly agree with this assessment.

If the African-American church is predominantly female, the mosque in the African-American community is predominantly male. According to Lincoln and Mamiya, "The phenomenon of more black males preferring Islam while more black females adhere to traditional black Christianity is not as bizarre as it sounds. It is already clear that in Islam the historic black church denominations will be faced with a far more serious and more powerful competitor for the souls of black folk than the white churches ever were. When is the question, not whether."[52] Jawanza Kunjufu notes, "I also don't think it is accidental that the gender ratio in the Christian Church is 75 percent female to 25 percent male, while it is exactly the opposite in Islam."[53] This statistic is partly explained by two factors: females are permitted to pray at home and are not required to attend the mosque, and black males are converting to Islam at faster rates than black females. This need to attract more women to the Muslim faith is pressing, but Ibn 'Umar reports that the Prophet Sallallahu Alehi Wasallam said: "Do not prevent the women from going to the mosques, although their houses are better for them."[54] This exemption is given to women because of their special role in the family and in Islamic society. If a woman is caring for children, pregnant, or experiencing monthly discomforts, she is exempt from going to the jummah or Friday prayer services. On the other hand, men do not have the same exemption.

Many African-American men have been inspired to revert[55] to Islam by reading the *Autobiography of Malcolm X,* listening to his speeches, and seeing Spike Lee's movie about Malcolm X. Malcolm is seen as a cultural hero and icon who supremely embodied manhood. Lincoln and Mamiya give other reasons for these reversions: (1) The Qur'an advocates self-defense while the Christian Bible counsels turning the other cheek; (2) black sports heroes such as Muhammad Ali and Kareem Abdul-Jabbar have further legitimated the Islamic option by converting to Islam and taking on Muslim names; (3) black parents who are not Muslims have given their children Muslim names to demonstrate their solidarity with some features of Islam, as a way of announcing their independence from Western social conventions, or as a means of identifying with an African cultural heritage; and (4) many black men have been attracted to Islam because of the dawah (propagation) efforts in prisons and on the streets, a ministry which is not as pronounced in most black Christian churches.[56]

In recent times, the tendency of black males to leave the church and revert to Islam has become a growing concern for some ministers and Christian organizations. Perhaps the most vocal and visible among this group is the Reverend Fred K. C. Price, who has criticized Sunni Muslims, the Nation of Islam, and Minister Louis Farrakhan in particular on radio and television programs. According to Price, he is doing "a consumer report" on Islam to warn males about the type of religion into which they are getting. His lecture series "Race, Religion, and Racism" was initially motivated by the existence of racism in white Christianity and the white church. Now that he has critiqued white Christianity, his attention has turned to Islam and Muslims. His concerns about Islam and Muslims are motivated by the exodus of black males from the church to the mosque, a trend he feels will create an entirely different black male and model of family life:

> I'm concerned because the racism in the church and in this nation historically has turned a lot of Black men sour on Christianity. So they are leaving and have left Christianity because they perceive Christianity as the White man's religion. It appears that the Nation of Islam, under the present directorship of Minister Louis Farrakhan, has the Black man at heart. . . . My purpose is not to tell you to go to Islam. My purpose is not to tell you to leave Christianity. My purpose is not to tell you to leave Islam. My purpose is not to tell you to come to Christianity. That's your decision. . . . But I think if you make a decision, you ought to have all the facts before you make it.[57]

Price's broadcasts from the Faith Dome in Los Angeles have stirred up a lot of controversy in Christian and Muslim communities. However, Price's concerns represent decades, if not centuries, of perceiving Islam as a threat to Christianity. These Crusade-type issues are now being dramatized in the black community, and this will continue as more and more African Americans struggle with the significance of Malcolm's and Martin's spiritual legacies for their lives.

In an article in *Newsweek* in October 1995, Carla Power and Allison

Samuels reported the following, which says something about Islam and the struggle for responsible black manhood on the streets of the inner cities and in prison:

> About one-third of the four million to five million Muslims in the United States are African Americans, and at its current rapid rate of growth, Islam will become the second largest religion in the United States by the year 2000. While still small compared with Christianity's overall numbers, the Muslim community's growth has been dramatic. In 1989, there were 2,000 declared Muslims in the armed services. This year there are 10,000. In Philadelphia, the number of Muslim blacks has risen from 40,000 to 60,000 in five years. In Chicago, there were only a handful of mosques twenty years ago; today there are 30. And a third of all blacks in the federal prison system are Muslim; most of them converted after being locked up.[58]

These patterns of growth are pertinent to any discussion of the relevance of Malcolm and Martin for the future of black men, black families, and the black struggle.

To understand the rapid rise of Islam in the African-American community, one has to put the phenomenon in some cultural and historical context. Power and Samuels further noted that "Islam is perceived as more compatible with Afrocentrism and, in some ways, as more masculine. Islamic clergy often emphasize that about a third of the slaves were shipped to America from Muslim countries. And since Islam rejects visual depictions of God, blacks can pray to a formless Allah instead of a blond, blue-eyed Jesus. Most important, Islam's emphasis on dignity and self-discipline appeals to many men in the inner city, where disorder prevails. Muslims are expected to pray five times a day, avoid drugs and alcohol, and take care of their families."[59] Malcolm's idea of manhood was strongly related to this understanding of Islam.

Given the high level of anxiety about Islam in certain churches, we can learn much from a comparative study of Martin and Malcolm. In these two great champions for justice and human rights, we find excellent role models for masculinity, fatherhood, and brotherhood, despite their different faith traditions. Indeed, Malcolm and Martin viewed each other as strong men, and their criticism of each other's religion did not diminish that respect.

The Million Man, Woman, and Family Marches: Revitalizing Manhood, Womanhood, and Family

In 1995, Louis Farrakhan called upon all black men in the United States to gather on October 16 for what he called the Million Man March. Unlike Martin's 1963 March on Washington, it was not a rally for civil rights legislation, jobs, or other demands on the government. It was to be a Day of Atonement for black men who were guilty of neglecting women and children. The message of the March on Washington was integrationism; the message of the Million Man March was in line with Malcolm's emphasis on self-determination for African-American men and women and the black nation.

The March on Washington involved 250,000 men and women of various races, religions, and classes who joined Martin in demanding to be allowed greater participation in society. The Million Man March represented a cross-section of the African-American male community. Estimates of attendance differed. On October 17, the *New York Times* reported the official estimate as 400,000. Other estimates stand at 400,000, 670,000, one million, and two million. Minister Farrakhan attacked the National Park Service's count of 400,000 as a racist effort to write the hundreds of thousands of black men at the march out of history. He threatened to sue. A reanalysis of the Park Service's photographs by Boston University's Center for Remote Sensing produced an estimate of between 670,000 and 1.04 million men. A *Detroit Free Press* headline four days after the march stated: "'New estimate: 870,000.' All of the men I've talked to who attended the March estimated the attendance figure as 'easily a million.'"[60]

The Million Man March was the largest gathering of black men in modern history. African Americans from all walks of life met to talk about what it means to be a man. As Maulana Karenga and Haki Madhubuti explained, "The Million Man March challenged African-American males to accept responsibility. . . . We challenge each Black man, in particular, and the Black community in general, to renew and expand our commitment to responsibility in personal conduct, in family relations, in obligations to the community, and to the struggle for a just society and a better world. And for us, to be responsible is to willingly and readily assume obligations and duties; to be accountable and dependable."[61] The agenda was one of self-determination and cultural identification.

The Million Man March was consistent with the civil and human rights struggles of African Americans. It did not seek to leverage any resources or legislation from the government; however, it sparked worldwide discussion about the plight of black males in particular and black families in general. It got African Americans to rethink the random acts of violence, the verbal and physical abuse of women and children, and other counterproductive and reactionary activities in families and communities. This event evoked powerful memories of Malcolm and Martin, and it attested to the power of their rich legacies.

Dignity and respect for black women and girls have always set the stage for the cultural and social transformation of the African-American community. For thirty-five years, Elijah Muhammad and Malcolm taught that "we must love, respect and protect our African women and children." As Muhammad said, "Until we learn to love and protect our women, we will never be a fit and recognized people on the earth. The white people here among you will never recognize you until you protect your woman. . . . She is your first nurse. She is your teacher. Your first lesson comes from your mother. If you don't protect your mother, how do you think you look in the eyes of other fellow human beings?"[62] Martin would have agreed fully with these comments, but his sense of what it meant to protect African-American women and families was different in some ways from that of Malcolm and Muhammad.

Black women are among the most exploited, oppressed, underpaid, and overworked groups in the United States. The African diaspora/nation within a nation, inside the United States, will be unable to develop without the education and liberation of women. Malcolm and Martin were equally conscious of this pressing need. As he traveled through the Middle East and Africa in 1964, Malcolm witnessed the impact of female education, or the lack of it, on the degrees of progress in various societies. This experience figured prominently in his increasingly positive and progressive attitude toward women and their roles in the public arena.[63]

The Million Woman March of October 25, 1997, was chaired by Phile Chionesu, a businesswoman and activist, and Asia Coney, a community activist. Their platform issues were as follows:

1. National support for Congresswoman Maxine Waters, in the efforts to effectively bring about a probe into the CIA's participation and its relationship to the influx of drugs into the African-American community in Los Angeles.
2. The development and completion of Black independent schools with a twenty-first-century focus from pre-k through 12th grade.
3. The formation of progressive mechanisms that will qualitatively ad-

dress the development and advancement of Black Women upon leaving the penal system.

4. The development of health facilities that can offer prevention and therapeutic treatment, and a major emphasis on alternative and traditional medicine.

5. The formation of Rites of Passage centers/academies which provide continual programming in addition to assigned enrollment periods.

6. The further development of Black Women, who are or who wish to become professionals, entrepreneurs, and/or politicians.

7. The further development of mechanisms that will assist Black Women who are "in transitional" experiences which will facilitate them more effectively and progressively.

8. The examination of Human Rights violations of Africans in the Americas and their effects.

9. The development of programming that will bring about a sincere and respectful environment that will foster the necessary interaction with our youth.

10. The formulation of progressive mechanisms to combat homelessness and the numerous circumstances that contribute to the plight of sisters/brothers who are without shelter.

11. The development of mechanisms to ensure that the gentrification of our neighborhood as it relates to public and private housing ceases.

12. The reclaiming of our elders' rights, who are entitled to the development of appropriate programs and support systems that will ensure that their quality of life is maintained, enhanced, and preserved.

In a broad sense, the Million Woman March focused on elders, family, culture, community, education, and economic development. The perennial micro issues of female/male relationships were subordinated to the macro issues of family, culture, and community. In a sense, the event contributed a female voice to the range of African-American concerns that Malcolm and Martin addressed decades earlier. The march also echoed the concerns of Ella Baker, Fannie Lou Hamer, and other black women of the 1950s and 1960s, all of whom challenged Malcolm and Martin on the issues of marital and family relationships.

Both of the gender-specific marches received criticism from those who were not fully represented. This criticism was clearly addressed in the Million Family March of October 16, 2000, which was inclusive of male and female, of family and community, and which extended beyond the boundaries of race and ethnicity. Themes of the Million Man and Million Woman Marches were revisited, couples were married, children played on the lawn, and adults and elders listened to speeches while purchasing clothing, jewelry, art, books, and other items. In the heart of the nation's capital, the Million Family March was a celebration of culture, family, and community in the same spirit as Kwanzaa.

Culture, Family, and the Beloved Community: Revisiting the Legacies of Malcolm and Martin

What manner of men were Malcolm and Martin? In the final analysis, their character, intellect, purpose, and leadership must be weighed in the balance of their religion and Sacred Texts, meaning the Qur'an for Malcolm and the Bible for Martin, for they were indeed religiously guided and inspired. The criterion that is appropriate for the evaluation of Martin Luther King Jr. in relation to manhood is Jesus Christ of Nazareth.[64] Likewise, the appropriate criterion for evaluating Malcolm X is Muhammad Ibn Abdullah of Mecca.[65] Jesus and Muhammad established a Sunnah (tradition) that their disciples and companions have long followed unconditionally. Hence, in the intergenerational transmissions of the faith, a Christian man is defined as "one who is like Christ," and a Muslim man is defined as "one who submits to the will of Allah" in the manner in which Muhammad submitted. Throughout their careers as imam and minister, respectively, Malcolm's and Martin's interpretation, approach, and applications of the faith were applauded and celebrated by many and questioned by others. Some ministers felt that the pastor's role was to "win souls for Christ" and not engage in secular forms of social change. Therefore, they questioned Martin's approach to the Social Gospel.[66] Mainstream Muslims challenged Malcolm X's interpretation of Islam while he was still with Elijah Muhammad. It was only when he converted to Sunni Islam that the religious critics started to lessen their attacks. However, his persistent advocacy of black nationalism did occasion some concerns among mainstream Muslims.[67]

Na'im Akbar lists five concerns that Malcolm, Martin, and other powerful black leaders had in common:

> First, they all demanded respect for black women, black family life, and working together. . . . Secondly, they all had faith in God. They all believed in a transcendent reality that their ancestors had conceptualized tens of thousand of years ago, long before there was a Pauline Theology or a man called Jesus. . . . Thirdly, they all recognized the power

and importance of moral values. They believed in moral excellence, not moral mediocrity. . . . The fourth thing that they all had in common is that they understood the importance of history as a context for analysis. . . . Finally, all the men we have discussed valued black life. They didn't listen to tales about being a reverse racist.[68]

Better descriptions of Malcolm and Martin cannot be found, even in the works of the most celebrated scholars. Indeed, Akbar captures the legacies of the two men and how they speak to black men, women, and families in contemporary America.

Martin and Malcolm were brilliant men driven by the courage of their faith and convictions. They were both family men, world citizens, international statesmen, and humanitarians. Their scopes and worldviews were global, and at the same time their commitments to the liberation of African Americans were national and unconditional. Martin and Malcolm were sterling models of the best in the Christian and Islamic liberation traditions, respectively. In a certain way, they were revolutionary twins on opposite sides of the same coin. When one attempts to uncover the essence of these two thinker-revolutionaries, their personas merge in a collective archetype premised on the liberation of the human spirit. In his famous eulogy of Malcolm, actor Ossie Davis expressed this sentiment, which could have been said of Martin as well: "And if you knew him you would know why we must honor him: Malcolm was our manhood, our living, black manhood! This was his meaning to his people. And, in honoring him, we honor the best in ourselves. . . . And we will know him then for what he was and is—a Prince—our own black shining Prince!—who didn't hesitate to die, because he loved us so."[69]

The hope of black men and families may well rest with the cultural nationalist perspective, one that was, for Malcolm, consistent with the values of both the African-American community and Pan Africanists. The cultural nationalists insist on cultural affirmation, not ambivalence or denial. The challenge is to reconcile the creative tension between black cultural independence and integration into the mainstream society. Do African Americans come to the table of equality and the bar of justice as Africans or Americans? These two cultural frames of reference are premised on qualitatively and quantitatively different philosophies and strategies of social change, as a careful study of Malcolm and Martin suggests.

Apparently, there has to be a more dynamic synergy between the transformation of black families and cultural affirmation. The black family exists as a matriarchal anomaly in a predominantly European society that is Judeo-

Christian and patriarchal. This phenomenon exists not because of African survivals but because it is fundamentally a reflection of capitalist and racial oppression. This must be transcended if we are to continue to build on the accomplishments of Malcolm and Martin.

Martin used the Gandhian method of passive resistance to change the hearts and minds of the white ruling class. He confronted hatred and violence with love and nonviolence. While this method brought the venom of white supremacy out in the open, it did not transform the venom of self-hatred in the subconscious of many African-American men and women. Today, we can witness the manifestations of this venom in the community pathologies of crime, violence, and a generalized disrespect for self. The challenge for the architects and leaders of nonviolence is to confront self-hatred and violence in the African-American community. In the spirit of Martin, we are compelled to ask ourselves: "How can agapic love and ahimsa be used to transform individuals and families in the African-American community?"

Bernard Lafayette, one of Martin's trusted lieutenants and former national program administrator for the Southern Christian Leadership Conference, still practices the philosophy of nonviolence. He also advocates its use at all levels of individual and communal life. Lafayette shared the following:

> Gandhi's technique is a strategy for those that oppose you, and those that are close to you. The majority of homicides are by persons that know each other. In my work with the Bloods and the Crips in Los Angeles, a member of the Bloods found out that he was a cousin to a member of the Crips. I said to him, even though you didn't know you were cousins, you should have known you were brothers. Nonviolence is based on putting love into action. If we love each other, sometimes things people say can really hurt. We must resist "acting out." The question is how do you restore relationships after the hurt and pain. Martin Luther King Jr. said, "I reject the behavior, but I love the person."[70]

Activists and scholars agree that the next stage of the human rights movement in the United States is the relentless struggle for economic justice. The creative tension between the integrationist and nationalist positions results from the primacy of race relations and how black communities are impacted by this. Both positions, boldly represented by Malcolm and Martin, agree with the goal of economic empowerment for black men, women, and families. Ostensibly, the question is whether African Americans can achieve economic empowerment without cultural empowerment. Stated differently, is cultural empowerment a necessary precondition for the collective achievement of economic self-determination?

Malcolm and Martin would agree that love is the key. Redemptive love starts with knowing and loving one's self. Then the love that grows out of self-knowledge and self-appreciation can be shared in forgiving and loving others.

5

The Character of Womanhood

The Views of Malcolm and Martin

The true worth of a race must be measured by the character of its womanhood.
Mary McLeod Bethune[1]

Wherever the spiritual values have been submerged, if not destroyed, by an emphasis upon material things, invariably, the women reflect it.
Malcolm X[2]

Women must be considered as more than "breeding machines." It is true that the primary obligation of the woman is that of motherhood, but an intelligent mother wants it to be a responsible motherhood—a motherhood to which she has given consent, not a motherhood due to impulse and to chance.
Martin Luther King Jr.[3]

Malcolm X and Martin Luther King Jr. lived and struggled in a male-dominated culture where gender roles and family life were defined in the most traditional terms.[4] Notions of what constituted true masculinity and femininity were seldom questioned, and the problem of female subordination permeated every level of American institutional life. The values and practices of this culture had an immense influence on how Malcolm and Martin viewed and related to women throughout their lives.[5]

There is no monolithic perspective on this issue because Malcolm's and Martin's notions of gender expanded a bit as they moved toward an informed and definitive internationalism. Even so, some claim that the two men remained essentially unconcerned with the oppression of females, while others view them as contributors, directly or indirectly, to the character and momentum of movements for women's liberation.[6] It is safer to say that Malcolm and Martin never stopped growing intellectually and spiritually around the whole question of what should be the roles of women in an enlightened and civilized society.

In Search of the Female Spirit: Earliest Attitudes toward Women

Malcolm's and Martin's earliest perceptions of and relationships to women began within the contexts of their home and family environments and were nurtured by their experiences with the black communities in which they were raised. In these related environs, they encountered from childhood black women who, despite being oppressed on account of race, sex, and class, were strong, assertive, and endowed with a spirit far more resilient than that of many black men. Malcolm and Martin first discovered such women in their mothers and sisters, and this is where one must begin in tracing the development of their attitudes toward and experiences with women in general.[7]

Louise Little and Alberta Williams King gave their sons their very first sense of the essence of womanhood and motherhood. These women exerted a quiet but powerful influence on their husbands and children within their homes. But Malcolm and Martin always knew that their fathers were the undisputed heads of their households. Earl Little and Martin Luther King Sr. were strong father figures who affirmed, even in subtle ways, biblical teachings that forbade women to usurp male authority. Malcolm recalled the many arguments that resulted from his mother's tendency to challenge his father, even on trivial matters. "Sometimes my father would beat her," Malcolm recounted, but the boy was apparently conscious of a shared love and strong bonds in his family life despite the occasional domestic violence. While Martin's parents "always lived together very intimately," and seldom argued, Martin Sr. could be as firm and intolerant as Earl Little when challenged by women in his home and church.[8]

Malcolm and Martin found in their mothers an essential quality of caring that helped sustain them whenever their fathers were impatient, hot-tempered, abrasive, and too heavy-handed as disciplinarians. Louise was known to protest whenever one of her children was being severely beaten by her husband, crying, "You'll kill that child, Early." In more forceful ways, Alberta demanded that her husband exercise control when using the belt on their children, as Daddy King reported: "Bunch insisted, though, as the children grew older that any form of discipline used on them by either of us had to be agreed upon by both parents. This often curbed my temper, but it also helped Bunch to understand the things that made me angry. We talked a lot about the future of the kids, and she was able to understand that even when I got very upset with them, it was only because I wanted them to be strong and able and happy."[9]

Alberta's role as a stabilizing force in the family could not have been more evident to young Martin, who once said, "Our mother has also been behind the scene setting forth those motherly cares, the lack of which leaves a missing link in life." Martin saw qualities in Alberta that he deemed worthy of emulation, and as his sister Christine observed, he "got his love, compassion and ability to listen to others from mother." He also inherited Alberta's short build, high forehead, full lips and nose, humility, keen sense of humor, and love for the arts. Perhaps more important, however, was his inheritance of Alberta's deep pride and intense dislike for systems of oppression, qualities that Louise Little displayed in supreme ways in her work with Marcus Garvey and in her desire to maintain her family without public assistance after Earl's death in 1931. Although Louise later broke under the pressure of raising her children alone, Malcolm, who knew her spirit as well as Martin understood Alberta's, attributed her mental illness mostly to a racist system that was too powerful for any one person to overcome.[10] Unfortunately, Malcolm's sense of his mother's struggle to survive with dignity never translated into a deep interest in the liberation of women.

What appeared most influential for Malcolm and Martin were the values they learned from their mothers. The stories that Louise shared with Malcolm and his siblings about their ancestry, coupled with her own determination to be upright and prosperous, obviously had some impact at a time when her children struggled with feelings of inadequacy and low self-esteem. Malcolm later remembered how his mother, in dresses that "were all faded out and gray," frequently "bent over the stove, trying to stretch what little we had," thus revealing a willingness to be self-sufficient. "I have rarely talked to anyone about my mother," he declared, "for I believe that I am capable of killing a person, without hesitation, who happened to make the wrong kind of remark about my mother."[11] Perhaps Martin would not have chosen the same words to express his love for Alberta, but he was equally appreciative of what she tried to teach him about history and self-respect when he was only six. As he himself put it: "My mother took me on her lap and began by telling me about slavery and how it ended with the Civil War. She tried to explain the divided system of the South—the segregated schools, restaurants, theaters, housing; the white and colored signs on drinking fountains, waiting rooms, lavatories—as a social condition rather than a natural order. Then she said the words that almost every Negro hears before he can yet understand the injustice that makes them necessary: 'You are as good as anyone.'"[12]

Martin also learned lessons of this nature from his maternal grandmother, Jennie C. Parks Williams, and his aunt, Ida Worthem. The tales that Mama Williams and Aunt Ida told Martin and his siblings grounded them in the same sense of values that Louise gave her children. Thus Martin, like Malcolm, came to respect the women in his home as more than merely cooks, housekeepers, and childbearers. Indeed, the women in the King and Little households were strong spiritual forces, defenders of family honor, and repositories of the accumulated lore of the folk. The absence of a strong grandmother like Jennie in Malcolm's childhood was telling enough, but he was not deprived of an understanding of the many burdens that black women had been forced to bear since slavery, for his own mother personified them in more than superficial ways.[13] Their mothers' struggles, values, and characters became the standard for Malcolm's and Martin's later reflections on the sanctity of family life and on how women might best exemplify the qualities of wife and mother.

The boys' attachment to their mothers was such that they initially found it difficult to leave home for extensive periods. Louise had suffered "a complete breakdown" by the time Malcolm reached age twelve, and her confinement to the State Mental Hospital at Kalamazoo, Michigan, meant that her children had to grow up in foster homes. Even before that time came, Malcolm had begun to rely heavily on his older sister Hilda, who became what he termed "my second mother." Malcolm found a measure of relief as he was nurtured by Hilda and occasionally visited by his sister Ella from Boston, who took him in at age fourteen, but his growing sense of masculinity made it impossible for him to obey and to avoid arguments with them. Moreover, the absence of Louise Little as the central force in the family wounded Malcolm's spirit. "As bad as I was, as much trouble and worry as I caused my mother," he conceded, "I loved her." Malcolm visited his mother until 1952, when her complete failure to respond to him left him with a sadness of heart with which Martin, in his more stable two-parent family, could never have identified. "I can't describe how I felt," asserted Malcolm years later. "The woman who had brought me into the world, and nursed me, and advised me, and chastised me, and loved me, didn't know me. It was as if I was trying to walk up the side of a hill of feathers. I looked at her. I listened to her 'talk.' But there was nothing I could do."[14]

Martin's periods of separation from his mother as a teenager occasionally brought loneliness but were considerably less painful. He had spent far more time as a child with Alberta than he had with his father, for she was with him and his siblings during Daddy King's frequent trips to church conferences. The letters that fifteen-year-old Martin sent to his mother in the summer of 1944, when he was working on a tobacco farm in Simsbury, Connecticut, reveal a closeness between the two that never wavered. While pursuing seminary and graduate studies in the North in the late 1940s and early 1950s, Martin never hesitated to contact Alberta whenever he needed advice and reinforcement. "I often tell the boys around the campus I have the best mother in the world," he said in a letter to Alberta during his Crozer years. Unlike Malcolm, Martin was never cut off from the wisdom and caring spirit typically passed from mother to son. Alberta's powerful influence on Martin's early life, the nurturing he received from his grandmother and aunt, and the intimate companionship with his older sister Christine made the young man less prone than Malcolm to abuse and to speak derisively of women.[15]

The girls Malcolm and Martin dated as teenagers contributed to their understanding of their own masculinity and gender roles. In Boston, Malcolm had a brief relationship with Laura, who closely resembled his mother and who figured prominently in the shaping of his sense of how black men should treat black women. Blinded by the intertwining myths of sex and race, Malcolm dumped Laura, his black girlfriend and dance partner, for a white girl named Sophia, causing psychic pain from which he and Laura never recovered. Laura turned to liquor, dope, and "selling herself to men," leaving Malcolm with deep feelings of guilt. "To have treated her as I did for a white woman made the blow doubly heavy," Malcolm sadly recalled. "The only excuse I can offer is that like so many of my black brothers today, I was just deaf, dumb, and blind."[16] The burden of shame Malcolm carried would have been easily understood by Martin, who knew how black women struggled to maintain self-esteem in a society where the highest standards of beauty were associated with white womanhood.

As Malcolm and Martin matured, they confronted different realities that impacted their perceptions of and experiences with women. In Malcolm's case, life in the streets proved pivotal, as Rufus Burrow Jr. explains: "Having become 'street wise' through his experiences in Harlem and the Roxbury area of Boston, there solidified within him a fairly typical view of women in general and Black women in particular. Some of this was learned through various experiences he had with women (including his mother and half-sister), although much of his attitude toward women was shaped and influenced by other Black men."[17] Clenora Hudson-Weems echoes this assertion, but suggests also that Malcolm's belief in female subordination resulted from other forces that would have influenced Martin or any other black male in the 1940s:

> During his early years, before his lengthy incarceration for burglary charges, Malcolm Little's attitude toward women in general was negative. Unfortunately, his opinion of women reflects the social influences which shape the attitudes of many Africana men living in a capitalist society. From very early in his adult life, he was the pimp, the hustler, the parasite and the thief, who callously used women for personal gains. Malcolm regarded women as objects reflecting his sexual prowess, most of whom were not to be trusted. He perceived women as capable of depriving men of their masculinity. Hence, out of fear, he would not allow himself to become too emotionally involved with women.[18]

Malcolm clearly held a more negative perception of women than Martin. Noting that "the value given to women was as a commodity either to be exploited or displayed as an ornament," he declared, in words that would never have been used by Martin, "I wouldn't have considered it possible for me to love any woman." He added, "I'd had too much experience that women were only tricky, deceitful, untrustworthy flesh. I had seen too many men ruined, or at least tied down, or in some other way messed up by women." The time Malcolm spent with female prostitutes in a rooming house in New York, together with what he observed with adulterous women, left him even more apt to subscribe to a stereotypical view of the female character:

> It was in this house that I learned more about women than I ever did in any other single place. It was these working prostitutes who schooled me to things that every wife and husband should know. Later on, it was chiefly the women who weren't prostitutes who taught me to be very distrustful of most women; there seemed to be a higher code of ethics and sisterliness among those prostitutes than among numerous ladies of the church who have more men for kicks than the prostitutes have for pay. And I am talking about both black and white. Many of the black ones in those wartime days were right in step with the white ones

in having husbands fighting overseas while they were laying up with other men, even giving them their husbands' money. And many women just faked as mothers and wives, while playing the field as hard as prostitutes—with their husbands and children right there in New York.[19]

Living and functioning in a different social circle, where most young ladies personified class and the will to achieve and prosper, Martin never really displayed the same inclination to judge women collectively in a negative fashion. After all, many of the symbols of success and progress that surrounded Martin in the first twenty years of his life—the teachers, business persons, artists—were black women. The young man learned, much earlier than Malcolm, to believe in the female capacity for impeccable character and great achievement.

But Martin and Malcolm were similar in some ways when it came to their views on and relationships with females. Both appreciated beautiful, well-dressed, elegant, and intelligent young ladies, but Martin generally showed more respect for them. Also like Malcolm, Martin had to overcome self-doubts before casting himself wholeheartedly into the social scene, dating Madeline Knight, Betty Milton, Gloria Royster, Juanita Sellers, and other girls from fine families in the Atlanta area. By the time he reached Boston University in 1951, Martin had become "a ladies' man" in the eyes of many who knew him. But despite his male chauvinism, he was always courteous and gracious to even the most unattractive women. "He would scout all of the schools to find the best looking black girls," one friend reported, "and he'd pick out the best one for himself."[20] At this point in his life, Martin's tendency to view women largely as sex objects was as evident at times as Malcolm's.

This inclination to think of females in sexual terms must have been reinforced by their relationships with white girls. This would have been only natural for young black men who had been deeply conscious of the insepa-rable links between race and sex from childhood and who were undoubtedly exposed to the stereotypical view, widely held in black communities, that white women found black men, with their qualities of physical dexterity and bodily finesse, to be sexually desirable. Breaking with the society's taboos and official sanctions against race-mixing, Malcolm and Martin seriously dated white women, apparently with little or no regard in those days for how their actions affected black women around them. Malcolm never forgot the feelings of attraction between himself and Sophia, the white woman who was for him a commodity, a status symbol, and a source of material gain. The relationship strengthened both Malcolm's belief that white women had an insatiable appetite for black men and his distrust of women in general. Moreover, his experiences with Sophia and other white women gave him a certain perspective on the morality of white society as a whole. "I got my first schooling about the cesspool morals of the white man from the best possible source, from his own women," Malcolm remembered. Aware of white housewives and mothers who operated as professional callgirls and who participated in wife-swapping, exposure Martin did not have, Malcolm concluded, clearly at the risk of overgeneralization, that white women were more immoral than black women.[21]

Martin was less likely to draw such a conclusion, despite the fact that he understood as well as Malcolm the part played by white women in upholding the structures of white supremacy. Both arrived at an early sense of the atrocities that had been committed against black men in the name of white womanhood since slavery, an awareness heightened by their own experiences with racist white females. A white woman slapped Martin when he was only eight years old, an experience with which Malcolm could have identified and one that would have convinced any perceptive child that white women were as much a reflection of the racist society as white men.[22] But Martin appeared more open than Malcolm to the possibility that genuine romantic relationships could occur between black men and white women. Martin's love affair with a white girl at Crozer, which contrasted sharply with Malcolm's sexual relationship with Sophia, probably would have ended in marriage had it not been for J. Pius Barbour, a black pastor with whom he associated, and other friends in the ministry. The King scholar David Garrow has reported:

> King dated regularly during his Crozer years, but one of his companions, a white girl of German origin whose mother worked at Crozer, raised concern in the eyes of Barbour and other friends. Barbour heard about the couple's serious romantic involvement, and told King in no uncertain terms of the difficulties an interracial relationship would face. King refused to reconsider the liaison; he and the girl were in love with each other, and even had talked about marriage. King's closest friends, like Ed Whitaker, knew the couple was "very serious" and considered the girl a "lovely young woman," but seconded Barbour's stern advice. If King wanted to return South to pastor, as he often said, an interracial marriage would create severe problems in the black community as well as the white. Another black student, Cyril Pyle, put it

more bluntly. "I told him it was a dangerous situation and it could get out of hand and if it did get out of hand it would affect his career." Barbour insisted to King that marrying the young white woman would be a tremendous mistake, and he urged both of them to reconsider. Finally, after a six-month involvement, the couple took the advice of King's friends and ended their relationship on amicable but painful terms.[23]

Any idea that this relationship affirmed the stereotype of black men finding white women sexually irresistible would most likely have been denied by Martin. As a Morehouse student a few years earlier, the young man had stated in a letter to an Atlanta newspaper, "We aren't eager to marry white girls, and we would like to have our girls left alone by both white toughs and white aristocrats." Malcolm's experiences in the streets led him to see the issue differently. He recalled that black men eagerly fixed their fantasies upon the white woman as an irresistible sex symbol, a tendency which he declared had grown out of a lack of self-respect and respect for black women: "That was why the white prostitutes made so much money. It didn't make any difference if you were in Lansing, Boston, or New York—what the white racist said, and still says, was right in those days! All you had to do was put a white girl anywhere close to the average black man, and he would respond. The black woman also made the white man's eyes light up—but he was slick enough to hide it."[24]

Malcolm and Martin found greater outlets for their sexist tendencies when they became ministers because both the Nation of Islam and the black Baptist Church stood on strong patriarchal traditions. In both the temple and the church, women were prevented from becoming ministers and virtually barred from major leadership positions, and the best evidence of Malcolm's and Martin's acceptance of such structures was their refusal to protest against them. Long before he was married, Malcolm was a strong supporter of special classes for Muslim females, "where the women and girls of Islam are taught how to keep homes, how to rear children, how to care for husbands, how to cook, sew, how to act at home and abroad, and other things that are important to being a good Muslim sister and mother and wife." Malcolm and the Muslims assigned women subordinate roles in the home and the temple, but insisted that they be honored by black men and protected from white men. "The Muslim sisters, both married and single, were given an honor and respect that I'd never seen black men give to their women, and it felt wonderful to me," Malcolm reported.[25]

Much less attention was devoted to the need to honor and protect black women in the black Baptist circles in which Martin functioned, but the attitude toward female subordination was as strong in many cases as that of the Muslims. The writings of Paul and other parts of the Bible were commonly quoted to deny women pastoral leadership and the privilege of usurping authority over men in any sphere of human activity. Although Martin's liberal theological education led him to raise critical questions about so much of the biblical fundamentalism and the traditional church practices to which he was exposed as a boy, this questioning attitude did not blossom into a strong belief in the essential equality of men and women.[26] Apparently, Martin's opinion of women reflected the cultural influences that also shaped Malcolm and most other black men in the first half of the twentieth century.

But in their capacities as ministers, Malcolm and Martin related to women in different ways. While both chose to remain single during the first five years of their ministries, Malcolm seems to have done so out of the conviction that a wife would have interfered with his service to Elijah Muhammad. "I had always been very careful to stay completely clear of any personal closeness with any of the Muslim sisters," he recounted, adding, "My total commitment to Islam demanded having no other interests, especially, I felt, no women. In almost every temple at least one single sister let out some broad hint that she thought I needed a wife. So I always made it clear that marriage had no interest for me whatsoever; I was too busy."[27] In contrast, Martin always dated with the clear intention of finding a wife, for he knew that this was a precondition for any successful pastorate in black Baptist churches.

In 1956, two years before taking a wife, Malcolm gave several lectures on black women at the Philadelphia Temple that would have made Martin or any other thoughtful black man grimace. Describing black women as "the greatest tool of the devil," Malcolm went on to use them as scapegoats for the many evils perpetrated against black men over time by the racist system. In a moment of sheer excitement, he asserted: "How do you think this black man got in this state? By our women tricking him and tempting him, and the devil taught her how to do this. The trickiest in existence is the black woman and the white man. If you go to court with your wife, she will always win over you because the devil can use her to break down more of our black brothers. . . . It is this evil black woman in North America who does not want to do right and holds the black man back from saving himself." Noticing a visitor walking out during this speech, Malcolm shouted: "Look at the sister who just got up and walked out. Hair five different shades. She's living in a perilous time to imitate that devil woman and when she hears a warning, instead of listening, trying to find out how she can change her ways, she walks out angry."[28] Although insulting remarks of this nature were never made publicly by Martin, the young man, who was emerging as a leader of the Montgomery bus boycott when Malcolm gave the Philadelphia lectures, was as uncomfortable as the Muslim spokesman with black women who appeared to challenge or undermine the masculinity of black men.

Their sexist views were clearly rooted in the patriarchal language and doctrine of the particular religious institutions they represented. James H. Cone is right in saying that Malcolm's blatantly negative attitude toward women resulted from a combination of "patriarchal religious doctrine" and "a misogynic view derived from the ghetto." Also, Malcolm obviously drew on the Bible in ways that were rather uncharacteristic of Martin. "Since the time of Adam and Eve in the garden," Malcolm proclaimed, "woman has led man into evil and the one she was created to serve became her slave. She rules him entirely with her sex appeal, her clothes are designed by man to accentuate those portions of her body related to sex, and when he fully dresses she undresses."[29]

Malcolm insisted that the creator had designed completely different and separate spheres of activity and influence for men and women, a perspective Martin apparently accepted but never seriously advanced given his belief that the responsibilities of men and women should often coincide in the home and in society. An important dimension of Malcolm's emphasis on the separate spheres of the genders was his conviction that men and women are naturally distinct physically and emotionally, a position he set forth in powerful terms in his temple lectures in the 1950s, and one which led even his fellow Muslims to label him "anti-woman." Malcolm later recalled: "Every month, when I went to Chicago, I would find that some sister had written complaining to Mr. Muhammad that I talked so hard against women when I taught our special classes about the different natures of the two sexes. Now, Islam has very strict laws and teachings about women, the core of them being that the true nature of man is to be strong, and a woman's true nature is to be weak, and while a man must at all times respect his woman, at the same time he needs to understand that he must control her if he expects to get her respect."[30]

Issues of power, politics, and male egoism were obviously at the center of Malcolm's and Martin's sexist attitudes. The need to assert male authority over women in word and deed was common to both, and in this regard they reflected a larger culture which legitimized established gender conventions and virtually demanded that men and women conform to them.

Male-Dominated Households: The Gender Roles of Malcolm and Martin

The idea that men who seriously give themselves to a cause do not need a family permeates patriarchal cultures. Malcolm and Martin entertained this idea at times, but nothing could have been further from the truth. They were the sort of men who needed the intimate companionship and nurturing attentiveness of a wife, of someone with whom they could bond in heart, mind, body, and spirit. Malcolm had more difficulty admitting this than Martin. Haunted by memories of Earl and Louise Little arguing and fighting, and doubtful about his own ability to be answerable to a woman, Malcolm was thirty-two before he overcame what seemed to be a fear of marriage.[31] This was not the case with Martin, who had many reasons, aside from what he knew about his parents' relationship, to believe in the power of matrimony.

Martin was only twenty-four when he exchanged vows with Coretta Scott, a gifted singer from Marion, Alabama, on June 18, 1953. She shared not only Martin's southern sense of place and his love for southern religion, food, music, and storytelling but also his dedication to the freedom and uplift of black people.[32] The list of things that Malcolm had in common with Betty Sanders, whom he married on January 14, 1958, was not as extensive. Both had come from Michigan, and, like Martin and Coretta, they were committed to the black struggle, as their affiliations with the Nation of Islam more than adequately demonstrated. Betty had joined the temple in Harlem under Malcolm's leadership in 1956, and Malcolm's decision to marry her signaled the beginning of a change in his attitude toward women in general.[33] For Betty, the marriage proved, among other things, that Malcolm could engage in a positive, sharing relationship with a woman:

> We laughed about his single days and his apprehension about letting a woman know where he was at all times. He didn't know where that fear of a woman having control came from. But after we were married it became very easy for him to volunteer information. He said that any mature man knows that if he is married to a woman and is concerned about her, she would also be concerned about him—about his coming and going. So sharing became very easy. He said it was the only civilized thing to do in a committed relationship. And if I left the house and

didn't say where I was going or when I was coming back, he was up-set.[34]

The marriages of Malcolm and Martin were not without priceless moments and memories of companionship. Harmonious love and friendship between them and their wives allowed for a lot of teasing, laughter, and serious conversation. Often referring to Betty as "the sweetest woman in the world," as "a good Muslim woman and wife," and as "the only person I'd trust with my life," Malcolm "felt genuine admiration for her, even awe," according to Alex Haley. Betty recalled the times when Malcolm teased her about her inability to sing, but Malcolm's devotion to her and their four daughters more than confirmed her view that "he had a serious regard for marriage":

> He also used to do tender, little things that I suppose every woman looks for in her husband. When he was gone for long intervals he used to leave money in different places around the house. I used to get a letter that said, "Look in the top desk drawer in the back. There's some money there for you to buy something, and a love letter too." I would go look and maybe he'd have the money in an envelope with a picture of himself. Sometimes there would just be money and sometimes there really would be a love letter. It got so that as soon as he left the house, I would start looking in all the secret places, but I never found anything. A few days later, though, I'd get a letter telling me where to look—and it was never in a place he'd used before.[35]

Martin's relationship with Coretta was equally warm and fulfilling at times. He was to her a very kind, sensitive, and generous person, who could be both playful and serious with her and their four children. "He always made me feel like a real woman because he was a real man in every respect," Coretta once said of her husband. Martin sometimes teased Coretta about her upbringing in the rural South, and they both joked about spending their honeymoon at a funeral parlor because of restrictions that barred blacks from hotels in Alabama. For Martin, Coretta possessed stunning beauty, character, intelligence, and personality, qualities he associated with "the ideal minister's wife."[36] Moreover, Martin could be as considerate as Malcolm when it came to showering his wife with praise and gifts.

But the roles these men assumed in their homes vividly reflected the influence of their family backgrounds and the perceptions of gender differences so prevalent in the society and culture generally. Convinced that women were ideally suited to maintain the home and care for children, they, much like their fathers, automatically expected their wives to submit to them. Concerning Malcolm, biographer Bruce Perry has written: "Unlike his father, Malcolm didn't beat his wife. But he was a domineering husband. The strictures he imposed upon Betty, who later characterized their impact as 'traumatic,' were consistent with those to which she had been conditioned by a lifetime of parental, pedagogical, and Islamic discipline. In public, she deferred to him and let him speak for her. Sometimes, she called him 'Daddy.' He called her 'Girl.'"[37] Apparently, Martin was not as domineering, but this had more to do with his gentle nature than with any particular perspective on gender equality in the home.

Betty's own testimony supports Perry's statement regarding her husband. She remembered that during their "little family talks," Malcolm often began by telling her what he expected of a wife. "But the first time I told him what I expected of a husband," she noted, "it came as a shock." On another occasion, Betty said, "I thought Malcolm was a little too strict with me. For example, he didn't want me to associate with anyone. He just wanted me to be for him. He didn't even want me to have women friends." Although Martin was not as strict in his dealings with Coretta, he was equally susceptible, in practice if not in principle, to the notion of the submissive wife. Even during their courtship, reminisced Coretta, Martin "was very definite that he would expect whoever he married to be at home waiting for him." "I want my wife to respect me as the head of the family," he sometimes remarked. "I am the head of the family." The couple would then laugh at the slightly pompous comment, and Martin would say: "Of course I don't really mean that. I think marriage should be a shared relationship."[38]

It would be a mistake, and perhaps even oversimplification, to conclude that Malcolm's and Martin's relationships with their wives reflected a one-sided view of women. Both were known to express conflicting feelings when pressed on the issue, and their ideas often failed to cohere with the practical sides of their lives. Even as Malcolm followed the traditions of male dominance in the home and in society, he sometimes said that his marital relationship to Betty should be a mutual exchange and an equal partnership.[39] Coretta noticed the same tendencies in Martin:

> Martin had, all through his life, an ambivalent attitude toward the role of women. On the one hand, he believed that women are just as intelligent and capable as men and that they should hold positions of authority and influence. But when it came to his own situation, he thought

in terms of his wife being a homemaker and a mother for his children. . . . At the same time, Martin, even in those days, would say, "I don't want a wife I can't communicate with." From the beginning, he would encourage me to be active outside of the home, and would be very pleased when I had ideas of my own or even when I could fill in for him. Yet—it was the female role he was most anxious for me to play.[40]

The idea of separate roles for men and women played out in somewhat different ways in the households of Malcolm and Martin. Malcolm never cooked, and he vehemently criticized any wife who failed to have a clean house and a hot meal "when a poor, scraggly husband comes in tired and sweaty from working like a dog all day, looking for some food." In contrast, Martin, especially before becoming active in the civil rights movement, spent one day a week doing the cooking, the dishes, the heavy cleaning, and the washing. It was his way of easing some of the burdens that rested on Coretta's shoulders. She remembers the many times she arrived home after a day of shopping and attending to other matters to be greeted by her husband with a warm smile, a kiss, and the aroma of smothered cabbage, fried chicken, pork chops, pigs' feet, ham hocks, cornmeal bread, and other southern-style foods. "Though Martin helped so much in the house the first year we were married," said Coretta, "all the domestic work did not make him self-conscious. He was too sure of his manhood."[41]

Because of Betty's and Coretta's independent-mindedness and strong wills, Malcolm and Martin found it virtually impossible to confine them to the private sphere of the home. Convinced that women were as capable as men of working in the public arena, fighting for equal rights and social justice, Betty and Coretta got involved in social causes, frequently over the objections of their husbands. Betty's determination was such that she and Malcolm occasionally argued, and she left home three times:

I shared Malcolm, but I don't know if he could have shared me to the same extent. He was possessive from the beginning to the end, though I think he learned to control it. I started traveling and doing curriculum development and setting up classes for the women at the various mosques. I really wanted to work, though Malcolm didn't want me to, but he agreed to let me do this volunteer work—organizing the women's classes. I used to beg. "Oh please," I'd say. "I want to work. I want to work." And he would take that to mean I was unhappy, that maybe I didn't love him. "You want to do what?" he would say whenever I said I wanted to work. "Here, read these three books and give me a report. I'll need the first one tonight." All my stress was over the fact that I wanted to work, and he wouldn't even entertain the idea. He didn't want anybody to have any influence over me that would compete with his. Each time I left him, that's why I left—he would not hear of my working.[42]

Martin and Coretta must have also had their disagreements over such matters at times, but they never separated. Coretta complained to friends about her husband's insistence that she confine her attention to the home and not become involved in the struggle. "I wish I was more a part of it," she commented sadly on one occasion. Andrew Young noted that "Martin didn't want her to get too active," mainly because he felt that the children needed Coretta desperately in his absence. Bernard Lee echoed this view, declaring that Martin was "absolutely a male chauvinist. He believed that the wife should stay home and take care of the babies while he'd be out there in the streets."[43] Clearly, Martin could be as narrow in his perspective as Malcolm when it came to the involvement of women in public affairs.

But Betty and Coretta transcended the very private, restricted roles assigned to them and made important contributions to the freedom of their people. Betty's efforts to educate black women in the Nation of Islam, which occurred behind the scenes, were a vital part of that group's overall struggle to raise the social, political, and economic awareness of African Americans as a whole. Coretta participated in civil rights marches, communicated the values of the freedom movement through her singing, worked with the Women's International League for Peace and Freedom, and occasionally spoke at anti-war rallies.[44] Long before womanism emerged as a concept and as the symbol of a new culture of resistance in the African-American community, Coretta and Betty were insisting that the struggle against racism, sexism, classism, and violence could not be won without the full participation of women.

But their greatest contributions to the struggle came through their roles as supportive wives. They explained the struggle to their children in the absence of Malcolm and Martin, communicated important telephone messages to and from their husbands, spared them all household chores, and watched their health with eagle eyes. When Malcolm was forced out of the Black Muslim movement in December 1963, at a time when he was seeking an even greater role in the freedom movement, Betty's fierce loyalty could not have been more evident to him. As Malcolm himself explained: "I never would have dreamed that I would ever depend so much upon any woman for strength as I now leaned upon Betty. There was no exchange between us; Betty said nothing, being the caliber of wife that she is, with the depth of understanding that she has—but I could feel the envelopment of her comfort. I knew that she was as faithful a servant of Allah as I was, and I knew that whatever happened, she was with me."[45]

As Malcolm revised his religion and political philosophy during the last year of his life, adopting a more international perspective, Betty's devotion never faltered. Her willingness to grow intellectually with Malcolm showed that she did not put her interests and self-fulfillment above or against those of her husband, a consideration that applies also in the case of Coretta and Martin. Malcolm appreciated the fact that Betty came to see with him the value of participating in the broader human community and struggle, a development that undoubtedly contributed to Malcolm's increasingly positive and flexible attitude toward women. He noted: "I never had a moment's question that Betty, after initial amazement, would change her thinking to join mine. I had known a thousand reassurances that Betty's faith in me was total. I knew that she would see what I had seen—that in the land of Muhammad and the land of Abraham, I had been blessed by Allah with a new insight into the true religion of Islam, and a better understanding of America's entire racial dilemma."[46]

Coretta's decision to surrender much of her own ambition for her husband was as much an act of self-sacrifice as Betty's. "As Martin was being made ready to be the leader and the symbol of the Negro movement," she noted, "so was I being prepared to be his wife and partner." Coretta considered it a great privilege, indeed a blessing, "to be a co-worker with a man whose life would have so profound an impact on the world." "It was the most important thing I could have done, and I wanted to do it," she observed. The fact that Coretta and her husband, in the words of Martin, "went down this path together" more than adequately justifies the claim that she was "an exemplar of a black wife and mother whose serenity was honed by adversity and by the insults and the injuries visited upon her race in the South." The feeling of harmony between the couple, much like that between Betty and Malcolm, could not have been greater during those times when Coretta encouraged Martin, embraced him, comforted him, and accepted him in spite of his mistakes. It is not insignificant that Martin dedicated his first book, *Stride toward Freedom: The Montgomery Story* (1958), to "Coretta, my beloved wife and co-worker."[47]

The charge that Malcolm's and Martin's frequent absences made their marriages only marginally and sporadically happy is open to serious debate. Bruce Perry claims that Malcolm rarely spent time with Betty, that he actually neglected her, for he was away from home "for days, weeks, sometimes months at a time":

> The babysitter never saw him hug or kiss Betty, whom he would later claim was the only woman he had ever thought about loving. He ridiculed women who expected "kissing and hugging," which he characterized as Hollywood-created wants. At times, he slept in his attic studio, into which he retreated nightly, or almost nightly, to work and study. . . . On several occasions, he cited a passage from the Qur'an that says that if a woman is disobedient, her husband should punish her by banishing her from his bed until she submits to his will. . . . Malcolm's marriage was no more unhappy than those of other public figures who shun intimacy for the love of the crowd. . . . Malcolm denied his wife the warmth and emotional support his mother and sister had unwittingly denied him. He controlled her the way they had controlled him. His male chauvinism was the predictable result of past tyranny.[48]

Although Martin tended to be quite affectionate toward Coretta, frequently embracing and kissing her, the marriage suffered because he was seldom at home. Working "twenty hours a day," traveling "325,000 miles" and making "450 speeches a year throughout the country on behalf of the Negro cause," Martin acknowledged, "I have to be out of town more than I'm in town, and this takes away from the family so much." But as was the case with Malcolm, he attributed his frequent absences not to a desire to get away from his wife but to the demands of the freedom cause. Moreover, both men insisted that their wives understood their absences and that these women, in their supportive roles, viewed themselves as making perhaps their best contributions to the liberation of their people.[49]

But the long periods that Malcolm and Martin were away from home must have been the source of some arguments with their wives. This would have been only natural given Betty's and Coretta's belief in strong and secure two-parent families. The situation for Malcolm had to be even more pressing, since he did not have the kind of extended family Martin had to draw on for assistance.[50] Be that as it may, Betty and Coretta were equally mindful of the difficulties their husbands faced in finding a proper balance between the public realm of politics and social involvement and the private realm of family, intimate relationships, and the raising of children. They were not able to shield their husbands from the excessive demands on their time and energy. Both Malcolm and Martin lost so much time in which they would have found fulfillment as husbands, but it was virtually impossible for them to adjust to this role in light of their many responsibilities as national and international figures.[51] Betty and Coretta accepted this as part of the sacrifices they had to make for a better society and world, and yet they cherished those times when their husbands came home. Concerning Malcolm, Betty once stated, "I felt that the time that he did have was spent constructively. Looking back now, I remember that whenever Daddy was home the whole house was happy. It wasn't a time for a lot of big, knockdown, drag-out fights that some people have. Daddy would be home tomorrow and there was always something special cooked, little extra touches added to the house. Measuring it in terms of quality, I think he spent as much time with his family as any other man."[52]

Coretta has voiced the same sentiments regarding Martin as a family man. She asserts that the time Martin spent with her and the children was "quality time. When daddy was home it was something special," she explained.[53] But questions have been raised about the levels of intimacy and passion that Coretta and Martin brought to their relationship on such rare occasions, especially since Martin is said to have slept occasionally with other women during his travels.[54] David J. Garrow alleges that Martin had "occasional one-night stands" and that the civil rights activist's long-standing sexual involvement with one particular woman, not his wife, "became the emotional centerpiece" of his life. Such extramarital affairs, if in fact they occurred, are difficult to understand in view of both Martin's professed love for Coretta and his eagerness in offering advice to women on the virtues of virginity, marital fidelity, and honest communication in marriage.[55] However, they could possibly be perceived as largely a product of Martin's cultural background, for he had always lived among black church members who were willing to tolerate sexual transgressions and other moral failures on the part of preachers if they were tactful and if there were no questions about their abilities to preach, their love for the folk, and their willingness to serve. Even so, it is difficult to refute the claim that Martin's many adulteries reflected an attitude toward his wife and women in general that was unhealthy, particularly when judged by the society's standards of monogamy. At the same time, one must remember that the racism Martin fought was far more evil and immoral than any imperfections he had.[56]

In Malcolm's case, the private man did not contradict the public persona when it came to faithfulness in marriage. This accounted in part for Betty's determination to stay with him despite the many difficulties they faced. When women made passes at Malcolm, he is said to have "treated this like water off a duck's back." "His devotion to his wife, Betty, was deep," stated one source, "although he wasn't the kind of man who kept saying, 'I love you.'" Governed by the "strictures against infidelity in Islamic religion," and perhaps more sensitive to public opinion than Martin, Malcolm was, according to Betty, "very straitlaced and disciplined," an advocate of the kind of Puritanism that ultimately led to his break with his adulterous leader. Alex Haley remembered one occasion when Malcolm's devotion to Betty was tested but not subdued:

> I remember a late afternoon when we happened to be interviewing in a Philadelphia hotel room. A pretty lady volunteer telephoned, then visited, bringing only half of some important typing she was doing for Malcolm and saying that he should pick up the rest at her apartment later. It was obvious to us both. She had eyes for Malcolm. He fretted and stewed and finally asked me to take a taxi and make the pick-up. When I returned to my room the phone was ringing, with Malcolm demanding, "What else did you do, because anything you did wrong was in my name." I told him that as mad as that woman had been when I turned up, there was no way anybody could have damaged his name with her. . . . "I must be purer than Caesar's wife," Malcolm would often say, hypersensitive that any hint of wrongdoing could so easily become gossip capable of damaging his public image and credibility.[57]

Some of the problems in Malcolm's and Martin's marriages probably stemmed from their attitudes toward money. Alex Haley recounts that "neither could have been much less concerned about acquiring material possessions," mainly because they understood their leadership in sacrificial terms. Betty often said that her husband's "unselfish, total concern for black people had certain drawbacks because it left him with practically nothing of his own." Bruce Perry writes, "He warned about leaders who took advantage of their position, often at the instigation of their wives." Even when Malcolm had "virtually unlimited access to the ever-expanding Muslim treasury," which paid all of his expenses, he gave Betty very little money to spend. Malcolm's unwillingness "to salt away any nest egg for his rapidly growing family," coupled with his failure at times to appreciate the extent of Betty's sacrifices, inevitably resulted in arguments and tension in his family. Perry reports that

Malcolm admitted he was not easy to live with and that not many women would have tolerated his behavior, which sometimes reduced Betty to tears. She tried hard to please him. She wore ankle-length dresses, even after the Nation of Islam decreed that skirt hems could rise to just below the knee. She wore a scarf on her head, even inside the house. She kept her home and her children spotlessly clean. She did her best to preserve the facade of the happy household. But the unhappiness showed through; tacitly, she eventually acknowledged it herself. . . . Eventually, the marriage nearly broke up, ostensibly over the issue of money.[58]

Although Coretta was not as dependent upon her husband as Betty, serious marital differences existed because Martin gave away more money than he accepted, and he demanded that his family "live in the most modest circumstances possible." He only accepted one dollar as an annual salary for his work as president of the Southern Christian Leadership Conference (SCLC), and this was for tax and insurance purposes. He donated his $60,000 Nobel Peace Prize to the movement in 1964, which upset Coretta. Since visiting India in 1959, Martin had tried desperately to follow as much as possible the lifestyle of Mohandas K. Gandhi, who gave up suits in favor of the simple dress worn by the untouchables. Influenced by the Gandhian view of simplicity of living, he "even considered the idea of changing his style of dress to a simpler one," a consideration that refuted the claim, made by some of his critics, that he was "exploiting the racial situation for personal gain." In any case, it was always difficult for Coretta to accept what she perceived to be Martin's excessive generosity toward others when it came to the material things of life.[59]

The idea that the altruistic ethic must always take priority over selfish ambition and material gain was one of the many lessons that Malcolm and Martin taught their wives. They also taught them that the essential quality of life rests not in its longevity but rather in the extent to which it is sacrificed for the common good, a lesson that became a source of strength for Betty and Coretta as each was compelled to deal philosophically with her husband's untimely death. But there were other lessons that related more specifically to African Americans and oppressed peoples as a whole. Noting that "life with Malcolm was one long, endearing learning experience," Betty credited her husband with introducing her "to a whole new way of thinking not only about myself, but also about the global condition of our people." She also insisted that Malcolm "taught me what every female ought to learn; to live and to love as a woman, to be true to myself and my responsibilities as a mother, and to use my spiritual, material, and intellectual capacities to help build a better human society." Martin did the same for Coretta. Betty and Coretta discovered in their husbands men who did not separate wholesome family life from mission.[60]

This helps explain why these women became preservers and promoters of their husbands' legacies. Speaking of the remarkable revival of interest in her husband in the early 1990s, Betty asserted, "I didn't have to rediscover Malcolm" because he "has always lived inside of me," a point more than sufficiently supported by her efforts to spread Malcolm's message through her work as a mother, an activist, and an educator.[61] The same holds true for Coretta, who, in 1968, founded the Atlanta-based Martin Luther King Jr. Center for Nonviolent Social Change, Inc., a multimillion-dollar building-crypt-park complex. Through lectures, workshops, symposia, and the publication of Martin's papers, the King Center advances the philosophy of nonviolence as a means of resolving conflict between individuals, social groups, and nations.[62]

But Betty and Coretta built on their husbands' legacies through their activism on behalf of women's rights worldwide. Betty's outspokenness on this issue, together with her educational and cultural contributions at Medgar Evers College in New York, supports Angela Davis's claim that she was deeply "affected by the changing economic roles of women as well as by the rise and circulation of feminist ideas." The same holds true for Coretta, who maintains, "Freedom, self-determination and world peace are nothing if not women's issues and they cannot be achieved without the active involvement of women." Thus, she and Betty are recognized not only as "mothers of the civil rights movement" but also as models of womanhood throughout the world.[63] This much and more was said of Betty when she died in 1997.

Beyond Traditional Female Roles: On Women in the Freedom Movement

Studies of the long struggle of African Americans for freedom and justice have been distorted and limited due to what has been termed "the great man approach to history." From Richard Allen and Frederick Douglass up to Malcolm X and Martin Luther King Jr., the contributions and leadership of men have been stressed to the neglect of important roles assumed by black women.[64] Malcolm and Martin failed to sufficiently acknowledge and address this pattern of omission, despite their familiarity with the activities of Sojourner Truth, Harriet Tubman, Ida B. Wells Barnett, and other women who helped pave the way for their movements. Their failures at this level supports the contention that they were "sexist men" and that "their sexism hindered greatly their achievement of the freedom for which they fought."[65]

In the 1950s and 1960s, black women did not attain the prominence and popularity bestowed upon leaders like Malcolm and Martin. Although women sometimes pressed for more gender inclusiveness in the black freedom struggle, more often in private meetings with male leaders, they, operating in a culture in which nineteenth-century Victorian images of womanhood still loomed large, found themselves relegated to traditional roles in most cases:

> The supportive roles that women played in the movement paralleled the roles of many mothers in the family. They offered emotional and spiritual comfort and support to members of organizations and groups; they performed duties of a secretarial nature; and grassroots campaigning. They offered nurturance in the form of procuring, preparing, and serving victuals and they provided the leadership with ideas, strategies, and tactics. The point being made is that men were the ones chosen to deal with the external society and women performed much of the groundwork in preparation for the efforts of these men.[66]

Several considerations accounted for the reluctance of most black females to publicly challenge patterns of gender exclusiveness in the movement in the 1950s and 1960s. First, they understood the need for black unity in the struggle against white supremacist policies and practices. Second, there was the fear that the white power structure would exploit the issue to divide African Americans and to distort the goals of the movement. Third, black women wanted to avoid even the suggestion that they identified with the emerging movement spearheaded by middle-class white women, most of whom refused to actively support black freedom. Finally, some black women believed that racism, not gender discrimination, was the greatest source of the oppression of their people.[67] All of these considerations would have won approval from Malcolm and Martin, both of whom failed to fully grasp the interconnectedness of racism and sexism.[68]

The very thought of women becoming prominent leaders in the movement was never entertained seriously by Malcolm or Martin. Although Malcolm emphatically stated that "you don't have to be a man to fight for freedom," he, especially as a Black Muslim, opposed the idea of putting women "on the front lines" of the struggle. His belief that black manhood was somehow undermined when black women were allowed to confront the oppressor in the streets was not surprising given his subscription to the teachings of Elijah Muhammad, "whose political-religious vision and whose personal life were thoroughly shaped by male supremacy." Declaring that Muslims do not "send our women" into "the lair of the beast," Malcolm deplored the fact that black women were being brutalized in civil rights campaigns led by Martin. "They had water hoses turned on our women, stripping off the clothes of our women," he said of the Birmingham situation in 1963. Concerning the Selma campaign of 1965, he was equally blunt as he scolded "that poor fool Black man" for "standing on the sidelines" being nonviolent while racists knocked "Black women down in front of a camera":

> I saw . . . on the television where they took this Black woman down in Selma, Alabama, and knocked her right down on the ground, dragging her down the street. . . . It showed the sheriff and his henchmen throwing this Black woman on the ground—on the ground. And Negro men standing around doing nothing about it saying, "Well, let's overcome them with our capacity to love." What kind of phrase is that? "Overcome them with our capacity to love." [Applause] And then it disgraces the rest of us, because all over the world the picture is splashed showing a Black woman with some white brutes, with their knees on her holding her down, and full grown Black men standing around watching it.[69]

Martin obviously held a different but not necessarily more positive view when it came to female involvement in civil rights campaigns. He knew that Gandhi had involved women in his satyagraha campaigns in India, that many had actually gone to jail with men, and he had no problem with female activists as long as they were not too assertive.[70] This became apparent to the longtime activist Ella J. Baker, who was chosen as interim director of the Southern Christian Leadership Conference in 1959. Her tenure with the organization was brief because she was not a preacher, and she refused to submit to Martin and his male staff members. "I . . . knew from the beginning that having a woman be an executive of SCLC was not something that would go over with the male-dominated leadership," she reminisced. "And then, of course, my personality wasn't right. . . . I was not afraid to disagree with the higher authorities."[71]

Reports of this nature also came from Dorothy Cotton and Septima Clark, who served on the SCLC executive staff in the 1960s. "I did have a decision-making role," remarked Cotton, who became director of the Citizenship Education Program, "but I'm also very conscious of the male chauvinism that existed." She continued, "Black preachers are some of the most chauvinistic of them all."[72] Clark, who supervised leadership training for SCLC, offered reflections on Martin and the other male preachers in the SCLC that are revealing enough to merit extended quotation:

> I was on the Executive Staff of SCLC, but the men on it didn't listen to me too well. They liked to send me into many places, because I could always make a path in to get people to listen to what I have to say. But those men didn't have any faith in women, none whatsoever. They just thought that women were sex symbols and had no contribution to make. That's why Rev. Abernathy would say continuously, "Why is Mrs. Clark on this staff?" . . . I had a great feeling that Dr. King didn't think much of women either. He would laugh and say, "Ha, ha, ha. Mrs. Clark has expanded our program." That's all. But I don't think that he thought too much of me, because when I was in Europe with him, when he received the Nobel Peace Prize in 1964, the American Friends Service Committee people wanted me to speak. In a sort of casual way he would say, "Anything I can't answer, ask Mrs. Clark." But he didn't mean it, because I never did get the chance to do any speaking to the American Friends Service Committee in London or to any of the other groups. . . . The way I think about him now comes from my experience in the women's movement. But in those days, of course, in the black church men were always in charge. It was just the way things were.[73]

Black female activists clearly had problems with the male leadership of the movement. The male-centered structure and thrust of the Nation of Islam made it impossible for Malcolm to escape their criticism. Martin was even more vulnerable because of the perception that he was the most important among the leaders in the struggle. "I was not a person to be enamored of anyone," commented Ella Baker in response to questions about Martin and the male staff of the SCLC. Her lack of a feeling of "special awe for King," coupled with her disagreement with the SCLC's plan to take over the newly formed Student Nonviolent Coordinating Committee (SNCC) in 1960, led to her early departure from the SCLC. Although Fannie Lou Hamer, a heroine of the movement in Mississippi, was not as critical of Martin, she thought that he was too quick to compromise at times, and she was known to mimic him.[74] Rosa L. Parks, Dorothy Cotton, Septima Clark, Gloria Richardson, and other female activists were never really comfortable standing in the shadows of men like Martin and Malcolm.

The problem stemmed primarily from differences over what actually constituted the best and most effective leadership model for African Americans. In conformity with a centuries-old tradition in African-American religious institutions, Malcolm and Martin encouraged and exemplified to the fullest the male-dominated charismatic leadership model. In Martin's case, this model was most problematic for two reasons. First, it was inconsistent with his beloved community ideal, which, as he so often suggested, was gender inclusive. Second, it was at odds with his professed opposition to W.E.B. Du Bois's "talented tenth" idea, which, as Martin saw it, left "no role for the whole people."[75] Be that as it may, certain women in the movement made no secret of their opposition to the traditional type of "leader-follower relationship" that favored men like Martin and Malcolm. Critical of "men who wanted to lead but were unable to confront their fears," and convinced that "leadership came from actual work and commitment and was not preordained by sex," Fannie Lou Hamer called for a "partnership" between black women and black men "in the interest of the family and the future of their people."[76] Having similar views, Ella Baker opted for "a group-centered leadership," thus heightening her conflict with Martin. Baker maintained: "Instead of trying to develop people around a leader, the thrust, in my direction, should be that the first consideration is to try to develop leadership out of the group and to spread the leadership roles so that you develop—in other words, you're organizing people to be self-sufficient rather than to be dependent upon the charismatic leader, or the Moses-type leader."[77]

Baker held that the kind of leadership model embodied by towering male figures like Malcolm and Martin proved counterproductive for several reasons. First, it was sexist, elitist, and exclusionary by its very nature. In the 1950s and 1960s, it excluded women and youth, discouraged leadership potential at the grassroots level, and allowed too few persons to make decisions for the masses. Thus, a more democratic model was needed, one that would have represented a shift away from the old patriarchal lines of authority to the values of equality and diversity. Second, Baker felt that under the male-dominated charismatic leadership model, authority did not come from the people but was imposed upon them. Third, the creative energies and potential of the masses were stifled. Fourth, both the levels of hierarchy inherent in civil rights organizations and the internal struggle for personal advantage were reinforced. Fifth, the media created charismatic male leaders. Sixth, such a model was inconsistent with the ideals of the movement. Finally, Baker believed that the assassination of a charismatic leader could possibly plunge the masses into chaos and destroy the movement, a conviction difficult to refute since the mass protest phase of the civil rights struggle virtually died with Martin in 1968.[78]

In any case, Septima Clark agreed wholeheartedly with Baker's reasoning and joined her in encouraging more grassroots leadership:

> When I heard men asking Dr. King to lead marches in various places, I'd say to them, "You're there. You going to ask the leader to come everywhere? Can't you do the leading in these places?" I sent a letter to Dr. King asking him not to lead all the marches himself, but instead to develop leaders who could lead their own marches. Dr. King read that letter before the staff. It just tickled them; they just laughed. I had talked to the secretaries before about it, and when the letter was read they wouldn't say a word, not one of them. I had a feeling that they thought Dr. King would have to do the leading. If you think that another man should lead, then you are looking down on Dr. King. This was the way it was.[79]

Baker's and Clark's idea of "group-centered leadership" was more in line with the communal values of the black heritage, with the concept of movement by and for the people, than the leadership model symbolized by Malcolm and Martin. Thus, Baker's characterization of Martin's leadership style as "unhealthy, unrealistic, and ideologically backward" must not be casually dismissed in discussions concerning the present and future course of the African-American struggle. Baker's model helps explain why SNCC, which originated out of her efforts, was much more successful than the SCLC in enhancing women's roles and those of grassroots persons in general. But the Baker model must not be embraced uncritically and without a careful study of the history of the black struggle. Hard questions of this sort must be answered: What are the strengths and weaknesses of the Baker leadership model? Is it as practical as Martin's and Malcolm's, especially given the propensity of African Americans throughout our history to await a Moses or some other male figure to deliver them from oppression?[80] As in all social movements, isn't there still a need for a central figure who can fearlessly and intelligently articulate the feelings, hopes, and dreams of the black masses?

Perhaps Diane Nash Bevel is more correct in saying that African Americans must not continue to organize around leadership models and ideologies, both of which become rigid, but around issues and values that automatically trigger an assertion of broadly based leadership.[81]

While refusing to see the movement as merely an extension of Malcolm's and Martin's personalities, black female activists generally admired these men and shared with them a determination to end racism. But in the areas of basic philosophy and methods, Gloria Richardson, who led the struggle for freedom and economic justice in Cambridge, Maryland, in the early 1960s, stood closest to Malcolm, flatly rejecting tactical nonviolence, the emphasis on integration, and the compromising style of Martin and other established civil rights leaders.[82] Ella Baker "supported nonviolent resistance as a valuable weapon in the fight for civil rights," but was more in agreement with Malcolm's ethic of self-defense than with Martin's nonviolent absolutism. "I have not seen anything in the nonviolent technique that can persuade me against challenging someone who wants to step on my neck," she maintained. "If necessary, if they hit me, I might hit them back." Fannie Lou Hamer conversed with Malcolm and marched with Martin, but she was closer to the latter in terms of basic ideas and methods.[83] Rosa Parks, Dorothy Cotton, and Septima Clark appreciated Malcolm's prophetic challenge to white supremacy, but stood with Martin in basic outlook and methods. "I adored him," declared Clark concerning King on numerous occasions. "I supported him in every way because I greatly respected his courage, his service to others, and his nonviolence."[84]

Malcolm and Martin tended to speak highly of certain women in the movement while either ignoring or criticizing others. Both respected the Christian commitment and profound courage of Rosa Parks, whose act of defiance gave rise to the Montgomery bus boycott in 1955. Martin was touched deeply by the fact that "she chose to stand her ground and say with those who have prophesied of old, 'Before I'll be a slave I'll be buried in my grave and go home to my Lord and be free.'" He and Malcolm also felt similarly regarding the incredible strength and sublime spirit of Ella Baker, whom Martin called "a very able person and a stimulating speaker."[85]

But in contrast to Martin, who questioned Gloria Richardson's political strategy and said nothing about Fannie Lou Hamer, Malcolm praised Richardson's grassroots activism and labeled Hamer "the country's number one freedom-fighting woman." Malcolm never referred publicly to the activities of Dorothy Cotton and Septima Clark, but Martin had a deep affection for both, calling Clark "the Mother of the Movement."[86] Both men were impressed with the contributions of young black women like Diane Nash Bevel, whom Martin highly praised for her work within the context of the student movement:

> In the midst of the student sit-ins of early 1960, Mrs. Bevel distinguished herself as the driving spirit in the nonviolent assault on segregation at lunch counters in her work as part of the Youth Division of the Nashville Christian Leadership Conference. As the nonviolent revolution gained momentum, Mrs. Bevel forsook her education and began to work full-time in the movement as Student Secretary of NCLC. When the original Freedom Ride bogged down in Birmingham, Alabama, after the Mother's Day Massacre, it was Mrs. Bevel who organized the continued ride that led to the ultimate nationwide support of the Freedom Ride and its concentration at Jackson, Mississippi. Mrs. Bevel was present during most of the mob violence that followed the attack on the Reverend Abernathy's First Baptist Church in Montgomery. Her courage and demeanor in such trying circumstances betrayed a maturity far beyond her years. Mrs. Bevel returned to Nashville and worked there as Coordinator for the Freedom Ride through Nashville and Convener of the Freedom Ride Coordinating Committee. When the necessity of Freedom Rides abated, Mrs. Bevel transferred her energies to Mississippi and voter registration work in the heart of the Delta.[87]

It was impossible for Malcolm and Martin to be completely oblivious to the fact that black female activists were as courageous and determined as they themselves were. Indeed, these women were leaders in the best sense of the word because they often prefigured Martin in addressing issues for the benefit of African Americans and the larger society as well. The Women's Political Council, headed by Jo Ann Robinson, actually took the lead in launching the Montgomery boycott, which catapulted Martin to national and international prominence. This group was as significant as Rosa Parks in giving Martin "the right to practice his nonviolence." After the boycott, Ella Baker gave Martin the idea that led to the founding of the SCLC.[88] Fannie Lou Hamer and other women in the Mississippi Freedom Democratic Party (MFDP) "were already clearly on record as opposing" the Vietnam War before Martin "made his own public declaration." Black females in the National Welfare Rights Organization (NWRO) had actually conceived the idea of a poor people's campaign before Martin acted on it in 1967. All of these women, like Martin and Malcolm, worked out of black religious institutions and out of a sense of tradition, for they saw what they were doing as part of a heritage that stretched back to Sojourner Truth and Harriet Tubman.[89]

The consciousness of working out of a vital core of values and traditions could not have been stronger for those women who were song leaders in the movement. Black females played a greater role than males "in passing down culture through the teaching and singing of old slave spirituals and the impromptu formation of new songs dealing with current trials and tribulations." Women such as Mahalia Jackson, Fannie Lou Hamer, and Bernice Johnson Reagon were particularly important in this regard, for they passed down traditions and taught ethics and values through their songs and stories, thus becoming cultural leaders, carriers, and communicators.[90] Malcolm appears to have been less appreciative of such contributions than Martin, despite the fact that both saw cultural communication as one of the chief responsibilities of black women.[91] Both admired and respected Mahalia Jackson, but Martin, whose mother and spouse were freedom singers, had a better grasp of the significance of her gospel songs for the cultural and spiritual dimensions of the movement.[92] "This world-famous gospel singer has willingly lifted her great voice over and over again in an inspiring appeal for moral, spiritual, and financial support of this great thrust of today's freedom champions," said Martin after Jackson's powerful rendition of the song "How I Got Over," at the March on Washington in August 1963.[93] Shortly thereafter, Martin wrote Mahalia about both that particular performance and her many contributions to the freedom cause:

[Y]ou have been fighting in the struggle so long. It really has been difficult to say to you how much you mean and have meant to the Negro revolution and especially SCLC. . . . You have been that kind of quiet reassuring friend in the dark hours of indecision and disappointment as well as sharing the golden moments of triumph. As long as I live I shall never forget the March on Washington. You are without a doubt the world's greatest gospel singer. You have sung before kings and potentates, but never have you sung the Lord's song like you did that day. When I got up to speak, I was already happy. I couldn't help preaching. Millions of people all over this country have said it was my greatest hour. I do not know, but if it was, you, more than any single person, helped to make it so. . . . Mahalia, you have been a blessing to me and SCLC; you have been a blessing to Negroes who have learned through you not to be ashamed of their heritage; you have been a blessing to this generation whose good fortune it is that your life has touched theirs.[94]

Martin never commented publicly on Fannie Lou Hamer's and Bernice Johnson Reagon's contributions through the power of singing, but there is no reason to doubt that he respected them as artists devoted to the struggle. In contrast, Malcolm was more likely to respect these women as activists rather than as song artists.[95]

The scores of ordinary women who struggled and sacrificed daily for the freedom of their people should have gotten more public recognition from Malcolm and Martin. Malcolm often encountered such women as he walked the streets of New York, as he appeared in Muslim temples, and as he traveled throughout the country. Martin marched with black women from all levels of society, and his SCLC benefited spiritually and materially from their resources. The civil rights leader delighted in referring to the "elderly toil worn Negro woman" in the Montgomery protest whose words "My feets is tired, but my soul is at rest" became the "boycotter's watchword," but he heaped far more praise on men. Martin was almost as silent as Malcolm when it came to the proper public acknowledgment of the many poor and unlettered women who made sandwiches, helped with publicity, ran mimeograph machines, passed out flyers, attended mass meetings, and went to jail for the cause. The untold number of women who contributed through communal mothering, who cared for the children of other women when they were jailed, conformed very much to Martin's and Malcolm's image of womanhood at its best, but these men took such roles for granted.[96]

The extent to which Malcolm and Martin supported black women's organizations is yet another matter that deserves serious consideration. Malcolm was highly interested in the work of Fannie Lou Hamer, Annie Devine, Victoria Gray, and other women in the MFDP, but he had little to offer them beyond strong words of support. Martin, too, supported the MFDP's challenge to discrimination in the national Democratic Party, and some of his Nobel Prize money went to the National Council of Negro Women (NCNW), an organization headed by Dorothy I. Height and devoted to the uplift of black women at all levels of the society. Interestingly enough, Height was the only female activist with whom Martin worked in the American Negro Leadership Conference on Africa (ANLCA), an organization started in New York in 1962 to bring the African-American and African struggles closer together.[97]

Black women brought a more inclusive vision of community to the struggle than Malcolm and Martin ever embraced. Like Martin, they had a moral vision of community that was also teleological, but it involved the full participation of women. Moreover, some black female activists held that race, gender, and class were inseparably linked, and that all had to be carefully and consistently addressed together in order for the fullness of Martin's beloved community ideal to be actualized.[98] It was virtually impossible for Malcolm and Martin to escape the challenge of this more powerful and inclusive communitarian ideal. This challenge was much more evident for Malcolm, who, as a spokesman for the Nation of Islam, differed substantially with female activists on the need for community across racial boundaries. Malcolm constantly advocated the separation of the races and was especially critical of black women who married white men. At that time, such relationships probably reinforced his belief that black women and white men were merely co-conspirators in a scheme to emasculate black men.[99] Constantly raving about the white man's long history of raping black women, Malcolm pointed to the mixed marriages of the playwright Lorraine Hansberry and the singer-actress Lena Horne to highlight the absurdity of the integrationist viewpoint.[100] Hansberry eventually confronted Malcolm about the attacks, and that particular confrontation, along with the challenge presented by Martin and other women in the movement, accounted to some degree for the Muslim spokesman's gravitation, in the last year of his life, toward the idea that intermarriage is one of many "strides toward oneness" among human beings.[101]

This gradual change of heart on the question of intermarriage may have been part of Malcolm's conscious quest for an international perspective that embraced a more positive view of women. Rufus Burrow Jr. has identified those influences, aside from considerable study and reflection, that led Malcolm to reassess his thinking about women in 1964: "One should underscore the fact that after his trip to Mecca and his travels throughout Africa and the Middle East he began making an earnest effort to turn the corner on male-female relations in the Black community. Since he did not live long enough to work through the implications of this it is difficult to know just what his revised view would have been."[102] The same could easily be said of Martin, who, by early 1968, would have agreed with the claim that societies throughout the world were guilty of mistreating women.

Malcolm's shift from what James H. Cone calls "ultrasexist views" toward a positive perception of women and their roles in the society and culture was further stimulated by his belief that his leader, Elijah Muhammad, had sexually misused several young black females. After his break with Muhammad, and the subsequent formation of his Muslim Mosque, Inc., and the Organization of Afro-American Unity, Malcolm spoke of phasing women such as Gloria Richardson and Maya Angelou into leadership roles, much to the disgust of some of his male followers.[103] Moreover, Malcolm began to assert publicly that women had to be an essential part of any society's effort to revolutionize itself, a position reinforced by his conversations with Maya Angelou and Shirley Graham Du Bois, the widow of W.E.B. Du Bois, in Ghana:

> One thing I became aware of in my traveling recently through Africa and the Middle East, in every country you go to, usually the degree of progress can never be separated from the woman. If you're in a country that's progressive, the woman is progressive. If you're in a country that reflects the consciousness toward the importance of education, it's because the woman is aware of the importance of education. But in every backward country you'll find the women are backward, and in every country where education is not stressed it's because the women don't have education. So one of the things I became thoroughly convinced of in my recent travels is the importance of giving freedom to the woman, giving her education, and giving her the incentive to get out there and put that same spirit and understanding in her children. And I frankly am proud of the contributions that our women have made in the struggle for freedom and I'm one person who's for giving them all the leeway possible because they've made a greater contribution than many of us men.[104]

Although Martin did not phase women into stronger leadership positions in his SCLC in the late 1960s, his support for the ordination of female preachers, a rarity for men in black Baptist circles at that time, more than adequately demonstrated that he, too, was moving away from the sexism of his past. Like Malcolm, Martin also developed a greater appreciation for the contributions that women were making worldwide in the struggle against various forms of oppression. He suggested as much in an address at the fiftieth anniversary celebration of the Women's International League for Peace and Freedom, which was held in Philadelphia in October 1965. As Martin increasingly encountered courageous female activists like Adelaide Tambo of South Africa, whose sacrifices to end apartheid were far greater than that of many men, it was only natural for the civil rights leader to grow in terms of his perspective on male-female relationships. This growth on Martin's part was not particularly surprising to Septima Clark, who observed that he had "changed the lives of so many people" in the movement "that it was getting to the place where he would have to see that women are more than sex symbols."[105]

The fact that Malcolm and Martin were beginning to connect their growing global visions to the plight of women toward the end of their lives is highly commendable. There is no reason to doubt that they were driven to do so by very practical considerations. In other words, they came to see that the struggle for freedom and justice was too difficult and demanding to exclude the full participation of any person merely on the basis of gender.

Beyond Male Chauvinism: Feminist and Womanist Perspectives on Malcolm and Martin

Malcolm and Martin did not live to see the flowering of feminism in the 1970s and the rise of womanism in the 1980s.[106] However, both witnessed the beginnings of the women's movement in the 1960s, and their silent reaction to it contrasted sharply with Betty's and Coretta's open acceptance of certain feminist ideas. According to Cone, "There were many reasons why Martin and Malcolm turned a deaf ear to the burgeoning women's movement, the most important of which were its perceived identification with 'bored white middle-class suburban housewives,' its rejection by many black women, the myth of the black matriarchy, and the widespread belief that race, not gender, was the primary factor determining the life chances of black people." It is also possible that Malcolm and Martin saw in the emerging women's movement a force that could potentially threaten the unity and effectiveness of the black freedom movement.[107]

Over the past three decades, Malcolm and Martin have been the focus of some criticism from female thinkers and writers who feel that society's need to honor these men has blinded too many to their moral shortcomings regarding women. The radical feminist theologian Mary Daly recognized this in 1973 and reminded the academic community that Malcolm and Martin actually perpetuated sexism, a claim slightly marred by her own failure to properly address the problem of white women's involvement in maintaining the structures that have oppressed black women and men for centuries. In any case, Daly's thoughts about Malcolm and Martin have not been seriously advanced by other white feminists, who sense their own vulnerability to criticism from the African-American community, but her claims do coincide with what has become the standard criticism of these men among certain black womanists.[108]

But despite their familiarity with and reflections on the problem of sexism in the freedom movement of the 1950s and 1960s, black womanist thinkers have not yet produced major critical works on Malcolm and Martin. Only scattered references to Malcolm and Martin appear in their writings, with Martin getting most of the attention because of the Christian roots he shares with womanist theologians and ethicists and because of the perception that his ethics are more relevant or applicable than Malcolm's to the struggles of black women.[109] In the first major treatment of womanist ethics, which appeared in 1988, Katie G. Cannon ignored Malcolm and concluded that Martin's ideas concerning the *Imago Dei,* community, and love grounded in justice and social change represent core values for African-American women in their continuing efforts to eliminate sexism and to liberate the black community as a whole. Eschewing Malcolm's concept of retaliatory violence, Jacquelyn Grant suggests that Martin's idea of redemptive suffering is relevant to the survival ethic of black women. Cheryl Townsend Gilkes's reference to Martin as an important source of the Afrocentric vision of Alice Walker, who has made communal self-love, the vitality of African-American culture and history, and unified black struggle central themes in her writings, is even more interesting and perplexing, especially since Malcolm is more commonly associated with Afrocentrism as a mode of thinking and viewing the world.[110]

Black female thinkers and writers tend to be far more objective than Mary Daly in their statements about Malcolm and Martin. Pauli Murray discusses the prophetic power of both and parallels Martin's famous "I Have a Dream" speech "with the 'spirit-filled utterances' of the apostles on the day of Pentecost." Murray's deep roots in the Christian faith, highlighted by years of service as an Episcopal priest, helps explain why she rejected much of the philosophy and methods of Malcolm in favor of those of Martin. But even as she praised Martin as a symbol "of the Christian hope for human freedom and reconciliation," and expressed passionate devotion "to his cause," Murray lamented his refusal to acknowledge "the role of women in the civil rights movement."[111]

The same might be said, with some qualifications, of womanists such as

Cheryl J. Sanders, Delores S. Williams, and Kelly Brown Douglas. These thinkers are quite mindful of the meaning and significance of Malcolm and Martin for the struggle of black women, despite the fleeting attention that these men receive in their works. Sanders sees Malcolm and Martin as two among many African-American leaders who embodied and exemplified empowerment ethics over the course of history. For Sanders, Malcolm stands as "a significant symbol of remoralization and empathy in the context of the Islamic faith," and she celebrates his rise "from a life of poverty and crime to become a great moral, religious, and cultural leader." In a different vein, Sanders views Martin as "the dominant voice of black Christian protest in the twentieth century." But she is equally mindful of Malcolm's and Martin's failure to sufficiently include women in their moral visions. Her understanding of the Christian life leads her to be more critical of Martin on this matter, and she does not condone or excuse his "moral errors" as they relate to womanizing and plagiarism. A similar approach was taken recently by Cheryl A. Kirk-Duggan, who refuses to "excuse King's sexism or his adultery," but who acknowledges that his "sexism softened somewhat eventually, but not to the extent of his historical ancestors who supported women's rights—Frederick Douglass and W.E.B. Du Bois."[112]

Sanders challenges the academic community with a question that few black womanist ethicists and theologians have sought to address up to this point: "What critique does the womanist perspective bring to bear upon African-American male ethical leadership in light of Martin King's legacy?" Sanders raised this question several years ago, but there has been little response from womanist theologians and ethicists. While Martin's and Malcolm's contributions to African-American theology and ethicists are mentioned in some of the most recent works by womanists, such treatments are heavily marred by the lack of a decisively critical focus.

Delores Williams perceives Malcolm and Martin as activists who represented the best in terms of sacrificial leadership. Both are included among what Williams calls "black salvation-bearers," despite the limitations of their philosophies and methods for addressing womanist concerns. Williams obviously has problems with the male-dominated model of leadership these men exemplified, but she is also concerned about the whole question of the relevance of Martin's ethics of redemptive suffering and community for African-American Christian women. She fears that Martin's notion "of the value of the suffering of the oppressed in oppressed-oppressor confrontations" could possibly lead black women to "passively accept their own oppression and suffering." Moreover, she feels that Martin's beloved community ideal, as set forth in his time, was essentially sexist.[113]

Kelly Brown Douglas approaches both the strengths and limitations of Malcolm's and Martin's perspectives from a different angle. She views the two men "as the catalyst that forced Black theologians to say something definite about Christ's relationship to a Black people fighting for life, dignity, and freedom." In Douglas's thinking, Malcolm taught black men and women that Christ was black and that reverence for the white Christ was "a severe impediment to their freedom" and "a betrayal of their own Black heritage." While Martin was not concerned so much with the color of Christ's skin, Douglas maintains, he did reflect "the religion of the Black Christ" in his concept of God as coworker and fellow sufferer with black people, in his thoughts on the meaning of freedom, and in his belief that Christianity is compatible with protest activity. But Douglas rightly concludes that the black Christ images of Malcolm and Martin promote masculinist perspectives and are devoid of an appreciation for the unique experiences of black women. Consequently, there is need for "a womanist understanding of the Blackness of Christ" that critiques the maleness of black theology, an understanding that "emerges as womanist theology engages a social-political analysis of wholeness and a religio-cultural analysis."[114]

Douglas's critique of the male-centered Christ of Malcolm and Martin stands in stark contrast to Flora Wilson Bridges's largely uncritical treatment of the two leaders' spirituality. Mindful of the concerns raised by Douglas, Bridges still concludes that Malcolm and Martin were "giants of the African-American spiritual tradition" and that their spirituality, rooted in a solid core of cultural values, heavily informed their "prophetic visions of the ideal community." Bridges's assessment of Malcolm and Martin on this level is praiseworthy, but it suffers somewhat from the absence of a strong critical focus. While it is true that Malcolm's and Martin's belief in and quest for a communitarian ideal hinged on powerful spiritual and moral foundations, their sexist tendencies prevented them from achieving the best possible wedding between spirituality and social transformation.[115]

Some black female thinkers feel that Malcolm is more commonly used than Martin to project masculinist notions and pervasive patterns of male dominance in the culture. This certainly holds true for Nikki Giovanni, Angela Davis, and Patricia Hill Collins. Giovanni is as mindful as Maya Angelou of the reciprocal roles that the two men played in the black struggle, and she appreciates Malcolm for embodying "our dreams of transformation and redemption," but she denounces images of the Muslim leader, especially in Spike Lee's film, that degrade black women while reinforcing prevailing customs of male supremacy in heterosexual partnerships.[116]

Angela Davis has written in more poignant terms about the "hero-fixated male supremacy" reflected in Lee's film and "shaped by contemporary social and technological forces":

I express my anxiety in the face of the one-dimensional iconization of Malcolm X, and it is because the iconization tends to close out possibilities of exploring other implications of Malcolm's legacy that are not heroic, nationalistic, and masculinist. From the vantage point of an African-American feminist with revolutionary aspirations toward socialism that refuse to go away, I acknowledge that I am also a product of that historical moment, informed in part by Malcolm's discourse, his oratory, and his organizing. . . . I am therefore repelled by the strong resonances of unquestioned and dehistoricized notions of male dominance in this contemporary iconization of Malcolm X. . . . This is not to imply that Malcolm was not as much a perpetrator of masculinist ideas as were others of his era—men and women alike. What disturbs me today is the propensity to cloak Malcolm's politics with insinuations of intransigent and historical male supremacy that bolster the contemporary equation of nationalism and male dominance, touted as representative of progressive politics, with black popular culture.[117]

Patricia Hill Collins shares Davis's contention that Malcolm "espoused a version of black nationalism that was strongly male-oriented." "Much of Malcolm X's symbolism and many of the metaphors he used to describe Black oppression were derived from the experiences of Black men," says Collins. "Malcolm X typically described political struggles confronting Black people as confrontations between the 'white man' and the 'Black man.'"[118] Noting that "Malcolm X had relatively little to say about gender oppression and its effects on African-American men and women," Hill argues that it is only logical to "question what version of Black community control Malcolm X had in mind for the economic, political and social development of African-American communities. Would the vision of 'strong' Black men offering benign leadership to Black women who willingly accepted their gender subordination be part of the separate Black nation?"[119]

Other questions are being raised today regarding the extent to which

Malcolm and Martin would have embraced feminist and womanist concerns had they lived. It is virtually impossible to refute Angela Davis's observation that "within the context constructed by ubiquitous images of Malcolm as the *essential Black man,* the juxtaposition of the words 'Malcolm' and 'feminist' rings strange and oxymoronic." But this does not keep Davis from wondering, on the basis of her reading of Patricia Robinson's analysis of Malcolm and females, where Malcolm might stand today on the issue of women's liberation: "Is it possible that if Malcolm had not been shot down on February 21, 1965, he might be identifying with the global feminist movement today? Would he have allowed his vision to be disrupted and revolutionized by the intervention of feminism? Or, in order to discuss the feminist implications of his legacy, is it even necessary to argue about the positions Malcolm X, the man, might have assumed?"[120]

Davis believes that Malcolm possibly could have grown to the point of overcoming the kind of sexist views that prevented him from seeing the human struggle in its wholeness. With piercing clarity, she writes:

> We might be able to liberate Malcolm's legacy from the rigid notions of male dominance that were a part of the ideological climate in which he grew to maturity. His willingness to reevaluate his political positions, for instance, suggests that he might—given exposure to newer ideological circumstances—also have reconfigured his relationship with his family, and that if [Betty] Shabazz were hypothetically to reencounter Malcolm during these contemporary times, she might find more of what she seeks today in the man than the historical Malcolm was capable of providing.[121]

Patricia Hill Collins agrees with Angela Davis. Collins explains that "Malcolm was beginning to turn his attention to issues new to him, such as global human rights, that had important implications for women. . . ." She adds, "The logic Malcolm X followed in thinking about other issues might have led him to a Black feminist analysis of Black oppression and liberation."[122] The same conclusion has been drawn in some circles regarding Martin. Dorothy Cotton speculates that the civil rights activist would have embraced the struggle against sexism, though "he would have had a lot to learn and a lot of growing to do as the Women's movement took on the momentum that it has taken on." Concerning Martin, she continues, "No, I don't think he would have resisted. I really don't, because he died saying we've gotta take all oppressed people, and my hope and dream—and maybe it's fantasy—but it is that he would have seen that women are an oppressed class. I don't know how he could have preached what he preached and could not have seen that, too, but it might have been a painful lesson he had to learn. But I think he would have learned it. He would have had to."[123]

Questions about the relevance and implications of Malcolm's and Martin's ideas for the shaping of an ethic of liberation for women will remain. Both spoke to the issues of freedom, equal opportunity, self-determination, and the moral obligation to resist evil and injustice in all forms, and in this sense their ideas and methods have meaning for feminists and womanists in their continuing struggle. Womanists such as Emilie Townes, Gloria Joseph, Delores Williams, Kelly Brown Douglas, and Cheryl Sanders clearly realize this, and this explains their willingness to draw on the wisdom of Malcolm and Martin. But these men must be read critically and selectively because their experiences were never the same as those of women, and because they never addressed the issues of wholeness or universality in the ways that black womanists are speaking to them today. In fact, black womanists are still their own best source when it comes to interweaving a concern for matters of race, gender, and class as they bear upon the welfare and survival of African Americans.[124]

The best lesson to be learned today, after reflecting critically upon Malcolm's and Martin's legacies, is that a devotion to black liberation should not result in alienation from the women's movement. Some black males in the academy are now joining womanist thinkers in reevaluating the meaning and significance of Malcolm and Martin for the liberation of all African Americans from racism and sexism. Rufus Burrow Jr., Garth Baker-Fletcher, Noel L. Erskine, and James H. Cone are but a few.[125] With increasingly loud voices, they are echoing the womanist argument that both sexism and patriarchal structures must be eliminated as a precondition for the liberation of all African Americans.

A New Spirit of Resistance

Malcolm and Martin on Children and Youth

Every time I see a young person who has come through the system to a stage where he could profit from the system and identify with it, but who identifies more with the struggle of black people who have not had his chance, every time I find such a person I take new hope. I feel a new life as a result of it.
Ella J. Baker[1]

I knew back in 1961 and '62 that the younger generation was much different from the older, and that many students were more sincere in their analysis of the problem and their desire to see the problem solved.
Malcolm X[2]

The blanket fear was lifted by Negro youth. When they took their struggle to the streets, a new spirit of resistance was born.
Martin Luther King Jr.[3]

Children and youth are among the most unsung heroes and heroines of the freedom movement of the 1950s and 1960s. Despite their many contributions at various levels of the struggle, they, much like women, have rarely been taken seriously and recognized in a society in which the lives and accomplishments of Malcolm X and Martin Luther King Jr. are commonly celebrated with unbounded enthusiasm. Although the voice and moral vision of the youngest soldiers in the cause of freedom have been virtually muted and unheeded, the silence is now being broken by the mounting interest in the strategic roles played by students in the civil rights movement.[4]

Malcolm and Martin held traditional views of children and youth that grew largely out of their sense of their own upbringing. Having grown up in a culture where elders and ancestors were seen as the chief sources of wisdom and insight, and where childhood and adolescence were most often associated with obedience and dependency, these men tended to view the feelings, perceptions, and actions of young people through the lenses of paternalism. Moreover, their attitudes toward children and youth figured prominently in their perceptions of what should be the direction and outcome of the struggle for liberation and survival.

The Burden of Parenthood: Malcolm and Martin as Fathers

The experience of fatherhood was as indispensable to Malcolm's and Martin's happiness, health, and survival as their roles as husbands. In other words, they needed children as much as they needed wives. Both decided very early in their marriages that they would have lots of children, plans to which Betty and Coretta initially objected.[5] But Betty, who was not "liberated" as that term would be understood by the generation of women who followed her, surrendered to Malcolm's desire and actually enjoyed all of her pregnancies. To their union, six girls were born. Attallah was born in 1958, Qubilah on Christmas Day in 1960, Ilyasah in 1962, Gamilah in 1964, and the twins, Malaak and Malikah, in November 1965, nine months after Malcolm's assassination. In a slightly earlier time frame, Martin and Coretta gave birth to two girls and two boys. Yolanda came in 1955, Martin in 1957, Dexter in 1961, and Bernice in 1963. Born in periods when Malcolm and Martin were increasingly subjected to the pressures of a tension-packed struggle for racial justice and equality, their children provided much-needed warmth and gave them a type of humaneness that brought them closer to the masses of the folk.[6]

Although sensitive to the notion that a man who devotes himself wholeheartedly to a cause does not need a family, Malcolm and Martin eagerly and graciously accepted fatherhood as a gift from God. Both remained undeterred by its many challenges and inspired by its possibilities for their own emotional and spiritual development. Betty shared the following concerning Malcolm's response to the birth of each of his first four daughters, testimony quite touching and meaningful since the Muslim leader grew up without a father himself: "I suppose people who only knew Malcolm from his public appearances and fiery speeches couldn't even imagine what he was like as a father. Malcolm had a very beautiful reaction to becoming a father. I don't think he really accepted the fact that I was going to have a baby until she arrived, but once she was here and he realized that he'd made the baby and the baby looked like him—the gentleness he showed was really so profound."[7]

Martin reacted similarly, for he was always "very attentive and concerned" throughout Coretta's pregnancies and during the first year of each of his children's lives. According to Coretta, "We were both excited and happy, especially because, at one point, there was some question about whether or not we could have children." She told *Good Housekeeping* magazine in 1964, "Martin often talked about how he loved children, and said that if we could not have any, we would adopt some. Now our marriage was complete."[8] As fathers, both Martin and Malcolm were clearly driven by this sense of the importance of children in building strong marital and family relationships as well as community and shared values.

In typical male fashion, each wanted his first child to be a son. As it turned out, both had girls.[9] As the first of his children, Attallah taught Malcolm a lot about parenting and provided some of the love and reinforcement he needed as he met his many daily responsibilities as a minister in the Nation of Islam. Yolanda, affectionately called Yoki by the family, served the same purpose for Martin as he pursued his many duties as a pastor and later as a civil rights leader. Coretta has reported, "Martin always said that Yoki came at a time in his life when he needed something to take his mind off the tremendous pressures that bore down upon him. When he came home from the stress and turmoil that he was suddenly plunged into, the baby was there cooing and cuddly and trustful and loving. There is something renewing about a small child—something he needed very much, because two weeks after Yoki was born, a seamstress named Rosa Parks refused to give up her seat on a Montgomery bus, and the Movement was born."[10]

The inordinate amount of time Malcolm and Martin spent in the public sphere robbed them of precious moments with their children. Bruce Perry suggests that Malcolm was never able to strike a proper balance between his public roles as a minister and activist and his private life as a father, a problem that helps explain what Perry identifies as his ambivalent relationship to his daughters:

[H]e neglected his . . . children. Even when he was home, he was stingy with the amount of time he devoted to his family. He would withdraw into his attic study, or someone would hustle the children into the basement playroom, so that he could work without being distracted. One visitor was struck by the way the children, who missed Malcolm when he was away, seemed to vanish after they were ushered out of the living room. There was no noise. No toys were visible. . . . Yet Malcolm cared very much about his young ones. When they accompanied him to public functions, he was heedful of their needs. They'd come and grasp his hand or wrap a little arm around his tall leg. He'd bend down and smile or speak softly to them.[11]

Always on the run, Martin had a more difficult time than Malcolm when it came to negotiating the boundaries between his public and private obligations. Both men admitted that they felt guilty about devoting too little time to their children. They were seldom present to answer their children's questions, to counsel them in their troubles, or to embrace them and whisper comforting words when they had bad dreams. "That's not good, I know," said Malcolm on one occasion as he reflected on the fact that he spent virtually no time shopping with his girls. "I've always been too busy." Martin called his frequent absences from his children "one of the most frustrating aspects of my life." "He wanted so badly to share with the children more," Coretta once observed. "He wanted to be like his father, always by his children's side." She added: "Martin knew his parents would support him all the way. Whenever he had an assembly recitation to do in school, or was going to sing in the choir or play football—anything—Mamma and Daddy King were sure to be in the audience rooting for him. Daddy King always felt that it was his duty to be present whenever one of his children was doing something special. If he could not go, Mamma King would attend."[12]

The Kings and Shabazzes were made to understand that the time and energy their fathers gave to the struggle were necessary to improve the quality of life for themselves and other black people. Betty's adeptness in explaining Malcolm's sacrifices brought some relief to the children as they struggled to understand why he was so unlike other fathers. Malcolm once stated with pride, "I have children from this size on down, and even in their young age they understand." He continued, "I think they would rather have a father or brother or whatever the situation may be who will take a stand in the face of any kind of reaction from narrow-minded people, rather than to compromise and later on have to grow up in shame and in disgrace." Martin made similar comments about his children, with whom he and Coretta frequently discussed the civil rights struggle. "I think that in some ways they understand," he remarked, "even though it's pretty hard on them."[13]

A number of humorous and touching stories developed out of the children's efforts to understand their fathers' frequent absences. "At times funny things would happen when he was home," said Betty of Malcolm.

"When the children were quite young and saw Daddy on television, they couldn't quite put the two things together, since sometimes Daddy was there watching himself on the screen. One of the children would look at the picture, go to the television to take a closer look, and then come back and look at Daddy." Stories shared about Martin's children are more plentiful and considerably more revealing. One day early in December 1961, as six-year-old Yoki wept out of fear that her father would not be released from jail in time for Christmas, four-year-old Martin III sat on the bed embracing and consoling his sister. "Don't cry, Yoki," the child uttered. "Daddy will be back. He has to help the people. He has already helped some people, but he has to help some more and when he finishes, he'll be back, so don't cry, Yoki." The point eventually sank in because a few days later, when Coretta explained to Yoki why Atlanta's Funtown was closed to black children, and how her father's going to jail would change that situation, the little girl responded: "Well, that's fine, Mommy. Tell him to stay in jail until I can go to Funtown." On yet another occasion, after Martin III and Dexter accompanied their father on a people-to-people tour through rural Georgia, Dexter, visibly tired and perplexed, told his mother, "I don't see how my daddy can do so much and talk to so many people and not even get tired at all!"[14]

The times Malcolm and Martin spent with their children were filled with fun and pleasant memories. Attallah, whose likeness to Malcolm in looks and temperament clearly equals Yolanda's resemblance to Martin, remembers how excited she and her sisters were "when our father telephoned our mother to say he was coming home." Ilyasah would "always go and sit by the door to wait," she recalls. Upon entering his home, she continued, Malcolm would "put all four of us up on his two big knees and just talk and talk to us and laugh a lot. I remember just his presence was so very calming for us kids." At other times, Malcolm read aloud to the girls as they sat on his lap, played with them, took them to the beach, or bought them something they liked. Alex Haley recounted Malcolm's sadness one night when he had overlooked buying a present for Attallah on her fourth birthday, "and how he beamed when I surprised him with my intended gift, a black walking doll, and insisted that it be his gift instead."[15] Malcolm's children remained a part of the center of his world, even as he gave of himself unselfishly for the freedom of his people.

The bond between Martin and his children was equally strong. Crowded as his travel schedule was, Martin always spent the major holidays at home with his family. On such occasions, the King home was literally filled with excitement, joy, and a mood of playfulness, as Coretta pointed out in an interview in 1964: "The children are wild about him. Whenever their daddy comes home, they run to meet him, shouting and jumping all over him. He has a habit, which they dearly love, of letting them stand on the steps leading to the second floor and catching them as they jump down into his arms. When they were babies, he used to put them up on top of the refrigerator. They would hurl themselves into his arms without even seeming to look. I died a thousand deaths each time they played this little game. I just knew that, one of those times, someone was going to get hurt. Of course, that never happened."[16]

Martin found great relief from many of the daily pressures of the movement by joking, swimming, bike riding, playing kissing games, and wrestling in bed with his children. "I might come into my bedroom and find all our family sitting on top of him," Coretta recounted. "Occasionally, on rainy days, when Martin was in town and he happened to be at home," she added, "you could hear me saying over and over, 'Martin, please don't play ball in the house.'"[17] In more serious moments, the civil rights leader, like Malcolm, read to his children and responded to any questions or comments they had.

Malcolm and Martin were held in high esteem and virtually worshiped by some around the world, but to their children they were simply Daddy.[18] Attallah and Yolanda were well aware of their fathers' fame, but they could not understand why people went to such great lengths to touch or to speak to them. Moreover, they wondered why their fathers were always in the public eye and why they had to be protected from classmates, the media, and other curious persons. In any case, the spiritual and emotional bond between Malcolm and Martin and their children became symbolic of how these leaders related to their people as a whole.

It is also important to note that the images of Earl Little and Martin Luther King Sr. figured to some extent into their sons' relationships with their own children. This became evident in Malcolm's and Martin's perceptions of parent-children relationships. Like their fathers, both regarded strong and responsible parenthood as the key to the strict but well-organized upbringing of children. While they were not as free-handed as their fathers when it came to the use of the belt, Malcolm and Martin believed in corporal punishment as a way of disciplining children, but only as a last resort. When their children were naughty, a sharp look of disapproval more than substituted for a spanking. "Malcolm came down hard on parents who let their children run the streets till midnight," writes Bruce Perry, "with apartment keys strung around their neck."[19] Concerning Malcolm's role as a disciplinarian, one heavily influenced by his Islamic faith, Betty asserted:

> My husband had very definite opinions about raising children. He be-
> lieved that parents should provide proper images for their children and
> should give them guidelines as to what they can and cannot do. Some of
> his basic aims were to see that our girls are taught to face reality, to
> accept themselves, to be able to function under supervision. . . . He
> believed that children should have a belief in a tradition and that this
> should come originally from the home. He did not believe in spoiling
> children. Many times people would tell our girls that they didn't have to
> do something because he was their father. He always put a stop to this,
> saying that other people will spoil your children and be the first to
> criticize them for their apparent lack of training.[20]

Martin had essentially the same perspective, grounded, as it was, in the values of the black church. He felt that "children should be raised moder-ately, neither overly inhibited nor allowed to run wild." Major family prob-lems were inevitable, he maintained, when children were allowed freedom of expression without discipline and a sense of responsibility. As was the case with Malcolm, Martin insisted that children should always respond to par-ents with respect, obedience, and, when possible, a sense of family responsi-bility. This accounted in part for the spiritual quality that characterized his relationship with his children. Bernard Lee, a friend and coworker, remem-bered that "spirituality was always present" in the King home, "even when Martin disciplined his children. Things were often said about him by others that would normally break up a family unit, but that spirituality would exude and just take over."[21]

Malcolm and Martin sought to instill in their children a keen sense of spiritual and moral values. Of particular significance among these was the conviction that life is incomplete without an unselfish devotion to God, to the welfare of others, to the constant enlightenment of the mind, and to the pursuit of some ethical ideal, values they upheld in the stories they told their children and in their daily activities. The fact that Malcolm and Martin em-braced different religious traditions made no difference in this regard. Ac-cording to Betty Shabazz, Malcolm always insisted that his children be taught to properly relate in mind and spirit to themselves and to others, particularly among the oppressed. This concern was consistent with Mal-colm's efforts to educate his little ones regarding the history and traditions of their people. Betty declares: "Basically he wanted the children prepared to accept themselves, to function in a community, and to be able to support themselves. He also wanted them to be aware that it was a spiritual as well as a moral duty to help their brothers and sisters. This is how all the children were to be reared."[22]

Malcolm could hardly bear the thought of his children growing up ill-prepared to live in a world marred by evil and injustice. The teachings he shared with them, basically humanitarian in nature, were designed to equip them for a better life. His widow wrote: "Malcolm was a man who had lived in a society where such conditions prevailed that he didn't want his children or any Afro-American to grow up in." The same could be said of Martin, despite the fact that he had grown up in a family atmosphere where there was more security, serenity, and happiness than Malcolm ever experienced in childhood. Much like Malcolm, Martin saw proper teachings in the home and the best of formal education as essential avenues for his children to realize the fullness of what it means to function daily as human beings in a diverse, complex, and demanding world. This is why he discussed sex, religion, and politics with Yolanda, his oldest child. With this in mind, Yolanda noted how her father "taught us so much about life and people and living in particular—the things that he felt were necessary in leading a good life and a life that would contribute to society. I believe that I learned my lessons well and whatever I become, I owe it to the lessons that my father and my mother taught me."[23]

But Malcolm and Martin were different somewhat in their approaches to educating and preparing their children to contribute to the ongoing struggle against oppression. For most of his public life, Malcolm sent his children to schools run by the Nation of Islam, institutions that emphasized black contributions to civilization while portraying whites as savages bent on the destruction of dark humanity. Apparently he was educating his daughters during that time to assume productive roles in the black nation. In contrast, Martin enrolled his children in integrated schools. As he saw it, this was one way of preparing them to live in an integrated society, a thought Malcolm never seriously entertained until the last year of his life. Even so, Malcolm ultimately shared Martin's vision of their children living in a world "where they will not be judged by the color of their skin but by the content of their character."[24]

But they differed in the extent to which they exposed their children to protest activities. Although Malcolm secured memberships for his daughters in his Organization of Afro-American Unity (OAAU) in 1964, a group devoted to the liberation and uplift of his people, he seemed determined to protect them from blatant racism and from the daily demands and challenges of the freedom movement. That determination was heightened after his break with the Nation of Islam and the subsequent bombing of his home in February 1965, which drove him to pick up a gun in defense of his daughters. Martin was equally protective, but he explained racism and segregation as social problems, taught his children how to respond to the use of the word *nigger* without hostility, and even allowed them to occasionally accompany him during civil rights rallies and demonstrations. In December 1963, three months after four black girls were murdered by white racists in Birmingham, Yolanda and Martin III actually agreed to "accept one symbolic gift or toy" so that their parents could help "make a brighter Christmas for some of those who had suffered the loss of dear ones in the civil-rights crusade." This reinforced Martin's and Coretta's belief that their children were benefiting morally and spiritually from their struggle for racial and economic justice.[25]

But Martin's need to protect his children was stronger at times than his willingness to expose them to the energy and excitement of the movement. He and Coretta agreed that it would be unwise for them always to march and go to jail together while the children were so young. Faced daily with the threat of assassination, the couple also decided never to travel by plane together, except in unusual situations, for they felt that at least one of them should be in a position to take care of the children if tragedy struck. Martin was always sensitive to the fact that Yolanda and Martin III experienced the bombing of their home in 1957 and that all of his children were subjected to racial insults, verbal and physical attacks on their father, and the pain of their father's frequent incarceration, concerns that made him all the more determined to protect them while reinforcing in them a sense of self-worth in the face of the pressures of white society.[26] The difficulties he often felt in trying to do so were painfully illustrated in his effort to explain to Yolanda why the most popular amusement park in Atlanta was closed to children of her race, an experience that marked the child's "first emotional realization and understanding of being black in a white world":

> The family often used to ride with me to the Atlanta airport, and on our way, we always passed Funtown, a sort of miniature Disneyland with mechanical rides and that sort of thing. Yolanda would inevitably say, "I want to go to Funtown," and I would always evade a direct reply. I really didn't know how to explain to her why she couldn't go. Then one

day at home, she ran down stairs exclaiming that a TV commercial was urging people to come to Funtown. Then my wife and I had to sit down with her between us and try to explain it. I have won some applause as a speaker, but my tongue twisted and my speech stammered seeking to explain to my six-year-old daughter why the public invitation on television didn't include her, and others like her. One of the most painful experiences I have ever faced was to see her tears when I told her that Funtown was closed to colored children, for I realized that at that moment the first dark cloud of inferiority had floated into her little mental sky, that at that moment her personality had begun to warp with that first unconscious bitterness toward white people. It was the first time that prejudice based upon skin color had been explained to her. But it was of paramount importance to me that she not grow up bitter. So I told her that although many white people were against her going to Funtown, there were many others who did want colored children to go. It helped somewhat. Pleasantly, word came to me later that Funtown had quietly desegregated, so I took Yolanda. A number of white persons there asked, "Aren't you Dr. King, and isn't this your daughter?" I said we were, and she heard them say how glad they were to see us there.[27]

Malcolm and Martin knew that self-esteem, more than anything else, would be critical to their children's will to grow and to achieve the best that life had to offer. They wanted their children to have the same privileges that white children routinely enjoyed as they prepared themselves for productive life vocations. Malcolm wanted his daughters "to study music because he felt it would teach them precision, poise, timing and coordination." Martin's children were also encouraged to study vocal and instrumental music, especially since artistic genius of this nature ran deep in his family. He and Coretta often gathered with the children around the piano, singing freedom songs and hymns together.[28] Although concerned deeply about the careers that his children would later pursue, Martin was as reluctant as Malcolm to pressure them, fearing that this could possibly turn them away from the things he wanted so much.

The thought of their children growing up without a father frequently bothered them, especially since both men constantly lived under the threat of death. This accounted for the seriousness and the sense of urgency with which they sought to nurture and mold their children. The worst possible scenario occurred when Malcolm was assassinated in 1965 and Martin in

1968. Their deaths devastated their oldest daughters, Attallah and Yolanda, in part because their memories of their fathers were more vivid than those of their younger siblings. "Dear daddy, I love you so," said Attallah in a letter to Malcolm hours after he was murdered. "O dear, O dear, I wish you weren't dead." Betty Shabazz recalled:

> My three oldest daughters were very much aware of what had happened and they took it very hard, especially Attallah. We can talk and laugh now at some of her actions but they were difficult to know how to cope with at the time. She used to go to school and just sit there without even taking off her hat and coat. It took more than a year and a half before we could put up a picture of him. There was a time when we would avoid even looking at pictures of him on display on the street or in store windows. Now we have pictures all over the house.[29]

An hour after Martin's murder, Yolanda said a prayer that echoed the sentiments expresssed in Attallah's letter to her deceased father: "Dear Lord, please don't let my daddy die," she pleaded. Speaking with an interviewer in 1974, six years later, she wept and declared, "Sometimes there are things I would really like to talk to him about. I thought he was the best person in the world."[30]

Pleasant memories of Malcolm and Martin sustained their children as they grew. Nothing aroused their curiosity more than conversations about the things their fathers liked and disliked. This was especially true in the case of Malaak and Malikah, the twins who never touched Malcolm, and who had to be filled in by Betty and their older sisters. They "used to say, 'Remember the time daddy...,'" Attallah recalls, "and I was amused because they hadn't been there." The mere mention of Malcolm was enough to discipline the twins when they misbehaved, as Betty pointed out in 1969: "I can say to my three-year-old twins, Malaak and Malikah, who were born after he was assassinated, 'Do you think your father would like that?' And they can get very teary because they don't want to displease him, even though he's dead. One day one of the twins had a little friend over who said something about her father. Suddenly I noticed Malaak pulling her friend into the living room where she pointed to the large painting hanging there, letting her friend know that this was her father. I felt kind of misty behind that."[31]

Coretta kept her children's memories of their father alive through books about him. This was particularly helpful for Bernice, who was only five when Martin was killed. The images she got from seeing her father's face in books and on television reinforced her belief that he was somehow still alive, a conviction that made even more sense since she, like generations of her family, was taught that the spirits of deceased ancestors survive and maintain an interest and role in the affairs of the living.[32]

Andrew Young, who worked closely with Martin in the movement, also became a source of information for Martin III and Dexter. In 1974, Young told an interviewer for *McCall's* magazine that the boys talked about their father daily and that the kinds of questions they asked about him stirred the emotions almost beyond controllable limits: "They talk about him in a way that almost brings tears to my eyes sometimes. When we play basketball, they want to know: 'Was my daddy a good basketball player? Did he play tennis?' And it really chokes me up. You realize that they've been deprived of a relationship. That at this point in their lives when he would have meant so much to them, he is not there. They don't resent it, but they still hunger for him."[33]

But the children of Malcolm and Martin have done more than simply endure the crushing experience of the loss of their fathers. They have in some ways triumphed. Knowing that their fathers were murdered because of their pursuit of the highest ethical ideals, the youngsters have consciously labored to enhance their fathers' legacies through their own achievements. They all attended college and have chosen stimulating and challenging careers. The widest variety of careers are being pursued by Malcolm's daughters. Attallah does hundreds of theatrical performances each year and is a producer, writer, lecturer, hairstyling consultant, and clothing designer. Qubilah works as a journalist. Ilyasah holds a degree in biology, Gamilah is involved in theater arts and is a rap artist, Malaak has ties to the legal profession, and Malikah has training in architectural engineering.[34] Driven by Malcolm's conviction that all labor is significant, especially when it involves serving others and uplifting oneself, these young women are visible symbols of the fact that African Americans can achieve whatever they wish if given opportunities to do so.

The Kings have maintained high visibility. Yolanda is an actress, producer, and lecturer who "combines her commitment to Black people with her artistic talents." In a one-woman play, *Tracks: A Celebration of the Triumph of the Spirit of Martin Luther King Jr.*, which is centered around her father's teachings, Yolanda seeks to "educate and entertain" while inspiring people to continue the struggle for a better world. After completing graduate school at New York University, she cofounded a theater company, Christian Theater Artists. One of its most provocative productions, *Mah Soul Buck Naked in*

Heaven's Breeze, focuses on the gospel of Jesus Christ. In a recent essay, Yolanda spoke of her work as connecting her to "the social vision of her father." Martin III has been involved in Georgia politics, and in 1997 he founded Americans United for Affirmative Action, a coalition devoted to dispelling "the notion that his father's dream would not have countenanced racial preferences." He is now president of the Southern Christian Leadership Conference (SCLC), the civil rights organization founded by his father and other black ministers in 1957.[35] Under his leadership, the SCLC is addressing issues ranging from affirmative action to reparations, voting irregularities, job discrimination, and the conviction of white racists who killed African Americans during the civil rights movement of the 1950s and 1960s. Dexter was a music producer before succeeding his mother, Coretta, as chairman and CEO of the Martin Luther King Jr. Center for Nonviolent Social Change in 1995. Bernice King is an author, an ordained Baptist minister, and an assistant pastor in Atlanta who was listed among *Ebony*'s top black female preachers in 1997. Her sermons clearly echo many of the human rights concerns of her father. Moreover, she and her siblings have continued their father's tradition of marching in support of human freedom worldwide.[36]

The intense scrutiny and public castigation endured by the progenies of Malcolm and Martin in recent years is not unlike that experienced by other descendants of the powerful and the famous. In 1994, Malcolm's daughter Qubilah was charged with collaborating with a Jewish man to assassinate Minister Louis Farrakhan of the Nation of Islam in retaliation for her father's murder. After she admitted her role in the plot and agreed to undergo drug and psychiatric treatment, the government shelved Qubilah's case. In 1997, Qubilah's twelve-year-old son, Malcolm, named for his grandfather, set a fire in his grandmother's apartment, causing Betty Shabazz's death. Although the Kings have not been stained by tragedies of this nature, the criticism they receive from civil rights leaders, journalists, and others is in some cases far more unsympathetic than that endured by Malcolm's daughters. They are accused of cheapening and distorting their father's legacy by profiting financially from it, a charge open to debate.[37]

Far more significant is the manner in which Attallah and Yolanda have formed a partnership in spreading their fathers' messages through the prism of art. The two were introduced by a mutual friend in 1979, and they soon formed an eight-member theater troupe whose play, *Stepping into Tomorrow*, "is carrying their fathers' voices to schools, churches, and community centers across the country" through "a blend of music, drama, and comedy."

Attallah and Yolanda are particularly interested in presenting to the public "their *own* perceptions of their fathers," a concern that led them to write and stage *Of One Mind*. "Our fathers met and even shook hands, but they never really got to know each other," they explained in an interview. "The play expresses what we believe would have happened had our fathers lived." Attallah and Yolanda are also lecturing together at colleges and universities nationwide and abroad concerning the relevance of their fathers' visions for addressing contemporary human problems. There is a touch of irony in the fact that these women are experiencing a spirit of unity that their fathers never knew. Peter Bailey is right in saying, "Their friendship is a fine and fitting legacy."[38]

A New Generation of Freedom Fighters: On Children and Youth in the Struggle

Malcolm and Martin were deeply touched by the suffering of children in America and abroad. In 1964, Malcolm denounced in the strongest possible terms the beating of black children during civil rights campaigns in Mississippi and the killing of babies in the Congo with American bombs, tragedies that reminded him of the lengths to which oppressors will go to maintain the status quo. In 1967, Martin bitterly complained not only about the undernourishment and poor health of children in Mississippi and in Asia, Africa, and Latin America, but also about the destruction of Vietnamese children by American bombs. He grimaced at the thought of American troops wandering into the towns and seeing "thousands of children homeless, without clothes, running in packs on the streets like animals." "They see the children selling their sisters to our soldiers, soliciting for their mothers," he complained.[39] This concern for the welfare of children came naturally to Martin and Malcolm, since both had a remarkable ability to empathize with poor and oppressed people at all levels.

But this shared concern did not lead them to the same position regarding the use of children in protest activities. Malcolm and his Muslim associates criticized Martin and other black leaders vehemently for "putting the lives of black children on the line" while "they sip cocktails in the lounges of Fifth Avenue." Martin was apparently more open to the involvement of children in the freedom cause, but his deep concern for their physical and psychological well-being always made it difficult for him to actively solicit their direct involvement in public protests. In 1957, Martin was deeply moved by "Negro children" in Little Rock, Arkansas, who "walked with fortitude through the ranks of white students—often hostile and jeering—at Central High School."[40] The civil rights leader appeared more apt than Malcolm to believe that children had something to gain in terms of spiritual and psychic benefits from direct participation in a movement that would shape their future in positive and perhaps even in unimaginable ways.

Black Muslim teachings concerning the place of children in a society accounted for Malcolm's position on the matter. He simply could not see the logic of involving children in struggles that go on in the public arena. Although Martin confronted the same attitude in black churches, he did not accept it uncritically since he, in stark contrast to Malcolm, had developed a sense of his own moral responsibility in a racist society while hardly in his teens. Furthermore, his own perspective benefited from what he observed during the Montgomery movement, his first effort at social protest, when children and youth walked proudly with adults rather than submit to segregated buses.[41] The mere sight of hundreds of youngsters patiently and wholeheartedly devoting themselves to the principles and disciplines of nonviolence in Montgomery left an indelible mark on Martin's consciousness, contributing in some measure to the spirit of his comments to the 26,000 black high school and college students who gathered in Washington, D.C., in October 1959 to demonstrate their support for the 1954 Supreme Court decision against segregation in public schools:

> I cannot help thinking—that a hundred years from now the historians will be calling this not the "beat" generation, but the generation of integration. The fact that thousands of you came here to Washington and that thousands more signed your petition proves that this generation will not take "No" for an answer—will not take double talk for an answer—will not take gradualism for an answer. It proves that the only answer you will settle for is total desegregation and total equality now. . . . What this march demonstrates to me, above all else, is that you young people, through your own experience, have somehow discovered the central fact of American life—that the extension of democracy for all Americans depends upon the complete integration of Negro Americans.[42]

Although impressed with this trend toward political activism among black students, Martin did not involve them in the founding and early development of the SCLC in the late 1950s. It is difficult to avoid the conclusion that he assumed that youth were not prepared intellectually and spiritually to assume major roles in an organization designed to coordinate local protest activities throughout the South.

The involvement of students in sit-in demonstrations in North Carolina, Tennessee, Alabama, and other states in February 1960 brought criticism from Malcolm and warm expressions of support and praise from Martin. Martin saw great potential in this new phase of the struggle, when young people enlisted in large numbers for the first time, and he talked to numerous student activists about how they might best assist the cause. In a lengthy statement, the civil rights leader ignored the attacks of Malcolm, who denounced the sit-ins as a futile effort on the part of students to force themselves on white society, and publicly endorsed the movement:

> An electrifying movement of Negro students has shattered the placid surface of campuses and communities across the South. Though confronted in many places by hoodlums, police guns, tear gas, arrests, and jail sentences, the students tenaciously continue to sit down and demand equal service at variety store lunch counters, and extend their protest from city to city. In communities like Montgomery, Alabama, the whole student body rallied behind expelled students and staged a walkout while state government intimidation was unleashed with a display of military force appropriate to a wartime invasion. Nevertheless, the spirit of self-sacrifice and commitment remains firm, and the state governments find themselves dealing with students who have lost the fear of jail and physical injury.[43]

The efforts of students to desegregate lunch counters triggered memories of earlier trends in militant activism among African-American youth. In fact, Martin refused to separate the sit-ins from the movements of young black soldiers to achieve major social reforms in the immediate aftermath of World War II and from the activities of black students in support of the Supreme Court decision of 1954. Indeed, Martin associated a spirit of youthful militancy and energy with these developments that Malcolm was often hesitant to acknowledge as a Black Muslim leader:

> It was the young veteran who gave the first surge of power to the postwar civil rights movements. It was the high school, college, and elementary school young people who were in the front line of the school desegregation struggle. Lest it be forgotten, the opening of hundreds of schools to Negroes for the first time in history required that there be

young Negroes with the moral and physical courage to face the challenges and, all too frequently, the mortal danger presented by mob
resistance. There were such young Negroes in the tens of thousands,
and no program for integration failed for want of students. The simple
courage of the students . . . should never be forgotten. In the years 1958
and 1959 two massive Youth Marches to Washington for Integrated
Schools involved some forty thousand young people who brought with
them nearly five hundred thousand signatures on petitions gathered
largely from campuses and youth centers. This mass action infused a
new spirit of direct action challenging government to act forthrightly.
Hence for a decade young Negroes have been steeled by both deeds and
inspiration to step into responsible action. These are the precedents for
the student struggle of today.[44]

After the sit-in movement of February 1960, Martin urged black students
in Durham, North Carolina, to form a coordinating council with members
from different schools and cities, advice that was well received and followed.
Martin wanted the student movement to fall under the leadership of his
SCLC, but "many student leaders expressed the desire to keep the movement
as much 'student-led' as possible." This proved to be a wise move on their
part because Martin was cautious and hesitant when the students challenged
him, in October 1960, to become personally involved in intensive sit-ins at
stores in Atlanta.[45] Although he participated and was arrested with students,
he found it difficult at times to relate to a younger generation that increasingly viewed him and the preachers of the SCLC as being too conservative in
philosophy and methods.

When students met at Shaw University in Raleigh, North Carolina, in
April 1960 to start the Student Nonviolent Coordinating Committee
(SNCC), Martin, driven in part by a spirit of paternalism, saw yet another
chance to reassert "control over the southern black struggle." But students
resisted Martin's "efforts to subvert their autonomy," and so did Ella Baker,
their advisor, "who understood the psychological need of student activists to
remain independent of adult control." Although the students expressed their
commitment to the nonviolent principles "popularized by King, yet they
were drawn to these ideas not because of King's advocacy but because they
provided an appropriate rationale for student protest."[46] Baker's philosophical influence on SNCC members was considerably greater than that of both
Martin and Malcolm, for she became their "constant mentor" and "official

adult advisor." Moreover, the students shared Baker's "philosophy of community development and leadership," one that strongly opposed the male-dominated charismatic leadership model exemplified by Martin and Malcolm.[47]

The courage and determination displayed by students during the sit-ins help explain why Martin was challenging even children to become more active in the struggle by the end of 1960. In a letter to the children at the Jesse Crowell School in Albion, Michigan, he said: "There is a great need for some of you to help win this fight to make our great nation exactly what we want it to be. I need the help of all of you. But you must have some ability by which your efforts can be made useful. In this way, you too can help in the great struggle for human dignity. I know you will not fail in your responsibility as the citizens and leaders of tomorrow. The whole country looks to you to help the nation successfully reach the goals we want to reach."[48]

The militant character of the youth wing of the civil rights movement took shape during the "freedom rides" in May 1961, when black and white students traveled by bus from Washington, D.C., through points in the South to protest segregation in interstate travel. SNCC was heavily involved in this "series of assaults on southern segregation," a movement that "for the first time brought student protesters into conflict with the Kennedy administration." For different reasons, Malcolm and Martin refused to participate. Although opposed to the integrationist agenda of the freedom riders, Malcolm offered his blessings to one of his young female followers who went South to work with SNCC. Martin chaired the Freedom Rides Coordinating Committee and provided moral, spiritual, and financial assistance, but, because he was still on probation for a 1960 traffic arrest in Georgia, he decided against riding with the students. This decision brought him once again into conflict with youth in the movement, and meetings did little to resolve the differences. "We're all on probation," shouted the youngsters during one meeting, as they pressured Martin to become a freedom rider. In "a flash of anger," Martin responded: "Do not tell me when my time has come! Only God can tell me that! How dare you try and tell me!"[49]

But the freedom rides impacted Malcolm's and Martin's perceptions of youth in positive ways. Even as Malcolm attacked the philosophy behind the freedom rides, he was compelled to admit at times that youngsters in that movement were infused with a special pride and militancy. The Muslim leader associated the freedom rides and other forms of activism among students in 1961 with a trend worldwide among young people:

In foreign countries the students have helped bring about revolution—it was the students who brought about revolution in the Sudan, who swept Syngman Rhee out of office in Korea, swept Menderes out in Turkey. The students didn't think in terms of the odds against them, and they couldn't be bought out. . . . In America students have been noted for involving themselves in panty raids, goldfish swallowing, seeing how many can get in a phone booth—not for their revolutionary political ideas or their desire to change unjust conditions. But some students are becoming more like their brothers around the world.[50]

Martin felt that the freedom rides and other youth activities in 1961 proved that young people were providing the nation with a new and more vigorous kind of leadership. "They took nonviolent resistance, first employed in Montgomery, Alabama, in mass dimensions," he wrote, "and developed original forms of applications—sit-ins, freedom rides, and wade-ins." "Inspired by the boldness and ingenuity of Negroes," he added, "white youth stirred into action and formed an alliance that aroused the conscience of the nation." The interracial nature of the freedom rides afforded Martin with further proof that youngsters were choosing the beloved community over segregation and that they were determined to replace the old order with one quite different and better.[51] Moreover, he saw as vividly as Malcolm the ways in which the concerns of student activists in America found affinity with those of young people in other parts of the world, though he expressed this in somewhat different terms:

The dynamism of the student movement can be understood only if we realize that it is part of a revolt of all youth—Negro and White—against a world they never made; a revolt not alone to achieve desegregation but a social order consistent with the high principles on which the nation was founded. Youth has moved out to take over leadership from what it perceives to be faltering hands. Negro youth has surged into a vanguard position because it has the most desperate need and has been gripped by a sense of destiny. . . . The Negro student knows he is not alone but is fortified by support of tens of millions of white and Negro citizens of all ages, of all classes, of all political persuasions. He is deadly serious and fiercely determined. . . . He is part of a worldwide thrust into the future to abolish colonialism and racism; to replace institutionalized handicaps with free opportunity.[52]

Malcolm's and Martin's reflections on youth activism in the early 1960s were heavily informed by their exposure to the kind of powerful intellectual exchanges that occurred in colleges, universities, and seminaries. Malcolm lectured at black and white schools throughout the country, and his mere presence always generated vigorous debate. Martin taught social philosophy at Morehouse College, his alma mater, and lectured frequently in various academic settings. Thus he and Malcolm developed a keen sense of the dynamic forces, intellectual and otherwise, that shifted the student movement from the campuses in cities and small towns to the rural areas of the Southland.[53]

The youth wing of the civil rights struggle matured during campaigns in Albany, Georgia, and Birmingham, Alabama. The Albany Movement, which emerged out of the arrests of freedom riders and the efforts of students from Albany State College to integrate bus terminal facilities, began in the fall of 1961, as SNCC organizers launched a voter registration drive among African Americans at the grassroots level. Some of the members of SNCC were openly hostile when local leaders invited Martin and his SCLC to Albany, apparently to bring new vitality and visibility to a faltering campaign. Martin's decision to go to jail with student protesters did not change this situation. Rifts developed between SNCC and SCLC over Martin's leadership style, his plan to attack segregation on all fronts, his decision to obey a court injunction halting demonstrations for ten days, and what was perceived as his tendency to receive credit for work done by the students. The "irreconcilable differences and disagreements" became public and contributed to both the failure of SCLC's offensive and the departure of Martin and his aides from the Albany campaign in 1962. Malcolm joined the students in blaming Martin for what many critics saw as the Albany fiasco.[54]

Martin went to great lengths to divert attention away from his problems with youth in Albany to other concerns that were causing dissatisfaction among young blacks generally throughout the South. "Part of the impatience of Negro youth stems from their observation that change is taking place rapidly in Africa and other parts of the world and comparatively slowly in the South," he complained in May 1962. Instead of lashing out at students who questioned his leadership style and strategies, Martin praised them for their opinions and debates concerning "the moral and practical soundness of nonviolence." He observed, "The striking quality in Negro students I have met is the intensity and depth of their commitment. I am no longer surprised to meet physically attractive, stylishly dressed young girls whose charm and personality would grace a junior prom and to hear them declare in unmistakably sincere terms, 'Dr. King, I am ready to die if I must.'"[55]

This vibrant and distinguishing quality among young African Americans became even more evident as students helped prepare the ground for SCLC's assault on the discriminatory practices of Birmingham's white business community in 1962 and 1963. Martin praised the students at Miles College for their part in mobilizing the black community in "a determined withdrawal of business" from stores that refused to employ or serve blacks. Significantly, the Birmingham protest provided the opportunity for both Martin and Malcolm to publicly assess the value of children to the struggle. Hundreds of black children took to the streets, unperturbed by attack dogs, cattle prods, and the high-pressure water hoses used against them, and chanting, singing, and marching with a kind of courage and determination that recalled Stephen of Cloyes and the great Children's Crusade of the Middle Ages.[56] Malcolm seemed quite unimpressed. Knowing that Martin, James Bevel, and others in SCLC had devised the crusade to breathe new life into a waning movement, the Muslim leader was furious, declaring, in a burst of anger, that "real men don't put their children on the firing line."[57]

Malcolm's reaction to the Birmingham decision did not surprise Martin, especially since hundreds of children had been brutalized and arrested. Major media sources joined Malcolm in deploring the use of children in Birmingham, forcing Martin to ask where these writers had been "when our segregated social system had been misusing and abusing Negro children": "The children themselves had the answer to the misguided sympathies of the press. One of the most ringing replies came from a child of no more than eight who walked with her mother one day in a demonstration. An amused policeman leaned down to her and said with mock gruffness: 'What do you want?' The child looked into his eyes, unafraid, and gave her answer. 'Feedom,' she said. She could not even pronounce the word, but no Gabriel trumpet could have sounded a truer note."[58]

Martin and his aides anticipated what he termed "a heavy fire of criticism" for involving children, but they were not deterred by their critics. Noting that young people had provided the spark in "most of the recent direct action crusades," Martin insisted that "we needed this dramatic new dimension":

> Our people were demonstrating daily and going to jail in numbers, but we were still beating our heads against the brick wall of the city offi-

cials' stubborn resolve to maintain the status quo. Our fight, if won, would benefit people of all ages. But most of all we were inspired with a desire to give our young a true sense of their own stake in freedom and justice. We believed they would have the courage to respond to our call. . . . Looking back, it is clear that the introduction of Birmingham's children into the campaign was one of the wisest moves we made. It brought a new impact to the crusade, and the impetus that we needed to win the struggle.[59]

The children's crusade in Birmingham overwhelmed Martin, reinforcing his belief that young people were a resource that could no longer be ignored in the struggle. "I have stood with hundreds of youngsters and joined in while they sang 'Ain't Gonna Let Nobody Turn Me 'Round,'" he remarked. "A few minutes later, I have seen those same youngsters refuse to turn around from the onrush of an attack dog, refuse to turn around before a pugnacious Bull Connor in command of men armed with power hoses."[60] The fact that children barely old enough to attend school responded with courage and enthusiasm was, in Martin's opinion, more than an adequate answer to critics like Malcolm:

> Even children too young to march requested and earned a place in our ranks. Once when we sent out a call for volunteers, six tiny youngsters responded. Andy Young told them that they were not old enough to go to jail but that they could go to the library. "You won't get arrested there," he said, "but you might learn something." So these six small children marched off to the building in the white district, where, up to two weeks before, they would have been turned away at the door. Shyly but doggedly, they went to the children's room and sat down, and soon they were lost in their books. In their own way, they had struck a blow for freedom. The children understood the stakes they were fighting for. . . . The movement was blessed by the fire and excitement brought to it by young people such as these.[61]

The differences between Malcolm and Martin over the relationship of young people to the freedom movement did not fade with time. Conflict erupted again during the March on Washington in the summer of 1963, when the youngsters of SNCC insisted on making a speech that criticized President John F. Kennedy and his administration for dragging their feet on civil rights matters. When conservative leaders and Martin's associates urged the students to purge the speech of its militancy, Malcolm reacted angrily, charging that white liberals were using blacks as "puppets" and "clowns."[62] Martin ignored the attacks, apparently feeling that any response on his part would be used by the press to further divide his people.

The thought of black children losing their lives in the South haunted both Malcolm and Martin, but this seems to have had little to do with their different attitudes toward youth involvement. Far more important were their different perspectives on where responsibility for transforming society rested and on whether young blacks should be taught nonviolence in a disturbingly violent culture. In any case, both men were deeply touched when the bombing of Birmingham's Sixteenth Street Baptist Church resulted in the deaths of four black girls in September 1963. Malcolm charged that the girls, who had been "praying to the same god the white man taught them to pray to," had been "blown apart by people who claimed to be Christians." The government's claim that it could not find the murderers added insult to injury for him.[63] Martin eulogized the girls, calling them "the martyred heroines of a holy crusade for freedom and human dignity." He was convinced that their deaths carried a message for blacks and whites who passively accepted injustice, and he reasoned that God had the power to will some good out of what he termed "one of the most vicious, heinous crimes ever perpetrated against humanity":

> The innocent blood of these little girls may well serve as the redemptive force that will bring new light to this dark city. The holy scripture says, "A little child shall lead them." The death of these little children may lead our whole Southland from the low road of man's inhumanity to man to the high road of peace and brotherhood. These tragic deaths may lead our nation to substitute an aristocracy of character for an aristocracy of color. The spilt blood of these innocent girls may cause the whole citizenry of Birmingham to transform the negative extremes of a dark past into the positive extremes of a bright future. Indeed, this tragic event may cause the white South to come to terms with its conscience.[64]

Malcolm's increasing exposure to young activists in colleges and in the streets made it more and more difficult for him to conform to Elijah Muhammad's policy of complete non-involvement in the struggle for civil rights. He was also pushed along by Black Muslim youth, many of whom had been inspired by Malcolm to join the Nation of Islam and had quietly expressed the need for more progressive thought and action. Moreover, it was clear by the summer of 1963 that Malcolm's influence among black young-sters in the northern ghettoes surpassed that of Martin, as John Lewis of SNCC observed, "I could see Malcolm's appeal, especially to young people who had never been exposed to or had any understanding of the discipline of nonviolence—and also to people who had given up on that discipline. There was no question Malcolm X was tapping into a growing and understandable feeling of restlessness and resentment among America's blacks. Earlier that year, when Dr. King delivered a speech in Harlem, a section of the audience jeered him, chanting, 'We want Malcolm! We want Malcolm!'"[65]

When Malcolm finally declared his independence from the Nation of Is-lam in March 1964, he had developed a perspective on youth in the civil rights movement that more closely approximated Martin's. In other words, he had begun to see even integration-inclined young activists as freedom fighters of great renown. That perspective expanded even more as Malcolm engaged students intellectually and spiritually at Jeddah, Saudi Arabia, the University of Ghana, and other academic institutions abroad and in the United States.[66] The same could be said in some sense of Martin, who always bonded in mind and spirit with young people and who saw students moving beyond a reliance on the principles of the movement to develop their own constructive vision.

The great potential Malcolm and Martin saw in the energy and imagina-tion of students virtually defied the limits placed on age, beauty, and talent. Both ultimately concluded that the forthrightness and unbridled militancy of students constituted America's best hope for becoming a better and more inclusive society. This helps explain why Malcolm met with a delegation from SNCC in the fall of 1964, a meeting that "marked the beginning of a relationship that had a major influence on SNCC and its successors, notably the Black Panther Party for Self-Defense, and shaped the entire Black Power movement." Even more significant was the fact that Malcolm actually praised black and white students who had launched a voter registration drive among African Americans in the South, and he vowed to work with student groups in Harlem to see that "every black face behind every door is registered to vote."[67] Involved in efforts of this nature himself, Martin observed with profound interest this change in Malcolm's outlook. But Martin found it difficult to abandon the notion that Malcolm, given his propensity for explo-sive rhetoric, might have a negative rather than a positive influence on young-sters in the movement.

One of Malcolm's goals in 1964 was to achieve through his newly formed

Organization of Afro-American Unity (OAAU) what Martin was still trying to accomplish through his SCLC, namely, the mobilization of young people for a massive assault on the structures of injustice. "We will have a youth group," said Malcolm at the founding rally of the OAAU in June 1964, and "it will be designed to work out a program for youth in this country, one in which the youth can play an active part":

> We've already issued a call for the students in the colleges and universities across the country to launch their own independent studies of the race problem in the country and then bring their analyses and their suggestions for a new approach back to us so that we can devise an action program geared to their thinking. The accent is on youth because the youth have less stake in this corrupt system and therefore can look at it more objectively, whereas the adults usually have a stake in this corrupt system and they lose their ability to look at it objectively because of their stake in it.[68]

The voting rights campaign in Selma, Alabama, in 1965 revived some of the sharpest disagreements between Malcolm and Martin about the importance of children and youth to the freedom cause. Malcolm was invited to Selma during the campaign by members of SNCC, who were growing increasingly unhappy with Martin's strategy and methods, and the invitation may have been designed to upstage the civil rights leader. Martin was in jail at the time. Several hundred young blacks showed up at the Brown's Chapel African Methodist Episcopal Church to hear Malcolm, despite the skepticism of Martin's aides in SCLC, who thought the Muslim leader might cause a riot. Malcolm recalled, "When I got to Selma I talked to these children. I talked to them. And, you know, I have to say this. I have to expose the man. King's men didn't want me to talk to them. They told me they didn't mind me coming in and all that but they wished that I wouldn't talk to the children. Because they knew what I was going to say. [Laughter] But the children insisted that I be heard. Otherwise, I wouldn't have gotten a hearing at all. And some of the—many of the students from SNCC also insisted that I be heard. This is the only way I got to talk to them."[69]

The treatment of black children during the Selma campaign shook Malcolm, as he later spoke of how they were "run down the road by brute policemen who are nothing but Klansmen." A twelve-year-old girl informed him that cattle prods had been used on her head while she was in jail. But Malcolm refused to blame Martin and the SCLC staff for the brutality, choosing instead to say that they had not acted in wisdom: "Don't you know it's a disgrace for the United States of America to let—to have Martin Luther King, my good friend, the Right Reverend Dr. Martin, in Alabama, using school children to do what the federal government should do. Think of this. Those school children shouldn't have to march. Why Lyndon Johnson is supposed to have troops down there marching. Your children aren't supposed to have to get out there and demonstrate just to vote. Is it that bad? It shows our so-called leaders have been out-maneuvered."[70]

Martin found much to be proud of in the young warriors who joined his nonviolent army in Selma. He actually befriended Sheyann Webb, who was eight, and her friend Rachel West, who was nine, and whose display of commitment and courage exceeded that of many adults who refused to march due to a fear of economic reprisals. "Just keep your marching shoes on," Martin said time and time again to Sheyann and Rachel, "because I'll be calling on you." The girls later collaborated on a book in which Rachel recalled their relationship with Martin during the Selma campaign:

I remember he said something about our singing, shook hands with us and then asked our names. Then he leaned down closer and said to us, "What do you want?" And we said, "Freedom." "What's that?" he says. "I couldn't hear you." So we say, louder this time, "Freedom." And he shakes his head and kind of smiles a little. "I still don't believe I heard what you said." So we laugh, and then real loud we yelled, "We want freedom." "I heard you that time," he says. "You want freedom? Well, so do I." We got to be friends from then on. Every time he'd see us he'd play that little game with us, asking what we wanted, pretending he couldn't hear what we'd say until we were shouting at the top of our lungs, "Freedom." Sometimes during the rallies at Brown Chapel, when Shey and I would sing, he would call us over where he would be sitting at the altar and lift us up on his lap and we'd sit there with him until it was time for him to speak. I'm sure many of the other people envied us. We'd be sitting up there so proud! During the rallies, Shey and I were always at the church early and often we'd be back of the altar listening to Dr. King and the other leaders discussing strategy.[71]

After Selma, the students in SNCC increasingly moved away from Martin's ideas and methods toward those of Malcolm. John Lewis, a member of SNCC's board, was the only leader in the group whose admiration for Martin remained unshakable. As a leader in the Nashville sit-ins in 1960,

Lewis, a student at American Baptist Theological Seminary, had met Martin in Montgomery, and he considered the civil rights leader "a Moses" who used "organized religion and the emotionalism within the Negro church as an instrument, as a vehicle, toward freedom." Lewis's view of Martin was such that he seemed unable at times to separate the actual man from the romantic image. But he did not have the same regard for Malcolm, whom he erroneously dismissed as having no role in the civil rights movement. Others in SNCC embraced Malcolm and saw Martin as part of the problem, as Lewis points out: "The resentment among the SNCC rank and file against Dr. King was almost as strong as the disgust with President Johnson. Both men represented a system that SNCC was fed up with. More than ever, there was pressure put on me—chiefly from Stokely and Courtland Cox—to resign from that board, something I would not dream of doing. I'd been on that board since 1962. I thought it was important to maintain a liaison with Dr. King and the SCLC. . . . Beyond that, I had an extremely deep relationship with Dr. King, and I was not going to give that up. Ever."[72]

Jim Foreman of SNCC strongly disliked Martin, especially since the civil rights leader often received credit that he felt rightfully belonged to student activists. Foreman recommended that SNCC challenge Martin's leadership in the South, a position that even SNCC militants like Stokely Carmichael deemed unwise. Feeling that such a move would be self-defeating, Carmichael suggested that "SNCC should exploit the enthusiasm created by King's presence." As he himself put it, "People loved King. . . . I've seen people in the South climb over each other just to say, 'I touched him! I touched him!' I'm even talking about the young. The old people had more love and respect. They even saw him like a God. These were the people we were working with and I had to follow in his footsteps when I went in there. The people didn't know what was SNCC. They just said, 'You one of Dr. King's men?' 'Yes, Ma'am, I am.'"[73]

The chasm between Martin and the youth in the movement grew even wider when Carmichael and Willie Ricks raised the "black power" cry during a march in Greenwood, Mississippi, in the summer of 1966. Malcolm had been dead for more than a year, but his spirit must have lingered among the youngsters who shouted the slogan. Martin, who walked with the demonstrators, immediately had reservations about the slogan, mainly because he felt that it would alienate white allies, give the impression that movement leaders were advocating black domination, and be interpreted as a call for violence and separatism. He agreed with the concept of black power, but preferred another choice of words.[74] Little did Martin know at that time that the young people, reacting to the shooting of James Meredith, a leader in the desegregation of the University of Mississippi, were actually clamoring for an end to the nonviolent phase of the struggle.

Malcolm had consistently predicted that such a time would come. He had looked forward to the day when young blacks would fight back, and he would have seen this as a hopeful sign. Having a different outlook, Martin feared that in an atmosphere of persistent, unprovoked violence against African Americans, the young people would abandon the nonviolent ethic. In 1966 and 1967, the civil rights leader was constantly confronted by youngsters in the North and South who declared that his methods were anachronistic. His attempts to reason with some young people on the question proved futile at best, especially since the American government was sanctioning the use of violence in Vietnam. The riots that followed in Chicago, Detroit, and other northern ghettoes confirmed Martin's deepest fears, as children and youth took to the streets hurling bricks, bottles, and Molotov cocktails. Another challenge came as Martin led a march in Memphis during the sanitation strike in March 1968. A group of youngsters rioted and shouted, "Black power," a development that left Martin deeply depressed, especially since he had never led a march in which violence occurred.[75]

But Martin's faith in the young remained largely undaunted. However, he was disturbed that the alienation of young people in the society had forced some to be indifferent to the freedom movement. During the last year of his life, he identified three principal groups of youth: "The largest group is struggling to adapt itself to the prevailing values of our society. . . . But even so, they are a profoundly troubled group, and are harsh critics of the status quo." Martin identified the second group as "the radicals," who "range from the moderate to the extreme in the degree to which they want to alter the social system." He called the third group "the hippies," whose "extreme conduct illuminates the negative effect of society's evils on sensitive young people."[76] Even so, he felt that young people would continue to assume leadership in the transformation of society's values and institutions.

Malcolm and Martin saw this as occurring worldwide as well. Malcolm said as much in December 1964, when questioned about his views concerning extremism in the cause of freedom and justice. He declared, "In my opinion the young generation of whites, blacks, browns, whatever else there is, you're living at a time of extremism, a time of revolution, a time when there's got to be a change. People in power have misused it, and now there has to be a change and a better world has to be built, and the only way it's going to be built is with extreme methods."[77]

But the Muslim activist felt that youngsters in Africa and Asia were more involved than those in the United States in revolutionary causes. He did not hesitate to point out that "many of the Congolese revolutionaries are children," and that the guerrillas "being caught by the American soldiers in South Vietnam" are "young people." "Most students are potential revolutionaries," he asserted. "Your Western countries don't have trouble because you have brainwashed them. But in Asia and Africa, students are more politically mature." Convinced that revolutionary action among youth in America had been consciously stifled by those in power, Malcolm cautioned students to develop an independence of thought and action:

> [T]he students have been deceived somewhat in what's known as the civil rights struggle, which was never designed to solve the problem. The students were maneuvered in the direction of thinking the problem was already analyzed, so they didn't try to analyze it for themselves. . . . In my thinking, if the students in this country forget the analysis that has been presented to them, and they went into a huddle and began to research the problem of racism for themselves, independent of politicians and independent of all the foundations (which are a part of the power structure), and did it themselves, then some of their findings would be shocking, but they would see that they would never be able to bring about a solution to racism in this country as long as they are relying on the government to do it. The federal government itself is just as racist as the government in Mississippi, and is more guilty of perpetrating the racist system.[78]

Martin shared much of Malcolm's perspective on the revolutionary activities of students in Africa and Asia. The civil rights leader suggested this much and more in his statements on the world's youth. "Many of the students" in America, "when pressed to express their inner feelings," he commented, "identify themselves with students in Africa, Asia, and South America." Having communicated with students at universities in South Africa, Martin saw in them the greatest possibilities for the transition from apartheid to true democracy in that country.[79] He also observed that black youth in the civil rights movement had been inspired by both African students and leaders who had successfully fought European colonial domination:

The liberation struggle in Africa has been the greatest single international influence on American Negro students. Frequently I hear them say, if their African brothers can break the bonds of colonialism, surely the American Negro can break Jim Crow. African leaders such as President Kwame Nkrumah of Ghana, Governor-General Nnamdi Azikiwe of Nigeria, Dr. Tom Mboya of Kenya, and Dr. Hastings Banda of Nyasaland are popular heroes on most Negro college campuses. Many groups demonstrated or otherwise protested when the Congo leader, Patrice Lumumba, was assassinated. The newspapers were mistaken when they interpreted these outbursts of indignation as "communist-inspired."[80]

Aware of the possible consequences of oppression for succeeding generations, Malcolm and Martin saw great promise in the growing tendency on the part of young black and white Americans to realize the ways in which their destiny intersected with that of other youngsters around the globe. Their recognition that young whites would have to make greater sacrifices in the interest of human freedom was only natural, given the depth of their prophetic insight and their understanding of the structures of oppression. According to Imam Benjamin Karim, Malcolm reasoned that "the white college student was more receptive to change than were his parents. He believed, and tried to emphasize to white students, that they could not follow in the path of their elders and survive in today's world. To illustrate his point, he reminded them of former Prime Minister Macmillan's press conference in New York in which he 'spoke of the changing geography of the world, of the decline of empires, saying that in his own lifetime he had seen England, and other Western powers, shrink from vast empires to second-rate powers.'"[81]

Malcolm's experiences during the last year of his life further convinced him that young whites would be more progressive on the race issue than their parents and grandparents. Although he had been heckled by white students who were exposed to him during his years with the Nation of Islam, many young whites who heard him speak after the split applauded him.[82] Moreover, Malcolm encountered white students who proved their loyalty to the struggle in practical ways. "In many parts of the African continent I saw white students helping black people," he said in February 1965. "I think there are many whites who are sincere, especially at the student level," he said on another occasion. "They just don't know how to show their sincerity." Malcolm was convinced that with young whites, pragmatism or the sense of inevitable change would ultimately assume priority over racial and political conservatism. He asserted: "There are many white people in this country, especially the younger generation, who realize that the injustice that has been done and is being done to black people cannot go on without the chickens coming home to roost eventually. And those white people, even if they are not morally motivated, their intelligence forces them to see that something must be done."[83]

Malcolm urged white students to form groups "ancillary to his own and work among whites to combat prejudice," a suggestion that Martin would not have opposed.[84] But Martin placed more emphasis than Malcolm on the need for interracial student groups to fight inequality and injustice. Having seen white students struggling with blacks in Mississippi and other parts of the South for voting rights and other social justice issues, Martin insisted, "It is extremely significant that in many places the Negro students have found white allies to join in their actions." The civil rights leader tried to reason with young black power advocates who distrusted white students and wanted them out of the movement. At the same time, he understood this attitude on the part of young black militants, especially since many young white people joined the movement "with a kind of messianic faith that they were going to save the Negro and solve all of his problems very quickly." Martin assessed the problem with white student activists in these terms:

> They tended, in some instances, to be rather aggressive and insensitive to the opinions and abilities of the black people with whom they were working; this has been especially true of students. In many cases, they simply did not know how to work in a supporting, secondary role. I think this problem became most evident when young men and women from elite northern universities came down to Mississippi to work with the black students at Tougaloo and Rust colleges, who were not quite as articulate, didn't type quite as fast and were not as sophisticated. Inevitably feelings of white paternalism and black inferiority became exaggerated. The Negroes who rebelled against white liberals were trying to assert their own equality and to cast off the mantle of paternalism.[85]

Although concerned that "the alliance of responsible young people which the movement represented" was falling apart by the late 1960s, Martin remained hopeful that black and white youth might play a leading role "in the shaping of a new world." He and Malcolm could not have been closer at this level of their thinking. Both would be shocked that at the beginning of the twenty-first century, young whites are reported to be more racist than their elders.[86]

Malcolm and Martin ultimately saw their struggles and sacrifices in terms of how they would benefit future generations. Malcolm "was obsessed with the idea that his children and upcoming generations should not have to face the kind of conditions that his generation faced," according to Betty Shabazz. He apologized to youngsters for the complacency and indifference of much of his own generation and, as one of his Muslim associates reports, "he was also optimistic about new black leaders rising up to take his place and the place of others." Martin felt likewise, asserting, on one occasion, "I want young men and young women who are not alive today but who will come into this world with new privileges and new opportunities—I want them to know and see that these new privileges and opportunities did not come without somebody suffering and sacrificing for them."[87]

It is equally true that Malcolm and Martin felt that youngsters in the movement had much to teach their elders. "Children have a lesson adults should learn, to not be ashamed of failing, but to get up and try again," Malcolm once said. "Most of us adults are so afraid, so cautious, so safe, and therefore so shrinking and rigid and afraid that it is why so many humans fail. Most middle-aged adults have resigned themselves to failure." Martin could not have agreed more. Confronted almost daily with the student protester who winked "at the disapproval of a cautious Dean or an ultra-conservative college president," Martin reasoned. "For once, it could be possible to instruct one's own parents, instead of the other way around."[88]

Characterizing Malcolm and Martin: Youthful Reflections from the Head and Heart

Magazine columnist Joe Wood rightly argues, "Dead folks' spirits can be molded to fit many different political agendas."[89] The sheer weight of this statement becomes evident when one realizes that young people from the ultraconservative camp to those who identify with the most radical elements of social movements have turned to Malcolm and Martin for inspiration and a sense of direction over the last six decades. The murder of the two men in the 1960s evoked a range of emotional responses from young people. Some black youngsters wept in silence and called for reconciliation and peaceful coexistence between the races, while others publicly expressed their anger and clamored for the violent overthrow of the racist system. Malcolm was remembered as one who had done so much to raise the consciousness of young blacks regarding their oppressive conditions and the need to change them. Martin was memorialized as a nonviolent soldier who had walked with black children and youth in the cause of freedom. The young of all ages rioted in the hours after Martin's assassination in April 1968, and children in many schools nationwide expressed their loss in poems and other writings.[90]

The reactions to the killing of Malcolm and Martin were far more diverse among young whites. Most were too much a part of the racist system to really agonize over the tragedies, and some actually rejoiced. Ossie Davis, the internationally known black actor, producer, and playwright, who eulogized Malcolm in Harlem on February 27, 1965, received letters from a sixth-grade class of white boys and girls who wondered why he would bestow such an honor upon "a man like Malcolm X."[91] Most white children at that time were not prepared to surrender the racist label they had attached to the Muslim activist. Although a few young whites were deeply saddened by Martin's murder, his struggle on behalf of his people meant that most were not morally and intellectually inclined to see him as being any less of a threat to themselves than Malcolm.

The ideas of Malcolm and Martin became the focus of intense study and discussion among some black and white youngsters in the 1960s and 1970s. The resurgence of black nationalism in this time frame resulted from the ideological influences of students who idolized Malcolm, as evidenced by even a superficial study of Maulana "Ron" Karenga's "US" and the Black Panther Party.[92] Even students in traditionally black colleges in the South explored Malcolm's "ideas as ideological reference points for their engagement in political activities which featured Black Nationalism." For young socialists, black and white, Malcolm was proof that many of the ideas embraced by Fidel Castro could be applied in the United States. In February 1967, Robert L. Allen wrote in the *National Guardian*, "Thousands of young Negroes have read the speeches and autobiography of Malcolm X, and have been deeply influenced by his ideas. Throughout the country a new generation of militant black youths are turning to Malcolm's life and work for inspiration and guidance. Their hope is to bring the revolt of the world's oppressed into the stronghold of the oppressor."[93]

Even young African Americans who had been confronted with negative or distorted images of Malcolm began to reevaluate their thinking. "Like many young black people brought up in a conservative, brainwashed home, I was isolated from the true character of Malcolm's ideas," asserted Tony Thomas of the Organization of Afro-American Students at American University in March 1968. Betty Shabazz was pleased that her husband's ideas had "struck a responsive chord" among black youth, noting that they, like Malcolm, refused to accept the old expression that "You can't fight the system." Malcolm's widow received countless letters in the late 1960s and the 1970s from black teenagers about her husband's contributions to the human struggle. Many of these students vowed to keep Malcolm's memory alive through educational activities and schools named in his honor.[94]

The attention given to Martin's ideas and methods among young blacks and whites was equally impressive. Courses on the subject had been developed in colleges and seminaries by the mid-1970s. Martin's daughter Yolanda, who was attending Smith College in Massachusetts during this period, was constantly asked to explain the African-American struggle and her father's role in it: "At Smith anytime anything came up involving Black people, including ideological differences between Daddy and Malcolm X, I was expected to comment on it." She quickly learned to say, "No comment," when approached with such questions, insisting that "Daddy didn't need defending by me." Although questions about the relevance of Martin's ideas continued to surface in debates among young people, the general view was that he had given his life for a noble cause. This perspective helps explain why some black youngsters strongly influenced by Martin were calling for a national holiday in his memory a decade before the issue was seriously discussed in the halls of the U.S. Congress.[95]

The attitudes of young Americans concerning Malcolm and Martin in the 1980s were impacted by a wave of political and religious conservatism. Reaganite Republicanism brought not only a resurgence of raw racism, new attacks on affirmative action guidelines and policies, and an assault on liberalism, but also challenges to the images of Malcolm and Martin as cultural heroes.[96] Although African-American students struggled to keep memories of Malcolm alive, only faint echoes of his voice could be heard in the national public discourse. In contrast, discussions of Martin among the young were often clouded by charges that the civil rights leader was a womanizer and traitor to his country, allegations pushed by conservative media sources, white scholars, and politicians like Jesse Helms and Pat Buchanan.[97] Strangely enough, such claims surfaced amidst the congressional debates concerning the King national holiday in the early 1980s, and they continued even as Stevie Wonder mobilized youngsters in an impassioned plea to Congress to support the holiday bill. The honor was bestowed upon Martin by a Senate vote in 1983, a development that occurred partly because young people continued to view him as "a symbol of hope" and refused to let the dreamer and his ideas die.[98]

But the "new racism" that surfaced on predominantly white campuses in the 1980s, and extended through the 1990s, seemed to call into question many of the values of Malcolm and Martin.[99] Black students across the country confronted violence, ostracism, and racist flyers from white classmates who resented efforts to promote diversity and multiculturalism through curricula, faculty recruitment, the establishment of black cultural centers, and other areas of campus life. It was in this atmosphere that Malcolm's message resonated with new vitality among black students, "enjoying a prominence he never knew as a preaching prophet." The X symbol and the face of Malcolm appeared on the caps, jackets, T-shirts, and bags of children and youth, a trend reinforced by the appearance of Spike Lee's film on Malcolm in 1992. This "renaissance of Malcolm X" was further strengthened by the exposure of black students to Afrocentric perspectives in university and seminary classrooms. Rejecting black neoconservative voices like Thomas Sowell, Clarence Thomas, Shelby Steele, and Ward Connerly, many black students expressed pride in Malcolm "as an ancestral champion of our rights as African Americans." "Malcolm has come to symbolize the frustration, rage, and impatience of a new generation of African Americans who feel locked out of the system," concluded the black scholar Manning Marable of Columbia University in 1992. Such a perspective on the Muslim leader was largely grounded in the sense that the civil rights revolution led by Martin helped some African Americans while leaving the masses of the poor behind. Moreover, this view owed much to the conviction that Malcolm's self-defense ethic was far more healthy, psychologically and physically, for African Americans than Martin's nonviolent ethic, a position held by the New Black Panther Party today.[100]

In the 1990s, many African-American youths were guilty of what Patricia Hill Collins termed "transporting Malcolm X uncritically into our own time." While there were African Americans who felt that Malcolm "did more harm than good" to "the nonviolent quest for civil rights led" by Martin, many young blacks offered a contrary opinion. "People are waking up to the fact that what Malcolm said was right," shouted Tyrell Diggs, a twenty-three-year-old Texan in 1992. Similar statements concerning Martin could be heard among schoolchildren during Black History Month celebrations, but seldom by blacks of Diggs's generation.[101]

The disagreements between the young concerning the importance of Malcolm and Martin have continued unabated since their deaths. There has long been the tendency to put the two leaders on opposite sides of the pole—to make one more acceptable than the other. That tendency played out in strange and subtle ways during exchanges that occurred between Martin's daughter Yolanda and her black classmates during her first year at Smith College. Arriving at a time when bitterness and hostility existed between black and white students, Yolanda, who chose to avoid the conflict as much as possible, was told that she "wasn't militant enough." "I knew you would be a Tom," one black student bellowed. The conversation then turned to the subject of her father, who, as the student put it, "wasn't like Malcolm X."[102] Benjamin Davis, a twenty-one-year-old college student, expressed the conviction in a 1992 interview that "most people have unfairly classified Malcolm X as a hatemonger in order to lend credence to King's 'gentle' civil rights movement." A conversation between youngsters in a Chicago store concerning the riots in Los Angeles in April 1992 took an interesting turn "when someone in the group wondered aloud what Martin Luther King Jr. would have done." "Forget King," cried one teenager. "Suppose Malcolm X was there." The group then "erupted in this chorus of 'Yeah' and 'That's right.'"[103] Clayborne Carson is right in saying that Malcolm and Martin still symbolize opposing ideological positions "that divide African Americans. Their clashes set the tone for internecine battles that have continued to disrupt Black communities. Which path to social justice is correct? By any means necessary? Or nonviolence? Integration or separation?"[104]

These questions form the broad outlines of the discussions among young people concerning Malcolm and Martin today. Such discussions, which occur in classrooms and on the streets, are important in that they are keeping alive conversation about the best means to win freedom. They are also significant for other reasons. "It is ironic that Black youth in their search for a more militant icon than King have not only resurrected Malcolm X but forced scholars to pursue a more serious presentation of King's thinking and activities," writes William Sales.[105] Be that as it may, the tendency to choose one leader over the other is counterproductive if it grows out of a rank oversimplification of, a misrepresentation of, and a lack of familiarity with both. This is too often the case with young blacks who pick Malcolm over Martin and young whites who select Martin over Malcolm. To be sure, there are limited truths implicit in the philosophies and methods of both, and each has something to tell us in the continuing struggle to shape a new world for young people. Because they were rapidly moving toward each other ideologically at the time of Malcolm's death, it is impossible to embrace one without the other. Attallah and Yolanda, the daughters of Malcolm and Martin, put it best when explaining *Of One Mind*, a play about the "similar goals" of their fathers: "We want people to learn from our play that to be pro-Malcolm X doesn't mean that one has to automatically be anti-Martin Luther King Jr. or vice versa."[106]

Young people will continue to disagree concerning the intellectual meaning and cultural significance of Malcolm and Martin. The situation could not be otherwise in an emotionally charged society in which many of the problems the two men addressed still haunt children and youth. Joe Wood's assertion that "Malcolm's spirit wears the face of each of its interpreters" applies to Martin as well. But young people would do well to remember that while their interpretations of both men may be full of information and hard insights, they are also marred by flaws and distortions.[107]

Teaching Malcolm and Martin: Revisiting Their Legacies for Young People

The legacies of Malcolm and Martin provide rich and powerful sources of wisdom and insight for young people of all ages, races, nationalities, and religious and political persuasions. Both men spoke consciously and directly to virtually every formidable problem confronting young people today, from the question of violence and human destruction to the issues of drug and alcohol abuse, sexual promiscuity and teenage pregnancy, self-esteem and community identity, and multicultural education. Both shared ideas about how future generations might deal with the stark realities and challenges of a rapidly changing world. Michael E. Dyson has this and more in mind when he explores the relevance of both Malcolm and Martin for the young hip-hop generation.[108]

Several levels of relevance surface when Malcolm's and Martin's legacies for young people are seriously considered. One relates to the pervasive problem of violence in the culture and how it might be confronted and addressed. Intragroup violence and murders among young black males, many of which are drug- and gang-related, have reached epidemic proportions since the 1950s and 1960s. Statistics show that homicide is the leading cause of death among black males between the ages of fifteen and twenty-four and that the violent crime victimization rate of black youths is 20 to 30 percent higher than that of whites. Violence among young whites is equally problematic, as the recent school shootings in Pearl, Mississippi, Jonesboro, Arkansas, Littleton, Colorado, and other small towns demonstrate. Much of the problem stems from the gratuitous violence on television, in movies, and in other areas of our popular culture. But perhaps more important are the many mixed messages about violence that children and youth receive from parents, national leaders, and adults generally. Consistently exposed to violent clashes in the home between parents, to a nation that cherishes its nuclear arsenal and uses its military might at the slightest provocation, and to men and women who turn to violence to deal with conflict in the workplace, it is not surprising that many teenagers are ignoring the teachings of adults on nonviolence while using violence to settle their own disputes.[109]

Malcolm and Martin strongly opposed the forms of youth violence that pervade society and culture today. They constantly urged young people, particularly in the African-American community, to develop the kind of self-respect and sense of responsibility that render violence unnecessary. Malcolm saw cultural awareness programs as being enormously important in this regard, and he included them in his OAAU to assist children and youth "who get into trouble" due to acts of violence.[110] Martin agreed with such an approach, but, in ways atypical of Malcolm, he also called upon educational institutions at all levels to stress the nonviolent resolution of conflict. By sharing his story, we teach the young that compassion, peacemaking, and community are far more ethical and beneficial than revenge, violence, and discord.[111] In keeping with this conviction, the King Center for Nonviolent Social Change has published *An Infusion Model for Teaching Dr. Martin Luther King Jr.'s Nonviolent Principles in Schools.*[112]

The false images of the "violent Malcolm" and the "nonviolent Martin" have been projected in ways that only confuse and mislead the young. Malcolm's ability to transcend a violent past to become a great leader remains a powerful lesson to youngsters who feel that their dignity rests on their capacity to strike out at others. Children need to know that while Malcolm and Martin were exposed to violence throughout their lives, they did not turn to acts of violence as leaders of their people. They were willing to die by violence, but refused to kill. Equally significant is the fact that during their years of involvement in the freedom struggle, gang activity and other forms of intragroup violence among young African Americans declined significantly. Although Malcolm affirmed in uncompromising terms the right to self-defense, a position consistent with American values, he agreed very much with Martin's image of the society in which people coexist peacefully.[113]

The young in our society need to know that Malcolm and Martin stood against crime and the scourge of drugs and alcohol. This is especially important in a nation where one in every three young black males encounters the criminal justice system and where African Americans in general are disproportionately represented in prisons. With the rapid increase of illegal drug use and related crime, fueled by high rates of poverty and the lack of education and sufficient job opportunities, there are more young black men in prison than in college.[114] Malcolm and Martin never envisioned such a disturbing situation, and both would view it as one dimension of the society's racist assault on African Americans. Moreover, both were aware of the extent to which young black men, even in their own time, were the victims of racial profiling, police corruption, injustice in the court system, and capital punishment.

Having spent years in prison due to his own involvement in drug abuse and crime, Malcolm is a superb example of how young criminals might transform themselves and become productive citizens.[115] In much stronger language than Martin, Malcolm attacked the system for making drugs highly available to young blacks and for turning them to prostitution and other criminal acts, and he committed his OAAU to fighting such evils. He even encouraged black youngsters to chase the drug pushers out of Harlem, a challenge that is still relevant, since law enforcement officials so often fail to eliminate the problem in inner-city areas. Echoing Malcolm's insistence that "the Negro is not criminal by nature," that "criminality is environmental, not racial," Martin also placed much of the burden for eliminating drugs and crime on the shoulders of young blacks, though he also recognized, at the same time, that such efforts would be largely futile as long as racial discrimination and economic injustice existed.[116] African-American Muslims and Christians are beginning to reflect Malcolm's and Martin's hopes and dreams for young blacks through their joint efforts to address the drug activity and criminal justice issues that have already destroyed too many lives.[117]

More attention should be devoted to what Malcolm and Martin said about the devastating impact of poverty and economic injustice on children and youth. Nothing could be more relevant in a world where an estimated 10 million children die annually of starvation, malnutrition, and other poverty-related causes.[118] Insisting that "an outsider can't take care of your children as well as you can," Malcolm urged African Americans to develop their own businesses, to hire one another, to be supportive of each other in business ventures, to be frugal, and to provide for the basic needs of their offspring. He knew that the economic marginalization that put millions of young people at risk stemmed largely from a vicious system of economic exploitation, a view heightened by his sense of his own struggle with grinding poverty in childhood. Martin could not have agreed more, and he advocated controllable birth rates and massive federal expenditures to help meet the needs of children who are undernourished, ill housed, shabbily clad, and without proper medical care.[119] The strong emphasis that he and Malcolm put on responsible parenthood and the economic well-being of young people remains a challenge in a society where teenage pregnancy runs high and where children are increasingly neglected, abandoned, or born with HIV or a crack addiction.

That challenge is no less formidable when it comes to racism. Malcolm and Martin warned black and white youngsters that racism was the greatest threat to their futures and that their failure to deal promptly and constructively with this corrosive evil would virtually ensure the decline and ultimate fall of America. Both men held that racism could be eliminated in time if youngsters developed a healthy and positive self-love, a love for God and for spiritual values, and an altruistic concern for all humans. Malcolm felt that white students might better attack the problem by challenging it in their own communities, although he was ultimately as receptive as Martin to interracial student groups designed to fight racism.[120] Unfortunately, their advice regarding the need to create a society free of racial discrimination remains virtually unheard of among most young, educated whites. Blacks, Jews, and other minorities are still verbally and physically attacked on predominantly white campuses, and some young whites are openly involved with the Skinheads, the Aryan Nations, Neo-Nazis, the Ku Klux Klan, paramilitary groups, and other forces of hatred.[121]

Perhaps the best answer to the range of problems and challenges confronting young people today rests in what Malcolm and Martin would call "a revolution of values and priorities." Both felt that such a revolution could occur if the society truly invested in the intellect and character of the young and of generations yet unborn. For them, this invariably involved exposure to the type of education that encourages critical thinking and the importance of translating new ideas and visions into practical action. While challenging students with the ideal of the intellectual-activist type, Malcolm and Martin knew that revolution must be brought into the educational system before it can be successful in the social, political, and economic spheres of a society.[122] But the American system of education is not yet devoted to promoting the kind of critical thinking and/or revolutionary training that Malcolm and Martin advocated. In most instances, the young are taught to be accommodationists, not critical thinkers and social change agents.

The ideas, activities, and contributions of Malcolm and Martin are not being properly taught in schools. Consequently, youngsters from the preschool to the college levels are deprived of important lessons from the two men about social evil and how it might be challenged and transcended. The position that most among the white, educated cultural elite are taking on the issues of multicultural education and political correctness suggests that this lack of exposure will not end without a struggle comparable to what took place in the 1950s and 1960s. In keeping with the spirit of Malcolm and Martin, youngsters would do well to place greater demands on the American educational and religious establishments, insisting that they be prepared intellectually and ethically to create a world in which people can live and function without fear of human differences. This is the task to which youngsters are called today.

The Great Debate

Multiethnic Democracy or National Liberation

What to the American slave is your Fourth of July? I answer: a day that reveals to him, more than all other days in the year, the gross injustice and cruelty of which he is the constant victim. To him, your celebration is a sham: your boasted liberty, an unholy license; your national greatness, swelling vanity.
Frederick Douglass[1]

I still think today as yesterday that the color line is a great problem of this century. But today I see more clearly than yesterday that back of the problem of race and color, lies a greater problem which both obscures and implements it: and that is the fact that so many civilized persons are willing to live in comfort even if the price of this is poverty, ignorance and disease of the majority of their fellowmen.
W.E.B. Du Bois.[2]

In 1998, Black Entertainment Television aired a special program titled "What If Malcolm and Martin Had Lived?" The program raised another question: "What if Malcolm and Martin had joined forces in the human rights struggle?" These two questions elicited powerful ideas, sentiments, and call-in questions from the viewing audience. In addition to eliciting strong sentiments from the general population, the Great Debate over El-Shabazz and King is also reflective of the emerging scholarship. Scholars are starting to realize that King and El-Shabazz cannot be studied separately. They must be seen in relationship to each other. In the struggle to overcome human oppression, it is not an existential choice of "either King or El-Shabazz" but an affirmative choice of "both King and El-Shabazz." James Cone writes, "Martin's and Malcolm's movement toward each other is a clue that neither one can be fully understood or appreciated without serious attention to the other. Again, they 'complemented' and 'corrected' each other;

each spoke a truth about America that cannot be fully comprehended without the insights of the other. Indeed, if Americans of all races intend to create a just and peaceful future, then they must listen to both Martin and Malcolm."[3]

The Historical and Socio-Existential Roots of the Great Debate

Perhaps the most fruitful analysis of the King and El-Shabazz phenomenon is the holistic model, which takes into account the interconnections and unity of their ideas. What appears to be a juxtaposition of King and El-Shabazz is in essence an interconnection. They are really opposite sides of the same coin. If we use the geometry of a circle to illustrate the holistic model, by analogy King's approach of integration represents 180 degrees of the circle, and El-Shabazz's approach of nationalism represents the other 180 degrees. Each leader represents a constituency and reality construction that constitutes 180 degrees of the circle of the total human rights struggle. Therefore, if their followers united today, the circle of human liberation would be complete.

They are often viewed as theological and philosophical opponents: King the eloquent orator for Christianity and integration, and El-Shabazz the eloquent debater for Islam and nationalism. The creative and dynamic tension between their respective paradigms mirrors the historiography of the protracted struggle of African Americans for freedom, justice, and equality. This clash of ideas also reflects a cosmic and historical Great Debate between the thesis of a multiethnic democracy and the antithesis of national liberation. The Great Debate is rooted in a long history of African-American leaders who offered essentially different diagnoses of the afflictions of their people and who proposed fundamentally different prescriptions for those afflictions. This tradition of debate extends as far back as the late eighteenth century, when the Christian preachers Jupiter Hammon and Richard Allen advocated different approaches to the problem of slavery. Hammon urged blacks to accommodate and to "bear slavery with patience," and Allen called for agitation on the part of northern free blacks while boycotting slave-made goods.[4]

Echoes are also detected in debates that occurred between black leaders in the 1840s. In 1841, the Baptist layman and integrationist William Whipper published letters accusing blacks who started separate and independent churches and other institutions of succumbing to the evils of "color-phobia" and "complexional distinctions," a position firmly rejected by the black nationalist called Sidney, who supported the creation of black churches and who insisted that African Americans must rely on their own values, perceptions, energies, and resources to overcome oppression. Also in the 1840s, the integrationist Frederick Douglass (1818–95) clashed with the nationalist Henry H. Garnet (1815–82) over the question of the practicality and morality of violence in the struggle against slavery. Douglass rejected violent rebellion and called for moral suasion and abolitionist agitation, while Garnet urged slaves to rise up and destroy their masters. These leaders actually set the boundaries and identified the critical issues for debates between Booker T. Washington and W.E.B. Du Bois, King and El-Shabazz, and King and the Bookerite and Baptist leader Joseph H. Jackson.[5]

The debate between Washington and Du Bois is most commonly viewed as establishing the context for the later debate between El-Shabazz and King. King himself confronted questions about this, but he once noted, "The debate between Booker T. Washington and W.E.B. Du Bois was much more vigorous than the debate taking place today." One scholar suggests that the debate between Martin and Malcolm was not as intense as that between Martin and the progressive accommodationist Joseph H. Jackson, who opposed King's nonviolent activism and civil disobedience. The contention is that the clash between King and Jackson, not that between King and Malcolm, was "in spirit a feud," "a replay of the Booker T. Washington–William E. B. Du Bois conflict."[6]

Because of his extraordinarily long life, Du Bois (1868–1963) was a contemporary of Booker T. Washington (1856–1915), King, and El-Shabazz. In this regard his life is unique in the annals of the Great Debate. If the Great Debate is the dialectical tension between assimilation vs. nationalism, then his life went through each of these stages, from the founding of the National Association for the Advancement of Colored People (NAACP) to his later involvement with Pan-Africanism and socialism and his citizenship in the Republic of Ghana.[7] Du Bois's ultimate goal was a multiethnic democracy in which race, class, gender, and religion would not be barriers to equal opportunity in society. His call for a sustained struggle to gain civil rights and political power clearly contradicted Booker T. Washington's insistence that African Americans abandon these pursuits while accommodating the racist and oppressive society.

El-Shabazz and King boldly recapitulated the classical arguments for equality, freedom, and justice within the confines of their own theoretical frameworks. King argued from the Christian and integrationist background, and El-Shabazz articulated arguments from the Islamic and nationalist traditions. Their unimpeachable logic resonated with freedom-loving people around the world. In a certain way, they were fraternal twins cosmically linked in the intergenerational transmission of Maat (truth, justice, righteousness, peace, balance, and harmony).[8]

What is the Great Debate? It is the historical and existential debate between two dominant schools of thought with respect to the freedom and human rights struggle of Africans on the continent and in the African diaspora. In the nineteenth century, the debate was largely between assimilation and repatriation. In the twentieth century, the debate was largely between integration and nationalism. As global African historiography marches into the twenty-first century, these two historical and existential schools of thought are converging and intersecting. Both traditions are starting to embrace more passionately the need for African self-determination. The integrationists and the nationalists are beginning to find common cultural, economic, and political grounds. It further appears that there is a dialogue between these two schools of thought on the questions of cultural identity, economic self-determination, and unity.

The Great Debate is treated here as a function of the dialectical tension between the advocates for a multiethnic democracy and the advocates for African national liberation. King's movement and vision focused on a multiethnic democracy that ultimately would advance the United States toward a beloved community of brotherhood and sisterhood. The civil rights movement functioned as the womb that carried the embryo of this futuristic multiethnic democracy, for it was King's unshakable belief that only "just and moral means could achieve just and moral ends."[9] From a Hegelian perspective, he believed the ends preexisted in the means. Stated differently, the means are the ends in process. With this in mind, the idea with King was that only an integrated and nonviolent struggle (means) could result in an integrated society or a beloved community (ends).

El-Shabazz's vision and movement were rooted in a universal Islam and Pan-African nationalism aimed at uniting all Muslims and all Africans. As he saw it, this Pan-Islamic and Pan-African strategy would ultimately set the stage for the unity of the human family. His conversion to mainstream Islam taught him the oneness of Allah, the oneness of creation, and the oneness of the human family.[10] Out of this realization, El-Shabazz's goal was the creation of one world with peace and justice for all, a vision similar to the one promoted by King.

History without sociology is empty, and sociology without history is blind. Before we proceed with any further analysis of the Great Debate, it is absolutely necessary to say more in terms of putting this phenomenon in proper historical context. El-Shabazz made an excellent case for historical analysis: "Of all our studies, history is best qualified to reward our research. And when you see that you've got problems, all you have to do is examine the historic method used all over the world by others who have problems similar to yours. Once you see how they got theirs straight, then you know how you can get yours straight."[11] El-Shabazz fully appreciated the power of historiography as a guiding instrument in restoring, analyzing, and organizing the collective memory of his people.

The late John Henrik Clarke, a close friend of El-Shabazz, conceptualized the role of history in this manner: "The history of Africans in the Americas and in the Caribbean Islands is incomplete without an examination of the African past. This background is indispensable to an intelligent approach to African-American history. . . . History is a clock that people use to tell their political and cultural time of day. It is also a compass that people use to find themselves on the map of human geography."[12] Therefore, this study of the Great Debate as a phenomenon and unit idea is informed and guided by historiography and the sociology of knowledge.

The Great Debate is the ideological and philosophical dialogue that emerged when Africans were alienated from their homelands by military conquest, slavery, and colonization. It is also the Zeitgeist (spirit of the times) in the historiography of Africans as they struggled to reconcile the creative tensions between assimilation and repatriation in the eighteenth and nineteenth centuries and integration and nationalism in the twentieth century. The sociology of knowledge mode of analysis is premised on three fundamental propositions: (1) all knowledge is a social product; (2) all knowledge is derived from specific categories or social class positions (cultural and social groups, etc.); and (3) all knowledge is constructed in the process of social interaction.[13] This theoretical framework for the sociology of knowledge can be found in Karl Mannheim's classic work, *Ideology and Utopia*. It is an accepted axiom of social science that human beings are not born with knowledge of their culture. The acquisition of knowledge is experiential (direct and indirect), existential, and cumulative.

The cognitive categories and social character of human knowledge are differentiated and stratified by one's culture, socioeconomic status, ideological orientation, religious beliefs, and core values. Ethnicity and race in this case are social products of culture and socialization. Therefore, if all knowledge is a social product, race and racism are social artifacts and not genetic transmissions or biological traits.[14]

Frantz Fanon pointed out the interconnection between racism and culture. He maintains that "the racist in a culture with racism is therefore normal. He has achieved a perfect harmony of economic relations and ideology. The idea that one forms of man, to be sure, is never totally dependent on economic relations; in other words—and this must not be forgotten—on relations existing historically and geographically among men and groups." Fanon elaborates this thesis to a point of closure: "To study the relations of racism and culture is to raise the question of their reciprocal action. If culture is the combination of motor and mental behavior patterns arising from the encounter of man with nature and with his fellow-man, it can be said that racism is indeed a cultural element. There are thus cultures with racism and cultures without racism."[15] The dynamics of the interactions between culture and racism, then, must be kept in mind. It informs with clarity the details of a sociology of knowledge analysis of the genesis of the religious and ideological socialization of El-Shabazz and King.

An application of the sociology of knowledge to the global African situation can be found in Andrew Jackson's dissertation, "The Sociology of Pan-Africanism" (1974), which examines Pan-Africanism within the contexts of culture, society, political ideology, economic organization, and social movements. This work is considerably more relevant to a study of El-Shabazz than it is to an examination of King's politics.

King and El-Shabazz were differentiated by socioeconomic status, formal education, geography, and religion. King was shaped by life in the segregated South, the Baptist faith, Ebenezer Baptist Church, integrationism, Morehouse College, Crozer Theological Seminary, and the Boston University School of Theology.[16] El-Shabazz was shaped by his Garveyite parents, broken family life, the streets of the North, prison, the Nation of Islam, and ultimately Sunni Islam.[17] Each man's stages of development prepared him for his particular destiny. Moreover, both were brilliant leaders who were at the right place at the right time, and they were more than equal to the task at hand.

The fundamental alienation of Africans from their minds, names, religions, lands, and culture occurred when Africa was invaded by foreigners. The first wave came from the Arabian peninsula (the Hyskos), followed by the Greeks and Romans from the Western world during the period of ancient

Kemet (Egypt).[18] Next came the Arabs, spreading the Islamic religion.[19] Then Europeans began colonizing and capturing slaves, thus creating the trans-Atlantic slave trade and eventually colonialism and neocolonialism.[20] When African captives were transported and enslaved on foreign soil, the African community was compartmentalized into two global regions, the continent and the African diaspora. This remained uppermost in both El-Shabazz's and King's thinking as they fashioned a philosophy and method that embraced the need for the liberation of all peoples of African descent.

While most Africans remained on the continent under colonialism, and continued the intergenerational transmission of the culture and history of their ancestors, those who were enslaved lost physical contact with the indigenous cultures of the African motherland. Alienation of Africans by foreign cultures from the white Western world became the crucible that gave birth to the Great Debate. The cultural and psychological ramifications of these fundamental alienations are found in W.E.B Du Bois's concept of the double consciousness:

> After the Egyptian and Indian, the Greek and Roman, the Teuton and Mongolian, the Negro is a sort of seventh son, born with a veil, and gifted with second-sight in this American world,—a world which yields him no true-consciousness, but only lets him see himself through the revelation of the other world. It is a peculiar sensation, this double-consciousness, this sense of always looking at one's self through the eyes of others, of measuring one's soul by the tape of a world that looks on in amused contempt and pity. One ever feels his two-ness, . . . an American, a Negro; two souls, two thoughts, two unreconciled strivings; two warring ideals in one dark body, whose dogged strength alone keeps it from being torn asunder.[21]

The double consciousness is useful in understanding the conscious and subconscious dimensions of the psychological impulse of the Great Debate. These connections are essential to any serious understanding of the El-Shabazz/King dialectic.

Africans in the United States are as ambivalent about their cultural identity as they are about their citizenship as Americans. Always mindful of this ambivalence, King elaborated further on the Du Boisian concept of the double consciousness:

> Every man must ultimately confront the question "Who am I?," and seek to answer it honestly. One of the first principles of personal adjust-

ment is the principle of self-acceptance. The Negro's greatest dilemma is that in order to be healthy he must accept his ambivalence. The Negro is the child of two cultures—Africa and America. The problem is that in the search for wholeness all too many Negroes seek to embrace only one side of their natures. Some, seeking to reject their heritage, are ashamed of their color, ashamed of black art and music, and determine what is beautiful and good by the standards of white society. They end up frustrated and without cultural roots. Others seek to reject everything American and to identify totally with Africa, even to the point of wearing African clothes. But this approach leads also to frustration because the American Negro is not an African. The old Hegelian synthesis still offers the best answer to many of life's dilemmas. The American Negro is neither totally African nor totally Western. He is Afro-American, a true hybrid, a combination of two cultures.[22]

El-Shabazz's perspective on the double consciousness was quite different, since he essentially rejected the claim that his people were truly Americans:

And I believe this, that if we migrated back to Africa culturally, philosophically, psychologically, while remaining here physically, the spiritual bond that would develop between us and Africa through this cultural, philosophical and psychological migration, so-called migration, would enhance our position here, because we would have our contacts with them acting as roots or foundations behind us. You never will have a foundation in America. You're out of your mind if you think that this government is ever going to back you and me up in the same way that it backed others up. They'll never do it. It's not in them.[23]

James Cone takes the double consciousness model a step further while specifically relating it to the Great Debate between the two leaders:

Martin and Malcolm represented the two sides in W.E.B. Du Bois's concept of double identity—they represented, respectively, the American and African, the two warring ideas struggling to make sense out of the involuntary presence of Africans in North America. During the early part of their participation in the black freedom movement, their answers to Du Bois's question, "What am I?" were clear, emphatic, and opposite: "American" was Martin's answer and "African" was Malcolm's. The battle between them, to a large extent, was fought in the white media, which portrayed them as adversaries. But they were not.

On the contrary, they were like two soldiers fighting their enemies from different angles of vision, each pointing out the other's blind spots and correcting the other's errors. They needed each other, for they represented—and continue to represent—the "yin and yang" deep in the soul of black America.[24]

These two classical arguments are the epitome of the Great Debate at the cultural and psychological levels of consciousness. They are also indicative of the "identity crisis" faced by many African Americans daily. Hence, this "identity crisis," as Malcolm and Martin often noted, has produced psychological conflicts that are deeply rooted in the collective unconscious of African Americans. These subterranean traumas have made personal, collective, and cultural identity extremely difficult.[25] Moreover, this social-psychological dynamic has contributed to the complexity of developing strategies of African-American unity for the achievement of freedom, justice, and equality. It has further exacerbated the economic, legal, moral, political, and social dimensions of this situation. The polarities of this dialectical problem circumscribe a continuum ranging from a thesis of assimilation into white Anglo-Saxon culture to an antithesis of repatriation back to the African motherland. Malcolm and Martin reflected this in remarkable ways.

At the level of individual consciousness, the antecedent of the Great Debate is the ancient psychological question "Who am I?" Similarly, at the level of collective consciousness, the antecedent of the Great Debate is the ancient sociological question "Who are we?" In the context of African culture, this existential dilemma is resolved in the proposition that "I am because we are." It is the "we are" and not the "I am" that has primacy in the cultural construction of African social reality, as El-Shabazz often declared. The interaction between individual identity and collective identity gives birth to the Great Debate phenomenon. This complex phenomenon has cultural, economic, philosophical, political, psychological, religious, and sociological dimensions. All of these dimensions are negatively or positively affected by alienation, ambivalence, anxiety, duality, and marginality in the individual and collective psyche. Oppressed Africans around the world experience a psychological civil war with the individual psyche and a violent sociological war of "economic exploitation, political oppression, and social degradation in society."[26] This repression of the African personality and freedom is the essential impulse for the Great Debate.

A careful examination of the African struggle for freedom and human rights will reveal two general orientations: (1) adaptation and inclusion in the dominant society, and (2) cultural resistance and separation from the dominant society. The leadership and movements within these two orientations are differentiated and stratified by socioeconomic class, ideology, and values. In general, integrationist movements originate from the African middle class, and nationalist movements originate from the masses. However, intellectuals tend to provide the leadership for both orientations.[27]

The Great Debate between El-Shabazz and King was not only driven by religion and ideology; it had a powerful class dimension as well. King was from the black middle class, and El-Shabazz identified himself as a member of the working class. Their different class identifications and religious, cultural, and political ideologies reflected their social reality constructions. In part for rhetorical purposes, El-Shabazz highlighted the class differences that had divided African Americans since slavery, making it clear that he was a man of the masses:

> You have to read the history of slavery to understand this. There were two kinds of Negroes. There was that old house Negro and the field Negro. And the house Negro always looked out for his master. When the field Negroes got too much out of line, he held them back in check. He put them back on the plantation. . . . And today you still have house Negroes and field Negroes. I'm a field Negro. If I can't live in the house as a human being, I'm praying for a wind to come along. If the master won't treat me right and he's sick, I'll call the doctor to go in the other direction. But if all of us are going to live as human beings, then I'm for a society of human beings that can practice brotherhood.[28]

The class contradictions between the religion and ideology of King and of El-Shabazz were clear and profound. They fundamentally determined their paradigms and epistemologies. On the issue of culture, the differences were not a matter of kind but of degree. They both were fully incorporated into African-American culture, but often at different levels due to class distinctions.

Historically, the parameters of the Great Debate are circumscribed by the creative and dialectical tension between integration and nationalism within the African-American diaspora. It is at this point of contention that the Great Debate between King and El-Shabazz intersect with the ebb and flow of African world historiography. Their ideas and beliefs intersect like the confluence of the Blue and White Nile Rivers in the city of Khartoum, Sudan, and after their respective enlightenments, their ideas and beliefs climax in a synthesis and flow in the same stream as the Nile River flows from the point of confluence into the Mediterranean Ocean.

The Great Debate is clearly dramatized in the unique plight of the African diaspora in the United States. However, it is also manifested in the African motherland. Jacob Carruthers succinctly states the issues:

> The dialogue among African thinkers about getting out of the mess in which African peoples have been for the last "2000 seasons" (to use Armah's idea) has been remarkably consistent. When Harold Cruse, in his *Crisis of the Negro Intellectual,* identified the two streams of thought among African Americans, he aptly captured the essence of the worldwide African debate. For him, the integrationist and the nationalist streams represented the most fundamental division among us. We must, of course, point out that among continental Africans the nationalist designation has absorbed the former integrationists who indeed have in many cases dominated the African nations. So much is this the case that today the more proper designations of the two camps should be something like African traditionalists vs. European assimilationists, i.e., those who want to resume African civilization after a long disruption vs. those who want to continue to Europeanize Africa as rapidly as possible.[29]

King envisioned a multiethnic democracy that would ultimately transform the United States and the "world house" into a beloved community with equal rights, social justice, shared power, and respect for human differences. El-Shabazz envisioned the global unity of the Muslim ummah and the African world community which would ultimately set the stage for the unity of the human family. Both men did a critical analysis of the particular contradictions within the United States and also of the universal contradictions within the international community of nations, and this heavily informed their pursuits of the ideal nation and world.

These two leaders began to converge on ultimate goals but consistently differed on methods and strategies. El-Shabazz stated the case in this manner:

> All of our people have the same goals, the same objective. That objective is freedom, justice, equality. All of us want recognition and respect as human beings. We don't want to be integrationists. Nor do we want to be separationists. We want to be human beings. Integration is only a method that is used by some groups to obtain freedom, justice, equality and respect as human beings. Separation is only a method that is used

by other groups to obtain freedom, justice, equality or human dignity.
. . . Our people have made the mistake of confusing the methods with
the objectives. As long as we agree on objectives, we should never fall
out with each other just because we believe in different methods or
tactics or strategies to reach a common objective.[30]

The historical progression of the freedom, civil rights, and human rights
struggles of Africans in the United States has been arduous and protracted.
Various leaders and organizations has stood on the stage of history, advocating different ideologies, objectives, and tactics. The final destination of complete freedom with justice and peace has not been achieved. An enormous
amount of work remains to be done at the individual and collective levels,
work that essentially builds on what King and El-Shabazz achieved.

King asked, "Where do we go from here?" A careful and systematic examination of the philosophies and approaches of King and El-Shabazz can
shed new light on this enduring question. El-Shabazz answered the question
in these terms:

First, we need some friends. We need some new allies. The entire civil
rights struggle needs a new interpretation, a broader interpretation. We
need to look at the civil rights thing from another angle—from the
inside as well as the outside. To those of us whose philosophy is black
nationalism, the only way you can get involved in the civil rights
struggle is give it a new interpretation. That old interpretation excluded
us. It kept us out. So, we're giving a new interpretation to the civil rights
struggle, an interpretation that will enable us to come into it, take part
in it.[31]

For El-Shabazz, that new interpretation involved changing the focus from
civil rights to human rights and advancing the movement beyond an interracial struggle based in the United States to a struggle for self-determination
involving people of color worldwide, especially on the African continent.

As African Americans struggle to make a living and to liberate themselves
from all forms of oppression, a keen understanding of the essential concepts
and strategies of King and El-Shabazz can be useful in exposing some of the
pitfalls along the pathway to liberation. Many tend to think that their respective visions of freedom and the methods each chose in his mutual pursuits of
equality and justice spoke to separate realities. This view, though questioned
and rejected in many circles, will continue to stimulate debate.

The vast majority of African Americans have no intention of emigrating to

Africa for dual citizenship or permanent residence, as El-Shabazz often advocated, nor are they prepared to embrace uncritically King's message of assimilation and integration. Therefore, it stands to reason that there should be a unified struggle in the United States around issues of civil and human rights. King's movement focused on civil rights, integration, and human solidarity. El-Shabazz's movement focused on human rights, Muslim solidarity, and Pan-African unity between the continent and the diaspora. The new dialectical equation for human freedom must strike a balance between the thesis of civil rights and the antithesis of human rights. It must further strike a balance between the thesis of integration and the antithesis of nationalism. The creative synthesis between these two sets of polarities is self-determination. In this sense, it is a form of self-determination that is operative in both the mutual power sharing of integration and the economic self-reliance of black nationalism. Indeed, this is one point at which elements of El-Shabazz's and King's approaches merge to form a creative union.

The archetypical Great Debate focused on repatriation back to the motherland of Africa or assimilation into the American culture and society. These were the two existential choices facing the African slaves before the Civil War and the ex-slaves/sharecroppers during and beyond Reconstruction. The core issues were compensation for labor and the restoration of culture and land. In the period extending from the late eighteenth up to the early twentieth century, Paul Cuffee, Martin Delany, Henry M. Turner, Marcus Garvey, and others who advocated repatriation wanted land to build a nation-state on the African continent, a position Malcolm later advanced with piercing clarity. It was out of this kind of thinking that Sierra Leone was established in 1787 and Liberia in 1822 and that the push for separate territory on the part of the Nation of Islam and the Republic of New Africa occurred much later.

Martin Delany (1812–85) was the quintessential Pan-Africanist of the nineteenth century. He advocated emigration to Africa as the only realistic solution to the problem of racial oppression and white supremacy in the United States. Delany maintained that Africans in the United States had to establish a homeland on the African continent. In this setting, he reasoned, they would be able to live in peace and practice the principles of self-determination and self-reliance, a view that prefigured Malcolm:

> Every people should be the originators of their own designs, the projectors of their own schemes, and creators of the events that lead to their destiny—the consummation of their desires. Situated as we are, in the

United States, many, and almost insurmountable, obstacles present themselves. We are four-and-a-half million in numbers, free and bond; six hundred thousand free, and three-and-a-half million bond. . . . We have native hearts and virtues, just as other nations; which in their pristine purity are noble, potent, and worthy of example. We are a nation within a nation;—as the Poles in Russia, the Hungarians in Austria, the Welsh, Irish, and Scotch in the British dominions.[32]

Delany clearly thought that freedom, justice, and equality were only achievable in a situation where African Americans had their own government. As long as they were under the oppressive hegemony of white supremacy, he maintained, vertical social mobility and freedom were not possibilities. El-Shabazz and King often said this much and more, especially as they came to grips with the intensity of white America's personal and institutional racism in their own times.

Delany was initially opposed to the efforts of the American Colonization Society to repatriate the free blacks to Africa before the end of slavery because he believed that this proposal was a trick by the white supremacists to eliminate strong leadership among African people in the United States. Delany had reasons to feel this way, since most of the Africans who were active in the abolition movement were free. With this class of blacks shipped back to Africa, there would have been fewer voices to agitate for the emancipation of the chattel slaves. With the passage of the Fugitive Slave Law (1850), Delany's attitude changed, for this law declared open season on all Africans, whether they were runaway slaves or free. The law read in substance, "And be it further enacted, that when a person is held to service or labor in any State or Territory of the United States, the person or persons to whom such services or labor may be due, or his, her, or their agent or attorney, duly authorized, by power of attorney, in writing, acknowledged and certified under the seal of some legal office court of the State or Territory in which the same may be executed, may pursue and reclaim such fugitive person."[33] In opposing this and other laws that sought to strengthen the slave system, Delany called to mind El-Shabazz, who attacked laws in his own time which, in his estimation, reinforced the structures of segregation.

Edward Blyden (1832–1912), another Pan-African and patriot in the repatriation movement, contributed to the advancement of Liberia as a republic. Liberia became the designated homeland of African slaves from the United States. In some ways it became for Blyden a model for the kind of separate nation that all uprooted and displaced Africans had to establish as a precondition for freedom and self-determination. Anything less, he reasoned, would only ensure the physical, spiritual, and psychological destruction of the race. In any case, by equating land with freedom, and by highlighting the need for *all* Africans to govern themselves, Blyden, like Delany, prefigured Malcolm in striking ways.

The case for assimilation and integration was argued by Frederick Douglass, a major spokesman for the abolitionist movement. Douglass declared, in words that anticipated King's position, that

> I shall advocate for the Negro, his most full and complete adoption into the great national family of America. I shall demand for him the most perfect civil and political equality, and that he shall enjoy all the rights, privileges and immunities enjoyed by any other members of the body politic. I weigh my words and I mean all I say, when I contend as I do contend, that this is the *only solid, and final* solution of the problem before us. . . . Save the Negro and you save the nation, destroy the Negro and you destroy the nation, and to save both you must have but one great law of Liberty, Equality, and Fraternity for all Americans without respect to color.[34]

Thus the archetypical Great Debate was demonstrated in the Delany vs. Douglass contest. Delany and Douglass worked together at one point but went their separate ways when their ideological differences became too sharp. The differences were clearly Afrocentricity vs. American-centeredness. Obviously, Delany, like Blyden, epitomized the Afrocentric outlook. According to Theodore Draper, "Delany himself liked to boast that 'there lives none blacker than himself.' Frederick Douglass is supposed to have said: 'I thank God for making me a man simply.' Delany always 'thanks Him for making him a black man.'"[35]

Perhaps the most widely known Great Debate occurred between Booker T. Washington and W.E.B. Du Bois. In his famous "Atlanta Exposition" speech in 1895, Washington advised African Americans to "Cast down your bucket where you are . . . , cast it down in making friends, in every manly way, of the people of all races by whom we are surrounded. Cast it down in agriculture, in mechanics, in commerce, in domestic service, and in the professions. . . . In all things that are purely social we can be as separate as the fingers, yet one as the hand in all things essential to mutual progress."[36] This speech, according to some scholars, signaled the beginning of the "age of

Washington." Between 1895 and 1910, Washington was the undisputed black leader in the United States, especially in the thinking of most whites.

While Washington stressed industrial education and accommodation for the masses, Du Bois emphasized the creation of a Talented Tenth, a professional class that would agitate for civil rights, including the right to vote and to become doctors, lawyers, educators, and businessmen. In Du Bois's estimation, "The Negro race, like all races, is going to be saved by its exceptional men. The problem of education, then, among Negroes must first of all deal with the Talented Tenth; it is the problem of developing the Best of this race that they may guide the Mass away from the contamination and death of the Worst, in their own and other races. Now the training of men is a difficult and intricate task. Its technique is a matter for educational experts, but its object is for the vision of seers."[37] Both El-Shabazz and King subscribed to variants of the Talented Tenth idea in practice, even as they tended to reject it in principle.

King summarized the Great Debate between Washington and Du Bois as follows:

> For decades the long and winding trails led to dead ends. Booker T. Washington, in the dark days that followed Reconstruction, advised them: "Let down your buckets where you are." Be content, he said in effect, with doing well with what the times permit you to do at all. However, this path, they soon felt, had too little freedom in its present and too little promise in its future. . . . Dr. W.E.B. Du Bois, in his earlier years at the turn of the century, urged the "talented tenth" to rise and pull behind it the mass of the race. His doctrine served somewhat to counteract the apparent resignation of Booker T. Washington's philosophy. Yet, in the very nature of Du Bois's outlook there was no role for the whole people. It was a tactic for an aristocratic elite who would themselves be benefited while leaving behind the "untalented" 90 percent.[38]

In "Who Won the Great Debate—Booker T. Washington or W.E.B. Du Bois?" Charles P. Henry asks some fundamental questions raised by this classic debate, which has long pitted black leaders on different sides of the ideological spectrum against one another: "The debate between Washington and Du Bois has remained with us throughout the twentieth century precisely because it is more than a debate over industrial or technical education versus the liberal arts or even economics versus politics. It is obvious to most that other types of education are needed just as both economic and political action lead to black progress. It is a debate over the fundamental character of American society. Are blacks to be fully absorbed in it or can they transform it? If they cannot transform it, can they retain a separate identity? Is it possible to be a part of the system and not be co-opted by it?"[39] This statement highlights questions that cannot be avoided in any discussion of the El-Shabazz/King dialectic. The transformation of the American economic, political, and social system, and the concomitant struggle of African Americans for a separate and self-determining cultural identity, are the cornerstones of the Great Debate between King and El-Shabazz.

They recapitulated and transformed the classic archetypical (Delany vs. Douglass) and prototypical (Washington vs. Du Bois) debate tradition. As the Zeitgeist moved the thesis of assimilation into the white American culture, and the antithesis of emigration back to Africa or elsewhere toward a synthesis, King transformed the assimilation thesis into integration, and El-Shabazz transformed the emigration antithesis into separation within the United States. As noted previously, the assimilation thesis and the emigration antithesis clearly dominated the eighteenth and nineteenth centuries, as earlier references to Hammon, Allen, Whipper, Douglass, Garnet, Delany, and Blyden indicate. During the twentieth century, the dominant movement was the thesis of integration and the antithesis of separation or nationalism, as shown in the differences between Marcus Garvey and A. Philip Randolph, and El-Shabazz and King.

The integrationist argument is rooted in the power of the Constitution to guarantee freedom, justice, and equality for all citizens, including African Americans. It challenges the fundamental class, race, and gender contradictions that were built into the framing of the Constitution. The American Revolution of 1776 did not eliminate chattel slavery in the thirteen colonies. A bloody internecine civil war had to be fought to reconcile these fundamental contradictions. In a word, the integrationist argument challenges the very foundation of America's claim to be a democratic society. Not only did King challenge the white supremacy version of democracy practiced in the United States; he also challenged the moral claims of the United States to be a society premised on Judeo-Christian values. Therefore, he argued his case based on the Bible and the Constitution.

On the other hand, the nationalist argument questions the relevance of the Constitution, and holds that the U.S. government is either unwilling or unable to fully include blacks in the democratic process in an integrated fashion.

Nationalists further argue that as long as white supremacy and a distorted democracy coexist, the African nation in America will never participate in the full range of freedom, justice, and equality.[40] Their core argument, as Malcolm often stated, is reparations for centuries of chattel slavery and the possibility of repatriation to the African motherland or some other separate territory. If reparations are given, the nationalist desire to build a nation-state within the borders of the United States on arable land is seen as a short-range objective. The classical case for this proposition was eloquently stated by Malcolm's leader, Elijah Muhammad: "We want our people in America whose parents or grandparents were descendants from slaves to be allowed to establish a separate state or territory of their own—either on this continent or elsewhere. We believe that our former slave-masters are obligated to provide such land and that the area must be fertile and minerally rich. We believe that our former slave-masters are obligated to maintain and supply our needs in this separate territory for the next 20 or 25 years until we are able to produce and supply our own needs."[41]

The long-range goal for many nationalists has long been the eventual return to the African motherland as citizens of an existing African country or having African nations designate land so that African Americans can develop a nation on African soil. Of course, the contradictions built into the creation of the Republic of Liberia and the Republic of Sierra Leone must be studied carefully in order to anticipate the practical problems of such a gigantic venture. El-Shabazz fell short at this point.[42] In any case, both nationalists and integrationists still have much to contribute to a serious and fruitful debate over this matter.

Integration, Black Nationalism, and Pan-Africanism

In his political manifesto, "The Ballot or the Bullet" (1964), El-Shabazz declared himself a "Black Nationalist freedom fighter." He further asserted that "though Islam is my religious philosophy, my economic, political and social philosophy is Black Nationalism."[43] This clear articulation of his purpose and interest set into motion a dialectical proposition that he clarified, defined, and reformulated until his assassination on February 21, 1965. El-Shabazz attempted to define, refine, and clarify his philosophy of black nationalism in this speech. He declared: "The political philosophy of black nationalism means that the black man should control the politics and the politicians in his own community. . . . The economic philosophy of black nationalism is pure and simple. It only means that we should control the economy of our community. . . . The social philosophy of black nationalism only means that we have to get together and remove the evils, the vices, alcoholism, drug addiction, and other evils that are destroying the moral fiber of our community."[44]

El-Shabazz's philosophy of black nationalism was a constant mode of analysis and pronouncement in most of his speeches after he left the Nation of Islam. When he traveled to Africa, especially Ghana, he internationalized his philosophy of black nationalism and moved toward Pan-Africanism. The establishment of the Organization of Afro-American Unity was the organizational manifestation of this commitment. Also, he constantly expressed the conviction that his religion was Islam. In this regard, it is important to remember that his concept of Islam changed when he abandoned the theology of the Nation of Islam and embraced Sunni Islam.

Pan-Africanism was axiomatic to the cultural, economic, philosophical, political, and social dimensions of El-Shabazz's ideology. It shaped his worldview and provided an international framework for his philosophy of black nationalism.[45] After he was excommunicated from the Nation of Islam and had declared his independence from Elijah Muhammad, he "returned" to the Garveyite philosophy of his parents. His father and mother had been active members of the Universal Negro Improvement Association, which was founded and led by Marcus Garvey (1887–1940). The most significant articulation of El-Shabazz's rediscovery of Pan-Africanism can be found in a letter he wrote from Ghana in 1964: "Being in Ghana now, the fountainhead of Pan-Africanism, the last days on my tour should be intensely interesting and enlightening. . . . Just as the American Jew is in harmony (politically, economically and culturally) with world Jewry, it is time for all African-Americans to become an integral part of the world's Pan-Africanists, and even though we might remain in America physically while fighting for the benefits the Constitution guarantees us, we must 'return' to Africa philosophically and culturally and develop a working unity in the framework of Pan-Africanism."[46] In the last year of his life, El-Shabazz advocated Pan-African ideas that were a synthesis of the classical period of Pan-African thought (1850–1920), the W.E.B. Du Bois Pan-African Congresses, and the vision of Kwame Nkrumah.

Revolution: Methods and Goals

King advocated a philosophy of nonviolence rooted in the Christian love ethic. All too often his philosophy is seen exclusively as passive resistance in nonviolent demonstrations, marches, sit-ins, prayer vigils, mass meetings, and other tactics. However, the Gandhian philosophy, as King understood it, has a deeper psychological and spiritual power. In order to practice this method, one must be fearless. One must also be nonviolent in thought, word, and deed. In other words, nonviolence becomes a way of life, a part of both the inner and outer self. It is not a set of tactics used only in a political situation. If we can appreciate this understanding of nonviolence, as advanced by both Gandhi and King, then we can start to think about its applications in daily relationships with family members, friends, and associates. Nonviolent love is a transcendent and highly inclusive idea. One must love the divine and the whole of creation, but hate all forms of negative behavior and energy. This is a manifestation of negative karma. It is no accident that Gandhi developed his ideas from karma yoga and Hindu culture. King, an eclectic philosopher and theologian, adapted these Eastern ideas to a Western Judeo-Christian culture. This is why he put such a strong emphasis on the Sermon on the Mount in the Book of Matthew, often mentioning Gandhi in his references to that part of the Bible.

King also advocated a revolution of values. He was opposed to a revolution based on immorality and violence. He once observed: "I am convinced that if we are to get on the right side of the world revolution, we as a nation must undergo a radical revolution of values. We must rapidly begin the shift from a 'thing-oriented' society to a 'person-oriented' society. When machines and computers, profit motives and property rights are considered more important than people, the giant triplets of racism, materialism, and militarism are incapable of being conquered."[47] El-Shabazz essentially agreed with this call for a revolution of values in the United States, despite the different language he commonly used to express this conviction.

El-Shabazz's concept of revolution was based on land. He argued that land is the basis of freedom, justice, and equality. His rebuttal to King's thesis is revealing: "Revolution is always based on land. Revolution is never based on begging someone for an integrated cup of coffee. Revolutions are never fought by turning the other cheek. Revolutions are never based upon love-your-enemy and pray-for those-who-spitefully-use-you. And revolutions are never waged singing 'We Shall Overcome.'" In his call for revolution based on love of self, El-Shabazz called to mind the nineteenth-century black nationalist Alexander Crummell.[48]

Thus El-Shabazz saw revolution as a function of a group seizing land and building a separate nation-state. King saw revolution as a revolution of values, which would ultimately lead to a transformation of human relationships and society. To King, relationships were primary while institutions and social structure were secondary. The different ways in which El-Shabazz and King defined *revolution* needs to be explored in greater detail if we are to truly understand the points at which their visions intersected and diverged.

Psychology and the psychological dimensions of the struggle played an enormous role in the thinking of King and El-Shabazz. Both men realized that in the final analysis, the mind of the oppressed and the mind of the oppressors had to be transformed if true freedom was to be realized. Whether the oppression assumed the form of slavery, colonization, segregation, institutionalized racism, capitalism, or white supremacy, the fundamental economic, political, and psychological contradictions are the same, namely, human bondage.

It is safe to conclude that King and El-Shabazz were both revolutionaries. King's vision of revolution was based on Christianity and Gandhian nonviolence, and El-Shabazz's on Islam and Pan-Africanism. In both cases, however, the ideal involved a total transformation of persons and of society as a whole in the interest of human liberation.

Diversity and Unity: Toward a Creative Synthesis

In the last three years of their lives, El-Shabazz and King reached a deeper understanding of the fundamental class dimension of the oppression of African Americans. This paradigm shift moved them closer to each other's perspectives. Although many of their differences in philosophy and methods remained constant, one could clearly see the emergence of unity within diversity. In fact, one could argue that there was unity without uniformity. Some of the areas of consensus were opposition to the Vietnam War, the call for human rights, identification with the struggles in Africa, internationalism, interfaith dialogue, and religious tolerance. Through introspection and protracted struggle, King and El-Shabazz arrived at the same position on the Vietnam War. They opposed it as conscientious objectors, based on religious and moral convictions.[49] King saw the war as "evil, unjust and futile." His reasons for opposing the war were carefully expressed in terms that reflected his sense of sheer urgency:

> Somehow this madness must cease. We must stop now. I speak as a child of God and brother to the suffering poor of Vietnam. I speak for those whose land is being laid waste, whose homes are being destroyed, whose culture is being subverted. I speak for the poor of America who are paying the double price of smashed hopes at home and death and corruption in Vietnam. I speak as a citizen of the world, for the world as it stands aghast at the path we have taken. I speak as an American to the leaders of my own nation. The great initiative in this war is ours. The initiative to stop it must be ours.[50]

El-Shabazz's opposition to the Vietnam War was an extension of the beliefs and practices of the Nation of Islam. Under the category of "What the Muslims Believe," Elijah Muhammad stated: "We believe that we who declare ourselves to be righteous Muslims should not participate in wars which take the lives of humans. We do not believe this nation should force us to take part in such wars, for we have nothing to gain from it unless America agrees to give us necessary territory wherein we may have something to fight for." Here El-Shabazz stood in a tradition as old as the nationalist David Walker and as recent as the nationalists Paul Robeson and Muhammad Ali, all of whom questioned the wisdom of fighting wars for the United States.[51]

In 1953, shortly after El-Shabazz was released from prison, he was visited by FBI agents, who asked why he had not registered for the Korean War draft. He replied that he did not know ex-convicts were required to register. They informed him that his criminal record did not exempt him from military service. Malcolm reported, "So I went straight from there to the draft board. When they gave me a form to fill out, I wrote in the appropriate places that I was a Muslim, and that I was a conscientious objector. . . . They asked if I knew what 'conscientious objector' meant. I told them that when the white man asked me to go off somewhere and fight and maybe die to preserve the way the white man treated the black man in America, then my conscience made me object."[52] He did not hear anything else from the draft board until he was classified as 5-A seven years later.

It is worth noting that El-Shabazz's attitude toward fighting for the United States and his resistance to the draft started when he was still in Jahiliyah (state of ignorance—during his years of criminal activities), a point that is also significant in any discussion of the position he took on Vietnam. When he received a draft notice in 1943, he went to the induction center in New York and pretended to be mentally ill:

> Suddenly, I sprang up and peeped under both doors, the one I'd entered and another that probably was a closet. And then I bent and whispered fast in his ear. "Daddy o, now you and me, we're from up North here, so don't you tell nobody. . . . I want to get sent down South. Organize them nigger soldiers, you dig? Steal us some guns, and kill up crackers! . . ." That psychiatrist's blue pencil dropped, and his professional manner fell off in all directions. He stared at me as if I were a snake's egg hatching, fumbling for the red pencil. I knew I had him. . . . A 4–F card came to me in the mail, and I never heard from the Army any more, and never bothered to ask why I was rejected.[53]

There is every reason to believe that, like Elijah Muhammad and numerous Black Muslims, Malcolm would have chosen to go to prison rather than go to war for the United States. This would have been consistent with the black nationalist tradition.

When Muhammad Ali poetically asserted that he "had no quarrel with the Viet Cong," American public opinion, politicians, the draft board, and the World Boxing Association turned against him. He recalled in his autobiography, "I had filed for draft exemption as a conscientious objector, telling the government that as a minister in the Nation of Islam . . . to bear arms or kill is against my religion. And I conscientiously object to any combat military service that involves the participation in any war in which the lives of human beings are being taken."[54] Muhammad Ali was not as fortunate as his mentor, El-Shabazz. He was persecuted by the military establishment, the legal system, and certain conservative and racist politicians. Moreover, he was stripped of his heavyweight boxing title and prevented from making a living as a professional boxer. Ali decided to resist the draft after seeing a photograph in a magazine. He recalled, "Up to the time of my statement, outwardly at least, the extent of my involvement in the war had been as a TV spectator. But I had seen bodies of dead Viet Cong laid out along a highway like rows of logs and a white American officer walking down the aisle of the dead taking the 'body count.' The only enemy alive was a little naked girl, searching among the bodies, her eyes wide, frightened. I clipped out the picture; and the face never quite left my mind."[55]

The bold and courageous stand that Ali took brought charges of a severe criminal offense. One of the officers at the induction station said, "Perhaps you don't realize the gravity of the act you just committed. Or maybe you do. But it is my duty to point out to you that if this should be your final decision, you will face criminal charges and your penalty could be five years in prison and a ten thousand dollars fine."[56] But like El-Shabazz, and with the blessings of King, Ali never wavered in his determination to resist. King commented, "No matter what you might think about Mr. Muhammad Ali's religion, you have to admire his courage." Ali's case (*Clay v. U.S.*) was appealed for six years before reaching the Supreme Court. *The Autobiography of Malcolm X* and Elijah Muhammad's *Message to the Black Man in America* were submitted as evidence. Ali won the appeal by a vote of 8–0. Thurgood Marshall was "recused from the case because he had been Solicitor General when the case began."[57]

El-Shabazz and King were largely in agreement about the international dimensions of the human struggle. Their passports to international statesmanship came in 1964. With El-Shabazz, it was the pilgrimage to Mecca; with King it was the Nobel Peace Prize. King said in his acceptance speech,

Civilization and violence are antithetical concepts. Negroes of the United States, following the people of India, have demonstrated that nonviolence is not sterile passivity, but a powerful moral force which makes for social transformation. Sooner or later, all the people of the world will have to discover a way to live together in peace, and thereby transform this pending cosmic elegy into a creative psalm of brotherhood. . . . If this is to be achieved, man must evolve for all human conflict a method which rejects revenge, aggression and retaliation. The foundation of such a method is love.[58]

In the same spirit of global brotherhood and peace, El-Shabazz wrote in a letter from Mecca:

America needs to understand Islam, because this is the one religion that erases the race problem from its society. Throughout my travels in the Muslim world, I have met, talked to, and even eaten with people who would have been considered "white" in America, but the religion of Islam in their hearts has removed the "white" from their minds. They practice sincere and true brotherhood with other people irrespective of their color. . . . Before America allows herself to be destroyed by the "cancer of racism" she should become better acquainted with the religious philosophy of Islam, a religion that has already molded people of all colors into one vast family, a nation or brotherhood of Islam that leaps over all "obstacles" and stretches itself into almost all the Eastern countries of this earth.[59]

The Nobel Prize and the pilgrimage gave King and El-Shabazz international legitimacy. From these noble heights, they could speak truth to power and organize and mobilize public opinion around issues of social justice on a global scale. King's public opposition to the war in Vietnam came after he received the Nobel Prize, and he had authority and power at this point. He was no longer the regionally based Southern Baptist minister but a world citizen and statesman who had the ear of leaders on every continent.

The pilgrimage allowed El-Shabazz to shed the stigma of being a racist. Now that he had embraced true and mainstream Islam, that label no longer could be used to define him. He was free of the stigma and devoid of the authoritarian control of the NOI. Now he could inject himself into the mainstream of the African-American civil and human rights struggle. However, he did not have enough time to cultivate bonds of trust and mutual cooperation to the extent that he had planned on both the national and international levels. If King and El-Shabazz had operated from the same agenda, the centuries-old Great Debate would have shifted even further toward a Great Dialogue.

James Cone has suggested that El-Shabazz and King represented the yin and yang of the double consciousness. But how does this principle relate to the Great Debate? The concepts of the yin/yang in Taoism and Maat in Kemetian (Egyptian) philosophy posit that spirit is primary and matter is secondary. This is the exact opposite of the materialist worldview, which posits that matter in motion is primary and consciousness is secondary. Huston Smith writes:

> Another feature of Taoism is its notion of the relativity of all values, and, as its correlative, the identity of opposites. Here Taoism is tied in with the traditional Chinese yin/yang. . . . This polarity sums up all of life's basic oppositions: good/evil, active/passive, positive/negative, light/dark, summer/winter, male/female. But though the halves are in tension, they are not flatly opposed; they complement and balance each other. Each invades the other's hemisphere and takes up its abode in the deepest recess of its partner's domain. And in the end both find themselves resolved by the circle that surrounds them, the *Tao* in its eternal wholeness. In the context of that wholeness, the opposites appear as no

more than phases in an endless cycling process, for each turns inces-
santly into its opposite, exchanging places with it. Life does not move
onward and upward toward a fixed pinnacle or pole. It bends back
upon itself to come, full circle, to the realization that all is one and all
is well.[60]

Historically, the Great Debate has been the driving force of the African
human rights struggle on the continent and in the diaspora. Moreover, the
Great Debate points to ideas that are dynamic and progressive, representing
both existential and cosmic reality construction. In the dynamics of mind and
body psychology, the Great Debate drama occurs at the levels of mind, body,
and soul. As soul force (truth force) interacts with social forces, which in
essence means "speaking truth to power," the Great Debate drama is cathartic in the resolution of societal conflicts and contradictions. The Great Debate is a historical debate predicated on the best and final solution to the
oppression and repression of African peoples.

Africans throughout the world share not only a common ancestry and
condition but also ideas and a sense of bonds with and obligations toward
each other. The sense of alienation and rootlessness among blacks in the
diaspora is more intensely based on the geographical and historical distance
from the African continent, which is essentially the cultural center of gravity
of all Africans. But the cultural norms, traditions, and values found among
Africans on the continent are often the standards by which African arche-
types are measured for all Africans. It is on the African continent where one
can still find the intergenerational transmissions of culture, customs, knowledge, language, and wisdom that can be traced back to antiquity or to the
very origins of human beings.

As dialecticians and students of history, King and El-Shabazz anchored
themselves within the ebb and flow of the historiography peculiar to their
respective ideologies. As stated, Christianity, Gandhian nonviolence, and
Thoreau's civil disobedience clearly informed the Hegelian dialectics of
King.[61] On the other hand, Sunni Islam, the Nation of Islam, Marcus Garvey, and Pan-African Nationalism informed and guided the dialectics of
El-Shabazz.[62] The Hegelian dialectics of King was also informed by the conviction that truth comes from various sources. This explains his sustained efforts to combine truths from a range of Christian and non-Christian sources
into an intelligible whole. In a different vein, Malcolm's dialectics emerged
out of the conviction that truth for people of African descent rests within the
confines of an Islamic and Pan-African worldview.

Modern scholarship suggests that it is almost impossible to discuss King without cross-referencing El-Shabazz and vice versa. In other words, the contention is that they exist in the historiography of African world history in a symbiotic dualism. In the beginning, the creative tension in this symbiotic duality was antagonistic in philosophy and methods: integration vs. separation and nonviolence vs. self-defense or counterviolence. As both activists matriculated in the crucible of social practice, the antagonistic dimensions of their ideologies and methodologies became less strident and more harmonious. On a more transcendent level, the ebb and flow of their dialectical logic created existential points of balance in the principles of peace, freedom, human rights, justice, internationalism, and unconditional love for humanity.

The Great Debate: Enduring Legacy and Pedagogy

The current generations of students are the children and grandchildren of the generations that came of age during the 1960s. Unfortunately, these students do not have a direct or primary knowledge about the legacies of King and El-Shabazz. Their knowledge is a product of intergenerational transmissions from conversations with the elders, reading books, or exposure to the mass media. Hence, this secondary knowledge, and in some instances tertiary knowledge, is the source of their appreciation or understanding of the contributions of these revolutionary leaders and thinkers.

Because of these historical and sociological realities, students have associated and constructed different ideas, images, and impressions of King and El-Shabazz, many of which portray them as something other than what they actually were. It is both the duty and responsibility of the elders to correct the mistaken ideas, images, and impressions among the young generations, and, at the same time, inspire them to build an ideology that will reconcile the creative and historical tensions between the ideologies of King and El-Shabazz. One of the challenges for the emerging King and El-Shabazz scholarship is to close the gap between their diverse but complementary ideologies. Hence, these two champions must be seen both in debate and in dialogue. Such a format can provide a cultural and intellectual bridge into the twenty-first century for those seeking freedom, justice, and equality in the world for all human beings.

New and creative pedagogical methods must be utilized in order to facilitate accurate conceptions of the Great Debate between Martin and El-Shabazz.[63] After teaching black nationalism for a few years at a historically white college and for many years at a historically black college, it occurred to me in 1985 that students could get a more in-depth understanding of the ideas of King and El-Shabazz if they were able to debate current issues and problems from the perspectives of these two thinkers and activists. This conviction led me to begin an annual Great Debate Series at Tennessee State University in 1985. El-Shabazz's advice to young people further underscores this idea that youngsters can better understand him and King when they bring their own informed and creative insights to a serious assessment of the relevance and implications of these leaders' ideas for addressing contemporary human problems: "One of the first things I think young people, especially nowadays, should learn how to do is see for yourself and listen for yourself and think for yourself. Then you can come to an intelligent decision for yourself. But if you form the habit of going by what others think about someone, instead of going and searching that thing out for yourself and seeing for yourself, you'll be walking west when you think you're going east, and you'll be walking east when you think you're going west."[64] Debating is a method by which students can learn how to think for themselves. It involves critical thinking, logic, presentation of evidence, and extensive research. From a psychological perspective, debate builds character, confidence, self-esteem, and the capacity for critical and analytical thinking, qualities that both King and El-Shabazz would cherish and consider essential to the molding of strong personalities.

The vision to create the Great Debate at Tennessee State was sparked by the fact that both King and El-Shabazz were extraordinary debaters and orators. Both honed their skills of critical analysis, argumentation, and persuasion through the exercise of debate techniques. After El-Shabazz began reading in prison, debate gave him an opportunity to analyze, refine, and articulate his thoughts:

[R]ight there, in the prison, debating, speaking to a crowd, was as exhilarating to me as the discovery of knowledge through reading had been. Standing up there, the faces looking up at me, the things in my head coming out of my mouth, while my brain searched for the next best thing to follow what I was saying, and if I could sway them to my side by handling it right, then I had won the debate—once my feet got wet, I was gone on debating. Whichever side of the selected subject was assigned to me, I'd track down and study everything I could find on it. I'd put myself in my opponent's place and decide how I'd try to win if

I had the other side; and then I'd figure a way to knock down those points.[65]

El-Shabazz later debated at such prestigious universities as Harvard, Oxford, Columbia, and Yale. This was a quantum leap for someone with only an eighth-grade formal education. El-Shabazz's epistemology and theoretical paradigm were premised on canons and sources that were not in currency in the Western academies, including the works of J. A. Rogers and the canons of Fard Muhammad.

The Oxford Union debate was perhaps one of the high points of his career. The proposition for the debate was "Extremism in defense of liberty is no vice, and moderation in the pursuit of justice is no virtue." This proposition was popularized by Barry Goldwater in his acceptance speech at the 1964 Republican National Convention. El-Shabazz adopted it and related it to the particular context of his people, who were often accused of being both too extreme and too moderate in their quest for freedom and justice.

The Great Debate at Tennessee State University is informed by two hypothetical questions: What would have happened if King and El-Shabazz had become allies or comrades in the struggle, and what would their positions be on a given issue today? There is clearly a certain timelessness about the ideas of El-Shabazz and King that makes them relevant today and in the future, especially since the struggle for black liberation in particular, and human liberation in general, will continue in the twenty-first century.

The format of the Great Debate is similar to the intercollegiate and interscholastic debates on college and high school campuses. Students participate as a team. Each team represents one of three perspectives: King, El-Shabazz, or the synthesis of elements of both personalities, philosophies, and methods. Similar to the traditional debates, teams present their cases as opening, rebuttal, cross-examination, and closing arguments. Unlike the traditional debates, they employ the dialectical method of thesis (King), antithesis (El-Shabazz), and synthesis (commonalities and unities in the perspectives of King and El-Shabazz). The object is to discover the synthesis. These Great Debate arguments are adjudicated by a panel of judges chosen from the campus and the broader community.

As the African global struggle evolves over time and space, the pressing need for the political and economic liberation of all Africans will make the distance between the assimilation/integration perspective and the emigration/nationalist perspective increasingly less significant. And as this evolution continues, eventually the quantitative and qualitative differences will be transformed and an ideology should emerge that is more holistic and inclusive. Most scholars of El-Shabazz and King have concluded that both men had come to entertain this possibility between 1963 and 1965, a development that helps explain their coming closer together in their analysis and vision for the future of African Americans. Hence, in the last years their differences were confined essentially to the areas of methods or tactics, rather than goals and strategies.

King and El-Shabazz operated from their own paradigms and perspectives. However, they were responding to the same cultural and societal dynamics. Thus, as black oppression and victimization created the context for their movements, they had to adapt their emerging perspectives to cognitively mediate and sociologically negotiate these unfolding conditions. As the exigencies of the vanguard position shifted, there was cleavage in both the integrationist and nationalist movements. The antithesis of Sunni Islam inside the Nation of Islam was in creative tension with the Lost-Found Nation of Islam of Fard Muhammad. Similarly, the antithesis of black power inside the civil rights movement was in creative tension with King's thesis of integration/Gandhian nonviolence. Hence the macrodialectics between the integrationist and the nationalist movements was also manifested as the microdialectics within each movement. Both movements were strongly challenged by the push and pull of cultural, economic, political, religious, and social forces that threatened to transform them into their ideological opposites. It was only the relative persistence of external and internal possibilities and realities that allowed each movement to persist in its original ideological form and purpose.

"Ballot or Bullet": The Great Debate and Democratic Trends from John F. Kennedy to Albert Gore

The Great Debate is deeply concerned about the shifting trends in the American democratic process since the election of President Kennedy in 1960. This process has reflected the very best in terms of integrity and fairness at times, but there are also periods in which it has suffered serious setbacks. This is clearly borne out by the circumstances surrounding the 2000 presidential election. To be sure, the long road from Kennedy and Richard Nixon to Albert Gore and George W. Bush reveals much about the problems that confront any quest for multiracial democracy in a race-conscious society.

"Politics is nonviolent warfare," said Richard Gephardt, House Democrat and minority leader, on an episode of *Meet the Press*. His comment, which would not have been accepted uncritically by El-Shabazz and King, was about Gore's demands for a recount of the ballots cast in Florida in the 2000 presidential election. Gore was engaged in a hotly contested presidential election with Bush, and the very foundation of American democracy was challenged. The demands for a recount of the ballots in Florida motivated many legal minds and scholars to revisit the *Federalist Papers,* for this document contains the debates, intent, and spirit of the founding fathers who crafted the U.S. Constitution. Most assuredly, the possibility that Congress or the Supreme Court would ultimately determine the next president vindicated many of El-Shabazz and King's fears about the possible threats to the disfranchisement of African Americans.

If history is prologue, then the 1960 election between Kennedy and Nixon elucidated the strategic significance of the black vote as it unfolded in the 2000 presidential election. El-Shabazz and King noted how crucial the black vote was for Kennedy, and both sensed that this same pattern would be reflected in future elections. In his celebrated and often quoted "Ballot or Bullet" speech, El-Shabazz observed:

> These 22 million victims are waking up. Their eyes are coming open. They are beginning to see what they used to only look at. They're becoming politically mature. They are realizing that there are new political trends from coast to coast. As they see these new political trends, it's possible for them to see that every time there's an election the races are so close that they have to have a recount. They had to recount in Massachusetts to see who was going to be governor, it was so close. It was the same way in Rhode Island, in Minnesota, and in many other parts of the country. And the same with Kennedy and Nixon when they ran for president. It was so close they had to count all over again. Well, what does this mean? It means that when white people are evenly divided, and black people have a bloc of votes of their own, it is left up to them to determine who's going to sit in the White House and who's going to be in the dog house.[66]

El-Shabazz pointed out that the white votes for Kennedy and Nixon were evenly divided in 1960. Kennedy won by a narrow margin, partly because 60–80 percent of African Americans voted for him. In this political context, the black vote held the balance of power. Few if any could have predicted at that time that the black vote would be an even more critical issue in the 2000 presidential election and that what Malcolm termed the "political maturity" of African Americans would be severely tested.

Traditionally, African Americans had voted Republican. Their reasoning was that the Republican Party was the party of Abraham Lincoln, and Lincoln issued the Emancipation Proclamation which freed African slaves in those states which seceded from the Union. Also, the 1954 *Brown vs. Board of Education* decision, which ended segregated public schools, was given during the Eisenhower Republican administration. How was Kennedy able to woo African Americans from the Republican Party? According to Chuck Stone, Kennedy responded to a situation involving the unjust arrest and persecution of Martin Luther King Jr. during the sit-in demonstrations.

> On Wednesday, October 26, 1960, he called Mrs. Martin Luther King Jr., to express his deep concern about a four-month prison sentence meted out to her husband in Georgia on a technical charge of not possessing a driver's license. No other important political figure had publicly expressed any dismay at this latest miscarriage of white Southern justice, and Kennedy's call to Mrs. King electrified the black community. . . . King's father, the Reverend Martin Luther King Sr., who had earlier endorsed Nixon—some suspected because of an entrenched Southern Baptist lack of affection for Catholicism—quickly changed political horses. "Because this man was willing to wipe the tears from my daughter's eye, I've got a suitcase full of votes and I'm going to take them to Mr. Kennedy and dump them in his lap," he declared. Kennedy's phone call broke the ice. He was now the Negro's friend. Other Baptist ministers followed the Reverend King's endorsement, and the Negro vote was no longer in doubt.[67]

Kennedy won by a margin of 112,827 votes out of 68,770,294 votes cast. Therefore, with an organized bloc of votes, coupled with a political consciousness that was both astute and mature, African Americans exploited political trends and swung the election in their favor. Technicalities and voter irregularities prevented this from happening in the 2000 election.

There are parallels between the Kennedy vs. Nixon election in 1960 and the Gore vs. Bush election in 2000. More than 90 percent of African Americans voted for Gore. This allowed him to win the popular vote, but he failed to receive enough electoral votes to win the White House. In terms of popular votes, Gore received 50,158,094 and Bush 49,820,518. However, in the all-important electoral votes, Bush received 271 to Gore's 267. In the Florida vote recount, Bush finished with 2,912,790 votes—537 more than Gore received. The recount would have been different had there not been efforts on the part of some of the authorities in Florida to dilute the power of the black vote. Many African Americans spoke of being harassed at polling places, of being told that they were not properly registered and of being told that unfounded prison records negated their voting privileges. Some were turned away from polling places, and others were told that the polling places were closed. The outcome of the election supports El-Shabazz's and King's claim that democracy in America is often unfair and unrepresentative of the masses. Both men understood that powerful corporate interests and political maneuverings can sometimes undermine healthy participatory democracy, and Bush's rise to the presidency supports this view. Thus the quest of El-Shabazz and King for a democracy in which every voice can be heard remains our own quest today.

When Gore did not carry his home state of Tennessee, and the Supreme Court ended the recount in Florida by a vote of 5–4, the African-American swing vote was effectively neutralized. George W. Bush became the nation's forty-third president, thus frustrating the hopes of many African Americans who fear that the America for which El-Shabazz and King so gallantly fought will become even more of an illusive dream. Bush appointed African Americans to powerful cabinet positions: General Colin Powell became secretary of state; Condoleezza Rice, national security advisor; and Roderick Paige, secretary of education. Even so, most African Americans view Bush's rise to the presidency as an unwelcomed challenge to the dreams and hopes of El-Shabazz and King. This perspective among American blacks was significantly reinforced by Bush's refusal to support wholeheartedly the world conference on racism in Durban, South Africa, in October 2001 and by the administration's failure to address seriously such issues as racial profiling, affirmative action, and the unfair treatment of blacks and other minorities by the criminal justice system. This situation is not likely to change as long as a conservative Republican agenda is put forth.

Rep. John Lewis (D-Ga.), a close companion of Martin Luther King Jr., made a poignant observation to *Newsweek* about the 2000 presidential election:

What's happening in Florida and in Washington is more than a game for pundits. The whole mess reminds African Americans of an era when we had to pass literacy tests, pay poll taxes and cross every "t" and dot every "i" to get to be able to vote. You had black men and women, graduates of the best universities in the country, failing literacy tests. A man was once asked how many bubbles were in a bar of soap. For all the political maneuvering and legal wrangling, many people have missed an important point: the story of the 2000 election is about more than George W. Bush and Gore. It's about the right to vote. And you cannot understand the true implications of this campaign and the subsequent litigation without grasping how deeply many minorities feel about the seemingly simple matter of the sanctity of the ballot box.[68]

"Democrats take the African-American voters for granted, and Republicans ignore them." This is a popular proverb in the African-American community, one that El-Shabazz and King would affirm without hesitation. Both men ultimately questioned the significance of the two-party system for African Americans. They taught us a powerful lesson that was rekindled in our minds by the circumstances surrounding the 2000 election, namely, that we must not allow any one party to assume our overwhelming support unless it is willing to speak strongly on our behalf when we feel disfranchised. Gore and the Democratic elite abandoned blacks who were disfranchised in Florida. Nevertheless, most African Americans vote for Democrats out of habit and because they are perceived as the lesser of two evils. In most instances, they vote for the Democratic candidate, but the same vote is a vote against the Republican candidate. In a sense, the vote is both proactive and reactive.

An important question for a study of this nature is what will happen to El-Shabazz's and King's legacy in this period of mounting political conservatism. Will the Bush administration be a positive force in the pursuit of King's dream, or will it turn us further in the direction of the nightmare about which El-Shabazz spoke? Black leaders are now strongly divided in terms of their answers to these questions. Most envision the increasing erosion of affirmative action and civil rights initiatives, and a few predict an improved quality of life for all African Americans. Whatever the case may be, we must never forget El-Shabazz's and King's insistence on the need to take charge of our own political destiny.

Beyond the 2000 Election: El-Shabazz, King, and the Question of Reparations

W.E.B. Du Bois said in his classic work, *The Souls of Black Folk* (1903), "The problem of the twentieth century is the problem of the color line—the relation of the darker to the lighter races of men in Asia and Africa, in America and the islands of the sea. It was a phase of this problem that caused the Civil War; and however much they who marched South and North in 1861 may have fixed on the technical points of union and local autonomy as a shibboleth, all nevertheless knew, as we know, that the question of Negro slavery was the real cause of the conflict." Du Bois made this observation at the beginning of the twentieth century. His words resonated in the 1950s and 1960s, as El-Shabazz and King urged America to transcend the color bar by compensating African Americans for the exploitation, physical and psychological torture, and humiliation they had endured for centuries. The same has occurred with the recent resurgence of the Reparations Movement. This movement seeks compensation for the pain and suffering of African Americans from the vestiges of slavery and colonization.[69] John Conyers (D-Mich.) has tried to get the House of Representatives to pass a bill that will establish a commission to study the effects of slavery on African Americans. The original bill is H.R. 891, and the current version is H.R. 40, introduced in 1995. H.R. 40 states: "A Bill to acknowledge the fundamental injustices, cruelty, brutality, and inhumanity of slavery in the United States and the 13 American colonies between 1619 and 1865, and to establish a commission to examine the institution of slavery, subsequent *de jure* and *de facto* racial and economic discrimination against African Americans, and the impact of these forces on living African Americans, and to make recommendations to the Congress on appropriate remedies, and for other purposes."[70]

With this in mind, one might conclude that the battle for reparations will be waged on different fronts in a protracted struggle. The issue has economic, legal, moral, political, and social ramifications on an international scale of justice, especially since the African continent is involved. At this stage of the dialectics, the mass movement is led by the National Coalition of Blacks for Reparations in America (N'COBRA), which is working in conjunction with Conyers and his political colleagues.

In more recent times, the battle has been joined by Randall Robinson of TransAfrica, whose work on behalf of people of African descent builds on the legacies of El-Shabazz and King. Robinson has written a powerful book, *The Debt: What America Owes Blacks* (2000). In addition to this project, Robinson has assembled a "dream team" of black attorneys known as the Reparations Assessment Group: Johnnie Cochran, Charles J. Ogletree, Alexander J. Pires Jr., Richard Scruggs, Dennis C. Sweet III, and Willie E. Gary. In a key address given at the 43rd Annual Meeting of the African Studies Association

(ASA), Randall Robinson asserted that the team will focus especially on the period extending from 1619 to 1965. Slavery started in the United States in 1619, and African Americans were disenfranchised up to the passage in 1965 of the Voting Rights Act.[71] El-Shabazz and King also saw this time frame as critical to any effort to compensate African Americans for their centuries of labor, pain, and suffering.

The Emancipation Proclamation (1863) and the Civil War (1861–65) supposedly freed some four million Africans from slavery. N'COBRA has examined the freedom of Africans during Reconstruction (1865–77) from the standpoint of kugichagulia, or self-determination. The question looms: What *choices* did the liberated African nation within America have at the end of the Civil War? Apparently the answer is not one-dimensional, for blacks had "(1) the right to return to Afrika as we were victims of warfare and illegal kidnapping; (2) the right to emigrate to another place, as our families were cruelly fragmented and scattered throughout the diaspora; (3) the right to seek admissions, as citizens, into the American community and strive for multiracial democracy; and (4) the right to remain where we were, negotiate with the native peoples of this land, and establish our nation in an independent separate territory; for we had been legally constructed *outside* the American community and found ourselves on soil claimed by the United States in great numbers and severed homeland ties."[72] Ostensibly, these *choices* are more indicative of a nationalist perspective, such as that advanced by El-Shabazz. However, the third choice of striving for multiethnic or multiracial democracy is congruent with an integrationist perspective, such as that set forth by King.

Henry M. Turner, the African emigrationist and controversial bishop in the African Methodist Episcopal Church, was the first to seriously raise the issue of reparations for centuries of African slavery. In a 1900 publication, Turner, with sentiments that later echoed through the speeches of El-Shabazz and King, declared:

> We have worked, enriched the country and helped give it a standing among the powers of the earth, and when we are denied our civil and political rights, the fool Negro who has no more sense than a jackass, yet he wants to be a leader, ridicules the idea of asking for a hundred million dollars to go home, for Africa is our home, and is the one place that offers us manhood and freedom, though we are subjects of nations that have claimed a part of Africa by conquest. A hundred million dollars can be obtained if we, as a race, would ask for it. The way we

figure it out, this country owes us forty billions of dollars, and we are afraid to ask for a hundred million.[73]

In his call for reparations, Turner established himself, along with W.E.B. Du Bois, William M. Trotter, and others, as Booker T. Washington's ideological nemesis. Washington did not push for reparations, and this, in conjunction with his politics of accommodationism and gradualism, convinced Turner that Washington was ill-prepared to lead African Americans to the next stage in their struggle for liberation and self-determination. Be that as it may, Turner, in promoting reparations as a critical part of the liberation agenda, helped set the stage not only for El-Shabazz and King, both of whom supported reparations for various reasons, but also for the current Great Debate among African-American leaders and thinkers regarding this question.

Reparations became the rallying cry in many circles in the 1950s and 1960s, as nationalists and integrationists set forth different strategies for freedom and competing visions of what would constitute the ideal society for African Americans. The legal, political, moral, and ethical issues surrounding the reparations question were entertained on some levels, though perhaps not as intense as they are today. One might say that the issue of reparations, as understood by El-Shabazz, King, and others in the 1960s, is raised to a higher level of intensity, clarity, and sophistication today by Randall Robinson and the attorneys, intellectuals, and politicians associated with this movement.

Like Marcus Garvey and Elijah Muhammad, El-Shabazz connected the call for reparations with the quest for a separate homeland. This position was advanced as an article of faith by the Black Muslims or Nation of Islam during El-Shabazz's years with the group. In their major periodical, *Muhammad Speaks,* this position is set forth in these terms: "We want our people in America whose parents or grandparents were descendants from slaves to be allowed to establish a separate state or territory of their own—either on this continent or elsewhere. We believe that our former slavemasters are obligated to maintain and supply our needs in this separate territory for the next 20 or 25 years until we are able to produce and supply our own needs."[74] Although El-Shabazz did not emphatically link this call for reparations to a desire for a separate homeland after he broke with the Nation of Islam, he did not abandon the basic principle that slavery and colonization alienated and appropriated the values of African labor, culture, and land in the interest of capitalism and white supremacy. He was convinced that any serious quest for reparations had to embrace some form of restitution for Africa from the

United States and European countries involved in the slave trade.[75] Moreover, he argued that the vestiges of slavery and colonization persist in the forms of alienation, apartheid, discrimination, exploitation, neocolonialism, oppression, and segregation.

King's position was embedded in his relentless moral, economic, political, and social campaigns to dismantle the institutional and structural inequities in the American society and culture. Unlike many nationalists, King's support for reparations was not grounded in a call for a separate homeland for African Americans. In explaining his support for both affirmative action and reparations in some form, King used terms like "special measures for the deprived," "compensatory measures," and "adequate compensation for the exploitation and humiliation of the Negro."[76] Moreover, his last crusade, the Poor People's Campaign (1967–68), conducted on a national level, and his involvement with the Memphis Sanitation Strike (1968), waged on a local level, echoed both his own position and some of the concerns being raised by advocates for reparations today.

Generally speaking, King, like El-Shabazz, saw the struggle as a dialectical tension between capital and labor or between the rich and the poor. Thus he called for a radical redistribution of economic power—of wealth and income. This amounted to a call for reparations not only for African Americans but for all oppressed people in American society. It is also important to point out that King always focused on the universality of contradictions, particularly as they related to questions of race and economics. For example, he once noted: "A true revolution of values will soon look uneasily on the glaring contrast of poverty and wealth. With righteous indignation, it will look at thousands of working people displaced from their jobs with reduced incomes as a result of automation while profits of the employers remain intact, and say: 'This is not just.' It will look across the ocean and see individual capitalists of the West investing huge sums of money in Asia, Africa and South America, only to take the profits out with no concern for the social betterment of the countries, and say: 'This is not just.'"[77] Convinced that reparations are consistent with the Christian ethic, King fought to give peasants and workers around the world economic opportunity, dignity, and the proper compensation for the full value of their labor.

In April 1969, James Foreman of the Student Nonviolent Coordinating Committee, still agonizing over the King assassination a year earlier, issued this manifesto: "We are therefore demanding of the white Christian churches and Jewish synagogues which are part and parcel of the system of capitalism, that they begin to pay reparations to black people in this country. We are demanding $500,000,000 from the white Christian Churches and the Jewish synagogues. . . . Fifteen dollars for every black brother and sister in the United States is only a beginning of the reparations due us for people who have been exploited and degraded, brutalized, killed and persecuted."[78] Foreman's bold action drew adverse reactions from other leaders in the civil rights movement, especially moderate ones. But it afforded an important historical link between El-Shabazz's and King's call for reparations in the 1950s and 1960s, and the current efforts of Randall Robinson and others, who are making the reparations issue a part of their push for a more positive shift in national public policy.

The outcome of the efforts of Robinson and other pro-reparations advocates is clearly unpredictable. Undoubtedly, they will continue to be challenged by both white and black political conservatives and even by elements of the so-called Christian Right. To be sure, the vast majority of white Americans will continue to oppose any proposal for reparations, and many will dismiss it as a move toward reverse discrimination. If the Bush administration sets the tone for action with respect to reparations, which looms today as an unrealistic expectation, then the issue will do more to enhance than to heal what social scientists and public policymakers call "the current racial divide."

The reparations movement has now reached international status, a development that speaks to the vitality of the legacy of both King and El-Shabazz. The United Nations convened a World Conference against Racism, Racial Discrimination, Xenophobia, and Related Intolerance in Durban, South Africa, on August 28–September 3, 2001. Initially, President George W. Bush indicated that no American delegation would be sent if the agenda called for a discussion of reparations and Zionism. This position was modified, and Secretary of State Colin Powell sent a low-level delegation. The Palestinian delegation's request for a declaration defining Israel as an apartheid state and Zionism as racism triggered a walkout by the delegations of Israel and the United States. Equally significant was the United Nation's resolution stating its determination to see that all nations, groups, and individuals who are victims of crimes based on "race, colour, caste, descent, ethnicity, or indigenous or national origin are provided reparations."[79] A greater tribute to the legacies of El-Shabazz and King could not have been given, despite the fact that the resolution was not consciously drafted in their honor.

8

Reluctant Admiration

What Malcolm and Martin Thought about Each Other

> While we did not always see eye to eye on methods to solve the race prob-
> lem, I always had a deep affection for Malcolm and felt he had the great
> ability to put his finger on the existence and root of the problem.
> **Martin Luther King Jr.**[1]

> But I have no comment to make about my good friend, Dr. King.
> **Malcolm X**[2]

> I went to Atlanta and interviewed for *Playboy* Dr. Martin Luther King. He
> was privately intrigued to hear little-known things about Malcolm X that I
> told him; for publication, he discussed him with reserve, and he did say
> that he would sometime like to have an opportunity to talk with him.
> Hearing this, Malcolm X said drily, "You think I ought to send him a tele-
> gram with my telephone number?" But from other things that Malcolm X
> said to me at various times, I deduced that he actually had a reluctant ad-
> miration for Dr. King.
> **Alex Haley**[3]

Malcolm X and Martin Luther King Jr. are often referred to as the most
important black leaders in the United States in the 1950s and 1960s. They are
perceived as having stood at opposite extremes within the ranks of black
leadership, representing profoundly different organizations and political-
religious perspectives. Their disagreements concerning love and hate, violence and nonviolence, separatism and integration, and the relevancy of the
Christian faith in the black freedom struggle not only prevented them from
becoming closely connected by friendship and association but were also of
enormous significance in determining how they viewed and related to each
other. Such disagreements have left many with the impression that Malcolm
and Martin were "adversaries in a great Manichaean contest, the forces of

light against the forces of darkness, with the future course of black protest at stake." This image has been created in the public imagination by the American mass media and reinforced in the writings of misinformed scholars and therefore must not be taken seriously by those who wish to understand the true nature of Malcolm's and Martin's relationship, as well as their meaning and significance for their people's historic struggle.[4]

The relationship between Malcolm and Martin passed through two stages. The first lasted from 1957 until March 1964. During most of this time, Malcolm was a minister in Elijah Muhammad's Black Muslim Movement, based in Harlem, and Martin was the president of the Southern Christian Leadership Conference (SCLC) and a co-pastor at his father's church in Atlanta, Georgia. The second stage began on March 26, 1964, when Malcolm and Martin met briefly in Washington, D.C., and it ended with Malcolm's death on February 21, 1965. The difference between the two periods is suggested by the manner in which the two men softened their criticisms of each other in the last eleven months of Malcolm's life, and also by the ways in which they moved closer together, personally and philosophically.[5]

Following Different Paths: Public Disagreements and Personal Attacks

Malcolm had little to say regarding Martin's philosophy and methods during the 1950s. Malcolm was seldom mentioned in the press prior to the 1959 television production, "The Hate That Hate Produced," and at such times he was careful not to allow media sources and the white power structure to use him against the civil rights movement and its leadership.[6] Martin followed the same policy with respect to Malcolm, for both understood that a public airing of their differences could only result in more disunity among African Americans.

The initial concern for Malcolm was to create bridges of understanding and goodwill between the Black Muslims and Martin's SCLC. He tried unsuccessfully to start a dialogue with Martin's movement in 1957. In March 1958, Elijah Muhammad sent a letter to Martin, inviting him to appear before the Muslims and other citizens "in a free rally in our great Temple #2 in Chicago's exclusive Hyde Park District." Martin responded three weeks later, expressing deep gratitude for the invitation, but declining it because he had "accepted as many speaking engagements that my schedule will allow for the remainder of the year." Malcolm did not question Martin's unavailability, but he began to criticize the SCLC and other civil rights organizations that appeared to place more value on white liberal support than on establishing strong links with the more militant wing of the black freedom struggle. "Most organizations that represent the so-called Negro," said Malcolm in a 1959 interview, "usually we find when we study them that though they are supposed to be for us, the leadership or the brain-power or the political power or whatever power that runs it usually is the white man."[7]

As the civil rights movement escalated, Malcolm made other attempts to open the lines of communication between the Black Muslims and Martin's group. In July 1960, he personally invited Martin to attend an "Education Rally" in Harlem, noting, "Since so much controversy has been spoken and written about Mr. Muhammad and his 'Black Muslims,' we invite you as a spokesman and fellow leader of our people to be among our invited guests, so you can see and hear Mr. Muhammad for yourself and then make a more intelligent appraisal of his teachings, his methods, and his program."[8] However, his letter did not arrive at Martin's office until after the program had occurred.

On yet another occasion, Malcolm challenged Martin to "come to Harlem and prove that 'peaceful suffering' is the solution to the atrocities suffered daily by Negroes throughout America." Martin ignored the challenge, leading the Muslims to announce that they would hold a rally in Atlanta to show that black southerners were "tired of suffering, peacefully or otherwise." Malcolm's intention at this point was not to alienate Martin as a spokesman for African Americans, for he constantly urged black leaders to forget their "petty differences" and to "reason together and keep open minds." He was convinced that Martin and other moderate civil rights leaders were avoiding him out of a fear "of irking their white bosses or embarrassing their white liberal friends."[9]

But there were clearly larger issues involved. Malcolm and the Black Muslims and Martin and the Southern Christian Leadership Conference were divided by too many political, philosophical, and religious differences to feel comfortable meeting and talking together. The Muslims' stress on black supremacy, black self-love, self-defense, racial separatism, and Islam as the "natural religion" of black people was too much at odds with Martin's emphasis on human equality, universal agape love, nonviolence, integration, and the redemptive power of the Christian faith. Black Muslimism is what made Malcolm such a conundrum for Martin, and that, along with Martin's unwavering devotion to Christian ethics, helps explain why each leader remained the other's "ideological nemesis."[10]

The issue of integration figured prominently in the conflict. Malcolm was both amazed and troubled that "the goal of Dr. Martin Luther King is to give Negroes a chance to sit in a segregated restaurant beside the same white man who has brutalized them for four hundred years." Convinced that the separation of the races afforded the best and only solution, the Muslim minister predicted in 1963 that black Americans would denounce and abandon Martin once they realized that whites had no intention of honoring the promise of integration. Martin thought otherwise, and he ridiculed Malcolm and the Black Muslims for their black supremacist ideas and their call for blacks to "live in a separate state."[11] The civil rights leader dismissed Malcolm's dream of a separate black nation as both unrealistic and undesirable.

The two men were equally critical of each other with respect to the love ethic. Malcolm frequently referred to Martin as that "foremost exponent of love, who gets his head bashed in while he is preaching brotherhood." In Malcolm's view, Martin's advocacy of universal agape love played "into the hands of the white oppressors" because it disarmed "the Negro" and fitted "into the stereotype of the Negro as a meek, turning-the-other-cheek sort of creature." Disturbed by this tendency to identify love with weakness, Martin insisted that Malcolm failed to understand the true nature of love and its relationship to power: "Well, I don't think of love, as in this context, as emotional bosh. I don't think of it as a weak force, but I think of love as something strong and that organizes itself in powerful direct action." Martin went on to say that Malcolm and the Muslims had "heard those things about my being soft, my talking about love, and they transfer their bitterness toward the white man toward me."[12]

Malcolm was not prepared to embrace Martin's concept of an unconditional love of the enemy. He criticized Martin for teaching African Americans to love whites before they actually learned to love themselves. "Most of the Negroes you see running around here talking about 'love everybody'—they don't have any love whatsoever for their own kind," Malcolm asserted in 1963. "When they say, 'Love everybody,' what they are doing is setting up a situation for us to love white people." In an equally telling remark, Malcolm declared that "Martin Luther King isn't preaching love—he's preaching love the white man." On yet another occasion, he insisted, "I do not agree with Martin Luther King that one should love a racialist whether he is lynching you or whatever he is doing."[13] For Malcolm, such a concept seemed all the more absurd since whites, in his estimation, lacked the moral capacity to respond in positive ways to acts of love from black people.

While agreeing with Malcolm on the necessity for black self-love, Martin was too devoted to Christian ethics to accept what he saw as the Black Muslim counsel of hostility toward all whites. "At times the public expressions of this group have bordered on a new kind of race hatred," he complained, though he readily admitted, "I can well understand the kind of impatience that leads to this kind of reaction." At one point, after seeing Malcolm on television, Martin commented: "When he starts talking about all that's been done to us, I get a twinge of hate, of identification with him. But hate is not the only effect."[14]

Malcolm's uncompromising stand on the question of violence made conversation and cooperation with Martin virtually impossible. In conformity with Black Muslim philosophy, Malcolm affirmed without question the right of every moral and rational person to practice self-defense or counterviolence. Reducing nonviolence to "a begging, hat-in-hand, compromising approach," he and his fellow Muslims slammed Martin in 1960 for making potential black freedom fighters defenseless and transforming them into "contented, docile slaves." Malcolm echoed this charge in 1963: "Any Negro who teaches other Negroes to turn the other cheek is disarming that Negro. Any Negro who teaches Negroes to turn the other cheek in the face of attack is disarming that Negro of his God-given right, of his moral right, of his natural right, of his intelligent right to defend himself. Everything in nature can defend itself except the American Negro. And men like King—their job is to go among Negroes and teach Negroes 'Don't fight back.'"[15]

Martin countered with the claim that Malcolm and the Black Muslims actually confused the meaning of the nonviolent ethic—that they mistakenly equated it with passive acquiescence or resignation. For the sake of clarity, Martin noted: "Now my feeling has always been, again, that they have never understood what I was saying, because they don't see that there's a great deal of difference between nonresistance to evil and nonviolent resistance. And certainly I'm not saying that you sit down and patiently accept injustice. I'm talking about a very strong force, where you stand up with all your might against an evil system, and you're not a coward; you are resisting but you come to see that tactically as well as morally it is better to be nonviolent."[16]

Martin's insistence that his nonviolence was squarely in the tradition of both Jesus and Gandhi was casually discounted by Malcolm, who argued that the man from Nazareth and the Indian leader acted out of strength rather than weakness. He questioned the view that Jesus advocated absolute nonviolence, noting that "in the Book of Revelation, they've got Jesus sitting on a horse with a sword in his hand, getting ready to go into action." In terms equally forthright, Malcolm rejected the notion that Martin was an "American Gandhi": "If you tell someone he resembles Hannibal or Gandhi long enough, he starts believing it—even begins to act like it. But there is a big difference in the passiveness of King and the passiveness of Gandhi. Gandhi was a big dark elephant sitting on a little white mouse. King is a little black mouse sitting on top a big white elephant."[17]

In an interview given in 1964, almost a year after this statement, Malcolm reasoned that "Christian-Gandhian philosophy" is "criminal" if it upholds "turning the other cheek." Strangely, he seemed more willing to compare Martin to Chief Albert J. Luthuli, the black South African who preached nonviolence, than to Gandhi, whom he read about and appeared to hold in high esteem.[18] Concerning Luthuli, who won the Nobel Peace Prize in 1960, Malcolm stated: "He is just another Martin Luther King who is used to keep the oppressed people in check and keep them from using bona fide methods to produce bona fide results. I think the real leaders in South Africa are Sobukwe and Mandela. They are in tune with the times."[19]

Malcolm's point was that Kingian-Luthulian methods were out of touch with the revolutionary spirit of the times, all the more because they conformed to the ground rules of white liberal establishments. Malcolm consistently said this about Martin's methods. He held that Martin's nonviolent approach had won wide acceptance not because most African Americans affirmed it but because deceitful white liberals sanctioned and encouraged it: "White people follow King. White people pay King. White people subsidize King. White people support King. But the masses of black people don't support Martin Luther King. King is the best weapon that the white man, who wants to brutalize Negroes, has ever gotten in this country, because he is setting up a situation where, when the white man wants to attack Negroes, they can't defend themselves, because King has put this foolish philosophy out—you're not supposed to defend yourself."[20]

Convinced that nonviolence hindered rather than enhanced the black freedom struggle, Malcolm scoffed at those who associated Martin with that grand tradition of black heroism. "Any man that propagates that kind of doctrine among Negroes is a traitor to those people," he declared in 1963. Referring to Martin as "a fool," Malcolm argued that "you need somebody who is going to fight; you don't need any kneeling-in or crawling-in." In even harsher terms, he denounced Martin as "a false shepherd" and a classic "Uncle Tom" who had sold out to "white devils": "Just as Uncle Tom, back during slavery, used to keep the Negroes from resisting the bloodhound or resisting the Ku Klux Klan by teaching them to love their enemies or pray for those who use them despitefully, today, Martin Luther King is just a twentieth-century or modern Uncle Tom or religious Uncle Tom, who is doing the same thing today to keep Negroes defenseless in the face of attack that Uncle Tom did on the plantation to keep *those* Negroes defenseless in the face of the attack of the Klan in that day."[21]

Martin never responded publicly to such attacks, but "they alarmed and saddened him." However, he was certain that "all this talk about my being an Uncle Tom" would eventually fade "and that nonviolence would triumph." On rare occasions, he did denounce Malcolm's call for blacks to buy guns and form self-defense teams as "irresponsible" and "demagogic," and he accused the Black Muslims of engaging in "an unconscious advocacy of violence." But the violence of the white South against African Americans made it increasingly difficult for Martin to counter Malcolm.[22]

Nothing disturbed Malcolm more than what he perceived as glaring inconsistencies in Martin's advocacy of nonviolence. Of particular concern for him was Martin's failure to properly emphasize the need for blacks to practice nonviolence with each other, an issue quite pressing in view of the readiness and the frequency with which blacks killed and maimed "their own kind." Of Martin, he complained: "He doesn't tell them, 'Don't fight each other.' 'Don't fight the white man' is what he's saying in essence, because the followers of Martin Luther King will cut each other from head to foot, but they will not do anything to defend themselves against the attacks of the white man."[23]

But Malcolm's criticism at this point misfired, since Martin's nonviolent campaigns so often created a unity and sense of common purpose among blacks that undermined and discouraged intraracial violence. Also problematic was Malcolm's claim that Martin was "justified in teaching Black people to turn the other cheek" only if he taught whites the same. The sheer depth of racism in white society, and the dangers that would have awaited Martin and his staff, rendered absurd Malcolm's suggestion that "the leaders of the nonviolent movement" should go "into the white community and teach nonviolence."[24] Moreover, Malcolm's suggestion on this matter was quite inconsistent with his own belief, stated consistently during his Black Muslim years, that whites were morally incapable of responding to the challenge of nonviolence.

The whole question of the morality and practicality of violence vis-à-vis that of nonviolence stood at the center of this ideological conflict. Malcolm was not persuaded by Martin's contention that violence is essentially immoral because it is rooted in hatred rather than love, and because it increases the existence of evil and prevents the creation of bridges of understanding and community between persons. Equally questionable for Malcolm was Martin's conviction that violence is impractical because it leads to more violence, fails to appeal to the conscience of the perpetrators of violence, and can only result in the extermination of the black minority by a well-armed and violent white majority. The Muslim leader insisted that resistance to oppression does not become any more *immoral* by virtue of it being armed, and neither is it necessarily *moral* because it is nonviolent. He further held that questions about the *practicality* and *impracticality* of violence constituted a non-issue in a society where African Americans were constantly brutalized by whites. Convinced that his people would never win genuine freedom and self-respect by embracing Martin's concepts of nonviolence and undeserved, redemptive suffering, Malcolm urged them to strike back when attacked by the white man. "When you're dealing with an enemy who doesn't know what nonviolence is," he explained, "as far as I'm concerned you're wasting your time."[25]

Malcolm rejected the idea that the odds would be against blacks in an armed struggle, and he attacked Martin for trying "to get Negroes to forgive the people who have brutalized them for four hundred years." But his assault on Martin's methods was undermined by his failure to implement his own call for "reciprocal bleeding" or counterviolence into a concrete plan of action. Martin recognized as much, and he challenged Malcolm's call for African Americans to respond violently to white racists who used clubs, dogs, cattle prods, and other instruments of violence against them. Said Martin of Malcolm: "I have often wished that he would talk less of violence, because violence is not going to solve our problem. And in his litany of articulating the despair of the Negro without offering any positive, creative alternative, I feel that Malcolm has done himself and our people a great disservice. Fiery, demagogic oratory in the black ghettoes, urging Negroes to arm themselves and prepare to engage in violence, as he has done, can reap nothing but grief."[26]

Malcolm was not pleased with these remarks, which Alex Haley recorded in a 1965 interview for *Playboy*. After telling Malcolm what Martin had said, Haley wrote:

The only time I have ever heard Malcolm X use what might be construed as a curse word, it was a "hell" used in response to a statement that Dr. Martin Luther King made that Malcolm X's talk brought "misery upon Negroes." Malcolm exploded to me, "How in the hell can my talk do this? It's always a Negro responsible, not what the white man does!" The "extremist" or "demagogue" accusation invariably would burn Malcolm X. "Yes, I'm an extremist. The black race here in North America is in extremely bad condition. You show me a black man who isn't an extremist and I'll show you one who needs psychiatric attention!"[27]

Martin's faith in the power of nonviolence to transform persons and the society as a whole was never really shared by Malcolm, who maintained, "There's no such thing as a nonviolent revolution." When reminded of Arnold Toynbee's view that nonviolence, as taught and practiced by Martin, would be "one of the savings of Christianity in the Western world," Malcolm responded sarcastically: "It probably would be the savings of Christianity in the Western world, even if it wasn't the savings of the Negroes." The Muslim leader dismissed as fantasy Martin's insistence that the salvation of African Americans, and indeed the entire human race, depends on the extent to which nonviolence figures into the arena of human relations.[28]

But both men questioned whether nonviolence could survive among a people who were increasingly victimized by white mobs. Martin remained hopeful that such would be the case, but Malcolm warned white America not to assume that blacks would continue to be passive, patient, and long-suffering. Convinced that "Martin Luther King is at the end of his rope," Malcolm cautioned:

If white people get the impression that Negroes all endorse the old turn-the-other-cheek cowardly philosophy of Dr. Martin Luther King, then whites are going to make the mistake of putting their hands on some Black man, thinking that he's going to turn the other cheek, and he'll end up losing his hand and losing his life in the try. So it is always better to let someone know where you stand. And there are a large number of Black people in this country who don't endorse any phase of what Dr. Martin Luther King and these other twentieth-century Uncle Toms are putting in front of the public eye to make it look like this is the way, this is the behavior, or this is the thought pattern of most of our people.[29]

The sheer power of this statement had become most evident by the mid-1960s, as blacks rioted in Los Angeles, Chicago, Detroit, New York, and scores of other American cities. These riots were to some degree a testimony to the influence of Malcolm and the black power movement that followed him, and Martin knew it. Speaking in 1964, the civil rights leader seemed to suggest that Malcolm was one reason for the many riots in the northern ghettoes. "More riots have occurred in the North because the fellow in Harlem, to name one Northern ghetto, can't see any victories," he said. He went on to say that Malcolm "remains throttled, as he has always been, by vague, intangible economic and social deprivations." In another statement, Martin appeared less direct: "Though it is never expressly stated, there are numerous indications that in some strange way, the Negro leadership is fundamentally responsible for the acts of violence and rioting which have occurred within these Negro communities." However, he quickly added, "The longer our people see no progress, or halting progress, the easier it will be for them to yield to the counsels of hatred and demagoguery."[30]

The attacks Malcolm and Martin made against each other did not result from a deep hatred. Rather, they were indicative of the strong dislike each had for the other's philosophy and methods. Even so, it is difficult to avoid the notion that there were petty, personal jealousies that were not particularly malicious in nature, feelings reinforced by the media's picture of them as adversaries.[31] Malcolm resented the attention that the media gave Martin, especially since he himself was the target of so much bad press. He once lashed out at the press in New York City for ignoring the positive side of the message that Muslims had to share while exaggerating Martin's importance: "When an integrationist like King or someone else comes into the city, if he talks to five people this will be blown up in the press and it will be made to appear that this is the man who represents the black masses, and that all of the black masses endorse the type of peaceful suffering, hat-in-hand, tongue-in-cheek doctrine that is usually displayed on these occasions."[32]

There were other matters about Martin that Malcolm found hard to accept. Martin was obviously the most prominent black leader in terms of visibility and influence. He had personal access to numerous celebrities and world leaders and could prevail upon the great and powerful to act. Furthermore, he was more successful than Malcolm in developing a consistent, overall philosophy, program, and movement for black liberation. But this did not keep Martin from becoming slightly rankled at times over Malcolm's celebrity. Despite his many privileges and accomplishments, Martin played second fiddle to Malcolm in the black ghettoes of the North. Martin and other moderate civil rights leaders were not pleased that the Muslim spokesman had the ear and the strong support of a ghetto lumpenproletariat whom they discussed but never reached completely.[33]

Martin and his aides categorically refused to include Malcolm's name among "the most responsible Negro leaders," a tendency Malcolm publicly welcomed since he equated "being responsible" with selling out to the system. However, privately he was hurt by the rejection. "I don't see why they hate me," he said sadly to Ossie Davis. "I raise hell in the backyard and they run out front and The Man puts money in their hands." Malcolm's biographer Peter Goldman has given an interesting account of the Muslim minister's reaction to being avoided by Martin and other civil rights leaders: "They placed him in moral Coventry, and it wounded Malcolm; something in him wanted acceptance, though never at the price he would have had to pay. 'He really hungered to be recognized as a national leader,' one friend said. 'It hurt him when first Kennedy and then Johnson would call King, Wilkins, Young, and Farmer to the White House. He wanted it to be a fivesome instead of a foursome.'"[34]

Malcolm's reputation as a skillful and effective debater made him all the more intimidating in the minds of Martin and his aides. Although Malcolm's formal education was limited to the eighth grade, Martin, who held a Ph.D., absolutely refused to challenge him in a debate. During business trips to Atlanta, Malcolm occasionally appeared at the main office of the Southern Christian Leadership Conference on Auburn Avenue to chat with Martin, but Martin was always away. Martin rejected invitations to debate Malcolm in California in 1962. Dora McDonald, Martin's secretary, gave this explanation: "On the question of debating with Malcolm X, Dr. King has taken a consistent position of not accepting such invitations because he feels that it will do no good. He has always considered his work in a positive action framework rather than engaging in consistent negative debate." The East Bay Ministerial Fellowship of Berkeley, California, responded with disappointment, noting in a letter to Martin, "We have indicated to CBS and NBC that you have declined their kind offer of discussion with Malcolm X, minister of the New York Temple of Islam Movement." Martin also threatened to withdraw from a David Susskind television panel if Malcolm were invited. Malcolm found such actions particularly amusing, and he once implied, slightly grinning, that Martin could not possibly win in a debate with him: "Why King? Because integration is ridiculous, a dream. I am not interested in dreams, but in the nightmare. Martin Luther King, the rest of them, they are thinking about dreams. But then really King and I have nothing to debate about. We are both indicting. I would say to him: 'You indict and give them hope. I'll indict and give them no hope.'"[35]

Malcolm and Martin knew that any debate between them would be exploited by their enemies to the detriment of the black liberation cause. Both wished to avoid the kind of negative publicity that the racist elements in society so often used to cloud the real issues and to divide those struggling for positive change. But they were also mindful of the benefits that the movement could derive from the kind of honest, constructive criticisms they directed at each other. Malcolm put it best when questioned about his role as a critic of Martin and other civil rights activists: "I think all of us should be critics of each other. Whenever you can't stand criticism you can never grow. I don't think that it serves any purpose for the leaders of our people to waste their time fighting each other needlessly. I think that we accomplish more when we sit down in private and iron out whatever differences that may exist and try and then do something constructive for the benefit of our people. But on the other hand, I don't think that we should be above criticism."[36]

But their roles as critics of each other led at times to hard feelings. Malcolm was passionately denounced by many blacks who were loyal to Martin. Martin felt the wrath of those who saw their only hope in Malcolm. The most unfortunate displays of anger and intolerance were aimed at Martin, who, during several trips to Harlem, never missed an opportunity to counter Malcolm's influence. He knew that Harlem was Malcolm's stomping ground, but he felt that something had to be done to prevent the Muslim spokesman from instigating a tragic cycle of violence there, especially since Harlem, with the largest population of blacks in the country, was so critical to the outcome of the freedom struggle.[37] But many Harlemites resented Martin's attempts to move on Malcolm's turf. Martin knew this, and he wondered whether Malcolm and other black nationalists were in some way responsible for several attacks on his person in Harlem. In September 1958, while autographing copies of his first book in a Harlem department store, the civil rights leader was stabbed with a letter opener by Izola Curry. Martin later speculated, "It may be that she had been around some of the meetings of these groups in Harlem, Black Nationalist groups, that have me all the time as a favorite object of scorn, and hearing this over and over again she may have responded to it when I came to Harlem," though he quickly added, "It may be that she was just so confused that she would have done this to anybody whose name was in the news. We will never know."[38]

There was absolutely no proof that Malcolm contributed to the Curry attack, but he definitely helped create the atmosphere that led to attacks on Martin during later visits to Harlem. In June 1963, as Martin drove through Harlem, he was greeted with boos and his car windows were splattered with eggs. Visibly "shaken and hurt" because "these were Negroes throwing eggs at me," Martin seemed certain that Malcolm was behind the incident:

> I think that was really a result of the Black Nationalist groups, and a feeling—you know, they've heard all of these things about my being soft and talking about love and the white man all the time. . . . And I think it grows right out of that. In fact Malcolm X had a meeting the day before and he talked about me a great deal and said—told them that I would be there the next night, and said: "You ought to go over there and let old King know what you think about him." And he had said a great deal about nonviolence, criticizing nonviolence, and saying that I approved of Negro men and women being bitten by dogs and the fire hoses, and I say go on and not defend yourself. So I think this kind of response grew out of the build-up and the—all of the talk about my being a sort of polished Uncle Tom.[39]

Malcolm vehemently denied being involved. "I frankly hold the police responsible for giving out misinformation designed to misinform the public about a religious group which they know has never been involved in any acts of aggression against anyone," he observed. "We express ourselves verbally against anyone with whom we don't agree, but we never attack anyone physically unless we are attacked ourselves."[40] But Malcolm's shadow continued to haunt Martin. In July 1964, in the wake of the Harlem riots, Martin was attacked by angry blacks. He went to Harlem for a series of meetings with New York mayor Robert F. Wagner and Jewish leaders, hoping to find a solution to the crisis. Malcolm was touring Africa and the Middle East at the time, but his presence was felt in a most painful manner. Stephen B. Oates reports, "The trip was a disaster. While King toured the riot sites, embittered Harlemites booed him and spouted anti-Semitic vitriol that made him grimace. At the same time, local Negro leaders fumed that no 'outsider' imported by the Mayor had the right to invade their territory and tell them what to do. . . . King was greatly troubled."[41]

Various media sources contributed immensely to the split between Malcolm and Martin and their followers. In late 1963, *Newsweek* made much of the claim that African Americans had ranked Martin and the SCLC far above Malcolm and the Black Muslims in terms of effectiveness and popularity. Malcolm casually dismissed this as yet another ploy to make African Americans embrace nonviolence. But he was clearly upset when a *New York Times* poll among blacks in New York showed that 75 percent had named Martin as "doing the best work for Negroes," while only 6 percent had chosen him. "Brother," remarked Malcolm to Alex Haley, "do you realize that some of history's greatest leaders never were recognized until they were safely in the ground."[42] Considering the widespread interest shown in him since his death, he could not have been more prophetic.

When Martin received the Nobel Peace Prize in December 1964, newspaper reporters and others who covered his activities saw other opportunities to exploit the differences between him and Malcolm. Malcolm was approached for his reaction to the tribute to Martin, and he found it impossible to hide his bitterness. "He got the Peace Prize, and we got the problem," he told Claude Lewis of the *New York Post*. "Black people in this country have no peace and have not made the strides forward that would in any way justify receiving a reward by any of us," Malcolm said to a student at Harvard University. When Martin's admirers staged a rally in Harlem to celebrate his award, Malcolm and a few of his followers appeared "and watched in heavy silence from a back row." Refusing to join the rejoicing, Malcolm asserted: "I don't want the white man giving me medals. If I'm following a general, and he's leading me into battle, and the enemy tends to give him rewards, or awards, I get suspicious of him. Especially if he gets a peace award before the war is over."[43]

The Nobel Peace Prize further convinced Malcolm that Martin was simply dancing to the tune piped by the money of white liberals. "The white liberals have a guilt complex about the Negro," he shouted. "They love people like King who salve that guilt feeling a little. That's why they finance him. He's their darling." At another point Malcolm said, "White people in the South are praying in the secrecy of their closets that King never dies. King is the best thing that ever happened to white folks."[44] In a 1964 interview with Claude Lewis, Malcolm was even more specific:

King himself is probably a good man, means well and all that. But the danger is that white people use King. They use King to satisfy their own fears. They blow him up. They give him power beyond his actual influence. Because they want to believe within themselves that Negroes are nonviolent and patient, and long-suffering and forgiving. White people want to believe that so bad, 'cause they're so guilty. But the danger is, when they blow up King and fool themselves into thinking that Negroes are really nonviolent, and patient, and long-suffering, they've got a powder keg in their house. And instead of them trying to do something to defuse the powder keg, they're putting a blanket over it, trying to make believe that this is no powder keg; that this is a couch that we can lay on and enjoy.[45]

Martin was not deterred by claims that he was a tool of the white liberal establishment, because he felt that his challenge to white America was as great, if not greater, than that of Malcolm. Even so, despite all the public disagreements and the name-calling that occurred between them, their greatest battles were not with each other but with a white society that failed to accept the full humanity of their people.

On King's Civil Rights Campaigns: Amazing Successes or Unqualified Failures?

It has been said that "Malcolm X in sum prepared the way for Martin Luther King's rebellion." This holds true in some respects, but the fact remains that the two leaders always differed in their perspectives on the meaning and significance of the modern civil rights movement. From the time of the Montgomery bus boycott in 1955–56, Malcolm had serious reservations and questions about the philosophical underpinnings, the interracial character, the objectives, and the direction of civil rights campaigns led by Martin. However, he refused to make those reservations and questions a matter of public record before 1960. When questioned in the late 1950s about Martin's leadership role in the Montgomery protest, Malcolm typically avoided any mention of Martin while shifting the attention to Rosa Parks, who courageously refused to surrender her bus seat to a white male passenger. Reflecting on why he refused to publicly attack Martin's role in civil rights campaigns in the 1950s, Malcolm observed: "Now my feeling was that although the civil rights 'leaders' kept attacking us Muslims, still they were black people, still they were our own kind, and I would be most foolish to let the white man maneuver me against the civil rights movement."[46]

Malcolm's silence regarding civil rights campaigns led by Martin had ended by 1962, when Martin joined various sectors of the black community in Albany, Georgia, in an across-the-board, full-scale offensive against the entire system of segregation there. Martin's activities in that city were consistent with what he perceived as the goal of the civil rights movement as a whole, namely, the creation of the beloved community, or a completely integrated society grounded in love and justice. After a series of blunders that "highlighted his vulnerabilities as a strategist and as a leader," Martin and the SCLC pulled out of Albany, leaving blacks there to carry on the struggle. Malcolm denounced Martin's efforts in Albany, insisting, "They didn't get anything but their heads whipped." "When Martin Luther King failed to desegregate Albany, Georgia," he bellowed, "the civil rights struggle in America reached its low point. King became bankrupt almost, as a leader."[47] As the images of Martin and other civil rights leaders were "shattered" in Albany, Malcolm continued, they "began to lose their prestige and influence" as well as their control over the black masses:

> The black masses across the country at the grassroots level had already begun to take their cases to the streets on their own. The government in Washington knew that something had to be done to get the rampaging Negroes back into the corral, back under the control of the white liberals. . . . The government propaganda machine began encouraging Negroes to follow only what it called "responsible" Negro leadership, and by "responsible" Negro leaders the government actually meant, *Negro leaders who were responsible to the government,* and who could therefore be controlled by the government, and be used by that same government to control their impatient people.[48]

Martin had a different assessment of the Albany campaign. While admitting that mistakes had been made and that the movement had failed to achieve its goals, he argued that "Albany was far from an unqualified failure." Martin wrote: "Though lunch counters remained segregated, thousands of Negroes were added to the voting-registration rolls. In the gubernatorial elections that followed our summer there, a moderate candidate confronted a rabid segregationist. By reason of the expanded Negro vote, the moderate defeated the segregationist in the city of Albany, which in turn contributed to his victory in the state. As a result, Georgia elected its first governor pledged to respect and enforce the law equally."[49]

Malcolm's strongest attacks on Martin's activities in the South came in 1963, when Martin and his staff were heavily involved in Project Confrontation in Birmingham, Alabama. This was Martin's third major attempt at social protest, an effort aimed at patterns of segregation in Birmingham's business community. While disagreeing with the goal of Project C, which he saw as *integration,* Malcolm was most upset because women and children were encouraged to participate in the street demonstrations, a move all the more troubling given the brutality that Eugene "Bull" Connor and other law enforcement officials meted out to the demonstrators. "Martin Luther King is a chump, not a champ," Malcolm cried. "Any man who puts his women and children on the front lines is a chump, not a champ."[50]

Malcolm's relentless assault caused some anxiety among those who felt that radical groups like the Black Muslims could benefit if Project C failed. "One urgent question raised by the Birmingham episode is what form the inevitably growing Negro protest is going to take," wrote Anthony Lewis in a *New York Times* article. "Will it be the peaceful route of the Rev. Dr. Martin Luther King, Jr? Or will it be the road of black nationalism preached by the Black Muslims?" This question haunted President John F. Kennedy and Burke Marshall, the assistant attorney general for civil rights, both of whom believed that violence could possibly "follow the failure of moderate efforts" by Martin and others in Birmingham.[51]

The outcome of Project C remained in serious doubt until May 10, 1963, when an accord was reached between Martin and his staff and the business and industrial community. Birmingham's businessmen agreed to desegregate the facilities of downtown stores and to upgrade and hire blacks on a nondiscriminatory basis, and steps were taken to release all jailed protesters and to prevent further protests. Martin called the pact "a fresh, bold step toward equality," and he predicted that "Birmingham will one day become a model in southern race relations." In contrast, Malcolm saw the Birmingham campaign as a failure. "And many of you saw on television, in Birmingham, how the police had these big vicious dogs biting Black people," he declared in a speech at the London School of Economics. "They were crushing the skulls of Black people. They had water hoses turned on our women, stripping off the clothes from our own women, from our children." Malcolm's response to black psychologist Kenneth B. Clark, who viewed Martin's efforts in Birmingham as "a success," was even more dynamic: "What kind of success did they get in Birmingham? A chance to sit at a lunch counter and drink some coffee with a cracker—that's success? A chance to—thousands of little children went to jail; they didn't get out, they were bonded out by King. They had to *pay* their way out of jail. That's not any kind of advancement or success."[52]

Disappointed that Martin was "satisfied in making a compromise or deal with the same ones" who "brutalized thousands of black people," Malcolm further denounced the Birmingham pact as "a sellout" rather than a positive gain. Moreover, he chastised Martin and others for believing that the recent election of Albert Boutwell, a white moderate, as mayor of Birmingham would ensure the fulfillment of the terms of the agreement:

Negroes in Birmingham are in worse condition now than they were then because the line is more tightly drawn. And to say that some moderate—to say that things are better because a different man, a different white man, a different Southern white man is in office now, who's supposed to be a moderate, is to tell me that you are better off dealing with a fox than you were when you were dealing with a wolf. The ones that they were dealing with previously were wolves, and they didn't hide the fact that they were wolves. The man that they got to deal with now is a fox, but he's no better than the wolf. Only he's better in his ability to lull the Negroes to sleep, and he'll do that as long as they listen to Dr. Martin Luther King Jr.[53]

For Malcolm, the violent clashes that occurred between blacks and whites in Birmingham immediately after the agreement attested not only to Martin's lack of ingenuity but also to the absurdity of his nonviolent tactics. The Muslim leader noted how "the Negroes in Birmingham" exploded and "began to stab the crackers in the back and bust them up 'side their head."[54] The problems in Birmingham were further exacerbated, Malcolm estimated, by a growing rift between Martin and other civil rights moderates over financial contributions from white liberals:

After Martin Luther King had been released from his Birmingham jail cell in May, he traveled from coast to coast in a fund-raising campaign for his Southern Christian Leadership Conference. Roy Wilkins then began to attack King, accusing him of stirring up trouble, saying that after the NAACP would bail out King and the other demonstrators, then King would capitalize on the trouble by taking up all the money for his own organization, leaving the NAACP to hold the bag at a great financial loss. . . . As King, Wilkins, and other civil rights leaders began to fight publicly among themselves over the money they were trying to get from the white liberals, they were destroying their own leadership "image."[55]

Martin refused to publicly address Malcolm's attacks, choosing instead to point to the triumph of nonviolence over the forces of segregation in Birmingham. But even if Malcolm exaggerated in dismissing the Birmingham campaign as a fiasco, he was essentially right about the tensions that existed within the ranks of black leadership. Martin hoped that the planned March on Washington, designed to mobilize the nation around the issues of jobs and freedom, would ease these tensions while heightening the sense of unity and common purpose among black leaders and all the black organizations on the civil rights front. Occurring on August 28, 1963, the event attracted roughly 250,000 participants, uniting in one luminous action black and white, rich and poor, and representatives of the Catholic, Protestant, and Jewish faiths.[56] The magnificent display of unity across racial, class, and religious boundaries, coupled with the dynamic speeches and the rousing singing, moved the nation in profound ways, but Malcolm, who was also in Washington, remained unimpressed and as critical as ever.

Malcolm denounced the March on Washington in a press conference the night before it occurred, labeling it as "nothing but a circus" or "a picnic." He was clearly incorrect in saying that the "march talk" germinated among the grassroots in the streets before Martin and other moderate civil rights leaders took it over and purged it of its militancy. He was more on the mark in arguing that white liberals assumed control of the march and that "the White House, with a fanfare of international publicity, 'approved,' 'endorsed,' and 'welcomed' a March on Washington." Malcolm declared: "They controlled it so tight, they told those Negroes what time to hit town, how to come, where to stop, what signs to carry, what song to sing, what speech they could make, and what speech they couldn't make; and then told them to get out of town by sundown. And every one of those Toms was out of town by sundown."[57]

For Malcolm, the event was "a takeover," "a sellout," "that Farce on Washington," led by "black and white clowns." He was unmoved by Martin's celebrated "I Have a Dream" speech, and he later insisted that "the Negro leaders have to come out of the clouds, and wake up, and stop dreaming and start facing reality." Malcolm also stated emphatically that "this dream of King's is going to be a nightmare before it's over, only he's too dumb to know it." Such a prediction was impossible to ignore, especially when a black church in Birmingham was bombed less than a month after the March on Washington, causing the deaths of four girls. The bombing raised more questions in Malcolm's mind about the significance of the great march. "Imagine, marching to Washington," he declared, "and getting nothing for it whatsoever." This assessment was obviously rejected by Martin, who contended that the enormous gathering in Washington "was the living, beating heart of an infinitely noble movement."[58]

A shift in Malcolm's attitude toward Martin and the civil rights movement began when he was forced out of the Nation of Islam in December 1963, less than four months after the March on Washington. "For years, I had attacked so many so-called 'black leaders' for their shortcomings," Malcolm conceded. "Now, I had to honestly ask myself what I could offer, how I was genuinely qualified to help the black people win their struggle for human rights." He officially declared his independence from the Black Muslims on March 8, 1964, noting in a press conference four days later in New York, "I myself intend to be very active in every phase of the American Negro struggle for *human rights*."[59]

Martin had privately predicted a split between Malcolm and Elijah Muhammad, but soon after it happened, he asserted:

> The recent declaration by Malcolm X of his break with Mr. Muhammad holds no particular significance to the present civil rights efforts of the American Negro. The program of "reciprocal bleeding" and the irresponsible prophecy of widespread violence that he espouses offers little comfort or hope of relief to the dilemma of the Negro community. It is regrettable that Malcolm X has publicly confessed to such a negative and desperate course of action. I must honestly say that this new turn of events is not so much an indictment against him as it is against a society whose ills in race relations are so deep rooted that it produces a Malcolm X. The critical significance of his present statements is that they challenge the national community of the United States to support the efforts of the Negro in his struggle for full citizenship while the masses are responsive to disciplined and responsible nonviolent leadership now at its helm. If sizeable tangible gains are not made soon across the country, we must honestly face the prospect that some Negroes might be tempted to accept some oblique path such as that Malcolm X proposes.[60]

Claude Lewis reported that "Malcolm began to say kinder things about Martin Luther King Jr." after breaking with the Black Muslims. Malcolm was known to "laugh at King" and to refer to him jokingly as "Rev. Dr. Chickenwing," but his criticism of King became less intense and less frequent, a development not surprising given Malcolm's struggle to find a respectable place within the ranks of the freedom movement. "Minister Malcolm has made public his intentions not to attack any person who is engaged in the struggle, nor any organization that is engaged in the struggle," wrote James Shabazz, the secretary of Malcolm's newly formed Muslim Mosque, Inc. in May 1964. "Certainly he is looking forward to the day (in the near future) when all leaders and organizations will be able to present a United Action Front."[61]

In June 1964, as the vicious forces of segregation rose up against Martin and other nonviolent protesters in St. Augustine, Florida, Malcolm displayed this changing spirit and attitude, stating in a June 30 telegram to King: "We have been witnessing with great concern the vicious attacks of the white racists against our poor defenseless people there in St. Augustine. If the Federal Government will not send troops to your aid, just say the word and we will immediately dispatch some of our brothers there to organize self-defense units among our people, and the Ku Klux Klan will then receive a taste of its own medicine. The day of turning the other cheek to those brute beasts is over." Malcolm knew that Martin would not respond affirmatively to this offer of assistance, but the fiery Muslim merely wanted to express his solidarity with the African Americans who were risking their lives for freedom and justice. He knew as well as Martin the benefits of collective struggle, but he was still unwilling to join the movement on Martin's terms. The efforts in St. Augustine struck Malcolm as yet another failure, an assessment not entirely rejected by Martin, who left that city "depressed, sad, and angry." But the fact remains that Malcolm was beginning to see the movement as a whole in a more positive light.[62] His Muslim Mosque and Organization of Afro-American Unity, both formed in 1964, provided new vehicles through which his people could participate in that movement without relying on the support of white liberals.

The relationship of the African-American struggle to movements of the oppressed worldwide became even more important to Malcolm and Martin in 1964. This mounting concern on their part resulted not only from their deepening and expanding involvements but also from considerable travel, observation, study, and reflection. This concern found some reinforcement when Martin was awarded the Nobel Peace Prize. The civil rights leader viewed the award in terms of its international implications:

> I would like to think that the award is not a personal tribute, but a tribute to the entire freedom movement, and to the gallant people of

both races who surround me in the drive for civil rights which will make the American dream a reality. I think that this internationally known award will call even more attention to our struggle, gain even greater sympathy and understanding for our cause, from people all over the world. I like to think that the award recognizes symbolically the gallantry, the courage and the amazing discipline of the Negro in America, for these things are to his eternal credit. Though we have had riots, the bloodshed that we would have known without the discipline of nonviolence would have been truly frightening.[63]

Malcolm was less clear and consistent in his perception of the meaning and significance of Martin's Nobel Prize. In a December 1964 interview with Claude Lewis, he seemed to agree with much of Martin's assessment: "Well, to me it represented the fact that the struggle of the Negro in this country was being endorsed at the international level and that it was looked upon as a problem that affects the peace of the world. And it was looked upon as a human problem or a problem for humanity, rather than just a Mississippi problem or an American problem. To me, King getting that Nobel Peace Prize—it wasn't King getting it—it represented the awareness on the part of the world that the race problem in America could upset the peace of the world. And this is true."[64]

At other times, Malcolm suggested that the awarding of the medal to Martin was a move on the part of the white Western world to keep the African-American struggle nonviolent and under its control. The same had occurred in 1960 with the black movement in South Africa, Malcolm argued, when the nonviolent leader Albert J. Luthuli was given the Nobel Peace Prize as a statement against Nelson Mandela and other militants, who had recently shifted to armed struggle:

If you read the testimony of Mandela in court, he brought out the fact that at that point the brothers in South Africa had begun to realize that they had to go into action, that nonviolence had become outdated; it only helped the enemy. But at the same time the enemy knows that once eleven million people stop being confined to a nonviolent approach against three million, you're going to have a different situation. They had to use their new modern tricks, so they ran down and got one of the Africans and gave him a glorious peace prize for being nonviolent, and it lent strength to the nonviolent image, to try and keep them a little nonviolent a little while longer. And it's the same way in the States. The black man in the States has begun to see that nonviolence is a trick that is put upon him to keep him from even being able to defend himself.[65]

For Malcolm, then, the most important development in 1964 was not so much the recognition that the freedom movement gained through Martin's Nobel Prize or the Civil Rights Act but, rather, his own success, through "An Appeal to African Heads of State" and other efforts, to internationalize the struggle:

In my opinion, the greatest accomplishment that was made in the struggle of the black man in America in 1964 toward some kind of real progress was the successful linking together of our problem with the African problem, or making our problem a world problem. Because now, whenever anything happens to you in Mississippi, it's not just a case of somebody in Alabama getting indignant, or somebody in New York getting indignant. The same repercussions that you see all over the world when an imperialist foreign power interferes in some section of Africa—you see repercussions, you see the embassies being bombed and burned and overturned—nowadays, when something happens to black people in Mississippi, you'll see the same repercussions all over the world.[66]

Malcolm felt that Martin and other black leaders were limiting the struggle by identifying it with civil rights rather than human rights: "Civil rights means you're asking Uncle Sam to treat you right. When you expand the civil rights struggle to the level of human rights, you can then take the case of the black man in this country before the nations in the UN."[67] Malcolm's desire to internationalize the African-American freedom struggle was no stronger than Martin's, though the Muslim activist, unlike the civil rights leader, clearly underestimated the influence of the United States in the UN. Moreover, Malcolm refused to acknowledge that Martin, too, spoke frequently of human rights, especially when stressing the theological and moral justifications for his crusade against racial segregation.

The debate over what form the freedom movement should take carried over into the Selma campaign of 1965, which was aimed at securing voting rights for African Americans. Martin led the campaign and was still determined to isolate Malcolm from the front lines of the civil rights struggle. As white mob violence against the protesters escalated in Selma, Malcolm found it impossible to remain silent. His patience ran out on January 18, 1965, when the American Nazi Party chief George Lincoln Rockwell and the local segregationist Jimmy G. Robinson confronted Martin in Selma, and Robinson knocked the civil rights leader to the ground. Less than a week later, Malcolm sent the following telegram to Rockwell:

This is to warn you that I am no longer held in check from fighting white supremacists by Elijah Muhammad's separatist Black Muslim movement, and that if your present agitation against our people there in Alabama causes physical harm to Reverend King or any other black Americans who are only attempting to enjoy their rights as free human beings, that you and your Ku Klux Klan friends will be met with maximum physical retaliation from those of us who are not handcuffed by the disarming philosophy of nonviolence, and who believe in asserting our right of self-defense—by any means necessary.[68]

The extent to which Malcolm would have acted on this warning remains questionable, but he clearly showed that he was concerned about the racist assault on Martin and other blacks in Selma. Knowing full well that Martin would not agree with retaliatory violence or counterviolence in the Selma movement, Malcolm later admitted that the telegram to Rockwell was primarily designed to get the civil rights leader's attention:

I was curious to find out how Dr. King would react, if he were told. See, I saw him getting knocked down on television, I saw the man knock him in the mouth. Well, that hurt me, I'll tell you. Because I'm black and he's black—I don't care how dumb he is. Still, when I see a black man knocked in the mouth, I feel it, because it could happen to you or me. And if I were there with King and I saw someone knocking on him, I'd come to his rescue. I would be misrepresenting myself if I made you think I wouldn't. Yes, and then I'd show him, see, he's doing it the wrong way—this is the way you do it.[69]

On February 4, 1965, less than three weeks before he was killed, Malcolm traveled to Selma to observe firsthand the events there. He was apparently invited by members of the Student Nonviolent Coordinating Committee, some of whom felt that they had been shunted aside by Martin and his SCLC staff. Although Malcolm insisted, "I wasn't trying to interfere with King's program, whatever it was," his unannounced appearance "sent SCLC officials in a tailspin."[70] Some weeks later, while testifying in the *Williams v. Wallace* case, which involved an SCLC suit against Alabama authorities, Martin expressed regret that the recently assassinated Muslim spokesman had invaded "my own territory down here." Martin told the court: "I couldn't block his coming, but my philosophy was so antithetical to the philosophy of Malcolm X—so diametrically opposed, that I would never have invited Malcolm X to come to Selma when we were in the midst of a nonviolent demonstration, and this says nothing about the personal respect I had for him. I disagreed with his philosophy and his methods."[71]

The highlight of Malcolm's visit to Selma was his appearance at the Brown Chapel African Methodist Episcopal Church. Before Malcolm spoke, Martin's aides, James Bevel and Andrew Young, tried to coach him concerning what he should and should not say, insisting that his mere presence could incite acts of violence. Malcolm listened quietly, then bluntly reminded them, "Nobody puts words in my mouth." The speech he gave was greeted with heavy silence from the ministers of SCLC and furious applause from the youngsters of SNCC. "I'm 100 percent for the effort being put forth by the black folks here," Malcolm said. "I believe they have an absolute right to use whatever means are necessary to gain the vote." After reminding the audience, "I do not believe in nonviolence," Malcolm made it clear that other more militant forces would emerge if the whites in Selma did not accept Martin's approach. Slightly raising his voice, he noted: "Dr. King and his followers are very intelligently trying to impress the people of this area that they should give the Black man the right to vote. Now, if the people in this area are not intelligent enough themselves to recognize what they consider an intelligent approach, then I think the intelligence of the Black people in this area will compel them to devise another method that will get results."[72]

After his speech, Malcolm had a brief and friendly conversation with Coretta Scott King, Martin's wife, assuring her, "I want Dr. King to know that I didn't come to Selma to make his job difficult." He added, "I really did come thinking that I could make it easier," and continued, "If the white people realize what the alternative is, perhaps they will be more willing to hear Dr. King." She thanked him and agreed to pass on his message. Martin himself seemed both puzzled and pleased with Malcolm's words, and sometime later he told David Halberstam, "You know, right before he was killed he came down to Selma and said some pretty passionate things against me, and that surprised me because after all it was my territory down here. But afterwards he took my wife aside, and said he thought he could help me more by attacking me than praising me. He thought it would make it easier for me in the long run."[73]

Malcolm and Martin were apparently mindful of the reciprocal roles they assumed in their people's quest for freedom, justice, and equal opportunity. Despite their many differences, ideological and otherwise, they *needed* each other, *learned* from each other, and helped *make* each other. Malcolm frequently mentioned how he and the Black Muslims had a very special role to play not only in making white America more sensitive to the civil rights cause but also in preparing the ground so that Martin, Roy Wilkins, Whitney Young, and other more moderate civil rights leaders would be heard.[74] "The Black Muslim Movement did make that contribution," Malcolm observed on one occasion. "They made the whole civil rights movement become more militant, and more acceptable to the white power structure. The white man would rather have them than us."[75] Martin, too, often spoke of the significance of the alternative roles presented by himself and Malcolm, indicating how each articulated different dimensions of the anguish and goals of black Americans. "If our white brothers dismiss as 'rabble-rousers' and 'outside agitators' those of us who employ nonviolent direct action, and if they refuse to support our nonviolent efforts," Martin declared, "millions of Negroes will, out of frustration and despair, seek solace and security in black nationalist ideologies."[76]

Malcolm and Martin were determined not to allow the forces of white power to exploit their differences and alternative roles as a means of undermining the black freedom movement. Malcolm frequently reminded his people of the "divide and conquer" tactics of the oppressor, noting, in terms that would have been acceptable to Martin, that as long as African Americans agree on their objectives, they should never "fall out with each other" over methods or tactics:

America's strategy is the same strategy as that which was used in the past by the colonial powers: divide and conquer. She plays one Negro leader against the other. She plays one Negro organization against the other. She makes us think we have different objectives, different goals. As soon as one Negro says something, she runs to this Negro and asks him, "What do you think about what he said?" Why, anybody can see through that today—except some of the Negro leaders. . . . All of our people have the same goals, the same objective. The objective is freedom, justice, equality. All of us want recognition and respect as human beings.[77]

Malcolm's and Martin's stated differences at the levels of philosophy and methods, despite appearances to the contrary, stimulated healthy debate and forced many to ponder the ethical dimensions of the violence/nonviolence dialectic. Moreover, their differences helped bring energy, clarity, and a keener sense of direction to a movement that at times appeared ineffectual, misguided, and futile. Malcolm brought a spirit of militant defiance and uncompromising zeal to the struggle that Martin understood but could not provide himself, and Martin contributed an altruistic vision and an ethical ideal that Malcolm thought about but refused to embrace uncritically. Thus, Colin Morris was right in saying that "American Negroes needed both Martin Luther King Jr. and Malcolm X, just as India had to have both Gandhi and Nehru."[78]

Toward Common Ground: The Last Year, 1964–1965

After roughly four years of verbal clashes through the media, Malcolm and Martin met face-to-face for the first and only time in Washington, D.C., in the spring of 1964. Peter Goldman describes the circumstances under which the brief meeting, initiated by Malcolm, occurred: "In March 1964, just after Malcolm had quit the Nation, he visited the U.S. Senate to take in a day of the civil-rights filibuster and later slipped into the back row at a King news conference off the floor. King afterward left by one door; Malcolm popped out another into his path. 'Well, Malcolm, good to see you,' King said. 'Good to see you,' Malcolm grinned. Reporters crowded around. Flash bulbs flared. 'Now, you're going to get investigated,' Malcolm teased, and then they parted."[79]

An encounter of this nature could not have occurred between bitter enemies. The two leaders actually greeted each other in the ancient tradition of hospitality. The playful manner in which Malcolm greeted Martin must have diffused any anxiety that both must have felt. David L. Lewis claims that the significance of the meeting became more evident as Malcolm and Martin publicly expressed solidarity on a pressing issue facing black America: "The civil rights propaganda value of this meeting was considerable, as both men pledged to concert their efforts to pressure Congress into passing the pending civil rights legislation. Practically, however, it represented little in the way of intrinsic collaboration. Ideologically, they still appeared to be antithetical personalities. But Malcolm X was a mind in flux, finally liberated from the cult of white deviltry preached by Elijah Muhammad."[80]

The friendly nature of the meeting disturbed a number of white liberals, who shuddered at the mere thought of an alliance between Malcolm and

Martin. The pictures taken on that occasion, which showed them smiling and shaking hands, were not a pleasant sight to those who were determined to exploit their philosophical differences. Abram Eisenman of the *Savannah Sun and Shoppers' Guide* wrote Martin, inquiring about the implications of the pictures. Martin quickly responded:

> I can assure you that there are no implications of an agreement of basic philosophy. I am still strongly opposed to the Black Muslim philosophy and to Malcolm X's constant attempt to exploit the despair of the Negro. I am committed to nonviolence as a philosophy and method. I think it is the best method available to Negroes in their fight for freedom. . . . In fact, my position is always that of kindness and reconciliation. I am constantly seeking to communicate with and persuade those that are not willing to follow the nonviolent philosophy. I would go so far as to say that I would gladly shake hands with Governors Wallace and Barnett and greet them with a kind smile. This would in no way be indicative of my sharing their segregationist views.[81]

It is widely held that Malcolm and Martin moved along converging paths, personally and ideologically, after the Washington meeting. James Baldwin said, "By the time each met his death, there was practically no difference between them." John A. Williams reports that in a conversation he had with Malcolm in Lagos in early 1964, "It was apparent that the distance that seemed to have existed between himself and King was small indeed, although he never gave up the idea of self-defense for blacks. . . . Malcolm was even willing to sing 'We Shall Overcome,' just so long as all who were singing had .45's firmly in hand."[82]

Malcolm's travels abroad in the spring and summer of 1964 were important in bringing him and Martin closer together, particularly at the point of ideology. After visiting Egypt, Lebanon, Nigeria, Ghana, Morocco, and Algeria, Malcolm made the pilgrimage to Mecca, where he saw Islam practiced with no distinctions based on race. This experience compelled him to cease making blanket judgments of white people. At the same time, Martin was moving toward a more explicit and enlightened globalism, and he thought it a propitious sign that Malcolm was getting beyond a simple skin-racism to a more sophisticated and inclusive view of the world. As the two men graduated to a higher level of analysis of the economic roots of racism, classism, and imperialism, and as they came to a greater sense of the unity of the struggles of the oppressed worldwide, they stimulated each other's increasing sophistication and radicality. In response to the challenge presented by Malcolm, Martin affirmed that "Black is beautiful," became more critical of the complacency and indifference of the black middle class, moved beyond integration as a panacea to stress economic justice and international peace, and became less cautious about emphasizing the need for black power and black unity. As a result of Martin's challenge, Malcolm supported the voter registration drives of civil rights organizations, ceased to oppose integration and intermarriage, and began to entertain the possibility of blacks and progressive-minded whites working together.[83]

The view that Malcolm and Martin reevaluated their presuppositions and moved toward each other on the question of integrationism vs. separatism should not be accepted without some points of clarification. Although Malcolm embraced integrationism in principle, he felt that such a state of existence was not genuinely possible as long as whites either rejected it or sought to dictate the terms on which it could occur. Moreover, he believed that whites could make an immeasurable contribution to the struggle not by seeking to integrate with blacks but by working among themselves to eliminate racist attitudes toward people of color generally, a point he emphatically made in early 1965: "Whites who are sincere don't accomplish anything by joining Negro organizations and making them integrated. Whites who are sincere should organize among themselves and figure out some strategy to break down prejudice that exists in white communities. This is where they can function more intelligently and more effectively, in the white community itself, and this has never been done."[84]

Obviously, Martin did not agree entirely with this point of view, though he clearly saw the need for whites to purge their own communities of the cancer of racism. At the same time, he and Malcolm wondered if whites were willing to develop the spirit and to readjust qualities necessary to take on such a noble task, especially since so many of the actions and attitudes of white liberals feebly echoed those of die-hard white supremacists. "The vast majority of white Americans are racists," Martin sadly mused in 1966. But despite the depth of racism in the United States, Martin never embraced racial separatism as a personal ethic. Thus, James H. Cone's suggestion that he *accepted* "temporary segregation" as "probably the only means of overcoming powerlessness in the black community" is almost impossible to sustain under close examination. When Martin spoke of "temporary segregation" as a "contemporary way station on the road to freedom," and an avenue "to the integrated society," he was merely stating that such a scenario would possibly be necessary, not that he found it morally acceptable, desirable, or preferable.[85]

One might also argue that Martin was simply stating what he had believed but refused to emphasize publicly from the early stages of the civil rights movement, namely, that black unity is a precondition for interracial solidarity and cooperation. He was never totally oblivious to the fact that without unity, his people could only come into an integrated situation as powerless individuals and not as a collectivity with strong communal values. Malcolm raised this same issue in 1964, noting, "There can be no white-black solidarity until there's first some black solidarity." This critical need for black unity helps explain why Malcolm and Martin called upon their people, with a deep sense of urgency by 1965, to ground themselves in a keener understanding of who they are as a group. According to Coretta Scott King, both had "the fierce desire that the black American reclaim his racial pride, his joy in himself and his race—in a physical, a cultural, and a spiritual rebirth."[86]

As Malcolm and Martin mitigated the extremes of their original positions to embrace aspects of each other's perspectives, they reached a common mind on the oppression of blacks in America and its links to that of Africans and people of color generally. They consistently argued that a truly democratic America for blacks and whites would be possible only within the confines of a world devoid of racial oppression, economic injustice, poverty, and wars of aggression. This view undergirded their opposition to South African apartheid, to colonialism in Africa and other parts of the Third World, and to the war in Vietnam. According to James Baldwin, "The fates of both men were radically altered (I would say, frankly sealed) the moment they attempted to release the black American struggle from the domestic context and relate it to the struggles of the poor and the non-white all over the world."[87]

But such a move came naturally for Malcolm and Martin, both of whom exhibited an amazing capacity to empathize with others. The similarities between them, in terms of personality, reinforced their movement toward each other on a range of issues. They also helped make it possible for the men to complement and correct each other without being threatened at the levels of their most fundamental convictions and claims.[88] This point has been made repeatedly by many who sensed an often unarticulated bond of empathy between the two men.

Alex Haley, a friend of both Malcolm and Martin, often spoke of a kind of "reluctant admiration" the two leaders had for each other. Haley recounted that "both men were intensely interested in each other but their images were such that they were supposed to be adversaries." Haley shared the following reflections concerning his visits with Martin and Malcolm in 1964: "Dr. King would always let maybe an hour pass before he'd casually ask, 'By the way, what's Brother Malcolm saying about me these days?' I'd give some discreetly vague response, and then back in New York, I'd hear from Malcolm, 'All right, tell me what he said about me!' to which I'd also give a vague reply. I'm convinced that privately the two men felt mutual admiration and respect."[89]

Malcolm's admiration for Martin seemed all the more interesting and significant in view of the Muslim leader's negative attitude toward black preachers. Haley's recollection of Malcolm's and Martin's affection for each other is supported by the testimony of Coretta Scott King: "Martin believed that Malcolm X was a brilliant young man who had been misdirected. They had talked together on occasion and had discussed their philosophies in a friendly way. At the same time, I know that, though he never said so publicly, Malcolm X had deep respect for Martin. He recognized that Martin was unique, not alone in talent or eloquence, but in fearlessness and courage. Malcolm admired manhood and he knew how supremely Martin exemplified it."[90]

It is most unfortunate that Malcolm and Martin never had the chance to meet and to discuss at length the future course of the black freedom movement. Shortly after Malcolm broke with the Black Muslims, Martin said that he would talk to him about his position on guns, but he never did. Martin and some of his aides made plans to go to New York to meet with Malcolm at the end of the Selma campaign in 1965, mainly because they thought the Muslim activist could be helpful when they moved their civil rights crusade to the northern ghettoes. "We were trying to build a coalition," reported Ralph D. Abernathy, Martin's closest friend and associate. "We knew he wanted to be supportive of our movement, and, although we did not agree with his total philosophy, we thought it would be good to talk with him. Before we were able to arrange the trip to New York, Malcolm X was killed."[91]

Malcolm apparently raised the possibility of meeting with Martin as well. According to the black psychologist Kenneth B. Clark, "Malcolm began to express his respect for the point of view of Martin Luther King. . . . He wanted the opportunity to be able to talk with Martin face to face. . . . He asked if I could arrange for him to speak with Martin Luther King and James Baldwin. I told him I would do my best to arrange for such a meeting. We agreed that prior to such a meeting, we would have a personal talk at my office at City College. It was arranged for a certain Tuesday. The Sunday before that Tuesday, Malcolm X was assassinated."[92]

Malcolm and Martin reportedly had a telephone conversation on February 14, 1965, during which they agreed to meet and talk. William Kunstler, the famous attorney who knew both men, speculated that this conversation may have sealed Malcolm's fate: "There was sort of an agreement that they would meet in the future and work out a common strategy, not merge their two organizations—Malcolm then had the Organization of Afro-American Unity and Martin, of course, was the president of the Southern Christian Leadership Conference—but that they would work out a method to work together in some way. And I think that that quite possibly led to the bombing of Malcolm's house that evening in East Elmhurst and his assassination one week later."[93]

It is tantalizing to speculate on where Malcolm's and Martin's relationship would have gone had they actually met and discussed their philosophies and objectives extensively. Malcolm had ceased to attack Martin in strong terms, and Martin was becoming less concerned about maintaining the kind of character profile that the media and liberal whites in general assigned to him. Such changes led Clarence Jones to assert that "it was not beyond the realm of possibility that in the building of a coalition within the Negro freedom movement, Dr. King and Malcolm X might find a common basis of action." What they would have accomplished had they formed an alliance will remain a matter of heated speculation.[94]

There remained enormous differences between Malcolm X and Martin Luther King Jr. at the levels of education, status, and achievements. But they were drawn together in a dialectic of social activism by the nourishment they shared in black folk traditions, by their essential quality of caring, by their common devotion to the liberation of the oppressed, by the ideas and convictions they shared, by the mutual admiration and respect they felt, and by the impelling moral, spiritual, and intellectual power they received from each other. Therefore, their contributions and their legacies cannot be evaluated and appreciated separately.

The Demise of a Potential Leader: Martin on the Death of Malcolm

The assassination of Malcolm X wounded and disturbed Martin. The civil rights leader reacted to the tragedy at press conferences and in newspaper and radio interviews. In an interview in Los Angeles on February 24, 1965, three days after Malcolm was murdered, Martin expressed regret that numerous commitments would prevent him from attending the funeral in New York, but he promised, "I will certainly extend my sympathy to his wife and to his family and, as I said, this has come as a great shock to so many of us, and although we had constant disagreements, I had a deep affection for Malcolm X, and I am very sorry about this whole thing." The telegram Martin sent to Mrs. Malcolm X carried essentially the same message and more: "I was certainly saddened by the shocking and tragic assassination of your husband. . . . He was an eloquent spokesman for his point of view and no one can honestly doubt that Malcolm had a great concern for the problems that we face as a race. While I know that this is a difficult hour for you, I am sure that God will give you strength to endure. I will certainly be remembering you in my prayers and please know that you have my deepest sympathy. Always consider me a friend and if I can do anything to ease the heavy load that you are forced to carry at this time, please feel free to call on me."[95]

By the time of his death, Malcolm had been examined psychologically and judged a fanatic who expounded unpalatable theories of race in a period of social chaos. He was much maligned and badly understood, and Martin knew this. But Malcolm had deeply impressed Martin with his capacity to grow in mind and spirit. While Martin regretted the brutal manner in which the Muslim leader was killed, he felt that "it is even more unfortunate that this great tragedy occurred at a time when Malcolm X was reevaluating his own philosophical presuppositions and moving toward a greater understanding of the nonviolent movement and toward more tolerance of white people, generally."[96] Coretta Scott King echoed this sentiment in 1969, a year after her own husband's death:

> The death of Malcolm X affected me profoundly. Perhaps that was because I had just met him, and perhaps it was because I had begun to understand him better. Martin and I had reassessed our feelings toward him. We realized that since he had been to Mecca and had broken with Elijah Muhammad, he was moving away from hatred toward internationalism and against exploitation. In a strange way, the same racist attitude which killed others who were working for peaceful change also killed Malcolm X. . . . I said to Martin, "What a waste! What a pity that this man who was so talented and such an articulate spokesman for black people should have to die just as he was reaching for something of real value."[97]

Martin never seriously considered how an insensitive federal government and mass media helped create the climate for Malcolm's assassination. The civil rights leader apparently assumed that Malcolm died at the hands of black men, an assumption quite common at a time when Malcolm and the Black Muslims attacked each other with the vigor of scorpions. Martin commented: "The American Negro cannot afford to destroy its leadership any more than the Congo can. Men of talent are too scarce to be destroyed by envy, greed and tribal rivalry before they reach their full maturity. Like the murder of Lumumba, the murder of Malcolm X deprives the world of a potentially great leader. I could not agree with either of these men, but I could see in them a capacity for leadership which I could respect, and which was only beginning to mature in judgement and statesmanship."[98]

For Martin, the assassination of Malcolm symbolized the kind of vicious cycle of violence that had long afflicted America and the Western world as a whole. He expressed this view in several statements which made clear his high regard for Malcolm. On the day Malcolm died, Martin stated: "We must face the tragic fact that Malcolm X was murdered by a morally inclement climate. It reveals that our society is still sick enough to express dissent through murder. We have not learned to disagree without being violently disagreeable. This vicious assassination should cause our whole society to see that violence and hatred are evil forces that must be cast into unending limbo."[99]

Martin's reaction to Malcolm's death approximated that of many Harlemites, who regarded the fallen leader as a hero in the style of Greek tragedy, but a hero nonetheless.[100] The civil rights leader had read a lot about Malcolm's life and struggles. In an extensive statement, in which he demonstrated a broad knowledge of Malcolm's rise from poverty and crime to leadership in the Nation of Islam, Martin commented:

Malcolm X came to the fore as a public figure partially as a result of a TV documentary entitled, "The Hate That Hate Produced." That title points clearly to the nature of Malcolm's life and death. Malcolm X was clearly a product of the hate and violence invested in the Negro's blighted existence in this nation. He, like so many of our number, was a victim of the despair that inevitably derives from the conditions of oppression, poverty, and injustice which engulf the masses of our race. But in his youth there was no hope, no preaching, teaching or movements of nonviolence. He was too young for the Garvey movement, too poor to be a Communist—for the Communists geared their work to the Negro intellectuals and labor without realizing that the masses of Negroes were unrelated to either—and yet he possessed a native intelligence and drive which demanded an outlet and means of expression. He turned first to the underworld, but this did not fulfill the quest for meaning which grips young minds. It is a testimony to Malcolm's personal depth and integrity that he could not become an underworld Czar, but turned again and again to religion for meaning and destiny. Malcolm was still turning and growing at the time of his brutal and meaningless assassination. . . . In his recent visit to Selma, he spoke at length to my wife Coretta about his personal struggles and expressed an interest in working more closely with the nonviolent movement, but he was not yet able to renounce violence and overcome the bitterness which life had invested in him. There were also indications of an interest in politics as a way of dealing with the problems of the Negro. All of these were signs of a man of passion and zeal seeking a program through which he could channel his talents. . . . But history would not have it so. A man who lived under the torment of knowledge of the rape of his grandmother and murder of his father, under the conditions of the present social order, does not readily accept that social order or seek to integrate into it. And so Malcolm was forced to live and die as an outsider, a victim of the violence that spawned him, and with which he courted through his brief but promising life. . . . Surely the young men of Harlem and Negro communities throughout the nation ought to be ready to seek another way.[101]

A more perceptive, sensitive, and compelling statement cannot be found in even the most brilliant biographical treatments of Malcolm. Here lies further proof of the spiritual bond that united Martin and Malcolm, even as they struggled to maintain their own different qualities as men of ideas and as social activists.

Toward a Broader Humanism

Malcolm, Martin, and the Search for Global Community

However deeply American Negroes are caught in the struggle to be at last at home in our homeland of the United States, we cannot ignore the larger world house in which we are also dwellers. Equality with whites will not solve the problems of either whites or Negroes if it means equality in a world stricken by poverty and in a universe doomed to extinction by war.
Martin Luther King Jr.[1]

I believe in a society in which people can live like human beings on the basis of equality.
Malcolm X[2]

You know I work for the liberation of all people, because when I liberate myself, I'm liberating other people.
Fannie Lou Hamer[3]

The search for community constituted a lifelong quest for both Malcolm X and Martin Luther King Jr. That quest was largely spiritual in nature, occurring on both intellectual and practical levels. Their earliest understandings of community developed in the contexts of their family environments and the black communities in which they were raised. In time, their communitarian visions extended beyond these related environs to embrace people of various racial and ethnic backgrounds in the United States and abroad. In other words, they transcended the particularities of the African-American experience in favor of a broader humanism and a more insightful and precise universalism.

Malcolm and Martin had very definite ideas about the significance of community and how it might best be actualized. Both viewed community as the goal of human existence, as the highest ethical ideal, and as the key to human welfare and survival, but at times they doubted that such a state of existence could be realized in human history.[4] Perhaps more important, they disagreed to a great extent over the best means to achieve genuine human community, as indicated in earlier chapters in this work.

A Dream or a Nightmare: On the State of Black America

In the tradition of African-American leaders and thinkers before them, Malcolm and Martin devoted much time to assessing the impact of oppression on their people through the centuries. Their reflections on this issue grew not only out of their own experiences over time in black communities but also out of their readings of works by W.E.B. Du Bois, Carter G. Woodson, E. Franklin Frazier, James Baldwin, John Killens, and numerous other writers, who captured their people's pain and struggle in various literary forms.[5] This kind of exposure compelled Malcolm and Martin not only to struggle with the question of the meaning of African-American history and the black experience but also to frame thoughts concerning their people's mission and destiny.

They agreed that their people's plight resulted primarily from more than three hundred years of slavery and its tragic legacy of racism and segregation. Both spoke with telling insight of the physical, spiritual, and psychological pain experienced by millions of their African forebears on slave ships and on the plantations of the so-called New World. "Over 115 million African blacks . . . were murdered or enslaved," Malcolm angrily reflected, an experience all the more tragic since the enslavers "stripped us of all human characteristics" and "brought us down to the level of an animal." In terms equally compelling, Martin noted that "more than 75 million black people were murdered," and "families were torn apart, friends separated," and "cooperation to improve their condition carefully thwarted." "Considering what our forebears went through," he added, "it is a miracle that the black man still survives."[6]

Malcolm and Martin placed slavery in America within the broader context of human history, thus arriving at a keen sense of how the experiences of people of African ancestry compared with those of other enslaved peoples over time. While drawing parallels between the experiences of their forebears and those of the biblical Hebrews in Egypt, Malcolm and Martin, like the black nationalist David Walker more than a century earlier, concluded that slavery in America was unparalleled in terms of its cruelty and its impact on generations of human beings. "It is true that the type of slavery that was practiced in America was never practiced in history by any other country," Malcolm observed. Martin essentially agreed, noting, "Nobody in the history of the world has suffered like the black man."[7] To those who charged that other immigrants had come to America and succeeded where blacks had failed, Martin offered a direct rejoinder, one that Malcolm would have echoed without hesitation:

> The situation of other immigrant groups a hundred years ago and the situation of the Negro today cannot be usefully compared. Negroes were brought here in chains long before the Irish decided *voluntarily* to leave Ireland or the Italians thought of leaving Italy. Some Jews may have left their homes in Europe involuntarily, but they were not in chains when they arrived on these shores. Other immigrants came to America with language and economic handicaps, but not with the stigma of color. Above all, no other ethnic group has been a slave on American soil, and no other group has had its family structure deliberately torn apart.[8]

The fact that African Americans had always been treated as exiles or resident aliens, never as first-class citizens, was more than adequately documented in the works of historians and in folk testimony and art passed down from generation to generation. Having experienced racism from childhood, Malcolm and Martin understood the exile's lot, which helps explain why they were so deeply moved by the songs and stories of their slave forebears. "Everything that came out of Europe, every blue-eyed thing, is already an American," Malcolm explained in a 1964 speech. "And as long as you and I have been over here, we aren't Americans yet." For Malcolm, this sense of being a resident alien found powerful expression in the slave spiritual "Sometimes I Feel Like a Motherless Child." Martin could not have agreed more. In words strikingly similar to Malcolm's, the civil rights leader often alluded to how America had accepted, nurtured, and granted full rights and privileges to immigrants from various parts of the world, but had "never demonstrated the same kind of maternal care for her black exiles who were brought here in chains from Africa." "It is no wonder," Martin continued, "that in one of our sorrow songs, our forebears could sing out, 'Sometimes I Feel Like a Motherless Child.' What a great sense of estrangement, rejection, and hurt that could cause people to use such a metaphor."[9]

The power of this metaphor was not lost, since African Americans in the 1950s and 1960s lived under an oppression not far removed from that of the slaves. Malcolm often said as much and more, insisting in 1963 that America was "nothing other than a modern house of bondage" or "a modern Egypt." The fact that blacks were denied basic constitutional rights made his critique of society and culture all the more persuasive. Although Martin was less prone than Malcolm to identify African Americans in his time as *slaves,* he did view them as persons struggling under glaring forms "of political, social, economic, and intellectual bondage." "The central quality of the Negro's life is pain," Martin asserted, "a pain so old and so deep that it shows in almost every moment of his existence. It emerges in the cheerlessness of his sorrow songs, in the melancholy of his blues, and in the pathos of his sermons."[10]

Malcolm and Martin were never really comfortable with the widely held assumption that African Americans fared much better in the North than in the South. In fact, both knew that their people were the victims of a racist system that knew no regional boundaries. Rejecting the traditional image of the North as the Promised Land for African Americans, Malcolm often said that segregation and the economic exploitation of his people in the northern ghettoes were sufficient proof that "south of the Canadian border" was still "South." Martin used different words to make the same point. Referring to racism and segregation in the North as "hidden and subtle," and in the South as "overt and glaring," the civil rights leader maintained that "the racial issue confronting America is not a sectional issue but a national problem."[11] This became painfully real to Martin in 1966 in Chicago, where he and other freedom marchers faced white mobs more vicious than any he had seen in Alabama and Mississippi.

But the condition of blacks in the South presented a special problem for Martin, not only because of the blatant racism, the visible signs of segregation, and white mob violence, but also because of his deep sense of identification with that region. He sadly admitted that in the South "the scars of the slave system remained more visible and law and custom became one," thereby exposing his people to levels of public abuse and rejection that were not so clearly evident in other parts of the nation. "Many Americans are aware of the fact that, on the crooked scales of 'southern justice,' the life, liberty and human worth of a black man weigh precious little," he complained. The intensity of the oppression in the South reinforced Martin's belief that the greatest challenge to American democracy would be met there, a position Malcolm was not likely to accept uncritically given his view that parts of the North were worse for blacks than even some of the most oppressive areas of the South.[12]

The emotional and psychological impact of white supremacy and segregation on African Americans was a matter of great concern for both men, and they gave it attention appropriate to its seriousness. They attributed the pervasiveness of ignorance and self-hatred among their people—a condition that caused them to exalt whites while denigrating themselves and their own kind—to an inferiority complex born of centuries of oppression, a situation which explained Malcolm's preoccupation with the question of how to restore African Americans to their ancient glory. Describing the Negro as "deaf, dumb, and blind," and his plight as "miserable," Malcolm agonized over the extent to which his people hated themselves and their features while struggling to be shaped in the image of their oppressors. Martin remained sensitive to the problem as well, pointing especially to those blacks who "reject their heritage, are ashamed of their color, ashamed of black art and music," and who "determine what is beautiful and good by the standards of white society."[13]

The effort to achieve assimilation on all levels was, according to Malcolm and Martin, far more typical of the educated elite than of the masses of their people. As a Black Muslim minister, Malcolm constantly criticized what he labeled "the black bourgeoisie," who "look forward hopefully to the future 'integrated-intermarried' society promised them by the white liberals." Of the typical middle-class black, Malcolm said, "He'll pay three times as much as the house is worth just to live near his master, and then brag about 'I'm the only Negro out here.'"[14] Malcolm did not exclude Martin from this kind of indictment, especially since the civil rights leader was well educated, strongly backed by white liberals, and quite diligent in his pursuit of integration. But viewing himself as an exception among the black educated elite, Martin described many as being confused and set against themselves—as persons "caught in the middle with no cultural roots." Like Malcolm, he noted that such middle-class blacks are often cultivated as leaders by "the white establishment," but their poor self-image and "absence of faith in their people" make them susceptible to becoming collaborators with whites in the subjugation of the African-American community. Said Martin: "This kind of Negro leader acquires the white man's contempt for the ordinary Negro. He is often more at home with the middle-class white than he is among his own people, and frequently his physical home is moved up and away from the ghetto. His language changes, his location changes, his income changes, and ultimately he changes from the representative of the Negro to the white man into the white man's representative to the Negro. The tragedy is that too often he does not recognize what has happened to him."[15]

Malcolm and Martin had little patience for those educated and affluent African Americans who casually surrendered the communal values of their heritage in a desperate effort to prove their equality with whites. Malcolm characterized them as "patriotic individualists" who zealously pursued their own best interests while remaining essentially unconcerned with the struggles of "the downtrodden black masses." He was particularly critical of those privileged blacks who entered the ranks of leadership, and who "sell out our people for just a few crumbs of token recognition and token gains." "I'm surprised that the white man is dumb enough to believe these Uncle Toms, who stoop so low, like Judas, to be stool pigeons against their own kind," he declared. Although Martin was not as harsh and persistent in his criticism of privileged blacks as Malcolm, he, too, remained suspicious of those targeted for leadership in the African-American community, noting that "we've passed the stage now where white people in the power structure can pick our leaders." Moreover, the civil rights leader was deeply troubled by those among his people who struggled to compensate for an unconscious self-hatred through "conspicuous consumption," and who seemed "untouched and unmoved by the agonies and struggles of their underprivileged brothers." Martin considered this kind of "selfish detachment" disgraceful and inexcusable, especially since so many well-to-do African Americans owed their success to the support of the underprivileged:

> How many Negroes who have achieved educational and economic security have forgotten that they are where they are because of the support of faceless, unlettered and unheralded Negroes who did ordinary jobs in an extraordinary way? How many successful Negroes have forgotten that uneducated and poverty-stricken mothers and fathers worked until their eyebrows were scorched and their hands bruised so that their children could get an education? For any middle-class Negro to forget the masses is an act not only of neglect but of shameful ingratitude.[16]

So devastating were the effects of oppression on African Americans that the weakest in mind and spirit found more satisfaction in the prosperity of whites than in the good fortune of their own people. For Malcolm, such behavior constituted the most frustrating of all reminders that his people suffered from intense degradation and a damaged egoism, a problem that made it all the more difficult for him to accept Martin's belief that blacks should love their oppressors. But Martin was as serious and dynamic as Malcolm when denouncing envy and rivalry among African Americans. The civil rights leader once observed: "Too many Negroes are jealous of other Negroes' success and progress. Too many Negro organizations are warring against each other with a claim to absolute truth. The Pharaohs had a favorite and effective strategy to keep their slaves in bondage: keep them fighting among themselves. The divide and conquer technique has been a potent weapon in the arsenal of oppression."[17]

The effects of what Malcolm and Martin termed the "divide and conquer" strategy on African Americans could not have been more evident, especially since fighting and treachery occurred so frequently within the group. Both men expressed pain over the extent to which their people killed, maimed, and made mischief upon each other, problems that could not have been more discouraging for Malcolm since so many blacks claimed to be nonviolent and peaceful in their relations with whites. Noting that Harlem's hospitals were often filled with blacks who "got violent with each other," Malcolm insisted, "I don't think anything is more destructive than . . . black people fighting each other." In a speech to his people in New York in December 1964, the Muslim minister pressed the issue further: "If you and I here in Harlem, who form the habit oft times of fighting each other, who sneak around trying to wait for an opportunity to throw some acid or some lye on each other, or sprinkle dust on each other's doorsteps—if you and I were really and truly for the freedom of our people, we wouldn't waste all of that energy thinking how to do harm to each other."[18]

Martin's description of the problem clearly paralleled Malcolm's. "Unfortunately, a check of the hospitals in any Negro community on any Saturday night will make you painfully aware of the violence within the Negro community," he wrote. "By turning his hostility and frustration with the larger society inward, the Negro often inflicts terrible acts of violence on his own black brother."[19] For Martin, as for Malcolm, the problem was exacerbated by the many black men who physically and psychologically abused black women. In words that bring Malcolm and the Black Muslims to mind, Martin declared, "We must convey to one another that our women must be respected, and that life is too precious to be destroyed in a Saturday night brawl, or a gang execution."[20] The problem of intragroup violence reminded Martin and Malcolm of the enormous work that had to be done before their people were ready for a unified struggle.

The various ways in which African Americans responded to oppression remained central to Malcolm and Martin as they assessed the potential of the masses for a collective role in their liberation. To some extent, Malcolm shared Martin's view that African Americans confronted their plight "in three characteristic ways." Some chose "the way of acquiescence," tacitly adjusting "themselves to oppression"; others affirmed "physical violence and corroding hatred" as a means of self-affirmation and racial advancement; and still others embraced "the principle of nonviolent resistance," which "seeks to reconcile the truths of two opposites—acquiescence and violence—while avoiding the extremes and immoralities of both."[21] When exploring the values that each of these segments of the black community might contribute to the freedom cause, Martin was consciously Hegelian or dialectical, while relying, much like Malcolm, on wisdom born of experience and observation.

Those African Americans who acquiesced to or passively accepted their condition stood as a reminder of the degree to which oppression can sap the spirit of a people. Malcolm was unsparing in his criticisms of such blacks, accusing them of succumbing to fear, the white man's brainwashing, and the view that they constituted a powerless minority on the world stage. "Nobody can give you equality or justice or anything," he cried. "If you can't take it, you don't deserve it." Although Malcolm was justified in his attack on the passivity, quietism, and indifference among his people, his comments often bordered on the unreasonable, especially since he knew, as well as Martin, the extent to which African Americans were forced to employ the art of deception for the sake of sheer survival.[22] Moreover, Malcolm clearly displayed a tendency that Sterling Stuckey attributes to black nationalists throughout American history: an inclination "to exaggerate the degree of acquiescence to oppression by the masses of black people."[23] While such a tendency was not as typical of Martin, the civil rights leader was known to lash out at those African Americans who had been reduced to a state so low that they preferred "the fleshpots of Egypt to the challenge of the Promised Land." Having little faith in themselves and dependent in many cases on whites for food, jobs, and shelter, these blacks, according to Martin, were not prepared to take the necessary steps to overthrow white domination. Indeed, large numbers of them were more apt to find comfort in the conviction that prayer alone would change their condition, a position quite at odds with Martin's and Malcolm's belief that divine guidance had to be combined with human initiative and wise and sustained activism.[24]

Passive resignation on the part of middle-class blacks proved all the more difficult to rationalize, especially since they were in a better position than most of their people to demand change. Malcolm attributed their spirit of acquiescence largely to an intense desire not to be classified by whites "as extremist, or violent, or irresponsible." He also shared Martin's sense that considerable numbers of well-to-do blacks remained silent in the face of injustice for fear of losing what little economic security and social status they had. "Many of these Negroes are occupied in a middle-class struggle for status and prestige," Martin argued. "They are more concerned about 'conspicuous consumption' than about the cause of justice, and are probably not prepared for the ordeals and sacrifices involved in nonviolent action." He further observed: "All too often the Negro who gets a little money and a little education, ends up saying, 'I've got mine and it doesn't matter what happens to anybody else.' What I want to see in the black community is a middle class of substance, a middle class that is concerned about the problems of the masses of people. For let me assure you that we all go up together, or we all go down together."[25]

For Malcolm and Martin, the problem with "acquiescence" or "passive resignation" is that it robbed African Americans of pride and dignity while allowing the conscience of the oppressor to remain undisturbed. But the two men never fully agreed on the form that resistance to oppression should take. Malcolm often said that there was essentially no difference between acquiescence and Martin's ethics of nonviolence and unconditional love for the oppressor, a view he seemed to hold even after breaking with the Black Muslim movement. In contrast, Martin always saw himself as representing a middle way between the "do-nothingism" of the "complacent" and "the hatred and despair of the black Nationalist." Moreover, he maintained that Malcolm and other black nationalists, who revolted against "everything white," only continued the cycle of hatred and oppression, thus making cooperative and productive relationships between the races impossible.[26] But as the two leaders grew closer ideologically in the last year of Malcolm's life, they learned to affirm and value the reciprocal roles they played in the struggle while jointly criticizing those African Americans who acquiesced to the oppressive system.

Despite all of their talk about the pervasiveness of a servile spirit among African Americans, Malcolm and Martin had great faith in the power and potential of their people. Like so many black leaders before them, they could be quite critical of their people while emphasizing, in the same breath, their inherent worth and redeeming qualities. Malcolm never really abandoned the view that African Americans, when in touch with their truest selves, are greater in physical strength, fighting power, and courage than whites. Although Martin never publicly expressed such a view, he believed as strongly as Malcolm in the power of African Americans to transcend the physical scars and the psychological effects of white supremacy, while improving their menial social and economic condition. The capacity to triumph over seemingly invincible odds, as Martin frequently stated, had long been demonstrated by African Americans through the power song and humor and the ability to laugh in the face of misfortune. Indeed, this sense of the redeeming power and resiliency of black humanity figured prominently in Martin's thoughts as he propounded a concept of black messianism—as he pondered, in intellectual terms, the leadership his people could provide in shaping a new and more tolerant human spirit.[27]

Malcolm and Martin proposed certain prescriptions for the afflictions of their people. One approach for them necessarily involved African Americans developing a stronger and more positive view of themselves. Both believed that this could be achieved to a great extent through a reeducation process and a cultural revolution spearheaded by African Americans. As was the case with Malcolm, Martin believed that the struggle for what he called "a majestic sense of self-worth" had to necessarily focus on the training of black children, "a real challenge" not only for parents but "for Negro artists and entertainers as well as writers." In words that recall Malcolm's constant challenge to the race, Martin maintained: "Our children must be taught to stand tall with their heads proudly lifted. We need not be duped into purchasing bleaching creams that promise to make us lighter. We need not process our hair to make it appear straight. Whether some men, black or white, realize it or not, black people are very beautiful. Life's piano can only produce the melodies of brotherhood when it is recognized that the black keys are as basic, necessary and beautiful as the white keys."[28]

Malcolm and Martin knew that until their people revolutionized their thinking about themselves, their struggle for liberation would be abortive and spasmodic at best. But bringing African Americans to a consciousness of the greatness of their heritage, in Malcolm's estimation, did not necessarily include an emphasis on the value of their ancestors' experience in slavery. In contrast, Martin insisted that the spiritual resources and values for the African American's drive toward self-acceptance and self-appreciation existed in abundance in the heritage that stemmed from the slaves. He wrote: "Something of the inner spirit of our slave forebears must be pursued today. From the inner depths of our being we must sing with them: 'Before I'll be a slave, I'll be buried in my grave, and go home to my Lord and be free.' This spirit, this drive, this rugged sense of somebodyness is the first and most vital step that the Negro must take in dealing with his dilemma."[29]

It was evident to Malcolm and Martin that African Americans had already begun to think of themselves in new and more positive ways, a development reflected in their mounting moral and physical support for the freedom movement. Even as he brooded over the defects of his people, Malcolm recognized that they were "waking up" and developing "a new type of thinking." "There are 22 million African-Americans who are ready to fight for independence right here," he told a mostly white audience in April 1964, obviously overstating the case.[30] Always mindful that "there are Negroes who will never fight for freedom," Martin felt nonetheless that "a new Negro" had emerged as early as the Montgomery bus boycott. He spoke in poignant terms of his people's "new sense of dignity and destiny," of "the revolutionary reevaluation of the Negro by himself":

> The most important thing in this whole movement is what has happened to the Negro. For the first time, the Negro is on his own side. This has not always been true. But today the Negro is with himself. He has gained a new respect for himself. He believes in himself. World opinion is on his side. The law is on his side and, as one columnist said, all the stars of heaven are on his side. It seems to be historically true that once an oppressed people rise up there is no stopping them short of complete freedom. The Negro is eternally through with segregation; he will never accept it again, in Mississippi, Georgia, or anywhere else.[31]

For Martin, the "Southern Negro's new visibility" and "new sense of dignity," which proved "to him that many stereotypes he has held about himself and other Negroes are not valid," found most profound expression "in the words of the old Negro slave preacher that were uttered in the form of a prayer":

Lord we ain't what we ought to be;
We ain't what we want to be;

We ain't what we gonna be;
But thank God, we ain't what we was.[32]

It became increasingly clear to Malcolm and Martin that the self-doubt and self-rejection which had long afflicted their people would not be permanent. But the afflictions of African Americans also necessitated a moving beyond the disunity within their ranks. The need for his people to "work together in unity and harmony" could not have been more significant for Malcolm, considering his belief that the "battle" for independence was one "that we have to wage ourselves." In his opinion, African Americans had to assume a unity and identity over and apart from whites, a development that necessarily required a certain cultural distance or apartness. Martin agreed with much of this idea, despite his receptivity to white allies, and he and Malcolm called for the type of broad cooperation between blacks that transcended southern or northern regional self-consciousness. Martin challenged his people to "work passionately for group identity" and "group trust," asserting that "only by being reconciled to ourselves will we be able to build upon the resources we already have at our disposal." In the same vein, he, much like Malcolm, conceded: "This plea for unity is not a call for uniformity. There must always be healthy debate. There will be inevitable differences of opinion. The dilemma that the Negro confronts is so complex and monumental that its solution will of necessity involve a diversified approach. But Negroes can differ and still unite around common goals."[33]

This critical need for unity led Malcolm and Martin to affirm the need for the preservation of black institutions and organizations. On this issue, time did not change their minds. From his Black Muslim years through the founding of his Organization of Afro-American Unity in 1964, Malcolm held that only through their own infrastructures could African Americans realize the fullness of freedom and independence. Martin was inclined to agree when pressed on the matter, but he felt that all-black organizations necessarily provided "only a contemporary way station on the road to freedom."[34] Moreover, he, in contrast to Malcolm, felt that the church and other black institutions, traditionally the arenas for the preservation of basic communal values, afforded the best foundation for forging what both men called "a black united front," though such institutions, as Martin pointed out, had not always devoted the full weight of their resources to the struggle:

There are already structured forces in the Negro community that can serve as the basis for building a powerful united front—the Negro church, the Negro press, the Negro fraternities and sororities, and the Negro professional associations. We must admit that these forces have never given their full resources to the cause of Negro liberation. There are still too many Negro churches that are so absorbed in a future good "over yonder" that they condition their members to adjust to the present evils "over here." Too many Negro newspapers have veered away from their traditional role as protest organs agitating for social change, and have turned to the sensational and the conservative in place of the substantive and the militant. Too many Negro social and professional groups have degenerated into snobbishness and a preoccupation with frivolities and trivial activity. But the failures of the past must not be an excuse for the inaction of the present and the future. These groups must be mobilized and motivated. This form of group unity can do infinitely more to liberate the Negro than any action of *individuals*. We have been oppressed as a group and we must overcome that oppression as a group.[35]

But Malcolm and Martin often underestimated the problems that classism presented in any effort to unite African Americans. James H. Cone is essentially right in contending that these men failed "to identify classism as a problem as harmful to the cause of freedom as racism and sexism." Malcolm and Martin seemed to think that class consciousness among blacks would not be a serious problem once they came to terms with their shared experience of suffering based on race. "Actually, there's no such thing as an upper-class Negro," Malcolm shouted, "because he catches the same hell as the other class Negro." Martin's treatment at the hands of white bigots was the best proof of this, especially since he was a Ph.D. with middle-class roots. By the time each met his death, however, Malcolm and Martin had begun to consider more seriously the role of class in understanding how African Americans related to each other. This intellectual quest informed Martin's challenge to his people in early 1968, as he marched with sanitation workers and planned a massive Poor People's Campaign: "There is a need to unite beyond class lines. Negro *haves* must join hands with Negro *have-nots*. Our society must come to respect the sanitation worker. He is as significant as the physician, for if he doesn't do his job, disease is rampant."[36]

Equally important was the need for African Americans to transcend all religious barriers to group solidarity and cooperation. Malcolm and Martin could have done more to highlight this, but they appeared more concerned about being accepted and remaining in good standing in their own particular faith traditions. During the earliest stages of their careers as public figures, both men were even guilty at times of contributing to the kind of misunderstanding and intolerance that kept blacks of different religions from affirming each other, respecting each other, and working together. Malcolm always felt that, culturally speaking, most African Americans were essentially "Christian" in their religious beliefs and outlooks, whether they attended a church or not. This was always difficult for the Muslim spokesman to accept, even as he called upon blacks to forget their religious differences, and despite his conviction that a freedom movement could not be sustained among his people without some basis in spiritual values. Instead of consistently urging Christians, Muslims, and persons of other faiths in the black community to affirm the truths in their various religious traditions, Malcolm sought to inspire the type of revolution in black thinking that would ultimately lead his people to fully embrace Islam. While he was largely responsible for Islam's wave of popularity among African Americans in the 1960s and beyond, his tendency to criticize Christianity while being essentially uncritical of Islam made it virtually impossible for him to forge the kind of racial unity that he longed to see. The same could be said of Martin, who, despite being critical of Christianity and other religions, always suggested that his own faith embodied more truths than Islam and other religions. The spirit of self-righteousness that Malcolm and Martin often brought to their understanding of their own faiths, coupled with a range of differences rooted in religion, kept these leaders from forming the type of alliance that would have won over the masses at all levels of black society.[37]

Malcolm and Martin ultimately had in mind a level of character development that would also result in the moral elevation of their people. Both saw improvements in group morality as not only a partial prescription for the afflictions of African Americans but also as a means of solidifying their claim to the moral and spiritual high ground in their struggle against the personal and institutional racism of white America. This is why Malcolm insisted that the challenges before his people necessitated "not only physical but moral separation" from whites, a position he altered somewhat after breaking with the Black Muslims:

> This is why the Honorable Elijah Muhammad teaches the black people in this country that we must stop drinking, we must stop smoking, we must stop committing fornication and adultery, we must stop gambling and cheating and using profanity, we must stop showing disrespect for our women, we must reform ourselves as parents so we can set the

proper example for our children. Once we reform ourselves of these immoral habits, that makes us more godly, more godlike, more righteous. That means that we are qualified then, to be on God's side, and it puts God on our side. God becomes our champion then, and it makes it possible for us to accomplish our own aims.[38]

The issue of group morality could not have been more critical for Martin, especially since he, like Malcolm, saw a direct correlation between the ascension of the nation's material wealth and the decline of its moral values. Martin called on blacks as a whole to reject the false morality of the larger culture while raising the moral climate in their own neighborhoods, an effort that for him, as for Malcolm, was most essential in refuting white assertions of black inferiority. "Our crime rate is too high" and "our level of cleanliness is frequently far too low," Martin complained. "Even the most poverty-stricken among us can purchase a ten-cent bar of soap; even the most educated among us can have high morals." Martin knew as well as Malcolm that crime, family disorganization, illegitimacy, alcohol and drug addiction, and other vices among African Americans were largely the tragic by-products of racism and segregation, and both held that their people were primarily responsible for improving their own "general level of behavior."[39]

This effort to improve the personal and group standards of African Americans would necessarily require hard work and discipline. This was a central theme in Malcolm's teachings. Denouncing those blacks who "just cry over their condition," the Muslim activist called upon his people to meet the highest standards of excellence in whatever professions they chose to pursue. Having essentially the same outlook, Martin spoke of the need for his people "to aspire to excellence" in every field of endeavor—"not excellence as a Negro doctor or lawyer or a Negro craftsman, but excellence per se." "This is particularly relevant for the young Negro," he wrote, for whom "doors of opportunity are gradually opening now that were not open to our mothers and fathers." Convinced that young African Americans should "work assiduously" to improve their educational and cultural standards, Martin noted, "We already have the inspiring examples of Negroes," from ex-slaves to those in the professional ranks, "who with determination have broken through the shackles of circumstance" and "risen to the heights of genius" in their particular fields.[40]

Hard work and perseverance could not have been more important, since African Americans lacked sufficient measures of economic and political power. Malcolm and Martin felt that their people should establish their own economic base by practicing wise economy, a position not particularly under-mined by Martin's belief in the integrated society as the ideal. In terms fully acceptable to Malcolm, Martin urged his people to "patronize Negro busi-nesses." The civil rights leader denied that such a practice would lead to "a new type of isolationism," noting instead that black businesses were neces-sary "because we can't get jobs in these other places" or in "white busi-nesses." Calling to mind W.E.B. Du Bois and other nationalists before him, Martin went on to recommend that blacks pool their resources in "coopera-tive enterprises" for "the economic security of the race."[41] This same position was preached almost as an article of faith by the more nationalistic Malcolm X.

Both men also held that through political power their people could better participate in the decision-making processes that affected their destiny. In-sisting that economic and political power "are two kinds of power that count in America, with social power being derived from those two," Malcolm maintained that "our communities must be the sources of their own strength politically, economically," and otherwise.[42] Although Martin spoke at times of black power and white power intersecting, he was often as dynamic as Malcolm when expressing the need for African Americans to "unite around powerful action programs" of an economic and political nature to better their own condition. However, Martin opposed all-black political parties, as evidenced by his criticisms of the Freedom Now Party, which was formed in the 1960s. Noting, with some anger, that that particular organization had quoted him and used his photograph to "forward its aims," Martin declared in 1964:

> I am deeply disturbed that the party's *Illustrated News* [vol. 4, no. 14] has grossly misquoted me in saying that I tend to favor the formation of an all Negro political party. I do not now and I have never advocated the formation of an all Negro political party. I have always supported increased political participation and organization by Negroes, not in isolation, but along with the Labor Movement, the churches and liber-als to make firm an alliance which has proven its power by achieving in 1964 the passage of the most comprehensive Civil Rights Bill in our history. For I believe the fundamental political aim of the Negro people is to join with other progressive segments of this society to create a political force capable of the further democratization of our country. When the best elements of the trade union movement, the churches, the liberals, the intellectuals and other ethnic minorities join in such a po-

litical force, then, and only then, can there emerge that majority consensus capable of solving the basic social and economic problems this
nation faces.[43]

Malcolm was more receptive to the Freedom Now Party, though he wondered about any possible white liberal influence on it. As he saw it in 1963,
the Nation of Islam was the only "black party" that was truly worthy of the
name. While both he and Martin had doubts about the devotion of the
nation's two-party system to the civil rights cause, Malcolm was far more
critical than Martin of the Democrats, the Republicans, and any other political party that claimed to be racially inclusive while preserving white privilege
and the structures of white power.[44]

Malcolm and Martin believed that their people could learn a lot from
other oppressed groups, especially Jews, who had achieved strong economic
and political power against great odds. Even as Malcolm attacked those Jews
who exploited African Americans in various ways, he concluded that the Jew
has a "sense of his own value" that enables "him to act and think independently, unlike our people and our leaders."[45] Although Martin acknowledged
that "Negroes have been far more cruelly exploited and suffer an intensity of
discrimination Jews have never felt," he thought that, especially in the United
States, "the lesson of Jewish determination to use educational and social
action on a mass scale to attain political representation and influence [was]
worthy of emulation." However, Martin never meant to suggest, as Malcolm
typically did, that his people should rely exclusively on their own means for
economic and political advancement. While agreeing to some degree with the
idea that African Americans should "lift themselves up by their own bootstraps," Martin always pointed out that the federal government also had a
role in uplifting his people, especially since it had long helped sustain the
oppressive system. With this in mind, Martin asserted: "I do always point out
the other side—that the problem is that Negroes have not always had the
resources in many ways to just do it by themselves. And it is a cruel jest to say
to a bootless man that he ought to lift himself by his own bootstraps. And it's
even worse if you have a boot, and somebody's standing on the boot, and
they're telling you to lift yourself by your own bootstraps."[46]

Martin's call for federal assistance conflicted sharply with Malcolm's view
that the government was not prepared morally to solve the problems of African Americans. While both men criticized the Democratic and Republican
Parties and attacked the American judicial system, Martin, unlike Malcolm,
frequently made appeals to the courts and petitions to federal, state, and

municipal authorities in support of equal rights for his people.[47] These differences in philosophy and method were revealed most profoundly in Martin's emphasis on "the American dream" and Malcolm's frequent references to "the American nightmare." But there is a sense in which "the dream" and "the nightmare" always stood in tension with each other in the minds of Martin and Malcolm, for both were constantly compelled by ever-changing political and economic situations to distinguish between the *real* and the *ideal*—between what America *actually was* and what she could *possibly become*.[48]

Malcolm and Martin were most persuasive when contending that black liberation could not occur without the liberation of other oppressed peoples. This view actually solidified them in ways that ultimately made the differences between them seem small indeed. Both encouraged their people to transcend the artificial boundaries of race and ethnicity to engage in dialogue, mutual support, and economic and political alliances with Native Americans, Hispanic Americans, Asian Americans, and other oppressed groups. The various ways in which Malcolm and Martin expressed this vision, and expanded it to cover the oppressed worldwide, will be treated in subsequent parts of this chapter.

Ambivalence in the Soul: Malcolm and Martin on White America

Malcolm and Martin held that the oppression of their people over time could be explained largely through an analysis of the attitudes, values, and institutions of white America. Both focused on the history of whites in the United States with critical insight, noting particularly the glaring inconsistencies between their democratic and Christian claims and their institutionalization of a racist ethic. Malcolm considered it most ironic that the Founding Fathers wrote about freedom and basic human equality, while holding people of African descent in bondage. For Malcolm, nothing could have been more hypocritical, especially since whites, from the time of the American Revolution, fought desperately to establish and preserve their own freedom and autonomy. Martin echoed this view as he recalled Thomas Jefferson and others who gave expression to the American dream in the Declaration of Independence and the Constitution. "But ever since the Founding Fathers of this nation dreamed this dream," Martin maintained, "America has been something of a schizophrenic personality tragically divided against itself." While cherishing "the great principles of democracy," he added, whites had "sadly practiced the antithesis of those principles." In Martin's estimation, "slavery and racial segregation have been strange paradoxes in a nation founded on the notion that all men are created equal." He concluded that "it has been this terrible ambivalence in the soul of white America that has led us to the state we are in now," a view Malcolm accepted and articulated perhaps more than any other black leader of his time.[49]

Both leaders attributed white society's dominance over blacks not to intelligence and prudence but to cleverness, ferocity, and the persistent and illegitimate use of its collective power. This appeared most evident in the extent to which whites had used violence and deception to retard the social, political, and economic advancement of African Americans. As Malcolm reflected on this history, he reasoned that white Americans had "created one of the most criminal societies that has ever existed on the earth since time began," a perspective that reinforced his conviction that blacks should no longer accept passively the night-riding forays of terrorism and torture staged by Klansmen, the White Citizens Council, and other extremists. Malcolm shared with Martin the belief that much of the violence in the black community, as evident in riots and in the fighting and treachery that occurred within the race, resulted largely from the many ways in which blacks had been victimized by a violent white culture for centuries.[50]

The long history of violence against people of color in the United States led Malcolm and Martin to the conclusion that blacks are generally more humane than whites. As a Black Muslim leader, Malcolm constantly referred to whites as "beasts," "dogs," "swine," "devils," and "the enemy," suggesting that they were contemptible, vicious creatures determined to dominate and destroy people of color. Moreover, Malcolm maintained that whites had more than demonstrated that they, as a group, are morally incapable of practicing nonviolence and of coexisting peacefully with people unlike themselves. Thus he insisted that Martin's efforts to appeal to the moral conscience of white society through nonviolent action would only result in more misery for African Americans. "When you speak the language of morality, or the language of nonviolence," he declared in referring to whites, "you are speaking a language that they don't understand." This thought must have crossed Martin's mind at times as well, but the civil rights leader knew of white bigots who had been transformed into integrationists under the power of love and the nonviolent movement.[51] Consequently, Martin never completely surrendered his faith in the capacity of whites to change for the better. Even so, he believed that whites as a group had always been great purveyors of violence, and he constantly urged the most radical elements in the black community to reject the values of the larger culture while embracing a higher morality:

> One of the greatest paradoxes of the Black Power movement is that it talks unceasingly about not imitating the values of white society, but in advocating violence it is imitating the worst, the most brutal and the most uncivilized value of American life. American Negroes have not been mass murderers. They have not murdered children in Sunday school, nor have they hung white men on trees bearing strange fruit. They have not been hooded perpetrators of violence, lynching human beings at will and drowning them at whim.[52]

The suggestion here is that African Americans had much to lose by imitating whites at the levels of values and character. Malcolm was generally more forthright than Martin in making this assertion, but both believed that an obsession with war, wealth, and power had robbed whites collectively of genuine spirituality and of a sense of the sacredness of human personality. Thus, whites as a group were, in the minds of both, generally less congenial than blacks to the idea of interracial community. Malcolm insisted that white society had virtually nothing of value to offer humanity—that even her scientific and technological advancements had turned out to be unimpressive, dispensable, and designed to reinforce systems of oppression. "This man hasn't learned how to make paint yet that will last two years," said Malcolm on one occasion, and on another he implied that whites had created bombs and planes largely out of a fear of facing people of color in hand-to-hand combat. Although Martin saw much value in the scientific and technological revolutions spearheaded by whites, he was equally mindful that such contributions were resulting in a society in which "machines and computers, profit motives and property rights are considered more important than people." Thus, when Martin called for "a revolution of values to accompany the scientific and freedom revolutions engulfing the earth," for a movement beyond the principle that "self-preservation is the first law of life" to the idea that "other-preservation is the first law of life," white people were uppermost in his mind.[53]

But there was a certain credibility to Malcolm's and Martin's critiques of white society, mainly because they were also unsparing in their descriptions of the shortcomings of African Americans. Malcolm was as critical of apathy and cowardice among his people as he was of avarice and cruelty on the part of whites. This is equally true of Martin, who denied that "the Negro is a saint," and who insisted that black people were subject to the same frailties as other human beings. "No one can pretend that because a people may be oppressed, every individual is virtuous and worthy," Martin observed. Asserting that "Negroes are human, not super-human," he went on, in language typically used by Malcolm, to attack those African Americans "who will never fight for freedom," who "will seek profit for themselves alone from the struggle," and who "will cooperate with their oppressors." "Every minority and every people has its share of opportunists, profiteers, free-loaders and escapists," he further noted. But for all their shortcomings, many of them born of oppression, Martin recognized in his people "peculiar spiritual gifts" that made them far more apt than whites to successfully conduct a nonviolent struggle against injustice. Indeed, African Americans constituted for Martin that creative minority of which Henry David Thoreau had spoken, that minority which improves the state by resisting its evil system.[54]

Malcolm and Martin adamantly disagreed with those who identified the problem of racism exclusively with white southerners. In other words, both saw racial prejudice as the sickness of whites nationwide. Standing in the tradition of his slave forebears, who likened the heartlessness and brutality of slaveowners to the ways of wolves, bears, tigers, and other vicious animals that preyed on smaller and weaker ones, Malcolm used the images of the wolf and the fox to suggest, with some exaggeration, that there were no essential differences in the perceptions and attitudes of whites when it came to people of African descent:

> The South is no different from the North. Let me tell you the only difference. The white man in the South is a wolf. You know where he stands. When he opens his mouth and you see his teeth he looks vicious. Well, the only difference between the white man in the South and the white man in the North is that one is a wolf and this one is a fox. The fox will lynch you and you won't even know you have been lynched. The fox will Jim Crow you and you don't even know you're Jim Crowed. . . . The objective of the fox and the wolf is the same. They want to exploit you, they want to take advantage of you. Both are canines, both are dogs—there is no difference. Their methods might differ, but their objective is the same, and the southern white man and the northern white man are in the same category.[55]

With a boldness of vision uncharacteristic of Martin, Malcolm pushed his analysis further: "These Northern crackers are in cahoots with the Southern crackers, only these Northern crackers smile in your face and show you their teeth and they stick the knife in your back when you turn around." He added, "You at least know what that man down there is doing and you know how to deal with him." Although Malcolm had virtually no faith in the moral capacity of white southerners to overcome the crippling legacy of bigotry and injustice, he nevertheless found their approach to race relations less hypo-critical and perhaps more acceptable than that of whites in the North:

> The white Southerner, you can say one thing—he is honest. He bares his teeth to the black man; he tells the black man, to his face, that Southern whites never will accept phony "integration." The Southern white goes further, to tell the black man that he means to fight him every inch of the way—against even the so-called "tokenism." The advantage of this is the Southern black man never has been under any illusions about the opposition he is dealing with. . . . You can say for many Southern white people that, individually, they have been paternalistically helpful to many individual Negroes. But the Northern white man, he grins with his teeth, and his mouth has always been full of tricks and lies of "equality" and "integration."[56]

Martin could not have agreed more, despite his claim that the white South had historically been the main source of America's racism. While he recog-nized that black southerners were generally more humane than their white counterparts, he believed nevertheless that whites in the South had a capacity for honesty and a commitment to principle that surpassed that of northern whites—a capacity that, if properly cultivated, could contribute to a trans-forming impulse. Martin expressed the point in these terms:

> You know, when you can finally convert a white Southerner, you have one of the most genuine, committed human beings that you'll ever find. Did you ever notice that? You see, what the white South has going for it that the North doesn't have is that the average white Southerner has at least had individual contact with Negroes. It hasn't been person-to-person contact, but he's at least had individual contact with Negroes. Now, the thing to do is to transform that Lord-serving relationship into intergroup, interpersonal living. And when that happens, do you know that I really feel that the South is going to get ahead of the North. Because one thing about this brother down here is that he doesn't like us, and he lets us know it. . . . You do at least know how to deal with it. I've been up North, and I've found that you don't know how to deal with it, because you can't quite get at your target. He'll [white North-

erner] sit up there and smile in your face. You go down to see the officials and they'll serve you cookies and tea, and shake your hand and pose for pictures with you. And at the same time, keeping Negroes in ghettoes and slums. But down here, they won't take no pictures with us, they won't give us no tea and cookies, and they tell us on television that they don't like us. They don't hide it.[57]

During the first five years of his activities as a civil rights leader, Martin expressed levels of confidence in white southerners that Malcolm never had as a public figure. In December 1956, toward the end of the Montgomery bus protest, Martin spoke of "the great resources of goodwill in the Southern white man that we must somehow tap." During the three years that followed, he constantly affirmed his "faith in the South," asserting, "We are convinced that in our time the South can be a peaceful and integrated society." He believed that "the great majority of white Southerners" were "law-abiding citizens," that they were "prepared to accept and abide by the supreme law of the land," and he estimated that "only a small but determined minority resort to threats, bodily assaults, cross-burnings, bombings, shootings and open defiance of the law in an attempt to force us to retreat."[58] In taking such positions, Martin was being either naive or prudent, or perhaps some of both, especially since the very existence of white supremacist structures in the South depended on the strong support and often silent acquiescence of the white majority. In any case, his expressed optimism regarding the goodwill and moral sensibilities of most white southerners clearly conflicted with other statements he made over time, in which he accused them of numerous acts of defiance and lawlessness and of widespread physical and psychological violence against African Americans. As Martin became more radical in his outlook in the late 1960s, his faith in whites as a group waned significantly, and he ultimately arrived at a perspective on white southerners and northerners that more closely approximated that of Malcolm X.[59]

The white liberal establishment presented a special challenge for Malcolm and Martin as they considered the range of resources that had to be drawn on for the liberation of black America. This concern was clearly inescapable for both men, because white liberals provided much of the financial and moral support for the black freedom cause in the 1950s and 1960s. But Malcolm was never really comfortable with their involvement in the struggle, and he simply refused to actively solicit their support even after his split with the Black Muslims. The Muslim minister constantly denounced what he called "the old, tricky, blue-eyed liberals," accusing them of controlling the civil rights movement, of teaching blacks to be passive and long-suffering, and of confusing "the true wants of the American black man" by encouraging a meaningless search for integration. "I know that all that have come in here tonight don't call yourselves liberals," said Malcolm to a group of whites at a meeting in New York in April 1964. "Because that's a nasty name today. It represents hypocrisy." A year later, he reminded whites, "If you're not of the John Brown school of liberals, we'll get you later."[60] Although Martin echoed some of Malcolm's concerns regarding the hypocrisy of the white liberal establishment, the civil rights leader's criticisms were often muffled by his determination to preserve the vital and sometimes fragile alliance of Protestants, Catholics, and Jews who participated in his quest for a just and inclusive society. In an interview in September 1964, Martin observed: "I don't think one can put all Liberals in the same category. It is true that some of the so-called Liberals have been devoted more to order than to justice, and they have paternalistically sought to set the timetable for the Negroes' freedom. I don't think this is quite true of all Liberals. I think there have been some who have evinced a genuine sincerity."[61]

Martin never abandoned his call for a genuine liberalism, or "a real positive ethical Christian liberalism," "that firmly believes in integration in its own community as well as in the deep South." He believed deeply that some southern moderates and northern liberals had demonstrated their usefulness to the struggle, a position that clearly separated him from Malcolm. Martin pointed to Sarah P. Boyle, Ann Braden, Lillian Smith, Ralph McGill, and other southern moderates who "have written about our struggle in eloquent and prophetic terms," and he acknowledged Viola Liuzzo, James Reeb, and other northern liberals who had sacrificed their lives for the cause.[62] Even so, he chided those white moderates in the South who "are silent today because of fear of social, political and economic reprisals," and he insisted that a stronger and more uncompromising leadership was needed from white northern liberals if America was to become a truly democratic nation:

There is a dire need today for a liberalism which is truly *liberal*. What we are witnessing today in so many northern communities is a sort of quasi-liberalism which is based on the principle of looking sympathetically at all sides. It is a liberalism so bent on seeing all sides, that it fails to become committed to either side. It is a liberalism that is so objectively analytical that it is not subjectively committed. It is a liberalism which is neither hot nor cold, but lukewarm. We call for a liberalism from the North which will be thoroughly committed to the ideal of racial justice and will not be deterred by the propaganda and subtle words of those who say, "Slow up for a while, you are pushing too fast."[63]

The differences between Malcolm and Martin extended to the whole question of which roles white institutions might assume in the crusade for equal rights and social justice. Having witnessed the role of the white-controlled media in the freedom movement, both understood the power of those institutions. But it was impossible for them to avoid feelings of ambivalence and even anger toward the white press, universities, churches, and other institutions, especially since these institutions had been used at times to attack black leadership and to undermine the movement. Malcolm frequently urged whites and blacks to promote the freedom cause through their own separate institutions, for he believed that the society was not ready for truly integrated institutions. Furthermore, he believed that in a nation which thrives on white power, such institutions would only subject his people to continued white domination. While Martin envisioned a truly integrated society, these considerations were relevant for him as well. Integration for him never meant the destruction of black institutions and the complete assimilation of his people into white culture. Rather, it meant, in political terms, "Mutual acceptance, true inter-group and inter-personal living where there is shared power."[64] Even as Martin encouraged whites to join and work with black churches and civil rights organizations, he knew the importance of African Americans having control of their own institutions. Nothing could have been more justifiable in a society dominated by white power. Martin once expressed this point in response to a question raised to him concerning the need to support historically black colleges:

> There is no contradiction in believing in integration and supporting the Negro College Fund. You must remember that although Negro colleges are by and large segregated institutions, they are not segregating institutions. If these colleges are properly supported they will serve in an integrated society. Many of these colleges already have white students. It is not true to feel that as soon as integration becomes a thoroughgoing reality, the so-called Negro private colleges will close down. In supporting these Negro colleges we are only seeking to make sure that the quality and caliber of these schools are of such nature that they will be appealing to all people.[65]

Malcolm and Martin were open to the possibility of Americans, white and black, becoming a single people, as long as African Americans exercised a significant influence in determining the direction and destiny of the nation. Both felt that it would be impossible for the races to live in harmony, or to coexist peacefully, if whites remained committed to keeping America exclusively under their control. Although Malcolm thought such harmony possible if whites made reparations for the centuries of black slave labor, he considered their virtual destruction a greater possibility, which explains his conviction that his people should return to Africa culturally, philosophically, and psychologically, and also his emphasis on the need for the establishment of closer ties between African Americans and other people of color worldwide. Malcolm never completely surrendered the idea that the fate of whites is essentially one of doom, especially if they fail to atone or repent for wrongs visited upon people of color throughout the centuries. Indeed, the atonement theme literally permeates Malcolm's writings and speeches, connecting him in mind and spirit with Martin, who also envisioned God's judgment and wrath upon white America. However, Martin, not given to the kind of apocalyptic vision held by Malcolm, also believed that whites, through God's intercession and the redemptive work of committed human beings, could be saved from what he termed "tragic self-destruction in the quagmire of racial hate." It was in this connection that the messianic role of African Americans became so important for him.[66]

The Other Side of the Color Line: Images of the Dark World

The plight of Africans and of other people of color worldwide occupied a prominent place in the thinking of both Malcolm and Martin. Both men acknowledged bonds and obligations between the oppressed everywhere, even as they devoted most of their time, energy, and resources to addressing the peculiar needs and interests of African Americans. They believed that black freedom could not be attained independently of the freedom of other oppressed people, that there would be no successful revolution for African Americans as long as other people of color suffered on grounds of race and economics.[67]

Such a conviction did not signal a radical shift in the thinking of Malcolm and Martin. Both had grown up in environments in which the problems of oppressed people in various parts of the world were known and almost routinely discussed. Because he had been raised by a mother from the West Indies and a father from the Deep South, both of whom were Garveyites, and because he had associated with people of various races while hustling in Boston and New York, Malcolm's sense of the world was never limited merely to the African-American experience. His sense that people of color throughout the world experienced oppression came naturally and was heightened in prison as he read intensely about Africans, Asians, and other "non-European people," studies that made him mindful of his links with the dark world long before he became a Black Muslim minister. Martin developed a similar outlook before becoming a civil rights leader, largely because his family background and his training at Morehouse College, Crozer Theological Seminary, and Boston University encouraged an intense interest in world affairs.[68]

It is impossible to determine precisely the point at which Malcolm and Martin first stressed the need for people of color to find common ground. As a follower of Elijah Muhammad, Malcolm frequently spoke of the experiences of oppressed people across the globe, giving primary emphasis to the need for people of African descent to achieve solidarity.[69] Martin alluded at times to the common struggle of African Americans and other oppressed people in his early sermons at Dexter Avenue Baptist Church in Montgomery, Alabama. "The people of the Third World are now rising up," he explained in May 1956, "and at many points I feel that this movement in Montgomery is part of this overall movement in the world in which oppressed people are revolting against the imperialism and colonialism that have too long existed." This view was strengthened as Martin visited Ghana in 1957 and India in 1959. He saw "in Ghana a symbol of the hopes and aspirations of all our people," and in India he conversed with Indians and Africans who shared many of his views on the oppressed. "We were looked upon as brothers with the color of our skins as something of an asset," Martin recalled. "But the strongest bond of fraternity was the common cause of minority and colonial peoples in America, Africa and Asia struggling to throw off racialism and imperialism."[70]

Malcolm and Martin knew that African Americans had to experience a revolution in their thinking before seriously entertaining and acting on the concerns that they shared with other black, brown, red, and yellow peoples. In more specific terms, African Americans had to move toward a stronger group definition, a position the two leaders advanced with undeviating sincerity. For Malcolm, this necessarily meant dropping the word *Negro* as a group name and taking on an identity that more closely identified his people with Africa and people of color generally. Nothing could have been more important, since the word *Negro* stood as a reminder of slavery and racism and as a symbol of the cultural and spiritual pain endured by blacks in America. Malcolm declared that his people were not Negroes or Americans but Africans deep within their souls, a perspective that seemed at odds with his view that slavery had destroyed African culture and with his critique of more contemporary expressions of black art. On one occasion, Malcolm remarked: "We are just as much African today as we were in Africa four hundred years ago, only we are a modern counterpart of it. When you hear a black man playing music, whether it is jazz or Bach, you still hear African music. The soul of Africa is still reflected in the music played by black men. In everything else we do we still are African in color, feeling, everything. And we will always be that whether we like it or not."[71] Martin took a more dialectical approach in his reasoning on the matter, concluding that "we're not Anglo-Saxons and we're not Africans," we are "a true hybrid, a combination of cultures."[72] However, he could be as adamant as Malcolm when arguing that his people needed a healthy collective identity in order to find their rightful place in the broader human struggle.

The larger issue here was the need for unity within the ranks of African Americans. Both men felt that without group solidarity, African Americans would not have the values needed to forge a proper spiritual bond with other oppressed people. This need for black unity became more pressing for Malcolm after his departure from the Nation of Islam in 1963. This is why he sent a letter to civil rights leaders in March 1964 requesting "forgiveness for the unkind things he had said" about them "in the past." He went on to call for "new areas for mutual cooperation" that would be "beneficial to our people and that should considerably shorten our struggle." To contribute to this new spirit of solidarity, Malcolm started the Organization of Afro-American Unity (OAAU) in June 1964, an organization "broad enough for all Afro-Americans who wanted to fight for freedom and human dignity 'by any means necessary.'" Martin responded gracefully to Malcolm's fresh initiative, and the two leaders had begun to entertain the possibility of meeting and discussing the future course of the freedom movement by early 1965.[73]

Their interest in bonds and obligations between African Americans and other people of color was consistent with their mounting political involvements worldwide and with their amazing capacity to identify with oppressed people across the boundaries of race and nationality. After severing ties with the Black Muslims, Malcolm constantly reminded his people that "no kind of action in this country" will ever "bear fruit unless that action is tied in with the overall international struggle." For him, that struggle primarily involved the "black, brown, red, and yellow peoples of the earth," who "had an oppressor in common, an exploiter in common—the European." As far as Malcolm was concerned, "What happens to a black man in America today happens to the black man in Africa. What happens to a black man in America and Africa happens to the black man in Asia and to the man down in Latin America. What happens to one of us today happens to all of us."[74]

Martin also recognized the extent to which people of color worldwide were victimized by what Malcolm termed "an international power structure" dominated by white "Western interests." Martin frequently referred to the long history of "the Western powers" as "colonial masters," noting in one instance, "In country after country we see white men building empires on the sweat and suffering of colored people." He and Malcolm regarded U.S. involvement in Vietnam as yet another example of a white Western power seeking to block the independence and self-determination of a people of color. For Martin, the American venture in Vietnam in the 1960s, much like President Harry Truman's and the U.S. government's refusal to recognize Vietnamese independence back in 1945, was indicative of "the deadly Western arrogance that has poisoned the international atmosphere for so long." Thus, one might question the claim that Martin did "not particularly think of the war in Vietnam as a racial one (although the phrase 'killing little brown children in Vietnam' slips in)," especially in view of his sensitivity to and reflections on the international ramifications of white supremacy.[75]

The extent to which the structures of white supremacy figured into the crisis situations in South Africa and the Middle East was considered on some level by Malcolm and Martin. The apartheid problem in South Africa was particularly important in this regard. Malcolm spoke of South Africa as a "place where racism is practiced openly by the government," and he denied that that country was considerably different from the United States. "The only difference," he maintained, is that "South Africa preaches and practices segregation whereas America preaches integration and practices segregation." Martin essentially agreed with this assessment, even as he labeled South Africa the "classic example of organized and institutionalized racism" and as the worst place in the world in the area of race relations. Describing South Africa's "national policy and practice" as "the incarnation of the doctrine of white supremacy in the midst of a population which is overwhelmingly black," Martin held that it was even more tragic that this "racist government" was "virtually made possible by the economic policies of the

United States and Great Britain, two countries which profess to be the moral bastions of our Western world." The collaboration of the major Western powers in maintaining South Africa was clear evidence to Martin, as it was to Malcolm, of how the structures of white supremacy functioned on a global scale.[76]

The degree to which this was true of the Middle East was open to serious debate. It was evident to Malcolm that race or color was at the center of the Arab-Israeli conflict, for he noted how the United States and other Western powers had supported European Jews in establishing a white nation (Israel) in the midst of the territory of a dark-skinned people. This tendency to view the Middle East situation in light of the color line proved inevitable for Malcolm the black nationalist, who visited parts of the Middle East as early as 1958 and as late as 1964. In contrast, Martin, from the time of Israel's 1956 war with Egypt, ignored any possible racial considerations while appearing to assume an essentially pro-Israel stance. The civil rights leader not only affirmed Israel's "territorial integrity" and "its right to a homeland" as incontestable. He is also said to have promoted "the legitimacy of Zionism within the black community." However, according to Rabbi Marc Schneier, Martin's pro-Israel and pro-Zionist outlook seemed to waver a bit after 1966, mainly because he was more interested in avoiding confrontations with young black nationalists, who "made alliance with brown-skinned Arabs more acceptable than a relationship with white Israelis." After Israel shot down Egyptian jets over Gaza in the Six Day War in 1967, Martin became more interested in supporting and maintaining friendships with both the Arab world and the Israelis. Subsequently, he either remained largely silent on the Middle East crisis, followed a path of neutrality, or called for a negotiated settlement that would benefit both sides. At one point, Martin and his SCLC produced a statement supporting both "Israel's right to exist as a state in security" and the Arab world's need to be freed from "a state of imposed poverty and backwardness." It was clear to Martin by 1967 that Israel and the Arabs had much to gain by working together. Thus he refused to endorse anti-Semitism or anti-Israel and anti-Arab sentiments.[77]

Martin's attitude toward the Arab-Israeli conflict shifted over time for reasons which have not yet been seriously addressed. Rabbi Schneier's suggestion that Martin "did not want to give ammunition to those anti-Israel propagandists who were beginning to dominate certain segments of the black community" is well taken but not very persuasive. Martin, especially during the last three years of his life, was not known to sacrifice principle in order to avoid conflict with radical elements in either the black or white communities. He felt that he had nothing of value to gain from this, an attitude which helps explain the drop in financial and moral support for his SCLC in 1967–68. The fact is that Martin came to better understand the Arab cause and to see that both sides in the Middle East conflict had legitimate goals. He also came to see that Israel was possibly more guilty of aggression in some cases than her Arab neighbors, often resorting to war instead of pursuing the full limits of much-needed diplomacy. Moreover, it is possible that Martin did ultimately see color or race as an issue in the Middle East crisis, especially since these concerns were occasionally raised in the black community by nationalists and others. This would have caused Martin to reconsider what had initially been his seemingly unwavering support for the Israeli cause. For those Jews who took a nondialectical approach to reasoning regarding the Middle East crisis, or who took any sympathy at all for Arabs as anti-Israeli, Martin's shifting position must have been most disturbing. In any case, the positions he and Malcolm took on the whole question of the racial implications of the conflict in the Middle East serve to impress upon one the seeming timelessness of certain concerns among black people regarding people of color worldwide. To be sure, Malcolm and Martin anticipated the current debates in the African-American community and at the world conference on racism in South Africa about Israel's often violent confrontations with the Palestinians.[78]

But Malcolm and Martin did not agree completely in their analyses of how American blacks and other people of color might work together to eliminate the structures of white supremacy. Doubtful that African Americans as a group were prepared to take the kind of revolutionary action that wins genuine freedom, Malcolm placed great stress on the need for them to learn from their dark brothers and sisters in the so-called Third World. The Muslim leader had absolutely no doubt about the abilities of Africans, Asians, and other people of color abroad to lead their own struggles while providing an example for his people in America, especially since people of color abroad had strong self-identities and a tendency to use any means necessary to secure perfectly legitimate ends. This explains Malcolm's tendency to see African revolutions as a model for black revolutions worldwide. In sharp contrast, Martin envisioned the possibility of African Americans serving as the vanguard in a struggle to liberate the dark world from high levels of poverty, illiteracy, and the subversive impact of racism, colonialism, and neocolonialism through nonviolent means. In 1967, he wrote: "The hard cold facts today indicate that the hope of the people of color in the world may well rest on the American Negro and his ability to reform the structure of racist imperialism from within and thereby turn the technology of the West to the task of liberating the world from want."[79]

Many African Americans, and most certainly the highly privileged, were not favorably disposed to the idea that they should feel a closer identification with other people of color than with whites in the United States. This deeply frustrated Malcolm, who, unlike Martin, attributed his people's serious lack of raw militancy to both their Christian faith and their failure to realize their true links with the dark world:

> Here in America, we have always thought that we were struggling by ourselves, and most Afro-Americans will tell you just that—that we're a minority. By thinking we're a minority, we struggle like a minority. We struggle like we're an underdog. We struggle like all the odds are against us. This type of struggle takes place only because we don't yet know where we fit in the scheme of things. We've been maneuvered out of a position where we could rightly know and understand where we fit into the scheme of things. It's impossible for you and me to know where we stand until we look around on this entire earth.[80]

For Malcolm, "the power of the oppressed black, brown, red and yellow people began at the Bandung conference, which was a coalition between the Arab and the Asian and the African." "The African-Asian-Arab bloc," he continued, "was the bloc that started the real independence movement among the oppressed peoples of the world." Malcolm further reminded his people that the Bandung conference

> actually serves as a model for the same procedure you and I can use to get our problems solved. At Bandung all the nations came together, the dark nations from Africa and Asia. Some of them were Buddhists, some of them were Muslims, some of them were Christians, some were Confucianists, some were atheists. Despite their religious differences, they came together. Some were communists, some were socialists, some were capitalists—despite their economic and political differences, they came together. All of them were black, brown, red or yellow. . . . The number-one thing that was not allowed to attend the Bandung confer-

ence was the white man. He couldn't come. Once they excluded the white man, they found that they could come together.[81]

Malcolm's faith in the potential of such alliances was further stimulated with China's explosion of an atomic bomb in 1964. In his view, this was "the greatest event" for people of color—"a great contribution to the struggle of oppressed people in the world."[82] But Malcolm seemed unmindful of the many obstacles that prevented the cementing of special ties between the African-American freedom movement and the struggles of people of color in other parts of the world, a problem Martin never had, despite his belief that the oppressed everywhere were a part of one family. Even as Martin met Asians and Africans who expressed solidarity with his people's cause in America, he knew also that many of them, and indeed others throughout the dark world, considered themselves superior to African Americans. Moreover, he appeared more apt than Malcolm to acknowledge publicly the points at which the interests of African Americans and those of other people of color across the globe diverged. Thus, Martin did not talk as much as Malcolm about the possibility of an international alliance of black, brown, red, and yellow peoples against white supremacist attitudes and structures.

The two men did become essentially one in their efforts to enlighten people of color everywhere about the growing race problem in the world. In December 1964, Martin "met with representatives from the total colored community of London"—with persons from India, Pakistan, Africa, and the West Indies—"to deal with" this problem "in a forthright and determined manner." Malcolm pursued a similar venture in France and England in 1964 and early 1965 with little success, mainly because the power elite in both countries interfered with his efforts.[83] Large numbers of blacks in America would have had difficulty grasping the full significance of such efforts at that time, but racist and colonial leaders in the United States and abroad did not. Proof of this surfaced in February 1965, when Malcolm was denied entrance into France to address both the Federation of African Students and the Committee of Members of the Afro-American Community in Paris. To be sure, Malcolm's and Martin's efforts to work with people of color throughout the world to eliminate racism and colonialism made conflict with the white world inevitable. As they incurred the hatred of white people worldwide, they became marked men and were ultimately silenced as various ruling elites moved against them.

The need for American blacks to form coalitions with other people of

African descent could not have been more pressing for Malcolm and Martin. Both consistently spoke of a special kinship among people of African ancestry everywhere, even as they saw the need for coalitions between the oppressed generally. They also visited African countries, met and conversed with Kwame Nkrumah and other African leaders and freedom fighters, provided moral support for anticolonial struggles throughout Africa and the black diaspora, and desperately sought to influence U.S. policy toward all people of African descent worldwide.[84] Convinced that "the same pulse that beats in the Black man on the African continent today is beating in the heart of the Black man in North America, Central America, South America, and in the Caribbean," Malcolm established his OAAU "as an American base for worldwide black liberation." Moreover, he urged African Americans not to support America's wars against people of African ancestry, and in July 1964 he appealed to African heads of state for support in his effort to take the plight of his people in America before the United Nations.[85] Such actions accounted largely for Malcolm's significance as the foremost molder of black nationalist thought in his generation.

Martin found Malcolm's views on black America's relationship to Africa to be quite reasonable but somewhat different from his own. Martin did not form an organizational channel comparable to the OAAU, but he did work with the American Committee on Africa (ACOA) and the American Negro Leadership Conference on Africa (ANLCA), New York-based organizations designed to encourage a more positive and constructive relationship between African Americans, the United States, and African countries. Although Martin agreed in principle with Malcolm's eight-page memorandum to the African heads of state, calling for the United Nations to condemn America's treatment of African Americans, the civil rights leader was more inclined to see liberation coming through the struggle in America. This helps explain why Martin refused to join Malcolm in pressing for a full recognition of their people's civil rights through the UN, a worldwide body which, in Martin's estimation, was dominated in the first place by the United States and other Western powers. Even so, Martin never abandoned the idea that Africans and African Americans should work together for the total liberation of people of African descent, especially since they, as Malcolm frequently said, shared much in terms of their origins, condition, and destiny. Thus, Martin called upon the U.S. government to include more American blacks in its diplomatic missions to Africa, to join the UN in applying diplomatic and economic pressure against colonial powers that oppressed and exploited Africans, and to develop a kind of "Marshall Plan" to benefit all of Africa economically.[86]

The ways in which Africans and blacks in the diaspora were influencing each other in the struggle seemed less important to Malcolm than to Martin. Malcolm persisted in seeing the most significant influence coming from the African side. This helps explain why he sought to pattern his OAAU after the Organization of African Unity (OAU), which consisted of independent African states. At the same time, he held that blacks in the diaspora had much to gain from the movement of African nations toward independence. "Just as a strong China has produced a strong Chinaman, a strong Africa will produce a respected black man anywhere that black man goes on this earth," Malcolm maintained. "It's only with a strong Africa, an independent Africa and a respected Africa that wherever those of African origin or African heritage or African likeness go, they will be respected."[87] Martin said as much and more, even as he spoke of African Americans as a possible instrument through which Africans might rise above the hatred and violence inspired by tribal loyalties to a state of nonviolent coexistence.

Malcolm's and Martin's deep concern for Africa and the liberation of all people of African ancestry did not lead them to the same conclusion regarding the need for African Americans to return to the motherland. At times, Malcolm envisioned the necessity for a repatriation of American blacks, but in the last year of his life he decided that it was more realistic and desirable for them to remain in America physically, while returning to Africa psychologically, culturally, spiritually, and philosophically. Although Martin did not speak in these terms, he did see the need for an exchange of cultural concerns between American blacks and Africans. This attitude was only natural for one who ultimately felt no dilemma or tension between being fundamentally *American* and having a commitment to *African* liberation.[88]

Because Malcolm's and Martin's views on Africans and blacks in the diaspora overlapped at many points, the words *nationalist* and *integrationist,* when perceived as mutually exclusive, are simply inadequate for understanding them. To say that Malcolm was a Pan-Africanist and Martin was not is equally inadequate and misleading, especially in view of their emphasis on the common cultural characteristics and problems shared by all people of African ancestry. Unlike Malcolm, Martin was never a full-blown black nationalist or a Pan-Africanist, but his perspective clearly contained elements of

Pan-Africanism and black nationalism. Perhaps more important is the fact that both he and Malcolm ultimately transcended the limits of black nationalism and Pan-Africanism to embrace the idea of the essential oneness of humanity.[89]

Clamoring for World Community: The Visions of Malcolm and Martin

Malcolm and Martin became essentially one in their desire for world peace and community, despite the somewhat different ways in which they articulated and pursued that ideal. This assertion is not likely to be understood by those who persist in placing the two men at different extremes on the ideological spectrum, with one spouting unpalatable theories of racial separatism and the other a palatable gospel of love and racial harmony. The fact is that Malcolm ultimately rejected the black supremacist mythology of the Nation of Islam, and he also moved beyond the boundaries of Sunni Islam, black nationalism, Pan-Africanism, and an Afro-Asian political perspective to embrace an enlightened globalism.[90] Consequently, his message became broad enough to resonate with Martin's and with the ideas and hopes of freedom-loving people everywhere. Before Malcolm and Martin died, they felt virtually no tension between their struggle for the liberation of African Americans and their devotion to an inclusive and just world. Malcolm's universalism stemmed directly from his conversion to Sunni Islam and the teachings of the Prophet Muhammad, and Martin's stemmed from the message of Jesus Christ as understood in the black Christian tradition.

Malcolm's and Martin's interest in and contributions to human community grew largely out of their experiences as black men in a racist society, as well as from considerable travel, observation, study, and reflection. Both men spent time in Africa, Europe, and other parts of the world, connecting in mind and spirit with people of different racial, ethnic, religious, and national backgrounds. They also read widely and interacted with people at all levels, from professors and students in academic circles to ordinary citizens in the streets. Such experiences reinforced their belief that a truly democratic America for blacks and whites would be possible only within the confines of a genuinely democratic and peaceful world, a conviction that undergirded their sense of purpose and mission.[91]

Martin's moral vision of reconciliation and community on a global scale appeared more teleological than Malcolm's, for the Baptist preacher said more than the Muslim minister about how the oppressed should relate to their oppressors after the oppressed are liberated and empowered. But this should not obscure the fact that both men ultimately gave expression to a communitarian ideal that transcended all artificial human barriers. "I care about all people," Malcolm declared toward the end of his life. On another occasion, he expressed a willingness to practice "brotherhood with anyone really interested in living according to it."[92] The idea of whites and people of color living in harmony was not repulsive to him, though he insisted, as did Martin, that such a state of existence could not occur as long as whites remained obsessed with world domination. But in contrast to Malcolm, Martin employed the metaphors of "the beloved community," "the great world house," and "the worldwide neighborhood" in articulating his vision of global community in intellectual and theoretical terms. In more specific terms, Martin commented: "We have inherited a large house, a great 'world house' in which we have to live together—black and white, Easterner and Westerner, Gentile and Jew, Catholic and Protestant, Moslem and Hindu—a family unduly separated in ideas, culture and interest, who, because we can never again live apart, must learn somehow to live with each other in peace."[93]

Malcolm essentially agreed with Martin's insistence that racism, poverty, and war are the greatest barriers to human community. Both saw white supremacy as a world problem, but their prophetic critiques of the problem centered mostly on the United States and South Africa, where organized and institutionalized racism existed in the most glaring forms.[94] Having changed his own philosophical posture on race, in that he no longer included all whites indiscriminately in the same category, Malcolm denounced the practice of judging a person on the basis of color rather than "his deeds, his behavior, his intentions."[95] To further demonstrate his own change of heart, he ceased his opposition to interracial marriages and began to think seriously about the possibility of white allies in the struggle to overcome oppression in all forms. Thus, Malcolm's philosophical differences with Martin on the question of race became small indeed, a development that must have accounted in part for their agreement to meet and discuss the problem in 1965. Also convinced that the content of character, not color, should be the yardstick for judging human beings, Martin's acceptance of what he termed "the basic fact of the interrelated structure of reality" became the grounds on which he rejected all barriers that separated or fragmented people. At times, he seemed more convinced than Malcolm that whites and people of color everywhere had to affirm and work with each other in order to survive.[96]

Malcolm and Martin placed a special burden for eliminating racism on the shoulders of white people, especially since they had long been the major and most consistent promoters of the problem worldwide. Malcolm presented the Islamic paradigm as an alternative to white world supremacy. In words almost identical to those used by Martin, the Muslim leader highlighted the need for whites "to readjust their thinking of superiority toward the darker-skinned people." This invariably meant that whites had to develop not only new and more positive ways of viewing and relating to people of color but also more creative, constructive, and imaginative approaches to institutional and cultural transformation. Malcolm and Martin held that the failure of whites to make such changes would only result in a race war, a confrontation all the more tragic since whites constituted a microscopic minority on the world scale.[97]

But convincing whites of the need for a broader and more inclusive atti-tude toward humanity would not be easy because, as Malcolm put it, they "are extremely intelligent on most subjects until it comes to race." Malcolm and Martin knew that whites were far more likely to respond to challenges to racism with guilt and denial rather than with attitudinal and structural changes. The failure of whites and people of color to deal honestly and forth-rightly with each other on the question of race led Malcolm to describe the 1960s as "the era of hypocrisy."[98] Martin was equally mindful of the extent to which hypocrisy and the techniques of deception reinforced white su-premacist attitudes and structures. Whatever may be said about the pragma-tism of Malcolm's and Martin's positions, both realized that in a just world racial differences should never be a determinant in forging strong and inti-mate human relationships.

The degree to which poverty and economic injustice divided humanity could not have been more evident to Malcolm and Martin. Both were greatly disturbed by the vast gulf between the "haves" and the "have-nots," between the wealthy few and the masses of the poor.[99] Furthermore, they understood the relationship between racial injustice and economic injustice—that racism flourishes because economic and social systems profit from it. From Mal-colm's and Martin's points of view, much of the hunger, malnutrition, homelessness, disease, and death among the poor of all colors resulted from a vicious capitalistic system dominated by the white West. Malcolm therefore denied that one could be a capitalist and a freedom fighter at the same time, and Martin viewed the capitalistic ethic—which encourages cut-throat com-petition, selfish ambition, and the profit motive—as antithetical to the very spirit of human community.[100]

Both ultimately decided that socialism was more consistent with their quest for a world free of economic and political oppression. Malcolm had in mind a type of socialism that squared with African and Islamic communal values: a social, political, and economic philosophy that not only inspired antiracism but also afforded "better housing and better education and better food and better clothing" than the "vulturistic" capitalistic system. Martin spoke in terms of democratic socialism, "the political and economic ideology most congenial with his view of the distinctively Christian goal of society, 'the Beloved Community,' the term he used more often and usually synonymously with the more traditional concept, 'the Kingdom of God.'" [101] Having seen democratic socialism at work in Norway and other Scandinavian countries in 1964, Martin felt that it provided some useful insights for creating a world free of racial oppression and class exploitation.

Malcolm and Martin differed at points on how poverty and economic injustice could be addressed and perhaps even eliminated globally. Malcolm believed that people of color in various parts of the world were capable of solving these problems for themselves, but only if left alone by the imperialists of the white world. In other words, the policy of some nations extending their authority over others by territorial acquisition and the establishment of economic and political hegemony had to end. Malcolm never wavered in his conviction that a people's control of their own land is always of primary importance in any effort to eliminate poverty and economic injustice from their ranks, especially given the tremendous acceleration in the growth rate of the world's population. Although Martin agreed with certain aspects of this position, particularly as they related to land as the basis of independence and social uplift, he differed with Malcolm in that he placed much of the responsibility for ridding the world of poverty and economic exploitation on the shoulders of America, Britain, Russia, Canada, Australia, and the nations of Western Europe. Martin felt that such nations had to "see it as a moral obligation to provide capital and technical assistance" to underdeveloped countries, a tendency quite unusual in a world in which wealthy nations used foreign aid as a means to control poor nations. [102]

The elimination of violence and human destruction as a barrier to world community was as essential for Malcolm as it was for Martin. Both men abhorred war and were disturbed by the possibility that human beings would ultimately choose violent coannihilation over peaceful coexistence, though it is equally true that Malcolm, unlike Martin, saw violent revolution as possibly the only way for poor and oppressed people to secure their rightful place in the human family. However, while believing that "there will ultimately be a clash between the oppressed and those that do the oppressing," Malcolm reasoned that such a clash would not be "based upon the color of the skin." His belief that many whites would be inclined to join blacks who used "any means necessary" to protect themselves was an admission of enormous significance, especially for one who had long denounced integration efforts.[103]

The claim that Malcolm was more violent than Martin, that he preferred violence as an ethic to be embraced in human interactions, is virtually impossible to sustain, especially since the Muslim leader never resorted to such means himself. Indeed, Malcolm shared Martin's view that war and human destruction are shaky foundations for creating a truly harmonious and peaceful world, a position all the more significant in view of the existence of nuclear weapons and humanity's capacity for self-destruction. When it came to the destructive capacity of nuclear weapons across the world, Malcolm was often as much of a realist as Martin.[104]

This perspective accounted in large measure for Malcolm's and Martin's opposition to U.S. involvement in Vietnam. Both saw the Vietnam War as a conflict that could possibly result in a confrontation with China and eventually become a world war. Considering the many weapons of mass destruction, nothing could have been more devastating for the human family. Interestingly enough, many of Malcolm's and Martin's concerns about U.S. policy in Vietnam have been vindicated by recent revelations regarding the slaughter of thousands of Vietnamese on both sides during the Johnson administration.[105] But when it came to the international implications of the Vietnam conflict, despite their passionate, informed critiques, they remained essentially unheard. Perhaps more important, however, is the fact that Malcolm and Martin dared to put their reputations and even their lives at risk because they believed that their nation's role in Vietnam and in other volatile areas of the world could not be justified on moral grounds, an achievement that should not be casually ignored, since many black leaders in their time were hesitant to address international issues of war and peace.

Martin's more moderate approach and methods afforded him more opportunities than Malcolm had to spread the message of world peace and cooperation among whites in the United States and Europe. Often limited in terms of his appearances in both these contexts, and always preoccupied with concerns confronting African Americans specifically and people of color generally, the Muslim activist seemed not as prone as Martin to address problems such as the Berlin Wall. Martin actually spoke on the problem in Berlin in 1964, arguing that the Wall symbolized "the divisions of men on the face of the earth." Predicting that the Wall would one day collapse, as it did almost thirty years later, Martin reminded the Germans on both sides that "there is one Lord, one faith, and one baptism which binds us in a common history, a common calling, and a common hope for the salvation of the world." Martin's challenge to those barriers that separated whites from each other spoke to the depth of his world vision. Perhaps his most brilliant and moving statement of that vision was given some three years later, as he pictured a world in which all humans are related to and dependent upon each other:

> We are made to live together because of the interrelated structure of reality. Did you ever stop to think that you can't leave for your job in the morning without being dependent on most of the world? You get up in the morning and go to the bathroom and reach over for the sponge, and that's handed to you by a Pacific Islander. You reach for a bar of soap, and that's given to you at the hands of a Frenchman. And then you go to the kitchen to drink your coffee for the morning, and that's poured into your cup by a South American. And maybe you want tea: that's poured into your cup by a Chinese. Or maybe you are desirous of having cocoa for breakfast, and that's poured into your cup by a West African. And then you reach over for your toast, and that's given to you at the hands of an English-speaking farmer, not to mention the baker. And before you finish eating breakfast in the morning, you've depended on more than half of the world. This is the way our universe is structured, this is its interrelated quality. We aren't going to have peace on earth until we recognize this basic fact of the interrelated structure of all reality.[106]

Religion figured prominently in the shaping of Malcolm's and Martin's visions of world community. Early in his public life, Malcolm described Elijah Muhammad's concept of a separate black nation as a "religious solution." But later his discovery of what he termed "true Islam" led him to accept the idea that human community across color barriers could exist. In other words, Malcolm's break with Elijah Muhammad set the stage not only for his rapid development as a Sunni Muslim and a Pan-Africanist but also for his increasing maturation as an internationalist. During the last year of his life, he repeatedly told his listeners, "It is only being a Muslim which keeps me from seeing people by the color of their skin."[107] Martin said this much and more about the Christian ethic, and both he and Malcolm were convinced that religion had to become a tremendous force in humanity's efforts to build bridges of understanding and goodwill across the boundaries of race, ethnicity, class, and nationality. But strangely, the two men failed to properly address religious bigotry and intolerance as a problem as harmful to the quest for world community as racism, poverty, and war.

For Malcolm and Martin, humanity's respect for differences within its ranks ultimately depended upon a revolution of values and priorities. Both believed that the dignity and worth of individuals had to assume priority in the human consciousness over the material things of life, and that egoistic impulse and selfishness had to give way to humility and a greater reliance on the ethic of altruism. In broader terms, they wanted finally to see a world striving for spiritual and communal values that recognize and respect the image of God in all humans, a goal not merely to will, but to study and strive for unceasingly.

Malcolm's and Martin's visions of a world in which diversity is affirmed, respected, and celebrated remain unfulfilled. Racism, classism, violence and human destruction, sexism, religious bigotry and intolerance, homophobia, and other evils that polarize the human family are at least as pervasive today as they were in the 1950s and 1960s. Echoes of the tragic divisions within the human family are as real as the practices of "ethnic cleansing" in the Balkans, as the civil wars in Africa, as the demoralization of the untouchables in India, as the religious bigotry and conflict in Northern Ireland and the Middle East, and as the persistent and gruesome hate crimes aimed at Jews and peoples of color throughout Europe and the United States.[108] Internet resources, satellite communications, and high-speed travel are making the world smaller and bringing people of diverse cultures and interests together physically, but terrorism, intolerance, and discord remain vital tendencies in the human spirit. These realities suggest the need for the ongoing appropriation of Malcolm's and Martin's ideas for ethical resources.[109]

Malcolm and Martin never surrendered their respect for the fundamental values of democratic society. They wanted a world of shared commitments centered around the principles of power-sharing, individual choice, mutual respect and obligation, interpersonal and intergroup living, and a healthy respect for human rights. They sought to function on all fronts—cultural, economic, political, psychological, spiritual, social, intellectual, and otherwise—with the goal of striking down all obstacles to human community. They reminded us in dynamic and even subtle ways that humans have believed perfectly only when they wish for themselves what they desire for other humans.[110] Although Malcolm was assassinated before his growing world vision could be concretized into specific goals and objectives, he and Martin remain central characters in our seemingly never-ending quest to discover our legitimate, moral selves.

Strangely, our world is still delicately poised between the colored and the uncolored, the rich and the poor, the warmongers and the peacemakers, and the cross and the crescent. The artificial separation of the human family by geography, culture, language, religion, space, and time still looms in a new world order that is being increasingly ushered in by technology. In the global realm of political economy, we observe "wars and rumors of wars," a situation not likely to change in the twenty-first century. We are still haunted by the fundamental question: Can humanity make its rapidly paced information-driven and technologically defined global community into an international beloved community? Or is this a utopian dream?

Human community in its fullness is not likely to become a historical reality. The capacity for sin and evil precludes any possibility of such a state of existence. Malcolm and Martin knew this, and yet they reminded us that we are called to pursue the highest communitarian ideal even when faced with human imperfections and apparent irreconcilable differences. Like them, we must never cease to look for those catalytic moments that might propel peace, harmony, and wholeness in our world. At the same time, we must recognize that cheap attempts at reconciliation and community between people are insufficient for the shaping of a new humanity.

The vicious attacks on the World Trade Center and the Pentagon on September 11, 2001, serve as yet another reminder of the abysmal failure of humans to create strong bridges of understanding, cooperation, and community. Sadly, many commentators are highlighting these tragedies, which claimed the lives of almost 3,000 in New York, Washington, D.C, and Pennsylvania, as another chapter in the long conflict between the cross and the crescent, between the Christianity of America and the West and the Islam of the East. Christians and Muslims in parts of the world are using their religions to solidify loyalty to their causes, and political leaders on both sides are calling the conflict a case of good versus evil. Muslims in Afghanistan, Indonesia, and other countries are raising the banner of anti-Americanism and are clamoring for a "holy war" or "jihad" against the United States; Christians in this country are evoking images of the Crusades as they urge the political leadership to bomb Islamic nations allegedly associated with violent attacks on U.S. interests here and abroad. All this can only exacerbate the threat to world peace and community. Moreover, these developments suggest that the problem of the twenty-first century will remain not only what W.E.B. Du Bois would call "the problem of the color line" but also the problem of the religion divide. In this global context of heightened tensions and hostility, we are compelled to revisit the ideas of Malcolm and Martin, particularly in terms of their relevance for addressing both race and religion as barriers to world community.

Malcolm and Martin warned us that America, due to years of arrogant and misguided foreign policy, would one day face judgment and the wrath of God. Both would see these attacks of September 2001, as largely a consequence of U.S. colonialist and imperialist policies and practices. Moreover, both would call upon America not only to take bold and positive diplomatic steps to eliminate terrorism but also to change its image in the eyes of the world. If we are to be true to the legacies of Malcolm and Martin, we must realize that it is not ultimately about blame and retaliation but about accountability and responsibility. America must not only face the irony of its complicity in the historic problems that led to the attacks but must also devise better ways of relating to a world in which there are many different religions, ideologies, value systems, and ways of thinking and living. Malcolm and Martin were not obsessed with a desire to Islamize or Christianize the world, but they consistently pointed to the need to humanize it and to rid it of the threats posed by the military mentality and weapons of mass destruction. Both men challenged this country to commit itself to moral leadership in the struggle against violence and oppression on a global scale. This invariably means replacing the culture of arrogance and imperialism with one that respects the dignity and worth of persons and the rights of nations to share fully in the fruits of freedom, peace, and self-determination. This is Malcolm's and Martin's message to the contemporary world.

Notes

Introduction

1. Our perspectives on this matter have been reinforced by a reading of Kateregga and Shenk, *A Muslim and a Christian in Dialogue,* 9–20.

2. These arguments are skillfully and persuasively advanced in Dyson, *Making Malcolm;* Ivory, *Toward a Theology of Radical Involvement.*

3. See Goldman, *Death and Life,* 74; Baldwin, "Reassessment," 103.

4. Bey, "The Renaissance of Malcolm X," 38–39.

5. Wilmore, *Black Religion and Black Radicalism,* 260; Cone, *Martin and Malcolm and America,* 246–71.

6. Wilmore, *Black Religion and Black Radicalism,* 260.

7. Paris, "The Bible and the Black Churches," in Sandeen, *The Bible,* 140–44; Ramsay, *Four Modern Prophets,* 1–7, 29–49; Cone, *Martin and Malcolm and America,* 244–318. My understanding of ethical prophecy came from my reading of Rufus Burrow Jr.'s 1998 unpublished manuscript, "David Walker and Ethical Prophecy."

8. Breitman, *By Any Means Necessary,* 35, 40, 140, 152; Breitman, *Malcolm X Speaks,* 24, 162; Washington, *A Testament of Hope,* 242, 370, 447–48; Martin, "King and Interfaith Dialogue," 34–48.

9. This idea of Malcolm as "religious revolutionist" is strongly developed in DeCaro, *Malcolm and the Cross.* The impact of Malcolm's conversion to orthodox Islam on the development of his internationalism is briefly but brilliantly treated in McCloud, *African-American Islam,* 35–38. For other references to the subject, see Malcolm X, *Autobiography,* 323–69, 381.

10. See Steve Clark, *February 1965,* 53–64; King, "Statement on the Legitimacy of the Struggle in Montgomery, Alabama," 4 May 1956, 1; Baldwin, *To Make the Wounded Whole,* 163–244; Baldwin, *Toward the Beloved Community,* 1–63.

11. Breitman, *By Any Means Necessary,* 33–107; Milne, "Malcolm's Sister Fights On," 48; Baldwin, *To Make the Wounded Whole,* 184–224; Baldwin, *Toward the Beloved Community,* 13–56; Herman, "Malcolm X Launches New Organization," 1.

12. Breitman, *By Any Means Necessary,* 183–84; Breitman, *Malcolm X Speaks,* 197, 212–13, 216; King, *Where Do We Go from Here?* 167–91; King, *The Trumpet of Conscience,* 21–34, 67–78.

13. Breitman, *By Any Means Necessary,* 184; I. F. Stone, "The Pilgrimage of Malcolm X," 4–5.

14. Quoted in Baldwin, *Toward the Beloved Community*, 41, 208n.66.

15. See Cleage, "Myths about Malcolm X," in Clarke, *Malcolm X*, 16–18.

16. Malcolm X, *Autobiography*, 274.

17. For sources that consider geography significant for understanding Malcolm and Martin, see Cone, *Martin and Malcolm and America*, 247; Bradley, "My Hero, Malcolm X," 490.

18. See McCloud, *African-American Islam*, 35–38.

19. This was true of Malcolm throughout his public life, despite the fact that he was deeply involved with a Black Muslim movement that claimed, at least in principle, to be religious and not political in its outlook. See Breitman, *By Any Means Necessary*, 158.

20. Breitman, *Malcolm X Speaks*, 8, 107, 207–8; Breitman, *By Any Means Necessary*, 53, 56, 66, 80, 119, 141, 149; Lomax, *When the Word Is Given*, 81, 85, 153; Karim, *End of White World Supremacy*, 102–3, 108–9; Malcolm X, *Malcolm X on Afro-American History*, 3, 68–69; Malcolm X, *Autobiography*, 414–15; Ayres, *The Wisdom of Martin Luther King Jr.*, 144–46; Coretta Scott King, *My Life*, 240–41; King, "The Dignity of Family Life," 7–8. King published an entire book of sermons on man and manhood. See King, *The Measure of a Man*, 9–56.

21. The discussion and critique provided in this work go far beyond what one finds in Cone, *Martin and Malcolm and America*, 273–80.

22. Bey, "The Renaissance of Malcolm X," 38–39, and Dyson, *Making Malcolm*, vii–184.

23. See Cone, *Martin and Malcolm and America*, 3–4, 270–71.

24. Baldwin agrees with Sterling Stuckey's contention that this "great debate" found classic expression in the conflicts between Samuel Cornish and William Whipper, Frederick Douglass and Henry Highland Garnet, and Douglass and Martin Delany, African-American leaders who predated Du Bois and Washington by more than a generation. See Stuckey, *Slave Culture*, 158–66, 203–6; Stuckey, *Ideological Origins*, 26–27.

25. See Cone, *Martin and Malcolm and America*, 246–71.

26. James H. Cone uses this interpretive model to the extreme, a mistake that makes it very difficult for him to arrive at a creative synthesis of elements of Malcolm's and Martin's ideologies. See ibid., 1–17, 246–70. Unlike Malcolm, Martin essentially rejected the Cartesian model or the nondialectical approach to reasoning. See Ayres, *Wisdom of King*, 58–59; King, "See You in Washington," 3–4.

27. Sterling Stuckey draws the same conclusions regarding Martin Delany and Frederick Douglass, and I am indebted to him for these ideas. See Stuckey, *Ideological Origins*, 26–27; King, *Where Do We Go from Here?* 123–28; King, "Suggested Preamble for the SCLC."

28. See Baldwin, "Reassessment," 103–10; Baldwin, "Malcolm X and Martin Luther King Jr.," 395–416.

Chapter 1. Out of the Dark Past

1. *New National Baptist Hymnal*, 477.

2. Breitman, *By Any Means Necessary,* 56.

3. King, "True Dignity," 8–9.

4. Asante, *Malcolm X as Cultural Hero,* 25–35; Baldwin, *There Is a Balm in Gilead.* For some of Malcolm's and Martin's best statements on black culture, see Breitman, *By Any Means Necessary,* 53–55, 63; Malcolm X, *Malcolm X on Afro-American History,* 1–74; King, "True Dignity"; King, "An Autobiography of Religious Development," in Carson et al., *Papers of Martin Luther King Jr.* (hereafter referred to as Carson, *Papers*), 1:359–63; King, *Where Do We Go from Here?* 102–66.

5. The best source for studying Malcolm's early life is Malcolm X, *Autobiography,* with the assistance of Haley, 1–56. The most important sources on King's early years are King, "An Autobiography of Religious Development," 359–63; King Sr., *Daddy King,* with the assistance of Riley, 87–139; Farris, "The Young Martin," 56–57; Alberta W. King, recording, "Dr. Martin Luther King Jr."; Baldwin, *Balm,* 91–127; Bennett, *What Manner of Man,* 4–7.

6. Malcolm X, *Autobiography,* 9–22; King, "An Autobiography of Religious Development," 359; Baldwin, *Balm,* 19–21.

7. Malcolm X, *Autobiography,* 12–13, 15–16, 26–27, 30–169; Franklin, *From Slavery to Freedom,* 370–71; Freeman, interview with King, 1–5; King, "Speech at a Mass Meeting," 3; Baldwin, *Balm,* 20–23; King, *Stride toward Freedom,* 90–91.

8. Bruce Perry makes the unpersuasive claim that Malcolm's "public career was a lifelong quest to resolve the terrible tensions of his youth." Malcolm's "prime strategies for doing so," according to this source, "were to fashion for himself an identity that was unequivocally black, and to project his own psychic divisions and nightmares onto the scapegoat enemy, the white man." See Perry, *Malcolm;* Malcolm X, *Autobiography,* 1–39; O'Meally, "Malcolm X," 4; King, "An Autobiography of Religious Development," 362–63; Freeman, interview with King, 4–5; Reddick, *Crusader without Violence,* 59–60; Washington, *A Testament of Hope,* 342–43; Baldwin, *Balm,* 20–23.

9. Freeman, interview with King, 3; Baldwin, *Balm,* 22–23; King, "An Autobiography of Religious Development," 362–63.

10. Breitman, *Malcolm X Speaks,* 4–8, 24, 40, 48, 50–51, 72–87, 169–72; Malcolm X, *Autobiography,* 213–68; Freeman, interview with King, 1–5; King, *Where Do We Go from Here?* 102–3, 124, 131–32, 159–91; King, *Why We Can't Wait,* 23, 61, 87; King, "Our Struggle," 3; *The Early Days.*

11. Some of the most brilliant reflections on the cultural interaction between African Americans from the North and South in the early twentieth century can be found in Stuckey, *Slave Culture,* 304–8. Many of the Littles' relatives were descendants of ex-slaves who moved from rural Georgia in large numbers and settled in cities like Boston. See Malcolm X, *Autobiography,* 5–9, 11, 19–20, 33–35; Baldwin, *Balm,* 16–63, 167–68; King, "An Autobiography of Religious Development," 359–63; Fluker, *They Looked for a City,* 82–98.

12. Malcolm X, *Autobiography,* 1–7; King, *Stride toward Freedom,* 19–20; Baldwin, *Balm,* 121–24.

13. Malcolm X, *Autobiography*, 1–9; Cone, *Martin and Malcolm and America*, 41–46; I. F. Stone, "The Pilgrimage of Malcolm X," 3; Baldwin, *Balm*, 16–17, 163–67, 275–330.

14. Malcolm X, *Autobiography*, 9, 20, 188. Some of the best sources for studying the persistence of African-based folk beliefs and practices among slaves and their descendants are Stuckey, *Slave Culture*, 3–97, 99–111, 304–6; Puckett, *Folk Beliefs of the Southern Negro;* Levine, *Black Culture*, 55–80. Malcolm's propensity toward visions and signs finds support in his own account of a vision he had in prison one night after he prayed to Allah to give him relief from his confusion.

15. Martin later noted, "I guess this is why today I am such a strong believer in personal immortality." See King, "An Autobiography of Religious Development," 362; Levine, *Black Culture*, 58. Stuckey sheds more light on this tradition in his discussion of the slave priest, whose position and influence among his people established him as an elder—as one who, in a manner that calls to mind the ancestral spirits, was able to "relate this world to the otherworld, to mediate between the living and the dead, in order to prevent or lessen hardship for the living." See Stuckey, *Slave Culture*, 255, 333–34.

16. Malcolm X, *Autobiography*, 6–8, 15, 22; King Sr., *Daddy King*, 127, 130–31; Farris, "The Young Martin," 56–58; C. S. King, *My Life*, 91; Freeman, interview with King, 2; King, "An Autobiography of Religious Development," 359–63.

17. For important distinctions between shouting and holy dancing, see Johnson, *God Struck Me Dead*, 10–12. The connection between shouting, the holy dance, and African spirit possession is clearly established in Stuckey, *Slave Culture*, viii, 10–17, 97; Baldwin, *"Invisible" Strands in African Methodism*, 137–40, 217–25; Malcolm X, *Autobiography*, 5; Baldwin, *Balm*, 31.

18. Regionalism has been excessively stressed as a factor in explaining the differences in the personalities of Malcolm and Martin. The fact that one was born and raised in the North and the other in the South is not as significant as we have been led to believe, especially since black oppression and the consistent cultural interaction between African Americans transcended regional boundaries. One work that clearly overemphasizes regionalism as a force in the moral, spiritual, and intellectual formation of Malcolm and Martin is Cone, *Martin and Malcolm and America*, 41, 58–60, 310. Cone seems to employ a Cartesian model or a paradigm of dualism in treating Martin and Malcolm, and this leads to rank oversimplifications. Another source that seems to exaggerate the cultural differences between black northerners and black southerners during the 1940s, the period of Malcolm's and Martin's movement from childhood to adolescence, is Sernett, *"Bound for the Promised Land,"* 122–79.

19. When one considers the impact that the presence of a thriving black middle class in Atlanta must have had on the outlook and aspirations of the Kings, Martin Sr.'s agreement with Earl Little on sacred dance becomes all the more interesting. After all, black middle-class values so often militated against the affirmation of some of the most vital cultural forms in the African-American community. Apparently, the Kings refused to absorb wholeheartedly the middle-class ethos. Baldwin, *Balm*, 31, 49; King, "An Autobiography of Religious Development," 359–60.

20. Malcolm X, *Autobiography*, 6–7; King, *Stride toward Freedom*, 19; King, "An

Autobiography of Religious Development," 11–13; King Sr., *Daddy King,* 126; Farris, "The Young Martin," 57.

21. Malcolm X, *Autobiography,* 10, 14, 16–22; Baldwin, *Balm,* 31. Speaking of the Gohannas, who were also raising a nephew called "Big Boy," Malcolm recalled: "I had watched them lead the jumping and shouting when my father preached." Malcolm's description of the leaping, swaying, and chanting of the Gohannas calls to mind the ceremonies that occurred among slaves and free blacks and their descendants at the annual Big Quarterly celebrations in Wilmington, Del., throughout the nineteenth century. See Baldwin, *"Invisible" Strands in African Methodism,* 126–41; King, "An Autobiography of Religious Development," 360.

22. Malcolm X, *Autobiography,* 5; Evans and Alexander, *Dexter Avenue Baptist Church,* 69; Baldwin, *Balm,* 180–81.

23. Malcolm X, *Autobiography,* 14–20, 26, 35, 151–52, 154–55, 164. The only extant source that treats Malcolm's religious life from childhood until his death is DeCaro, *On the Side of My People,* 38–55. Also see King, "An Autobiography of Religious Development," 361; *The Early Days;* Smith, *A History of Ebenezer Baptist Church, Atlanta, Georgia,* 3; King, *Why We Can't Wait,* 89–90; Baldwin, *Balm,* 94–95, 160–74; King Sr., *Daddy King,* 84–86. Lerone Bennett Jr. describes A. D. Williams as "a keen-witted pioneer who was unusually successful in accumulating worldly goods and diffusing the spiritual insights of the Negro religious tradition." See Bennett, *What Manner of Man,* 7.

24. A genuine sense of community prevailed despite the fact that there were "local Uncle Tom Negroes" who had once funneled stories about Earl Little's "revolutionary beliefs to the local white people." See Malcolm X, *Autobiography,* 3, 11, 14–15, 19.

25. Solid treatments of the role of family in shaping Malcolm's and Martin's lives are extremely rare. Most works which focus on Malcolm's and Martin's family backgrounds and ties, particularly those by white scholars, reflect a lack of insight into how the black extended family network nurtured and sustained both, even as tensions surfaced in their nuclear families. Having no deep roots in the traditions of the black extended family, white scholars, consciously or unconsciously, have subscribed to what Wallace Charles Smith calls "the pathological-dysfunctional school" of thought in their approaches to Malcolm's and Martin's family contexts—a school of thought which concludes that the black family structure is "unstable, disorganized, and unable to provide its members with the social and psychological support and development needed to assimilate fully in American society." Moreover, this school of thought marginalizes the black family, denies or minimizes its constructive capacity, and does not account for the strong presence of friends, neighbors, and others with whom a sense of family so often existed in Malcolm's and Martin's early years. It is also based on an ethnocentric idealization of the Western nuclear family model and is racist and elitist. This explains in part the insufficient attention given to the most positive sides of Malcolm's and Martin's family life in sources such as Perry, *Malcolm,* 2–52; Branch, *Parting the Waters,* 39–66; Garrow, *Bearing the Cross,* 32–38. The best model for understanding Malcolm's and Martin's family life is what Smith terms "the cultural relativity school" of thought—one which holds that the black family

structure has been influenced by African traditions and has long been a functional entity. One source that draws on the insights of "the cultural relativity school" of thought in analyzing Martin's family as a support system and a bulwark of black achievement and survival is Baldwin, *Balm,* 91–158. One scholar's claim that Taylor Branch "gets closer to examining more of" Martin's "complex family dynamics than does Baldwin" clearly borders on the absurd, especially since Baldwin devotes far more attention to the King family than any other scholar. See *Trinity Seminary Review,* spring 1992, 44–46. Also see Smith, *The Church in the Life of the Black Family,* 34–40.

26. "Rev. and Mrs. King Return to Atlanta," 3. The King family established a tradition of naming children after relatives, thereby increasing the spiritual significance of their names. See King Sr., *Daddy King,* 87–88; Baldwin, *Balm,* 102, 160–62. One of the most brilliant discussions of naming practices as they carried over from Africa into the culture of the slaves and their descendants in America is Stuckey, *Slave Culture,* 195–98. Ebenezer Baptist Church in Atlanta served as a kind of extended family for the Kings. For useful insights for placing Martin in this context, see Roberts, "A Black Ecclesiology of Involvement," 40–41.

27. Malcolm X, *Autobiography,* 5, 14–15, 19–20; Baldwin, *Balm,* 32, 163–64, 291–97. One scholar's description of the voice of the old-time Negro preacher as "a marvelous instrument" could have been applied to Earl Little and Martin Luther King Sr. as well. See Johnson, *God's Trombones,* 5. Martin clearly had more exposure to black sacred music as a child than did Malcolm, especially since Alberta Williams King frequently sang and played the piano at home, at Ebenezer Baptist Church, and at other churches throughout Atlanta and beyond. See King Sr., *Daddy King,* 127; C. S. King, *My Life,* 93; Farris, "The Young Martin," 56.

28. Malcolm X, *Autobiography,* 28–114; King, *Stride toward Freedom,* 212; Farris, "The Young Martin," 57–58; Baldwin, *Balm,* 32–34; Garrow, *Bearing the Cross,* 34; Harris, *The Rise of the Gospel Blues,* 98–99, 149, 185; Spencer, *Blues and Evil,* xv–xvi; C. S. King, *My Life,* 75, 99.

29. Harris, *The Rise of the Gospel Blues,* 103, 125, 182–83; Levine, *Black Culture,* 182–84; Garrow, *Bearing the Cross,* 34; Farris, "The Young Martin," 57–58; Baldwin, *Balm,* 33. Coretta Scott King reports that Martin "loved to dance and was a good dancer. He loved people and enjoyed parties and, especially, good conversation. He loved music too." See C. S. King, *My Life,* 75, 99.

30. Malcolm X, *Autobiography,* 52, 57–60, 62–75.

31. This view of African Americans permeates black literature, going at least as far back as the early nineteenth century. See Wiltse, *David Walker's Appeal,* 25; Stuckey, *Ideological Origins,* 12; Stuckey, *Slave Culture,* 126; Levine, *Black Culture,* 333–34, 397–440.

32. Levine, *Black Culture,* 429–38; Malcolm X, *Autobiography,* 23–24. For a rich discussion of Joe Louis as a cultural hero, see Moses, *Black Messiahs and Uncle Toms,* 155–82.

33. Malcolm X, *Autobiography,* 124; King, "The Negro and the Constitution," in Carson, *Papers,* 1:109–11. Lawrence Levine declares, "The qualities of the exaggerated hero could be found in almost any type of twentieth-century black tale." Figures

like Old Doc, the Trickster John, and Stagolee often manifested superhuman powers in the folktales. Stagolee, goes one tale, "was undoubtedly the baddest nigger that ever lived"—one who could defeat white men and even frighten death. See Levine, *Black Culture,* 403–7; Lester, *Black Folktales,* 113–35.

34. Stuckey, *Slave Culture,* 4–10; Levine, *Black Culture,* 81–135, 298–440; Brewer, *American Negro Folklore,* 3–46; Faulkner, *The Days When the Animals Talked;* Malcolm X, *Autobiography,* 82–84; King, "An Autobiography of Religious Development," 359; Perry, *Teaching Malcolm X,* 28; Baldwin, *Balm,* 33–34. One family member claims that Martin got his storytelling ability and sense of humor from his mother, who had "many wonderful stories to tell." See C. S. King, *My Life,* 92.

35. The role of folk wit and humor in the cultural experience of African Americans is brilliantly treated in Levine, *Black Culture,* 81–190, 298–366.

36. Such a conclusion can be made on safe grounds, given the fact that Malcolm and Martin spent a lot of time listening to the stories of their elders. See Malcolm X, *Autobiography,* 82–84, 90–91, 114; King, "An Autobiography of Religious Development," 359; Baldwin, *Balm,* 33–34, 38, 304–10.

37. Malcolm X, *Autobiography,* 76, 88, 104, 106, 110, 113, 119, 146, 277. Referring to Malcolm's later years as an activist, one source likens him "to the 'trickster' figure popular in black folk culture." See Coughlin, "Politics and Commerce in the Rebirth of Malcolm X," A8. In one of the best essays available on Malcolm's relationship to black folk culture, Perry concludes that Malcolm was "like the African diasporic Trickster figure who, personified in various animal forms, used his wit to overcome positions of disadvantage" (Perry, *Teaching Malcolm X,* 172).

38. Levine, *Black Culture,* 102–33, 309. For rich insights into the manner in which the weak have employed deception to protect themselves against the strong, see Thurman, *Jesus and the Disinherited,* 58–73.

39. King, "True Dignity," 7. Martin was known to keep a copy of Thurman's *Jesus and the Disinherited* with him as he traveled across the country during his years as a civil rights leader. Thurman's chapter on deception (58–73) probably influenced Martin's understanding of how the weak have employed deception to protect themselves. For an interesting discussion of the connection between Martin's philosophy of nonviolence and the Brer Rabbit ethos, see McKinney, "Brer Rabbit and Brother Martin Luther King Jr."

40. Malcolm X, *Autobiography,* 3, 6–8, 40; Baldwin, *Balm,* 34–35, 37–38, 40. For important insights into the historical and cultural significance of food for African Americans, see Paige, *Aspects of African-American Cookery.*

41. Malcolm X, *Autobiography,* 7–9; Baldwin, *Balm,* 34–35.

42. Malcolm X, *Autobiography,* 6; King, *Stride toward Freedom,* 90; Baldwin, "The Making of a Dreamer," 641; Baldwin, *Balm,* 123.

43. Malcolm X, *Autobiography,* 40. Some of the most profound comments on the festive and celebrative side of African-American culture can be found in Cox, *The Feast of Fools,* 18, 28. Also see King, "Prelude to Tomorrow," 4–5; Baldwin, *Balm,* 34; Breitman, *Malcolm X Speaks,* 26, 39; Breitman, *By Any Means Necessary,* 47; King, *Why We Can't Wait,* 55.

44. Breitman, *Malcolm X Speaks,* 21, 51, 53–56, 63, 68–70, 78–80, 94–98, 124.

Referring to his early years, Malcolm noted, with some exaggeration, "I didn't really have much feeling about being a Negro, because I was trying so hard, in every way I could, to be white." It is more accurate to conclude that Malcolm's craving in those years was for acceptability and not so much to be white. Also see King, *Stride toward Freedom*, 90.

45. Malcolm X, *Autobiography*, 55; Garrow, *Bearing the Cross*, 40–41, 45.

46. This tendency among the oppressed is explored to some degree in sources such as Veblen, *The Theory of the Leisure Class*, 60–80, and Frazier, *Black Bourgeoisie*, 180–85. King was familiar with Frazier's discussion of how middle-class African Americans so often try to compensate for their unconscious self-hatred through conspicuous consumption. See "Excerpts from an Interview with Martin Luther King Jr.," in Warren, "Who Speaks for the Negro?" 14–15; Baldwin, *Balm*, 49.

47. Quoted in Carson, *Papers*, 1:111–12, 115.

48. Malcolm X, *Autobiography*, 36–37. Recent accounts claim that the white teacher who challenged Malcolm's early desire to become a lawyer was not Mr. Ostrowski, as he reported, but Richard Kaminska, who died in 1969. The questions surrounding the incident are not insignificant, especially since it is "usually described as the first defining moment in the life of Malcolm X." See B. Perry, *Malcolm*, 42–43; Gilchrist, "The Rebirth of Malcolm X," 5G.

49. Carson, *Papers*, 1:327–29.

50. Asante, *Malcolm X as a Cultural Hero*, 25–34; Baldwin, *Balm*, 63–90, 274–75.

51. Carson, *Papers*, 1:108–11; "Contest Winner, M. L. King Jr.," 2; Washington, *A Testament of Hope*, 342–43; Baldwin, "The Making of a Dreamer," 646. Malcolm apparently turned to criminal activity because he did not have the kind of spiritual base and nurturing community that sustained Martin. See Malcolm X, *Autobiography*, 46–150.

52. Carson, *Papers*, 1:121–24, 127–42, 359–63; Malcolm X, *Autobiography*, 159, 171–92; Williams, "Molding Men: At Morehouse College, Middle-Class Blacks Are Taught to Lead"; Farris, "The Young Martin," 58; King, *Stride toward Freedom*, 91; King, "A Talk to a Seventh Grade Class at George A. Towns Elementary School"; Baldwin, *Balm*, 25–29; *Atlanta Constitution*, 6 August 1946, 6; "Rev. M. L. King Jr. Speaker for Cultural League," 3. King often preached while pursuing his undergraduate degree at Morehouse, and there is reason to believe that his sermons occasionally addressed issues relating to race and culture. See "Rev. M. L. King Jr. to Preach Sunday Morning at Ebenezer," 3; "Rev. M. L. King Jr. to Fill Pulpit at Ebenezer Sunday," 2.

53. The Negro Cultural League was quite active in Atlanta in the 1940s, addressing issues that were of particular importance to middle-class blacks. Martin's appearance before this group strengthens the claim that he was deeply interested in black culture and history before he became a civil rights leader. See "The Rev. M. L. King Jr. Guest Speaker for Cultural League," 3; "Cultural League Meets Tonight," 15 June 1948, 1. One source indicates that the Negro Cultural League conducted weekly meetings at the league's center, 149 Auburn Avenue, not far from the Kings' residence

and Ebenezer Baptist Church. See "Cultural League Meets Tonight," 1 June 1948, 3. Martin apparently wrote two drafts of this essay on "The Purpose of Education." See Carson, *Papers,* 1:122–24. This essay on "The Economic Basis of Cultural Conflict" appeared in the first volume of the *Annual Sociology Seminar Digest,* published in early 1948 by members of the Graduate Seminar in Sociology at Morehouse College. See "M. L. King Jr. Contributes to Sociology Digest,"1.

54. It is not excessive to suggest certain comparisons between the educational experiences of Martin and Malcolm, especially because "instructors for the educational rehabilitation programs" at the Norfolk Prison Colony "came from Harvard, Boston University, and other educational institutions in the area." See Malcolm X, *Autobiography,* 158–83.

55. Malcolm found much reinforcement for his views on ancient peoples and cultures in works by Will Durant, Gregor Mendel, and H. G. Wells. Undoubtedly, his readings concerning Herodotus must have been enormously important in establishing his sense of Africans as the creators of human civilization. See ibid., 176–77.

56. Sterling Stuckey insists that Du Bois's *Souls of Black Folk* ranks among the most important works on slave culture. See Stuckey, *Slave Culture,* 254, 259, 270–71. Malcolm refers to Fannie Kimball in his account of his life, but he probably meant Frances Kemble. See Malcolm X, *Autobiography,* 176–77. Although Malcolm read extensively about slavery, he never abandoned the view that that institution destroyed the cultural traditions that his ancestors brought from Africa. See Breitman, *By Any Means Necessary,* 28, 54; Malcolm X, *Malcolm X on Afro-American History,* 16–17, 31–37. It would have been impossible for Malcolm to read *The Souls of Black Folk,* as he claimed, without coming across Du Bois's powerful statements on the preacher, the music, and the frenzy.

57. See Herskovits, *The Myth of the Negro Past.* Since Herskovits's time, the study of Africanisms in black culture in America has remained what one scholar calls a "controversial area of inquiry." See Holloway, *Africanisms in American Culture,* ix–xx.

58. See Carson, *Papers,* 1:127, 131. Martin had apparently read parts of Herskovits, *Life in a Haitian Valley.* Also see King, "The Meaning of Hope," 16; Baldwin, *Balm,* 57.

59. Martin's and Malcolm's reading of Du Bois and other sources on black history and culture in the late 1940s was not informed by a broad knowledge of slave sources. This is not surprising. Slave testimony—as revealed through autobiographies, narratives, tales, letters, and other sources—was still virtually ignored in scholarly circles, a problem that existed until the 1970s. Studies of slave life and culture drew almost exclusively on the diaries of slaveowners and the written accounts of missionaries and of travelers like Fredrika Bremer and Frederick Law Olmstead. Moreover, studies of the slaves as artists and craftspersons were essentially nonexistent. The creative abilities and skills that slaves brought to their work with wood, metal, leather, and textiles had not been seriously studied. Had Martin and Malcolm had the chance to study slave sources and the many contributions of slaves as artists and craftspersons, their reflections on *The Souls of Black Folk* would have been more perceptive and refined.

Even so, Martin's perspective on the pivotal role of Du Bois as an interpreter of African-American history and culture ultimately became quite sophisticated, a point that cannot be made of Malcolm. See King, "Honoring Dr. Du Bois," 104–11.

60. King, "An Autobiography of Religious Development," 363; King, "My Call to Preach," 7 August 1959; C. S. King, *My Life,* 96, 107; Farris, "The Young Martin," 58; Baldwin, *Balm,* 279, 322–25, 327; Lincoln, *Black Muslims,* 140–54; Malcolm X, *Autobiography,* 213–68.

61. Clark, *King, Malcolm, Baldwin,* 35–39; Malcolm X, *Autobiography,* 202–3, 221–24, 244, 254, 396; Lomax, *When the Word Is Given,* 19, 22–25, 35–36; Karim, *End of White World Supremacy,* 25, 29–34, 77; Perry, *Malcolm X: The Last Speeches,* 39, 43, 103–4.

62. King, *Stride toward Freedom,* 16; Baldwin, *Balm,* 36–41, 118; Malcolm X, *Autobiography,* 33–34, 41, 97, 272, 380.

63. Baldwin, *Balm,* 24–25; Brock, "The Dialectical Perspective," 4–5.

64. King, *Strength to Love,* 149–50; Baldwin, "The Making of a Dreamer," 646n.22. Reinhold Niebuhr's Christian Realism also proved useful to King in understanding the ambiguities and contradictions of life, especially since Niebuhr underscored the paradoxical or dialectical nature of human beings, taking into account their capacities for both good and evil. See Ansbro, *Martin Luther King Jr.,* 119–28, 151–60; Smith and Zepp, *Search for the Beloved Community,* 71–97, 114–18. One of Martin's most important statements on the dialectical nature of the self appears in *The Measure of a Man,* 9–56. This point is made evident throughout Malcolm X, *Malcolm X on Afro-American History,* 3–74.

65. See Ansbro, *Martin Luther King Jr.,* 162; Baldwin, *Balm,* 23.

66. King, *Stride toward Freedom,* 91. Martin's interests along these lines obviously surfaced at a time when the initial surges of civil rights militancy were occurring with black soldiers who were returning from World War II, determined not to accept the brutal oppression and segregation they had known before undertaking their military assignments. Ward and Badger, *The Making of Martin Luther King,* 1, 18–20. Also see King, "Application for Admission to Crozer Theological Seminary," in Carson, *Papers,* 1:144; Ansbro, *Martin Luther King Jr.,* 1–36, 110–62; Smith and Zepp, *Search for the Beloved Community,* 47–118.

67. Carson, *Papers,* 1:121, 334, 354; Baldwin, "The Making of a Dreamer," 650; quoted in Carson, *Papers,* 2:163.

68. Du Bois, *The Negro,* 146. Du Bois set forth such a vision as early as 1897, asserting, "We are the first fruits of this new nation, the harbinger of that black tomorrow which is destined to soften the whiteness of the Teutonic today." In 1903, Du Bois declared, "Negro blood has a message for the world." See Du Bois, *The Conservation of Races,* 12; Franklin, *The Souls of Black Folk,* 215. For other sources that advance Du Bois's black messianic vision, see Du Bois, *The Gift of Black Folk,* 287, 320, 339; Du Bois, *Dusk of Dawn,* 139; Du Bois, "What the Negro Has Done for the United States and Texas," in Foner, *W.E.B. Du Bois Speaks,* 93.

69. Martin actually read Thoreau's treatise while at Morehouse. Thoreau's essay was first published in January 1848 under the title "On the Relation of the Individual to the State." In it, Thoreau justified his successive refusals to pay state taxes in

Massachusetts on the basis of the existence of African slavery, the terrible treatment of American Indians, and America's imperialistic ventures in the Mexican War. King, *Stride toward Freedom,* 91; Ansbro, *Martin Luther King Jr.,* 110–14; Bedau, *Civil Disobedience,* 15–26; Jack, *The Gandhi Reader,* 312–16.

70. Niebuhr, *Moral Man and Immoral Society,* 252–54.

71. Toynbee envisioned history not simply as the rise and fall of civilizations, but also in terms of the rise of a creative minority to change the world for the better. In this regard, he reminds one of Thoreau. See Toynbee, *A Study of History,* 129; King, *Stride toward Freedom,* 224.

72. Garrow persuasively argues that "King did not at any time during his divinity and graduate school education adopt a belief in pacifism, Gandhi, or nonviolence." Garrow goes on to report that during the early stages of the Montgomery bus protest, Martin even considered taking up arms when "white harassment and violence was targeted against the protest leaders and their homes." See Garrow, "The Intellectual Development of Martin Luther King Jr.," 10–11. Malcolm apparently became familiar with the works of Du Bois, Thoreau, and Gandhi while in prison, and he studied Toynbee after becoming a Muslim minister. There is no record of him having studied Niebuhr. See Malcolm X, *Autobiography,* 155, 176–77, 244. For one of Malcolm's most interesting comments about Toynbee, see B. Perry, *Malcolm X,* 102–3.

73. Malcolm X, *Autobiography,* 193–98; King, *Stride toward Freedom,* 21–22; C. S. King, *My Life,* 106–7.

74. Malcolm X, *Autobiography,* 213–24; C. S. King, *My Life,* 97, 106–9; Pulpit Committee of the Dexter Avenue Baptist Church to King, 10 March 1954; King to Dexter Avenue Baptist Church, 14 April 1954.

75. This contention finds support in Kly, *The Black Book;* Walton, *The Political Philosophy of Martin Luther King Jr.*

76. An excellent discussion of how Malcolm and Martin provided their people alternative means of securing the same goals is afforded in David E. Luellen's 1972 dissertation, "Ministers and Martyrs."

77. Huggins, "Martin Luther King Jr.," 480–81; Malcolm X, *Autobiography,* 314–16, 385.

78. Malcolm X, *Autobiography,* 248–49, 276, 282–83; Lomax, *When the Word Is Given,* 169–72; Breitman, *Malcolm X Speaks,* 4–6; *The Early Days.*

79. King, *Stride toward Freedom,* 67–68; King, "Answer to a Perplexing Question," 7–8; King, "An Address to the Ministers' Leadership Training Program," 2.

80. Breitman, *By Any Means Necessary,* 35–67; Breitman, *Malcolm X Speaks,* 21–22; Breitman, *The Last Year of Malcolm X,* 70–124; Herman, "Malcolm X Announces Rally to Launch New Organization."

81. *Early Days;* King, "Is the Universe Friendly?" 5–6; King, "The Meaning of Hope," 16–17; King, "A Knock at Midnight," 13; Malcolm X, *Malcolm X on Afro-American History,* 17, 54; Smylie, "On Jesus, Pharaoh, and the Chosen People"; Malcolm X, *Autobiography,* 4–5; Lomax, *When the Word Is Given,* 175–76.

82. King, "Is the Universe Friendly?" 6; King, "The Meaning of Hope," 16–17; Baldwin, *Balm,* 302; Lomax, *When the Word Is Given,* 173; Breitman, *Malcolm X Speaks,* 12; Lincoln, *Black Muslims,* 147–53.

83. King, "Is the Universe Friendly?" 6; Franklin, *Souls of Black Folk,* 338, 342; Johnson, *God's Trombones,* 2–3; Stuckey, *Slave Culture,* 256–57.

84. Johnson, *God's Trombones,* 2–3, 5; Franklin, *The Souls of Black Folk,* 342. For a brief but probing remark on the failure of scholars to locate Malcolm in the fecund soil of the black preaching tradition, see Baldwin, review of *On the Side of My People,* by Louis A. DeCaro, 701. Also see Stuckey, *Slave Culture,* 256–57.

85. King, "Field of Education a Battleground," 1–4; King, "Revolution in the Classroom," 1–8; King, "An Address," 1; Breitman, *By Any Means Necessary,* 43–45; Malcolm X, *Malcolm X on Afro-American History,* 14, 18–22, 64–65.

86. King, "Field of Education a Battleground," 4; King, "An Address," Syracuse University, 1; Malcolm X, *Autobiography,* 270; King, *Where Do We Go from Here?* 122–23, 131–32.

87. Malcolm X, *Malcolm X on Afro-American History,* 3, 19. Malcolm's most extensive statements on the role of blacks in the ancient civilizations of Egypt, Ethiopia, and the Kingdoms of the Sudan, which drew on the scholarship of Du Bois, Woodson, and Rogers, are provided in ibid., 18–28, 53, 56, 65. Also see Stuckey, *Slave Culture,* 276–78; Sertima, *Great African Thinkers,* 19–73; Okafor, "Diop and the African Origin of Civilization"; Sertima, "Egypt Revisited"; Ravitch, "Multiculturalism: E Pluribus Plures," 347–48, 352; Asante, "Multiculturalism: An Exchange," 271; Asante, *Kemet, Afrocentricity, and Knowledge,* 6–190.

88. King, "Honoring Dr. Du Bois," 104–11; Malcolm X, *Autobiography,* 176, 182, 184, 260, 270–71, 365, 405; Malcolm X, *Malcolm X on Afro-American History,* 53. Although Malcolm found hopeful signs in educators like C. Eric Lincoln and Kenneth B. Clark, and in writers like James Baldwin, John Killens, and Louis Lomax, he felt that all too many black intellectuals attached more importance to their own careers and to collegiality with whites than they did to black causes.

89. Malcolm X, *Autobiography,* 182, 184, 246–48, 265, 270.

90. Malcolm X, *Malcolm X on Afro-American History,* 15.

91. King, "Address at a Mass Meeting," Clarksdale, Miss., 7; King, "Address at a Mass Meeting," Eutaw, Ala., 3–4. For a comprehensive view of leading theories and practices of multicultural education from scholars of various ethnic and racial backgrounds, see Sleeter and McLaren, *Multicultural Education.* Also see a series of essays under the title "Multiculturalism Revisited," in *Academe,* May/June 1996, 10–28.

92. King, *Where Do We Go from Here?* 126–27; King, "The Meaning of Hope," 16. In 1961, Martin noted with pride that "greats" like Harry Belafonte, Sidney Poitier, and Sammy Davis "actively participate" in the struggle, "as artists and as citizens, adding the weight of their enormous prestige and thus helping to move the struggle forward." See King to Davis, 28 March 1961. The King collections at both Boston University and the King Center in Atlanta include numerous letters Martin received from and exchanged with black artists. For examples, see Cole to King, 25 June 1963; King to Jackson, 10 January 1964; King to Cole, 18 July 1963. One interesting letter, from the mother of Gladys Knight, requested Martin's assistance in making it possible for her sixteen-year-old daughter to sing at the inaugural ball of President-Elect John F. Kennedy. See Knight to King, 10 January 1961.

93. Breitman, *By Any Means Necessary,* 55. Malcolm used the words *puppets* and

clowns in a television interview in November 1963, literally days before his split with the Nation of Islam, to describe some of the most popular black artists whom he felt had been hand-picked by white liberals to be leaders. Had he studied closely the career of the intellectual-singer-activist Paul Robeson, an African Methodist, his view of the potential role of artists as leaders in the struggle would have been more enlightened. See Gil Noble's 1963 videotape interview *Like It Is.*

94. Breitman, *By Any Means Necessary,* 63–64.

95. Karim, *End of White World Supremacy,* 25; B. Perry, *Malcolm X,* 31; Malcolm X, *Malcolm X on Afro-American History,* 17, 32. Malcolm himself often attacked black intellectuals who rejected their own people and elements of their own culture out of a desire to be shaped in the image of whites, a tendency quite unexpected in light of his own rejection of the rich emotional heritage of people of African descent. See Malcolm X, *Autobiography,* 182, 226, 247, 260; King, "President's Address," 12.

96. Malcolm made similar statements in "The Ballot or the Bullet" and "The Black Revolution," speeches made in 1964. See Breitman, *Malcolm X Speaks,* 9, 38, 50, 52.

97. Angelou, *All God's Children Need Traveling Shoes,* 133–34. Significantly, Malcolm's response was different in December 1964, about seven months later, when the Student Nonviolent Coordinating Committee Freedom Singers appeared in Harlem. The group danced and sang songs in honor of African freedom fighters such as Oginga Odinga, Jomo Kenyatta, and Patrice Lumumba. See Breitman, *Malcolm X Speaks,* 105–6, 114.

98. Angelou, *All God's Children Need Traveling Shoes,* 134. Malcolm probably had this experience in mind a few months later when he told a Detroit audience: "When I was in Africa in May, I noticed a tendency on the part of the Afro-Americans to—what I call lollygag." They "were just socializing, they had turned their back on the cause over here, they were partying, you know." Breitman, *Malcolm X Speaks,* 159. Malcolm also refers briefly to the experience in Ghana in Malcolm X, *Autobiography,* 361.

99. For brilliant insights that are useful for understanding black sacred and secular dance as expressions of freedom—as the "ultimate emblem of the freedom of creative soul force," see Stewart, *Soul Survivors,* 68–70, 119–25. Also see *Martin Luther King Jr., 1929–1968,* 69–70.

100. Stuckey convincingly argues that Paul Robeson remains perhaps the only black nationalist to escape this tendency. See Stuckey, *Slave Culture,* ix, 304–58.

101. King, "True Dignity," 7; King, *Why We Can't Wait,* 61. King held that African-American songs, "ranging from the spirituals of the slaves through the folk music of the freedom riders," were evidence of both the power and the cultural significance of the movement. Equally important in this regard were "the genius of playwrights" and "the sensitivity of artists"—which "made the world aware of the crippling crisis through which the black American has moved." See King, "Message for My People," 1.

102. Malcolm X, *Malcolm X on Afro-American History,* 17; Breitman, *By Any Means Necessary,* 53. One scholar, who associated with and wrote extensively about Black Muslims in the 1960s, "was struck by" the group's "coldness to Africa and African ways." He concluded "that in their own way the Black Muslims are as much

in flight from Negritude as was Booker T. Washington." See Essien-Udom, *Black Nationalism,* 240–52; Stone, "The Pilgrimage of Malcolm X," 4–5.

103. Malcolm X, *Autobiography,* 352, 365, 405; King, *Where Do We Go from Here?* 53, 59–60, 109, 121, 127; King to Courlander, 30 October 1961; King, "Address at a Mass Meeting," Clarksdale, Miss., 19 March 1968, 7; King, "Address at a Mass Meeting," Eutaw, Ala., 20 March 1968, 3–4.

104. Breitman, *By Any Means Necessary,* 53–55.

105. Baldwin, *Balm,* 36; Breitman, *By Any Means Necessary,* 53–55; King, "Address at the Chicago Freedom Movement Rally," 10 July 1966, 4.

106. Lomax, *When the Word Is Given,* 171; Breitman, *By Any Means Necessary,* 5–6; Breitman, *Malcolm X Speaks,* 10–11, 210–11.

107. King, *Why We Can't Wait,* 33–35; King, *Where Do We Go from Here?* 125; King to Mr. Cummings, 22 December 1961. Dyson boldly claims that King embraced an "enlightened black nationalism," a position difficult to defend given King's consistent critique of that philosophy. See Dyson, *I May Not Get There with You,* 101–20.

108. Warren, "Who Speaks for the Negro?" 15–16; C. S. King, *My Life,* 260.

109. Martin was really closer to Malcolm on this question than we have been led to believe, especially after 1964. In 1964, Martin asserted that "The Negro is an American. We know nothing about Africa, although our roots are there in terms of our forebears." But by 1967, under the influence of the Black Power Movement, he was urging his people to accept their ambivalence. Employing the Hegelian Dialectic, he held that the Negro is neither completely African nor completely American, but "the child of two cultures." See Warren, "Who Speaks for the Negro?" 15–16; King, *Where Do We Go from Here?* 53; King, "See You in Washington," 3–4; Baldwin, *To Make the Wounded Whole,* 22–23; Breitman, *Malcolm X Speaks,* 36, 48, 52, 72–87, 90, 95, 101, 103, 210–11; C. S. King, *My Life,* 260; Montgomery, "Malcolm X a Harlem Idol on Eve of Murder Trial"; Malcolm X, *Autobiography,* 351–52, 356–58, 360–62.

110. Breitman, *Malcolm X Speaks,* 59–61; C. S. King, *My Life,* 260; King, *Why We Can't Wait,* 89–93.

111. J. Franklin, "The Forerunners," 35; Breitman, *By Any Means Necessary,* 80; Malcolm X, *Malcolm X on Afro-American History,* 54.

112. Perry, *Malcolm X,* 158–59; Clark, *February 1965,* 28; Breitman, *By Any Means Necessary,* 183–84; King, *Where Do We Go from Here?* 167–91.

113. Dyson, *Making Malcolm.* vii–xxvi, 21–76, 129–44; Perry, *Teaching Malcolm X,* 93–103, 153–58; Lentz, *Symbols, the News Magazines, and Martin Luther King,* 237, 340–42; Ivory, *Toward a Theology of Radical Involvement,* 13–14; Baldwin, *To Make the Wounded Whole,* 286–301.

114. Dyson, *Making Malcolm,* 21–76, 145–73; Baldwin, *Balm,* 243–52; Baldwin, *To Make the Wounded Whole,* 286–301; Asante, *Malcolm X as Cultural Hero,* 25–44; McCartney, *Black Power Ideologies,* 93–96, 183–89; Baker-Fletcher, *Xodus,* 70–110; Perry, *Malcolm;* Downing, *To See the Promised Land;* Kenneth Smith, "The Radicalization of Martin Luther King Jr.," 270–88; Macinnes, "Malcolm, the Lost Hero"; Bradley, "My Hero, Malcolm X"; Dyson, *I May Not Get There with You,* 1–8; Ivory, *Toward a Theology of Radical Involvement,* 13–14.

115. "Malcolm Called a Martyr Abroad"; Hansen, "Rowan's Smear of Malcolm X," 4; "Now It's Negroes vs. Negroes in America's Racial Violence"; Rowan, "Will Malcolm X Movie Be Truthful or Just a Fiction?" Rowan's constant denunciations of Malcolm attest not only to his refusal to consider how the black leader transcended his criminal past but also to his inability to identify with a certain dimension of the black experience. For scathing critiques of Rowan's attacks on Malcolm, see G. Wilson, "Look Homeward, Mr. Rowan"; Vernon, "A 'Left-Wing' Smear of Malcolm X: Repeat Time-Worn Slanders"; "Rips Rowan's Stand"; "An Ill Wind"; "Rowan Should Read about Malcolm X." In 1970 Geller reported, "There are certain elements of the black community who have an intense dislike for Malcolm X," a point that should not be accepted uncritically. See Geller, "Malcolm X Display Might Have Inspired Bombing," 3.

116. Jackson, *A Story of Christian Activism,* 486; Loury, "Performing without a Net," in Curry, *The Affirmative Action Debate,* 60.

117. "Malcolm X: The Complexity of a Man in the Jungle," 1; Barnes, "The Impact of Malcolm X," 4; "Remember Brother Malcolm," 4–10; Geller, "Malcolm X Display Might Have Inspired Bombing," 3; Bradley, "My Hero, Malcolm X"; "Malcolm X: Warrior, Diplomat, Minister—Apostle of Manhood, Dignity, and Freedom," 1–7; Rowan, "Will Malcolm X Movie Be Truthful?," 5D.

118. Macinnes, "Malcolm, the Lost Hero," 4–5; Bradley, "My Hero, Malcolm X"; Asante, *Malcolm X as Cultural Hero,* 25–34; "School Dedication," 23; Cone, *Martin and Malcolm and America,* 290–93; Baldwin, *To Make the Wounded Whole,* 290–91; "Dream Realized at Last for a Memorial to King," 8A.

119. "Speakers Pay Tribute to Malcolm X"; Schroth, "Malcolm X Is Alive"; "Remembering Malcolm X at 60"; Baldwin, *To Make the Wounded Whole,* 290–91; Jones, "Heirs and Keepers in the '90s," 37–39; Long, "BSAC Honors King's Birthday by Celebrating Universal Rights," 2.

120. Smylie, "On Jesus, Pharaoh, and the Chosen People"; Wiltse, *David Walker's Appeal,* 20; Stuckey, *Ideological Origins,* 36–37; Moses, *Black Messiahs and Uncle Toms,* 155–82. James H. Cone's contention that "Martin and Malcolm, despite the excessive adoration their followers often bestow upon them, were not messiahs" is not persuasive, and it seems to suggest some unfamiliarity with much of African-American cultural and political history. See Cone, *Martin and Malcolm and America,* 315. Also see Dyson, *Making Malcolm,* 79–184; Baldwin, *Balm,* 243–52; Franklin, "The Forerunners," 35; Perry, *Teaching Malcolm X,* 171.

121. In a moment of stern prophecy, Malcolm declared that after his death, "the white man, in his press, is going to identify me with 'hate.' . . . He will make use of me dead as he has made use of me alive, as a convenient symbol of 'hatred.'" Malcolm could not have been more prophetic. See Malcolm X, *Autobiography,* 388; Metcalfe, "How Blacks Remember Malcolm X," 23.

122. Smith, "Equality and Justice," 4–5, 7; Harding, *Martin Luther King Jr.,* vii–x, 1–44. Harding echoes a concern consistently raised by other King scholars; namely, the tendency of Americans to freeze Martin at the Washington monument in 1963, where he envisioned little white boys and girls holding hands with little black boys and girls. Thus, the post-1963 life of Martin, during which he attacked economic

injustice and U.S. involvement in the Vietnam War, gets largely excluded from national celebrations. See Ivory, *Toward a Theology of Radical Involvement,* 13–14; Smith, "Equality and Justice," 4–5, 7.

123. Hunter, *Culture Wars,* 17; Baldwin, *To Make the Wounded Whole,* 294. "Convenient hero" comes from Harding, *Martin Luther King,* 58.

124. Fackre, *The Religious Right and Christian Faith,* 14, 28. Also see "Group Criticize Civil Rights Appointee," 11A. The argument here is based on Martin's assertion, made in the "I Have a Dream" speech in Washington, D.C., in 1963, that one should be judged by the content of one's character and not by the color of one's skin. But Martin clearly supported affirmative action as an avenue toward equal opportunity for all Americans. See King, *Why We Can't Wait,* 136–41.

125. Pappas, *Plagiarism and the Culture War,* 174.

126. Jones, "Martin Luther King: Black Messiah or White Guardian?" 6 April 1986.

127. "What's Ahead for Affirmative Action," 6–10; Coleman, "Affirmative Action Wars," 30–37; Charles, "The New Al Sharpton," 34–38.

128. Smith, "Equality and Justice," 5; Baldwin, *To Make the Wounded Whole,* 291–93; "Movement Revives Memory of Activist Malcolm X," 29. In May 1994, Rep. Charles Rangel of New York asked Congress to designate May 19 as a national holiday in Malcolm's memory, but no serious movement has been made regarding this request. See *Jet,* 9 May 1994, 12; Metcalfe, "How Blacks Remember Malcolm X," 23.

129. Dyson, *Making Malcolm,* xiii, 79–184; "The Legacy of Malcolm X"; Simanga, "Against the Silence," 10–11; Erickson, "Malcolm X," C1–C2; Vern Smith et al., "Rediscovering Malcolm X"; Begley et al., "African Dreams," 43; Wood, "Looking for Malcolm"; Bey, "The Renaissance of Malcolm X," 38–39.

130. Bradley, "My Hero, Malcolm X"; "Daughter's View of Malcolm X," 15A; Angela Davis, "On Malcolm X," 35–36; "Black Students Complain of Georgia School Dress Code," 24; Frady, "Reflections"; Dyson, *Making Malcolm,* xiii; Dyson, *I May Not Get There with You,* 177–78, 183–88, 190; "Labeling King, Malcolm," A11.

131. Rowan, "Will Malcolm X Movie Be Truthful?" 5D; Perry, *Malcolm.*

132. Michael Dyson offers a brilliant discussion of what he calls "Malcolm's cultural renaissance" or "his improbable second coming." See Dyson, *Making Malcolm,* xiii; Baldwin, *To Make the Wounded Whole,* 299–300. Martin's extramarital affairs are discussed at some length in Garrow, *Bearing the Cross,* 361–62, 374–75; Branch, *Parting the Waters,* 239, 242, 860–62; Abernathy, *And the Walls Came Tumbling Down,* 434–36, 470–75; Dyson, *I May Not Get There with You,* 155–74. For information on Martin's plagiarism, see Waldman, "To Their Dismay, King Scholars Find a Troubling Pattern," A1, A6; DePalma, "Plagiarism Seen by Scholars in King's Ph.D. Dissertation," 1, 10; Garrow, "How King Borrowed," C1, C5; Raymond, "Discovery of Early Plagiarism," A1, A8; Carson, "Documenting Martin Luther King's Importance—and His Flaws," A52. For the most scathing assault on King's plagiarism and on the intellectual standing and capacity of both King and his professors at Boston University, see Pappas, *Plagiarism and the Culture War.*

133. Erickson, "Malcolm X," C1; Coughlin, "Politics and Commerce in the Rebirth of Malcolm X," A8, A14; Dyson, *I May Not Get There with You,* 250–81.

134. Dyson, *Making Malcolm,* 144; Trescott, "The Battle over Malcolm X," G1, G8; Benjamin, "Spike Lee: Bearing the Cross"; Giovanni, *Racism 101,* 63–73; "Denzel Washington Gets Bid for a Second Oscar in Spike's 'Malcolm X' Film," 52. For critical reflections on the merchandising of Malcolm by Lee and others, see Coughlin, "Politics and Commerce," A8, A14. Lee's defense of his efforts appears in sources such as "Lee Urges Blacks to Skip School to See 'Malcolm X,'" 18.

135. Gilchrist, "The Rebirth of Malcolm X," 1G, 5G; Gilchrist, "A Message from Malcolm," 1E, 3E; L. Johnson, "'Malcolm X' Film May Stimulate Black Studies," 4B; Wickham, "Only Lee Could've Created This Movie," 15A. Other more favorable or less critical statements on the Spike Lee film can be found in Angela Davis, "On Malcolm X," 35–37; Lester, "Malcolm X as Icon," 255–57; "The Honorable Louis Farrakhan Speaks on the Malcolm X Movie." The most objective appraisal of the film is offered in Dyson, *Making Malcolm,* 129–44.

136. Dyson, *Making Malcolm,* 128. For some of the problems Lee encountered in producing the Malcolm X film, see "Black Celebs 'Bail Out' Director Spike Lee's 'Malcolm X' Film Project," 30, 32; "Lee Blasts 'Malcolm X' Box-Office Ticket Mix-Up," 36; Perkins and Williams, "The Malcolm X Movie"; Coughlin, "Politics and Commerce," A8; Ahmad, "Malcolm X Documentary Set for PBS," 1A, 13A; Gilchrist, "The Rebirth of Malcolm," 5G.

137. Rowan, "Will Malcolm X Movie Be Truthful?" 5D; Dyson, *Making Malcolm,* vii–xxvi; Harding, *Martin Luther King,* 68; Baldwin, *To Make the Wounded Whole,* 301.

Chapter 2. Al-Qur'an and Sunnah

1. Ali, *The Meaning of the Holy Qur'an,* 1342–43.

2. Breitman, *By Any Means Necessary,* 305.

3. Hoskins, *"I Have a Dream,"* 10.

4. Ali, *The Meaning of the Holy Qur'an,* 1714.

5. Chapnick, *Malcolm X: The Great Photographs,* 162.

6. The El-Shabazz stamp contributed greatly to creating a positive image of Islam in the United States. It opened the door for the U.S. government to issue an Eid stamp in 2001. Eid is the celebration of the end of Ramadan, which is the month of fasting, and the end of the Hajj or Muslim pilgrimage to Mecca.

7. The acronym *pbuh* stands for "peace and blessings be upon him." It is expressed after speaking or writing the names of Prophets such as Adam, Noah, Abraham, Moses, Jesus, and Muhammad.

8. The term *mainstream Islam* was suggested by Dr. Awadh Amir Binhazim of Meharry Medical College, in Nashville. He feels that it is a better term than *Sunni* or *orthodox Muslim.* According to Dr. Binhazim, this terminology seems to be the consensus among modern Islamic scholars. On the other hand, the terms *orthodox* and *fundamentalist* Muslim are inventions of Western observers of Islam. From a universal Islamic perspective, the terms *Sunni* and *Shia Muslim* tend to balkanize the Muslim ummah (world community of Muslims) into denominations and sects. Essentially,

this phenomenon is more peculiar to the Christian World Community than to the Muslim ummah.

9. A'La Mawdudi, *Towards Understanding Islam*, 11.

10. See Evanzz, *The Judas Factor*; Goldman, *Death and Life*; Breitman, Porter, and Smith, *The Assassination of Malcolm X*.

11. Malcolm X, *Autobiography*, 84–107.

12. Garvey, comp., *Philosophy and Opinions of Marcus Garvey*, 13.

13. Vincent, "The Garveyite Parents of Malcolm X."

14. See El-Amin, *Religion of Islam*, 3–6; Shaheed, *Taqwiyat-ul-Iman*, 46–55.

15. Ali, *The Meaning of the Holy Qur'an*, 1013, 1342–43.

16. See, e.g., Wolfenstein, *The Victims of Democracy*; Evanzz, *The Judas Factor*; Perry, *Malcolm*; Kly, *The Black Book*; T'Shaka, *The Political Legacy of Malcolm X*; Goldman, *Death and Life*.

17. Shabazz, "The Legacy of My Husband, Malcolm X," 172; Shabazz, "Loving and Losing Malcolm," 50.

18. Ali, *The Meaning of the Holy Qur'an*, 106.

19. See Zen, *The Pillars of Islam and Iman*; Khan, *Sahih Al-Bukhari*; Abd Al-Ati, *Islam in Focus*, 1–32; and Haykal, *The Life of Muhammad*.

20. B. Perry, *Malcolm X: The Last Speeches*, 156–57.

21. Merton, *Gandhi on Nonviolence*, 44; King, *The Words of Martin Luther King Jr.*, 15–25.

22. See Imam Muhammad, *Prayer and Al-Islam*; Shu'aib, *The Prescribed Prayer Made Simple*; Malcolm X, *Autobiography*, 331–33. Elijah Muhammad states, "We must study the words and the different positions taken by the Muslim in his daily prayer. This helps us to understand the true way to worship Allah (God)." Muhammad, *Message to the Blackman in America*, 139. As a whole, members of the Nation of Islam don't make salat. They make only duas. In some places, members of the NOI do perform jummah prayer (Friday community prayer), and in other places they do not. El-Amin, *The Religion of Islam and the Nation of Islam*, 32–33.

23. Sakr, *Sujood: Prostration*, 58–63.

24. *The World Almanac and Book of Facts 1997*, 646.

25. Jaaber, *Final Chapter*, 49.

26. Al-Amin, *Revolution by the Book*, 63.

27. Ibid., 61–62.

28. Shariati, *Hajj*, x.

29. See Essien-Udom, *Black Nationalism: A Search for an Identity*.

30. Lincoln, *Black Muslims*, xii.

31. Gallen et al., *Malcolm X as They Knew Him*, 136.

32. Malcolm X, *Autobiography*, 318–63.

33. Jaaber, *Final Chapter*, iv.

34. Breitman, *Malcolm X Speaks*, 59–60.

35. See Williams, *The Destruction of Black Civilization*; Ben-Jochannan, *African Origins of the Major "Western Religions,"* 195–245; Asante, *Afrocentricity*, 2–7.

36. Selsam and Martel, *Reader in Marxist Philosophy*, 226–27.

37. Seale, *Seize the Time*, i–ii, 3–4, 30–31, 63, 72, 82–84.

38. Clark, *February 1965*, 24.

39. Dyson, *Making Malcolm*, 24.

40. Rashad, *Islam, Black Nationalism, and Slavery*, 192.

41. See Al-Mansour, *Seven African Arabian Wonders of the World*, 115; Mazarui, *The Triple Heritage*.

42. See Felder, *The Original African Heritage Study Bible*, 23–25; Blyden, *Christianity, Islam, and the Negro Race*; Rashad, *Islam, Black Nationalism, and Slavery*, 15.

43. Muslim scholars make a distinction between three grouping of Arab tribes: Perishing Arabs, Pure Arabs, and Arabized Arabs. See the scholarship of Al-Faruqi and Al-Faruqi, *The Cultural Atlas of Islam*, 7–12; Al-Mubarakpuri, *Ar-Raheeq Al-Makhtum*, 15–22; Rashad, *Islam, Black Nationalism, and Slavery*, 14–16.

44. Diop, *The African Origin of Civilization*, 123–28.

45. Al-Faruqi and Al-Faruqi, *Cultural Atlas of Islam*, 7–10.

46. Al-Mubarakpuri, *Ar-Raheeq Al-Makhtum*, 34–64.

47. Ali, *The Meaning of the Holy Qur'an*, 651.

48. Al-Mubarakpuri, *Ar-Raheeq Al-Makhtum*, 56–60.

49. Ibid., 67–72.

50. Qutb, *Milestones*, 88–89.

51. Rogers, *Sex and Race: Negro-Caucasian Mixing*, 1:95.

52. Malcolm X, *Autobiography*, 176.

53. See Rodney, *How Europe Underdeveloped Africa*.

54. Haddad, "A Century of Islam in America," 1; Nyang, "Islam and the African-American Experience," 39.

55. Sertima, *They Came before Columbus*, 1; "Afrique Histoire," 33.

56. See Muhammad, *Message to the Blackman in America*.

57. Abd Al-Ati, *Islam in Focus*, 12–13.

58. Farley, "Moslem Faithful in U.S.A. Tackle Misconceptions"; Goldman, "Mainstream Islam Rapidly Embraced by Black Americans," 1; Blum, "Islam Challenges Black Churches," 13A; Kaba, "Today, Islam," 33–37.

59. Essien-Udom, *Black Nationalism*, 20.

60. See Muhammad, *Message to the Blackman in America*, 31; *The Final Call*, "Saviours" Day ed., 43; El-Amin, *Religion of Islam*, 3–9.

61. Imam Muhammad, *A Light Shineth from the East*, 9–34.

62. *Original African Heritage Study Bible*, 14–15.

63. King, *Where Do We Go from Here?* 75.

64. Imam Muhammad, *A Light Shineth from the East*, 9–34.

65. Vincent, "The Garveyite Parents of Malcolm X."

66. Malcolm X, *Autobiography*, 155–68.

67. Ibid., 188.

68. Muhammad, *Message to the Blackman in America*, 31.

69. Muhammad, *The Supreme Wisdom*, 31.

70. Muhammad, *Message to the Blackman in America*, 116.

71. Gallen et al., *Malcolm X as They Knew Him*, 15.

72. Clarke, *Malcolm X: The Man and His Times*, 286.

73. Muhammad, *Message to the Blackman in America*, 161–71.

74. Malcolm X, *Autobiography*, 305.

75. Hadid, interview with Imam Warith Deen Mohammed, 10 February 1993.

76. Breitman, *Malcolm X Speaks*, 20.

77. Hadid, interview with Muhammad.

78. Ibid.

79. King, *Why We Can't Wait*, 86–87.

80. King, *Where Do We Go from Here?* 123.

81. Breitman, *Malcolm X Speaks*, 21.

82. Ali, *The Meaning of the Holy Qur'an*, 469.

83. Hadid, interview with Mohammed.

84. Ali, *The Meaning of the Holy Qur'an*, 442.

85. Ibid., 857–58.

86. Zeno, *The Pillars of Islam and Iman*, 207–8.

87. Malcolm X, *Autobiography*, 324.

88. Goldman, *Death and Life*, 178.

89. Al-Hussein and Sakr, *Introducing Islam to Non-Muslims*, 7; Kly, *The Black Book*, 24.

90. Al-Mubarakpur, *Ar-Raheeq Al-Makhtum*, 19.

91. Rashad, *Islam, Black Nationalism, and Slavery*, 2.

92. Jaaber, *Final Chapter*, 44–50.

93. Clarke, *Malcolm X: The Man and His Times*, 245.

94. Breitman, *Malcolm X Speaks*, 199.

95. The term *ummah* refers to group affiliations and has been employed to designate a community, a nation, or a generation. In Qur'anic usage, however, the term has a somewhat more precise meaning, referring to the "community of believers" who struggle in unison to submit to the Will of Allah. In this sense, the ummah is composed of many particular groups who can put aside their individual identities and mutual suspicions in order to uphold what is right, forbid injustice, and worship Allah in congregation. See McCloud, *African-American Islam*, 4.

96. See Azzam, *The Eternal Message of Muhammad*.

97. Siddiqi, *Muhammad: The Benefactor of Humanity*, 302.

98. *'Asabiya* is an Arabic concept that was ardently asserted by Ibn Khaldun, an Arab social historian of the thirteenth century. As used by Khaldun, *asabiya* refers to kinship relations, which exert themselves in a feeling of tribal solidarity, common ethical understandings and, ultimately, in a community identity. Though Khaldun generally restricts the concept to kinship relations, the term can be usefully extended to encompass group affiliations that are somewhat broader in character affiliations that comprise national and cultural identities. In this broader usage, *asabiya* designates a key theme in the history of African-American Islam—namely, the theme of nation-building. See McCloud, *African-American Islam*, 4.

99. Ali, *The Meaning of the Holy Qur'an*, 1662–65.

Chapter 3. Of Their Spiritual Strivings

1. Franklin, *The Souls of Black Folk,* 387.

2. Breitman, *By Any Means Necessary,* 140.

3. Ayres, *Wisdom of King,* 98.

4. The best study of Malcolm's and Martin's challenge to American religion and institutions is Cone, *Martin and Malcolm and America.*

5. Wilmore, *Black Religion and Black Radicalism* (1972), 260.

6. Malcolm X, *Autobiography,* 5–6, 14–15, 35; Evans and Alexander, *Dexter Avenue Baptist Church,* 69; Baldwin, *Balm,* 31, 180–81; King Sr., *Daddy King,* 60.

7. Earl Little's funeral was not held in a church, a practice virtually nonexistent among African-American Christians, especially at that time. Malcolm, even at the tender age of six, found this odd. "That surprised me, since my father was a preacher, and I had been where he preached people's funerals in churches. But his was in a funeral home." Malcolm X, *Autobiography,* 4, 10; Carson et al., *Papers of Martin Luther King Jr.* (hereafter referred to as Carson, *Papers*), 1:1.

8. DeCaro, *On the Side of My People,* 51–52; Carson, *Papers,* 1:1.

9. Malcolm never really made such an admission, which seems ironic, since many of the nationalist values he later espoused were grounded in black church traditions. A serious study of the life and contributions of Malcolm X supports Wilmore's contention that "black pride and power, black nationalism and Pan-Africanism have had no past without the black church and black religion." Wilmore, *Black Religion and Black Radicalism* (1973), xiii.

10. Carson, *Papers,* 1:360–61.

11. Malcolm once stated that some of the same African Americans who shouted when his father preached appeared "more intelligent" when they met to discuss Garvey's UNIA, a point that gives credence to this view. See Malcolm X, *Autobiography,* 5–6; Evans and Alexander, *Dexter Avenue Baptist Church,* 69; Carson, *Papers,* 1:44; Baldwin, *Balm,* 163; King Sr., *Daddy King,* 127; C. S. King, *My Life,* 93.

12. Malcolm X, *Autobiography,* 4, 6. Martin's view of the typical black Baptist preacher was not radically different, for he saw this figure as "anti-intellectual and prone to establish or maintain emotionalism as the chief sign of salvation." See Carson, *Papers,* 1:44n.139, 363.

13. One source claims that "Malcolm's unusual religious orientation was Christian only in a very limited sense" because his family remained largely "indifferent to established religious groups." See DeCaro, *On the Side of My People,* 51–52. For interesting studies of Martin's faith journey, beginning with childhood, see Carson, *Papers,* 1:362–63; see also Downing, *To See the Promised Land,* 37–145. Downing applies James Fowler's faith development model and the psychosocial theories of Erik H. Erikson to the faith pilgrimage of King.

14. Malcolm X, *Autobiography,* 5; Carson, *Papers,* 1:361.

15. Malcolm X, *Autobiography,* 2–5.

16. Karim, *End of White World Supremacy,* 25.

17. King, *Where Do We Go from Here?* 41.

18. Malcolm X, *Autobiography,* 5; Carson, *Papers,* 1:361–62.

19. It is difficult to believe Malcolm's claim, in an interview with Alex Haley, that these experiences were not considerations in his "moving away from Christianity." See Clark, *King, Malcolm, Baldwin,* 35; Malcolm X, *Autobiography,* 16–17; Carson, *Papers,* 1:112.

20. Malcolm X, *Autobiography,* 39, 112, 118, 120–23, 128, 141; Gallen et al., *Malcolm X as They Knew Him,* 123. DeCaro advances a different view from mine in a recent study of Malcolm's religious life. DeCaro concludes that because Malcolm "was reared in a community where most people were Christians, he was quite familiar with black Christianity, but his family's religion was eclectic and it was quite inexact for Malcolm to refer to himself later as having been 'a brainwashed black Christian.'" This author seems to suggest that Malcolm's earliest religious life developed outside the traditions of the black religious experience, and particularly the black church, a view that can be challenged on safe grounds. See DeCaro, *On the Side of My People,* 48–50, 52, 67–68.

21. Carson, *Papers,* 1:30.

22. Malcolm X, *Autobiography,* 315.

23. See ibid., 153–54, 156–92; R. Franklin, "The Three Faces of Malcolm X," 14; Carson, *Papers,* 1:38.

24. Malcolm X, *Autobiography,* 156–57; K. Clark, *King, Malcolm, Baldwin,* 37.

25. Lincoln, *Black Muslims,* 69, 76–79, 116–17, 126–27, 146–54; Lomax, *When the Word Is Given,* 197, 202; Karim, *End of White World Supremacy,* 23–66; Lomax, *To Kill a Black Man,* 71–72; Clark, *King, Malcolm, Baldwin,* 38.

26. Clark, *King, Malcolm, Baldwin,* 38. This contention is borne out in Baldwin, *Balm,* 159–228.

27. See Wilmore, *Black Religion and Black Radicalism* (1983), 152–53; Baer and Singer, *African-American Religion in the Twentieth Century,* ix–xxiii, 28–64.

28. One argument developed by Christian authors Cross and Scott is that by ignoring the Christian traditions of their parents, Malcolm and other revolutionaries "threw out the baby with the bathwater." "In the search for truth and justice," they continue, "they forgot that the Bible is the heritage of Black as well as White and the greatest power for social and personal change the world has ever known." See Cross and Scott, *What's Up with Malcolm,* 9–73; Carson, *Papers,* 1:363; Baldwin, *Balm,* 166–67.

29. Malcolm X, *Autobiography,* 154–55, 172; Carson, *Papers,* 1:44, 363; Freeman, interview with King, 1; King Sr., *Daddy King,* 23–136; King, *Stride toward Freedom,* 18–20.

30. Malcolm X, *Autobiography,* 164, 186–87, 191; Carson, *Papers,* 1:43; King, *Strength to Love,* 147; Smith and Zepp, *Search for the Beloved Community,* 12.

31. Malcolm X, *Autobiography,* 155, 177. For excellent accounts of how spiritual values influenced Thoreau's and Gandhi's crusades against injustice, see Bedau, *Civil Disobedience,* 7–9, 15–48; Chatterjee, *Gandhi's Religious Thought,* 1–181; King, *Stride toward Freedom,* 91, 96.

32. Malcolm remembered reading Will Durant's *Story of Civilization,* H. G. Wells's *Outline of History,* and J. A. Rogers's three-volume work *Sex and Race.* See Malcolm X, *Autobiography,* 176–77, 186, 191. Also see the paper Martin completed

on the sacred rituals of Christian Churches during his Morehouse years in Carson, *Papers*, 1:127–42.

33. Malcolm X, *Autobiography*, 164. The most brilliant and extensive treatment of Malcolm's relationship with Christians and Christianity is provided in DeCaro, *Malcolm and the Cross*.

34. See King, *Why We Can't Wait*, 89–92.

35. Ansbro, *Martin Luther King Jr.*, 1–2; King, *Strength to Love*, 149; King, *Stride toward Freedom*, 95–96; Malcolm X, *Autobiography* 181.

36. See Carson, *Papers*, 1:162–433.

37. Ibid., 363, 384.

38. Malcolm X, *Autobiography*, 193–238.

39. Stone, "The Pilgrimage of Malcolm X," 5; Carson, *Papers*, 2:82–87, 95–107, 110–12, 141–51, 165–70, 204, 207, 228–33, 248–55, 269–79.

40. This point has been made concerning Elijah Muhammad, but it applies in equal measure to Malcolm. See Chapman, *Christianity on Trial*, 60. For insights into Malcolm's use of the Bible to the advantage of Islam, see Lomax, *When the Word Is Given*, 134–36, 163, 166, 168, 178, 180–81, 192–93, 205; Karim, *End of White World Supremacy*, 16–17, 33, 36–37, 40–43, 49, 53–58, 64, 68, 72–73, 101, 103–4, 125–27, 131–32; Epps, *Speeches of Malcolm X at Harvard*, 116–19; Malcolm X, *Malcolm X on Afro-American History*, 17; Clark, *King, Malcolm, Baldwin*, 44; Gallen, *A Malcolm X Reader*, 107–8; Goldman, *Death and Life*, 78–79.

41. This seemingly contradictory or ambivalent approach to the Scriptures was quite typical of Elijah Muhammad and his ministers. See Chapman, *Christianity on Trial*, 61; Karim, *End of White World Supremacy*, 16–17. Malcolm was most creative when using the Babylonian Captivity to explain what had happened to African Americans. On one occasion he said: "We were *brought* here, and those who brought us here, tell us daily, 'Sing. Sing for us. Dance for us. Clown for us. Make us laugh. . . . Sing us one of the songs of Zion. Sing us one of those spirituals, or some of those blues.'" Malcolm added: "And the answer came back, 'How shall we sing the Lord's song in a strange land?' How can *we* intelligently sing the Lord's song in this strange land?" Quoted in Goldman, *Death and Life*, 78–79.

42. Karim, *End of White World Supremacy*, 72; Epps, *The Speeches of Malcolm X at Harvard*, 116–19; Lomax, *When the Word Is Given*, 163.

43. Clark, *King, Malcolm, Baldwin*, 44.

44. King, *Stride toward Freedom*, 211–12; King, *Strength to Love*, 14, 132; Washington, *A Testament of Hope*, 280–81, 482, 495; Baldwin, *Balm*, 43, 85, 244, 295; King, "Excerpts from a Speech," delivered at the Ford Hall Forum, Boston, 1.

45. This is clear from a reading of Goldman, *Death and Life*, 79; Raboteau, *A Fire in the Bones*, 17–36; Johnson, *African-American Christianity*, 1–17; Fulop and Raboteau, *African-American Religion*, 101–4. For a source that questions the relevance of the Exodus story for African Americans, see W. Jones, *Is God a White Racist?* 18, 113–14, 116–18, 123, 162, 190.

46. Lomax, *When the Word Is Given*, 63, 134–36, 163; Epps, *Speeches of Malcolm X at Harvard*, 118–20; Malcolm X, *Autobiography*, 191, 222–23, 241, 254, 304; Gallen et al., *Malcolm X as They Knew Him*, 118–19.

47. King, *Strength to Love*, 9, 18, 26–75, 115–37; King, *Why We Can't Wait*, 89; Washington, *A Testament of Hope*, 15–16, 47, 88, 90, 216, 250–51, 255–56, 284, 295–96, 298, 491–92, 538; King, "Advice for Living," October 1957, 53.

48. King, "An Address at the Ministers' Leadership Training Program," 5; Baldwin, *To Make the Wounded Whole*, 57.

49. Malcolm X heavily influenced Albert B. Cleage Jr.'s argument that Jesus was black in a literal-historical sense, and also James H. Cone's view of Jesus' blackness as an ontological symbol. See Cleage, *The Black Messiah*, 3–200; Cleage, *Black Christian Nationalism*, 44–76, 104–19; Cone, *Black Theology and Black Power*, 5–61; "James Cone Interview," 9–12. Also see Cone, *A Black Theology of Liberation*, 107–50; Jones, *Is God a White Racist?* 7–158; Witvliet, *The Way of the Black Messiah*, 3–265; Jones, *The Color of God*, 1–119; Gaines, "Renegade Reverend," 22.

50. Malcolm X, *Autobiography*, 244; Karim, *End of White World Supremacy*, 68, 70–73, 76, 131–32; Lomax, *When the Word Is Given*, 192–94; Epps, *Speeches of Malcolm X at Harvard*, 118–19; King, *Strength to Love*, 26–55; Breitman, *Malcolm X Speaks*, 112, 162. Interestingly enough, black folklore since slavery has defined whites as goats and African Americans as sheep. This kind of symbolic and cryptic language permeated some of the sermons of the slave preacher Brudder Coteny, and Malcolm's use of it further attests to his links with African-American traditions. See Williams, "De Ole Plantation," 8–10; Genovese, *Roll, Jordan, Roll*, 265–66; Goldman, *Death and Life*, 79.

51. Malcolm was as ambivalent on this question as he was in his approach to the Bible. At points in his early speeches he spoke of God as having raised up Moses "from among the lowly Hebrew slaves," and in other instances he suggested that Moses and the prophets were not Jews but Muslims. See Lomax, *When the Word Is Given*, 113, 134; Karim, *End of White World Supremacy*, 76.

52. King, *Strength to Love*, 150–51. Martin's Christology merits far more attention than it has been given so far by scholars. The most interesting treatments so far can be found in Temme, "Jesus as Trailblazer," 75–80; Fluker, *They Looked for a City*, 174–77; Ivory, *Toward a Theology of Radical Involvement*, 79–84; Baldwin, *To Make the Wounded Whole*, 61–63.

53. Malcolm X, *Autobiography*, 374, 376; Karim, *End of White World Supremacy*, 76. Malcolm held that ancient Egypt and Ethiopia were black civilizations, a position that finds support in the works of W.E.B. Du Bois, Cheikh Anta Diop, and Afrocentrists such as Molefi Kete Asante. See Stuckey, *Slave Culture*, 277–78; Okafor, "Diop and the African Origin of Civilization," 252–68; Sertima, *Great African Thinkers*, 35–73; Asante, *Kemet, Afrocentricity, and Knowledge*, 3–168. Malcolm's claim that Augustine was a black African should not be casually dismissed, for that claim was made as early as 1837 by *Colored American*, a New York–based black newspaper, and as recently as 1997 by the womanist theologian Cheryl Kirk-Duggan. See Lynch, *Edward Wilmot Blyden*, 57; Kirk-Duggan, *Exorcizing Evil*, 349n.49; Breitman, *By Any Means Necessary*, 25; Lomax, *When the Word Is Given*, 40–41, 161.

54. King, "Discerning the Signs of History," 4–5; Baldwin, *Balm*, 226–27.

55. Karim, *End of White World Supremacy*, 79.

56. King, "The Sword That Heals," 14; Baldwin, *Balm,* 236–37; Ansbro, *Martin Luther King Jr.,* 157–58; Lincoln, *Black Muslims,* 72. Martin's thoughts on the scarcity of higher human values and virtues among whites were undoubtedly influenced by the Christian realism of Reinhold Niebuhr, who drew clear distinctions between individual morality and societal morality—between the behavior of a person as an individual and the behavior of social groups. See Niebuhr, *Moral Man and Immoral Society,* xi–xii, 257. For an interesting treatment of Malcolm's and Martin's views on the relationship between religion and race, see Hatch, "Racism and Religion: The Contrasting Views of Benjamin Mays, Malcolm X, and Martin Luther King Jr.," 26–36.

57. Lincoln, *Black Muslims,* 27; Cone, *Martin and Malcolm and America,* 169; Malcolm X, "The Truth about the Black Muslims," 1–3.

58. Lomax, *When the Word Is Given,* 41, 160–61; Malcolm X, *Autobiography,* 22, 222, 224, 252–302, 311, 313, 317, 393; Lincoln, *Black Muslims,* 148.

59. Malcolm X, *Autobiography,* 226. Louis Lomax and C. Eric Lincoln have pointed to the virtual absence of a liturgy in the Black Muslim temples in Malcolm's time. See Lomax, *When the Word Is Given,* 21–22; Lincoln, *Black Muslims,* 108–13; Baldwin, *Balm,* 181–91, 236; King, *Stride toward Freedom,* 35–38, 58–63, 177–78; C. S. King, *My Life,* 260.

60. King, "Address to the Initial Mass Meeting of the Montgomery Improvement Association," 4; King, *Stride toward Freedom,* 224; Baldwin, *Balm,* 226–27, 238–43; King, "Discerning the Signs of History," 4–5.

61. Breitman, *Malcolm X Speaks,* 12; Malcolm X, *Autobiography,* 405; Clark, *February 1965,* 182; Cone, *Martin and Malcolm and America,* 255–56.

62. Shabazz to Lewis, 15 May 1964; Breitman, *Malcolm X Speaks,* 24–25; Clark, *February 1965,* 201, 230; C. S. King, *My Life,* 261.

63. King, "President's Address," 2; Breitman, *Malcolm X Speaks,* 59–60.

64. Maglangbayan, *Garvey, Lumumba, Malcolm,* 71–73.

65. Gallen et al., *Malcolm X as They Knew Him,* 247; Washington, *I Have a Dream,* 191–92; Baldwin, *To Make the Wounded Whole,* 301; Washington, *A Testament of Hope,* 371; Breitman, *By Any Means Necessary,* 84, 86; Karim, *End of White World Supremacy,* 6–7, 117. Like Martin, Malcolm did not think of life as an inexhaustible well, and this is why death presented no fears. For both men, death was equated in a strange way with freedom, calling to mind slave thought generations earlier. See Faulkner, *The Days When the Animals Talked,* 36–39.

66. Washington, *A Testament of Hope,* 41–42.

67. Gayraud S. Wilmore makes this point regarding Martin, but it applies also to Malcolm. See Wilmore, *Black Religion and Black Radicalism* (1983), 174. Malcolm's impact on religion and theology in America is largely ignored even in DeCaro, *On the Side of My People,* 129–300. The best available studies of Malcolm's and Martin's influence on religion and theology in America are "James Cone Interview," 9–11; Cone, "The Theology of Martin Luther King Jr.," 21–36; Cone, "Black Theology in American Religion," 759–71; Cone, *Martin and Malcolm and America,* 295–97.

68. Malcolm X, *Autobiography,* 197, 202–3, 214, 221–22; Washington, *A Testament of Hope,* 365.

69. Malcolm X, *Autobiography*, 183–84. Apparently, this was a subject about which both Malcolm and Martin had scant knowledge. Both were deceased long before the most thorough and reliable scholarship on Islam and resistance among African slaves in antebellum America first appeared. See Austin, *African Muslims in Antebellum America*, 3–759; Turner, *Islam in the African-American Experience*, 11–46; Diouf, *Servants of Allah*, 145–78.

70. Malcolm X, *Autobiography*, 177; Malcolm X, *Malcolm X on Afro-American History*, 54, 65; Breitman, *By Any Means Necessary*, 80.

71. King, *Where Do We Go from Here?* 56.

72. Malcolm X, *Malcolm X on Afro-American History*, 34–37. Malcolm's perspective on the slave spirituals was clearly ambivalent, for at times he suggested that that music was something other than great art. Even so, music provided the lenses through which he and Martin interpreted certain essentials of slave culture.

73. Ibid., 32.

74. Courlander, *Negro Folk Music, U.S.A.*, 41–42; Malcolm X, *Malcolm X on Afro-American History*, 32, 34–37; King, *Why We Can't Wait*, 61; King, *The Trumpet of Conscience*, 3–4; Cone, *The Spirituals and the Blues*, 88–90. Malcolm's view that the language of escape in the spirituals revealed the slaves' deep longing to return to Africa finds support in Fisher, *Negro Slave Songs in the United States*, 129, 146, 156, 178. Also see Malcolm X, *Malcolm X on Afro-American History*, 32, 34–35; King, *The Trumpet of Conscience*, 3–4; Courlander, *Negro Folk Music, U.S.A.*, 41–43; Cone, *The Spirituals and the Blues*, 88–90.

75. Lincoln, *Black Muslims*, 152–53. Malcolm occasionally visited and spoke at black churches, and was therefore quite mindful of the manner in which most of them operated. The fact that Malcolm often joined others in the Nation of Islam in "fishing" for Muslim converts on the grounds of black churches on Sunday mornings is certainly an indication of the lack of respect he had for those institutions. See Karim, *End of White World Supremacy*, 16–17, 77–78, 109–10; Malcolm X, *Autobiography*, 109–10, 221–24.

76. Karim, *End of White World Supremacy*, 25, 109–10; Malcolm X, *Autobiography*, 197, 221–22, 224, 302, 311, 313, 317, 371; Lincoln, *Black Muslims*, 72–90, 151–54.

77. King, *Stride toward Freedom*, 35–36; King, *Why We Can't Wait*, 67; Baldwin, *Balm*, 7–8, 159–228; C. S. King, *My Life*, 260.

78. King, "Annual Address," delivered at the First Annual Institute on Nonviolence, 2; King, "Our Struggle," 3–6.

79. King, *Why We Can't Wait*, 87. King made a similar comment in a speech called "A Challenge to the Churches and Synagogues." See Ahmann, *Race: A Challenge to Religion*, 164–65. King knew that the ethics of love and nonviolence as defined by Gandhi were already expressed in the symbols and philosophic language of his people, especially in the South, where a strong "tradition of Christian stoicism" existed. He noted on some occasions that nonviolence "is consistent with the deeply religious traditions of Negroes," and on other occasions that "it is important to recall that Negroes created the theory of nonviolence as it applies to American conditions."

King, "The Burning Truth in the South," 3; King, "Negroes Are Not Moving Too Fast," 10; Huggins, "Martin Luther King," 480–81.

80. Quoted in Washington, *A Testament of Hope,* 346–47. King had a high regard for the normative authority of the early church. The strict discipline and devotion of the early Christians in the face of the unjust laws and persecution of the Roman Empire were a tremendous source of inspiration for the civil rights leader's nonviolent campaigns. See Baldwin, *Balm,* 203.

81. King, *Where Do We Go from Here?* 125.

82. Stone, "The Pilgrimage of Malcolm X," 3; Gallen et al., *Malcolm X as They Knew Him,* 113, 126; Perry, *Malcolm X: The Last Speeches,* 31; King, "A Proposed Statement to the South," 3; C. S. King, *My Life,* 260.

83. Washington, *A Testament of Hope,* 346–47, 356; Ansbro, *Martin Luther King Jr.,* 180; King, "Advice for Living," February 1958, 84; King, "Advice for Living," April 1958, 104.

84. Malcolm X, *Autobiography,* 178–79, 191, 197, 202, 221–22, 374–76, 394.

85. Breitman, *Malcolm X Speaks,* 40. For references to King's relationship with Graham, see Edward L. Moore's 1979 dissertation, "Billy Graham and Martin Luther King Jr.," 453–80; Washington, *A Testament of Hope,* 298–99.

86. Washington, *A Testament of Hope,* 299. This statement of King was made in response to criticism he received from conservative white churchmen in Alabama. He may well have directed it at the white fundamentalist preacher Jerry Falwell, who, in a 1965 sermon called, "Ministers and Marches," denounced King and other black preachers for their social and political involvements. See Conway and Siegelman, *Holy Terror,* 85–86.

87. This atonement theme is almost as strong in Martin's writings and speeches as it is in Malcolm's. King consistently spoke of God's judgment upon the Christian Church, even as he praised certain segments of that institution for its vitality and contributions to humanity. His capacity to be critical of the church, an institution with which he identified, shows that he was much more objective in his perspective on religion than Malcolm, who was known for his essentially uncritical view of Sunni Islam. See King, *Why We Can't Wait,* 89–92; Washington, *A Testament of Hope,* 345–47; Karim, *End of White World Supremacy,* 121–48; Malcolm X, *Autobiography,* 375–76.

88. Malcolm X, *Autobiography,* 249; Lomax, *When the Word Is Given,* 161; Gallen et al., *Malcolm X as They Knew Him,* 113.

89. King, "Guidelines for a Constructive Church," 4–5; King, *Why We Can't Wait,* 65, 67; King, "Answer to a Perplexing Question," 8, 10–11. King held that preachers of the otherworldly gospel tended to teach that prayer alone would solve the problems of their people, a message he dismissed as not religion but superstition. See King, *Strength to Love,* 131–32; Ayres, *Wisdom of King,* 98.

90. Malcolm X, *Autobiography,* 216; Lincoln, *Black Muslims,* 152–53.

91. King, "Answer to a Perplexing Question," 7–8.

92. King, "An Address to the Ministers' Leadership Training Program," 2; Lincoln, *Black Muslims,* 148. Also see Breitman, *By Any Means Necessary,* 101.

93. Gallen et al., *Malcolm X as They Knew Him,* 116.

94. Clark, *February 1965,* 240, 250, 271, 279; Perry, *Malcolm X: The Last Speeches,* 116, 125, 131–32.

95. See Breitman, "Reviews and Reports," 1–2. Malcolm was also frequently referred to as "the St. Paul of the Black Muslim movement," and one scholar wrote an entire chapter in a book called, "From Moses to Malcolm X." See Lomax, *When the Word Is Given,* 17, 35–58.

96. Breitman, *Malcolm X Speaks,* 9–10, 12, 24; C. S. King, *My Life,* 261–62; Malcolm X, *Autobiography,* 405, 431–33; Breitman, *By Any Means Necessary,* 16, 77, 99–100; Karim, *End of White World Supremacy,* 14–15. Albert Cleage Jr. devoted a chapter to Malcolm and Martin each in his first book, *The Black Messiah,* 186–213.

97. DeCaro, *On the Side of My People,* 51; Carson, *Papers,* 1:195–209, 211–25, 236–42, 294–327, 416–33.

98. Clark, *King, Malcolm, Baldwin,* 12–13; Gallen et al., *Malcolm X as They Knew Him,* 84. These conclusions are based on definitions of "interfaith dialogue" and "ecumenism" as set forth in Martin, "King and Interfaith Dialogue," 34–35. For important references to Malcolm and Martin in an important work on black ecumenism, see Sawyer, *Black Ecumenism,* 11, 29, 31, 37–64, 66–67, 69, 91, 105, 178–79, 184, 186–87.

99. Karim, *End of White World Supremacy,* 28–32.

100. King, "Advice for Living," September 1958, 68.

101. See Martin, "King and Interfaith Dialogue," 35; Newfield, "Blacks and Jews," 1, 3, 15.

102. David Lewis, *King: A Critical Biography,* 125; Baldwin, "Reassessment," 104; Baldwin, "Malcolm X and Martin Luther King Jr.," 395; King, "More than Any Other Person in History," 2; King, "Address on Gandhi," 22 March 1959.

103. Martin, "King and Interfaith Dialogue," 43–47; Clark, *King, Malcolm, Baldwin,* 40–41, 46–47; Breitman, *By Any Means Necessary,* 4, 26; Lomax, *When the Word Is Given,* 201; Breitman, *Malcolm X Speaks,* 204–5; Karim, *End of White World Supremacy,* 93–95, 105.

104. King, *Stride toward Freedom,* 208; Ansbro, *Martin Luther King Jr.,* 180; King and Walker to the Student Interracial Ministry Committee, 29 March 1961; Martin, "King and Interfaith Dialogue," 43–47. King's refusal to dialogue with Malcolm and the Nation of Islam continued through the early 1960s. See Malcolm X to King, 21 July 1960; Ballou, secretary to King, to Malcolm X, 10 August 1960; McDonald, secretary to King, to Clark, 26 November 1962; Clark to King, 4 December 1962.

105. King to Resnikoff, 17 September 1961.

106. King to Eisenman, 3 April 1964; Eisenman to King, 9 April 1964; King, "Statement on Malcolm X," 16 March 1964; Cone, *Speaking the Truth,* 167.

107. *Like It Is,* videotape; "Draft of Statement Regarding SCLC's Participation at National Conference on New Politics," September 1967, 1; Schneier, *Shared Dreams,* 39–40, 158, 168–69.

108. King to Fey, 23 June 1962; King, "Statement on Interfaith Conference on Civil Rights," 15 January 1963.

109. Agronsky et al., interview, *Face the Nation,* 7.

110. King, "Address on Gandhi," 7–11; King, "My Jewish Brother," 1, 12; *Orbis Books,* 3; Money to Baldwin, 17 June 2001.

111. This development in Malcolm's consciousness is brilliantly treated in McCloud, *African-American Islam,* 35–38. Also see Clark, *February 1965,* 46, 84–85, 201; Gallen et al., *Malcolm X as They Knew Him,* 235; Malcolm X, *Autobiography,* 375; Shabazz to Lewis, 15 May 1964; Breitman, *By Any Means Necessary,* 77, 152; Breitman, *Malcolm X Speaks,* 24–25; K. Clark, *King, Malcolm, Baldwin,* 12; Adams, "Malcolm X 'Seemed Sincere' about Helping Cause: Mrs. King," 28, 30.

112. King, *Where Do We Go from Here?* 167; King, "President's Address," 6; King, "Pathos and Hope," 2; King, "An Address to the American Jewish Congress," 6–7; Baldwin, *To Make the Wounded Whole,* 40–41; Clark, *King, Malcolm, Baldwin,* 12–13.

113. Karim, *End of White World Supremacy,* 96; Breitman, *Malcolm X Speaks,* 4. It could be argued that Malcolm had come to such a conclusion as early as his Black Muslim years, for he often said that "our" struggles "do not mean Muslim nor Christian, Catholic nor Protestant, Baptist nor Methodist." See Lomax, *When the Word Is Given,* 150; S. Clark, *February 1965,* 182; Breitman, *By Any Means Necessary,* 6, 26–27, 36, 39–40, 57, 111–12, 180.

114. King, *Where Do We Go from Here?* 167–68; Karim, *End of White World Supremacy,* 97–98.

115. Breitman, *By Any Means Necessary,* 122–23; Karim, *End of White World Supremacy,* 33–37, 40–72; Lomax, *When the Word Is Given,* 134–38, 205–6; Breitman, *Malcolm X Speaks,* 162; S. Clark, *February 1965,* 83; Gallen et al., *Malcolm X as They Knew Him,* 182.

116. Such statements confirm Peter Paris's view that King "remained a universalist in his views about religion." See Washington, *A Testament of Hope,* 242; Paris, review of *Martin and Malcolm and America,* by James H. Cone, 88; King, "Address on Gandhi," 10–11; King to Fey, 23 June 1962.

117. Franklin, "Three Faces of Malcolm X," 14.

118. Flewellen, "March Support Swells," 3, 23; Mitchell and Waldron, "Minister Louis Farakhan Sets the Record Straight," 11–12.

119. Flewellen, "March Support Swells," 3, 23.

120. Ibid.

121. Ibid.

122. Sadler, *Atonement: The Million Man March,* Introduction; "Farrakhan Urges Marchers to Return Home and Make a Positive Difference," 10–11; Baker-Fletcher, *Black Religion and the Million Man March,* 1–166.

123. Harding, *Martin Luther King: The Inconvenient Hero,* 139–41.

124. Caldwell, "The Significance of the March," 17; Rifkin, "'Million Man March' Divides Black Religious Community," 3. It is ironic that the National Baptist preacher E. V. Hill, who has associated widely with Jerry Falwell, a white preacher who has never properly confessed to and received forgiveness for his segregationist views in the 1960s and his support of South African apartheid leaders in the 1980s, found it impossible to support the Million Man March because of its links to Minister

Farrakhan. This apparently holds true for other black ministers who have not hesitated to work with white churches and their leaders despite their long history of discrimination against African Americans. See Rifkin, ibid.

125. For interesting commentaries on the continuing waves of religious persecution in various parts of the world, see "Religious Persecution in China on Rise," B4; "Freedom of Faith for All Religions," 12A.

Chapter 4. In the Matter of Faith

1. An-Nawawi, *Riyadh-Us-Saleheen*, 1:180.

2. C. S. King, *The Words of Martin Luther King Jr.*, 65.

3. Breitman, *Malcolm X Speaks*, 197–98.

4. Merton, *Gandhi on Nonviolence*, 66.

5. Easwaran, *Gandhi the Man*, 168.

6. Ibid., 48.

7. Gallen et al., *Malcolm X as They Knew Him*, 138.

8. Khaldun, *The Maqaddimah*, 264–65; Basharat Ali, *Muslim Social Philosophy*, 47–50, 55–56.

9. Washington, *A Testament of Hope*, 46–47. King defined agapic love in many of his essays and speeches, such as "Nonviolence and Racial Injustice" and "An Experiment in Love," both of which are included in the Washington volume.

10. According to Dagobert D. Runes et al., *Dictionary of Philosophy*, "Manicheism is a religio-philosophical doctrine, which spread from Persia to the West and was influential during the third and seventh century. It was instituted by Mani (Grk. Manes, Latinized Manichaeus), a Magian who, upon conversion to Christianity, sought to synthesize the latter with the dualism of Zoroastrianism, not without becoming a martyr to his faith. To combat the powers of darkness, mother of light created the first man. As Buddha and Zoroaster, he worked illumination among men; as Jesus, the Son of Man, he had to suffer, become transfigured and symbolize salvation by his apparent death at the cross; as spirit of the sun he attracts all connatural light particles to himself" (187). Frantz Fanon explains this doctrine in these terms: "The colonial world is a Manichean world. It is not enough for the settler to delimit physically, that is to say, with the help of the army and the police force, the place of the native. As if to show the totalitarian character of colonial exploitation the settler paints the native as a sort of quintessence of evil. Native society is not simply described as a society lacking in values. It is not enough for the colonist to affirm that those values have disappeared from, or still better never existed in, the colonial world. The native is declared insensible to ethics; he represents not only the absence of values, but also the negation of values. He is, let us dare to admit, the enemy of values, and in this sense he is the absolute evil. . . . At times this Manicheism goes to its logical conclusion and dehumanises the native, or to speak plainly it turns him into an animal" (*The Wretched of the Earth*, 33–34). For important reflections on the roles of myth, symbolism, and utopia in religion, see Manheim, *Ideology and Utopia*.

11. Perry, *Malcolm X: The Last Speeches*, 156–57.

12. King, *Strength to Love*, 9–16.

13. Lomax, *To Kill a Black Man*, 209–10.

14. Karim, *End of White World Supremacy*.

15. Breitman, *Malcolm X Speaks*, 207.

16. Malcolm X, *Autobiography*, 2, 4.

17. See Carson, *Autobiography of Martin Luther King Jr.*

18. Malcolm X, *Autobiography*, 228.

19. See Moynihan, *The Negro Family*.

20. Collins, *Seventh Child*, 96; Malcolm X. *Autobiography*, 231.

21. C. S. King, *My Life*, 39–45.

22. Imran, *Ideal Woman in Islam*, 19.

23. See *The Open Bible*, 592; Koltuv, *Solomon and Sheba*.

24. Carson, *Autobiography of Martin Luther King Jr.*, 35.

25. C. S. King, *My Life*, 50, 53, 69.

26. Malcolm X, *Autobiography*, 231.

27. Sakr, *Matrimonial Education in Islam*, 5.

28. This is probably a typographical error. Perhaps the word should have been *mosque* rather than *Muslims*.

29. Betty Shabazz, "On Loving and Losing Malcolm," 54, 104.

30. *Matrimonial Education in Islam*, 28–29.

31. Shabazz, "On Loving and Losing Malcolm," 104.

32. Malcolm X, *Autobiography*, 298.

33. Collins, *Seventh Child*, 96.

34. Cone, *Martin and Malcolm and America*, 273–74.

35. Clark, *February 1965*, 254.

36. Billingsley, *Climbing Jacob's Ladder*, 84.

37. See Diop, *The African Origin of Civilization*; Diop, *Civilization or Barbarism*.

38. Rainwater and Yancey, *Moynihan Report and the Politics of Controversy*, 404.

39. King, *Where Do We Go from Here?* 104–5. Strong support for King's analysis can be found in Blassingame, *The Slave Community*, which is an excellent treatment of the subject. See also Latif and Latif, *Slavery*.

40. See Oliver Cox, *Caste, Class, and Race*; Dollard, *Caste and Class in a Southern Town*.

41. See Herskovits, *The Myth of the Negro Past*; Frazier, *The Negro Church in America*, 1; Edwards, *E. Franklin Frazier on Race Relations*, 191; Hill, *Rhetoric of Racial Revolt*.

42. Rainwater and Yancey, *Moynihan Report and the Politics of Controversy*, 403–4.

43. Malcolm X, *Malcolm X on Afro-American History*, 51.

44. Rainwater and Yancey, *Moynihan Report and the Politics of Controversy*, 404.

45. *Proceedings of the Black Family Summit*, 7–8.

46. Staples, *The Black Family*, 39–42.

47. King, *Where Do We Go from Here?* 105–6.

48. See Robert B. Hill, *The Strengths of Black Families*; Sudarkasa, "Interpreting the African Heritage in Afro-American Family Organization." Also see McAdoo, *Black Families*, 27–43.

49. Rainwater and Yancey, *The Moynihan Report and the Politics of Controversy,* 439.

50. See Ahmed, "Muslim Organizations in the United States"; Stone, "Estimate of Muslims Living in the United States," 11–36; McCloud, *African-American Islam,* 9–94.

51. Lincoln and Mamiya, *The Black Church in the African-American Experience,* 304.

52. Ibid., 391.

53. Jawanza Kunjufu, *Adam! Where Are You?* 29.

54. Sabiq, *Fiqh us-Sunnah: Supererogatory Prayer,* 2:50. The Arabic expression "Sallallahu Alehi Wasallam" means "peace and blessing be upon him." In chapters 2 and 4, I used the English abbreviation (pbuh) to indicate the same expression.

55. Muslims believe human beings are Muslims at birth. They change due to the religion of their parents or other environmental circumstances. This point is discussed in my chapter entitled, "Al-Qur'an and Sunnah: From Malcolm X to El-Hajj Malik El-Shabazz."

56. Lincoln and Mamiya, *The Black Church in the African-American Experience,* 391.

57. Graham, "Holy War: Rev. Fred Price is Fighting the Church over Racism," 48–49.

58. Power and Samuels, "Battling for Souls," 46.

59. Ibid., 47.

60. Smitherman, "A Womanist Looks at the Million Man March," in Karenga and Madhubuti, *The Million Man March,* 106.

61. See Karenga and Madhubuti, *The Million Man March: Day of Absence.* To compare the Million Man and Million Woman marches in terms of their goals, see also Coleman, "Reflections on the Million Woman March," 76–79.

62. Elijah Muhammad, *Message to the Blackman in America,* 58–59.

63. Breitman, *By Any Means Necessary,* 179.

64. The character of Jesus Christ is that of a righteous Prophet in Islam. For examples see Ata ur-Rahim, *Jesus: A Prophet of Islam;* Ragg and Ragg, *The Gospel of Barnabas;* Yusseff, *The Dead Sea Scrolls.*

65. See Al-Mubarakpuri, *Ar-Raheeq Al-Makhtum;* Maulana Ali, *Muhammad the Prophet.*

66. Washington, *A Testament of Hope,* 289–302.

67. Clark, *February 1965,* 252; Breitman, *Malcolm X Speaks,* 212.

68. Akbar, *Visions for Black Men,* 83–85.

69. Davis, "Our Shining Black Prince," in Clarke, *Malcolm X,* xi–xii.

70. Hadid, interview with Bernard Lafayette Jr., March 1999.

Chapter 5. The Character of Womanhood

1. Quoted in Lerner, *Black Women in White America,* 583.

2. Malcolm X, *Autobiography* 354.

3. King, "Advice for Living," December 1957, 120.

4. What one scholar says of Malcolm is equally true of Martin, namely, that "rigid

notions of male dominance . . . were a part of the ideological climate in which he grew to maturity." See Davis, "On Malcolm X," 37.

5. No major studies exist concerning how Malcolm and King viewed and related to women at all levels of society. Some of the best available treatments of the subject are Shabazz, "Malcolm X as a Husband and Father," in Clarke, *Malcolm X: The Man and His Times,* 132–43; Hudson-Weems, "From Malcolm Little to El Hajj Malik El Shabazz," 26–31; C. S. King, *My Life,* 1–308; Powers, *I Shared the Dream,* 1–4, 91–321.

6. Daly, *Beyond God the Father,* 163–64; Cone, *Martin and Malcolm and America,* 273–80; Ansbro, *Martin Luther King Jr.,* xv; Baldwin, *To Make the Wounded Whole,* 294; Perry, *Teaching Malcolm X,* 199–205; Hudson-Weems, "From Malcolm X to El Hajj Malik El Shabazz," 26–31.

7. This contention is apparently supported by Burrow, "Some African-American Males' Perspectives on the Black Woman," 68. Also see Malcolm X, *Autobiography,* 140, 344, 430; King, *Stride toward Freedom,* 18–19.

8. Strangely enough, Malcolm knew that there was a deep love between his parents that virtually transcended the conflict that so often occurred between them. See Malcolm X, *Autobiography,* 2–10. I reject Bruce Perry's suggestion that Earl Little's abusive manner was symptomatic of an essentially dysfunctional family. See Perry, *Malcolm,* 6–14; Carson et al., *Papers of Martin Luther King Jr.* (hereafter referred to as Carson, *Papers*), 1:360; Baldwin, *Balm,* 106. L. D. Reddick, who knew the Kings well, described the King home as "father-centered," as a setting in which Daddy King's word, "considerate and benevolent as he tried to make it, was final." Martin Luther King Jr. reported that the same applied in the case of his father's pastoral role at Atlanta's Ebenezer Baptist Church. See Reddick, *Crusader without Violence,* 51; Griffin, interview with King, 2.

9. Perry, *Malcolm,* 6; King Sr., *Daddy King,* 131.

10. Carson, *Papers,* 1:360; Farris, "The Young Martin," 57; C. S. King, *My Life,* 76–77, 92; Baldwin, *Balm,* 106–7; King, *Stride toward Freedom,* 19; Malcolm X, *Autobiography,* 11–19, 22. It is reported that Louise Little actually contributed articles to the *Negro World,* Garvey's major periodical. Her pride in her African heritage was unmistakable, thus challenging any claim that she was "in conflict about color," favoring "her lighter-skinned relatives" over the darker ones. See Decaro, *On the Side of My People,* 41; Perry, *Malcolm,* 5.

11. "Alex Haley Remembers Malcolm X," 54; Malcolm X, *Autobiography,* 22, 395–96; Perry, *Teaching Malcolm X,* 28.

12. King, *Stride toward Freedom,* 19.

13. E. Franklin Frazier says much the same in his portrait of the "Negro grandmother" during slavery. I am indebted to him for much of this idea. See Frazier, *The Negro Family in the United States,* 114–16. Also see Perry, *Teaching Malcolm X,* 28; Carson, *Papers,* 1:359; Baldwin, *Balm,* 106–27; Malcolm X, *Autobiography,* 122, 163.

14. Malcolm X, *Autobiography,* 18–19, 21–22.

15. Carson, *Papers,* 1:1, 13, 19, 26, 29–30, 36–37, 105–6, 111–12, 115–17, 161;

King Sr., *Daddy King,* 13–15, 19–20, 68–72, 75, 83, 87, 90, 109, 130–31; Farris, "The Young Martin," 56–57; Baldwin, *Balm,* 103–27.

16. Perry, *Malcolm,* 54–55; Malcolm X, *Autobiography,* 57–70, 416.

17. Burrow, "Some African-American Males' Perspectives," 68.

18. Hudson-Weems, "From Malcolm Little to El Hajj Malik El Shabazz," 27.

19. Malcolm X, *Autobiography,* 92, 135–36, 228. In an important psycho-history of Malcolm, Wolfenstein suggests that Malcolm's negative views on women grew out of his early childhood relationship with his mother and father. According to this source, Louise Little, from Malcolm's early childhood perspective, was "the arche-typal verbally castrative woman." "Moreover," continues Wolfenstein, "because Earl Little left home on the day that he was killed as a result of a quarrel with Louise, Malcolm may have felt that she was partially responsible for his death." Building on Wolfenstein's suggestion, Burrow notes, "This means that Malcolm's view of women was a result of the displacement of his own repressed hostility onto women." In yet another study by Bruce Perry, there is the suggestion that Malcolm's "male chauvin-ism was the predictable result of past tyranny," i.e., the fact that his mother, Louise, and his sister Ella "denied him warmth and emotional support." See Wolfenstein, *The Victims of Democracy,* 264; Burrow, "Some African-American Males' Perspectives," 69; Perry, *Malcolm X,* 55, 190.

20. Garrow, *Bearing the Cross,* 36, 40–41, 45; Carson, *Papers,* 1:161.

21. Malcolm X, *Autobiography,* 31, 44, 46, 51, 67–70, 92, 94, 97, 122–23, 135; Carson, *Papers,* 1:121; Garrow, *Bearing the Cross,* 40–41, 97, 122–23, 135; Hudson-Weems, "From Malcolm Little to El Hajj Malik El Shabazz," 28. For a source that questions much of Malcolm's own account of Sophia, see Perry, *Malcolm,* 56–57.

22. Freeman, interview with King, 4–5; Baldwin, *Balm,* 21–22; Reddick, *Crusader without Violence,* 59–60. Malcolm's childhood exposure to white women who called blacks "niggers" would have made it possible for him to identify with any insult Martin received from white women even in the South. See Malcolm X, *Autobiogra-phy,* 27, 29–30.

23. Malcolm tended at this point in his life to reduce such relationships to "taboo lust." See Malcolm X, *Autobiography,* 94, 97, 122; Garrow, *Bearing the Cross,* 40–41. The advice King got from Barbour and other friends was reflected years later in the suggestions he made to blacks and whites who planned to marry interracially. See King, "Advice for Living," March 1958, 92; King, "Advice for Living," October 1958, 138.

24. Carson, *Papers,* 1:121; Malcolm X, *Autobiography,* 94.

25. Goldman, *Death and Life,* 75–76; Malcolm X, *Autobiography,* 197, 230.

26. Carson, *Papers,* 1:361–63.

27. Malcolm X, *Autobiography,* 228–29, 232, 298.

28. "Malcolm X: FBI Surveillance File," 1978, reel #1.

29. Ibid.; Cone, *Martin and Malcolm and America,* 275–76.

30. Cone, *Martin and Malcolm and America,* 275; Malcolm X, *Autobiography,* 228, 298.

31. Perry, *Malcolm,* 172; Malcolm X, *Autobiography,* 230–32; Shabazz, "Mal-colm X as a Husband and Father," 134. "One of the things my husband said before

he got married," recalled Betty Shabazz, "is that it would be very difficult for him to tell a wife where he was, where he was going, when he was coming back. . . . It was basically that fear of a woman having control." See Shabazz, "Loving and Losing Malcolm," 107.

32. King was known to say during his periods of dating, "I must have a wife who is as dedicated as I am. I will be the pastor of a large black church in the South. That's where I plan to live and work. I want the kind of wife who will fit into that kind of situation." One King scholar has observed, "Because of her own family conflicts in Perry County, Alabama," Coretta had "decided to become something of an activist herself. She had made up her mind that she would not marry a man unless he held an active and strong stance in racial matters." See Downing, *To See the Promised Land,* 171; C. S. King, *My Life,* 58, 67–72.

33. Perry, *Malcolm X,* 172–73; DeCaro, *On the Side of My People,* 318n.14; Gallen et al., *Malcolm X as They Knew Him,* 15–16; Wood, *Malcolm X in Our Own Image,* 131–32; Clarke, *Malcolm X: The Man and His Times,* 132–33. Wolfenstein claims that by 1956 or 1957, "Malcolm's irrational misogyny was beginning to break down. . . . On the one hand, there was the progressive impact of Islamic Belief," and "on the other, there was Betty, whose good character, intelligence, and beauty Malcolm found . . . increasingly difficult to resist." See Wolfenstein, *The Victims of Democracy,* 264.

34. Shabazz, "Loving and Losing Malcolm," 107; "Alex Haley Remembers Malcolm X," 54, 118; Shabazz, "Malcolm X as a Husband and Father," 133–34; Shabazz, "Remembering Malcolm X, 61."

35. Angelou, *All God's Children Need Traveling Shoes,* 139; "Alex Haley Remembers Malcolm X," 118; Malcolm X, *Autobiography,* 235, 415, 422, 429–30; Shabazz, "Malcolm X as a Husband and Father," 133–35. Bruce Perry claims that Malcolm's "inability to trust apparently made it difficult for him to confide" in Betty, a questionable contention. See Perry, *Malcolm,* 190; Shabazz, "Remembering Malcolm X"; Shabazz, "The Legacy of My Husband," 176, 178.

36. C. S. King, *My Life,* 24, 71–72, 87–88; Baldwin, *Balm,* 131. A completely different picture of Martin and Coretta's marriage has emerged from interviews with some of Martin's friends and associates. One says that Martin "was so harassed at home," that Coretta "was as much a part of his depression as his staff." The account goes on to note that had Martin "lived, the marriage wouldn't have survived, and everybody feels that way." See Garrow, *Bearing the Cross,* 617, 683n.39. For other insights that are useful for analyzing this relationship, see Carson, *Papers,* 2:220; C. S. King, *My Life,* 53–54.

37. Perry, *Malcolm,* 188–89. See also Shabazz, "Malcolm X as a Husband and Father," 134; Shabazz, "Loving and Losing Malcolm," 107; C. S. King, *My Life,* 58, 87–88; Baldwin, *Balm,* 132; Cone, *Martin and Malcolm and America,* 274.

38. Malcolm X, *Autobiography,* 94, 228; B. Perry, *Malcolm,* 188; Cone, *Martin and Malcolm and America,* 274–75; C. S. King, *My Life,* 87–88. According to L. D. Reddick, King was convinced that "biologically and aesthetically women are more suitable than men for keeping house." See Reddick, *Crusader without Violence,* 5; Shabazz, "Remembering Malcolm X," 61.

39. Shabazz, "Loving and Losing Malcolm," 107; Shabazz, "Malcolm X as a Husband and Father," 135.

40. C. S. King, *My Life,* 57–58.

41. Shabazz, "Malcolm X as a Husband and Father," 135; Malcolm X, *Autobiography,* 234; Baldwin, *Balm,* 131–32; C. S. King, *My Life,* 86–87. For important references to how Betty served her husband in their home, see Shabazz, "The Legacy of My Husband," 176, 178.

42. Shabazz, "Loving and Losing Malcolm," 107, 109. See also Davis, "On Malcolm X," 37.

43. Garrow, *Bearing the Cross,* 375–76, 617, 669n.7.

44. Shabazz, "Loving and Losing Malcolm," 107–8; Malcolm X, *Autobiography,* 229–31; David Lewis, *King: A Critical Biography,* 288, 290; Carson, *Papers,* 3:386; Oates, *Let the Trumpet Sound,* 381, 431, 440; C. S. King, *My Life,* 12, 91–92.

45. Malcolm X, *Autobiography,* 310.

46. Ibid., 344.

47. Baldwin, *Balm,* 141–51; Lentz, *Symbols, the News Magazines, and Martin Luther King Jr.,* 299. The most intense discussions of Coretta's role as supportive wife are afforded in C. S. King, *My Life;* King Sr., *Daddy King,* 151–52, 168, 172, 174–75, 181–82, 189–93; Vivian, *Coretta.*

48. Perry, *Malcolm,* 188–90, 326–27. Perry's comments regarding Malcolm's frequent absences from home are supported in Malcolm X, *Autobiography,* 235; Shabazz, "Malcolm X as a Husband and Father," 134; Shabazz, "Loving and Losing Malcolm," 107.

49. See Washington, *A Testament of Hope,* 341; Baldwin, *Balm,* 135; Garrow, *Bearing the Cross,* 375; Shabazz, "Malcolm X as a Husband and Father," 134; Malcolm X, *Autobiography,* 235, 395, 422, 429–30; B. Perry, *Malcolm,* 189. Alex Haley reported that both Malcolm and Martin were "obsessed with their work but felt guilty about being away from their families." See "Alex Haley Remembers Malcolm X," 118.

50. Betty said in an interview that "her husband's relatives, many of whom still live in Michigan, were not much help" to her and her children. "When the children wanted aunts or uncles," she continued, "my friends became that because we didn't know that much about Malcolm's family because they didn't come near us." Concerning Malcolm's brothers Wilfred and Philbert Little, Betty declared: "They elected to stay in the Black Muslim movement and not support their brother. Even in death, they did not support him." Martin's family situation was much better because his parents, aunts, and uncles were always there to help Coretta with the children. See Gilchrist, "Some Worry the Leader's Message Will Be Lost," 5G; Baldwin, *Balm,* 149.

51. Baldwin, *Balm,* 134–35; "Alex Haley Remembers Malcolm X," 118; Shabazz, "Malcolm X as a Husband and Father," 134. Martin was known to receive letters from friends who wondered "how one can effectively play the role of Pastor, Husband, Father and Public Leader when every role demands so much from the individual." For example, see Carson, *Papers,* 3:441.

52. Shabazz, "Malcolm X as a Husband and Father," 134; Shabazz, "Remembering Malcolm X," 61. Betty recalls that Malcolm enjoyed "coming home to a house

filled with the odor of baked bread." See Shabazz, "The Legacy of My Husband," 176.

53. Baldwin, *Balm,* 135–36; C. S. King, *My Life,* 200.

54. Garrow, *Bearing the Cross,* 374–75. The charge that King had extramarital affairs has been widely discussed, particularly by white scholars, since the 1980s. Such accounts appeal to the soap opera mentality so pervasive in our society. The fact that white male writers like David J. Garrow and Taylor Branch, who have given excessive attention to King's sexual liaisons, have received Pulitzer Prizes for their works is quite interesting, thus calling to mind William Styron's winning of a Pulitzer Prize for a work that claims that Nat Turner had an unconquerable lust for a white woman. See Garrow, *The FBI and Martin Luther King Jr.,* 103, 124–26, 130; Branch, *Pillar of Fire,* 197, 207, 518, 525, 533; Branch, *Parting the Waters,* 239, 242, 860–62; Styron, *The Confessions of Nat Turner,* 108, 168, 344, 349, 351, 370; Clarke, *William Styron's Nat Turner,* viii, 6. Aside from the aforementioned works by Garrow and Branch, other sources that make significant references to King's extramarital affairs are Gallen and Friedly, *Martin Luther King Jr.,* 66, 623–26; Abernathy, *And the Walls Came Tumbling Down,* 434–36, 470–75; Sanders, *Empowerment Ethics,* 97–98; Oates, *Let the Trumpet Sound,* 265, 283; Powers, *I Shared the Dream,* 145–48, 156, 161–62, 172–74, 185, 226–27; Baldwin, *Balm,* 155.

55. Garrow, *Bearing the Cross,* 375. In his monthly column in *Ebony* entitled "Advice for Living," printed from August 1957 to December 1958, Martin frequently urged readers to follow the highest standards of honesty and integrity in their courtships and marriages. For examples, see King, "Advice for Living," April 1958 and June 1958. In his May 1958 column, he declared that "good morals and knowing how to make a home . . . are the things that ultimately count in making a meaningful relationship." The vast gulf between his ideas and lifestyle, particularly as related to marriage, obviously indicates that he, like all humans, was to some extent a creature of contradictions. If pressed on the inconsistencies between what he taught and how he lived with respect to marriage, he, being the intellectual that he was, could have easily explained within the context of Reinhold Niebuhr's concept of the dialectical or paradoxical nature of humans, which holds that persons are capable of both enormous evil and amazing goodness. See King, "Advice for Living," May 1958, 112.

56. Cone, *Martin and Malcolm and America,* 276. Referring to the "storm of controversy" provoked in the 1980s and 1990s by the revelation of "King's many adulteries," Arnold Rampersad perceptively states that "although King had been a minister and had based his career as a Civil Rights activist on moral grounds, virtually none of his colleagues and admirers took this revelation (if it was a revelation to them) as reason enough to break with him, or with his memory as an icon of morality. . . . Even his widow has been steadfast in her loyalty to King either by ignoring or by denying the evidence of his infidelities." See Rampersad, "The Color of His Eyes: Bruce Perry's Malcolm and Malcolm's Malcolm," in Wood, *Malcolm X in Our Own Image,* 132. Another scholar contends that "King was never at ease with the apparent conflict between the depersonalization caused by sexual promiscuity and his own teachings concerning the necessity of respecting persons." See Baker-Fletcher, *Somebodyness,* 183.

57. MacGregor, "The Week in Books," 47; Rampersad, "The Color of His Eyes," 132–33; Shabazz, "Loving and Losing Malcolm," 109; "Alex Haley Remembers Malcolm X," 118.

58. "Alex Haley Remembers Malcolm X," 118; Shabazz, "Malcolm X as a Husband and Father," 138. This observation is supported by Malcolm's own testimony. For example, see Clark, *February 1965*, 192; Malcolm X, *Autobiography*, 294–95, 422, 430; B. Perry, *Malcolm*, 189–90.

59. Garrow, *Bearing the Cross*, 374; Washington, *A Testament of Hope*, 371; Abernathy, *And the Walls Came Tumbling Down*, 480–82; Branch, *Pillar of Fire*, 197. Coretta reports that Martin believed that "much of the corruption in our society stems from the desire to acquire material things—houses and land and cars." He "would have preferred to have none of these things." C. S. King, *My Life*, 2–3, 88, 164–65. King often lashed out at persons who were "too prone to judge success by the index of" their "salaries and the size of the wheel base on" their "automobiles, and not by the quality of" their "service and relationship to humanity." He felt that this tendency grew out of an obsession with the capitalistic ethic. See King, *Strength to Love*, 102.

60. For Malcolm and Martin, this lesson was especially important for African Americans generally because of the need for their collective struggle against white racism and oppression. See Shabazz, "Malcolm X as a Husband and Father," 138, 142–43; C. S. King, *My Life*, 2–3, 91–92, 301, 312–14; Shabazz, "Loving and Losing Malcolm," 51–52, 109–10, 112; Shabazz, "The Legacy of My Husband," 176; Baldwin, *Balm*, 145–46. Betty often recalled those times when Malcolm read to her and instructed her in other ways, but she also mentioned the lessons Malcolm learned from her. See Shabazz, "Remembering Malcolm X," 61; DeCaro, *On the Side of My People*, 292–93.

61. Shabazz, "Loving and Losing Malcolm," 50, 52; Laughinghouse, "Mothers of the Civil Rights Movement," 35, 38–39; Coleman, "A Mother's Struggle."

62. "Martin Luther King Jr.: His Widow Keeps His Dream Alive"; "'The Woman behind the King Anniversary' Featured in January *Ebony* Magazine," 10; Baldwin, "The Making of a Dreamer," 639–40; Laughinghouse, "Mothers of the Civil Rights Movement," 35–37; Norment, "Coretta Scott King," 116–18.

63. Laughinghouse, "Mothers of the Civil Rights Movement," 35–39; Shabazz, "The Legacy of My Husband," 182; A. Davis, "On Malcolm X," 37; Coleman, "A Mother's Struggle." Also see King, "South Africa: Selected Quotes, 1973–1986," 30–31; C. S. King, "Empowering Women Will Benefit Nation," 9A; Baldwin, *To Make the Wounded Whole*, 239–42; Baldwin, *Toward the Beloved Community*, 82, 113, 116–17, 122–27, 145, 161, 163; C. S. King, "U.S. Needs More Willing Women Participants in Foreign Policy," 9A.

64. Crawford et al., *Women in the Civil Rights Movement*, xix; Atwater, "Editorial: The Voices of African-American Women in the Civil Rights Movement," 539–40; Millner, "Recasting Civil Rights Leadership," 668; Sanders, *Empowerment Ethics*, 99; Cone, *Martin and Malcolm and America*, 271–80. In their efforts to reinterpret the historic civil rights struggle in light of the contributions of black women, the aforementioned works reflect a discernible shift in the scholarship. How-

ever, some revisionist works that claim to give a broader picture of leadership in the modern phase of the civil rights struggle fail to adequately treat women. For example, see Ward and Badger, *The Making of Martin Luther King Jr.,* 1–12.

65. Franklin, "The Forerunners," 35; Cone, *Martin and Malcolm and America,* 274. The power of this contention is not diminished by the fact that Martin was more apt than Malcolm to cite biblical passages—in letters, speeches, and sermons—that opposed female subordination. One such passage was Galatians 3:28, in which "Paul states that there is neither Jew nor Greek, there is neither slave nor free, there is neither male nor female for you are all one in Christ Jesus." See Carson, *Papers,* 3:378–79; King, *The Trumpet of Conscience,* 72.

66. Joseph and Lewis, *Common Differences,* 110. For a more lengthy treatment of the various roles assumed by females, see Lynne Olson, *Freedom's Daughters,* and Collier-Thomas and Franklin, *Sisters in the Struggle.*

67. Cone, *Martin and Malcolm and America,* 277; Nance, "Hearing the Missing Voice," 551. The failure on the part of some black women and men to see both racism and sexism as unquestionably evil and immoral, as being equally destructive of their people, is clearly indicative of how oppression from outsiders also has the effect of producing self-oppression within a group. Speaking generally of female activists, one source observes, "Even when Black women started complaining about their roles in the Civil Rights Movement organizations, their complaints were directed mainly at their roles within the groups themselves." See Joseph and Lewis, *Common Differences,* 110.

68. Cone, *Martin and Malcolm and America,* 273–74. On one occasion, King did describe "the striking similarity between Dr. Margaret Sanger's fight for recognition and the Negro's struggle for equality." In comparing the struggle of Sanger (1879–1966), the champion of the birth control movement in America, to that of his own people, King demonstrated that he was not completely oblivious to the relationship between sexism and racism in America. See "Martin Luther King Supports Voluntary Family Planning Legislation," *Congressional Record—Senate,* 10 May 1966, 10161.

69. Quoted in Mills, *This Little Light of Mine,* 144. Malcolm held that women should be protected from the white man's violence, not exposed to it as participants in demonstrations. Bayard Rustin said that in this respect, Malcolm X was "the great male feminist, and all the women loved him for it," a point open to debate. See Breitman, *Malcolm X Speaks,* 107, 113; Lomax, *When the Word Is Given,* 153; Elijah Muhammad, *The Supreme Wisdom,* 9; Goldman, *Death and Life,* 75–76; A. Davis, "Meditations on the Legacy of Malcolm X," in Wood, *Malcolm X in Our Own Image,* 36–37; Lincoln, *Black Muslims,* 150; S. Clark, *February 1965,* 61, 86–87; B. Perry, *Malcolm X: The Last Speeches,* 121. Kay Mills is right in saying that Malcolm and Martin "viewed men's role toward women as protector rather than as equal." See Mills, *This Little Light of Mine,* 141.

70. C. S. King, *My Life,* 162. Andrew Young reports that King "was somewhat uncomfortable around assertive women," a problem he attributed to King's "need to be free of that strong matriarchial influence" of his mother, Alberta King, who controlled Daddy King, the church, and Martin. Quoted in Giddings, *When and Where I Enter,* 312–13. More recent studies identify the chauvinism of male leaders as reflec-

tive of broader patterns of sexism in the movement and in the society. See John Lewis, *Walking with the Wind,* 92; Halberstam, *The Children,* 219, 532.

71. Dallard, *Ella Baker,* 76–77. See also Cone, *Martin and Malcolm and America,* 278; Garrow, *Bearing the Cross,* 141, 655n. 12; and Hine, *Hine Sight: Black Women,* 23. Martin's ambivalent attitude toward women clearly surfaced in his relations with Ella Baker. Despite the problems he had with her assertiveness, he insisted that women like her were essential to the success of the movement: "[T]he women of the nation and the south have a tremendous role to play in this tense period of transition. This is one of the reasons we employed a woman as associate director of the Southern Christian Leadership Conference. We felt the need of bringing together this vast wealth of latent potential." King to Whickam, 7 July 1958. See also Sandra Jones to King, 26 May 1961.

72. Quoted in Fairclough, *To Redeem the Soul of America,* 49–50, and Cone, *Martin and Malcolm and America,* 278. In *Bearing the Cross,* Garrow quotes Cotton as saying, "I'm always asked to take the notes, I'm always asked to go fix Dr. King some coffee. . . . I did it, too. . . . They were sexist male preachers" who "grew up in a sexist culture" (376).

73. Brown, *Septima Clark,* 77–79. See also Weisenfeld and Newman, *This Far by Faith,* 306–10, 312n.24; Fairclough, *To Redeem the Soul of America,* 49–50. James Lawson recalls that "Martin had real problems with having a woman in a high position." Cheryl Sanders rightly criticizes contemporary black male scholars who "seem to stumble over the question of [Martin's] relation to women and attitudes toward female leadership." See Garrow, *Bearing the Cross,* 141; Sanders, *Empowerment Ethics,* 97–98; Powers, *I Shared the Dream,* 125. Ralph Abernathy says essentially nothing about the great contributions that Baker, Cotton, and Clark made to the SCLC in his book *And the Walls Came Tumbling Down.*

74. Garrow, *Bearing the Cross,* 131–34, 141. According to one report, Baker's conflict with King and the SCLC accounted for the fact that she was not asked to speak at the celebrated March on Washington in 1963, where King delivered his speech "I Have a Dream." No women were chosen to be on the program initially, and Baker did not go to Washington. See Dallard, *Ella Baker,* 99; Grant, *Ella Baker: Freedom Bound,* 107–11; Mills, *This Little Light of Mine,* 44.

75. See Carson, *Papers,* 3:378–79; King, *Why We Can't Wait,* 33; Baldwin, *To Make the Wounded Whole,* 14. Martin and Malcolm seemed ambivalent in that both expressed a belief in social movements that draw on the values, energies, and resources of the masses, while embracing the traditional, male-dominated charismatic leadership model. See Baldwin, *Balm,* 269n.136; Breitman, *Malcolm X Speaks,* 3–17.

76. Nance, "Hearing the Missing Voice," 552–53; Reagon, "Women as Culture Carriers in the Civil Rights Movement," in Crawford et al., *Women in the Civil Rights Movement,* 213; Hamlet, "Fannie Lou Hamer: The Unquenchable Spirit," 569.

77. Britton, interview with Ella Baker, 37. See also V. Davis, "Midwifery and Grassroots Politics," 2–3. One scholar treats Baker's concept of leadership under the rubric of "participatory democracy." See Mueller, "Ella Baker and the Origins of 'Participatory Democracy,'" in Crawford et al., *Women in the Civil Rights Move-*

ment, 53–64. For other sources that devote attention to Baker's leadership model, see Atwater, "Editorial: The Voices of African-American Women," 541; Nance, "Hearing the Missing Voice," 552–53; Elliot, "Ella Baker: Free Agent in the Civil Rights Movement"; Dallard, *Ella Baker,* 76–77; Hine, *Hine Sight,* 23; Giddings, *When and Where I Enter,* 312; Cone, *Martin and Malcolm and America,* 278; Garrow, *Bearing the Cross,* 141, 655n.12; Baldwin, *Balm,* 269–70; Mills, *This Little Light of Mine,* 52; Hine and Thompson, *A Shining Thread of Hope,* 279.

78. V. Davis, "Midwifery and Grassroots Politics," 1–3, 11–24; Baldwin, *Balm,* 269–70; Hine, *Hine Sight,* 23; Hine and Thompson, *A Shining Thread of Hope,* 279; Mills, *This Little Light of Mine,* 52. Vanessa Davis is quite right in saying that Baker's leadership philosophy "was unique in the civil rights movement of the 1950s and 1960s."

79. Brown, *Septima Clark,* 77–78. King always thought of social movements as leader-centered in the traditional sense, as his reflections on the crusade against apartheid in South Africa indicate. See Baldwin, *Toward the Beloved Community,* 18–19, 35–36, 53.

80. Mills, *This Little Light of Mine,* 45; Baldwin, *Balm,* 243–72; Fairclough, *To Redeem the Soul of America,* 50; Oates, *Let the Trumpet Sound,* 124. Martin's own leadership evoked memories of his slave forebears yearning—as expressed in sermon, song, and tale—for a Moses "going down in Egyptland, telling old Pharaoh to let my people go." See Courlander, *Negro Folk Music, U.S.A.,* 42–43; Smylie, "On Jesus, Pharaoh, and the Chosen People."

81. Baldwin, *Balm,* 269; Kingsbury, "Author Discusses Nashville's Role in Civil Rights Movement," 3.

82. Martin was at times as critical of Richardson's confrontational, uncompromising style as he was of Malcolm's. One scholar notes that Richardson's "leanings were always more consistent with those of Malcolm X over Mohandas Gandhi or Martin Luther King Jr." See Millner, "Recasting Civil Rights Leadership," 671–72, 677–86. See also Foeman, "Gloria Richardson," 608, 610; "Mrs. Richardson Hails Support of Malcolm X," 4.

83. Dallard, *Ella Baker,* 78. "Thanks to the counsel of Dr. King and, probably, the overwhelming number of women involved," write two black female scholars, "the demonstrations remained nonviolent." See Hine and Thompson, *A Shining Thread of Hope,* 279. As one writer puts it, "Malcolm spoke a vastly different language than Martin Luther King or Fannie Lou Hamer; he urged his listeners to learn the language of the violent white racist." See Mills, *This Little Light of Mine,* 142, 177, 324–25.

84. Clark also credited King with making "black people aware of their blackness and not ashamed of being black," a comment she would have made without hesitation concerning Malcolm. See C. Brown, *Septima Clark,* 78; Weisenfeld and Newman, *This Far by Faith,* 307.

85. Malcolm X, *Autobiography,* 272; King, *Stride toward Freedom,* 43–47, 55, 63, 69; Friese, *Rosa Parks,* 66; Carson, *Papers,* 3:302; King, "Speech at a Rally," Crawfordville, Ga., 2; King to Whickam, 7 July 1958.

86. It is difficult to determine why King had virtually nothing to say about Fannie Lou Hamer. Given his belief that "the 'No D' is just as significant as the Ph.D.," it is

doubtful that he ignored her due to the fact that she was unlettered. However, it is reported that King's wife, Coretta, refused on one occasion to share a platform with Hamer for that reason. Hamer responded: "I may not have all the education but I do have common sense, and I know how to treat people." See Foeman, "Gloria Richardson," 610; Millner, "Recasting Civil Rights Leadership," 683; Cone, *Martin and Malcolm and America,* 278–79; Mills, *This Little Light of Mine,* 140, 144, 249, 325; Baker-Fletcher, *Somebodyness,* 157; King, *Where Do We Go from Here?* 132; Breitman, *Malcolm X Speaks,* 13; Weisenfeld and Newman, *This Far by Faith,* 300.

87. King to Paterson, 9 April 1962.

88. Garrow, *The Montgomery Bus Boycott and the Women Who Started It,* ix–x; Mills, *This Little Light of Mine,* 25; Weisenfeld and Newman, *This Far by Faith,* 308; Dallard, *Ella Baker,* 67.

89. Mills, *This Little Light of Mine,* 217. Referring to the Poor People's Campaign, Paula Giddings notes that the women of the NWRO "were peeved when King started to beat that drum without even acknowledging their efforts—or their knowledge of the issue. Yet King needed the NWRO, which by 1968 was ten thousand strong and had chapters throughout the country." See Giddings, *When and Where I Enter,* 312–13. These women have been appropriately referred to as "trailblazers" and "torchbearers" because their "heroic acts initiated specific events" and because they carried on the long-standing "struggle for reform." See Crawford et al., *Women in the Civil Rights Movement,* xv, xix.

90. Davis, "'Sisters and Brothers All': Gender, Race, Class, and Community Organizing in the Mississippi Freedom Democratic Party," 8n.6; Reagon, "Women as Culture Carriers in the Civil Rights Movement," in Crawford et al., *Women in the Civil Rights Movement,* 203–17.

91. Speaking of her husband, Betty Shabazz once wrote: "The black woman, he believed, is the sustainer of life, which she had to be because of circumstances, the emotional supporter of the family, the maintainer and teacher of culture, the vital force in any movement." See Shabazz, "The Legacy of My Husband," 180. For Martin's best statement on women as the bearers and communicators of vital cultural values and traditions, see King, "What a Mother Should Tell Her Child"; King, "Training Your Child in Love."

92. Malcolm made some very positive comments about Mahalia Jackson and her rise from poverty to fame as a gospel artist, but his negative view of the black church kept him from comprehending her full significance as a cultural leader, carrier, and communicator in the freedom movement. Martin was different precisely because of his lifelong association with and love for the black church. See Malcolm X, *Autobiography,* 221–22; Baldwin, *Balm,* 86, 270n.137, 291n.61.

93. King, "Statement Regarding Mahalia Jackson," 26 November 1963.

94. King to Jackson, 10 January 1964. King loved so many of the gospel songs sung by Mahalia Jackson, among which are "Precious Lord, Take My Hand," "How I Got Over," "Move On Up a Little Higher," and "Beulah Land." Baldwin, interview with Abernathy, 7 March 1987.

95. For some of the best discussions of Hamer as an artist, see Reagon, "Women as Culture Carriers in the Civil Rights Movement," 203–16; Mills, *This Little Light*

of Mine, 19–21, 41–42, 84–86, 306–7. The songs of the movement have become the inspiration for Reagon's rise as a brilliant cultural artist and historian. See Bernice Johnson Reagon's 1975 dissertation, "Songs of the Civil Rights Movement, 1955–1965." One scholar holds that King's "great insight and application of nonviolence" was essentially "a refining of the faith of the mothers" as expressed through "the symbols and songs of the movement." See Wade-Gayles, *My Soul Is a Witness,* 45, 58.

96. King, *Stride toward Freedom,* 10; King, "The Time for Freedom Has Come," 10 September 1961, 1. For insights into this role of communal or collective mothering, see Reagon, "Women as Culture Carriers in the Civil Rights Movement," 203–16; Davis, "'Sisters and Brothers All,'" 8. For one of King's references to the importance of recognizing mothers, see Carson, *Papers,* 3:266–67.

97. Breitman, *Malcolm X Speaks,* 107, 109, 111, 113–14; Mills, *This Little Light of Mine,* 140–44, 151, 161; C. S. King, *My Life,* 3; Baldwin, *Toward the Beloved Community,* 38, 40, 80.

98. Mueller, "Ella Baker and the Origins of 'Participatory Democracy,'" 51–68; V. Davis, "'Sisters and Brothers All': The Mississippi Freedom Democratic Party and the Struggle for Political Equality."

99. Perry, *Malcolm X: The Last Speeches,* 31; Lomax, *When the Word Is Given,* 156, 198–99; Gallen, *A Malcolm X Reader,* 102–3. Peter Goldman is right in contending that Malcolm "argued as heatedly as any unregenerate Southern segregationist that the real purpose of the integrationists was intermarriage." See Goldman, *Death and Life,* 72.

100. Stone, "The Pilgrimage of Malcolm X," 4–5; Lomax, *When the Word Is Given,* 199; Gallen, *A Malcolm X Reader,* 102; Goldman, *Death and Life,* 72.

101. Goldman, *Death and Life,* 72; Malcolm X, *Autobiography,* 425; Breitman, *Malcolm X Speaks,* 197. It is quite obvious that such a transition in thought was never necessary for King, who always affirmed the most intimate of relationships between the races on the grounds that there is "no justification in the Bible for" standing "against interracial marriages," and "that marriage is a mutual agreement between two individuals and not between two races," positions that Malcolm came to accept ultimately. At the same time, King made it clear to white women and whites in general that his quest for integration had nothing to do with promoting interracial marriages. See Martin Luther King, "Advice for Living," *Ebony,* February, March, June, and October 1958; Malcolm X, *Autobiography,* 425; King, *Where Do We Go from Here?* 89; King, "Speech at a Voter Registration Rally," Louisville, Kentucky, 2 August 1967, 2–3.

102. Burrow, "Some African-American Males' Perspectives," 69.

103. Cone, *Martin and Malcolm and America,* 275; Goldman, *Death and Life,* 245; Burrow, "Some African-American Males' Perspectives," 69; Breitman, *By Any Means Necessary,* 77. Gloria Richardson welcomed Malcolm's maturing perspective. See "Mrs. Richardson Hails Support of Malcolm X," 4.

104. Breitman, *By Any Means Necessary,* 179. Clenora Hudson-Weems argues that the "pronounced shift" in Malcolm's ideology during the last year of his life included, "among many things, a return to his positive attitude toward women." See Hudson-Weems, "From Malcolm Little to El Hajj Malik El Shabazz," 26, 29. Shirley

Graham Du Bois declares that "Malcolm X left Ghana for the United States with the song of unity on his lips," a spirit that undoubtedly had implications for his developing attitude toward women and their role in the struggle against oppression worldwide. See S. G. Du Bois, "The Beginning, Not the End," in Clarke, *Malcolm X: The Man and His Times,* 125.

105. Baldwin, interview with Abernathy, 7 May 1987; King, "Address at the Fiftieth Anniversary of the Women's International League," 1; Baldwin, *Toward the Beloved Community,* 30, 125, 170–75; King, "Epitaph for a First Lady"; C. Brown, *Septima Clark,* 79.

106. "Feminism" is most commonly used in reference to the white women's movement. The "womanist" concept has emerged since the late 1980s as a part of religious discourse. As Kelly Brown Douglas has stated, "Various black feminist ethicists, biblical scholars, and theologians have adopted the term 'womanist' as a way of indicating the distinctiveness of black women's experience in church and society. . . . Womanist symbolizes black women's resistance to their multidimensional oppression." See Douglas, "God Is as Christ Does: Toward a Womanist Theology," 7–8.

107. Cone, *Martin and Malcolm and America,* 274, 276; Davis, "On Malcolm X," 37; C. S. King, *My Life,* 193–95, 284–85.

108. See Daly, *Beyond God the Father,* 163–64; C. Brown, *Septima Clark,* 78; Joseph and Lewis, *Common Differences,* 110; Murray, *Autobiography of a Black Activist, Feminist, Lawyer, Priest, and Poet,* 23–24; Perry, *Teaching Malcolm X,* 199–205.

109. Sanders, *Empowerment Ethics,* 99–102; P. Collins, *Black Feminist Thought,* 197; Baldwin, *To Make the Wounded Whole,* 156–59; Baldwin, *Toward the Beloved Community,* 174.

110. Cannon, *Black Womanist Ethics,* 21–24, 163, 165–67, 169–74; Grant, "The Sin of Servanthood and the Deliverance of Discipleship," in Townes, *A Troubling in My Soul,* 213–14; Gilkes, "We Have a Beautiful Mother," in Sanders, *Living the Intersection,* 37. For impressive research that puts Martin, and to a much lesser extent Malcolm, in dialogue with Barbara Jordan around the communitarian ideal, see Holmes, "Barbara Jordan's Speeches," 180–202. Also see P. Collins, *Black Feminist Thought,* 197; Sanders, *Empowerment Ethics,* 100–101; Baldwin, *Toward the Beloved Community,* 174; Asante, *Malcolm X as Cultural Hero,* 25–34.

111. Murray, *Autobiography,* 232, 377, 383, 389, 394, 417; Murray, "Black Theology and Feminist Theology," in Cone and Wilmore, *Black Theology: A Documentary History,* 1:310–11; Collier-Thomas, *Daughters of Thunder,* 228, 253–54, 261, 300n.47.

112. Sanders concludes, "Because of the intensity and effectiveness of his outreach to poor black males in particular," Malcolm "provides a more convincing incarnation of the transformed, remoralized black male than King does." See Sanders, *Empowerment Ethics,* 4, 34, 97–102, 109–10, 123, 134n.19. See also Hayes, *And Still We Rise,* 57–59, 61, 63–64, 70–71; Terrell, *Power in the Blood?* 77–83; Kirk-Duggan, *Refiner's Fire,* 90–92.

113. Williams, *Sisters in the Wilderness,* 135–36, 200, 210, 275n.5; Williams, "Afrocentrism and Male-Female Relations," in Sanders, *Living the Intersection,* 46,

48; Baldwin, *Toward the Beloved Community,* 170–74. I would submit that while King himself was sexist, the communitarian ideal he articulated was not. It is clear that for him, community in the most genuine sense transcended all artificial human barriers. This is how he understood Paul's words in Galatians 3:28. See Williams, "Between Hagar and Jezebel," 1–20.

114. Douglas, *The Black Christ,* 6–7, 37–51, 97; Douglas, "God Is as Christ Does," 14–16.

115. Bridges, *Resurrection Song,* 121, 130–50.

116. Giovanni also lashes out at Lee for trashing King in his film, insisting that both King and Malcolm "gave their lives for the dignity and integrity of Black people." Giovanni, *Racism 101,* 64, 67, 70–73; Angelou, *All God's Children Need Traveling Shoes,* 129; Davis, "Meditations on the Legacy of Malcolm X," 36–46.

117. Davis, "On Malcolm X," 36–37.

118. See Coughlin, "Politics and Commerce in the Rebirth of Malcolm X," A14; Collins, "Learning to Think for Ourselves," in Theresa Perry, *Teaching Malcolm X,* 201. Patricia Collins's essay also appears in Wood, *Malcolm X in Our Own Image,* 59–85.

119. Collins explains that Malcolm identified two opposing categories of women: the "Eves" who deceptively challenged male authority by using their sexuality for personal gain, and the "Madonnas" or "archetypal wives and mothers who sacrifice everything for their husbands and children." See P. Collins, "Learning to Think for Ourselves," 199–202.

120. Davis, "Meditations on the Legacy of Malcolm X," 37–38. Also see Patricia Robinson, "Malcolm X, Our Revolutionary Son and Brother," in Clarke, *Malcolm X: The Man and His Times,* 56–63.

121. Davis, "On Malcolm X," 37. See also Davis, "Meditations on the Legacy of Malcolm X," 44–46.

122. Collins, "Learning to Think for Ourselves," 204. Collins declares that she sees "hopeful signs" in the last year of Malcolm's life. See also Coughlin, "Politics and Commerce," A14. James H. Cone also supports this view, despite his contention that Malcolm and Martin actually changed very little, when compared with Frederick Douglass and W.E.B. Du Bois, on the female question. See Cone, *Martin and Malcolm and America,* 274, 278.

123. Quoted in Raines, *My Soul Is Rested,* 433. See also Cone, *Martin and Malcolm and America,* 278, 280; Garrow, *Bearing the Cross,* 376. There is reason to believe that Septima Clark would have agreed with Cotton on King's capacity to come to terms with the women's movement, for she spoke of his tremendous ability to grow in mind and heart. See C. Brown, *Septima Clark,* 103. It is also important to note that as far back as the early 1950s, King was familiar with the theology of Georgia Harkness, one of the first women to teach at Garrett Seminary in Evanston, Ill. In a letter to Harkness, 8 November 1958, King wrote: "I have long admired your Christian witness and your sound theology."

124. It is important to point out, however, that Pauli Murray felt that King "demonstrated the power of love to transcend divisions of race, sex, or class." See Murray, *Autobiography,* 417.

125. Joseph and Lewis, *Common Differences,* 39. Burrow treats Malcolm in this regard, Baker-Fletcher and Erskine focus on King, and Cone treats both Malcolm and King. See Burrow, "Some African-American Males' Perspectives," 68–69; Baker-Fletcher, *Somebodyness,* 172–86; Erskine, *King among the Theologians,* 159–71; Cone, *Martin and Malcolm and America,* 273–80. For a brief but thoughtful comment on the shortcomings of Erskine's work, which seeks to put womanist thinkers in dialogue with King, see Sanders, *Empowerment Ethics,* 100.

Chapter 6. A New Spirit of Resistance

1. Quoted in Lerner, *Black Women in White America,* 352.

2. Breitman, *By Any Means Necessary,* 163; Breitman, *Malcolm X Speaks,* 220–21.

3. King, *The Trumpet of Conscience,* 45; Ayres, *Wisdom of King,* 239.

4. See Halberstam, *The Children,* 3–727, and Lewis, *Walking with the Wind,* 11–475.

5. Malcolm occasionally said that "he was going to have six girls before he had a boy." At other times he envisioned having more and more children as long as they were healthy, but Betty's reply "was that he was going to have them by himself." Martin approached Coretta with the idea of being the father of eight children, but the couple compromised and decided on four. See Betty Shabazz, "Malcolm X as a Husband and Father," in Clarke, *Malcolm X: The Man and His Times,* 136–37; King, *My Life,* 98; Baldwin, *Balm,* 133–34.

6. Shabazz, "Malcolm X as a Husband and Father," 135–37; Malcolm X, *Autobiography,* 234–35; Perry, *Malcolm,* 327–28; Pamela Johnson, "Daughters of the Revolution," 104–5; Shabazz, "The Legacy of My Husband," 172, 176; King, *My Life,* 98–99, 149, 165, 189, 204.

7. Shabazz, "Malcolm X as a Husband and Father," 135–36; Shabazz, "Loving and Losing Malcolm," 109.

8. King, *My Life,* 97–99; King, "My Dream for My Children," 144.

9. One scholar makes the unconvincing claim that "Malcolm defeminized his daughters with masculine names" because "he longed for a son. . . . He talked about having one who would bear his name and carry on his work after his death. At times, he predicted that his next child would be a boy; at other times, he prophesied that the boy would be his seventh child. He said he'd name him after Patrice Lumumba." See Perry, *Malcolm,* 328, and Breitman, *By Any Means Necessary,* 64–65. King's desire for a son as his first child was apparently as strong as Malcolm's, though both were more concerned about having healthy children than they were about the issue of gender. See Shabazz, "Malcolm X as a Husband and Father," 136; King, *My Life,* 98.

10. Shabazz, "Malcolm X as a Husband and Father," 136; C. S. King, *My Life,* 99. Coretta's statement here is supported by Martin's own reflections on the emotional strength he received from Yolanda in the earliest stages of the Montgomery protest. Martin called the child "the darling of my life" and "the boss of the family," and noted that "I'd come in night after night and see that little, gentle smile." See King, "Thou Fool," 10–11; Albert and Hoffman, *We Shall Overcome,* 20; Carson et al.,

Papers of Martin Luther King Jr. (hereafter referred to as Carson, *Papers*), 3:311; King Sr., *Daddy King,* 181.

11. Perry, *Malcolm,* 326–27.

12. Malcolm X, *Autobiography,* 423–24; Gallen et al., *Malcolm X as They Knew Him,* 247; Baldwin, *Balm,* 135; Shabazz, "Loving and Losing Malcolm," 107; "Alex Haley Remembers Malcolm X," 118; *Martin Luther King Jr.: A Personal Portrait,* videotape; C. S. King, *My Life,* 82.

13. Breitman, *Malcolm X Speaks,* 157–58; Clark, *February 1965,* 76; Barboza, *American Jihad,* 209; *Martin Luther King Jr.: A Personal Portrait,* videotape; Baldwin, *Balm,* 147; C. S. King, *My Life,* 256.

14. Shabazz, "Malcolm X as a Husband and Father," 135. Coretta felt that it was so important for their children "not to develop a fear of jail-going," which they normally would have associated with wrongdoing, "but rather to feel it a badge of honor." See King, *My Life,* 175–76, 283; *Martin Luther King Jr.: A Personal Portrait,* videotape; Baldwin, *Balm,* 147.

15. Bailey, "The Ties That Bind," 102; "Alex Haley Remembers Malcolm X," 118, 122; Shabazz, "Malcolm X as a Husband and Father," 134; Shabazz, "The Legacy of My Husband," 176; Gallen et al., *Malcolm X as They Knew Him,* 248.

16. King, "My Dream for My Children," 144. See also Johnson, "King's Children Tell How They Remember Him," 23.

17. King, *My Life,* 78. Yolanda recalls that "Daddy used to love to tell jokes—a whole lot of them. He could tell jokes with such a straight, poker face that it only added to the humor." See "I Remember Martin," 38. See also Johnson, "King's Children Tell How They Remember Him," 18–29; King, "My Dream for My Children," 144.

18. Shabazz, "The Longest Prayer," 154; P. Johnson, "Daughters of the Revolution," 98, 105; Bailey, "The Ties That Bind," 102; Pierce, "The Legacy of Martin Luther King," 28, 30, 32; King, *My Life,* 165–66.

19. Shabazz, "Malcolm X as a Husband and Father," 136; Shabazz, "The Legacy of My Husband," 176; Reddick, *Crusader without Violence,* 5–8; Baldwin, *Balm,* 156–57; Perry, *Malcolm: The Life of a Man,* 327.

20. Shabazz, "The Legacy of My Husband," 176. According to Betty Shabazz, Malcolm felt that she should be particularly "strict with Attallah because he could see a lot of wildness in her that needed strictness and proper direction. . . . He saw in her a lot of traits that he himself had possessed." See Shabazz, "Malcolm X as a Husband and Father," 136.

21. Reddick, *Crusader without Violence,* 5; Baldwin, *Balm,* 157; Smith, *The Ethics of Martin Luther King Jr.,* 94–98; Baldwin, interview with Bernard S. Lee; Baldwin, *To Make the Wounded Whole,* 136.

22. Shabazz, "Malcolm X as a Husband and Father," 136; Shabazz, "The Legacy of My Husband," 176, 178, 180. For interesting comments on the values that Malcolm sought to convey to his daughter, Attallah, see Barboza, *American Jihad,* 205–12.

23. Quoted in Pierce, "Widow of Malcolm X Tells of Life with Him, without

Him," 23; Johnson, "King's Children Tell How They Remember Him," 19. See also Baldwin, *Balm*, 140–41.

24. These views permeate much of Malcolm X, *Malcolm X on Afro-American History*, 3–74. Also see King, *My Life*, 196, 233; King, *Where Do We Go from Here?* 195–96; Washington, *A Testament of Hope*, 219; King, "My Dream for My Children," 77.

25. Breitman, *By Any Means Necessary*, 64; King, *My Life*, 16, 196–97, 260, 263–64; Johnson, "King's Children Tell How They Remember Him," 18–19; King, "My Dream for My Children," 144.

26. King, *My Life*, 4, 179, 195, 197, 234; Baldwin, *Balm*, 140.

27. Quoted in Washington, *A Testament of Hope*, 342.

28. Pierce, "Widow of Malcolm X Tells of Life with Him," 23; DeCaro, *On the Side of My People*, 293; "Memorable Photos of Martin Luther King Jr.: Pictorial Legacy Captures Charismatic Personality," 88; Shabazz, "The Legacy of My Husband," 178; *Martin Luther King Jr., 1929–1968: An Ebony Picture Biography*, 25; "Mother, Books Help Bunny Remember Her Father," 28.

29. A. Shabazz, "The Longest Prayer," 154. This piece is part of a more extensive work by Malcolm's daughter, Attallah, which was recently published. See also Johnson, "King's Children Tell How They Remember Him," 20–21; Malcolm X, *Autobiography*, 438; Shabazz, "Malcolm X as a Husband and Father," 142–43.

30. Johnson, "King's Children Tell How They Remember Him," 21; Pierce, "The Legacy of Martin Luther King," 32.

31. Quoted in Johnson, "Daughters of the Revolution," 105. Also see Shabazz, "The Legacy of My Husband," 176.

32. "Mother, Books Help Bunny Remember Her Father," 28; Johnson, "King's Children Tell How They Remember Him," 27–28; Baldwin, *Balm*, 165; King, *My Life*, 296, 300, 307–8.

33. Young quoted in Pierce, "The Legacy of Martin Luther King," 156.

34. Bailey, "The Ties That Bind," 107; Shabazz, "The Longest Prayer," 72–74, 154–55; "Alex Haley Remembers Malcolm X," 122; Johnson, "Daughters of the Revolution," 105; "People Are Talking About . . . ," 54.

35. Johnson, "Daughters of the Revolution," 98; Haywood, "Yolanda King Stars in One-Woman Show about Teachings of Her Father, Martin Luther King Jr."; C. Roberts and S. Roberts, "Martin Luther King III: Can He Step Forward?" 4–5; Sack, "Sheen of the King Legacy Dims on New, More Profitable Path," A16; King, "Back Talk: Creating Our Own Work," 232.

36. Norment, "New Generation of Kings Take Over"; Zaslow, "Straight Talk: Dexter Scott King Accepts Destiny," 22; "MLK's Daughter Preaches First Sermon at Ebenezer 20 Years after His Death," 6–7; "Fifteen Greatest Black Women Preachers: Experts and Leading Blacks Name Select Group of Ministers," 106; "The Rev. Bernice A. King Continues the Family's Preaching Legacy." For a book of sermons by Bernice A. King, which addresses the range of issues raised by Martin Luther King Jr., see Bernice King, *Hard Questions, Heart Answers*, 3–175. Also see "King Family Arrested and Jailed for Embassy Protest," 5; Baldwin, *Toward the Beloved Community*, 123; "Businessmen, King's Children Help Keep His Dream Alive."

37. Muhammad and Muhammad, "A Step toward Healing," 3; Dwyer et al., "Malcolm X Grandson Sorry: Psych Tests Ok'd in Shabazz Arson," 7; Bruni, "Widow of Malcolm X Burned, Badly, in Fire at Yonkers Home," A1, A14; Baker et al., "Betty Shabazz: Symbol of Pride Succumbs in Bx. to Burn Wounds," 3; Sack, "Sheen of the King Legacy Dims," A1, A16; Sack, "Kings Cheapen Legacy, Some Say." The most scathing critiques of the King family are afforded in Dyson, *I May Not Get There with You*, 256–81; Dyson, "Reaping Riches: Profiting from Dr. King's Dream"; Pappas, *Plagiarism and the Culture War*, 175–86.

38. Clayton, "The Daughters of Malcolm X and Martin Luther King Team Up to Bring a Play of Hope to Kids," 99–100; Bailey, "The Ties That Bind," 107–8; "Alex Haley Remembers Malcolm X," 122; P. Johnson, "Daughters of the Revolution," 98, 105; Baldwin, "Malcolm X and Martin Luther King Jr.: What They Thought about Each Other," 411–12; Waddle, "Reject Hate, Daughters of Black Leaders Urge," 1B, 2B.

39. Breitman, *Malcolm X Speaks*, 93, 107; King, *The Trumpet of Conscience*, 27, 61, 69; King, "What Are Your New Year's Resolutions?" 1; King, "Revolucio per Amo."

40. Lincoln, *Black Muslims*, 150; King, *Stride toward Freedom*, 10.

41. See Carson, *Papers*, 1:109–12, 121; King, "A Talk to a Seventh Grade Class at George A. Towns Elementary School." One source supports the notion that King was interested in youth involvement in the movement as early as 1956. He endorsed and served as honorary chairman of the "Enroll for Freedom Campaign," which was started by student activists in New York in that year. See Carson, *Papers*, 3:439.

42. Quoted in Washington, *A Testament of Hope*, 21. See also Ayres, *Wisdom of King*, 238–39; King, *The Trumpet of Conscience*, 46.

43. King was referred to in some circles as the "advisor to the current student sit-in movement." See Wynn, "Introduction of Dr. King," October 1960, 1. King was particularly impressed with the student movement in Nashville, calling it "the best organized and the most disciplined in the Southland." See Lewis, *Walking with the Wind*, 117; Washington, *A Testament of Hope*, 94; King, "People in Action," 3 February 1962, 3; King, "The Time for Freedom Has Come," 10 September 1961, 2; King, "Statement to the Press at the Beginning of the Youth Leadership Conference," 15 April 1960, 1.

44. King went even further: "These young people have connected up with their own history—the slave revolts, the incomplete revolution of the Civil War, the brotherhood of colonial colored men in Africa and Asia. . . . They are an integral part of the history which is reshaping the world, replacing a dying order with modern democracy. They are doing this in a nation whose own birth spread new principles and shattered a medieval social society then dominating most of the globe." See Washington, *A Testament of Hope*, 95, 97–98.

45. Garrow, *Bearing the Cross*, 128–29, 143–44.

46. Carson, *In Struggle*, 19. Garrow reports that King really wanted the students to "identify with SCLC," but he soon decided "that would not be in the best interests of the students or SCLC," especially given the opposition of Ella Baker and the manner in which the organizing conference had been structured. See Garrow, *Bearing the*

Cross, 132–33; Young, *An Easy Burden,* 164; Albert and Hoffman, *We Shall Overcome,* 146.

47. Vanessa Davis reports that Baker "served as a bridge" for the students in SNCC, keeping "them in touch with the older and more established civil rights leaders while at the same time encouraging them to be their own people and allow the communities that they were working with to do the same." Davis further notes that Baker "was accepted as a woman with wisdom beyond the years and experiences of the students, yet she always allowed the students to make their own decisions and choices." Baker told the youth in SNCC: "Don't let anyone, especially the older folks, tell you what to do. Think and act for yourselves. Hold onto your energy and your vision. Keep it pure. Keep it real." See Davis, "Midwifery and Grassroots Politics," 15–16; Lewis, *Walking with the Wind,* 114. Goldman observes, "Even SNCC, at the radical Left edge of the movement, held back from Malcolm's embrace; its kids were hardly less scornful of King—they called him 'De Lawd' behind his back." See Goldman, *Death and Life,* 142. Baker held that "King's charismatic style of 'Moses-type' leadership, drawing as it did on the preacher-congregation relationship, hindered as much as it encouraged the emergence of self-reliance and political independence among participants." See Albert and Hoffman, *We Shall Overcome,* 146.

48. King to the Student Body of Jesse Crowell School, Albion, Mich., 1 December 1960, 2.

49. Carson, *In Struggle,* 31; Goldman, *Death and Life,* 95. Another source notes that Martin, in response to pressure from the young freedom riders, "answered, with some irritation in his voice, 'I think I should choose the time and place of my Golgotha.'" See King, *My Life,* 183–86; Lewis, *Walking with the Wind,* 166–67; Halberstam, *The Children,* 270–73.

50. Breitman, *By Any Means Necessary,* 163; Breitman, *Malcolm X Speaks,* 220–21.

51. King, *The Trumpet of Conscience,* 45–56; Ayres, *Wisdom of King,* 238–39; King, "Statement at a Rally to Support the Freedom Riders," 21 May 1961, 2; King, "The Time for Freedom Has Come," 1–3; King, "Statement to Freedom Riders," 1–5; King, "Statement on Freedom Rides," 1; King, "After Desegregation—What?"; Washington, *A Testament of Hope,* 52, 214.

52. King spoke and wrote extensively about the important contributions of students to the freedom cause in the early 1960s. See King, "After Desegregation—What?" See also King, *The Trumpet of Conscience,* 37–50; Washington, *A Testament of Hope,* 160–66. Also see Gilbert, "King Urges Youth Join in New Order," 1.

53. Malcolm X, *Autobiography,* 285; Karim, *End of White World Supremacy,* 18–19; Epps, *Speeches of Malcolm X at Harvard,* 15–191; King to Chalmers, 20 September 1961; Sarrat to King, 2 January 1963; King to Long, 24 April 1962.

54. Watley, *Roots of Resistance,* 65–66, 69–70; Breitman, *Malcolm X Speaks,* 13.

55. King, "Regarding the Influence of African Movements on U.S. Students," 3; Washington, *A Testament of Hope,* 162; King, "The Time for Freedom Has Come," 2–4.

56. King, *Why We Can't Wait,* 51–52. The term *Children's Crusade* is actually used to describe the activities of African-American youngsters in the Birmingham

campaign, code named Project C (Confrontation). See C. S. King's commercial recording, *Free at Last! Free at Last! His Truth Is Marching On,* and *My Life,* 214.

57. Quoted in Oates, *Let the Trumpet Sound,* 251. Malcolm actually called King "a chump" for even entertaining such an idea. See Lomax, *When the Word Is Given,* 85. Malcolm agonized over the fact that attack dogs, clubs, and high-pressure water hoses had been used on children in Birmingham. See Karim, *End of White World Supremacy,* 140.

58. King, *Why We Can't Wait,* 97–98.

59. Ibid., 96–97. For one of King's most profound arguments in favor of the use of children in Birmingham, one in which he denied the charge that "we have revealed a want of family feeling or a recklessness toward family security," see Ayres, *Wisdom of King,* 36.

60. King, *Why We Can't Wait,* 61.

61. Ibid., 98.

62. Breitman, *Malcolm X Speaks,* 16–17; Myers, *Malcolm X: By Any Means Necessary,* 130–31.

63. Breitman, *Malcolm X Speaks,* 43; Clark, *February 1965,* 61.

64. Quoted in Washington, *A Testament of Hope,* 221–22. Also see King, "Eulogy for the Martyred Children," 1–3; King, *Why We Can't Wait,* 112; King, *The Trumpet of Conscience,* 76.

65. Lewis, *Walking with the Wind,* 204–5.

66. Pierce, "Widow of Malcolm X Tells of Life with Him," 27; Gallen et al., *Malcolm X as They Knew Him,* 41.

67. "Remembering Malcolm at 60," 3; Breitman, *By Any Means Necessary,* 162; "Malcolm Maps Negro Vote Drive," 3.

68. One scholar claims that "At the time of his death," Malcolm "was forging organizational links with what was to become an autonomous Black Student movement." See Sales, *From Civil Rights to Black Liberation,* 127–32; Breitman, *By Any Means Necessary,* 6–7, 10, 35, 62; Perry, *Teaching Malcolm X,* 34.

69. Clark, *February 1965,* 138–39; Watley, *Roots of Resistance,* 82–83. See also Perry, *Malcolm X: The Last Speeches,* 145–46.

70. Clark, *February 1965,* 217–18. See also Breitman, *By Any Means Necessary,* 172; Perry, *Malcolm X: The Last Speeches,* 143–44.

71. Nelson and Webb, *Selma, Lord, Selma,* 31, 33, 41–42.

72. Lewis, *Walking with the Wind,* 53, 56, 204, 362. It is difficult to understand how John Lewis could arrive at such a conclusion, especially since Malcolm did more to raise the consciousness of African Americans regarding themselves and the challenges before them than any other leader. See also Carson, *Our Struggle,* 21; Halberstam, *The Children,* 245.

73. Carson, *In Struggle,* 163–64. Foreman probably resented King more than any other young man in the movement. See J. Lewis, *Walking with the Wind,* 366–67.

74. King, *Where Do We Go from Here?* 28–66.

75. Breitman, *Malcolm X Speaks,* 49. Some young black militants heeded Malcolm's advice to "start rifle clubs to defend the Black community against police brutality and racial attacks." See "Remembering Malcolm at 60," 3; King, *Where Do We*

Go from Here? 25–27; King, *The Trumpet of Conscience,* 15, 23–24, 37–38, 76; Garrow, *Bearing the Cross,* 610–14, 617–22. King noted that in the course of riots, blacks had destroyed property but had not killed whites. However, he doubted that the lack of life-threatening violence against whites could be sustained if the spiral of poverty and racism remained untreated. See Washington, *A Testament of Hope,* 70.

76. King, *The Trumpet of Conscience,* 39–50.

77. Breitman, *By Any Means Necessary,* 182.

78. Clark, *February 1965,* 45; Breitman, *By Any Means Necessary,* 163–65; Breitman, *Malcolm X Speaks,* 137. Malcolm had great faith in the ability of youth to think and act for themselves. See Epps, *Speeches of Malcolm X at Harvard,* 135.

79. Quoted in Washington, *A Testament of Hope,* 161. Also see King, "Address to the World Assembly of Youth," 1–5; King, "Statement to the Press at the Beginning of the Youth Leadership Conference," 15 April 1960; Baldwin, *Toward the Beloved Community,* 57–61.

80. King, "Regarding the Influence of African Movements on U.S. Students." See also Washington, *A Testament of Hope,* 162; King, "The Time for Freedom Has Come," 3–4. Some of the students involved in the civil rights movement with King actually worked with Operation Crossroads Africa. See Robinson to King, 22 June 1965.

81. Karim, *End of White World Supremacy,* 18.

82. Ibid., 19, 104–5; Vernon, "Why Black Nationalism Upsets Liberals." As a member of the Nation of Islam, Malcolm expressed virtually no faith in young whites. He later recalled with regret his insulting remark to a white girl who asked him, "What can I do?" See Malcolm X, *Autobiography,* 289–90, 429; S. Clark, *February 1965,* 231.

83. Malcolm X, *Autobiography,* 429; S. Clark, *February 1965,* 231; Breitman, *Malcolm X Speaks,* 136, 224–25; Breitman, "Reviews and Reports," 4.

84. "Life of Malcolm X Receives Homage"; Montgomery, "Malcolm X a Harlem Idol on Eve of Murder Trial." Brief but important references to Malcolm's growing influence on young blacks and whites can be found in "Remembering Malcolm at 60," 3. One source reports that Malcolm came to see "all militant whites as possible allies." See "Malcolm X: The Complexity of a Man in the Jungle," 6.

85. Washington, *A Testament of Hope,* 98, 571–72; King, *Where Do We Go from Here?* 25–29, 36. Although he refused to belabor the point, King was as mindful as Malcolm X of the unconscious racism that often lurked in the hearts and the thinking of white students who participated in civil rights activities.

86. King, *The Trumpet of Conscience,* xi, 46–48; Ayres, *Wisdom of King,* 239; King, "After Segregation—What," 2. Also see "New Report Reveals Young Whites Are More Biased against Blacks than Older Whites Are"; "The Southern Poverty's Law Center's Intelligence Report," 1–2, 5, 26–29.

87. DeCaro, *On the Side of My People,* 293; Karim, *End of White World Supremacy,* 19; Clark, *February 1965,* 64; Breitman, *Malcolm X Speaks,* 145; King quoted in Ayres, *Wisdom of King,* 238.

88. Malcolm X, *Autobiography,* 413; King, "After Segregation—What," 1.

89. Wood, "Can Denzel Washington Make Malcolm Speak to a New Generation of Americans?" 39.

90. Nadle, "Burying Malcolm X"; Johnson, *Stokely Carmichael,* 115; "A Children's Tribute to Dr. King," 2.

91. Ossie Davis received no such letters from young African Americans. See Malcolm X, *Autobiography,* 453; Davis, "Why I Eulogized Malcolm X."

92. Cunnigen, "Malcolm X's Influence on the Black Nationalist Movement of Southern Black College Students," 32–43. Amiri Baraka "claimed Malcolm as an inspiration for the quasi-nationalist Black Arts Movement he helped found in the late sixties." Cultural nationalists like Baraka and Ron Karenga thought in terms of Malcolm as a cultural nationalist, and the Black Panthers linked him to their Marxist-oriented activism. See Wood, "Can Denzel Washington Make Malcolm Speak?" 39. For an interesting discussion that fails to seriously address the question of Malcolm's influence on both the United States and the Black Panthers, see Ngozi-Brown, "The US Organization, Maulana Karenga, and Conflict with the Black Panther Party," 157–67. More attention to Malcolm in relation to Marxist-oriented activism is given in Henderson, "The Lumpenproletariat as Vanguard? The Black Panther Party, Social Transformation, and Pearson's Analysis of Huey Newton."

93. Cunnigen, "Malcolm X's Influence on the Black Nationalist Movement," 32; Malcolm X, *Malcolm X Talks to Young People,* 23–29; Allen, "Malcolm X's Fatal Challenge to White Capitalism," 5. Also see Montgomery, "Malcolm X a Harlem Idol on Eve of Murder Trial," 46.

94. Barnes, "Nationwide Tributes to Malcolm X," 1; Shabazz, "The Legacy of My Husband," 173.

95. Bailey, "The Ties That Bind," 102; Johnson, "King's Children Tell How They Remember Him," 24, 26, 28.

96. See Lashley, "African Americans and the Reagan-Bush Years"; Smith, "Politics and African Americans: The Civil Rights Legacy of Ronald Reagan."

97. Baldwin, *To Make the Wounded Whole,* 295–97; Patrick Buchanan, "A Rascal's Bedroom Escapades Diminish His Status as a Saint," 5G; Garrow, "The Helms Attack on King," 12–15; "Pro and Con: A National Holiday for Martin Luther King Jr.?" 49.

98. "The Continuing Struggle for a National King Holiday"; "What Martin Luther King Jr. Means to Me"; Wheeler-Stewart, "Young Thoughts on King's Legacy," 3B.

99. See Short, "A 'New Racism' on Campus?"; Steele, "The Recoloring of Campus Life."

100. Smith et al., "Rediscovering Malcolm X"; A. Davis, "On Malcolm X," 35–36; Begley et al., "African Dreams"; Gilchrist, "The Rebirth of Malcolm X," G1; Bey, "The Renaissance of Malcolm X," 38; Coughlin, "Politics and Commerce," A14.

101. Quoted in Coughlin, "Politics and Commerce," A14; "Snarling at the White Man," 16–23; Bey, "The Renaissance of Malcolm X," 38. For an interesting source which includes letters written to King by children in the 1990s, see Colbert and Harms, *Dear Dr. King: Letters from Today's Children,* 5–59.

102. Erickson, "Malcolm X," C1; Pierce, "The Legacy of Martin Luther King," 30.

103. This tendency to pit Malcolm against Martin was reflected in *Do the Right Thing,* one of Spike Lee's films. See Carson, "A 'Common Solution': Martin and Malcolm's Gulf Was Closing, but the Debate Lives On," 44; Bey, "The Renaissance of Malcolm X"; Erickson, "Malcolm X," C1–C2; Bradley, "My Hero, Malcolm X," 488, 490; Walker, "The New Generation Speaks Out," 166.

104. Carson, "A 'Common Solution,'" 44.

105. Sales, *From Civil Rights to Black Liberation,* 217n.3.

106. Quoted in Bailey, "The Ties That Bind," 107; King, "Back Talk: Creating Our Own Work," 232.

107. Wood, "Can Denzel Washington Make Malcolm Speak?" 39.

108. See Dyson, *Making Malcolm,* 79–184; Dyson, *I May Not Get There with You,* 175–76; Dyson, *Between God and Gangsta Rap,* 97–108; Uehara et al., "African American Youth Encounters Violence," 768–81; King, "Understanding Violence among Young African American Males," 79–96.

109. James Alan Fox, dean of the school of criminology at Northeastern University in Boston, said in 1996, in reference to murders committed by teenagers, that the worst is yet to come. "It may be so bad by the year 2005," he declared, "that the 1990s are remembered as the good old days of relatively low murder rates." See Hedges, "Number of Kids Who Kill Growing," 1; Uehara et al., "African-American Youth Encounters Violence"; King, "Understanding Violence among Young African-American Males."

110. Breitman, *Malcolm X Speaks,* 20–22, 114; Breitman, *By Any Means Necessary,* 42, 51–56; King, *Where Do We Go from Here?* 125.

111. For interesting sources on how King's message of nonviolence relates to children, see Harding, *Martin Luther King,* 128–37; Colbert and Harms, *Dear Dr. King: Letters from Today's Children,* 5–59. For an important comment by President Bill Clinton on what King would say today to nine- and thirteen-year-olds who gun down each other, see "Clinton Speaks of King in Decrying Violence."

112. Despite the mounting cycles of violence among children, this infusion model has not been taken seriously in the nation's schools. This is all the more disturbing because the book can be duplicated for distribution on a purely not-for-profit basis. See *Infusion Model for Teaching Dr. Martin Luther King Jr.'s Nonviolent Principles in Schools.* One major contemporary black theologian has recommended "more dissemination of the teachings of non-violence by Dr. Martin Luther King Jr." "There are writings about King's life and work suitable for children, teenagers, and young adults," he declares. See Roberts, *The Prophethood of Black Believers,* 71.

113. Malcolm knew that such images would be promoted after his death in an effort to keep black people confused about the true meaning and significance of himself and Martin. See Malcolm X, *Autobiography,* 384, 387–88; Breitman, *Malcolm X Speaks,* 197.

114. See Askew and Wilmore, *From Prison Cell to Church Pew,* 6.

115. Sanders is right in saying that Malcolm "provides a more convincing incarnation of the transformed, remoralized black male than King does." See Sanders, *Empowerment Ethics,* 109–10.

116. Breitman, *By Any Means Necessary*, 50–53; Gallen et al., *Malcolm X as They Knew Him*, 88; King, "Advice for Living," September 1958, 68.

117. See Kelley, *Jailhouse Religion*, 2–179; Askew and Wilmore, *From Prison Cell to Church Pew*, 1–129; Askew and Wilmore, *Reclamation of Black Prisoners*, 1–125; Wilmore, *Black Men in Prison*, 1–161.

118. See the information provided in *Children and Poverty—An Episcopal Initiative: Biblical and Theological Foundations*, 1–8.

119. Breitman, *By Any Means Necessary*, 48–49; King, *Where Do We Go from Here?* 176–81; King, *Why We Can't Wait*, ix–xi, 136–39. Martin, to a greater degree than Malcolm, argued that birth control methods should be acceptable since "changes in social and economic conditions make smaller families desirable, if not necessary." See King, "Advice for Living," December 1957, 120; "Martin Luther King Jr. Supports Voluntary Family Planning Legislation," 10161.

120. Karim, *End of White World Supremacy*, 18; King, *Where Do We Go from Here?* 175–76; Breitman, *Malcolm X Speaks*, 221; King, *The Trumpet of Conscience*, 45–47.

121. See "New Report Reveals Young Whites Are More Biased against Blacks"; Pluta, "Combating Campus Prejudice"; "Aryan Nations Stage Alarming Comeback in 1994."

122. Breitman, *Malcolm X Speaks*, 220–21; Karim, *End of White World Supremacy*, 18; King, *Where Do We Go from Here?* 186; Malcolm X, *Malcolm X on Afro-American History*, 3–74; King, "Field of Education a Battleground," 1; King, "Revolution in the Classroom," 2–8.

Chapter 7. The Great Debate

1. Douglass, "Fourth of July Oration," 26.

2. Du Bois, *The Souls of Black Folk*, xiv.

3. Cone, *Martin and Malcolm and America*, 246.

4. Norwood, *The Story of American Methodism*, 171; Sernett, *African-American Religious History*, 33–42.

5. Stuckey, *Slave Culture*, 158–59, 187, 203–12, 231; Stuckey, *Ideological Origins*, 15–16, 19, 26, 150, 161–63, 252–60. *Bookerite clergy* is the term Gayraud S. Wilmore uses to describe those black preachers who, in the first half of the twentieth century, subscribed to Booker T. Washington's gradualism and progressive accommodationism. Joseph H. Jackson was among those black preachers who echoed Washington's philosophy in the 1950s and 1960s. See King, "Quest and Conflict," 6–9; Bennett, "From Booker T. to M.K.," 152–62; and Wilmore, *Black Religion and Black Radicalism*, 164–65, 168.

6. King, "Quest and Conflict," 7. See also Baldwin, *Balm.* 214; Baldwin, *To Make the Wounded Whole*, 9–19; King, interview on "Face the Nation," 13.

7. See Shirley Du Bois, *His Day Is Marching On*. Manning Marable presents a revisionist critique of the evolution of Du Bois's political ideology. Some historians and sociologists have emphasized Du Bois's "paradoxical" behavior, that he was, at various stages, a supporter of racial integration and voluntary racial segregation, an African nationalist, socialist, communist, and pacifist. This "paradox" begins to un-

ravel if one considers the central insight of Du Bois's close friend and colleague, Herbert Aptheker: "Du Bois was a Du Boisite. His political affiliations or affinities varied as times changes, as programs altered, and as he changed. . . . These were, however, political choices and not defining marks of his philosophical approaches. All his life Du Bois was a radical democrat." See Marable, *W.E.B. Du Bois,* ix.

8. Karenga, *Selections from the Husia,* 4.

9. Hoskins, *"I Have a Dream,"* 76.

10. Breitman, *Malcolm X Speaks,* 61.

11. Ibid., 8.

12. Clarke, *African People in World History,* 11.

13. Jackson, "The Restoration of Values," 1–10. See also Berger and Luckman, *The Social Construction of Reality.*

14. Cox, *Race Relations,* 21–40; also his magnus opus on the subject, *Caste, Class, and Race,* 321–52.

15. Fanon, *Toward the African Revolution,* 32, 40. See also Jackson, "The Sociology of Pan-Africanism."

16. Baldwin provides a fresh and incisive perspective on this thesis in two books, *There Is a Balm in Gilead* and *To Make the Wounded Whole.*

17. Rodnell Collins has provided an excellent primary source in *Seventh Child.* Collins is the son of Malcolm's sister Ella Collins. This biography goes beyond *The Autobiography of Malcolm,* written with the assistance of Alex Haley. Also see DeCaro, *On the Side of My People.* This is an excellent seminal work written by a non-Muslim.

18. See Williams, *The Destruction of Black Civilization;* Clarke, *Christopher Columbus and the Afrikan Holocaust.*

19. DeGraft-Johnson, *African Glory,* 58–76.

20. See Du Bois, *The Suppression of the African Slave-Trade;* Eric Williams, *Capitalism and Slavery;* Nkrumah, *Neo-Colonialism: The Last Stage of Imperialism.*

21. Du Bois, *The Souls of Black Folk,* 16–17.

22. King, *Where Do We Go from Here?* 53.

23. Breitman, *Malcolm X Speaks,* 210–11.

24. Cone, *Martin and Malcolm and America,* 270–71.

25. See Fanon, *Black Skin, White Masks;* Fanon, *The Wretched of the Earth.*

26. See Richards, *Let the Circle Be Unbroken;* Ani, *Yurugu: An African-Centered Critique.*

27. See Cruse, *Crisis of the Negro Intellectual;* Banks, *Black Intellectuals.*

28. Breitman, *By Any Means Necessary* 183–84. This fundamental class analysis of the plantation, and by logical extension the African-American community, appears also in his cultural and political manifesto entitled "Message to the Grassroots." This famous speech can be found in Breitman, *Malcolm X Speaks,* 3–17.

29. Carruthers, *MDW NTR: Divine Speech,* 1.

30. Breitman, *Malcolm X Speaks,* 51.

31. Ibid., 31; King, *Where Do We Go from Here?*

32. Delany, "The Condition, Elevation, Emigration, and Destiny of the Colored People," 97–98.

33. Moses, *Classical Black Nationalism*, 104.

34. Brotz, *African-American Social and Political Thought*, 7.

35. Draper, *Rediscovery of Black Nationalism*, 22.

36. Washington, "Atlanta Exposition Address," 357–58.

37. Du Bois, "The Talented Tenth," 518.

38. King, *Why We Can't Wait*, 33.

39. Henry, "Who Won The Great Debate?" 15.

40. Breitman, *Malcolm X Speaks*, 28–33.

41. Muhammad, *Message to the Blackman in America*, 161.

42. See Johnson, *Bitter Canaan*; Wilson, *The Loyal Blacks*.

43. Breitman, *Malcolm X Speaks*, 21, 24, 38. From a scholarly standpoint, it is worth noting that George Breitman deleted portions of this speech where Malcolm stressed his Muslim faith and his black nationalist philosophy. Breitman has also been criticized by other scholars for deleting portions of Malcolm's speeches in order to construct his own "image" of Malcolm as an emerging socialist. See, for example, Joe Goncalves's introduction to T'Shaka, *The Political Legacy of Malcolm X*, 9–11.

44. Breitman, *Malcolm X Speaks*, 38–41.

45. Essien-Udom and Essien-Udom, "Malcolm X: An International Man," in Clarke, *Malcolm X*.

46. Vincent, "The Garveyite Parents of Malcolm X"; Breitman, *Malcolm X Speaks*, 62–63.

47. King, "A Time to Break Silence," 240.

48. Breitman, *Malcolm X Speaks*, 50; Wilmore, *Black Religion and Black Radicalism*, 140–42.

49. A conscientious objector is legally defined as "One who, by reason of religious training and belief, is conscientiously opposed to participation in war. Such a person need not be a member of a religion whose creed forbids participation in war to be entitled to classification as a conscientious objector. . . . In lieu of active military service, such a person is subject to civilian work contributing to the national health, safety or interest." See Nolan and Nolan-Haley, *Black's Law Dictionary*, 304.

50. King, *The Trumpet of Conscience*, 31; King, "A Time to Break Silence," 231–44.

51. Muhammad, *Message to the Blackman in America*, 164; Baldwin, *To Make the Wounded Whole*, 280.

52. Malcolm X, *Autobiography*, 205.

53. Ibid., 108.

54. Muhammad Ali, *The Greatest*, 138, 186.

55. Ibid., 153.

56. Ibid., 203.

57. Armstrong and Woodward, *The Brethren: Inside the Supreme Court*, 157–60.

58. King, "Nobel Prize Acceptance Speech," 224–25.

59. Breitman, *Malcolm X Speaks*, 59–60.

60. Smith, *The World's Religions*, 214–15.

61. Ansbro, *Martin Luther King Jr.*, 119–28.

62. Turner, *Islam in the African-American Experience*, 174–223.

63. See Hilliard III, "Pedagogy in Ancient Kemet," in Karenga and Carruthers, *Kemet and the African Worldview*, 131–48; Freire, *Pedagogy of the Oppressed*.

64. Malcolm X, *Malcolm X Talks to Young People*, 49.

65. Malcolm X, *Autobiography*, 185.

66. Breitman, *Malcolm X Speaks*, 26.

67. Stone, *Black Political Power in America*, 49.

68. John Lewis, "It's About the Right to Vote."

69. From a legal standpoint, reparations constitute "payment for a debt owed; to repair a wrong or injury; to atone for wrongdoings; to make amends; to make one whole again; the payment of damages; to repair a nation; compensation in money or material payable for damages." See Black, *Black Law Dictionary*, 1298; "Reparations: Calculating the Incalculable," 1059; and Curry, *The Affirmative Action Debate*.

70. Lumumba et al., *Reparations Yes!* 97.

71. C. Stone Brown, "TransAfrica's Randall Robinson: Leading the Growing Reparations Movement."

72. Lumumba et al., *Reparations Yes!*

73. Quoted in Wilmore, *Black Religion and Black Radicalism*, 123–24.

74. Elijah Muhammad, *Message to the Blackman in America*, 161.

75. Malcolm's perspective agrees essentially with many of the points made in Barnett, *Payback? Racism, Reparations, and Accountability*, 1070–71; "Suit to Seek Reparations for Slavery," 1A, 2A.

76. King, *Why We Can't Wait*, 136–38.

77. King, *Where Do We Go from Here?* 178–79.

78. Foreman, *The Political Thought of James Foreman*, 63.

79. WCAR NGO *Forum Declaration*, Durban, South Africa, 3 September 2001, 31.

Chapter 8. Reluctant Admiration

1. Telegram from King to Mrs. Malcolm X, 26 February 1965.

2. Epps, *Speeches of Malcolm X at Harvard*, 181.

3. "Alex Haley Remembers Malcolm X," 122. See also Malcolm X, *Autobiography*, 403, 405.

4. Goldman, *Death and Life*, 74. Typical of such are Paris, *Black Leaders in Conflict*, 9–226; Bishop, *The Days of Martin Luther King Jr.*, 379. Bishop claims that Martin "had never admired Malcolm X, or Elijah, or any of the other militants whom he called 'the crazies.'" See also Cone, *Speaking the Truth*, 167; James Cone, interview, 9.

5. Malcolm and Martin have been described as "cordial adversaries" during much of this time. See Lewis, *King: A Critical Biography*, 125; Baldwin, "Malcolm and Martin," 94, 201; Williams, *The King God Didn't Save*, 77. My position on the two stages in Malcolm's and Martin's relationship is closer to claims made by Claude Lewis and David Gallen. It contrasts somewhat with the view advanced by James H. Cone. See Gallen et al., *Malcolm X as They Knew Him*, 78; Cone, *Martin and Malcolm and America*, 193; Baldwin, "Reassessment," 103–4.

6. This point is made in Cone, *Martin and Malcolm and America*, 193, 246; Gallen, *A Malcolm X Reader*, 168. Malcolm once noted, "The Deep South white press generally blacked me out." See Malcolm X, *Autobiography*, 272, 274; Lomax, *To Kill a Black Man*, 65.

7. Lewis, *King: A Critical Biography*, 125; Muhammad to King, 19 March 1958; King to Muhammad, 9 April 1958; Lomax, *To Kill a Black Man*, 74.

8. Malcolm X to King, 21 July 1960.

9. Ballou to Malcolm X, 10 August 1960; Lincoln, *Black Muslims*, 134, 148–49.

10. Baldwin, "Reassessment," 104; Lewis, *King: A Critical Biography*, 258, 271.

11. Gallen, *A Malcolm X Reader*, 106–7; Lomax, *When the Word Is Given*, 96, 99. Malcolm consistently argued that the offer of integration was "only a trick" to "lull Negroes to sleep, to lull them into thinking that the white man is changing and actually trying to keep us here." See Clark, *King, Malcolm, Baldwin*, 35–36, 45; Breitman, *Malcolm X Speaks*, 42, 196–97; Washington, *A Testament of Hope*, xxi; Lincoln, *Black Muslims*, 147–48.

12. Clark, *February 1965*, 178; K. Clark, *King, Malcolm, Baldwin*, 25; Washington, *A Testament of Hope*, 335. Martin recognized this same tendency in the German philosopher Friedrich Nietzsche, who equated love and the Hebraic-Christian ethic in general with weakness or a resignation of power. See Ansbro, *Martin Luther King Jr.*, 1–2, 7–8; Oates, *Let the Trumpet Sound*, 254; Baldwin, "Reassessment," 104–5, 111n.18.

13. Gallen et al., *Malcolm X as They Knew Him*, 138; Clark, *King, Malcolm, Baldwin*, 41–42; Goldman, *Death and Life*, 75; Clark, *February 1965*, 66.

14. Breitman, *Malcolm X Speaks*, 93, 145, 164, 177; Goldman, *Death and Life*, 68, 227. Also see "Excerpts from an Interview with Martin Luther King Jr.," in Warren, "Who Speaks for the Negro?" 7; Oates, *Let the Trumpet Sound*, 252; Gallen et al., *Malcolm X as They Knew Him*, 139, 207.

15. Breitman, *Malcolm X Speaks*, 52; Lincoln, *Black Muslims*, 147; Baldwin, *To Make the Wounded Whole*, 30; Clark, *King, Malcolm, Baldwin*, 42; Paris, *Black Leaders in Conflict*, 152–53.

16. Warren, "Who Speaks for the Negro?" 7. See also Baldwin, "Reassessment," 104, 111n.18; Baldwin, "Malcolm X and Martin Luther King, Jr.," 399–400. Martin's claim that Malcolm and his fellow Black Muslims distorted the meaning of nonviolent resistance by interpreting it as passive nonresistance was also made by the civil rights leader in reference to the Christian realist Reinhold Niebuhr. See Ansbro, *Martin Luther King Jr.*, 250. See also Jones, "Liberation Strategies in Black Theology," 38–46.

17. Breitman, *Malcolm X Speaks*, 112, 162; Oates, *Let the Trumpet Sound*, 251. See also "Angry Spokesman Malcolm X Tells Off Whites," 30; Baldwin, "Malcolm X and Martin Luther King Jr.," 401, 414n.27.

18. Breitman, *By Any Means Necessary*, 8–9. Malcolm credited Gandhi with twisting "a knot in the British Lion's tail," a comment quite interesting in light of his negative view of Martin's nonviolent methods. See Malcolm X, *Autobiography*, 177, 244, 272. One explanation for Malcolm's high regard for Gandhi is offered in Karim et al., *Remembering Malcolm*, 141.

19. Martin apparently had a much more positive image of Chief Albert J. Luthuli than Malcolm did. See Clark, *February 1965*, 68–69; Baldwin, *Toward the Beloved Community*, 17–19, 25–29, 35–36, 46–47, 53–55. For other remarks Malcolm made concerning Luthuli and Nelson Mandela, see Gallen et al., *Malcolm X as They Knew Him*, 175; Gallen, *A Malcolm X Reader*, 203; Breitman, *By Any Means Necessary*, 114.

20. Clark, *King, Malcolm, Baldwin*, 42–43; Karim et al., *Remembering Malcolm*, 141; Gallen, *A Malcolm X Reader*, 106, 200.

21. Karim, *End of White World Supremacy*, 69, 109, 116–17, 135, 140; "Emancipation II"; Breitman, *Malcolm X Speaks*, 12–13; Gallen, *A Malcolm X Reader*, 106; Baldwin, "Reassessment," 104, 111n.15.

22. Oates, *Let the Trumpet Sound*, 252, 254; Warren, "Who Speaks for the Negro?" 7; Baldwin, "Reassessment," 104; Haley, "Interview with Martin Luther King," 73–74; "King Views Malcolm X as Tragic," 35; Lomax, *To Kill a Black Man*, 80.

23. Clark, *King, Malcolm, Baldwin*, 42; Breitman, *Malcolm X Speaks*, 138.

24. Perry, *Malcolm X: The Last Speeches*, 149; Clark, *February 1965*, 142; Breitman, *Malcolm X Speaks*, 112, 139, 143–44; Breitman, *By Any Means Necessary*, 160.

25. King, *Stride toward Freedom*, 102–7; Ansbro, *Martin Luther King Jr.*, 231–33, 238; Clark, *February 1965*, 24–25; Breitman, *Malcolm X Speaks*, 34, 48–49, 109, 183; Breitman, *By Any Means Necessary*, 11, 42, 80–83; Gallen, *A Malcolm X Reader*, 107.

26. Gallen, *A Malcolm X Reader*, 107; Breitman, *By Any Means Necessary*, 154; Breitman, *Malcolm X Speaks*, 25, 48, 68, 117, 143; Cone, *Martin and Malcolm and America*, 266; Washington, *A Testament of Hope*, 365; Haley, "Interview with Martin Luther King," 74.

27. Malcolm X, *Autobiography*, 399.

28. Breitman, *Malcolm X Speaks*, 9, 56–57, 71, 112–13, 136, 153; Perry, *Malcolm X: The Last Speeches*, 103. Martin set forth this view throughout his writings and in his speeches and sermons. See King, *Stride toward Freedom*, 224; Baldwin, *Balm*, 229–72.

29. Perry, *Malcolm X: The Last Speeches*, 39–40. See also Clark, *February 1965*, 58; Gallen, *A Malcolm X Reader*, 107; Clark, *King, Malcolm, Baldwin*, 43.

30. Malcolm consistently predicted that riots would occur if the conditions under which his people lived in the ghettoes were not seriously addressed. See Breitman, *Malcolm X Speaks*, 25, 49, 67–68, 174–75, 190–91; Haley, "Interview with Martin Luther King," 73; Washington, *A Testament of Hope*, 362. Also see King, "Statement Regarding Riots in Rochester and New York City," 27 July 1964. In placing much of the blame on "extremists" like Malcolm X for the riots in northern ghettoes, Martin was echoing what many whites wanted to believe.

31. James H. Cone contends, "There was no animosity" between Malcolm and Martin, an argument some scholars find unacceptable. Stephen B. Oates reports, "Some of Malcolm's diatribes against King may have stemmed from jealousy." See Cone, *Martin and Malcolm and America*, 2; Oates, *Let the Trumpet Sound*, 252;

Baldwin, "Malcolm X and Martin Luther King Jr.," 401; Baldwin, "Reassessment," 105.

32. There is some truth to James H. Cone's claim that Malcolm's and Martin's "public comments about each other seemed to be based on media images rather than precise information," but Cone's suggestion that "both played roles assigned to them by the white public" needs further clarification. See Cone, *Martin and Malcolm and America*, 245–46; Gallen et al., *Malcolm X as They Knew Him*, 226; Karim, *End of White World Supremacy*, 86. Malcolm commonly attacked the press for unfair and misleading reporting. See Breitman, *Malcolm X Speaks*, 91–92, 165, 168.

33. Goldman, *Death and Life*, 16; Baldwin, "Reassessment," 105.

34. Malcolm X, *Malcolm X on Afro-American History*, 13; Breitman, *Malcolm X Speaks*, 134, 145, 182; Cone, *Martin and Malcolm and America*, 245, 268; Haley, "Interview with Martin Luther King," 73; Goldman, *Death and Life*, 17, 214, 232. Goldman claims that while visiting parts of Africa in 1964, Malcolm actually described himself as "the leader of 22 million American blacks."

35. Baldwin, "Reassessment," 105; Goldman, *Death and Life*, 16–17, 95; McDonald to Clark, 26 November 1962; Clark to King, 4 December 1962; *Harper's*, June 1964, 54–61.

36. Perry, *Malcolm X: The Last Speeches*, 87.

37. This need to undercut Malcolm's influence in Harlem, and in the black ghettoes of the North generally, became particularly pressing for Martin in July 1964, when riots broke out in parts of New York. See King, "Statement Regarding Riots in Rochester and New York City," 27 July 1964.

38. Warren, "Who Speaks for the Negro?" 5–6.

39. Ibid., 6. See also Oates, *Let the Trumpet Sound*, 253–54; Goldman, *Death and Life*, 86; Baldwin, "Malcolm X and Martin Luther King Jr.," 404–5.

40. "Muslims Pelt King; His Answer: Love"; Oates, *Let the Trumpet Sound*, 306.

41. Oates, *Let the Trumpet Sound*, 252, 306.

42. Ibid., 252; Malcolm X, *Autobiography*, 418–19. Malcolm frequently responded to such polls by saying that blacks distrusted and were seldom honest with white pollsters who approached them. See Breitman, *Malcolm X Speaks*, 65, 175; Clark, *February 1965*, 102, 218.

43. Gallen, *A Malcolm X Reader*, 200–201; Gallen et al., *Malcolm X as They Knew Him*, 172–73, 226; Goldman, *Death and Life*, 17, 237; Epps, *Speeches of Malcolm X at Harvard*, 181.

44. Southwick, "Malcolm X: Charismatic Demagogue," 740; Goldman, *Death and Life*, 230.

45. Gallen, *A Malcolm X Reader*, 206. See also Gallen et al., *Malcolm X as They Knew Him*, 172, 178; Clark, *February 1965*, 42, 217–18, 228; Karim et al., *Remembering Malcolm*, 141; Breitman, *By Any Means Necessary*, 8, 115; Breitman, *Malcolm X Speaks*, 12–16; Clark, *King, Malcolm, Baldwin*, 42–43; Cone, *Martin and Malcolm and America*, 245.

46. See Bennett, *Confrontation: Black and White*, 205–7, 211–13, 216, 276, 278, 290, 294; Malcolm X, *Autobiography*, 272.

47. Martin's efforts failed in Albany because of insufficient attention to such fac-

tors as timing, the rifts between the Southern Christian Leadership Conference and the Student Nonviolent Coordinating Committee, the methods of opposition, and court injunctions. See Watley, *Roots of Resistance,* 68–70; Goldman, *Death and Life,* 96; Breitman, *Malcolm X Speaks,* 13.

48. Karim, *End of White World Supremacy,* 140.

49. Martin cited other reasons why nonviolence had not been "soundly defeated," and why "our movement had been checked in Albany but not defeated." See King, *Why We Can't Wait,* 43–44. Scholars generally view Martin's movement in Albany as a failure, or as one of his "darkest hours." See Watley, *Roots of Resistance,* 70; Goldman, *Death and Life,* 100.

50. Watley, *Roots of Resistance,* 71; Cone, *Martin and Malcolm and America,* 193; Clark, *February 1965,* 61; Lomax, *When the Word Is Given,* 85.

51. *New York Times,* 19 May 1963, 10E; *New York Times,* 15 May 1963, 26; Cone, *Martin and Malcolm and America,* 264.

52. King, *Why We Can't Wait,* 105–6, 109; Gallen et al., *Malcolm X as They Knew Him,* 139; Clark, *February 1965,* 61.

53. Gallen et al., *Malcolm X as They Knew Him,* 140.

54. Breitman, *Malcolm X Speaks,* 14.

55. Karim, *End of White World Supremacy,* 141–42; Breitman, *Malcolm X Speaks,* 13–14.

56. King, *Why We Can't Wait,* 122–25; Bleiweiss, *Marching to Freedom,* 103–12.

57. Goldman, *Death and Life,* 107; Malcolm X, *Autobiography,* 282; Breitman, *Malcolm X Speaks,* 14–17; Karim, *End of White World Supremacy,* 142–43.

58. Malcolm X, *Autobiography,* 281; Karim, *End of White World Supremacy,* 144; Gallen et al., *Malcolm X as They Knew Him,* 78, 175; Goldman, *Death and Life,* 107; Breitman, *Malcolm X Speaks,* 16, 151; King, *Why We Can't Wait,* 123.

59. Malcolm X, *Autobiography,* 314; Breitman, *Malcolm X Speaks,* 18, 20.

60. King, "Statement on Malcolm X," 1.

61. See Gallen et al., *Malcolm X as They Knew Him,* 78; Lomax, *To Kill a Black Man,* 79; Baldwin, "Reassessment," 104; Shabazz to Lewis, 15 May 1964.

62. See Miller, *Martin Luther King Jr.,* 194–95; Fairclough, *To Redeem the Soul of America,* 191; Goldman, *Death and Life,* 17; Cone, *Martin and Malcolm and America,* 192–93, 266; Baldwin, "Reassessment," 104. See also Malcolm X to King, 30 June 1964; Breitman, *By Any Means Necessary,* 66, 77.

63. Haley, "Interview with Martin Luther King," 78; Washington, *A Testament of Hope,* 374–75.

64. Gallen et al., *Malcolm X as They Knew Him,* 172; Gallen, *A Malcolm X Reader,* 200.

65. Breitman, *By Any Means Necessary,* 114, 154; Clark, *February 1965,* 68–69. Malcolm refused to see the Nobel Peace Prize as an honor to be cherished: "They get a Negro and hire him and make him a big shot so he's a voice of the community and then he tells all of them to come on in and join the organization with us, and they take it over. Then they give him peace prizes and medals and things." See Breitman, *Malcolm X Speaks,* 95.

66. Malcolm was as critical of the Civil Rights Act of 1964 as he was of Martin's Nobel Award. The bill, he asserted, "has produced nothing where we're concerned. It was only a valve, a vent, that was designed to enable us to let off our frustrations." See Breitman, *Malcolm X Speaks,* 143, 151; Clark, *February 1965,* 39.

67. Breitman, *Malcolm X Speaks,* 34–35. See also 51, 53–54.

68. Clark, *February 1965,* 87, 277n.47; Breitman, *Malcolm X Speaks,* 201; Perry, *Malcolm X: The Last Speeches,* 119–120; Malcolm X, *Malcolm X on Afro-American History,* 43–44; Goldman, *Death and Life,* 228.

69. Malcolm X, *Malcolm X on Afro-American History,* 44.

70. Watley, *Roots of Resistance,* 82; Clark, *February 1965,* 114; Perry, *Malcolm X: The Last Speeches,* 120; Adams, "Malcolm X 'Seemed Sincere' about Helping Cause: Mrs. King," 28. Peter Goldman notes that the people of SNCC felt left out of the Selma campaign and that "their invitation to Malcolm had an edge of provocation to it." See Goldman, *Death and Life,* 230–31; Baldwin, "Malcolm X and Martin Luther King, Jr.," 396–97, 413n.15.

71. See King, "Testimony in *Williams vs. Wallace,*" 74–75. See also Garrow, *Protest at Selma,* 111–12, 272n.5.

72. Breitman, *Malcolm X Speaks,* 225; Goldman, *Death and Life,* 231–32; Baldwin, "Malcolm X and Martin Luther King Jr.," 398; Clark, *February 1965,* 24–25.

73. Malcolm had also planned to visit Martin at the Selma jail, but had to leave to catch a flight to London. See King, *My Life,* 259; Cone, *Martin and Malcolm and America,* 267; "Malcolm X Gives Views," 9.

74. Malcolm X, *Autobiography,* 427; Perry, *Malcolm X: The Last Speeches,* 172–73; Clark, *February 1965,* 24–25, 163, 274n.28; Breitman, *Malcolm X Speaks,* 171–72; Cone, *Martin and Malcolm and America,* 246–71; Goldman, *Death and Life,* 186, 232; Baldwin, "Reassessment," 106; Wilmore, *Black Religion and Black Radicalism,* 190.

75. Breitman, *Malcolm X Speaks,* 172. See also Clark, *February 1965,* 163; Perry, *Malcolm X: The Last Speeches,* 172. "Given a Martin Luther King Jr., there had to be a Malcolm X," said Martin's associate Wyatt Tee Walker. "In the earlier days, Dr. King was considered by most in the national community (circa 1960) a dangerous wild-eyed perverter of religion with demagogic power and obvious Communist sympathies." When Malcolm emerged with his explosive rhetoric, Martin "became more palatable to the American scene." See Walker, "Nothing but a Man," 30–31; Cone, *Martin and Malcolm and America,* 268.

76. King, *Why We Can't Wait,* 87. In his celebrated "Letter from the Birmingham City Jail" (1963), Martin spoke of standing between opposing forces in the African-American community; the complacent who refuse to struggle for freedom, and the extremists who offer a gospel of despair, hatred, and violence. See Washington, *A Testament of Hope,* 296–97; Cone, *Martin and Malcolm and America,* 265; Baldwin, "Reassessment," 106; Baldwin, *To Make the Wounded Whole,* 43. One source claims that "Malcolm X could articulate Black rage much better than . . . Martin Luther King Jr." See Lester, "Malcolm X as Icon," 256.

77. Breitman, *Malcolm X Speaks,* 51. The contention that Malcolm and Martin

had essentially the same goals has been consistently advanced since their deaths. See "Malcolm X and Martin Luther King Jr.: Violence versus Nonviolence," 168; Erickson, "Malcolm X," C1.

78. Morris, *Unyoung, Uncolored, Unpoor*, 91. James H. Cone is correct in his assertion that "uncompromising militancy was Malcolm's great contribution to the black freedom struggle." See Cone, *Martin and Malcolm and America*, 264.

79. Goldman, *Death and Life*, 95.

80. Lewis, *King: A Critical Biography*, 271.

81. King to Eisenman, 3 April 1964. See also Eisenman to King, 9 April 1964. James H. Cone rightly argues that white liberals were largely responsible for preventing Malcolm and Martin from working together. See Cone, *Speaking the Truth*, 167. Despite his view of Malcolm as a "tremendously intelligent and dedicated human being," Martin knew that any close association with the Muslim activist would possibly tarnish his image and jeopardize the financial and moral support he got from white liberals. "He always felt that they could not be on the same platform," Andrew Young said. See Cone, *Martin and Malcolm and America*, 255–56.

82. James Baldwin, "Malcolm and Martin," 94, 201; Williams, *The King God Didn't Save*, 77. The notion that Malcolm and Martin were moving closer together is widely accepted among scholars. See Cruse, *The Crisis of the Negro Intellectual*, 563–64; Lomax, *To Kill a Black Man*, 10–11, 131; Morgan, "Malcolm X's Murder," 310; Moses, *Black Messiahs and Uncle Toms*, 212, 224, 229; Baldwin, "Reassessment," 107–8; Cone, *Martin and Malcolm and America*, 253–59. Malcolm seems to have detected that Martin was becoming more radical. "Since I've gotten involved" in the mainstream of the freedom struggle, Malcolm said in 1964, "I am surprised at how militant some of these 'integrationists' are sounding; man, sometimes they put me to shame." Malcolm also insisted, "When Martin Luther King speaks of social disruption, he is saying the same thing when I say *bloodshed*. He uses big words, and I am direct and to the point." See Russell, "Exclusive Interview with Brother Malcolm X," 12. Martin never publicly acknowledged that he was moving toward Malcolm, despite David Halberstam's suggestion that the civil rights leader "sounded like a nonviolent Malcolm" in 1965. Halberstam declared that Martin "was much closer to Malcolm than he would admit and anyone would have predicted five years ago—and much farther from more traditional allies like Whitney Young and Roy Wilkins." See Halberstam, "The Second Coming of Martin Luther King," 47–48.

83. Breitman, *Malcolm X Speaks*, 197; "Brother Reveals Malcolm X Had Disavowed His Racist Philosophy in Later Life," 19; C. S. King, *My Life*, 260–61; Baldwin, "Reassessment," 108; Cone, *Martin and Malcolm and America*, 254–59; Moses, *Black Messiahs and Uncle Toms*, 212; King, *Where Do We Go from Here?* 23–166; Clark, *February 1965*, 242. Coretta Scott King reports that Martin "believed in nonviolent Black Power."

84. Breitman, *Malcolm X Speaks*, 221. Also see Cone, *Martin and Malcolm and America*, 256; Breitman, *By Any Means Necessary*, 58. One source rejects the view that Malcolm's pilgrimage to Mecca turned him into an integrationist, reducing it to the level of a myth. See Cleage, "Myths about Malcolm X," in Clarke, *Malcolm X:*

The Man and His Times, 14–15. See also Horton and Horton, "Race and Class," 155–57.

85. Quoted in Fairclough, "Was Martin Luther King a Marxist?" in *Martin Luther King Jr. and the Civil Rights Movement,* ed. Garrow, 2:304; Cone, *Martin and Malcolm and America,* 256. For the reference to Martin's idea of "temporary segregation," see "Conversation with Martin Luther King Jr.," 8. I agree with Lawrence Mamiya's contention that James Cone "tends to over-emphasize the idea of temporary segregation, which King mentioned only once in a speech." Mamiya goes on to say that Cone "is straining the material a bit to bring about a closer accommodation of Martin's and Malcolm's views." See Mamiya, review of *Martin and Malcolm and America,* by James H. Cone, 138. Cone's emphasis on Martin's reference to "temporary segregation" is embraced uncritically by some scholars. See Burrow, review of *Toward the Beloved Community,* by Lewis V. Baldwin, in the *Journal of Religion,* 445–47.

86. Breitman, *By Any Means Necessary,* 13; C. S. King, *My Life,* 260.

87. This is why both Malcolm and Martin counseled young men, especially in the black community, not to participate in the war efforts of the U.S. government. See Breitman, *By Any Means Necessary,* 48, 125; Breitman, *Malcolm X Speaks,* 140–41, 172; King, *The Trumpet of Conscience,* 50; King, *Where Do We Go from Here?* 167; interview with Cassius Clay and Martin Luther King Jr., 1; James Baldwin, "Malcolm and Martin," 201.

88. Cone, *Martin and Malcolm and America,* 246–71. The similarities between Malcolm and Martin have also been explored at some length in Goldman, *Death and Life,* 383–92; Lomax, *To Kill a Black Man,* 9–11; C. S. King, *My Life,* 260.

89. "Alex Haley Interview," 38; "Alex Haley Remembers Malcolm X," 122; Cone, *Martin and Malcolm and America,* 258–59; Malcolm X, *Autobiography,* 403, 405.

90. C. S. King, *My Life,* 261–62.

91. Goldman, *Death and Life,* 142; Baldwin, *To Make the Wounded Whole,* 41. Abernathy's account is corroborated to some extent by Goldman in *Death and Life,* 391.

92. Clark, *King, Malcolm, Baldwin,* 12–13.

93. Quoted in Gallen et al., *Malcolm X as They Knew Him,* 84.

94. *New York Times,* 29 July 1964, 40; Cone, *Martin and Malcolm and America,* 259; Goldman, *Death and Life,* 381, 391; Bailey, "The Ties That Bind," 78.

95. Press conference with Martin Luther King Jr., 24 February 1965, 1–2, 6; telegram from Martin Luther King to Mrs. Malcolm X, 26 February 1965. Betty Shabazz, Malcolm's widow, reported that she never received this telegram or any other statement from Martin concerning her husband's death, although Martin's family confirms that the telegram was sent. Perhaps it was intercepted by forces that had both Malcolm and Martin under surveillance. See Cone, *Martin and Malcolm and America,* 345n.28; "The Daughters of Malcolm X and Martin Luther King Team Up to Bring a Play of Hope to Kids," 104; Baldwin, "Reassessment," 103, 110; Wilmore, *Black Religion and Black Radicalism* (1983), 190.

96. Press conference with King, 24 February 1965, 6. One of Martin's associates went so far as to suggest that Malcolm was "beginning to examine a new non-violent approach" when he was murdered. No confirmation of this has been found. See "Bayard Rustin and Malcolm X," 4.

97. C. S. King, *My Life,* 261.

98. King, "People to People: The Nightmare of Violence," 26 February 1965, 2–3. These remarks raise questions about James H. Cone's conclusion that "if one used only Martin's public statements, the unavoidable conclusion would be that he did not consider Malcolm a significant, creative black leader." See Cone, *Martin and Malcolm and America,* 245.

99. King, "Statement Regarding the Death of Malcolm X," 1. See also "King and Roy: On Malcolm's Death"; press conference with King, 24 February 1965, 6.

100. See "What Harlemites Say about Malcolm X Slaying," 22. Other civil rights leaders also responded to Malcolm's death in a somewhat sympathetic fashion. See Wilkins, "No Time for Avengers," 8; Young, "To Be Equal: The Next Malcolm X," 8.

101. King, "People to People: The Nightmare of Violence," 26 February 1965, 1–3. Martin probably read Malcolm's interview with Alex Haley, which appeared in the May 1963 issue of *Playboy.* His deep knowledge of the Muslim leader's life history could not have resulted solely from watching the 1959 CBS documentary *The Hate That Hate Produced.* Malcolm's autobiography had not yet appeared in published form.

Chapter 9. Toward a Broader Humanism

1. King, *Where Do We Go from Here?* 167.

2. Breitman, *Malcolm X Speaks,* 197.

3. Crawford et al., *Women in the Civil Rights Movement,* 212. See also Lerner, *Black Women in White America,* 610.

4. One source contends that King believed that the beloved community "would be actualized within history, and he saw approximations of it already." Another argues that King "could not have expected that the perfect beloved community in its fullness could ever become an historical reality." While some scholars still question whether King really believed in the actualization of the beloved community in human history, this is not the case with Malcolm, who was clearly not as optimistic as King on this issue. See Smith and Zepp, *Search for the Beloved Community,* 156; Ansbro, *Martin Luther King Jr.,* 188. See also Fluker, *They Looked for a City,* 82–86; Baldwin, *Balm,* 1–339; Cone, *Martin and Malcolm and America,* 38–57.

5. Malcolm X, *Autobiography,* 176–78; Malcolm X, *Malcolm X on Afro-American History,* 14–74; Carson, *Autobiography of Martin Luther King Jr.,* 1–110; King, *Where Do We Go from Here?* 29, 53, 55, 59–61, 65–66, 106, 110–11, 121, 127; King to James Baldwin, 26 September 1961; King, "Honoring Dr. Du Bois"; Baldwin, *Balm,* 44–46.

6. Malcolm X, *Malcolm X on Afro-American History,* 55; King, "The Meaning of Hope," 1, 2. See also Breitman, *By Any Means Necessary,* 54; Lomax, *When the Word Is Given,* 137–39, 161–63; Baldwin, *Balm,* 46.

7. Malcolm X, *Malcolm X on Afro-American History,* 40; King, "The Meaning of Hope," 1–2.

8. King, *Where Do We Go from Here?* 103. See also King, "The Meaning of Hope," 1–2.

9. Breitman, *Malcolm X Speaks* 25–26, 172–73; Malcolm X, *Malcolm X on Afro-American History,* 36–37; King, "A Knock at Midnight," 14–16; King, "The Crisis of Civil Rights," 10; King, "An Address at a Mass Meeting," Montgomery, Ala., 16 February 1968, 4; Baldwin, *Balm,* 42.

10. Clark, *King, Malcolm, Baldwin,* 44; Breitman, *By Any Means Necessary,* 80–81; King, *Why We Can't Wait,* 23; King, *Where Do We Go from Here?* 102–3.

11. Breitman, *Malcolm X Speaks,* 55, 108–10, 139; King quoted in Washington, *A Testament of Hope,* 110.

12. King, "Who Is Their God?" 210; King, "When a Negro Faces Southern Justice"; King, "Statement regarding the Mississippi Freedom Democratic Party at the COFO Rally," 22 July 1964; Baldwin, *Balm,* 47; Breitman, *Malcolm X Speaks,* 139.

13. Breitman, *By Any Means Necessary,* 54–55, 181. See also Lomax, *When the Word Is Given,* 132, 197–99; Breitman, *Malcolm X Speaks,* 53, 168–69; King, *Where Do We Go from Here?* 122–25; Baldwin, *Balm,* 47–49, 57–58; Karim, *End of White World Supremacy,* 135.

14. Karim, *End of White World Supremacy,* 135; Lomax, *When the Word Is Given,* 198–99; Breitman, *Malcolm X Speaks,* 11.

15. Warren, "Who Speaks for the Negro?" 14–15; King, *Where Do We Go from Here?* 131, 160; Baldwin, *Balm,* 48.

16. Karim, *End of White World Supremacy,* 134–35; Lomax, *When the Word Is Given,* 156, 191, 198–99; S. Clark, *February 1965,* 243; King, *Where Do We Go from Here?* 131–32; Warren, "Who Speaks for the Negro?" 14–15; Baldwin, *Balm,* 48–49; King, "Crisis and Political Rally in Alabama," 163.

17. Breitman, *Malcolm X Speaks,* 50–51, 114, 145, 174, 176; Clark, *King, Malcolm, Baldwin,* 41–42; Gallen, *A Malcolm X Reader,* 106; King, *Where Do We Go from Here?* 124. Malcolm probably spoke more frequently on the divide and conquer tactics of the oppressor than Martin. See Breitman, *By Any Means Necessary,* 26–27; Malcolm X, *Malcolm X on Afro-American History,* 39–40.

18. Breitman, *Malcolm X Speaks,* 114, 138, 176. When Malcolm and Martin spoke of debased behavior among African Americans, of the violence and treachery that occurred within the group, they had the whole history of their people's contact with whites in view, which extended back to black involvement in the African slave trade and beyond. Malcolm's reflections on Africans "who sold us" to European traders were quite sparing. The same could be said of Martin, who once noted that "slavery was so divisive and brutal, so molded to break up unity, that we never developed a sense of oneness, as in Judaism." See Breitman, *By Any Means Necessary,* 122–23; Malcolm X, *Malcolm X on Afro-American History,* 39–40; Washington, *A Testament of Hope,* 369.

19. King, *Where Do We Go from Here?* 64, 125.

20. Ibid.; King, "President's Address," 12.

21. King, *Stride toward Freedom,* 211, 214; King, "Our Struggle," 3; King, "Some Things We Must Do," 7.

22. Breitman, *Malcolm X Speaks,* 42, 52, 93, 111, 118. See also Epps, *Speeches of Malcolm X at Harvard,* 189–90; Malcolm X, *Autobiography,* 76, 88, 104, 106, 110, 113, 119, 146, 277; Lincoln, *Black Muslims,* 169; Malcolm X, *Malcolm X on Afro-American History,* 36–37.

23. Stuckey, *Ideological Origins,* 11; Stuckey, *Slave Culture,* 125.

24. King, *Stride toward Freedom,* 211–12; King, "Our Struggle," 3; King, "Some Things We Must Do," 7; Baldwin, *Balm,* 52–53; King, *The Measure of a Man,* 54–55; King, *Strength to Love,* 131–32; Gallen, *A Malcolm X Reader,* 107–9; Breitman, *Malcolm X Speaks,* 70; Breitman, *By Any Means Necessary,* 140. Malcolm was more apt than Martin to trace a high degree of acquiescence to oppression by the masses of blacks back to slavery. The Muslim leader suggested at times that his slave forebears had passively endured treatment to which the American Indian offered the most violent resistance. In contrast, King noted that numerous slaves "fought, stole, sacrificed and died for their families," proving "that life is stronger than death." See Malcolm X, *Malcolm X on Afro-American History,* 41; King, "The Negro Family," 19–20.

25. Breitman, *Malcolm X Speaks,* 134, 174; Baldwin, *Balm,* 53–54; King, *Where Do We Go from Here?* 131–32. See also King, "The Negroes in America: The End of Jim Crow?" 5; King, "Address at a Mass Meeting," Selma, Ala., 16 February 1968, 8.

26. King, *Stride toward Freedom,* 212–14; Warren, "Who Speaks for the Negro?" 1–5; King to Kaplan, 6 March 1961; King, *Why We Can't Wait,* 87.

27. Breitman, *Malcolm X Speaks,* 33; Malcolm X, *Malcolm X on Afro-American History,* 68; Lincoln, *Black Muslims,* 148; Baldwin, *Balm,* 56–57, 230–43, 252–72.

28. Malcolm X, *Malcolm X on Afro-American History,* 1–74; Breitman, *By Any Means Necessary,* 53–56; King, *Where Do We Go from Here?* 122–23; King, "Advice for Living," May 1958, 112.

29. King, *Where Do We Go from Here?* 123.

30. Breitman, *Malcolm X Speaks,* 49–53, 67; Clark, *February 1965,* 64; Breitman, *By Any Means Necessary,* 11. Malcolm knew as well as Martin that there would always be African Americans who would refuse to struggle for freedom. In his more reflective moments, the Muslim leader said as much and more. See Perry, *Malcolm X: The Last Speeches,* 28–33, 121; K. Clark, *King, Malcolm, Baldwin,* 41–43; King, "The Sword That Heals," 14; Baldwin, *Balm,* 236–37.

31. King, "The Sword That Heals," 14; Bennett, "Rev. Martin Luther King Jr., Alabama Desegregationist, Challenges Talmadge"; King, "An Address to the National Press Club," 6–7; Washington, *A Testament of Hope,* 44, 76–77; Carson et al., *Papers of Martin Luther King Jr.,* 3:210, 237, 264, 280, 285, 301, 324, 452, 456.

32. King, "A Speech at a Dinner Honoring Him as a Nobel Peace Prize Recipient," 16; Oates, *Let the Trumpet Sound,* 253.

33. Breitman, *By Any Means Necessary,* 26–27, 58; King, *Where Do We Go from Here?* 123–24. Malcolm made the same point on numerous occasions, and he and Martin felt that black unity had to occur as a precondition for unity between the folk and whites. See Breitman, *Malcolm X Speaks,* 51.

34. Breitman, *By Any Means Necessary,* 33–67; Karim, *End of White World Supremacy,* 109–10, 115; K. Clark, *King, Malcolm, Baldwin,* 47. At times, King could be as unyielding as Malcolm in arguing that the development of "a sense of black consciousness and peoplehood" did not necessarily mean being anti-white. See Washington, *A Testament of Hope,* 317; King, *The Trumpet of Conscience,* 9.

35. King, *Where Do We Go from Here?* 123–25; Baldwin, *Balm,* 59.

36. Cone, *Martin and Malcolm and America,* 280; Breitman, *Malcolm X Speaks,* 174; quoted in *I Am a Man: Photographs of the 1968 Memphis Sanitation Strike and Dr. Martin Luther King Jr.,* 66.

37. King, "Advice for Living," September 1958, 68; King to Fey, 23 June 1962; Malcolm X, *Autobiography,* 222–23, 244, 254, 317, 375; Lomax, *When the Word Is Given,* 27–29, 121–24, 130, 160–64; Karim, *End of White World Supremacy,* 23–66.

38. Clark, *King, Malcolm, Baldwin,* 45. For some sense of the frequency with which Malcolm addressed moral issues among his people, also see Malcolm X, *Autobiography,* 223–24, 228–29, 298; Breitman, *By Any Means Necessary,* 49–52; Lomax, *When the Word Is Given,* 153; Karim, *End of White World Supremacy,* 83.

39. Washington, *A Testament of Hope,* 315; King, *Stride toward Freedom,* 223; King, "The Negro Family," 19–20; Karim, *End of White World Supremacy,* 119–20; Malcolm X, *Malcolm X on Afro-American History,* 31–32; Breitman, *Malcolm X Speaks,* 11–12; King, *Where Do We Go from Here?* 125.

40. Breitman, *Malcolm X Speaks,* 107–8; King, *Stride toward Freedom,* 222–24; King, *Where Do We Go from Here?* 126–28; Baldwin, *Balm,* 60–61.

41. Breitman, *By Any Means Necessary,* 45–49; Breitman *Malcolm X Speaks,* 202–3; King, *Where Do We Go from Here?* 128–34; C. S. King, *My Life,* 239; King, "President's Address," 13–14, 16.

42. Breitman, *By Any Means Necessary,* 45–49, 89; Allen, "Malcolm X's Fatal Challenge to White Capitalism," 5.

43. King, *Where Do We Go from Here?* 128–66; King, *Why We Can't Wait,* 67; Baldwin, *Balm,* 61–62; King, "Statement regarding the Freedom Now Party," 30 October 1964, 1.

44. *Like It Is,* videotape; Breitman, *Malcolm X Speaks,* 27–28, 30, 54–56, 110; Breitman, *By Any Means Necessary,* 23, 37, 90; King to Kennedy, 30 October 1956; Coleman B. Brown, "Grounds for American Loyalty," 123.

45. Malcolm X, *Autobiography,* 194, 286–87; Clark, *King, Malcolm, Baldwin,* 41, 46–47; Breitman, *Malcolm X Speaks,* 198.

46. Washington, *A Testament of Hope,* 212, 311, 609–10; King, *Where Do We Go from Here?* 153–54; Baldwin, *Balm,* 62; King, "Speech at an Operation Breadbasket Meeting," 5.

47. Interestingly enough, Malcolm refused to interpret his call for reparations for more than two centuries of slavery as simply another way of requesting government assistance for his people. See Malcolm X, *Malcolm X on Afro-American History,* 67–68; Breitman, *By Any Means Necessary,* 23, 46, 59, 123; Herman, "Malcolm X Launches a New Organization," 1; Breitman, *Malcolm X Speaks,* 25–30, 32–33, 55–56, 155; King, *Where Do We Go from Here?* 146–47; Washington, *A Testament of*

Hope, 142, 198; King, *Why We Can't Wait,* 20–21; Ansbro, *Martin Luther King Jr.,* 134–35.

48. James H. Cone skillfully uses the "dream" and "nightmare" metaphors to focus Martin's and Malcolm's "perspectives on America and to reveal something about the audiences to whom and for whom they spoke." See Cone, *Martin and Malcolm and America,* ix–x, 58–119; King, "The Negro and the American Dream," 1–5. This point concerning the tension between the "dream" and the "nightmare" should have been emphasized more in Cone, *Martin and Malcolm and America,* ix–x, 58–119.

49. Breitman, *Malcolm X Speaks,* 49; Malcolm X, *Malcolm X on Afro-American History,* 30–31; King interview, 28 July 1965, 2–3; King, "Address at a Mass Meeting," Montgomery, Ala., 16 February 1968, 4; Baldwin, *Balm,* 50.

50. Malcolm X, *Malcolm X on Afro-American History,* 30; Breitman, *By Any Means Necessary,* 41–42; Breitman, *Malcolm X Speaks,* 163–65; Karim, *End of White World Supremacy,* 119–20; King, *Where Do We Go from Here?* 64.

51. Lomax, *When the Word Is Given,* 24–25, 62, 199–200; Karim, *End of White World Supremacy,* 49–65; Lincoln, *Black Muslims,* 76; Cleage, "Myths about Malcolm X," 19–22; Breitman, *By Any Means Necessary,* 41–43; Breitman, *Malcolm X Speaks,* 42, 96, 108, 112; Lomax, *When the Word Is Given,* 199–211; Baldwin, *Toward the Beloved Community,* 41–42.

52. King, *Where Do We Go from Here?* 64.

53. King, "A Proposed Statement to the South," 3; Baldwin, *Balm,* 233–34; Malcolm X, *Autobiography,* 375, 395; Lomax, *When the Word Is Given,* 139; Malcolm X, *Malcolm X on Afro-American History,* 21; Breitman, *Malcolm X Speaks,* 36–38, 93–94, 148–50; King, *Where Do We Go from Here?* 167–68, 180–81, 186.

54. Breitman, *Malcolm X Speaks,* 134, 138, 159; Breitman, *By Any Means Necessary,* 42; Lincoln, *Black Muslims,* 143, 148; King, *Where Do We Go from Here?* 64; Baldwin, *Balm,* 236–37; King, "The Sword That Heals," 14; Ansbro, *Martin Luther King Jr.,* 111, 159.

55. Karim, *End of White World Supremacy,* 117–18; Breitman, *Malcolm X Speaks,* 28, 30, 42, 56, 106, 110; Malcolm X, *Autobiography,* 274–75. See also Flick and Powell, "Animal Imagery in the Rhetoric of Malcolm X," 435–45.

56. Breitman, *Malcolm X Speaks,* 110; Malcolm X, *Autobiography,* 274–75.

57. King, "An Address at a Mass Meeting," Marks, Miss., 19 March 1968, 5–6; King, "Civil Rights at the Crossroads," 4; Baldwin, *Balm,* 78–79.

58. King, "An Address at the First Annual Institute on Nonviolence and Social Change," 1–3; King, "Some Things We Must Do," 3; King to Boone, 9 May 1957; King, "An Address at the Freedom Fund Report Dinner of the N.A.A.C.P.'s 53rd Annual Convention," 3; King, "A Statement to the South and the Nation," 10 January 1957, 2–3; Baldwin, *Balm,* 67–68.

59. In 1963, King admitted that "Perhaps I was too optimistic; perhaps I expected too much." He further noted: "I suppose I should have realized that few members of the oppressor race can understand the deep groans and passionate yearnings of the oppressed race, and still fewer have the vision to see that injustice must be rooted out by strong, persistent and determined action." See King, *Why We Can't Wait,* 89.

60. Breitman, *By Any Means Necessary,* 7, 59. Breitman, *Malcolm X Speaks,* 34, 53–55, 173, 225; Malcolm X, *Autobiography,* 275; K. Clark, *King, Malcolm, Baldwin,* 47; Karim, *End of White World Supremacy,* 133–37.

61. "Interview with Martin Luther King Jr.," London, England, 2.

62. King, *Stride toward Freedom,* 32, 108–9, 163, 173; King, *Why We Can't Wait,* 89; King, "Address at the Golden Anniversary Conference of the National Urban League," 7–8; Baldwin, *Balm,* 80–82; King, "President's Address," 6; Washington, *A Testament of Hope,* 56, 576; King, "Address at the Prayer Pilgrimage for Freedom at the Lincoln Memorial," 2.

63. King, "Address at the Prayer Pilgrimage," 2.

64. Breitman, *By Any Means Necessary,* 7, 58; Breitman, *Malcolm X Speaks,* 5–6; Malcolm X, *Malcolm X on Afro-American History,* 46; King, "To Chart Our Course for the Future," 4–5.

65. King, "Advice for Living," October 1957, 53. This statement is one reflection of King's skill as a dialectical thinker. He generally opposed the "either-or" approach to reasoning and embraced the "both-and" approach. See Ayres, *Wisdom of King,* 58–59.

66. The contention that Malcolm was never open to whites and blacks becoming a single people is not supported by comments that he made during the last year of his life. See Breitman, *By Any Means Necessary,* 111, 123, 183–84; Breitman, *Malcolm X Speaks,* 5–6, 59–63, 72–87, 197, 210–11, 216; Lomax, *When the Word Is Given,* 202–6; Karim, *End of White World Supremacy,* 121–48; Washington, *A Testament of Hope,* 300; *Dr. Martin Luther King Jr.: An Amazing Grace,* film; King, "A Proposed Statement to the South," 3; Baldwin, *Balm,* 229–72.

67. See "James Cone Interview," 9; Baldwin, *Toward the Beloved Community,* 4; Baldwin, *To Make the Wounded Whole,* 163–317; Cone, *Martin and Malcolm and America,* 311–14; King, *Where Do We Go from Here?* 167–91; Breitman, *By Any Means Necessary,* 7–8, 184; Breitman, *Malcolm X Speaks,* 5–6, 72–87, 210–13.

68. Malcolm X, *Autobiography,* 2, 5–7, 176–92; Baldwin, *Toward the Beloved Community,* 8–9.

69. There are apparently some inconsistencies in Malcolm's accounts of just how important links with Africa were to the Nation of Islam. On one occasion, he observed: "One of the things that made the Black Muslim movement grow was its emphasis on things African." At another point, he declared that "Elijah Muhammad never made one statement that's pro-African. And he has never, in any of his speeches . . . , said anything to his followers about Africa." On yet another occasion, Malcolm insisted that Muhammad's "doctrine is as anti-Arab and anti-Asian as it is anti-white." "No Arab or Muslims were ever permitted in his temples or places of worship," Malcolm added. See Breitman, *Malcolm X Speaks,* 171–72; Clark, *February 1965,* 205, 249.

70. See C. S. King, *My Life,* 142–44; King, "Statement on the Legitimacy of the Struggle in Montgomery, Alabama," 4 May 1956, 1; Washington, *A Testament of Hope,* 24.

71. Malcolm raised this issue in a manner that recalled the controversies over names in the nineteenth and early twentieth centuries. See Stuckey, *Slave Culture,*

193–244; Breitman, *By Any Means Necessary,* 55–56; Malcolm X, *Malcolm X on Afro-American History,* 15–19, 27; Karim, *End of White World Supremacy,* 24, 91, 107; Breitman, *Malcolm X Speaks,* 36; Epps, *Speeches of Malcolm X at Harvard,* 76, 125, 161–62, 182.

72. Interestingly enough, Martin's thinking on a group name for his people seems to have shifted over time. In 1964, he insisted that "The Negro is an American"—that "his culture is basically American" and his "destiny is tied up with the destiny of America." "We know nothing about Africa," he added. His later tendency to embrace "both the African and American sides of his people's heritage" resulted largely from the challenge of Malcolm X and the black power movement. See Warren, "Who Speaks for the Negro?" 15–16; King, *Where Do We Go from Here?* 53; King, "See You in Washington," 3–4; Baldwin, *To Make the Wounded Whole,* 22–23.

73. "Malcolm X Woos Two Rights Leaders," 28; Herman, "Malcolm X Announces Rally to Launch New Organization," 1; Clark, *King, Malcolm, Baldwin,* 12–13.

74. Breitman, *By Any Means Necessary,* 153; Perry, *Malcolm X: The Last Speeches,* 14; Breitman, *Malcolm X Speaks,* 48.

75. Malcolm X, *Malcolm X on Afro-American History,* 13–14, 69–70; Clark, *February 1965,* 46–64, 106–70; B. Perry, *Malcolm X: The Last Speeches,* 109–81; King, *Where Do We Go from Here?* 173–76, 179; Washington, *A Testament of Hope,* 235; Halberstam, "When 'Civil Rights' and 'Peace' Join Forces," in Lincoln, *Martin Luther King, Jr.,* 207; King, *The Trumpet of Conscience,* 26; Breitman, *Malcolm X Speaks,* 218–19; Karim, *End of White World Supremacy,* 117.

76. Clark, *February 1965,* 35, 70; King, *Where Do We Go from Here?* 173; Baldwin, *Toward the Beloved Community,* 25–63.

77. *Like It Is,* videotape; Schneier, *Shared Dreams,* 160–65, 168–69; "Draft of Statement Regarding SCLC's Participation at National Conference on New Politics," September 1967, 1. Also see King, "My Jewish Brother," 1, 12; Ruskin to King, 30 November 1959.

78. Schneier, *Shared Dreams,* 160–65, 168–69.

79. Breitman, *Malcolm X Speaks,* 36–37, 72–87, 101, 103; Breitman, *By Any Means Necessary,* 18–19; Clark, *February 1965,* 31–32, 45; King, *Where Do We Go from Here?* 57.

80. Breitman, *Malcolm X Speaks,* 103, 117.

81. Ibid., 5, 130; Karim, *End of White World Supremacy,* 96–97.

82. Clark, *February 1965,* 31–32.

83. Radio interview with King regarding the Nobel Peace Prize, 1–2; Clark, *February 1965,* 38–41, 77, 110; Breitman, *Malcolm X Speaks,* 161.

84. Malcolm X, *Autobiography,* 370, 377; Breitman, *By Any Means Necessary,* 19, 114, 121–22, 136–37, 145–47, 153, 155–56, 171–74; Breitman, *Malcolm X Speaks,* 72–87; Clark, *February 1965,* 24, 38–40, 54–55, 62–63, 77, 79, 108, 121, 145; Lomax, *When the Word Is Given,* 181; Epps, *Speeches of Malcolm X at Harvard,* 158; Carson et al., *Papers of Martin Luther King Jr.,* 3:263; King to Sealy, 6 July 1965; King to Van Nuys, 29 April 1957; King, "My Talk with Ben Bella," 12; King, "Address at the Valedictory Service," University of the West Indies, Mona, Jamaica, 1–12; Baldwin, *To Make the Wounded Whole,* 163–244.

85. Clark, *February 1965,* 55; Milne, "Malcolm's Sister Fights On," 48; Breitman, *By Any Means Necessary,* 147; Breitman, *Malcolm X Speaks,* 72–87.

86. Baldwin, *Toward the Beloved Community,* 13–21, 32–57; press statement, "Stand on Sit-Ins," 19 February 1962, 1; Baldwin, *To Make the Wounded Whole,* 172; Breitman, *By Any Means Necessary,* 145; "U.S. Negroes' Goal: To Set Africa Policy."

87. Breitman, *By Any Means Necessary,* 36, 136, 146, 161; Clark, *February 1965,* 63.

88. Breitman, *Malcolm X Speaks,* 210; *National Review,* 29 December 1964, 2; Breitman, *By Any Means Necessary,* 5–6; King to the South African embassy, 9 February 1966; C. S. King, *My Life,* 239; Baldwin, *Toward the Beloved Community,* 60.

89. This problem of perceiving "nationalist" and "integrationist" as mutually exclusive is quite evident in the treatment of Malcolm and Martin by James H. Cone. See Cone, *Martin and Malcolm and America,* 3–37. King's relationship to Pan-Africanism should not be casually dismissed merely because he talked a lot about integration. One scholar claims that King "was not essentially a Pan-Africanist," despite the commonalities between his and W.E.B. Du Bois's positions. A former civil rights activist disagrees, arguing that "Dr. King was most certainly a Pan-Africanist." See Houser, "Freedom's Struggle Crosses Oceans and Mountains," in Albert and Hoffman, *We Shall Overcome,* 183; Baldwin, interview with the Reverend Clarence James, 7 February 1999. The view that King's thought was peppered with elements of Pan-Africansism is borne out in Baldwin, *Toward the Beloved Community,* 8–61, 187–88n.2, 189n.18; Baldwin, *To Make the Wounded Whole,* 163–218.

90. McCloud, *African-American Islam,* 35–37.

91. Breitman, *Malcolm X Speaks,* 216–17; Perry, *Malcolm X: The Last Speeches,* 181; King, *Where Do We Go from Here?* 167; King, *The Trumpet of Conscience,* 69–70.

92. Nadle, "Malcolm X: The Complexity of a Man in the Jungle," 6; Breitman, *By Any Means Necessary,* 184; Breitman, *Malcolm X Speaks,* 197.

93. Breitman, *Malcolm X Speaks,* 216; "Doubts and Certainties Link," 1–2; Baldwin, *Toward the Beloved Community,* 2–3, 56; King, *Where Do We Go from Here?* 167–68.

94. Breitman, *By Any Means Necessary,* 19, 114, 121–22, 153, 162, 169; "A Tribute to Malcolm X: How Ossie Davis Saw Him," 8; Lomax, *When the Word Is Given,* 181; Epps, *Speeches of Malcolm X at Harvard,* 158; Gallen et al., *Malcolm X as They Knew Him,* 175; Clark, *February 1965,* 35, 50, 68–71; King, *Where Do We Go from Here?* 173–74; Baldwin, *Toward the Beloved Community,* 1–63.

95. Malcolm X, *Autobiography,* 339–40, 345, 358; Breitman, *Malcolm X Speaks,* 96; "Brother Reveals Malcolm X Had Disavowed His Racist Philosophy in Later Life," 19; Hatch, "Racism and Religion: The Contrasting Views of Benjamin Mays, Malcolm X, and Martin Luther King Jr."; "First Time in Print: An Interview with Malcolm X," 5. Sterling Stuckey's contention that black nationalists have long had "a concern for values that go beyond race" is borne out by Malcolm's rejection of racism in the last year of his life. See Stuckey, *Slave Culture,* 229.

96. Breitman, *Malcolm X Speaks,* 197, 206–7, 216, 220–22, 224–25; Washington,

A Testament of Hope, 219; King, *The Trumpet of Conscience,* 69–70; "Doubts and Certainties Link," 1–2; King, "Speech at an Operation Breadbasket Meeting," 4.

97. Malcolm was obviously naive in thinking that Islam could be more effective than Christianity in eliminating racism as a global problem. King was far more perceptive concerning this matter, for he knew that both Christianity and Islam had long been connected with slavery and prejudice based on skin color. See Malcolm X, "Racism: The Cancer that is Destroying America," 302–6; Breitman, *Malcolm X Speaks,* 47, 216; "Doubts and Certainties Link," 1–2; Baldwin, *Toward the Beloved Community,* 56.

98. Epps, *Speeches of Malcolm X at Harvard,* 134; Gallen et al., *Malcolm X as They Knew Him,* 177–78; *National Leader,* 2 June 1983, 28.

99. Breitman, *Malcolm X Speaks,* 120–22; King, *Strength to Love,* 102.

100. This is what Malcolm had in mind when he referred to "An international power structure consisting of American interests, French interests, English interests, Belgian interests, European interests. . . . A structure, a house that has ruled the world up until now." See Perry, *Malcolm X: The Last Speeches,* 14; King, *Where Do We Go from Here?* 173–74, 186–88; "Many Memorial Meetings around Nation Pay Tribute to Memory of Malcolm X," 4; "Remembering Malcolm at 60," 3; "The Impact of Malcolm X: His Ideas Keep Spreading," 4; Allen, "Malcolm X's Fatal Challenge to White Capitalism," 5; King, *Strength to Love,* 102–3; King to Edward D. Ball, 14 December 1961.

101. Breitman, *Malcolm X Speaks,* 69, 120–22; Breitman, *By Any Means Necessary,* 180–81; "Remembering Malcolm at 60," 3; Smith, "The Radicalization of Martin Luther King Jr.," 270, 278.

102. Breitman, *Malcolm X Speaks,* 50, and King, *Where Do We Go from Here?* 178–79.

103. Breitman, *Malcolm X Speaks,* 164–65, 216–17; Breitman, *By Any Means Necessary,* 30, 41–42, 177; King, *Where Do We Go from Here?* 181–86, 191.

104. King, *Where Do We Go from Here?* 181–86; King, *The Trumpet of Conscience,* 67–78.

105. "LBJ Tapes Reveal Confusion about Vietnam."

106. King, "East or West—God's Children," 1–16; King, *Trumpet of Conscience,* 69–70.

107. Clark, *February 1965,* 46, 85, 185.

108. This problem of fragmentation in the global human family is stressed in Baldwin, *Toward the Beloved Community,* 138–39. For important reflections on how this problem continues to unfold with respect to women, see "Jewish Women Pray Aloud," 3A; "Push Renewed to Accelerate Women's Rights," 2A; "U.N. Conference Fends Off Efforts," 4A; "U.N. Delegates Struggle with Women's Rights," 4A.

109. No scholar has developed this point more persuasively than the black theologian James H. Cone. See Cone, *Martin and Malcolm and America,* 288–314. This point is made in reference to King in Baldwin, *Toward the Beloved Community,* 138–39.

110. This became Malcolm's motto toward the end of his life. See review of the *Autobiography* in the *New Yorker,* 13 November 1965, 246–47.

Bibliography

Books and Pamphlets

Abd Al-Ati, Hammudah. *Islam in Focus*. Edmonton, Alberta: Canadian Islamic Centre, 1963.

Abernathy, Ralph D. *And the Walls Came Tumbling Down: An Autobiography*. New York: Harper and Row, 1989.

Ahmann, Mathew, ed. *Race: A Challenge to Religion*. Chicago: Henry Regnery, 1963.

Akbar, Na'im. *Chains and Images of Psychological Slavery*. Jersey City, N.J.: New Mind Publications, 1984.

———. *Visions for Black Men*. Nashville: Winston-Derek, 1991.

A'La Mawdudi, Abul. *Towards Understanding Islam*. Malaysia: Polygraphic Press, 1982.

Al-Amin, Jamil. *Revolution by the Book*. Beltsville, Md.: Writers International, 1994.

Albert, Peter J., and Ronald Hoffman, eds. *We Shall Overcome: Martin Luther King Jr. and the Black Freedom Struggle*. New York: Pantheon Books, 1990.

Al-Faruqi, Isma'il R., and Lois Lamya Al-Faruqi. *The Cultural Atlas of Islam*. New York: Free Press, 1986.

Al-Hussein, Hussein Khalid, and Ahmad Hussein Sakr. *Introducing Islam to Non-Muslims*. Lombard: Foundation for Islamic Knowledge, n.d.

Ali, Abdullah Yusuf. *Holy Qur'an: Text, Translation, and Commentary*. Brentwood, Md.: Amana Corporation, 1989.

———. *The Meaning of the Holy Qur'an*. Brentwood, Md.: Amana, 1992.

Ali, Basharat. *Muslim Social Philosophy*. Karachi: Jamiyatul Falah, 1967.

Ali, Maulana Muhammad. *Muhammad the Prophet*. Lahore: Ahmadiyya Anjuman Isha 'At Islam, 1993.

Ali, Muhammad. *The Greatest: My Own Story*, with Richard Durham. New York: Ballantine Books, 1975.

Al-Mansour, Khalid Abdullah Tariq. *Seven African Arabian Wonders of the World: The Black Man's Guide to the Middle East*. San Francisco: First African Arabian Press, 1991.

Al-Mubarakpuri, Safi-Ur-Rahman. *Ar-Raheeq Al-Makhtum (The Sealed Nectar): Biography of the Noble Prophet*. Riyadh-Saudi Arabia: Maktaba Dar-us-Salam, 1996.

Angelou, Maya. *All God's Children Need Traveling Shoes.* New York: Vintage Books, 1986.

Ani, Marimba. *Yurugu: An African-Centered Critique of European Cultural Thought and Behavior.* Trenton, N.J.: Africa World Press, 1994.

An-Nawawi, Iman Abu Zakariya Yahya Bin Sharaf, comp. *Riyadh-Us-Salcheen.* Vol. 1. Karachi: International Islamic Publishers, 1983.

Ansbro, John J. *Martin Luther King Jr.: The Making of a Mind.* Maryknoll, N.Y.: Orbis Books, 1982.

Armstrong, Scott, and Bob Woodward. *The Brethren: Inside the Supreme Court.* New York: Avon Books, 1979.

Asante, Molefi Kete. *Afrocentricity.* Trenton, N.J.: Africa World Press, 1988.

———. *Kemet, Afrocentricity, and Knowledge.* Trenton, N.J.: Africa World Press, 1990.

———. *Malcolm X as Cultural Hero and Other Afrocentric Essays.* Trenton, N.J.: Africa World Press, 1993.

Askew, Glorya, and Gayraud S. Wilmore, eds. *From Prison Cell to Church Pew: The Strategy of the African American Church.* Atlanta: ITC Press, 1993.

———. *Reclamation of Black Prisoners: A Challenge to the African American Church.* Atlanta: ITC Press, 1992.

Ata ur-Rahim, Muhammad. *Jesus: A Prophet of Islam.* London: MWH London, 1977.

Austin, Allan D. *African Muslims in Antebellum America: A Sourcebook.* New York: Garland, 1984.

Ayres, Alex, ed. *The Wisdom of Martin Luther King Jr.* New York: Penguin Books, 1993.

Azzam, Abd-Al-Rahman. *The Eternal Message of Muhammad.* New York: Devin-Adair, 1964.

Az-Zubaidi, Al-Ilmam Zain-Ud-Din Ahmad bin Abdul-Lateef, and Muhammad Muhsin Khan, comp. *Sahih Al-Bukhari.* Riyadh-Saudi Arabia: Maktaba Darus-Salam, 1994.

Baer, Hans A., and Merrill Singer. *African American Religion in the Twentieth Century: Varieties of Protest and Accommodation.* Knoxville: University of Tennessee Press, 1992.

Baker-Fletcher, Garth K., ed. *Black Religion and the Million Man March.* Maryknoll, N.Y.: Orbis Books, 1998.

———. *Somebodyness: Martin Luther King Jr. and the Theory of Dignity.* Minneapolis: Fortress Press, 1993.

———. *Xodus: An African American Male Journey.* Minneapolis: Fortress Press, 1996.

Baldwin, Lewis V. *"Invisible" Strands in African Methodism: A History of the African Union Methodist Protestant and Union American Methodist Episcopal Churches, 1805–1980.* Metuchen, N.J.: Scarecrow Press, 1983.

———. *There Is a Balm in Gilead: The Cultural Roots of Martin Luther King Jr.* Minneapolis: Fortress Press, 1991.

————. *To Make the Wounded Whole: The Cultural Legacy of Martin Luther King Jr.* Minneapolis: Fortress Press, 1992.

————. *Toward the Beloved Community: Martin Luther King Jr. and South Africa.* Cleveland: Pilgrim Press, 1995.

Barboza, Steven. *American Jihad: Islam after Malcolm X.* New York: Image Books, Doubleday, 1994.

Bedau, Hugo A., ed. *Civil Disobedience: Theory and Practice.* New York: Pegasus, 1969.

Ben-Jochannan, Yosef. *African Origins of the Major "Western Religions."* New York: Alkebu-Lan Books, 1970.

Bennett, Lerone, Jr. *Confrontation: Black and White.* Chicago: Johnson Publishing, 1965.

————. *What Manner of Man: A Memorial Biography of Martin Luther King Jr.* New York: Pocket Books, 1968.

Berger, Peter L., and Thomas Luckman. *The Social Construction of Reality: A Treatise in the Sociology of Knowledge.* Garden City, N.Y.: Doubleday, 1966.

Billingsley, Andrew. *Climbing Jacob's Ladder: The Enduring Legacy of African American Families.* New York: Touchstone, 1992.

Bishop, Jim. *The Days of Martin Luther King Jr.* New York: G. P. Putnam's Sons, 1971.

Blassingame, John. *The Slave Community: Plantation Life in the Antebellum South.* New York: Oxford University Press, 1979.

Bleiweiss, Robert M., ed. *Marching to Freedom: The Life of Martin Luther King Jr.* New York: New American Library, 1969.

Blyden, Edward W. *Christianity, Islam, and the Negro Race.* 1887. Reprint, Edinburgh: Aldin Publishing, 1967.

Branch, Taylor. *Parting the Waters: America in the King Years, 1954–63.* New York: Simon and Schuster, 1988.

————. *Pillar of Fire: America in the King Years, 1963–65.* New York: Simon and Schuster, 1998.

Breitman, George. *The Last Year of Malcolm X: The Evolution of a Revolutionary.* New York: Pathfinder Press, 1967.

————, ed. *By Any Means Necessary: Speeches, Interviews, and a Letter by Malcolm X.* New York: Pathfinder Press, 1970.

————, ed. *Malcolm X Speaks: Selected Speeches and Statements.* New York: Merit, 1965.

Breitman, George, Herman Porter, and Baxter Smith, eds. *The Assassination of Malcolm X.* New York: Pathfinder Press, 1976.

Brewer, J. Mason. *American Negro Folklore.* New York: Quadrangle/New York Times Books, 1968.

Bridges, Flora Wilson. *Resurrection Song: African American Spirituality.* Maryknoll, N.Y.: Orbis Books, 2001.

Brotz, Howard, ed. *African American Social and Political Thought, 1850–1920.* 1966. Reprint, New Brunswick, N.J.: Transaction, 1995.

Brown, Cynthia Stokes, ed. *Septima Clark and the Civil Rights Movement: Ready from Within—A First Person Narrative.* Trenton, N.J.: Africa World Press, 1990.

Cannon, Katie G. *Black Womanist Ethics.* Atlanta: Scholars Press, 1988.

Carruthers, Jacob H. *MDW NTR: Divine Speech—An Historical Reflection on African Deep Thought from the Time of the Pharaohs to the Present.* Chicago: Karnack House, 1995.

Carruthers, Jacob H., and Maulana Karenga, eds. *Kemet and the African Worldview: Research, Rescue, and Restoration—Selected Papers of the Proceedings of the First and Second Conferences of the Association for the Study of Classical African Civilizations.* Los Angeles: University of Sankore Press, 1986.

Carson, Clayborne. *In Struggle: SNCC and the Black Awakening of the 1960s.* Cambridge: Harvard University Press, 1981.

———, ed. *The Autobiography of Martin Luther King Jr.* New York: Warner Books, 1998.

——— et al., eds. *The Papers of Martin Luther King Jr.* Vol. I, *Called to Serve, January 1929–June 1951.* Berkeley: University of California Press, 1992.

———. *The Papers of Martin Luther King Jr.* Vol. II, *Rediscovering Precious Values, July 1951–November 1955.* Berkeley: University of California Press, 1994.

———. *The Papers of Martin Luther King Jr.* Vol. III, *Birth of a New Age, December 1955–December 1956.* Berkeley: University of California Press, 1997.

———. *The Papers of Martin Luther King Jr.* Vol. IV. *Symbol of the Movement, January 1957–December 1958.* Berkeley: University of California Press, 2000.

Chapman, Mark L. *Christianity on Trial: African American Religious Thought Before and After Black Power.* Maryknoll, N.Y.: Orbis Books, 1996.

Chapnick, Howard, ed. *Malcolm X: The Great Photographs.* Text by Thulani Davis. New York: Stewart Tabori and Chang, 1992.

Chatterjee, Margaret. *Gandhi's Religious Thought.* Notre Dame, Ind.: University of Notre Dame Press, 1983.

Children and Poverty—An Episcopal Initiative: Biblical and Theological Foundations. Nashville: United Methodist Publishing House, 1996.

Clark, Kenneth B. *King, Malcolm, Baldwin: Three Interviews.* Middletown, Conn.: Wesleyan University Press, 1985.

Clark, Steve, ed. *February 1965: The Final Speeches—Malcolm X.* New York: Pathfinder Press, 1992.

Clarke, John Henrik. *African People in World History.* Baltimore: Black Classic Press, 1993.

———. *Christopher Columbus and the Afrikan Holocaust: Slavery and and Rise of European Capitalism.* Brooklyn: A and B, 1994.

———, ed. *Malcolm X: The Man and His Times.* New York: Collier Books, 1969.

———, ed. *William Styron's Nat Turner: Ten Black Writers Respond.* Boston: Beacon Press, 1968.

Cleage, Albert B., Jr. *Black Christian Nationalism: New Directions for the Black Church.* New York: William Morrow, 1972.

———. *The Black Messiah.* New York: Sheed and Ward, 1968.

Colbert, Jan, and Ann M. Harms, eds. *Dear Dr. King: Letters from Today's Children to Dr. Martin Luther King Jr.* New York: Colbert, 1998.

Collier-Thomas, Bettye. *Daughters of Thunder: Black Women Preachers and Their Sermons, 1850–1979.* San Francisco: Jossey-Bass, 1998.

Collier-Thomas, Bettye, and V. P. Franklin. *Sisters in the Struggle: African American Women in the Civil Rights–Black Power Movement.* New York: New York University Press, 2001.

Collins, Patricia Hill. *Black Feminist Thought: Knowledge, Consciousness, and the Politics of Empowerment.* New York: Routledge, 1991.

Collins, Rodnell P. *Seventh Child: A Family Memoir of Malcolm X,* with the assistance of A. Peter Bailey. Secaucus, N.J.: Birch Lane Press, 1998.

Cone, James H. *A Black Theology of Liberation.* Philadelphia and New York: J. B. Lippincott, 1970.

———. *Black Theology and Black Power.* New York: Seabury Press, 1969.

———. *Martin and Malcolm and America: A Dream or a Nightmare.* Maryknoll, N.Y.: Orbis Books, 1991.

———. *Speaking the Truth: Ecumenism, Liberation, and Black Theology.* Grand Rapids, Mich.: William B. Eerdmans, 1986.

———. *The Spirituals and the Blues: An Interpretation.* Westport, Conn.: Greenwood Press, 1980.

Cone, James H., and Gayraud S. Wilmore, eds. *Black Theology: A Documentary History, 1966–1979.* 2 vols. Maryknoll, N.Y.: Orbis Books, 1993.

Conway, Flo, and Jim Siegelman. *Holy Terror: The Fundamentalist War on America's Freedoms in Religion, Politics and Our Private Lives.* New York: Dell, 1984.

Courlander, Harold. *Negro Folk Music, U.S.A.* New York: Columbia University Press, 1963.

Cox, Harvey. *The Feast of Fools: A Theological Essay on Festivity and Fantasy.* New York: Harper and Row, 1969.

Cox, Oliver C. *Caste, Class and Race: A Study in Social Dynamics.* New York: Modern Readers Paperbacks, 1948.

———. *Race Relations: Elements and Social Dynamics.* Detroit: Wayne State University Press, 1976.

Crawford, Vicki L., et al., eds. *Women in the Civil Rights Movement: Trailblazers and Torchbearers, 1941–1965.* Brooklyn, N.Y.: Carlson, 1990.

Cross, Haman, Jr., and Donna E. Scott. *What's Up with Malcolm: The Real Failure of Islam,* with Eugene Seals. Chicago: Moody Press, 1993.

Curry, George E., ed. *The Affirmative Action Debate.* Reading, Mass.: Addison-Wesley, 1996.

Dallard, Shyrlee. *Ella Baker: A Leader behind the Scenes.* Englewood Cliffs, N.J.: Silver Burdett Press, 1990.

Daly, Mary. *Beyond God the Father: Toward a Philosophy of Women's Liberation.* Boston: Beacon Press, 1973.

DeCaro, Louis A. *Malcolm and the Cross: The Nation of Islam, Malcolm X, and Christianity.* New York: New York University Press, 1998.

———. *On the Side of My People: A Religious Life of Malcolm X*. New York: New York University Press, 1996.

DeGraft-Johnson, J. C. *African Glory: The Story of Vanished Negro Civilizations*. New York: Walker and Co., 1954.

Diop, Cheikh Anta. *Civilization or Barbarism: An Authentic Anthropology*. New York: Lawrence Hill, 1981.

———. *The African Origin of Civilization: Myth or Reality?* New York: Lawrence Hill, 1974.

Diouf, Sylviane A. *Servants of Allah: African Muslims Enslaved in the Americas*. New York: New York University Press, 1998.

Dollard, John. *Caste and Class in a Southern Town*. Garden City, New York: Doubleday, 1949.

Douglas, Kelly Brown. *The Black Christ*. Maryknoll, N.Y.: Orbis Books, 1994.

Downing, Frederick L. *To See the Promised Land: The Faith Pilgrimage of Martin Luther King Jr*. Macon, Ga.: Mercer University Press, 1986.

Draper, Theodore. *The Rediscovery of Black Nationalism*. New York: Viking, 1969.

Du Bois, Shirley G. *His Day Is Marching On: A Memoir of W.E.B. Du Bois*. Philadelphia: J. B. Lippincott, 1971.

Du Bois, W.E.B. *Dusk of Dawn: An Essay Toward an Autobiography of a Race Concept*. New York: Harcourt and Brace, 1940.

———. *The Conservation of the Races*. Washington, D.C.: American Negro Academy, 1897.

———. *The Gift of Black Folk: Negroes in the Making of America*. Boston: Stratford, 1924.

———. *The Negro*. 1915. Reprint, New York: Oxford University Press, 1970.

———. *The Souls of Black Folk*. 1903. Reprint, Greenwich: Fawcett, 1961.

———. *The Suppression of the African Slave Trade to the United States, 1638–1870*. 1896. Reprint, New York: Schocken Books, 1969.

Dyson, Michael E. *Between God and Gangsta Rap: Bearing Witness to Black Culture*. New York: Oxford University Press, 1996.

———. *I May Not Get There with You: The True Martin Luther King Jr*. New York: Free Press, 2000.

———. *Making Malcolm: The Myth and Meaning of Malcolm X*. New York: Oxford University Press, 1995.

Easwaran, Eknath. *Gandhi the Man: The Story of His Transformation*. Tomales, Calif.: Nilgiri Press, 1997.

Edwards, G. Franklin, ed. *E. Franklin Frazier on Race Relations*. Chicago: University of Chicago Press, 1968.

El-Amin, Mustafa. *The Religion of Islam and the Nation of Islam: What Is the Difference?* Newark, N.J.: El-Amin Productions, 1991.

Encyclopedia of Sociology. Guilford, Conn.: Dushkin, 1974.

Epps, Archie, ed. *The Speeches of Malcolm X at Harvard*. New York: William Morrow, 1968.

Erskine, Noel L. *King among the Theologians*. Cleveland: Pilgrim Press, 1994.

Essien-Udom, E. U. *Black Nationalism: A Search for Identity in America.* New York: Dell, 1964.

Evans, Zelia, and J. T. Alexander, eds., *The Dexter Avenue Baptist Church, 1877–1977.* Montgomery, Ala.: Dexter Avenue Baptist Church, 1978.

Evanzz, Karl. *The Judas Factor: The Plot to Kill Malcolm X.* New York: Thunder's Mouth Press, 1992.

Fackre, Gabriel. *The Religious Right and Christian Faith.* Grand Rapids, Mich.: William B. Eerdmans, 1982.

Fairclough, Adam. *To Redeem the Soul of America: The Southern Christian Leadership Conference and Martin Luther King Jr.* Athens: University of Georgia Press, 1987.

Fanon, Frantz. *Black Skin, White Masks.* New York: Grove Press, 1967.

———. *Toward the African Revolution.* New York: Grove Press, 1967.

———. *The Wretched of the Earth: The Handbook for the Black Revolution that Is Changing the Shape of the World.* New York: Grove Press, 1963.

Faulkner, William J. *The Days When the Animals Talked: Black American Folktales and How They Came to Be.* Chicago: Follett, 1977.

Felder, Cain H., ed. *The Original African Heritage Study Bible.* Nashville: James C. Winston, 1993.

Fisher, Miles M. *Negro Slave Songs in the United States.* New York: Carol, 1990.

Fluker, Walter E. *They Looked for a City: A Comparative Analysis of the Ideal of Community in the Thought of Howard Thurman and Martin Luther King Jr.* Lanham, Md.: University Press of America, 1989.

Foner, Philip S., ed. *W.E.B. Du Bois Speaks: Speeches and Addresses, 1920–1963.* New York: Pathfinder Press, 1970.

Foreman, James. *The Political Thought of James Foreman.* Detroit: Black Star, 1970.

Four Decades of Concern: Martin Luther King Jr. Atlanta: Martin Luther King Jr. Center for Nonviolent Social Change, 1986.

Franklin, John Hope. *From Slavery to Freedom: A History of Negro Americans.* New York: Alfred A. Knopf, 1974.

———, ed. *The Souls of Black Folk in Three Negro Classics.* New York: Avon Books, 1965.

Frazier, E. Franklin. *Black Bourgeoisie: The Rise of a New Middle Class in the United States.* New York: Collier Books, 1965.

———. *The Negro Church in America.* New York: Schocken Books, 1963.

———. *The Negro Family in the United States.* 1939. Reprint, Chicago: University of Chicago Press, 1968.

Freire, Paulo. *Pedagogy of the Oppressed.* New York: Herder and Herder, 1970.

Friese, Kai. *Rosa Parks: The Movement Organizes.* Englewood Cliffs, N.J.: Silver Burdett Press, 1990.

Fulop, Timothy E., and Albert J. Raboteau. *African American Religion: Interpretive Essays in History.* New York: Routledge, 1997.

Gallen, David, ed. *A Malcolm X Reader: Perspectives on the Man and the Myths.* New York: Carroll and Graf, 1994.

Gallen, David, and Michael Friedly. *Martin Luther King, Jr.: The FBI File.* New York: Carroll & Grad, 1993.

Gallen, David, et al. *Malcolm X as They Knew Him.* New York: Carroll and Graf, 1992.

Garrow, David J. *Bearing the Cross: Martin Luther King Jr. and the Southern Christian Leadership Conference.* New York: William Morrow, 1986.

———. *Protest at Selma: Martin Luther King Jr. and the Voting Rights Act of 1965.* New Haven, Conn.: Yale University Press, 1978.

———. *The FBI and Martin Luther King Jr.: From "Solo" to Memphis.* New York: W. W. Norton, 1981.

———, ed. *Martin Luther King Jr. and the Civil Rights Movement.* 18 vols. Brooklyn, N.Y.: Carlson, 1989.

———, ed. *The Montgomery Bus Boycott and the Women Who Started It: The Memoir of Jo Ann Gibson Robinson.* Knoxville: University of Tennessee Press, 1987.

Garvey, Amy J., comp. *Philosophy and Opinions of Marcus Garvey.* London: Frank Cass, 1967.

Genovese, Eugene D. *Roll, Jordan, Roll: The World the Slaves Made.* New York: Pantheon Books, 1972.

Giddings, Paula. *When and Where I Enter: The Impact of Black Women on Race and Sex in America.* New York: William Morrow, 1984.

Giovanni, Nikki. *Racism 101.* New York: William Morrow, 1994.

Goldman, Peter. *The Death and Life of Malcolm X.* Urbana: University of Illinois Press, 1979.

Grant, Joanne. *Ella Baker: Freedom Bound.* New York: John Wiley, 1998.

Haddad, Yvonne Y. *The Muslims of America.* New York: Oxford University Press, 1991.

Halberstam, David. *The Children.* New York: Random House, 1998.

Hamilton, Alexander, et al. *The Federalist Papers.* New York: New American Library, 1961.

Harding, Vincent. *Martin Luther King Jr.: The Inconvenient Hero.* Maryknoll, N.Y.: Orbis Books, 1996.

Harris, Michael W. *The Rise of the Gospel Blues: The Music of Thomas Dorsey in the Urban Church.* New York: Oxford University Press, 1992.

Hayes, Diana L. *And Still We Rise: An Introduction to Black Liberation Theology.* New York: Paulist Press, 1996.

Haykal, Muhammad Husayn. *The Life of Muhammad.* Indianapolis: North American Trust, 1976.

Herskovits, Melville J. *Life in a Haitian Valley.* New York: Alfred A. Knopf, 1937.

———. *The Myth of the Negro Past.* 1941. Reprint, Boston: Beacon Press, 1958.

Hill, Robert B. *The Strengths of Black Families: A National Urban League Research Study.* New York: Emerson Hall, 1972.

Hill, Roy L., ed. *Rhetoric of Racial Revolt.* Denver: Golden Bell Press, 1964.

Hine, Darlene C. *Hine Sight: Black Women and the Reconstruction of American History.* Bloomington: Indiana University Press, 1994.

Hine, Darlene C., and Kathleen Thompson. *A Shining Thread of Hope: The History of Black Women in America*. New York: Broadway Books, 1998.

Holloway, Joseph E., ed. *Africanisms in American Culture*. Bloomington: Indiana University Press, 1990.

Hoskins, Lottie, ed. *"I Have a Dream": The Quotations of Martin Luther King Jr.* New York: Grosset and Dunlap, 1968.

Hunter, James D. *Culture Wars: The Struggle to Define America—Making Sense of the Battles over the Family, Art, Education, Law, and Politics*. New York: Basic Books, 1991.

I Am a Man: Photographs of the 1968 Memphis Sanitation Strike and Dr. Martin Luther King Jr. Memphis: Memphis Publishing Company, 1993.

Imran, Muhammad. *Ideal Woman in Islam*. Lahore, Pakistan: Islamic Publications, 1993.

Infusion Model for Teaching Dr. Martin Luther King Jr.'s Nonviolent Principles in Schools: Grade Levels K-12. Atlanta: Martin Luther King Jr. Center for Nonviolent Social Change, 1990.

Ivory, Luther D. *Toward a Theology of Radical Involvement: The Theological Legacy of Martin Luther King Jr.* Nashville: Abingdon Press, 1997.

Jaaber, Heshaam. *The Final Chapter: I Buried Malcolm (El-Hajj-Malik El-Shabazz)*. Jersey City, N.J.: New Mind, 1992.

Jack, Homer A., ed. *The Gandhi Reader*. Bloomington: Indiana University Press, 1956.

Jackson, Joseph H. *A Story of Christian Activism: The History of the National Baptist Convention, USA, Inc.* Nashville: Townsend Press, 1980.

Johnson, Charles S. *Bitter Canaan: The Story of the Negro Republic*. New Brunswick, N.J.: Transaction, 1987.

Johnson, Clifton H., ed. *God Struck Me Dead: Voices of Ex-Slaves*. 1969. Reprint, Cleveland: Pilgrim Press, 1993.

Johnson, Jacqueline. *Stokely Carmichael: The Story of Black Power*. Englewood Cliffs, N.J.: Silver Burdett Press, 1990.

Johnson, James Weldon. *God's Trombones: Seven Negro Sermons in Verse*. 1927. Reprint, New York: Viking Press, 1969.

Johnson, Paul E., ed. *African American Christianity: Essays in History*. Berkeley: University of California Press, 1994.

Jones, Major J. *The Color of God in Afro-American Thought*. Macon, Ga.: Mercer University Press, 1987.

Jones, William R. *Is God a White Racist? A Preamble to Black Theology*. New York: Doubleday, 1973.

Joseph, Gloria I., and Jill Lewis. *Common Differences: Conflicts in Black and White Feminist Perspectives*. Boston: South End Press, 1981.

Karenga, Maulana. *Selections from the Husia: Sacred Wisdom of Ancient Egypt*. Los Angeles: Kawaida, 1984.

Karenga, Maulana, and Jacob H. Carruthers. *Kemet and the African Worldview: Research, Rescue, and Restoration*. Los Angeles: University of Sankore Press.

Karenga, Maulana, and Haki R. Madhubuti. *The Million Man March: Day of Absence*. Chicago: Third World Press, 1996.

Karim, Imam Benjamin, ed. *The End of White World Supremacy: Four Speeches by Malcolm X*. New York: Seaver Books, 1971.

Karim, Imam Benjamin, et al. *Remembering Malcolm*. New York: Carroll and Graf, 1992.

Kateregga, Badru D., and David W. Shenk. *A Muslim and a Christian in Dialogue*. Scottdale, Pa.: Herald Press, 1997.

Kelley, Anthony. *Jailhouse Religion: The Church's Ministry and Mission to the Incarcerated*. Nashville: Townsend Press, 1992.

Khaldun, Ibn. *The Maqqaddimah: An Introduction to History*. Translated by Franz Rosenthal. Princeton: Princeton University Press, 1958.

Khan, Muhammad Muhsin. *Sahih-Al-Bukhari*. Beirut: Dar Al Islam, n.d.

King, Bernice A. *Hard Questions, Heart Answers: Speeches and Sermons*. New York: Broadway Books, 1996.

King, Coretta Scott. *My Life with Martin Luther King Jr.* 1969. Reprint, New York: Henry Holt, 1993.

———, ed. *The Words of Martin Luther King Jr.* New York: Newmarket Press, 1987.

King, Martin Luther, Jr. *Strength to Love*. 1963. Reprint, Philadelphia: Fortress Press, 1981.

———. *Stride toward Freedom: The Montgomery Story*. New York: Harper and Row, 1958.

———. *The Measure of a Man*. 1959. Reprint, Philadelphia: Fortress Press, 1988.

———. *The Trumpet of Conscience*. San Francisco: Harper and Row, 1967.

———. *Where Do We Go from Here: Chaos or Community?* Boston: Beacon Press, 1968.

———. *Why We Can't Wait*. New York: New American Library, 1964.

King, Martin Luther, Sr., with the assistance of Clayton Riley. *Daddy King: An Autobiography*. New York: William Morrow, 1980.

Kirk-Duggan, Cheryl A. *Exorcizing Evil: A Womanist Perspective on the Spirituals*. Maryknoll, N.Y.: Orbis Books, 1997.

———. *Refiner's Fire: A Religious Engagement with Violence*. Minneapolis: Fortress Press, 2001.

Kly, Y. N., ed. *The Black Book: The True Political Philosophy of Malcolm X (El-Hajj Malik El-Shabazz)*. Atlanta: Clarity Press, 1986.

Kunjufu, Jawanza. *Adam! Where Are You? Why Most Black Men Don't Go to Church*. Chicago: African American Images, 1994.

Latif, Sulton A., and Naimah Latif. *Slavery: The African American Psychic Trauma*. Chicago: Latif Communication Group, 1994.

Lentz, Richard. *Symbols, the News Magazines, and Martin Luther King*. Baton Rouge: Louisiana State University Press, 1990.

Lerner, Gerda, ed. *Black Women in White America: A Documentary History*. New York: Vintage Books, 1972.

Lester, Julius. *Black Folktales*. New York: Grove Press, 1970.

Levine, Lawrence W. *Black Culture and Black Consciousness: Afro-American Folk Thought from Slavery to Freedom*. New York: Oxford University Press, 1977.

Lewis, David L. *King: A Critical Biography*. New York: Praeger, 1970.

Lewis, John, with the assistance of Michael D'Orso. *Walking with the Wind: A Memoir of the Movement*. New York: Simon and Schuster, 1998.

Lincoln, C. Eric. *The Black Muslims in America*. 1961. Reprint, Trenton, N.J., and Grand Rapids, Mich.: Africa World Press and William B. Eerdmans, 1994.

————, ed. *Martin Luther King Jr.: A Profile*. New York: Hill and Wang, 1986.

Lincoln, C. Eric, and Lawrence H. Mamiya. *The Black Church in the African American Experience*. Durham, N.C.: Duke University Press, 1990.

Lomax, Louis E. *To Kill a Black Man*. Los Angeles: Holloway House, 1968.

————. *When the Word Is Given: A Report on Elijah Muhammad, Malcolm X, and the Black Muslim World*. 1963. Reprint, Westport, Conn.: Greenwood Press, 1979.

Lumumba, Chokwe, et al. *Reparations, Yes!* Baton Rouge, La.: Malcolm Generation, 1995.

Lynch, Hollis R. *Edward Wilmot Blyden: Pan-Negro Patriot, 1832–1912*. New York: Oxford University Press, 1970.

Maglangbayan, Shawna. *Garvey, Lumumba, Malcolm: Black Nationalist Separatists*. Chicago: Third World Press, 1972.

Malcolm X. *Malcolm X on Afro-American History*. New York: Pathfinder Press, 1970.

————. *Malcolm X Talks to Young People*. New York: Pathfinder Press, 1992.

————. *Two Speeches by Malcolm X*. New York: Pathfinder Press, 1992.

————, with the assistance of Alex Haley. *The Autobiography of Malcolm X*. New York: Grove Press, 1965.

Malcolm X: The Great Photographs. Text by Tulami Davis. New York: Stewart Tabori and Chang, 1993.

Mannheim, Karl. *Ideology and Utopia*. New York: Harcourt, Brace and World, 1936.

Mao Tse-tung. *Four Essays on Philosophy*. Peking: Foreign Languages Press, 1968.

Marable, Manning W. *W.E.B. Du Bois: Black Radical Democrat*. Boston: Twayne, 1986.

Martin Luther King Jr., 1929–1968: An Ebony Picture Biography. Chicago: Johnson, 1968.

McAdoo, Harriette P., ed. *Black Families*. Beverly Hills, Calif.: Sage, 1988.

McCartney, John T. *Black Power Ideologies: An Essay in African American Political Thought*. Philadelphia: Temple University Press, 1992.

McCloud, Aminah B. *African American Islam*. New York: Routledge, 1995.

Merton, Thomas, ed. *Gandhi on Nonviolence*. New York: New Directions Books, 1965.

Miller, William R. *Martin Luther King Jr.* New York: Weybright and Talley, 1968.

The Million Man March–Day of Absence: Mission Statement. Los Angeles, 1995.

Mills, Kay. *This Little Light of Mine: The Life of Fannie Lou Hamer*. New York: Penguin Books, 1993.

Mohammed, Imam Warith Deen. *A Light Shineth from the East.* Chicago: WDM, 1980.

———. *Prayer and Al-Islam.* Chicago: Muhammad Islamic Foundation, 1982.

Morris, Colin. *Unyoung, Uncolored, Unpoor.* Nashville and New York: Abingdon Press, 1969.

Moses, Wilson J. *Black Messiahs and Uncle Toms: Social and Literary Manipulations of a Religious Myth.* University Park: Pennsylvania State University, 1982.

———. *Classical Black Nationalism: From the American Revolution to Marcus Garvey.* New York: New York University Press, 1996.

Moynihan, Daniel P. *The Negro Family: The Case for National Action.* 1965. Reprint, Westport, Conn.: Greenwood Press, 1981.

Muhammad, Elijah. *Message to the Blackman in America.* Chicago: Muhammad Mosque of Islam No. 2, 1965.

———. *The Supreme Wisdom: Solution to the So-Called Negroes' Problem.* Newport News, Va.: National Newport News and Commentator, 1957.

Murray, Pauli. *The Autobiography of a Black Activist, Feminist, Lawyer, Priest, and Poet.* Knoxville: University of Tennessee Press, 1987.

National Baptist Hymnal. Nashville: Tenn.: National Baptist Publishing Board, 1983.

Nelson, Rachel West, and Sheyann Webb. *Selma, Lord, Selma: Girlhood Memories of the Civil Rights Days as Told to Frank Sikora.* New York: William Morrow, 1980.

Niebuhr, Reinhold. *Moral Man and Immoral Society: A Study in Ethics and Politics.* New York: Charles Scribner's Sons, 1932.

Nkrumah, Kwame. *Neo-Colonialism: The Last Stage of Imperialism.* London: Heinemann, 1965.

Oates, Stephen B. *Let the Trumpet Sound: The Life of Martin Luther King Jr.* New York: Harper and Row, 1982.

Olson, Lynne. *Freedom's Daughters: The Unsung Heroines of the Civil Rights Movement from 1830 to 1970.* New York: Scribner, 2001.

The Open Bible. Nashville: Thomas Nelson, 1975.

Orbis Books: A World of Books that Matter. Spring–Summer. Maryknoll, N.Y.: Orbis Books, 2001.

Paige, Howard. *Aspects of African American Cookery.* Southfield, Mich.: Aspects, 1987.

Pappas, Theodore. *Plagiarism and the Culture War: The Writings of Martin Luther King Jr. and Other Prominent Americans.* Tampa, Fla.: Hallberg, 1998.

Paris, Peter J. *Black Leaders in Conflict: Martin Luther King Jr., Malcolm X, Joseph H. Jackson, and Adam Clayton Powell, Jr.* New York: Pilgrim Press, 1978.

Perry, Bruce. *Malcolm: The Life of a Man Who Changed Black America.* Barrytown, N.Y.: Station Hill Press, 1991.

———, ed. *Malcolm X: The Last Speeches.* New York: Pathfinder Press, 1989.

Perry, Theresa, ed. *Teaching Malcolm X.* New York: Routledge, 1996.

Powers, Georgia D. *I Shared the Dream: The Pride, Passion and Politics of the First Black Woman Senator from Kentucky.* Far Hills, N.J.: New Horizon Press, 1995.

Proceedings of the Black Family Summit. New York: National Urban League, 1985.

Puckett, Newbell N. *Folk Beliefs of the Southern Negro.* Chapel Hill: University of North Carolina Press, 1926.

Qutb, Sayyid. *Milestones.* Indianapolis: American Trust, 1991.

Raboteau, Albert J. *A Fire in the Bones: Reflections on African American Religious History.* Boston: Beacon Press, 1995.

Ragg, Lonsdale, and Laura Ragg. *The Gospel of Barnabas.* Chicago: Kazi, 1975.

Raines, Howell. *My Soul Is Rested: Movement Days in the Deep South Remembered.* New York: G. P. Putnam's Sons, 1977.

Rainwater, Lee, and William L. Yancey. *The Moynihan Report and the Politics of Controversy.* Cambridge: MIT Press, 1967.

Ramsay, William M. *Four Modern Prophets: Walter Rauschenbusch, Martin Luther King Jr., Gustavo Gutierrez, Rosemary Ruether.* Atlanta: John Knox Press, 1986.

Rashad, Adib. *Islam, Black Nationalism, and Slavery: A Detailed History.* Beltsville, Md.: Printers, Inc., 1995.

Reddick, Lawrence D. *Crusader without Violence: A Biography of Martin Luther King Jr.* New York: Harper, 1959.

Report of the National Advisory Commission on Civil Disorders. New York: Bantam Books, 1968.

Rice, F. Philip. *Intimate Relationships, Marriages, and Family.* Mountain View, Calif.: Mayfield, 1990.

Richards, Dona M. *Let the Circle Be Unbroken: The Implications of African Spirituality in the Diaspora.* Trenton, N.J.: Red Sea Press, 1989.

Roberts, J. Deotis. *The Prophethood of Black Believers: An African American Political Theology for Ministry.* Louisville: Westminster John Knox Press, 1994.

Robinson, Randall. *The Debt: What America Owes Blacks.* New York: Dutton, 2000.

Rodney, Walter. *How Europe Underdeveloped Africa.* Washington, D.C.: Howard University Press, 1974.

Rogers, J. A. *Sex and Race: Negro-Caucasian Mixing in All Ages and All Lands.* 3 vols. New York: Helga M. Rogers, 1967.

Runes, Dagobert D., et al. *Dictionary of Philosophy.* Totowa, N.J.: Littlefield, Adams, 1962.

Sabiq, As-Sayyid. *Fiqh Us-Sunnah: Supererogatory Prayer.* Vol. 2. Indianapolis: American Trust, 1989.

Sadler, Kim M., ed. *Atonement: The Million Man March.* Cleveland: Pilgrim Press, 1996.

Sakr, Ahmad H. *Matrimonial Education in Islam.* Lombard, Ill.: Foundation for Islamic Knowledge, 1991.

——. *Sujood: Prostration.* Lombard, Ill.: Foundation for Islamic Knowledge, 1997.

Sales, William W., Jr. *From Civil Rights to Black Liberation: Malcolm X and the Organization of Afro-American Unity.* Boston: South End Press, 1994.

Sandeen, Ernest R., ed. *The Bible and Social Reform.* Philadelphia: Fortress Press, 1982.

Sanders, Cheryl J. *Empowerment Ethics for a Liberated People: A Path to African American Social Transformation*. Minneapolis: Fortress Press, 1995.

————, ed. *Living the Intersection: Womanism and Afrocentrism in Theology*. Minneapolis: Fortress Press, 1995.

Sawyer, Mary R. *Black Ecumenism: Implementing the Demands of Justice*. Valley Forge, Pa.: Trinity Press International, 1994.

Schneier, Rabbi Marc. *Shared Dreams: Martin Luther King Jr. and the Jewish Community*. Woodstock, Vt.: Jewish Lights, 1999.

Seale, Bobby. *Seize the Time: The Story of the Black Panther Party and Huey P. Newton*. Baltimore: Black Classic Press, 1991.

Selsam, Howard, and Harry Martel. *Reader in Marxist Philosophy: From the Writings of Marx, Engels, and Lenin*. New York: International Publishers, 1963.

Sernett, Milton C., ed. *African American Religious History: A Documentary Witness*. Durham, N.C.: Duke University Press, 1985, 1999.

————. *"Bound for the Promised Land": African American Religion and the Great Migration*. Durham, N.C.: Duke University Press, 1997.

Sertima, Ivan Van, ed. *Great African Thinkers: Cheikh Anta Diop*. Vol. 1. New Brunswick, N.J.: Transaction Books, 1989.

————. *They Came before Columbus*. New York: Random House, 1976.

Shaheed, Shah Ismail. *Taqwiyat-Ul-Iman (Strengthening of the Faith)*. Riyadh-Saudia Arabia: Dar-Ul-Salaam, 1995.

Shariati, Ali. *Hajj*. Bedford, Ohio: Free Islamic Literature, 1978.

Shu'aib, Tajuddin B. *The Prescribed Prayer Made Simple*. Los Angeles: Da'awah Enterprises International, 1983.

Siddiqi, Naeem. *Muhammad: The Benefactor of Humanity*. Delhi: Markazi Maktaba Islam, 1994.

Sleeter, Christine E., and Peter L. McLaren, eds. *Multicultural Education, Critical Pedagogy, and the Politics of Difference*. New York: State University of New York, 1995.

Smith, Ervin. *The Ethics of Martin Luther King Jr*. New York: Edwin Mellen Press, 1981.

Smith, Esther M. *A History of Ebenezer Baptist Church, Atlanta, Georgia*. Atlanta: Ebenezer Baptist Church, 1956.

Smith, Huston. *The World's Religions*. San Francisco: HarperCollins, 1991.

Smith, Kenneth L., and Ira G. Zepp Jr. *Search for the Beloved Community: The Thinking of Martin Luther King Jr*. Valley Forge, Pa.: Judson Press, 1974, 1998.

Smith, Wallace Charles. *The Church in the Life of the Black Family*. Valley Forge, Pa.: Judson Press, 1985.

Spencer, Jon M. *Blues and Evil*. Knoxville: University of Tennessee Press, 1993.

Staples, Robert, ed. *The Black Family: Essays and Studies*. Belmont, Calif.: Wadsworth, 1971, 1986.

The State of Black America: National Urban League Report. New York: National Urban League, 1990.

Stewart, Carlyle F., III. *Soul Survivors: An African American Spirituality*. Louisville: Westminster John Knox Press, 1997.

Stone, Chuck. *Black Political Power in America*. New York: Bobbs-Merrill, 1968.

Stuckey, Sterling. *Slave Culture: Nationalist Theory and the Foundations of Black America*. New York: Oxford University Press, 1987.

———, ed. *The Ideological Origins of Black Nationalism*. Boston: Beacon Press, 1972.

Styron, William. *The Confessions of Nat Turner*. New York: New American Library, 1966.

Terrell, Joanne M. *Power in the Blood? The Cross in the African American Experience*. Maryknoll, N.Y.: Orbis Books, 1998.

Thurman, Howard. *Jesus and the Disinherited*. Nashville: Abingdon Press, 1949.

Townes, Emilie M., ed. *A Troubling in My Soul: Womanist Perspectives on Evil and Suffering*. Maryknoll, N.Y.: Orbis Books, 1993.

Toynbee, Arnold J. *A Study of History*. Vols. I–IV. New York: Oxford University Press, 1947.

T'Shaka, Oba. *The Political Legacy of Malcolm X*. Chicago: Third World Press, 1983.

Turner, Richard B. *Islam in the African American Experience*. Bloomington: Indiana University Press, 1997.

Veblen, Thorstein. *The Theory of the Leisure Class: An Economic Study of Institutions*. 1899. Reprint, New York: New American Library, 1953.

Vivian, Octavia. *Coretta: The Story of Mrs. Martin Luther King Jr.* Philadelphia: Fortress Press, 1970.

Wade-Gayles, Gloria, ed. *My Soul Is a Witness: African American Women's Spirituality*. Boston: Beacon Press, 1995.

Walton, Hanes, Jr. *The Political Philosophy of Martin Luther King Jr.* Westport, Conn.: Greenwood Press, 1971.

Ward, Brian, and Tony Badger, eds. *The Making of Martin Luther King Jr. and the Civil Rights Movement*. New York: New York University Press, 1996.

Washington, James M., ed. *A Testament of Hope: The Essential Writings and Speeches of Martin Luther King Jr.* New York: HarperCollins, 1986.

———. *I Have a Dream: Writings and Speeches that Changed the World*. San Francisco: HarperCollins, 1992.

Watley, William D. *Roots of Resistance: The Nonviolent Ethic of Martin Luther King Jr.* Valley Forge, Pa.: Judson Press, 1985.

WCAR NGO Forum Declaration: Resolutions. Durban, South Africa, 28 August–3 September 2001.

Webster's New Collegiate Dictionary. Springfield: Merriam, 1976.

Weisenfeld, Judith, and Richard Newman, eds. *This Far by Faith: Readings in African American Women's Religious Biography*. New York: Routledge, 1996.

Williams, Chancellor. *The Destruction of Black Civilization*. Chicago: Third World Press, 1974.

Williams, Delores S. *Sisters in the Wilderness: The Challenge of Womanist God-Talk*. Maryknoll, N.Y.: Orbis Books, 1993.

Williams, Eric. *Capitalism and Slavery*. 1944. Reprint, New York: Capricorn Books, 1966.

Williams, John A. *The King God Didn't Save*. New York: Coward-McCann, 1970.

Williams, John G. *"De Ole Plantation."* Charleston, S.C.: Walker, Evans and Cogswell, 1895.

Williams, Juan. *Eyes on the Prize: America's Civil Rights Years, 1954–1965*. New York: Viking Penguin, 1987.

Wilmore, Gayraud S. *Black Religion and Black Radicalism: An Examination of the Black Experience in Religion*. New York: Doubleday, 1973.

———. *Black Religion and Black Radicalism: An Examination of the Religious History of Afro-American People*. Maryknoll, N.Y.: Orbis Books, 1983; rev. ed., 1998.

———, ed. *Black Men in Prison: The Response of the African American Church*. Atlanta: The ITC Press, 1990.

Wilson, Ellen G. *The Loyal Blacks*. New York: Capricorn Books, 1976.

Wilson, William J. *When Work Disappears: The World of the New Urban Poor*. New York: Alfred A. Knopf, 1997.

Wiltse, Charles M., ed. *David Walker's Appeal to the Coloured Citizens of the World*. 1829. Reprint, New York: Hill and Wang, 1965.

Witvliet, Theo. *The Way of the Black Messiah: The Hermeneutical Challenge of Black Theology as a Theology of Liberation*. Oak Park, Ill.: Meyer, Stone, 1987.

Wolfenstein, Eugene V. *The Victims of Democracy: Malcolm X and the Black Revolution*. New York: Guilford Press, 1993.

Wood, Joe, ed. *Malcolm X in Our Own Image*. New York: St. Martin's Press, 1992.

World Almanac and Book of Facts (1977). Mahwah, N.J.: World Almanac Books, 1997.

Young, Andrew. *An Easy Burden: The Civil Rights Movement and the Transformation of America*. New York: HarperCollins, 1996.

Yusseff, Muhammad A. *The Dead Sea Scrolls, the Gospel of Barnabas, and the New Testament*. Indianapolis: American Trust, 1985.

Zeno, Muhammad bin Jamil. *The Pillars of Islam and Iman*. Riyadh-Saudia Arabia: Dar-Us-Salam, 1996.

Journal, Magazine, and Newspaper Articles

Adams, Alvin. "Malcolm X 'Seemed Sincere' about Helping Cause: Mrs. King." *Jet*, 11 March 1965, 28, 30.

Ahmad, Ishmael L. "Malcolm X Documentary Set for PBS: Producer Says Muslim's Message Is Not Lost." *St. Louis American*, 13–19 January 1994, 1A, 13A.

"Alex Haley Interview." *Black Scholar* 8, no. 1 (September 1976): 33–40.

"Alex Haley Remembers Malcolm X." *Essence* 14, no. 7 (November 1983): 52–54, 118, 122.

Allen, Robert L. "Malcolm X's Fatal Challenge to White Capitalism." *National Guardian*, 18 February 1967, 5.

"Angry Spokesman Malcolm X Tells Off Whites." *Life*, 31 May 1963, 30.

"Aryan Nations Stage Alarming Comeback in 1994." *Klanwatch: Intelligence Report—A Publication of the Southern Poverty Law Center* 77 (March 1995): 1, 5.

Asante, Molefi Kete. "Multiculturalism: An Exchange." *American Scholar* (Summer 1990): 267–76.

Atwater, Deborah F. "Editorial: The Voices of African American Women in the Civil Rights Movement." *Journal of Black Studies* 26, no. 5 (May 1996): 539–42.

Bailey, A. Peter. "The Ties That Bind." *Essence* 12, no. 9 (January 1982): 78–79, 102, 107–8, 111, 113.

Baker, K. C., et al. "Betty Shabazz: Symbol of Pride Succumbs in Bx. to Burn Wounds." New York *Daily News,* 24 June 1997, 3.

Baldwin, James. "Malcolm and Martin." *Esquire* 77, no. 4 (April 1972): 94–97, 195–96, 198, 201.

Baldwin, Lewis V. "The Making of a Dreamer: The Georgia Roots of Martin Luther King, Jr." *Georgia Historical Quarterly* 76, no. 3 (Fall 1992): 639–51.

———. "Malcolm X and Martin Luther King Jr.: What They Thought About Each Other." *Islamic Studies* 25, no. 4 (Winter 1986): 395–416.

———. "A Reassessment of the Relationship Between Malcolm X and Martin Luther King Jr." *Western Journal of Black Studies* 13, no. 2 (Summer 1989): 103–13.

Barnes, Elizabeth. "The Impact of Malcolm X." *Militant,* 6 March 1967, 4.

———. "Nationwide Tributes to Malcolm X." *Militant,* 4 March 1968, 1.

"Bayard Rustin and Malcolm X." *Militant,* 15 March 1965, 4.

Begley, Sharon, et al. "African Dreams." *Newsweek,* 23 September 1991, 42–50.

Bell, Carl C., and Esther J. Jenkins. "Preventing Black Homicide." In *The State of Black America*, National Urban League Report (1990): 143–55.

Benjamin, Playthell. "Spike Lee: Bearing the Cross." *Emerge* 2, no. 8 (November 1991): 26–27, 30–32.

Bennett, Lerone, Jr. "From Booker T to M.L." *Ebony* (November 1962): 152–62.

———. "Rev. Martin Luther King Jr., Alabama Desegregationist, Challenges Talmadge." *Ebony* 12, no. 6 (April 1957): 77, 79–81.

Bey, Lee. "The Renaissance of Malcolm X." *Chicago Sun Times,* 8 November 1992, 38–39.

"Black Celebs 'Bail Out' Director Spike Lee's 'Malcolm X' Film Project." *Jet,* 8 June 1992, 30, 32.

"Black Students Complain of Georgia School Dress Code." *Jet,* 18 October 1993, 24.

Blum, Edward, and Marc Levin. "Islam Challenges Black Churches." *USA Today,* 19 July 2000, 13A.

Booker, Simeon. "Ticker Tape: National Headliners." *Jet,* 9 May 1994, 12.

Bradley, David. "My Hero, Malcolm X: Some Boys Weren't Made to Be Credits to Their Race." *Esquire* 100, no. 6 (December 1983): 488–93.

"Brother Reveals Malcolm X Had Disavowed His Racist Philosophy in Later Life." *Jet,* 10 June 1985, 19.

Brown, C. Stone. "TransAfrica's Randall Robinson: Leading the Growing Reparations Movement." *New Crisis* 107, no. 6 (November/December 2000): 17–19.

Bruni, Frank. "Widow of Malcolm X Burned, Badly, in Fire at Yonkers Home." *New York Times,* 2 June 1997, A1, A14.

Buchanan, Patrick. "A Rascal's Bedroom Escapades Diminish His Status as a Saint." *Tennessean,* 22 October 1989, 5G.

Burrow, Rufus, Jr. "Some African American Males' Perspectives on the Black Woman." *Western Journal of Black Studies* 16, no. 2 (Summer 1992): 64–73.

"Businessmen, King's Children Help Keep His Dream Alive." *Jet,* 20 January 1986, 12–14.

Caldwell, Gilbert H. "The Significance of the March: From a Christian Perspective." *Final Call,* 27 September 1995, 17.

Carson, Clayborne. "A 'Common Solution': Martin and Malcolm's Gulf Was Closing, but the Debate Lives On." *Emerge* 9, no. 4 (February 1998): 44–46, 48–52.

———. "Documenting Martin Luther King's Importance—and His Flaws." *Chronicle of Higher Education,* 16 January 1991, A52.

Charles, Nick. "The New Al Sharpton." *Emerge* 6, no. 2 (November 1994): 34–38.

"A Children's Tribute to Dr. King." *Negro History Bulletin* 31, no. 5 (May 1968): 2.

Clayton, Dawn. "The Daughters of Malcolm X and Martin Luther King Team Up to Bring a Play of Hope to Kids." *People,* 5 September 1983, 99–100, 104.

"Clinton Speaks of King in Decrying Violence." *Jet,* 29 November 1993, 8–9.

Coleman, Paulette. "Reflections on the Million Woman March." *A.M.E. Church Review* 113, no. 369 (January–March 1998): 76–79.

Coleman, Trevor W. "Affirmative Action Wars." *Emerge* 9, no. 5 (March 1998): 30–37.

———. "A Mother's Struggle: Betty Shabazz Held Up a Family and a Legacy of Activism." *Emerge* 8, no. 10 (September 1997): 49–52, 54–56, 58.

Cone, James H. "Black Theology in American Religion." *Journal of the American Academy of Religion* 53, no. 4 (December 1985): 755–71.

———. "The Theology of Martin Luther King Jr." *Union Seminary Quarterly Review* 40, no. 4 (1986): 21–36.

"Contest Winner, M. L. King Jr." *Atlanta Daily World,* 16 April 1944, 2.

"The Continuing Struggle for a National King Holiday." *Ebony* 43, no. 3 (January 1988): 27–28, 30, 32.

"Conversation with Martin Luther King Jr." *Conservative Judaism* 22, no. 3 (Spring 1968): 1–19.

Coughlin, Ellen K. "Politics and Commerce in the Rebirth of Malcolm X." *Chronicle of Higher Education,* 7 October 1992, A8, A14.

"Cultural League Meets Tonight." *Atlanta Daily World,* 1 June 1948, 3.

"Cultural League Meets Tonight." *Atlanta Daily World,* 15 June 1948, 1.

Cunnigen, Donald. "Malcolm X's Influence on the Black Nationalist Movement of Southern Black College Students." *Western Journal of Black Studies* 17, no. 1 (Spring 1993): 32–43.

"Daughter's View of Malcolm X." *USA Today,* 16 November 1992, 15A.

Davis, Angela. "On Malcolm X." *Emerge* 4, no. 3 (December 1992): 35–37.

Davis, Ossie. "Why I Eulogized Malcolm X." *Negro Digest* 15, no. 4 (February 1966): 64–66.

"A Day of Pride, Prayer, Song Fills Mall." *New York Times,* 17 October 1995, A1.

"Denzel Washington Gets Bid for a Second Oscar in Spike's 'Malcolm X' Film." *Jet,* 8 March 1993, 52.

DePalma, Anthony. "Plagiarism Seen by Scholars in King's Ph.D. Dissertation." *New York Times,* 10 November 1990, 1, 10.

Douglas, Kelly Brown. "God Is as Christ Does: Toward a Womanist Theology." *Journal of Religious Thought* 46, no. 1 (Summer/Fall 1989): 7–16.

"Dream Realized at Last for a Memorial to King." *Tennessean,* 12 October 1996, 8A.

Dwyer, Jim, et al. "Malcolm X's Grandson Sorry: Psych Tests Ok'd in Shabazz Arson." New York *Daily News,* 3 June 1997, 7.

Dyson, Michael E. "Reaping Riches: Profiting from Dr. King's Dream." *Emerge* 11, no. 4 (February 2000): 48–55.

Elliot, Aprele. "Ella Baker: Free Agent in the Civil Rights Movement." *Journal of Black Studies* 26, no. 5 (May 1996): 593–603.

"Emancipation II." *America,* 1 June 1963, 790–91.

Erickson, Mark St. John. "Malcolm X, 1925–1965: Dark Prince of Civil Rights Struggle Still an Enigma 25 Years after His Death." *Daily Press,* 12 February 1990, C1, C2.

Farley, Christopher. "Moslem Faithful in U.S.A. Tackle Misconceptions." *USA Today,* 31 August 1989, D5.

"Farrakhan Urges Marchers to Return Home and Make a Positive Difference." *Jet,* 30 October 1995, 10–11.

Farris, Christine King. "The Young Martin: From Childhood through College." *Ebony* 41, no. 3 (January 1986): 56–58.

"Fifteen Greatest Black Women Preachers: Experts and Leading Blacks Name Select Group of Ministers." *Ebony* 53, no. 1 (November 1997): 102–4, 106, 108, 110, 112, 114.

"First Time in Print: An Interview with Malcolm X." *Militant,* 20 February 1967, 5.

Flewellen, Dionne. "March Support Swells: Momentum Picks Up as Min. Farrakhan, Rev. Chavis Criss Cross Country Gathering Support for Million Man March." *Final Call,* 27 September 1995, 3, 23.

Flick, Hank, and Larry Powell. "Animal Imagery in the Rhetoric of Malcolm X." *Journal of Black Studies* 18, no. 4 (June 1988): 435–51.

Foeman, Anita K. "Gloria Richardson: Breaking the Mold." *Journal of Black Studies* 26, no. 5 (May 1996): 604–15.

Frady, Marshall. "Reflections: The Children of Malcolm." *New Yorker,* 12 October 1992, 64–72, 74–81.

Franklin, John Hope. "The Forerunners." *American Visions* 1, no. 1 (January/February 1986): 26–35.

Franklin, Robert M. "The Three Faces of Malcolm X." *Harvard Divinity Bulletin* 21, no. 4 (1992): 14.

"Freedom of Faith for All Religions." *Tennessean,* 22 June 2000, 12A.

Gaines, Alayna A. "Renegade Reverend: Archbishop George Augustus Stallings, Jr. Preaches Inclusion to the Masses." *Emerge* 6, no. 6 (April 1995): 20–22, 24.

Garrow, David J. "The Helms Attack on King." *Southern Exposure* 12, no. 2 (March/April 1984): 12–15.

———. "How King Borrowed: Reading the Truth Between the Sermons and Footnotes." *Washington Post,* 18 November 1990, C1, C5.

———. "The Intellectual Development of Martin Luther King Jr.: Influences and Commentaries." *Union Seminary Quarterly Review* 40, no. 4 (1986): 5–20.

Geller, Laurence. "Malcolm X Display Might Have Inspired Bombing." *Manhattan Tribune,* 25 April 1970, 3.

Gilbert, Jack. "King Urges Youth Join in New Order." *Athens* (Ohio) *Messenger,* 30 December 1959, 1–2, 16.

Gilchrist, Brenda J. "A Message from Malcolm: Spike Lee's Movie Should Wake Us Up, Make Us Change." *Detroit Free Press,* 9 November 1992, 1E, 3E.

———. "The Rebirth of Malcolm X: Spike Lee's New Film About the '60s Martyr Stirs Hope, Fear and Painful Memories—Some Worry the Leader's Message Will Be Lost." *Detroit Free Press,* 8 November 1992, 1G, 5G.

Goldman, Ari L. "Mainstream Islam Rapidly Embraced by Black Americans." *New York Times,* 21 February 1989, 1.

Graham, Rhonda B. "Holy War: Rev. Fred Price Is Fighting the Church over Racism." *Emerge* 10, no. 3 (December/January 1999): 44–46, 48, 50–51.

"Group Criticize Civil Rights Appointee." *Tennessean,* 28 June 1997, 11A.

Haddad, Yvonne Y. "A Century of Islam in America." *Muslim World Today.* Occasional Paper, no. 4, Washington Islamic Affairs Programs, Middle East Institute (1986): 1–25.

Halberstam, David. "The Second Coming of Martin Luther King." *Harper's,* August 1967, 39–51.

Haley, Alex. "Interview: Malcolm X." *Playboy,* May 1963, 53–54, 56–60, 62–63.

———. "Interview: Martin Luther King Jr." *Playboy,* January 1965, 65–68, 70–74, 76–78.

Hamlet, Janice D. "Fannie Lou Hamer: The Unquenchable Spirit of the Civil Rights Movement." *Journal of Black Studies* 26, no. 5 (May 1996): 560–76.

Hansen, Joseph. "Rowan's Smear of Malcolm X." *Militant,* 15 March 1965, 4.

Hatch, Roger D. "Racism and Religion: The Contrasting Views of Benjamin Mays, Malcolm X, and Martin Luther King Jr." *Journal of Religious Thought* 36, no. 2 (Fall/Winter 1979–80): 26–36.

Haywood, Richette. "Yolanda King Stars in One-Woman Show About Teachings of Her Father, Martin Luther King Jr." *Jet,* 18 January 1993, 8–12.

Hedges, Michael. "Number of Kids Who Kill Growing." *Casper* (Wyoming) *Star-Tribune,* 19 May 1996, C2.

Henderson, Errol A. "The Lumpenproletariat as Vanguard? The Black Panther Party, Social Transformation, and Pearson's Analysis of Huey Newton." *Journal of Black Studies* 28, no. 2 (November 1997): 171–96.

Henry, Charles P. "Who Won the Great Debate: Booker T. Washington or W.E.B. Du Bois?" *Crisis* 99, no. 2 (February 1992): 12–13, 15, 17.

Herman, David. "Malcolm X Announces Rally to Launch New Organization." *Militant,* 22 June 1964, 1.

———. "Malcolm X Launches a New Organization." *Militant,* 13 July 1964, 1.

"The Honorable Louis Farrakhan Speaks on the Malcolm X Movie." *Final Call,* 30 November 1992, 20–21, 26.

Horton, James O., and Lois E. Horton. "Race and Class." *American Quarterly* 35, no. 1/2 (Spring/Summer 1983): 155–68.

Hudson-Weems, Clenora. "From Malcolm X to El-Hajj Malik El-Shabazz: Malcolm's Evolving Attitude toward Africana Women." *Western Journal of Black Studies* 17, no. 1 (Spring 1993): 26–31.

Huggins, Nathan I. "Martin Luther King Jr.: Charisma and Leadership." *Journal of American History* 74, no. 2 (September 1987): 477–81.

"An Ill Wind." *New York Amsterdam News,* 10 April 1965, 16.

"The Impact of Malcolm X: His Ideas Keep Spreading." *Militant* 6 (March 1967): 4.

"I Remember Martin." *Ebony* 39, no. 6 (April 1984): 33–34, 36, 38, 40.

"James Cone Interview: Liberation, Black Theology, and the Church." *Radix Magazine* 14, no. 2 (September/October 1982): 9–12.

"Jewish Women Pray Aloud at Wall, Defying Israeli Bill." *Tennessean,* 5 June 2000, 3A.

Johnson, Lucas L. "'Malcolm X' Film May Stimulate Black Studies." *Tennessean,* 6 September 1992, 4B.

Johnson, Pamela. "Daughters of the Revolution." *Essence* 17, no. 1 (May 1986): 97–107.

Johnson, Robert E. "King's Children Tell How They Remember Him." *Jet,* 3 February 1972, 18–29.

Jones, K. Maurice. "Heirs and Keepers in the '90s: Young Adults of Generation X Have Their Own Version of Martin Luther King Jr.'s Legacy." *Emerge* 4, no. 6 (April 1993): 37–39.

Jones, William R. "Liberation Strategies in Black Theology: Mao, Martin, or Malcolm?" *Chicago Theological Seminary Register* 73, no. 1 (Winter 1983): 38–48.

Kaba, Lansine. "Today, Islam, Which Has Been in Existence for Four Centuries, Is Growing Dramatically." *Afrique Histoire* 1, no. 4 (1983): 33–37.

King, Anthony E. O. "Understanding Violence among Young African American Males: An Afrocentric Perspective." *Journal of Black Studies* 28, no. 1 (September 1997): 79–96.

King, Charles H. "Quest and Conflict: The Untold Story of the Power Struggle between King and Jackson." *Negro Digest* (May 1967): 6–9, 71–79.

King, Coretta Scott. "Empowering Women Will Benefit Nation." *Tennessean,* 13 November 1990, 9A.

———. "My Dream for My Children." *Good Housekeeping,* June 1964, 77, 144–52.

———. "U.S. Needs More Willing Women Participants in Foreign Policy." *Tennessean,* 1 March 1988, 9A.

King, Martin Luther, Jr. "Advice for Living." *Ebony* 12, no. 12 (October 1957): 53.

———. "Advice for Living." *Ebony* 13: no. 2 (December 1957): 120; no. 4 (February 1958): 84; no. 5 (March 1958): 92; no. 6 (April 1958): 104; no. 7 (May 1958): 112; no. 8 (June 1958): 118; no. 11 (September 1958): 68; no. 12 (October 1958): 138.

———. "The Burning Truth in the South." *Progressive* 24, no. 5 (May 1960): 8–10.

———. "Honoring Dr. Du Bois." *Freedomways* 8, no. 2 (Spring 1968): 104–11.

———. "More than Any Other Person in History." *Peace News,* 13 January 1958, 2.

———. "My Jewish Brother." *New York Amsterdam News,* 26 February 1966, 1, 12.

———. "My Talk with Ben Bella." *New York Amsterdam News,* 27 October 1962, 12–13.

———. "Negroes Are Not Moving Too Fast." *Saturday Evening Post,* 7 November 1964, 8, 10.

————. "Our Struggle." *Liberation* 1, no. 2 (April 1956): 3–6.

————. "Revolucio per Amo." *Kontakto* 2 (1965): 4–7.

————. "The Sword That Heals." *Critic* 22 (June/July 1964): 6–14.

————. "When a Negro Faces Southern Justice." *New York Amsterdam News,* 16 April 1966, 31.

————. "Who Is Their God?" *Nation,* 13 October 1962, 209–10.

"King and Roy: On Malcolm's Death." *New York Amsterdam News,* 27 February 1965, 27.

Kingsbury, Paul. "Author Discusses Nashville's Role in Civil Rights Movement." *Vanderbilt Register* 1–14 June 1998.

"King Views Malcolm X as Tragic." *New York Amsterdam News,* 28 March 1964, 35.

Lashley, Marilyn E. "African Americans and the Reagan-Bush Years: Retreat of the Liberal State or Tyranny of Majority." *Western Journal of Black Studies* 18, no. 3 (Fall 1994): 132–40.

Laughinghouse, Amy. "Mothers of the Civil Rights Movement: Intimate Reflections from the Widows of Malcolm X, Martin Luther King Jr. and Medgar Evers." *Upscale* 8, no. 8 (May 1997): 34–41.

"LBJ Tapes Reveal Confusion about Vietnam: Ex-President Did Not Want Death Toll Known." *Tennessean,* 13 October 1996, 13A.

"Lee Blasts 'Malcolm X' Box-Office Ticket Mix-Up." *Jet,* 11 January 1993, 36.

"Lee Urges Blacks to Skip School to See 'Malcolm X' and Learn Black History." *Jet,* 14 September 1992, 18.

"The Legacy of Malcolm X: Nearly 30 Years after His Death, the Words of One of the Most Provocative Orators of the Black Nationalist Movement Strike a Responsive Chord." *Ebony,* May 1989, 156, 158, 160–61.

Lester, Julius. "Malcolm X as Icon." *Dissent* (Spring 1993): 255–57.

Lewis, Anthony. "Negroes Press Harder for Basic Rights." *New York Times,* 19 May 1963, 10E.

Lewis, John. "It's About the Right to Vote." *Newsweek,* 11 December 2000, 38.

"Life of Malcolm X Receives Homage." *Daily World,* 19 May 1970, 9.

Long, Perdeta A. "BSAC Honors King's Birthday by Celebrating Universal Rights." *Kaleidoscope,* 14 January 1997, 2.

Macinnes, Colin. "Malcolm, the Lost Hero." *Negro Digest* 16, no. 4 (May 1967): 4–5.

"Malcolm Called a Martyr Abroad." *New York Times,* 26 February 1965, 1.

"Malcolm Maps Negro Vote Drive." *New York Post,* 30 March 1964, 3.

"Malcolm's Sister Fights On." *New York Post,* 20 May 1970, 48.

"Malcolm X and Martin Luther King Jr.: Violence versus Nonviolence." *Ebony,* April 1965, 168–69.

"The Final Views of Malcolm X." *National Leader,* 2 June 1983, 9, 11, 28.

"Malcolm X: Warrior, Diplomat, Minister—Apostle of Manhood, Dignity, and Freedom." *Black Liberation Month News* (February 1985): 1–7.

"Malcolm X Woos Two Rights Leaders [Bayard Rustin and Rev. Milton A. Galamison]; Asks 'Forgiveness' for Past Remarks and Seeks Unity." *New York Times,* 19 May 1964, 28.

"Many Memorial Meetings around Nation Pay Tribute to Memory of Malcolm X." *Militant,* 6 March 1967, 4.

Martin, Sandy D. "King and Interfaith Dialogue, 1955–1968." *Journal of Religious Thought* 48, no. 2 (Winter/Spring 1991–92): 34–48.

"Martin Luther King Jr.: His Widow Keeps His Dream Alive." *Jet,* 20 January 1986, 10, 12–15.

"Martin Luther King Supports Voluntary Family Planning Legislation." *Congressional Record–Senate,* Washington, D.C., 10 May 1966, 10161.

McKinney, Don S. "Brer Rabbit and Brother Martin Luther King Jr.: The Folktale Background of the Birmingham Protest." *Journal of Religious Thought* 46, no. 2 (Winter/Spring 1989–90): 42–52.

"Memorable Photos of Martin Luther King Jr.: Pictorial Legacy Captures Charismatic Personality of Multifaceted Civil Rights Leader." *Ebony* 41, no. 3 (January 1986): 86–90, 92, 94, 96, 98, 100, 102–3.

Metcalfe, Ralph, Jr. "How Blacks Remember Malcolm X." *Jet,* 20 May 1971, 23.

Millner, Sandra Y. "Recasting Civil Rights Leadership: Gloria Richardson and the Cambridge Movement." *Journal of Black Studies* 26, no. 6 (July 1996): 668–87.

Milne, Emile. "Malcolm's Sister Fights On." *New York Post,* 20 May 1970, 48.

Mitchell, James, and Clarence Waldron. "Minister Louis Farrakhan Sets the Record Straight: His Relationship with Malcolm X." *Jet,* 5 June 2000, 4–7, 10–12, 14.

"M. L. King Jr. Contributes to Sociology Digest." *Atlanta Daily World,* 29 June 1948, 1.

"MLK's Daughter Preaches First Sermon at Ebenezer 20 Years after His Death." *Jet,* 11 April 1988, 6–7.

Montgomery, Paul L. "Malcolm X a Harlem Idol on Eve of Murder Trial." *New York Times,* 6 December 1965, 46.

"Mother, Books Help Bunny Remember Her Father." *Jet,* 3 February 1972, 27–29.

"Movement Revives Memory of Activist Malcolm X." *Jet,* 12 March 1990, 29.

"Mrs. Richardson Hails Support of Malcolm X." *National Guardian,* 21 March 1964, 4.

Muhammad, Donald, and Richard Muhammad. "A Step toward Healing." *Final Call,* 24 May 1995, 3, 8–9.

"Multiculturalism Revisited." *Academe* 82, no. 3 (May/June 1996): 10–28.

"Muslims Pelt King; His Answer: Love." *New York Post,* 1 July 1963, 3.

Nadle, Marlene. "Burying Malcolm X." *Village Voice,* 4 March 1965, 1, 10.

———. "Malcolm X: The Complexity of a Man in the Jungle." *Village Voice,* 25 February 1965, 1, 6.

Nance, Teresa A. "Hearing the Missing Voice." *Journal of Black Studies* 26, no. 5 (May 1996): 543–59.

Newfield, Jack. "Blacks and Jews: The Tragedy of Jackson, the Logic of Coalition." *Voice,* 20 March 1984, 1, 13, 15.

"New Report Reveals Young Whites Are More Biased against Blacks than Older Whites Are." *Jet,* 5 July 1993, 26–29.

Ngozi-Brown, Scot. "The US Organization, Maulana Karenga, and Conflict with the Black Panther Party: A Critique of Sectarian Influences on Historical Discourse." *Journal of Black Studies* 28, no. 2 (November 1997): 157–70.

Norment, Lynn. "Coretta Scott King: The Woman behind the King Anniversary." *Ebony* 45, no. 3 (January 1990): 116–18, 120–22.

———. "New Generation of Kings Take Over: Dexter King Named CEO of the King Center." *Ebony* 50, no. 3 (January 1995): 25–26, 28.

"Now It's Negroes vs. Negroes in America's Racial Violence." *U.S. News and World Report,* 8 March 1965, 6–7.

Nyang, Sulayman. "Islam and the African American Experience." *Islamic Horizons* 18, nos. 7–8 (July/August 1989): 38–43.

Okafor, Victor O. "Diop and the African Origin of Civilization: An Afrocentric Analysis." *Journal of Black Studies* 22, no. 2 (December 1991): 252–68.

"People Are Talking About . . ." *Jet,* 11 January 1993, 54.

Perkins, Ken P., and Bruce Williams. "The Malcolm X Movie: The Financial Configuration." *Dollars and Sense* 18, no. 6 (November 1992): 18–22, 24.

Pierce, Ponchitta. "The Legacy of Martin Luther King Jr." *McCall's,* April 1974, 28, 30, 32.

———. "Widow of Malcolm X Tells of Life with Him, without Him." *Jet,* 11 March 1965, 22–27.

Pluta, Joanna. "Combating Campus Prejudice: SGA Resolution Takes a Stance against Hatred." *Vanderbilt Hustler,* 20 October 1998, 1, 4.

Power, Carla, and Allison Samuels. "Battling for Souls." *Newsweek,* 30 October 1995, 46–47.

"Pro and Con: A National Holiday for Martin Luther King Jr.?" *U.S. News and World Report,* 29 August 1983, 49.

"Push Renewed to Accelerate Women's Rights Worldwide: Global Conference of Women Has Formidable Roadblocks." *Tennessean,* 4 June 2000, 2A.

Ravitch, Diane. "Multiculturalism: E Pluribus Plures." *American Scholar* (Summer 1990): 337–54.

Raymond, Chris. "Discovery of Early Plagiarism by Martin Luther King Raises Troubling Questions for Scholars and Admirers." *Chronicle of Higher Education,* 21 November 1990, A1, A8.

"Religious Persecution in China on Rise, Christian Group Says." *Atlanta Journal-Constitution,* 20 May 2000, B4.

"Remember Brother Malcolm." *Black Panther,* 19 May 1969, 1–11.

"Remembering Malcolm X at 60." *Atlanta Voice,* 25–31 May 1985, 3.

"Reparations: Calculating the Incalculable." *Christian Century* 117, no. 29 (25 October 2000): 1059.

"Rev. and Mrs. King Return to Atlanta." *Atlanta Daily World,* 7 July 1948, 3.

"The Rev. Bernice A. King Continues the Family's Preaching Legacy." *Ebony,* January 1995, 30, 32, 34.

"Rev. M. L. King Jr. Guest Speaker for Cultural League." *Atlanta Daily World,* 11 July 1948, 3.

"Rev. M. L. King Jr. to Fill Pulpit at Ebenezer Sunday." *Atlanta Daily World,* 21 August 1948, 2.

"Rev M. L. King Jr. to Preach Sunday Morning at Ebenezer." *Atlanta Daily World,* 24 July 1948, 3.

Rifkin, Ira. "'Million Man March' Divides Black Religious Community." *United Methodist Reporter of the Tennessee Conference* 142, no. 21 (13 October 1995): 3.

"Rips Rowan's Stand." *New York Amsterdam News,* 3 April 1965, 18.

Roberts, Cokie, and Steven V. Roberts. "Martin Luther King III: Can He Step Forward?" *Tennessean: USA Weekend,* 16–18 January 1998, 4–5.

Roberts, J. Deotis, Sr. "A Black Ecclesiology of Involvement." *Journal of Religious Thought* 32, no. 1 (Spring/Summer 1975): 36–46.

Rowan, Carl T. "Will Malcolm X Movie Be Truthful or Just a Fiction?" *Tennessean,* 6 September 1992, 5D.

"Rowan Should Read about Malcolm X." *Tennessean,* 10 September 1992, 8A.

Russell, Carlos E. "Exclusive Interview with Brother Malcolm X." *Liberator* 4, no. 5 (May 1964): 12–13.

Sack, Kevin. "Kings Cheapen Legacy, Some Say." *Tennessean,* 20 August 1997, 1A, 8A–9A.

———. "Sheen of the King Legacy Dims on New, More Profitable Path." *New York Times,* 19 August 1997, A1, A16.

"School Dedication." *Jet,* 22 November 1993, 23.

Schroth, Raymond A. "Malcolm X Is Alive." *America,* 22 April 1967, 594.

Sertima, Ivan Van. "Egypt Revisited." *Journal of African Civilizations* 4, no. 2 (November 1982): 4–122.

Shabazz, Attallah. "The Longest Prayer: The Eldest Daughter of Dr. Betty Shabazz Shares a Personal View of Her Extraordinary Mother's Final Days." *Essence* 28, no. 6 (October 1997): 72–77, 148, 154–55.

Shabazz, Betty. "Loving and Losing Malcolm." *Essence* 22, no. 10 (February 1992): 50–52, 54, 104, 107–10, 112.

———. "The Legacy of My Husband, Malcolm X." *Ebony* 24, no. 8 (June 1969): 172–74, 176, 178, 180, 182.

———. "Remembering Malcolm X." *Essence* 17, no. 10 (February 1987): 61.

Short, Thomas. "A 'New Racism' on Campus?" *Commentary* 86, no. 2 (August 1988): 46–50.

Simanga, Michael. "Against the Silence: Malcolm X Rising." *Southline* 2, no. 14 (14 May 1986): 10–11.

Smith, C. Calvin. "Politics and African Americans: The Civil Rights Legacy of Ronald Reagan." *Western Journal of Black Studies* 14, no. 2 (Summer 1990): 102–14.

Smith, Kenneth L. "Equality and Justice: A Dream or Vision of Reality." *Report from the Capital* 39, no. 1 (January 1984): 4–5, 7.

———. "The Radicalization of Martin Luther King Jr.: The Last Three Years." *Journal of Ecumenical Studies* 26, no. 2 (Spring 1989): 270–88.

Smith, Vern E., et al. "Rediscovering Malcolm X: Twenty-five Years after His Murder, His Message Has New Resonance for Blacks." *Newsweek,* 26 February 1990, 68–69.

Smylie, James H. "On Jesus, Pharaoh, and the Chosen People: Martin Luther King Jr. as Biblical Interpreter and Humanist." *Interpretation* 24 (January 1970): 74–93.

Southwick, Albert B. "Malcolm X: Charismatic Demagogue." *Christian Century* 80, no. 23 (5 June 1963): 740–41.

"Speakers Pay Tribute to Malcolm X." *Militant,* 15 March 1965, 1.

Steele, Shelby. "The Recoloring of Campus Life: Student Racism, Academic Pluralism, and the End of a Dream." *Harper's,* February 1989, 47–55.

Stone, I. F. "The Pilgrimage of Malcolm X." *New York Review* 5, no. 7 (11 November 1965): 3–5.

Temme, John M. "Jesus as Trailblazer: The Christology of Martin Luther King Jr." *Journal of Religious Thought* 42, no. 1 (Spring/Summer 1985): 75–80.

Trescott, Jacqueline. "The Battle over Malcolm X: Spike Lee vs. Amiri Baraka—Who Should Immortalize the Man on Film, and How?" *Washington Post,* 18 August 1991, G1, G8.

"A Tribute to Malcolm X: How Ossie Davis Saw Him." *Militant,* 27 February 1967, 8.

Uehara, Edwina S., et al. "African American Youth Encounter Violence: Results from the Community Mental Health Council Violence Screening Project." *Journal of Black Studies* 26, no. 6 (July 1996): 768–81.

"UN Conference Fends Off Efforts to Curb Women's Rights." *Tennessean,* 11 June 2000, 4A.

"UN Delegates Struggle with Women's Rights." *Tennessean,* 10 June 2000, 4A.

USA Today, 14 December 2000, 3A.

"U.S. Negroes' Goal: To Set Africa Policy." *U.S. News and World Report,* 11 January 1965, 60–61.

Vernon, Robert. "A 'Left-Wing' Smear of Malcolm X: Repeat Time-Worn Slanders." *Militant,* 24 May 1965, 3.

———. "Why Black Nationalism Upsets Liberals: James Wechsler's Attack on Malcolm X." *Militant,* 22 June 1964, 5.

Vincent, Ted. "The Garveyite Parents of Malcolm X." *Black Scholar* 20, no. 2 (March/April 1989): 10–13.

Waddle, Ray. "Reject Hate, Daughters of Black Leaders Urge." *Tennessean,* 27 January 1988, 1B–2B.

Waldman, Peter. "To Their Dismay, King Scholars Find a Troubling Pattern: Civil Rights Leader Was Lax in Attributing Some Parts of His Academic Papers." *Wall Street Journal,* 9 November 1990, A1, A6.

Walker, Nicole. "The New Generation Speaks Out." *Ebony* 53, no. 1 (November 1997): 166.

Walker, Wyatt Tee. "Nothing but a Man." *Negro Digest* 14, no. 10 (August 1965): 29–32.

Watson, Aaron. "Labeling King, Malcolm—The Dream: King, Malcolm, and Affirmative Action." *Atlanta Constitution,* 20 January 1992, A11.

"What Harlemites Say about Malcolm X Slaying." *New York Amsterdam News,* 27 February 1965, 22.

"What Martin Luther King Jr. Means to Me." *Ebony* 41, no. 3 (January 1986): 74–76.

"What's Ahead for Affirmative Action?" *Jet,* 10 July 1995, 6–10.

Wheeler-Stewart, Sherrel. "Young Thoughts on King's Legacy." *Tennessean,* 16 January 1989, 3B.

Wicker, Tom. "Kennedy Fears Negro Extremists Will Get Power If Moderates Fail." *New York Times,* 15 May 1963, 26.

Wickham, DeWayne. "Only Lee Could've Created This Movie." *USA Today,* 16 November 1992, 15A.

Wilkins, Roy. "No Time for Avengers." *New York Amsterdam News,* 6 March 1965, 8.

Williams, Linda. "Molding Men: At Morehouse College, Middle-Class Blacks Are Taught to Lead." *Wall Street Journal,* 5 May 1987, 1, 25.

Wilson, Gertrude. "Look Homeward, Mr. Rowan." *New York Amsterdam News,* 6 March 1965, 9.

"'The Woman behind the King Anniversary' Featured in January *Ebony* Magazine." *Jet,* 15 January 1990, 10.

Wood, Joe. "Can Denzel Washington Make Malcolm Speak to a New Generation of Americans?" *Rolling Stone,* 26 November 1992, 34–36, 39.

———. "Looking for Malcolm: The Man and the Meaning behind the Icon." *Village Voice,* 29 May 1990, 43–45.

Young, Whitney M., Jr. "To Be Equal: The Next Malcolm X." *New York Amsterdam News,* 6 March 1965, 8.

Zaslow, Jeffrey. "Straight Talk: Dexter Scott King Accepts Destiny." *Tennessean: USA Weekend,* 12–14 January 1996, 22.

Unpublished Manuscripts

Baldwin, Lewis V. "The Harmonies of Liberty: Malcolm X and the Black Nationalist Tradition." 2002. Author's collection.

———, ed. "The Boundaries of Law, Politics, and Religion: Revisiting the Legacy of Martin Luther King, Jr." 2001 Author's collection.

———, ed. "The Word Made Flesh: The Bible as a Source for Martin Luther King, Jr." 2002. Author's collection.

Burrow, Rufus, Jr. "David Walker and Ethical Prophecy." 1998. Author's collection.

Warren, Robert Penn. "Who Speaks for the Negro?" 1964. King Center Archives, Atlanta.

Ph.D. Dissertations

Brown, Coleman B. "Grounds for American Loyalty in a Prophetic Christian Social Ethic—with Special Attention to Martin Luther King Jr." Union Theological Seminary, 1979.

Davis, Vanessa L. "'Sisters and Brothers All': The Mississippi Freedom Democratic Party and the Struggle for Political Equality." Vanderbilt University, 1996.

Holmes, Barbara A. "Barbara Jordan's Speeches, 1974–1995: Ethics, Public Religion, and Jurisprudence." Vanderbilt University, 1998.

Jackson, Andrew. "The Sociology of Pan-Africanism." University of California, Santa Barbara, 1974.

Luellen, David E. "Ministers and Martyrs: Malcolm X and Martin Luther King Jr." Ball State University, 1972.

Moore, Edward L. "Billy Graham and Martin Luther King Jr.: An Inquiry into White and Black Revivalistic Traditions." Vanderbilt University, 1979.

Reagon, Bernice Johnson. "Songs of the Civil Rights Movement, 1955–1965: A Study in Culture History." Howard University, 1975.

Unpublished Papers and Statements

Brock, Krue. "The Dialectical Perspective of Martin Luther King Jr." Vanderbilt University, 1988.

Davis, Vanessa L. "Midwifery and Grassroots Politics: Ella Jo Baker and Her Philosophy of Community Development." Vanderbilt University, 1991.

King, Martin Luther, Jr. "Address on Gandhi." WILD Sound Atlanta #27B, Atlanta, 22 March 1959. Papers of Martin Luther King Jr. Special Collections, Mugar Memorial Library, Boston University.

———. "After Desegregation—What?" N.d. Archives of the Martin Luther King Jr. Center for Nonviolent Social Change, Atlanta.

———. "Epitaph for a First Lady: Eleanor Roosevelt." 24 November 1962. King Center Archives, Atlanta.

———. "Marriage Ceremony Remarks." Atlanta, n.d. King Center Archives, Atlanta.

———. "My Call to Preach." American Baptist Convention, 7 August 1959. King Center Archives, Atlanta.

———. "People in Action." Atlanta, 3 February 1962. King Center Archives, Atlanta.

———. "People to People: The Nightmare of Violence." 26 February 1965. King Center Archives, Atlanta.

———. "Regarding the Influence of African Movements on U.S. Students." Atlanta, May 1962. King Center Archives, Atlanta.

———. "Statement at a Rally to Support the Freedom Riders." First Baptist Church, Montgomery, Ala., 21 May 1961. King Center Archives, Atlanta.

———. "Statement Regarding Mahalia Jackson." Atlanta, 26 November 1963. King Center Archives, Atlanta.

———. "Statement Regarding the Freedom Now Party." Atlanta, 30 October 1964. King Center Archives, Atlanta.

———. "Statement on Interfaith Conference on Civil Rights." Chicago, 15 January 1963. King Papers, Boston University.

———. "Statement on Malcolm X." Atlanta, 16 March 1964. King Center Archives, Atlanta.

———. "Statement on the Freedom Rides." Atlanta, 31 May 1961. King Papers, Boston University.

———. "Statement on the Legitimacy of the Struggle in Montgomery, Alabama." Montgomery, 4 May 1956. King Papers, Boston University.

———. "Statement Regarding Riots in Rochester and New York City." New York, 27 July 1964. King Center Archives, Atlanta.

———. "Statement Regarding the Mississippi Freedom Democratic Party at the COFO Rally." Jackson, Miss., 22 July 1964, 1–2. King Center Archives, Atlanta.

———. "Statement to the Press at the Beginning of the Youth Leadership Conference." Raleigh, N.C., 15 April 1960. King Center Archives, Atlanta.

———. "Statement to the South and the Nation." Atlanta, 10–11 January 1957. King Center Archives, Atlanta.

———. "Suggested Preamble for the SCLC." N.d. King Papers, Boston University.

———. "The Time for Freedom Has Come." 10 September 1961. King Papers, Boston University.

———. "True Dignity." N.d. King Center Archives, Atlanta.

King, Martin Luther Jr., Randolph A. Philip, and Roy Wilkins. "Statement Regarding the Little Rock Decision to President Dwight D. Eisenhower," 23 June 1958. King Center Archives, Atlanta.

——— et al., comps. "Draft of Statement Regarding SCLC's Participation in the National Conference on New Politics: Resolution on the Middle East." Chicago, September 1967. King Center Archives, Atlanta.

Wynn, Daniel W. "Introduction of Dr. King," ca. October 1960. Wynn Papers, Amistad Research Center, Tulane University, New Orleans.

Unpublished Addresses and Speeches

Jones, William R. "Martin Luther King: Black Messiah or White Guardian?" First Unitarian Society, Minneapolis, 6 April 1986.

King, Martin Luther, Jr. "Address at a March in Detroit." Cobo Hall, Detroit, 23 June 1963. King Center Archives, Atlanta.

———. "An Address at a Mass Meeting." Clarksdale, Miss., 19 March 1968. King Center Archives, Atlanta.

———. "An Address at a Mass Meeting." Eutaw, Ala., 20 March 1968. King Center Archives, Atlanta.

———. "An Address at a Mass Meeting." Maggie Street Baptist Church, Montgomery, Ala., 16 February 1968. King Center Archives, Atlanta.

———. "An Address at a Mass Meeting." Marks, Miss., 19 March 1968. King Center Archives, Atlanta.

———. "An Address at a Mass Meeting." Selma, Ala., 16 February 1968. King Center Archives, Atlanta.

———. "An Address at the Chicago Freedom Movement Rally." Chicago, 10 July 1966. King Center Archives, Atlanta.

———. "An Address at the Freedom Fund Report Dinner of the NAACP's 53rd Annual Convention." Atlanta, 5 July 1962. King Papers, Boston University.

———. "An Address at the Golden Anniversary Conference of the National Urban League." New York, 6 September 1960. King Papers, Boston University.

———. "An Address at the Prayer Pilgrimage for Freedom at the Lincoln Memorial." Washington, D.C., 17 May 1957. King Center Archives, Atlanta.

———. "An Address at the Synagogue Council of America." Waldorf-Astoria Hotel, New York, 5 December 1965. King Center Archives, Atlanta.

———. "An Address at the Valedictory Service." University of the West Indies, Mona, Jamaica, 20 June 1965. King Center Archives, Atlanta.

———. "An Address." Syracuse University, Syracuse, N.Y., 15 July 1965. King Center Archives, Atlanta.

———. "An Address." The Fiftieth Anniversary of the Women's International League for Peace and Freedom, Philadelphia, 15 October 1965. King Center Archives, Atlanta.

———. "An Address." First Annual Institute on Nonviolence and Social Change, Montgomery Improvement Association, Holt Street Baptist Church, Montgomery, Ala., 3 December 1956. King Papers, Boston University.

———. "An Address." Initial mass meeting of the Montgomery Improvement Association, Holt Street Baptist Church, Montgomery, Ala., 5 December 1955. King Papers, Boston University.

———. "An Address." Occasion of the formation of the Gandhi Society for Human Rights, Sheraton-Carlton Hotel, New York, 17 May 1962. King Papers, Boston University.

———. "An Address to the American Jewish Congress." Americana Hotel, New York, 20 May 1965. King Center Archives, Atlanta.

———. "An Address to the Ministers' Leadership Training Program." Miami, 19–23 February 1968. King Center Archives, Atlanta.

———. "An Address to the National Press Club." Washington, D.C., 19 July 1962. King Papers, Boston University.

———. "An Address." United Nations Plaza, New York, 15 April 1967. King Center Archives, Atlanta.

———. "A Proposed Statement to the South." Southern Negro Leaders Conference on Transportation and Nonviolent Integration, Atlanta, 10 January 1957. King Papers, Boston University.

———. "A Speech at a Dinner Honoring Him as a Nobel Peace Prize Recipient." Dinkler Plaza Hotel, Atlanta, 27 January 1965. King Center Archives, Atlanta.

———. "A Speech at an Operation Breadbasket Meeting." Chicago Theological Seminary, 25 March 1967. King Center Archives, Atlanta.

———. "A Speech." Ford Hall Forum, Boston, 11 December 1960. King Papers, Boston University.

———. "A Talk to a Seventh Grade Class." George A. Towns Elementary School, Atlanta, 11 March 1964. King Center Archives, Atlanta.

———. "Beyond Discovery, Love: An Address." International Convention of Christian Churches (Disciples of Christ), Dallas, 25 September 1966. King Center Archives, Atlanta.

———. "Civil Rights at the Crossroads." Meeting of the shop stewards of Local 815, Teamsters and Allied Trade Council, New York, 2 May 1967. King Center Archives, Atlanta.

———. "East or West—God's Children." Berlin, 13 September 1964. King Center Archives, Atlanta.

———. "Field of Education a Battleground." United Federation of Teachers, New York, 15 July 1965. King Center Archives, Atlanta.

———. "Message for My People." Released by Associated Negro Press, New York, ca. 1 January 1966. King Center Archives, Atlanta.

———. "Moral and Religious Imperatives for Brotherhood." Congregation B'nai Jeshurun, New York, 9 February 1963. King Papers, Boston University.

———. "Prelude to Tomorrow: An Address." Operation Breadbasket meeting, Chicago, 6 January 1968. King Center Archives, Atlanta.

———. "President's Address." Meeting of the Southern Christian Leadership Conference, Second Anniversary of the Montgomery Bus Protest, Montgomery, Ala., 5 December 1957. King Papers, Boston University.

———. "Rally Speech." Gadsden, Alabama, 21 June 1963. King Papers, Boston University.

———. "Revolution and Redemption." European Baptist Assembly, Amsterdam, 16 August 1964. King Center Archives, Atlanta.

———. "Revolution in the Classroom." Georgia Teachers and Education Association, Atlanta, 3 April 1967. King Center Archives, Atlanta.

———. "See You in Washington." SCLC retreat, Ebenezer Baptist Church, Atlanta, 17 January 1968. King Center Archives, Atlanta.

———. "Some Things We Must Do." Montgomery, Ala., 5 December 1957. King Papers, Boston University.

———. "Speech at a Mass Meeting." Grenada, Miss., June 1966. King Center Archives, Atlanta.

———. "Speech at a Rally." Crawfordsville, Ga., 11 October 1965. King Center Archives, Atlanta.

———. "Speech at a Voter Registration Rally." Louisville, Kentucky, 2 August 1967. King Center Archives.

———. "Speech Made in Savannah." Savannah, Ga., 1 January 1961. King Papers, Boston University.

———. "Speech to a Northern Jewish Congregration." N.p., 13 January 1958. King Center Archives, Atlanta.

———. "The Church on the Frontier of Racial Tension: An Address." Gay Lectures, Southern Baptist Theological Seminary, Louisville, Ky., 19 April 1961. King Papers, Boston University.

———. "The Crisis of Civil Rights." Operation Breadbasket meeting, Chicago, 10 July 1967. King Center Archives, Atlanta.

———. "The Dignity of Family Life." Abbott House, Westchester County, N.Y., 29 October 1965. King Center Archives, Atlanta.

———. "The Negro and the American Dream." Local NAACP meeting, Charlotte, N.C., 25 September 1960. King Papers, Boston University.

———. "The Negro Family." University of Chicago, 27 January 1966. King Center Archives, Atlanta.

———. "The Negroes in America: The End of Jim Crow?" Transcription of a taped speech, n.d. King Center Archives, Atlanta.

———. "The Truth about the Black Muslims." Boston University School of Theology, 24 May 1960. King Papers, Boston University.

———. "To Charter Our Course for the Future: An Address." SCLC retreat, Penn Center, Frogmore, S.C., 29–31 May 1967. King Center Archives, Atlanta.

———. "To the South and the Nation." Atlanta, 10–11 January 1957. King Papers, Boston University.

Williams, Delores S. "Between Hagar and Jezebel: A Womanist Assessment of Martin Luther King Jr.'s Beloved Community." Vanderbilt Divinity School, Nashville, 13 January 1997.

Unpublished Sermons

King, Martin Luther, Jr. "A Knock at Midnight." Canaan Baptist Church, New York, 24 March 1968. King Center Archives, Atlanta.

———. "Answer to a Perplexing Question." Ebenezer Baptist Church, Atlanta, 3 March 1963. King Papers, Boston University.

———. "Discerning the Signs of History." Ebenezer Baptist Church, Atlanta, 15 November 1964. King Papers, Boston University.

———. "Eulogy for the Martyred Children." Sixteenth Street Baptist Church, Birmingham, 22 September 1963. King Papers, Boston University.

———. "Guidelines for a Constructive Church." Ebenezer Baptist Church, Atlanta, 5 June 1966. King Center Archives, Atlanta.

———. "Is the Universe Friendly?" Ebenezer Baptist Church, Atlanta, 12 December 1965. King Center Archives, Atlanta.

———. "The Meaning of Hope." Dexter Avenue Baptist Church, Montgomery, 10 December 1967. King Center Archives, Atlanta.

———. "Thou Fool." Mt. Pisgah Missionary Baptist Church, Chicago, 27 August 1967. King Center Archives, Atlanta.

———. "Training Your Child in Love." Ebenezer Baptist Church, Atlanta, 8 May 1966. King Center Archives, Atlanta.

———. "What a Mother Should Tell Her Child." Ebenezer Baptist Church, Atlanta, 12 May 1963. King Papers, Boston University.

Interviews

Agronsky, Martin, et al. Interview with Martin Luther King Jr. on *Face the Nation*. CBS, New York City, 16 April 1967. King Center Archives, Atlanta.

Baldwin, Lewis V. Interviews with Ralph D. Abernathy. Atlanta, 7 March 1987, 7 May 1987.

———. Interview with Clarence James. Lincoln University, Lincoln (Oxford), Pa., 7 February 1999.

———. Interview with Bernard S. Lee. Washington, D.C., 9 July 1986.

Britton, John. Interview with Ella Baker. Moreland-Spingarn Collection, Howard University, Washington, D.C., 19 June 1968.

"Doubts and Certainties Link." Transcript of an interview with Martin Luther King Jr. London, ca. February 1968. King Center Archives, Atlanta.

Freeman, John. Interview with Martin Luther King Jr. for BBC Television, *Face to Face,* London, 29 October 1961. King Papers, Boston University.

Griffin, Merv. Interview with Martin Luther King Jr., *Merv Griffin Show,* New York, 6 July 1967. King Center Archives, Atlanta.

Hadid, Amiri YaSin. Interview with Arun Gandhi. Scarritt-Bennett College, Nashville, 11 January 1998.

———. Interview with Bernard Lafayette Jr. Nashville, 15–16 March 1999.

———. Interview with Imam Warith Deen Mohammed. Tennessee State University, Nashville, 10 February 1993.

Interview with Cassius Clay and Martin Luther King Jr. Louisville, Ky., 29 March 1967. King Center Archives, Atlanta.

Interview with Martin Luther King Jr. Chicago, 28 July 1965. King Center Archives, Atlanta.

Press conference with Martin Luther King Jr. International Airport, Crown Room of Satellite no. 6, Delta Airlines, Los Angeles, 24 February 1965. King Center Archives, Atlanta.

Radio interview with Martin Luther King Jr. regarding the Nobel Peace Prize. Oslo, 9 December 1964. King Center Archives, Atlanta.

"Stand on Sit-Ins." Press statement by King, Atlanta, 19 February 1962. King Papers, Boston University.

Telephone interview with Attallah Shabazz, 2 February 1990.

Letters

Ballou, Maude L. W., secretary to King, to Malcolm X, 10 August 1960. King Center Archives, Atlanta.

Clark, Frank, to King, 4 December 1962. King Papers, Boston University.

Cole, Nat King, to King, 25 June 1963. King Center Archives, Atlanta.

Eisenman, Abram, to King, 9 April 1964. King Center Archives, Atlanta.

Jones, Sandra, to King, 26 May 1961. King Center Archives, Atlanta.

King to James Baldwin, 26 September 1961. King Papers, Boston University.

King to Edward D. Ball, 14 December 1961. King Center Archives, Atlanta.

King to Buford Boone, 9 May 1957. King Papers, Boston University.

King to Allan K. Chalmers, 20 September 1961. King Papers, Boston University.

King to Nat King Cole, 18 July 1963. King Papers, Boston University.

King to Harold Courlander, 30 October 1961. King Papers, Boston University.

King to Joseph B. Cummings Jr., 22 December 1961. King Papers, Boston University.

King to Sammy Davis, 28 March 1961. King Papers, Boston University.

King to the Dexter Avenue Baptist Church, Montgomery, Ala., 14 April 1954. King Center Archives, Atlanta.

King to Abram Eisenman, 3 April 1964. King Center Archives, Atlanta.

King to Dr. Harold E. Fey, 23 June 1962. King Papers, Boston University.

King to Georgia Harkness, 8 November 1958. King Center Archives, Atlanta.

King to Mahalia Jackson, 10 January 1964. King Center Archives, Atlanta.

King to Kivie Kaplan, 6 March 1961. King Papers, Boston University.

King to Earl Kennedy, 30 October 1956. King Papers, Boston University.

King to Herman Long, 24 April 1962. Amistad Research Center, Tulane University, New Orleans, Louisiana.

King to Elijah Muhammad, 9 April 1958. King Papers, Boston University.

King to Basil A. Patterson, 9 April 1962. King Papers, Boston University.

King to Bernard Resnikoff, 17 September 1961. King Papers, Boston University.

King to T. E. Sealy, 6 July 1965. King Center Archives, Atlanta.

King to South African Embassy, 9 February 1966. King Center Archives, Atlanta.

King to the Student Body of Jesse Crowell School, Albion, Mich., 1 December 1960. King Papers, Boston University.

King to Galal Kernahanof Van Nuys, 29 April 1957. King Papers, Boston University.

King to Katie E. Whickam, 7 July 1958. King Papers, Boston University.

King and Wyatt Tee Walker to the Student Interracial Ministry Committee, 29 March 1961. King Papers, Boston University.

Knight, Elizabeth, to King, 10 January 1961. King Papers, Boston University.

McDonald, Dora, secretary to Dr. King, to Frank Clark, 26 November 1962. King Papers, Boston University.

Malcolm X to King, 21 July 1960. King Center Archives, Atlanta.

Money, Roy, to Lewis V. Baldwin, 17 June 2001. Personal collection, Vanderbilt University.

Muhammad, Elijah, to King, 19 March 1958. King Papers, Boston University.

Pulpit Committee of the Dexter Avenue Baptist Church, Montgomery, Ala., to King, 10 March 1954. King Papers, Boston University.

Robinson, James H., to King, 22 June 1965. Amistad Research Center, Tulane University, New Orleans.

Ruskin, Isadore W., M.D., to King, 30 November 1959. King Papers, Boston University.

Sarrat, Reed, to King, 2 January 1963. Amistad Research Center, Tulane University, New Orleans.

Shabazz, James, to John Lewis, 15 May 1964. King Center Archives, Atlanta.

Young, Andrew J., to Harry Belafonte, 28 February 1966. King Archives, Atlanta.

Telegrams

Jackson, Mahalia, to King, Atlanta, 16 October 1964. King Center Archives, Atlanta.

King to Mahalia Jackson, Chicago, 29 July 1965. King Center Archives, Atlanta.

King to Mrs. Malcolm X, Faith Temple Church in Harlem, New York City, 26 February 1965. King Center Archives, Atlanta.

Malcolm X to King, St. Augustine, Fla., 30 June 1964. King Center Archives, Atlanta.

Book Reviews

The Autobiography of Malcolm X, by Malcolm X with Alex Haley. *New Yorker*, 13 November 1965, 246–47.

Baldwin, Lewis V. *On the Side of My People: A Religious Life of Malcolm X,* by Louis A. DeCaro. *Journal of American History* 83, no. 2 (September 1996): 701.

Breitman, George. "Reviews and Reports." *Militant,* 26 September 1966, 4.

Burrow, Rufus, Jr., *Toward the Beloved Community: Martin Luther King, Jr. and South Africa,* by Lewis V. Baldwin. *Journal of Religion* 77, no. 3 (1997): 442–48.

MacGregor, Martha. "The Week in Books." *New York Post,* 14 November 1965, 47.

Mamiya, Lawrence H. *Martin and Malcolm and America,* by James H. Cone. *Horizons* 19, no. 1 (Spring 1992): 138.

Paris, Peter. *Martin and Malcolm and America,* by James H. Cone. *Religious Studies Review* 20, no. 2 (April 1994): 88.

Microfilm

"Malcolm X: FBI Surveillance File." Reel no. 1. Wilmington, Del.: Scholarly Resources.

Films, Videotapes, Audiotapes, and Record Albums

Dr. Martin Luther King Jr.: Birth to Twelve Years Old. Recording of Alberta W. King, 18 January 1973. King Center Archives, Atlanta.

The Early Days. Taped sermon by Martin Luther King Jr., Mt. Pisgah Baptist Church, Chicago, 27 August 1967. King Center Archives, Atlanta.

Free at Last! Free at Last! His Truth Is Marching On. Coretta Scott King. Caedmon recording TC-1407, King Center Archives, Atlanta.

The Hate That Hate Produced. CBS News documentary, New York, 1959.

Like It Is. Videotaped interview with Malcolm X. Written, produced, and narrated by Gil Noble. WABC-TV, New York, November 1963. King Center Archives, Atlanta.

Martin Luther King Jr.: An Amazing Grace. McGraw-Hill Films, Del Mar, Calif., 1978.

Martin Luther King Jr.: A Personal Portrait. Videotape. Carroll's Marketing and Management Service, Goldsboro, N.C., 1966–67.

Index

Lewis V. Baldwin is professor of religious studies at Vanderbilt University. He is the author of six books, including *To Make the Wounded Whole: The Cultural Legacy of Martin Luther King Jr.* (1992) and *The Mark of a Man: Peter Spencer and the African Union Methodist Tradition* (1987).

Amiri Yasin Al-Hadid is professor and chair of Africana Studies and founder of the Great Debate Production and Honor Society at Tennessee State University.